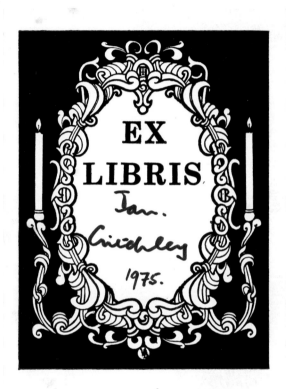

EX
LIBRIS

Ian.
Critchley
1975.

THE REGIMENTS DEPART

By the same author:

J. H. THOMAS: A LIFE FOR UNITY
OBJECTIVE EGYPT
THE FAREWELL YEARS: THE BUFFS 1948–67
AMIENS 1918

THE REGIMENTS DEPART

A HISTORY OF THE BRITISH ARMY,
1945–1970

GREGORY BLAXLAND

WILLIAM KIMBER
22A QUEEN ANNE'S GATE, LONDON, S.W.1

First published in 1971 by
WILLIAM KIMBER & CO. LIMITED
22A Queen Anne's Gate, London, S.W.1

© GREGORY BLAXLAND 1971

SBN 7183 0012 2

PRINTED IN GREAT BRITAIN
BY W & J MACKAY & CO LTD, CHATHAM

TO
THE REGIMENTS DEPARTED

PREFACE

I ATTEMPT in this book to describe the part played by the Army in the years of Britain's disengagement from Empire. Some may find it a sad story, for there are many departures to record, both of troops from lands left with poignant relics of British service and of famous names from the roll of regiments. Yet it may also be thought an honourable story. There have been many land-hungry bullies at large, eager to trade on Britain's earnest desire to hand over responsibility, and in nine countries British troops have had to resist attempts at a grab made either by outright on-slaught or by the attrition of murder and intimidation. The situations confronting the soldiers have varied between the desperate, the tense, exhausting, exasperating, embarrassing, and patently ridiculous, while at home they were subjected to frequent verbal sniping and were rarely cheered by a public uninterested in, and unappreciative of, the com-plexities of responsible withdrawal. They have needed courage and compassion, physical endurance and patience, defiance under massed attack and restraint under wild provocation, skill at diplomacy as often as at arms, discipline and humour. It is for the reader to judge whether these diverse virtues have been displayed.

This is not an official history. On the other hand it does aspire at being accurate and comprehensive within the limitations imposed by the rule that places official records in purdah for thirty years. The staple in-gredients come from the regiments themselves, all of whose secretaries have very kindly provided me with details of their units' movements. I have enlarged on their information by consulting the regimental maga-zines and much other literature at the Ministry of Defence Library (Army and Central), and I should not in fact have written this book without the encouragement and help given me from the start by the chief librarian Mr. D. W. King. I also owe a great deal to his two assistants, Mr. Potts and Mr. Woods, and to the library's historical narrator, Lieutenant-Colonel W. B. R. Neave-Hill. Another source of constant aid has been the Army Public Relations department.

Many people who played parts in the various campaigns have given me their aid by letter or interview. They have filled the gaps uncovered by published works, of which there are many large ones, notably in the operations in Palestine, Egypt, Cyprus and Borneo. I am greatly in-debted to these private contributors, the majority of whom are very busy men. Rather than make a parade of them here, I have indicated in

Appendix E, Sources, from what individuals and published works I obtained my material for each chapter. I am afraid I have not linked specific items of information to their sources because of a personal allergy to reference numerals in the text.

Some readers may be disappointed not to find battalions and regiments accorded their full titles on first appearance. I had intended to do this but found the text became too heavily encumbered and have instead adopted compromise, similar to that used in official war histories, between the full titles and the terse abbreviations of staff officialese; thus the 1st Battalion The North Staffordshire Regiment (The Prince of Wales's) becomes the 1st North Staffordshire and subsequently the North Staffords. Full regimental titles, both old and new, can however be found in Appendix A, from which the evolution of the Regular Army, between 1949 and 1970, can be traced. A guide to the service of each regiment can be obtained from the Index, where the theatres of operations visited by each are named.

It needs to be stressed that the accounts of the various campaigns are concerned primarily with the part played by the British Army and are not fully comprehensive. The contributions made by Colonial and Allied forces, the Police, the Royal Navy, the Royal Air Force, and civil and political agencies have been sketched in, but there has never been space to do them full justice. The picture may consequently appear somewhat lop-sided. This has to be accepted, and I hope that in cramming the post-war deeds of Britain's soldiers into a single book I do not make it appear that they won every war on their own.

For their permission to reproduce extracts from works shown I am grateful to Cassell and Company Ltd. and the agents of the late Lieutenant-General Sir Francis Tuker (Tuker's *While Memory Serves*), William Collins, Sons and Company Ltd. (*The Memoirs of Field Marshal Montgomery*), Faber and Faber Ltd. (Lawrence Durrell's *Bitter Lemons* and Julian Paget's *Last Post: Aden 1964–1967*), Thomas Nelson and Sons Ltd. and Major-General B. A. Coad (Lieutenant-Colonel G. I. Malcolm's *The Argylls in Korea*), the Editor of the *Sunday Telegraph* (General Sir Hugh Stockwell's articles of October–November 1966), Times Newspapers Ltd. (leading article in *The Times* of June 17, 1968), Field Marshal Sir Gerald Templer (letter in *The Times* of June 29, 1968), and to Brigadier J. W. Tweedie (private letter to the author).

CONTENTS

Contents

MAPS

1

Redeployment for Peace

I—THE COMMITMENT

THE defeat of Germany and Japan put the British Army in occupation of a larger part of the world than ever before. Its men numbered three million, and in battle dress, khaki drill, jungle green, or olive green, with on their heads a beret, balmoral, caubeen, bush hat, or more often the inelegant hybrid known as the cap G.S., they were strewn in winding chains from London to Tokyo, from the Baltic to the Caribbean. Some performed the traditional tasks of the British Army, keeping the peace within the Empire and garrisoning the links of strategic importance that littered school atlases with red dots; some were returning from incarceration as prisoners of war; some were on depot duty in Britain, and some were similarly employed in those other two great bases, Egypt and India, from which armies had burst out to drive the enemy from contemplation of victory to complete destruction. The most numerous and far spread were the men who had fought with these armies and were in occupation of Northern Africa, Italy, North-West Europe, and Burma when news of victory arrived. Scarcely pausing to shout hurrah, they rushed on to cope with the chaos wrought by the collapse of the enemy powers and to tackle the more lasting problems thrown up in the great eruption, while consumed themselves, in the majority of cases, with thoughts of their own resettlement.

The first expansion had been from Egypt, a British bastion of over fifty years' standing which had played so crucial a part in imperial strategy that troops had been sent for its defence even at the risk of imperilling the homeland. From here British troops deprived Italy of her colony of Libya, covering over 1,000 miles of coastline and stretching as far southwards into the hinterland of Africa, and they would obviously have to remain until Libya was independent and secure. Further westwards they had retrieved Tunisia and Algeria for France, and the only task left was to remove the remains of the depots and camps set up before the plunge into Europe.

Sicily and Italy were littered with the debris and weird little administrative units that denote the passing of an invading army. Italy had, by an act of political redemption, freed herself from the shame of punitive occupation, but was confronted with an invasion of Venezia Giulia, the north-east province she had won as the price demanded for participation in the First World War. Now Yugoslavia claimed it, and her troops entered Trieste before the arrival of the British Eighth Army. Political pressure, combined with a display of air power, forced them to relinquish the city, but the Yugoslavs did not drop their claim and the task of holding them back was not a commitment the British Army could abandon. The bulk of the Eighth Army had meanwhile brought their long journey to its close by entering Austria. The southern provinces formed the zone of occupation allotted the British, with one battalion on ceremonial duty in Vienna, when admitted by the Russians on July 30, 1945. There they would remain until a treaty was signed, and while the summer months lasted the troops did not mind how long they remained in this pleasant land.

Three divisions had been removed from the Eighth Army during the previous winter and shipped across to Greece, where an armed rising against the Greek Government followed the entry of the 2nd Parachute Brigade into Athens on the heels of the departing Germans. In subduing this rising these troops can be said to have fought the first of the post-war battles before the real war had come to its end. There was still plenty to be done by them after some sort of order had been restored, for communications were in chaos, the people near starvation, and rebellion liable to erupt again.

Whereas the British had advanced up Italy on the right of the Americans, they were on their left in the battle for North-West Europe, and consequently the north-west portion of Germany was the zone of occupation allotted them at the Yalta conference. It was about as large as England and Wales and contained the cities of Cologne, Hamburg, Kiel, and with usage rights granted to the Americans, the city-port of Bremen, from which the British Army's previous excursion across the Rhine, made in 1795, had ended in pitiful evacuation. Field Marshal Montgomery's 21st Army Group not only invaded this zone but expanded into that allotted the Russians and simultaneously raced on into Denmark to round up prisoners and receive a rapturous welcome from the people. Not until July 4, after withdrawal behind the agreed boundaries of occupation, did British troops make their first entry into

Berlin as a national contingent under the four-power Control Council. They were led by the 11th Hussars and were drawn from that most widely fought of all divisions, the 7th Armoured.

To revert to Egypt, whence the 7th Armoured had begun their odyssey, there had also been sproutings of troops into the Italians' East African possessions, and while only a mission needed to remain in Abyssinia, Eritrea and Somaliland were in a state of turbulence and had to be policed. Elsewhere in Africa the British Army had to provide a garrison for Khartoum, a command organisation for East and West Africa, and officers, N.C.O.s, and technicians for the Colonial forces.

East of Egypt, Palestine had been a magnet to British troops ever since the rebellion broke out there in 1936 and was bound to remain so until a political solution could be reached. Syria, Iraq, and even Persia had all been entered, either by force or invitation, but the army's commitments could be swiftly shed, and Aden and its Protectorate could be left to air control.

Further eastwards lay that great stronghold of British military might, India. It had formed the buffer against which the Japanese advance at last collapsed and the springboard from which Burma had been rewon. It had also despatched the expedition that had regained Malaya, without a fight as it turned out, and enabled Admiral Mountbatten to accept the surrender of the Japanese at Singapore on September 12. Meanwhile the Royal Navy had reclaimed Hong Kong, with aid from Commandos, and an Australian force North Borneo. The final act of Nemesis was the occupation of Japan, for a share of which a Commonwealth division, consisting of a British, Indian and Australian brigade, was formed in March 1946. The British representative was the 5th Infantry Brigade, made up of the 2nd Royal Welch Fusiliers, the 2nd Dorset, and the 1st Queen's Own Cameron Highlanders.

There were problems enough in the reoccupation of British territories after all the humiliations and tribulations inflicted by the Japanese. Even thornier problems, providing a foretaste of the fever with which a whole generation of British soldiers would have to cope, were encountered in the tasks of reoccupation Britain undertook for other countries. Only in Siam did the troops receive a warm welcome and restore a regime without arousing violence. In Indo-China they became embroiled with the rebel forces of Ho Chi Minh and can be said to have fired the opening rounds of the Vietnam war. Not until December were the French established in sufficient strength to assume control, and April 1946 had arrived before the rearguard of the British force withdrew, having had its total of casualties brought to over fifty. But only Indian troops were engaged here, partly for administrative convenience

3

and partly because all the British battalions were emaciated by a repatriation scheme that removed the seasoned elements in a single swoop.

The Dutch East Indies proved as dangerous to occupy as a roaring furnace. The Indonesian nationalist leader, Dr. Soekarno, had with the backing of the Japanese set up a republic, and although the British general, Sir Philip Christison, was admitted into Batavia, the capital of Java, on September 29, violent rioting followed the arrival of the first troops ashore, the 1st Seaforth Highlanders. Clumsy diplomacy by the Dutch increased the difficulties of the British, and most of the 23rd Indian Division had to be employed before Batavia was pacified. A ferocious battle for Sourabaya followed, in which armour, aircraft and naval guns were freely used and the whole of the 5th Indian Division committed. The equivalent of one more division had to be brought to Java before the nationalists could be persuaded to release their 129,000 hostages, former internees of the Japanese. Although Dutch troops began to arrive in March 1946, not until the end of November was the withdrawal of the British completed, and by now the Indonesians had won a substantial measure of independence, sending out a victory peal to stir the pulse of subject people all over the world.

The Indian troops had once again borne the brunt of this awful aftermath of Japanese occupation. Twenty-eight British officers and ten R.A.F. officers were killed in it, and twenty-two British soldiers, out of a total of 2,136 casualties suffered by the British force. The Seaforth were followed in by the 178th Assault and the 3rd Field Regiments, R.A., the 2nd West Yorkshire, the 5th Parachute Brigade, and the 2nd Buffs, and in Sumatra, where the fighting was less heavy, the 1st Lincolnshire and the 6th South Wales Borderers were the British battalions engaged. High valedictory tribute was paid the British and Indian troops, both by the Dutch Governor-General and by the Indonesian Prime Minister, Dr. Shahrir, who spoke of his admiration, even when an opponent, for 'your politeness, your kindness, and your dignified self-restraint'.

In no other part of the world could there be any immediate hand-over of responsibility, and this was a matter of regret to the British Government. Labour had come to power on July 26, 1945, and the Prime Minister was the man who had led the opposition against rearmament in 1935 and against national service in 1939, Mr. Clement Attlee. Disengagement was the foremost objective of the Government in matters military, and they pursued it not only from instinctive aversion to imperialism but from an urgent need to make economies at a time when the Exchequer was on the point of penury and had yet to bear the cost of the sweeping social measures that had been promised. The Army, it was clear enough, was to suffer its traditional fate on forcing the King's enemies to their knees, neglect.

The most enticing areas of disengagement were no less than the three countries that had contained the great bulk of Britain's army overseas before the war, India, Egypt, and Palestine, and indeed Mr. Ernest Bevin, the new Foreign Secretary, as good as promised that there would be no occupation without consent when he proclaimed his wish 'to leave behind for ever the idea of one country dominating another.' The National Government had in fact done much to dispel this idea during the Thirties. Only the urgency was new, and the confidence that solutions to baffling problems of sovereignty and security could be found.

In the event disengagement was achieved both from India and Palestine, although at dire cost to their inhabitants, as will be described in subsequent chapters. Over Egypt negotiations broke down, largely because the Egyptians demanded too much. The troops remained by the Suez Canal, employed on a function of dubious value affording little joy or comfort, and plans to transfer the Middle East base to Kenya, on which plenty of work had been done, were abandoned. The sky meanwhile was darkening over Europe, and prospects of an early withdrawal of troops from Greece or Venezia Giulia were fading. Having stubbornly resisted the pressure to end conscription, Attlee was persuaded to place it on a regular peacetime basis. In July 1947 the National Service Act was passed. It was to come into effect on January 1, 1949, from which date men called-up would have an obligation of a year's service with the colours and six on the reserve.

The prime mover of this measure was the Chief of the Imperial General Staff, Field Marshal Viscount Montgomery, as he records with some glee in the chapter of his Memoirs entitled *I Make A Nuisance Of Myself In Whitehall*. However, all his battles there were defensive ones, largely against continual demands that expenditure must be cut, and he was forced to see many of his battalions overrun. The structure of the army that survived needs to be studied in some detail, and if it might appear that the Field Marshal's renowned sense of balance lacked its customary inspiration, it must be remembered that no one, other than a clairvoyant, could predict at the close of 1947 the burdens the army would soon have to bear.

5

The planned strength of the Regular Army under the new National Service plan was 305,000, a figure that had eventually to be raised by over 100,000. This was much larger than the pre-war army, and yet the Infantry (including Foot Guards) was smaller, subsiding from over half the whole to barely a fifth. The totals (to the nearest hundred) in January 1939 were 108,000 out of 201,000. In March 1951, the earliest year obtainable, they were 88,100 out of 417,800, and by now there had been much rebuilding of the infantry, with national service increased to two years. Even so, a high proportion of the 88,100 were employed away from their regiments at headquarters, schools and base camps.

These figures tell a revealing story. They tell of the increased complexity of the soldiers' needs, which raised the strength of the services to 42 per cent of the whole and greatly swelled headquarters at all levels, and they tell of the conviction, typical of the optimism that always pervaded strategic planning, that the evacuation of India and Palestine would bring an end to the great imperial policing tasks, in which infantrymen played an even more predominant part than on the battlefield. They also tell of the collapse of the Cardwell System, which had given regiments of the Line content and stability for seventy years. Twenty-five years would be spent in groping for a suitable alternative.

The Cardwell System had come in two instalments, of which only the first had been introduced, in 1873, by Edward Cardwell himself, as Secretary of State for War during Gladstone's first ministry. Its object was to provide the hitherto nomadic regiments with permanent homes and to give the men better prospect of home service. Overseas garrisons were therefore reduced and battalions were paired together for alternate tours at home and abroad, and although these tours were to remain of up to twenty years' duration, the men were to be interchangeable between the two. At the same time the regiments were allotted static depots and recruiting areas and linked with Militia battalions to form administrative brigades. Those regiments bearing a number from 1st to 25th had had two battalions since the Indian Mutiny and could do their own internal pairing, as also could the 60th (King's Royal Rifle Corps) and Rifle Brigade, who each had four. The remainder, numbered 26th to 59th and 61st to 109th, had to form the most suitable partnerships they could—except for one regiment (for the number was odd), the 79th (Queen's Own Cameron Highlanders), who had to wait until 1897 before acquiring a second battalion.

6

Since the regiments retained the old nominal affiliations, which were observed in regimental titles but seldom on the ground, there were plenty of absurdities in the new scheme, as for instance the domiciling of the 31st (Huntingdonshire) Regiment at Kingston-on-Thames. However, the Tories dared not tamper with such a sacrosanct thing as regimental structure when in office from 1874–80, and it was left to another of Gladstone's War Ministers, Hugh Childers, to make the logical and outrageous decision to convert the brigades, regulars and militia, into large regiments in 1881. County titles were allotted, although the revered old numbers were retained as subsidiaries and never forgotten. Great was the outcry, great also the eventual gain. The tense ties of loyalty that had bound together the little nomad bands gradually took wider root and afforded the more mature and restful content derived from participation in the family life of a county.

Sixty-nine regiments of the Line emerged from this reorganisation, and with Foot Guards added, and six extra battalions retained after expansion for the South African War (by the Royal Fusiliers, Worcestershire, and Middlesex), there were 157 regular battalions available in 1914, which is not such a contemptible figure for an army of volunteers. The disbandment of the five regiments of Southern Ireland, the reduction of all line regiments to two battalions, and the addition of the Welsh Guards brought the total down to 138 by 1922. They were all still intact when war broke out in 1939, and although most of the home battalions were at little more than cadre strength, they could be speedily mobilised for war, as had happened when the 1st Division had been summoned to Palestine in 1936.

An infantryman had the right always to remain with his regiment during peacetime, and in some regiments it was regarded not just as a right but a duty, even to the extent that officers were discouraged from sitting for Staff College. After all the upheavals of war, there were many who looked forward to a return to this settled, orderly life, with its narrow bonds of comradeship. The first public indication that they were to be disappointed came on October 14, 1946, when a new system was announced in the House of Commons by Mr. Fred Bellenger, who had newly become War Minister on the retirement of the former miner, Mr. Jack Lawson, and had undoubted affection for the army. The Cardwell System, he said, had been found too rigid for modern needs and had to be modified. 'In view of the great traditions and fighting records of the various infantry regiments, however, it has been decided that the regimental system shall remain as a feature of the post-war Army.'

The modification was the formation of the Group. It replaced the regiment as the corps within which a soldier was liable for service and was soon to assume the name Cardwell had given his groupings, the Brigade. There were fifteen groups initially, one of which, the Machine Gun Group, was disbanded after a year. Three of the others had military affiliations: the Brigade of Guards, the Light Infantry, and the Motorised Infantry (later renamed the Green Jacket). The remainder were regional groupings, with the number of regiments in each ranging from eight in the Lancastrian Group to three each in the Welsh and Northern Irish. It was not long before officers and men were made depressingly aware that there could be complete fluidity of posting within each group. Group training centres were set up, and orders were issued standardising uniforms and depriving regiments of cherished idiosyncracies.

Worse was to follow, emphasising beyond all doubt that the golden days of the Cardwell System were gone beyond recall. At the close of 1946 orders began to be transmitted placing regular battalions in suspended animation. Twenty-three fell initially, and by October 1947 the War Office had been compelled to order the reduction of every regiment of the Line to a single battalion. Operational convenience was the governing factor in the choice of battalions, age no protection whatever. Thus many old battalions, including four that had served continuously since the reign of King Charles II—the 1st Queen's, 1st Buffs, 1st Royal Northumberland Fusiliers, and the 1st Royal Warwickshire (which Montgomery had commanded)—had the light of life snuffed out, while their junior partners survived. There were many heavy hearts in the breasts of those who valued tradition and believed, as every recruit was taught, that it had played its part in kindling the fighting spirit that so recently had plucked victory from defeat.

In the event every 1st Battalion struck down made a nominal come-back, in some cases after more than a year in limbo. Animation was restored by the predatory expedient of dispossessing the 2nd Battalion, which might be disbanded or amalgamated, as decided within the regiment, but either way would surrender its title to the 1st. In this way every regular battalion of the sixty-four regiments came to be numbered the 1st, and the only concession made to the junior partners of the Cardwell reforms was the insertion of their numbers in the full, formal title. Thus the famous, jealously preserved rivalry between the 43rd and the 52nd ended in mealy assimilation as the 1st Battalion The Oxfordshire and Buckinghamshire Light Infantry, 43rd and 52nd Foot, and the 91st Argyll became inextricably entwined with the 93rd Sutherland Highlanders.

For three regiments—the Lincolnshire (who as 10th Foot were the senior hitherto unhonoured), Leicestershire, and Hampshire—the accolade of Royal, conferred in December 1946, provided a ray of sunshine to lighten the gloom cast by the cuts and reorganisation. The Military Police, Pay Corps, Veterinary Corps, Educational Corps, Dental Corps, and Pioneer Corps also received the honour, and this emphasised a strange anomaly, for almost half the infantry regiments bore unadorned titles, even though they had each won upwards of sixty battle honours before the start of the Second World War. But it is certain that no jealousy was felt. Infantrymen were proud of their idiosyncracies, and such simple names as Suffolks, Devons, Cheshires, Gloucesters, Worcesters and Welch could generate as much pride and individuality as the old numbers that were still echoing around the barrack blocks. The echoes were growing in volume, as the older soldiers felt the need for reassurance in a changing world.

The Foot Guards survived intact and kept their ten battalions, of which the Grenadiers and Coldstream each had three, the Scots Guards two. On the other end of the line stood a new regiment, the Parachute Regiment, which had been formed in August 1942 and had to rely on secondment from other regiments until at last being allowed a permanent cadre, of soldiers in 1953 and of officers in 1958. It cannot have been easy to decide its peacetime establishment. Seventeen battalions had been raised during the war and had won great fame in battle; but there was reason to doubt their suitability for the humdrum duties of peace, especially after the mutiny at the squalid Muar camp, Malaya, in May 1946, as a result of which 250 men of one battalion received prison sentences, only to have them quashed a month later for technical irregularities during the trial. There was also the question of cost, both of their own equipment and of the aircraft with which to train them, and this no doubt sharpened the edge of the axe, for they were slashed to three battalions and an independent company of guardsmen. Nine battalions were still in existence when the order was made near the end of 1947, and it came as a bitter blow for their officers and men, most of whom were serving with the 6th Airborne in Palestine. The three surviving battalions were grouped into an independent brigade, numbered the 16th in memory of the 1st and 6th Airborne Divisions.

The combined total of British battalions therefore came to seventy-seven, and to this were added eight of the Brigade of Gurkhas, supplied by the four regiments belatedly salvaged from the Indian Army. They were not included in the strengths issued for the British Army, nor were the engineer, signals, and service units they were to raise, bringing their strength to 14,000, but they were an integral part of the British Army from January 1948 and were to prove a timely and most valuable addition.

The Royal Marines formed one further valuable reserve available to the War Office although administered by the Admiralty. They had assumed full responsibility for the provision of commandos, whose origin was among the first expressions of Churchillian defiance in 1940, and like the parachutists they were assigned a brigade of three units, each organised into troops and half-troops, the latter consisting of around thirty-five men. All had been formed during the war, following the Army's lead.

The Cavalry of the Line had experienced the convulsions of reduction in 1922, when its regiments were cut from twenty-eight to twenty. The latter were by now all happily ensconced in the Royal Armoured Corps, together with eight regiments of the Royal Tank Regiment, which was the same figure as in 1939, when they were termed battalions. Although aloof from the R.A.C. in matters of precedence, the two regiments of Household Cavalry fielded regiments of armoured cars, while also providing a combined mounted squadron for ceremonial duties, with the men alternating between the two. There were therefore thirty armoured regiments available, divided in the rough proportion of three to one between tanks and armoured cars, and the slender infantry force available for war in Europe could at least have more steel around it than in 1940.

Having borne an ever larger burden with the invention of every new engine of war, the Royal Regiment of Artillery at last managed to pass the anti-tank role on to the R.A.C., a switch completed in 1950. It was left with the imposing total of sixty-nine regiments, more than there were battalions of the Line. Fourteen of these were grouped with territorial regiments in Anti-Aircraft Command. Of the remainder, about half were field, a quarter medium and heavy, and a quarter field force anti-aircraft. Again the infantry were assured ample support if they became involved in full scale war—and the consequence was to be that the artillery would have to provide valuable support as infantrymen in unconventional wars.

No one had left such mark on the world as the Corps of Royal Engineers. Their bridges were to be seen in every country through which British soldiers had passed, and they long served the needs of the inhabitants. However, the days when specific, as opposed to fortuitous, aid to communities would be a set commitment of the sappers had not yet arrived, and the twenty-three regiments retained on the peace establishment catered for their widespread military roles; there was a fortress, a transportation, and a survey regiment among them, and eleven had training roles. There was also a wide miscellany of independent squadrons, ranging from postal to port operating.

The Royal Corps of Signals, to whom the R.E. had given birth in 1920, had greatly expanded and acquired as many regiments as its parent although as yet little more than half its size in officers and men. Great technical strides had been made during the war, and in the campaigns that lay ahead there would be problems more complex than found on the battlefield, calling for further development of the signaller's art.

Of the services, the youngest (formed in 1942) was the Corps of Royal Electrical and Mechanical Engineers and it was to become the largest, faced with a mounting welter of work by the strain on the equipment of an overstrained army. The R.E.M.E. had a complement of thirty-nine regular lieutenant-colonels by 1949, and it is indicative of the expansion made by the services that in the Royal Army Service Corps and the Royal Army Ordnance Corps the complement of lieutenant-colonels had grown since 1939, although they had provided most of the officers and men for the formation of the R.E.M.E. In the R.A.S.C., which had responsibilities for barrack and clerical services as well as supply and transport by wheel, hoof, and propeller, the number of lieutenant-colonels had risen from twenty-three to twenty-seven, and in the R.A.O.C. from twenty-four to thirty-one. The Royal Army Medical Corps had sixty-six lieutenant-colonels, and this figure was greatly to swell in the course of time, showing the Army Council's concern for the health of its flock. Most of course were specialists, the most erudite professionals the army had.

Such was the shape of an army fashioned for the needs of a nation that had shed its most taxing imperial responsibilities and was drawing closer to Europe instead. Its members were less stereotyped than of old, and although the horse still featured prominently in recreational activities, thanks largely to captures from the German Army, there were few commanding officers left who would dare admit ignorance in matters mechanical. It had also been placed on a more democratic basis. The R.M.A. Woolwich and the R.M.C. Sandhurst had been merged into the Royal Military Academy Sandhurst, and instead of extracting fees from the parents of most gentlemen cadets it had to be entered by cadets (no longer styled 'gentlemen') who were serving soldiers and would, in theory, be granted choice of regiment according to their grading in the final order. For the soldiers there were greater barrack comforts and relaxation of the rigid routine of roll calls, lights out, and instant rising at reveille, and lance-corporals could no longer be ordered not to walk out with privates. The soldier's life, the C.I.G.S. announced, was to be 'the good life'.

Yet there was a grave shortage of recruits, and prospects were dim of bringing the regular strength to the required 200,000. This was partly because it was a conscript army and consequently lacked glamour; battle dress remained the standard uniform even for ceremonial, and the only embellishment was a blue beret—or a different colour for a select few—in place of the cap G.S. There was also a high incidence of family separation, rising from the disruption of the old overseas stations and an endemic shortage of funds. Pay was meagre too, amounting to only 4/- a day for the regular recruit. But what was lacking most of all was belief in the role to be played by the new-style army. It would not be long in coming.

III—THE DISTRIBUTION

By July 1, 1948, the evacuation of Palestine was complete, following that of India, and the heaviest of the pre-war commitments were removed from the Army's shoulders. No troop movements had as yet been made to respond to the first of the big post-war threats, although the alarm bells were clanging in Berlin and Malaya. It is a suitable date therefore for an examination of the disposition of the eighty-five infantry battalions and thirty armoured regiments available, leaving aside the few remaining 2nd battalions not yet laid to rest, of whom the last—the 2nd Royal Scots and the 2nd King's Own—lingered on into 1949. It was the moment of lowest pressure for the army. It had crashed down the jagged slopes into the valley of peace and stood panting before the ascent up the mist covered crags ahead, not as yet realising that the speed of the descent was making these crags all the more formidable.

The central plank of British strategy—some might say its central flaw—was the maintenance of a powerful reserve in the Middle East. Palestine had been intended to fulfil this function, but the reserve had by its presence aggravated the unrest, with the result that it had been committed to preserving peace in its own homestead and been eventually removed with the remainder of the garrison. In Egypt the 10,000 troops allowed by treaty was 10,000 more than Egypt wanted, and the garrison had been cut to three battalions and two armoured regiments, together with artillery, which were now the main reserve. Libya similarly had a garrison of three and two, rather more closely tied to security duties. Cyprus should also have contained a reserve brigade, but there had been a suction of troops to Eritrea to quell the brigandage and terrorism waged by the Shiftas. The 1st South Wales Borderers, 2nd (soon to be 1st) Royal Berkshire, and 1st Loyals, together with the moribund 2nd King's Own, were engaged on this exacting task in the wild and torrid country next the Red Sea, and they were aided by armoured cars of the 15th/19th Hussars. There were also two battalions on policing duties in Somaliland and the usual garrison battalion in the Sudan, bringing the total in Africa to twelve battalions earmarked for survival and five armoured regiments.

In the Far East there were thirteen battalions, including all eight of the Gurkhas, split ten and three between Malaya and Hong Kong. There was no armour. The brigade in Japan had been withdrawn in February 1947.

There was a battalion in Jamaica, as before the war, with a new commitment in British Honduras. Gibraltar, with two battalions, was one of the few places with a surplus, and Malta was in the possession of Commandos.

On the mainland of Europe there were nine battalions divided evenly between Greece, Venezia Giulia, and Austria. Germany, including Berlin, had eighteen battalions and eight armoured regiments.

Thirty battalions and seventeen regiments are left as the quota in Britain and Northern Ireland. It is a speciously large total. Such was the plight of the infantry that fourteen battalions were performing the depot duties for the administrative brigades, training all recruits centrally under the one cap badge, and an armoured regiment was similarly employed, with others on territorial assistance. Most of the remainder had been heavily mulcted of men in order to bring overseas units up to strength. There was no operational organisation, not even a brigade headquarters—and this in a country which, although notorious for military unreadiness, had contained a field force of five infantry divisions, at the least, ever since the days of Haldane. Only the 1st, which bestrode the Middle East with headquarters at Tripoli, and the 2nd, which had dissolved in the Far East and been resurrected in Germany in February 1947, usurping the structure of the 53rd Welsh, were even in existence. The 3rd had moved from Germany to Egypt near the end of 1945 and there been disbanded in mid-1947; the 4th had ended the war in Greece and met its end there in March 1947; and the 5th, after fighting in many parts, had reached Germany before the war's end and had there fallen to disbandment in January 1948. Of the armoured divisions, only the 7th, in Germany, remained.

As substitute for the old home-based field force, Montgomery converted the Territorial Army, which had been reconstituted in March

1947, into the wider based Reserve Army by enlarging its regular staff and giving national-servicemen an obligation of three and a half years' part-time service with it on completion of their regular service. In this way it was planned to make nine divisions—six infantry, two armoured, and one airborne—fully operational as an immediate reserve. It was an imaginative scheme, but it had its drawbacks, one of which was the difficulty of recruiting territorials into a half-conscript force. Another was the delay in drafting in national-servicemen, which was widened by two extensions of their full-time commitment. Not until January 1951 did they begin to fill the ranks of the Reserve Army in any number, and four more years would be needed before the divisions could approach the standard of readiness required.

The first of these extensions, keeping the national-servicemen in the Regular Army eighteen months and keeping its strength well above 350,000, was obtained by the ever combative Field Marshal through a rather more sweeping threat of resignation than usual and through the powerful backing of his third War Minister, Mr. Emanuel Shinwell, who turned the trepidation his appointment roused at the War Office into devoted loyalty. Even so, Montgomery was forced to admit in his Memoirs, 'the Army was in a parlous condition, and was in a complete state of unreadiness and unpreparedness for war.' Having come to the War Office fired with the determination to prevent the drift that had set in after the end of the previous war, this must have been a sad disappointment to him.

How the soldiers rose from this parlous condition to confront the many-shaped dragons that waylaid them forms the subject of this book. But it is necessary first of all to follow them along the two thorny paths prepared for them during the pre-war era, leading to extrication from India and Palestine.

2

India

(1945–48)

FORTY-FIVE battalions of infantry were among the 45,250 British troops stationed in India and Burma prior to the outbreak of war in 1939, and they formed just under a quarter of the all-volunteer Army in India, providing a layer intermixed at brigade level in the ratio of two Indian units to one British. It was soldiering at its best, with its ceremonial and whirl of competitive events, its excursions to the hills for training or to the Frontier for active operations, and even for the private there were barrack comforts never to be found in England, savoured with the mysticism and wonder of life amid a people whose tranquillity and dignity in country districts contrasted so weirdly with the agitated blarings made on their behalf in the towns.

It had become apparent, by the autumn of 1945, that there could be no return to this life. The battalions themselves were in a crippled state, having suddenly had all men removed who had served three years and four months overseas, as a result of which they (the battalions) were removed from their Indian brigades. And India was in the grip of fever, with politicians clamouring for the independence that had been dangled before them for fifteen years and with hysteria brought to a new peak by the trial of three officers who had served with the Indian National Army. This was the force of renegades raised by the Japanese in conquered territory, and although brutality against their own compatriots featured among the charges, the accused were hailed as great heroes for having turned against the British Raj. It was a delicate situation for the famous soldiers at the top, Field Marshal Viscount Wavell as Viceroy and General Sir Claude Auchinleck, the Commander-in-Chief and revered father figure of the Indian Army, soon also to be Field Marshal. The fact that prison sentences were remitted to cashiering suggests that they were sensitive to the public clamour.

15

Such an award for treachery came as a poor stimulant to the morale of the forces at a time when a strong one was badly needed. There was a mutiny at an R.A.F. camp near Calcutta, which was proclaimed a strike and subdued by negotiation. The Royal Indian Air Force mutinied in sympathy: a comparatively mild affair which came to a mild ending. In February 1946 the Royal Indian Navy mutinied, and this was much more serious. It began at Bombay, with the hoisting of the flags of Congress and the Moslem League on the ships. The mutinous ratings then came ashore and began rioting and looting.

Resolute action by a battalion of Mahrattas returned them to ship. The 2nd Leicestershire were then brought in to contain them, wearing in their caps the Royal Tiger awarded them in 1829 for 'exemplary conduct in India'. On February 21 their pickets came under fire both from the ships and a naval barracks ashore. They had a prolonged fire fight with the mutineers during which they lost six men wounded, some by fire from an Oerlikon pom-pom. The 72nd Infantry Brigade, of the 2nd Queen's, 2nd Border, and 1st Essex, came into the city and spent a busy week in keeping sympathisers and hooligan bands off the streets.

On February 23, after Mosquitoes of the R.A.F. had dived threateningly over the mutineers, flags of surrender at last appeared. The Leicesters placed guards on the ships and moved into the barracks to round up shore-based sailors. This proved a difficult task, for the sailors lay grimly on their beds and had to be coaxed to their feet by gentle use of the bayonet. A few days later the Leicesters were playing them at football.

Mutiny also broke out at Karachi. It germinated at a shore establishment, H.M.I.S. *Himalaya*, on Manora island, and spread to a sloop in harbour, H.M.I.S. *Hindustan*. Warning of it was obtained by a shrewd piece of deduction on the part of the Military Police, and troops were deployed in time to prevent an attempt by the mutineers to break out of the dock area on the afternoon of February 21. A British brigade of the 1st Indian Airborne Division was summoned overnight and given the task of disarming the mutineers. The 2nd Black Watch were assigned the shore establishment, the 15th Parachute the sloop.

The Black Watch went in first. Using rescue craft of the R.A.F. they made an assault landing on Manora island as dawn was breaking and took the mutineers by surprise, encountering no opposition and gaining possession of the barracks without the firing of a round. The 15th Para found their mutineers ready and determined to fight. They waited until 10 a.m. to allow the ship's 4-inch guns to subside with the tide below the level of the wharf, and the brigade commander then made final appeal. The sailors opened up with an Oerlikon on the paras and with a 4-inch gun on an inshore barracks, the only target available to it. The paras replied with rifle fire from the roofs of warehouses, with mortar bombs, and with 75-mm. shells fired with great accuracy by a Royal Artillery troop. Practically every missile hit the ship, and after enduring the crash for twenty minutes the mutineers ran up a white flag. The paras went aboard to remove four dead and twenty-six wounded and round up the remainder of the crew. They had suffered two wounded themselves. A riot in Karachi followed, but was soon subdued.

1,300 miles eastwards the huge, tight-packed city of Calcutta had also been in ferment. Many vehicles had been burned in some previous riots, which had been conventional anti-British sprees, quelled by the police without great bloodshed. Now communal rivalry added its first lethal spark to this most combustible of communities. It began with a protest march by the Moslem League, which the students joined with all the verve to be expected. At nightfall the *goondas*—the teeming criminal riff-raff—took over and, half-naked, glistening and frenzied, filled the narrow streets with terror and the sound as of a thousand baying wolves.

Reinforced by their own Gurkha gendarmerie, the police held their own for twenty-four hours by use of tear gas and bullets. But by the evening of February 12 buses and tramcars were ablaze, the police were exhausted, and chaos was complete. Only now did the 2nd York and Lancaster debouch from the great walls of Fort William, in the city's centre, to occupy key places. The 2nd Green Howards then came in from the north and the 4th/3rd Gurkhas from the south; all night long they grimly paced the streets, sending mobs scurrying in droves in the early stages and subsequently hounding looters out of shop windows and isolating the fires still blazing in the wreckage-strewn streets. There were fresh eruptions next day, with the result that the 1st North Staffordshire were also brought in, and not until the fifth day of the rioting, February 15, had mob hysteria been drained out of the vast, sprawling city. It had been harrowing work stoically endured, for the youths that filled the bulk of the British battalions.

In March 1946 Attlee announced in the Commons that it was up to India to choose the type of government she wanted and that he was sending out a mission to help settle details. This at least brought the leaders of the Congress Party and of the Moslem League into consultation, but by attempting to lead the parties into partnership the mission widened the cleavage between the two, for to Moslems partnership spelt Hindu domination. The departure of the British mission was therefore soon followed by the first of those awful outbreaks of communal madness, the great killings. Nothing like it had occurred when that favourite Aunt Sally, the British presence, had been the target. The dispute now was about something more important, the life and death of the people who were to remain.

Calcutta was again the scene and the month August, during the heady, clammy humidity of the monsoon. The trouble began on the 16th, when the Moslems staged a protest meeting against the child of the mission, the Interim Government, and the Hindus sought to break it up, with Sikhs joining in just for the sake of joining in. The York and Lancasters and the Green Howards were again alerted, and the 7th Worcestershire too, and all three were summoned soon after dark. They rode in lorries with carrier escorts, and by now streets had been ravaged by wholesale looting, shops were ablaze, and large sections of the population had fled in panic, for the police had lost control of the situation much sooner than previously. A company commander of the York and Lancasters, Major Livermore, gained the impression on reaching the centre of the city that 'an armoured division had swept through on the tail of a heavy bombardment'. In the shacks and alleyways the corpses were beginning to accumulate, as yet undetected.

For the next five days these three battalions endured a strain not often surpassed in battle. They could remove hooligan mobs easily enough, by coming at them steadily with the steel of bayonet and helmet on prominent display, and in this manner established domination over the centre of the city, but the blood lust spluttered to and fro like a forest fire caught in a whirlwind and no sooner was one area of the enormous city pacified than the baying of murderers and screams of their victims would be heard from another. The police did their best with bullet and tear gas, the latter adding its fumes to the dust clouds of battle and the dark palls of smoke created by the arsonists, but the soldiers bore the main burden. The 1st/3rd Gurkhas came in to take their share on the 17th, and at dusk some light tanks of an Indian regiment arrived to cast their searchlights on the devastation and reveal contorted corpses and slinking forms defying the curfew. The Military Police played an important part, especially in providing refuge for the homeless.

The 2nd Royal Norfolk and the 2nd East Lancashire came from afar to ease the strain on the others, and by a supreme effort during the afternoon and night of the 18th quiet was restored to the city, to be broken by only a few squibs of violence next day. A different and more gruesome task of clearance now confronted the troops. So hectic had been the tempo that there had been no opportunity to remove the corpses. They littered most streets and were spread thick across more open spaces and the insides of hovels. They were of all ages, children included, and of either sex; very often the throat was slit and the belly ripped open, and some had been lying there for three days or more, rotting fast in the damp summer heat and drawing to Calcutta every vulture that flapped wing over Bengal. A military assessment, made in retrospect, put the number of dead at 4,000, with a further 10,000 injured and in dire need of treatment.

The task of removal fell on the three resident battalions, the York and Lancasters, Green Howards, and Worcesters. Major Livermore, of the first-named, has vividly described the 'awful 'ush' that descended when his commanding officer gave out orders for the task at 9 p.m. on the 19th, saying that it was to begin at once and that the locations of Moslem burial grounds and Hindu burning ghats would be notified. 'How the hell do I tell a Moslem from a Hindu when they've all been dead three days?' came a plaintive chirp, and its tone sent the tension bursting into a roar of laughter, ghoulish and pertinent though the query was. Gloom, the officers had instinctively decided, would only make the task more hideous.

Some Hindu sweepers were provided to assist in the task of removal and also some refuse lorries, but no drivers came with the latter and officers of the battalion took on this duty. A staff officer said of them, 'they drove their trucks till they were almost in a stupor; they stank so much that even their own men recoiled from them; they gave up wearing stench masks as these proved useless and breathed the foul air freely; they did not eat for two days but lived on cigarettes and neat gin.' The York and Lancasters had the hardest lot—Livermore removed 517 corpses from his company area in the course of two nights and days—and meanwhile other officers and men were still patrolling the foetid streets, moving away the debris and rubbish, shooing off vultures, bringing succour to the weak and destitute, and coaxing shopkeepers to re-open business. Thanks to the British soldier, Calcutta was spared the complementary horror beckoned by the killing, plague.

The madness spread. On September 1 Bombay erupted, and again the Leicesters were called out, to be kept fully deployed in support of the police for the next two months, with magistrates permanently attached so that the correct procedures for the transfer of responsibility could be observed. In October there was a massed flight of Hindus from Eastern Bengal, and revenge was taken on the Moslems with awful fury in Bihar and later at Garhmukteswar, 60 miles east of Delhi. In January 1947 the terror spread to the Punjab, fount of recruitment into the Indian Army, where Moslem and Sikh bands began to wage a bitter, organised war against each other. The Indian Army bore the main burden of its suppression and acted with firmness and impartiality which contrasted with the lack of either displayed by the police. Even politicians who had so often abused it were beginning to see the value of their army as the one possible means of preventing the disintegration of their country in anarchy and bloodshed. Hindus, Moslems, and Sikhs were still to be found within the one battalion, and in keeping religious prejudices subordinate to the traditions of the service a great deal depended on the five or six careworn British officers who might still remain.

Sensing that the problems of the Indian Army were all consuming at G.H.Q., the C.I.G.S. decided that British troops should have their own special representative there, and for this role he (Montgomery) chose a man who had served under him as a divisional commander, Major-General L. G. ('Bolo') Whistler; he was a man of great height and endearing personality, with a great reputation as a leader and no staff experience, and was formerly of the Royal Sussex Regiment. His was an advisory appointment, termed Major-General British Troops India, and he arrived to assume it on February 3, 1947. He found the troops of whom he was to act as guardian spread on either side of India in six independent brigade groups, with a dozen or so extra battalions and four armoured regiments allotted static internal security duties. The aims for their employment, for which Wavell obtained agreement in his last days as Viceroy, were to protect British nationals and if necessary evacuate them; to avoid involvement in the suppression of intercommunal disturbances; and to maintain the stability and integrity of the Indian Army.

On February 20, 1947, India took a leap nearer her destiny. Attlee announced the Government's 'definite intention' to complete 'the transfer of power into responsible Indian hands by a date not later than June 1948'. As a complement to this bold pledge Admiral Lord Louis Mountbatten was appointed Viceroy in place of Wavell.

The announcement sent fresh tremors through the zones of dispute between the religious factions, tying British troops closer to security tasks when plans for their disengagement should have been uppermost in mind. Calcutta was continually a-simmer, keeping the battalions there as busy as ever, and among other places affected by the fever it ran particularly high in Cawnpore, where the 2nd King's Own arrived to subdue the fury. The police staged a mutiny in the neighbouring province of Bihar and barricaded themselves inside two barracks, only to be cowed into swift and bloodless surrender by the 1st North Staffords, who a month later dissolved in suspended animation.

In the Punjab some help was given to the Indian Army in the increasingly daunting task of holding down the violence of civil war. The 2nd Suffolk and 2nd Black Watch provided a share of it and were touched by the eagerness of the welcomes they received. The people were, with good reason, in the grip of fear, and it was pathetic to see their faith in the *gora paltan*, the white regiment. Certainly the faith proved to be justified for the short period it could last. Warring bands of Sikhs and Moslems put away their weapons at the approach of the British, extended grave salaams, and spoke in grieved terms of the atrocities committed by the other side. Gifts flowed in for the peacekeepers from the grateful people. In place of prisoners, 'watches and clocks, trinkets and jewellery, silks and sovereigns, nuggets of gold' filled the guardroom cell of a mixed British and Indian engineer regiment commanded by Lieutenant-Colonel Mark Henniker.

On June 3 Mountbatten broadcast the great decision on which he had obtained agreement: there were to be two countries, India and Pakistan, with the latter divided between West and East, containing parts of the Punjab and Bengal, although not Calcutta. The Indian Army of course was condemned to partition too, right down to battalion level, and scarcely had G.H.Q. embarked on the intricacies of this heartrending problem than the idea of an orderly transition was shattered. The Viceroy had decided, rightly or wrongly, that speed was the best antidote to the violence that had begun to flare with renewed energy once the content of the announcement had been digested. On July 18 the British Parliament conferred independence on India and Pakistan by an Act, to come into force as soon as August 15 of that year, ten months earlier than pledged by Attlee.

There were some strange experiences for the British troops in those last two months as an occupying army, interspersed with the continual process of disbandment and departure, which reduced the total of fighting units from around thirty at the start of 1947 to fourteen by Independence day. They were concentrated now in six areas—around Lahore; Delhi and Meerut; Calcutta; Lucknow and Cawnpore; Bombay; and Bangalore—and from here they toured the countryside on flag marches in order to reassure the people, in traditional style, that peace could be preserved. They had a warmer reception than ever before, but they could not provide the reassurance most avidly sought: that they would be remaining to afford the protection so dearly needed. No one had imagined it would end like this.

The approach of Independence produced a great upsurge of emotion, and from a British viewpoint it reached its peak on the night before, August 13, without ceremony and in secret. The Union Jack over the Residency at Lucknow had flown night and day throughout the four and a half months of siege during the Mutiny, and it had been kept flying night and day ever since, over battlements that remained in their scarred and battered state. Near the end of July the last troops in occupation, the 1st Lancashire Fusiliers, departed, leaving only a caretaker in charge. Watched in stern silence by a few senior officers, he lowered the flag after dark on the 13th, through fear that rioters might next day attempt to make the capture for which so many Indians had striven in vain in 1857. Sappers later blew up the flag pole and its base to complete the disintegration of this proudest symbol of the British Raj.

August 14 was the official day of its expiry, and in Delhi and elsewhere there were combined parades of British and Indian troops, emphasising that in matters military cooperation between the old and the new countries could produce splendid results. With the arrival of midnight the new were born, and now it was India for the Indians and Pakistan for the Pakistanis.

The status of British troops changed from that of peacekeepers to guests in a foreign land, with responsibility only for the protection of British lives and property if the national security forces appeared to be incapable of providing it. The fear that British troops might be needed in this role had been much shrivelled by recent events, and it was found now that there were no grounds for it. Whistler, who became G.O.C. British Troops instead of a mere adviser, was therefore freed of his greatest anxiety and could concentrate on planning the evacuation, which was to be carried out from Bombay, Karachi and Calcutta.

Almost all the old Indian Army, which still included some 4,500 British officers out of an original 9,000, had been split between India and Pakistan. Some two and a half divisions remained to form the Punjab Frontier Force, and with the British troops they were all that was left under the command of Field Marshal Auchinleck, who had been appointed military overlord with the title Supreme Commander. This Punjab Frontier Force had the purely transitional function of preserving order during the settlement of the boundary line. It proved to be an appalling task for an expiring army. The civil war had slid in early August into a horrific affair of massed flights and of massed killings, of which some were conducted as sadistic ceremonial orgies, others with numb, callous indifference. The police were worse than useless; they were often seen helping the killers. For six weeks the slaughter lasted, over an area 500 miles from north to south, with people (in Pandit Nehru's words) gone completely mad and behaving like wild animals. The troops saved countless lives by resolute and tireless interventions, but eventually, inevitably the impartiality, particularly of the officers, was strained too far by the sight, and even more the reports, of the hideous things done to their own people. The British officers, of whom at least ten are reported to have been killed, were far too sparsely spread and too exhausted to prevent the cracks that appeared from widening towards cleavage. On September 2 this sad remnant of the old Indian Army was withdrawn and the force disbanded. Its officers and men had been asked too much, and it was not their fault that the last battle ended in defeat.

If the British Army, instead of being withdrawn, had been assigned a peacekeeping role in the Punjab, at least until the time limit prescribed by Attlee, June 1948, it could have performed a task in life-saving of which the extent could never have been assessed, far less recognised. But the policy was swift disengagement, regardless of the zone, and instead of performing this last service for India, the British troops busied themselves with preparations for their departure, leaving the Punjab Force to endure its agony alone. However, there were a number of occasions when they were able to prevent panic merely by their presence, and in the Punjab there were some exciting interventions as convoys drove through to collect families and other assortments from Kashmir. The Black Watch used their pipers to revive spirits numbed by demoralisation, and by this method a layer of supine humanity, which was blocking the railway line at Lahore station, was restored to animation and brought to its feet.

As the remnant of the old Indian Army fell apart in anguish, there was anguish too in the small portion of it transferred to British service. The ten regiments of the Brigade of Gurkhas had for long been beset with doubt about their future, and not until August 8, after Montgomery had come to India to discuss the matter, was it announced that six of them would be joining the new Indian Army and the remaining four the British. As in the reduction of the British Army, the location of battalions appears to have been a crucial factor—and in this instance a shrewd one —in the choice. One of the oldest regiments, the 2nd King Edward VII's Own, was among the British four. The others were the 6th, the 7th, and the 10th, and each had a battalion in Burma. The transfer was not officially made until January 1, 1948, and for the battalions in India there was a hard interim.

The split itself was one cause of anguish for this tight-knit band of mercenaries from Nepal, who had never before served under Indian officers. Another was the 'opt', the clause under which every individual, regardless of regiment, had to declare his preference for British or Indian service. This led to some intimidating and shameless electioneering by Indians within the battalions earmarked for British service, and the men were more vulnerable to it than they should have been, because most of the regular British officers had been posted to other arms, such as the R.A., R.A.S.C. or R.A.O.C., leaving few except young wartime commissioned officers with the battalions. They could do little to combat the wiles of agitators who preyed on the superstitions of the simple Gurkhas or the bludgeon tactics of Indian brigadiers and suchlike who sought to browbeat Gurkha officers into voting for their side. It was a sad state of affairs in a brigade renowned for the happy relationship between officers and men, and it brought one battalion to the point of mutiny. All the British ones left in India shrank sadly as a result of the opt, and the men that remained could not even obtain a new pair of socks.

On November 30 the Supreme Commander, Field Marshal Auchinleck, was forced into retirement by political pressure, and the 1st Royal Scots Fusiliers provided the guard of honour for that sad event, his departure from Delhi. They then departed themselves, completing the evacuation of the capital city.

1948 was to yield a harvest of evacuations, and the first of them was made by the 2nd Royal Berkshire from Burma on January 3. Burma's right to independence had long been conceded by the British Government, and although politicians had been shot dead during the advance to it, the British Army's role had been less onerous than in India. There had, however, been plenty of guard duties, discomfort and frustration. The Royal Berkshires departed quietly, on the day before independence, without ceremony and without message of tribute, even for the part they had played in freeing Burma from the Japanese. They left the three British Gurkha battalions behind, awaiting shipment to Malaya.

All that now remained of the old Army in India was a brigade in new India and a battalion in Pakistan; there was some uncertainty as to which would be the last to leave. In the event the 2nd Black Watch in Pakistan narrowly missed this honour, having bade farewell to their brigaded colleagues, the 1st Royal Scots and the 14th Field Regiment. They embarked at Karachi on February 26, having marched ceremonially into the city with pipes skirling and colours flying. The crowd was so huge that the police had great difficulty in clearing a passage for the battalion, and every window was crammed with waving figures. Many bemedalled old Musselmans were observed standing rigidly to attention as the colours passed. At Government House the battalion formed line—a short line, for its strength had dwindled pending disbandment—and accorded the Governor-General, Mohammed Jinnah, a royal salute. The latter expressed his thanks and best wishes in a brief speech.

There was further ceremony at the docks, where massed bands and a guard of honour, drawn from four battalions of Baluchis and Punjabis, were waiting. Touching tribute was paid by Major-General Mohammed Akbar Khan, who said that in thirty-five years' service he had 'come to know and to honour the sterling qualities of British soldiers and of the British nation as a whole. Your departure breaks an old association of friendship and comradeship.' The Begum Akbar Khan then garlanded the Commanding Officer and R.S.M. and the colours of the Black Watch were marched in slow time up the gangway of the ship, while the soldiers of all contingents stood at the present. Two days passed before the ship left harbour, after sad, grave farewells by the bearers.

At Bombay it fell to the 1st Somerset Light Infantry, after the departure of the 1st South Staffordshire and the 1st Essex, to perform the final rites. At 9 a.m. on February 28 they arrived with their colours in front of the Gateway of India, accompanied by a detachment of the Royal Military Police. Five guards of honour, provided by the Royal Indian Navy, the Bombay Grenadiers, Mahrattas, Sikhs, and Gurkhas, were drawn up to receive them with colours flying and music by the Royal Bombay Engineers. After an exchange of salutes and messages, the Somersets trooped their colours through the Gateway of India and embarked in launches to be taken out to H.M.T. *Empress of Australia*. General Whistler was the last to leave and all the way to the troopship he stood in the stern of his launch, motionless at the salute. From the quay, the compliment was returned by the Governor of Bombay and the G.O.C. Southern Command, representing new India.

It was in 1754 that two companies of the 39th Foot landed at Madras to earn the motto 'Primus in Indis' for eventual retention by the Dorset Regiment. Now the Somersets could claim to be 'Ultimus ex Indis' and they had achieved the distinction in a manner that reflected credit both on themselves and the British Army as a whole. It was something to have left this turbulent great land with precision and dignity; what was even more pleasing was the palpable sincerity of the honours accorded both the Somersets and the Black Watch by the new national armies they left behind. Here at least were twin elements of India and Pakistan bound by kindred ties that could, ironically, act as a curb on hot-headed belligerence.

The pangs of nostalgia felt at the ending of an era were apt to blur the more recent past. In most people's minds India was the land of Kipling, of the Durbar, and of Frontier wars, and so it would remain. Yet for the British Army the severest test, at least since the Mutiny, came in these final years of upheaval. A distinguished Gurkha officer, Lieutenant-General Sir Francis Tuker, had ample opportunity to test the quality of British troops when G.O.C.-in-C. Eastern Command, which included Calcutta. In his book *While Memory Serves* he praises the keenness, humour, and common sense of the youths who formed so large a part of the British battalions, and he gives honourable mention too to a corps that played a key, but seldom publicised, part, the Royal Military Police. In his opinion, 'Master Thomas's last appearance in India—and we must not forget his officers—has been quite the most successful of a long and chequered career of good-natured sinning and unwitting *faux pas*. The Indian is still fond of him, though his leaders would have been loath to admit it.'

3

Palestine

1—ROOTS (1917-45)

OF all burdens cast on soldiers by politicians surely none ever
chafed so painfully as that which grew out of the Balfour Declaration of November 1917, wherein the British Government expressed
favour for 'the establishment in Palestine of a National Home for the
Jews.' Palestine was at the time still under the dominion of the Turks.
It contained 600,000 Arabs and only 55,000 Jews, and there were
Arabs fighting on the British side and under British instigation to gain
independence. However, the League of Nations accepted the British
proposal after the war and entrusted Britain with the Mandate for
Palestine with the object of establishing this national home for the Jews.
It acknowledged the right of Jews to be consulted over matters of
government and ordered Jewish immigration to be given every facility.
No specific mention was made of the Arabs, their civil and religious
rights merely being recognised with those of other non-Jewish communities as if they formed a minority.

Not surprisingly the Arabs felt betrayed. They gave display of their
anger from 1920 onwards, and as the immigration of Jews gained
momentum from persecutions in Europe they were driven at length to
rebellion. It broke out in 1936, under the military leadership of
Fawzi Kawukji.

The Royal Air Force had, under the Trenchard scheme, assumed
responsibility for the security of Palestine, assisted by two battalions of
infantry. The Army now took over. Lieutenant-General Dill was
despatched from his Aldershot Command, with the 1st Infantry Division, and by the end of 1936 the rebellion had apparently been crushed
and the troops were homewards bound. The calm proved deceptive.
Rebellion broke out again, and large tracts of the Carmel and Judaean

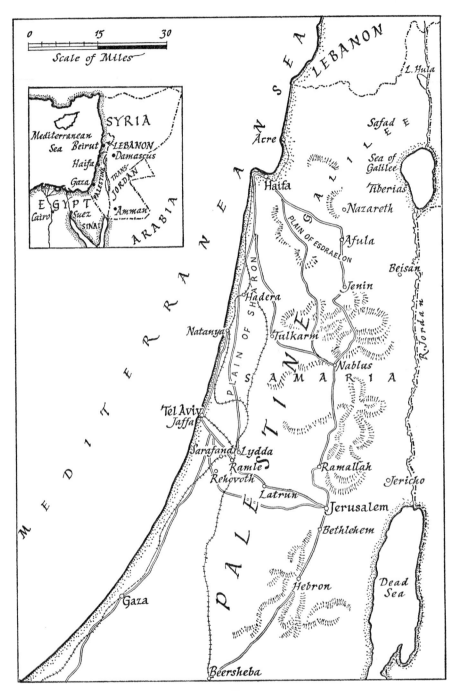

hills were in rebel hands before the army were called upon to make another large effort. By the end of 1938 the whole of Palestine had been placed under military control and the security force had swollen to seventeen battalions, drawn mainly from Egypt and India. They gradually gained the mastery over the rebels, thanks largely to some extensive road-building into the hills. Casualties were high. In 1938 alone 1,138 rebels were killed and they in turn killed 486 loyal Arabs, 292 Jews, and 69 policemen and soldiers.

While they were being defeated in the field, the Arabs won political success. In March 1939 the British Government issued a statement of policy, the famous 1939 White Paper. In violation of the terms of the mandate it restricted Jewish immigration to 75,000 over the next five years, after which there was to be no more without the consent of the Arabs—and that of course meant no more. The Jews were now the ones with the grievance, and the Arabs had shown what could be achieved by violence. Both these people had for centuries submitted to persecution as if it were their ordained lot. The intransigence and fury they displayed in rivalry came as a bewildering, if understandable, surprise for the British Government.

Since the earliest days of the mandate the Jews had had their people's army, the Hagana. It had the sanction of the British Administration but was not permitted weapons more lethal than shotguns, even when the Arabs began attacking Jewish settlements. A regular, illicitly armed spearhead was therefore formed, named the Palmach, and it was fashioned into a formidable instrument for night raiding under the tuition of an officer of the British Army, Captain Orde Wingate. From it there emerged a dissident, more violently minded group, the Irgun (or in full the Irgun Zvai Leumi), which carried the attack to British as well as Arab targets following the execution of a youth, Ben Yussef, merely for illegal firing. Operations were suspended when war began against the greatest of persecutors of the Jews, except by one further splinter group that disagreed with this policy, the Stern Gang. Most Jews cooperated with the British war effort, while chafing against the menial nature of the military employment offered them and making best use of many admirable opportunities to build up their stocks of arms and ammunition for the great fight that was to follow the liberation of Europe. Even before its full achievement the Irgun resumed operations with a few murderous attacks.

That the British Government regarded security as the paramount problem in Palestine was demonstrated by the appointment in 1944 of Field Marshal Viscount Gort as High Commissioner. However, he ruled as a civilian, not as a soldier, although vested with control of the armed forces as part of his normal duties. The seat of government was at Jerusalem, where the past always seemed to intrude upon the present, and just outside the city walls, near Government House, was the massive King David Hotel, which housed part of the government secretariat and Headquarters British Troops Palestine and Transjordan. Lieutenant-General J. C. D'Arcy was G.O.C.

Security was no great concern of the British troops when war ended. The Palestine Police was a powerful semi-military force, with stations organised as frontier forts, and it now formed a new department, the Police Mobile Force. Arabs and Jews served in it together under British officers of whom a large number had been in the service since its inception after the First World War; recruiting posed a problem, both of officers and men. Various colonial troops had been employed on guard duties as a wartime contribution, and of them the Transjordan Frontier Force would remain available both in a static and mobile role. The same applied to the Arab Legion, the British-officered force owing allegiance to King Abdulla of Transjordan, whose kingdom was well advanced on the road to independence from the confines of its mandate.

The 1st Infantry Division had by an odd coincidence returned to Palestine early in 1945, for a period of recuperation from Italy, and they were the only British fighting troops there when the war ended. Their first task was to intervene in Syria and the Lebanon, where violence flared between departing French troops and emergent nationalists. It was a delicate task, and was successfully achieved, bringing the division back by the end of July. In August the World Zionist Congress was held in London, and a resolution was passed demanding that Palestine be immediately established not just as a national home but as a Jewish state. It was obvious enough that Jews the world over were in truculent mood, their claims boosted by the horror revealed in the captured concentration camps.

There is no indication that the British military command as yet anticipated the wrath to come. True, the 6th Airborne Division arrived from Germany in the early autumn to occupy camps in southern Palestine, but they had the role of strategic reserve, and Palestine had the key function in the overall plan of housing this all-important reserve. It was contrary to the terms of the mandate that the country should be used for this purpose, and it rasped the nationalist instinct of the Jews to see their home used for the imperialist ends of their guardian. As a distant project, it was planned to build barracks, and as negotiations for the evacuation of Egypt progressed, so did the project for the development of Palestine mature, impervious to the mounting Jewish rage. In the meantime the brigades of 6th Airborne—the 2nd and 3rd Parachute and the 6th Airlanding—eked what comfort they could from their tented camps in the glaring Sharon Plain between Gaza and Tel Aviv. The 1st Division overlapped them astride the rugged hills to the east and were spread as far northwards as Haifa, around which the newly arrived 1st Guards Brigade could enjoy the beauty and grandeur of the Esdraelon Plain and its adjacent hills, a pleasant part even in the heat of summer and the chill of winter. There was no shortage of troops in this little land, of some 220 miles long and 62 broad, thanks to its suitability as a training ground for the Middle East reserve.

The Jews opened their offensive on the night of October 31 with an impressive crash of explosions that rocked the country from end to end. 153 breaches were blown in the railway line—out of 240 attempted— three police launches were sunk, Lydda station and goods yard were badly damaged, and some damage was done to the oil refinery at Haifa. The people's army, Hagana, and the rival commando groups, the Irgun and the Stern Gang, all claimed their different triumphs. They killed one soldier in the raids, one policeman, and two railway workers; but life had not been the objective.

Even more alarming than the damage, which caused a two-day blockage of the main line, were the difficulties encountered in the subsequent searches. Police and troops spent the hours from midnight onwards dashing around the countryside in hope of an interception. Only one capture was made. Later in the morning a police party, following a trail with tracker dogs, obtained daunting experience of the strength and width of the organisation. As they approached a Jewish village settlement, its school bells were rung and the inhabitants turned out in force to foil the scent and crowd the policemen into retreat. In marked contrast with the Arabs in the days of their rebellion, unity was the mightiest weapon wielded by the Jews.

The explosive demonstration had been timed to influence the policy statement the British Government were known to be preparing. It was issued by the Foreign Secretary, Ernest Bevin, on November 13, and whereas the 1939 White Paper had revoked the terms of the mandate, the

White Paper was now in turn revoked. The immigration of Jews was to be continued at the rate of 1,500 a year, which was a mere particle of the homeless unfortunates in Europe whose illegal shipment to Palestine was being condoned by countries not at all keen to support them. Both Jews and Arabs were angered, an inevitable result of any attempt at compromise. They had little faith in the Anglo-American Committee of Enquiry whose appointment was announced as part of the statement in hope of reaching a more durable solution.

Poor Gort had for some time been in the throes of a mortal illness, and he was succeeded, soon after the statement, by General Sir Alan Cunningham, whose war career had soared in Abyssinia and crashed in the Western Desert. He had the difficult task of enforcing the policy laid down by the Foreign Office while being directly responsible to the department concerned with the often conflicting matters of internal government, the Colonial Office. He was quick to make acquaintance with a remarkable phenomenon (as he himself termed it) of which it was hard to convince his masters in London: that the Jews and Arabs ignored each other's very existence.

The Jews lost no time in making protest against Bevin's statement, and in a manner more characteristic of Arabs. They broke into rioting in Jerusalem and in the city they had built themselves, Tel Aviv. It was soon brought under control in Jerusalem. In Tel Aviv the mob became increasingly violent, ransacking British shops, stoning vehicles and finally setting fire to the District offices. Only now, as darkness was falling (on November 14), were the military called in to the aid of the police, who had made some spirited charges with their batons but were now near the point of being overwhelmed.

C Company, 8th Parachute Battalion had been standing by in nearby barracks all day. Youthful veterans of European warfare, they were novices at the once familiar role of 'duties in aid' and had been training hard at it in recent weeks. They came in four uncovered 3-ton lorries, moving at 10 m.p.h. with horns blaring and the men displaying their bayonets and the signs with the message in three languages, 'DISPERSE OR WE FIRE'. The effect seemed magical. The crowd dissolved at speed and freed the gasping policemen from the pounding that had brought them almost to their knees in the main square. The soldiers leapt out to complete the clearance of the square and block the three roads leading into it, as a magistrate gave warnings by loud hailer. It was all achieved without hurt to either side.

Finding that the soldiers were coming no further after them, the youthful rioters recovered from the initial shock and began stoning them. Others continued the rampage around other parts of the town and set fire to the post office and other buildings. Lieutenant-Colonel G. Hewetson, commanding the 8th Para, at length called in his A and B Companies and set all three on the stern, deliberate tasks of clearing different streets. Their advances, in box formation, were violently contested here and there, and three shots had to be fired, one causing a fatal casualty, before defiance subsided—and they were fired with extreme reluctance, for men who had been fighting German soldiers shrank from shooting unarmed Jews. A curfew was imposed and broken next morning by a further outbreak of rioting and arson, which caused a few more shots to be fired. The equivalent of four more battalions of the Airborne were brought in and imposed a rigid curfew for four nights. There was no further show of defiance, either during the curfew hours or by day, and at dawn on the 20th the soldiers departed, leaving the citizens of Tel Aviv to their thoughts.

It is proof of the success of this operation that the Jews did not again resort to mass violence as a means of protest. None the less their fanaticism could never be quenched, as was shown near the end of November when searches were made for some armed men who had attacked two coastguard stations. They were tracked to two austere villages, 15 miles apart, and cordons were thrown, by the 1st Loyals and 2nd North Staffordshire, of 2nd Infantry Brigade, round the one and by the 8th Para round the other. When the police entered to carry out the search, they were fought with clubs and stones, and the troops had to contend with vast throngs from other villages, who tried to rush the cordons from within and without. The sequence was becoming familiar. Shots had to be fired, more troops rushed to the scene, and finally the soldiers had to take over the task of removing the villagers to cages for screening by the police. This involved lifting them, for resistance turned from active to passive on the intervention of the military. Eleven battalions became engaged and six Jews were killed—including a zealot who led a massed surge from horseback against a platoon of paratroops—before the task was done, with the removal of 150 suspects.

As was apt to happen to reserves in the Middle East, the 6th Airborne had become fully tied to the security of the region they occupied. Indeed, there was an urgent need for more reserves, and the 3rd Infantry Division were consequently rushed out from Germany. Their first task was to relieve the 1st, who were suffering from manpower problems brought about by demobilisation, and to this end the 185th Brigade, who were to be redesignated the 7th, came out in November and took over Jerusalem, of which the garrison always came directly under Force H.Q. The remainder of the division arrived in December and enabled the 1st to retire to Egypt for reorganisation, leaving behind the 1st Guards Brigade under the 3rd Division and four territorial battalions on static garrison duty.

Boxing Day was chosen for the next big effort by the Jews. Simultaneous nocturnal attacks were made, with varying success, at Jerusalem, Jaffa, Tel Aviv, and Lydda, with police stations and a R.E.M.E. armoury among the targets. There was then a pause until February when a series of blows was struck between the 20th and 26th. The last of them fell on three R.A.F. aerodromes, where the planes were dispersed in accordance with wartime custom. Seven were destroyed and eight damaged in a highly successful feat of sabotage, most being transport aircraft of the Airborne, and the raiders lost only one man.

They had less success at Sarafand on March 6, when they attacked the camp of the 3rd King's Own Hussars, who had taken part in the Syrian intervention with the 1st Division and had now joined 6th Airborne. The raiders came during the lunch break, disguised as British paratroops and riding in a stolen army truck. Amazingly, the gate was guarded only by Jewish policemen, who were surprised, overpowered, and in once case shot dead. The truck went to the ammunition tent, where an officer and some sentries were made prisoner. But the alarm was raised, and the raiders had to dash off with the truck half full and bullets pinging into and around it. They entrusted their prisoners to a time bomb, which mercifully destroyed nothing but the tent. The signals officer, Captain Barrow, rushed to the gate to intercept the truck. He physically overpowered one of the gangsters left there on guard, but had nothing with which to counter the fire directed at him and had to take cover. However, the truck had been badly damaged and some of its occupants hit, and it was later captured with two of the latter inside it. Apart from the Jewish policeman, the only casualty on the British side was the Y.M.C.A. canteen lady, one of a little band that throughout the campaign acted as a great prop to the troops' morale. She received a nasty wound from a bullet.

This raid was made on the arrival date of the Anglo-American committee of inquiry, and if the Jews sought to impress its members by a show of force, it was clearly the policy of the Administration to deny the Jews evidence of provocation or of oppressive treatment. Visibly, the police were in control, and the soldiers kept out of sight as far as they could, refraining from marching or driving through a town if there were any alternative. Off duty, soldiers still walked out unarmed, and in general they looked less warlike than the police. There was determination to avoid display of the type of militarism under which so many of the newly settled Jews had smarted.

There was in fact nothing very much the soldiers could do without information, and the supply of this desperately scarce commodity was primarily the responsibility of the police. Although on a looser basis than would be evolved in subsequent campaigns, military commanders at all levels kept in close touch with the police, waiting to hear how they could help, and the police for their part were conscious of the need to free as many troops as possible from the deadening burden of guard duties so that powerful columns could be kept at readiness for swift intervention. To achieve this the Supplementary Branch, supplying armed police guards, was raised, although without ever attaining the strength of 7,000 intended. Most of the men enlisted were Arabs, whose loyalty was subject to less strain than Jews.

The first big test for these hastily trained men came on the night of April 2, when further attacks were made on railway installations. One post was overpowered, but another held out and seriously hampered the plans of a gang over thirty strong. Rushed to the scene, some paratroops lost two vehicles and three men wounded by mines laid by the raiders to prevent interception—a common ploy—and others had difficulty in stopping the fire directed at them from every police post along the line. In the morning, thanks to some tracker work by dogs and the services of an observation plane, a section of the 8th Para had the rare experience of catching a gangster group in the open. It consisted of twenty-four members of the Irgun, lavishly armed with automatic weapons but wearied by their long journey back to base. Although outnumbered by three to one, the paratroops opened fire and inflicted such loss that the entire gang capitulated almost without a fight.

Shortly after this heartening success the 1st Division returned and relieved the 3rd, who themselves went to Egypt. The 1st were commanded now by the man who had led the 6th Airborne into Normandy, Major-General R. N. Gale. Most of his troops were the old originals of the 1st Division, others having come from Europe. The battalions had restocked with men, although it could only be a temporary replenishment in these difficult days when demobilisation was turning corporals into sergeant-majors overnight. Gale took over the northern sector, where one of his foremost tasks was to watch the coastline for the streams of pathetic human flotsam attempting illicit entry. His foremost aim was to establish sufficient trust in the minds of the Jewish authorities, in particular at Haifa, to enable guard commitments to be reduced. It was easier to achieve such a reduction in this part of Palestine, and he had considerable success.

The 6th Airborne received reinforcement in the form of the 1st Parachute Brigade, which thus joined the 2nd and 3rd. The Airlanding

Brigade was consequently removed from the division and sent to relieve the 7th Infantry at Jerusalem, where it was renamed the 31st Independent Infantry Brigade and lost its red berets, a sad wrench for the veterans of the 2nd Oxfordshire and Buckinghamshire Light Infantry, the 1st Royal Ulster Rifles, and the 1st Argyll and Sutherland Highlanders.

Taking advantage of the British reluctance to disrupt the normal flow of life, the Stern Gang struck a savage blow on April 25, no doubt as revenge for the previous setback. Liberty trucks still brought their loads of intending revellers to Tel Aviv. They were parked near the sea front under the protection of a guard of eight men, who when not on sentry occupied some tents that were overlooked by houses on three sides. Just after dark on the 25th the gangsters quietly entered one of these houses and held up its occupants. The men of the 5th Para on guard had no cause to know of this until automatic fire slashed at them from an upper window and a bomb landed in one of the tents. Next moment the gangsters were inside the tent, shooting at everyone until they raced off again with a haul of arms. Seven soldiers lay dead or dying. For the first time the word outrage acquired true meaning, and so outraged were some comrades of the dead that they indulged in their own private, but far from lethal, reprisal on a Jewish settlement. For this they were punished. There was no punishment for any Jew in Tel Aviv, except a brief curfew and a formal rebuke for the Mayor on his and his people's silence. It was delivered by Major-General A. J. H. Cassels, who had command of the division while Major-General E. J. Bols did a year's course at the Imperial Defence College.

On May 1 the recommendations of the Anglo-American committee were published. They included the admission of 100,000 Jews to Palestine and the ultimate establishment of a neutral form of government. There was a pause in violence while the Jews deliberated, and it conveniently coincided with the passing of the command of the troops from D'Arcy to Lieutenant-General Sir Evelyn Barker, who had held command, first of a division and then of a corps, from Normandy to Germany. A strong character, forthright and caustic, Barker had been awarded the nickname of 'Bubbles' when a newly joined subaltern in the K.R.R.C. It had stuck, in the clubby manner of the army, and was typically inappropriate.

The calm did not last long, and the G.O.C. was personally involved in the latest and most stormy point of contention, the fate of two men sentenced to death for their part in the raid on the 3rd Hussars' camp— for offenders against the Defence Emergency Regulations were tried by court martial, as had been the case before the war, and although the

High Commissioner had power of pardon and therefore of consent, the official onus of confirmation rested on the G.O.C. On June 16, three days after sentence had been passed, the Hagana did their best to destroy nine bridges, one with a time bomb that killed an R.E. officer, and on the 18th the Irgun brought off a more dramatic coup, the kidnapping of five British officers, of whom three were of the 6th Airborne, one of the R.E.M.E. and one of the R.A.F. It was made possible by the continued ban on the carrying of arms. The officers were having lunch in the officers' club, Tel Aviv, and the raiders merely burst in and dragged them away. Two were released after four days in shackles. The fate of the others, it was announced in a Kol Israel broadcast, depended on that of the two gangsters in the death cell.

Field Marshal Montgomery made a visit as C.I.G.S. at this time, meeting Barker at Lydda airport in company with the C.-in-C. Middle East, General Sir Bernard Paget. Much concerned by the indecision he saw emanating from Whitehall, he told Barker he must not be deterred from his duty by the threats to murder the officers, and according to his Memoirs, 'This did a good deal to strengthen his resolve.' But the iron hand was never as easy to apply as it appeared to Montgomery, and Barker commuted the death sentences to life imprisonment. The kidnapped officers were duly released. They were chloroformed by their captors and found themselves in coffins when they came round. They broke out and discovered they were in the streets of Tel Aviv, completely ignored by passers-by. This was common treatment from the people of Tel Aviv, even for a soldier bleeding to death. It was as though witnessing the results of a crime was tantamount to witnessing the crime itself, a thing no Jew would ever dare do.

Since so little cooperation in the search for gangsters was forthcoming, it was decided that a massed search of all organisations must be made, including that of the Jewish Agency, the official branch through which the promised establishment of the national home was to be made. At the same time a long list was prepared of suspects who were to be arrested. The operation was called Agatha, and it involved practically every army unit. It was carefully planned; there were no reconnaissances, and order groups were disguised as informal gatherings of officers lower in seniority than was the case. On Friday June 28 there was a lavish display of generals and brigadiers at Jerusalem Horse Show. Around 4 next morning members of the Royal Corps of Signals entered various telephone exchanges all over Palestine, placed their staffs under guard as courteously as possible, and obstructed all calls. Troops meanwhile were climbing out of lorries to march to their cordon stations, while in Jerusalem, Haifa, and Tel Aviv others quietly accompanied policemen in making entry into the houses of the people on the arrest list. Complete surprise was achieved.

The only opposition encountered came, as usual, from the village settlements or kibbutzes, those harsh clusters of austere buildings whose inhabitants seemed as dedicated to hatred as they were to work. There were some desperate scuffles to break cordon, resist arrest, or prevent entry to some secret store. Shots had to be fired at times, but certainly in the case of 6th Airborne, who were astride the heart of the resistance movement, no casualties were caused by bullets; it had been found that warning shots fired in the air, in violation of old principles, could be effective. Children presented the most trying problem of all. They were stirred to fury by their parents and often formed a protective screen in front of them, spitting at the troops and chanting venomous songs. Their removal by force was an embarrassing task, unleavened by the remotest flicker of humour on the part of those who had to be man-handled. Yells of 'Gestapo!' pierced the air, and however ludicrous the soldiers made the description appear, the Jews were determined to try every trick to make it fit.

2,718 persons were arrested as a result of this great swoop, and among them was Mr. Ben Gurion (who was soon released) and other leading members of the Jewish Agency, where many incriminating documents were found. On the heels of this blow to the political leadership came one at their recognised army, the Hagana. It stemmed from a small, chance discovery of arms in a village near Haifa. The 2nd Cheshire thereupon began a more thorough search. With the aid of mine detectors and by dint of sheer perseverance, thirty-three caches were unearthed from beneath the ground or in recesses in such buildings as nurseries and cowsheds. They contained close on 600 weapons, including brens and mortars, half a million rounds of ammunition, and a quarter of a ton of explosive.

Representatives of units in all parts of Palestine were brought to see the manner in which these arms had been concealed, and there was good prospect now of reducing the whole of Hagana to impotence. But the Irgun, with the professionalism gleaned from their experience of fighting the real Gestapo, were too skilled in the art of security to be seriously smitten by Agatha, and as if to prove it they staged the most resounding blow of all. They blew up the King David Hotel.

The deed was done on Monday, July 22, soon after noon. Either through complacency, or as part of the deliberate policy of playing down the emergency, the hotel still functioned as such, although most of its rooms were occupied as government or military offices. This made it easier to gain entrance and no great notice was taken of the workmen dressed as Arabs who unloaded several milk churns from a lorry and took them through the kitchen of the hotel's Regency Café into the basement. An officer who enquired their purpose was shot. A policeman who came to his aid was also shot; neither lived. A gun battle now began outside the hotel between the gangsters' covering party and some odd policemen and soldiers. The gangsters made their getaway after letting off a smoke bomb, leaving one dead and one wounded behind them. Warning soon arrived by telephone, through an accomplice of the gangsters, that the hotel should be evacuated. Nothing was done about it for fifteen minutes, by which time it was too late. It was a gigantic explosion. The hotel is a square, seven-storeyed building, and about a quarter of it, at one corner, was demolished. It contained the government secretariat. The military occupied a different part of the building, and among those sitting in their offices, rocked by the explosion, was General Barker.

The 9th Airborne Squadron, R.E., were summoned at once, and for days they toiled at the removal of the rubble, working on a shift system that allowed only eight hours' rest out of every twenty-four. They retrieved six survivors and ninety-one corpses, a number of the latter being of Jews.

The 31st Brigade threw a cordon and conducted a search with all possible speed, but they could do no more than arrest suspects for questioning. There was evidence enough to show, as was indeed the case, that the raid had been planned in Tel Aviv, and although this was a city of 170,000 inhabitants, nearly all Jewish, it was decided to seal the city, search every house, and screen every inhabitant. The operation was named Shark and was more ambitious than Agatha, for not only did the population have to be marshalled without warning, but such essential services as the provision of food, the removal of rubbish, and the care of the sick would have to be maintained by military means for at least four days. The conducting role was entrusted to 6th Airborne, taking such other troops under command as brought the total engaged to sixteen infantry battalions, three armoured and two artillery regiments, two field squadrons, a field ambulance, and a supplemented divisional column of the R.A.S.C. and Military Police; certainly the principle of concentration of force was observed. Tuesday, July 30, was picked as D Day, eight days after the terrible explosion.

It was of course an advantage that the sea flanked one side of the $3\frac{1}{2}$ miles of flats and houses that was Tel Aviv, and police and naval launches kept this flank under close watch. Approaching by converging routes, the brigades laid the outer cordon in darkness, and we learn from the Irgun commander, Menachem Begin, that he and his colleagues were caught inside it, having received no intimation of this massive assembly of troops. As dawn broke some troops paraded the streets to announce and enforce a curfew, while others took up position to form inner cordon rings, slicing the city into segments between which there could be no communication. Then the mammoth task of search and clearance began. Street by street, officer parties made entrance into each house, assembled the occupants in one room, checked their identity cards, and then searched every part of the house, accompanied, except in case of absolute refusal, by the householder. All except the very old and the very young were then taken to battalion headquarters for screening. For anyone arousing suspicion—as did those dressed as rabbis and the apparently disabled—there was a further journey to brigade headquarters. Here members of the Criminal Investigation Department, many of them newly arrived from England, made the final selections for despatch to the detention camp at Rafah. It was a laborious business.

The search lasted for three and a half days and was marked by an absence of the bitter and violent resistance encountered in the kibbutzes during operation Agatha. 787 people were removed to detention and five arms dumps were discovered, of which the largest was in the basement of the Great Synagogue. There was no breakdown of the supply and health services, and indeed no incident bringing disrepute on the troops. General Cassels had good cause to congratulate his men on the accomplishment of 'a long, difficult and laborious task involving great tolerance and cheerfulness on the part of everybody concerned.' But Begin had safely preserved his freedom by lying up in a secret cranny, and he claims to have lost only two high-ranking assistants, one of whom was detected beneath the disguise of a rabbi. The most wanted men had saved themselves because the emphasis had been on good manners, not on ruthlessness.

There were signs that the King David Hotel tragedy had caused genuine disgust against the terrorist groups within the Jewish movement. Indeed, Ben Gurion went as far as saying, 'The Irgun is the enemy of the people,' in an interview with a French journalist. It was the eternal hope of the British Administration that such expressions of censure should be turned to cooperation in the hunt for these alleged enemies of the people, and consequently the drive against Hagana, which had caused deep depression within the Jewish movement, was called off. Among the last finds made was one of fifty powerful weapons hidden deep below a henhouse, and the clue came from a police gundog after mine detectors had failed to react. It was frustrating for the security forces to be halted when such good progress was being made, but probably there was little to be gained from going on, for the fear of losing stocks of weapons that might be needed for a war of survival kept Hagana quiet from now onwards.

A further gesture was made in early November, following an unusually long lull. The release was ordered of a large number of the Jewish leaders who had been arrested during operation Agatha and had since been held in a camp at Latrun, where the 3rd Parachute Brigade had recently been called in to restore order out of what had become virtual anarchy, with even the identity of some of the prisoners unknown to the jailers. To many soldiers, from Montgomery downwards, the freeing of these men seemed a foolish act of weakness, and they could soon claim to be right, for before the end of November the Irgun and the Stern Gang together sprang to life again with some heavy assaults on that saboteur's sitting duck, the railway line. They achieved the derailment of several trains and spread such fear among the Arab engine drivers that the service had to be confined to daylight, with vast numbers of troops deployed on irksome protective duties. They also inflicted twenty-eight casualties, six of them mortal, in the course of three weeks. Two of the dead were sapper officers, killed trying to unravel anti-handling devices attached to mines.

Explosive was nectar to the erudite gangster, and now that he was finding as much joy in the crafty little explosion as in the mighty bang—turning as it were from gourmand to gourmet—perilous responsibility fell on the Royal Engineers, which was not shirked. There was a steady increase in the range of devilment concocted to fray the nerves and exhaust the patience of the occupying troops. The dumping of suitcases was one example, with inside them either a time bomb or a bomb primed to go off when the case was opened. Cars were used in a similar, if more grandiose, fashion, and being well equipped with stolen vehicles and uniforms, it was easy enough for the gangsters to place them in damaging positions without attracting much attention; alternatively the vehicle would be set in motion driverless at its target as a not very reliably guided missile. Then of course there were all sorts of refinements to be used as accompaniment to a simple road mine, and no sooner had the railway assaults subsided than there was a sudden increase of activity on the roads. As the troops became wary of booby traps so did the call for sappers expand—and it usually fell to an officer to neutralise the most wicked products on display.

There was a grim ending to this grim year of 1946. Just before Christmas a Jewish youth received eighteen strokes of the cane as part of a sentence passed on him as an armed member of an Irgun gang that bungled a raid on a bank at Jaffa. An officer—the brigade major of the

2nd Parachute Brigade—and three N.C.O.s were ambushed in different parts of the Tel Aviv district on the night of December 29. They were stripped, whipped, and left to be retrieved naked and almost dead.

Every soldier smarted under the sting of the blows. Forty-nine of them had been killed during the year and 122 wounded, while the police had lost twenty-eight killed and thirty-four wounded. Only twenty-five Jews were known to have been killed in action, and although death sentences had been passed on a further nineteen, not one had been carried out. Now came this humiliation. Yet reprisal could still not be traded for reprisal, and those few paratroopers who chose such a means to show the locals their sympathy for their brigade major encountered a chastening lack of sympathy when marched before their commanding officer. However, troops of the 1st Parachute Brigade were able to provide a consolation prize. They forced a car to a halt in the cordoning that followed the kidnappings, and in a battle with its occupants killed one and captured the other four. Several arms were also captured in this fight and two rawhide whips.

Changes of location afforded a means of upholding the morale of the troops. There were frequent movements within the command, including training visits to Transjordan, and there was also plenty of traffic between Palestine and Egypt. Thus the 9th Infantry Brigade came from the latter in December and relieved the disbanding 31st Brigade at Jerusalem. Between January 18 and 22, 1947, the 1st and 6th Airborne Divisions exchanged areas, and the whole of Palestine throbbed with the movement of troops, unimpeded by bombs or mines. The 6th Airborne lost the 2nd Para Brigade in transit, due for return to England. The inter-divisional boundary consequently shifted northwards, and the Gaza area was taken over by what remained of the moribund 3rd Division. From March this amounted only to their Royal Artillery, supplemented by the 61st Lorried Infantry Brigade, late of 1st Armoured Division.

The exchange of areas had the disadvantage, particularly at divisional and brigade headquarter level, that carefully cultivated relationships with the police and civil authorities had to be regrown. Indeed, it made General Gale 'sad and distressed', according to his *Call To Arms*—not because his 1st Division were the losers both in environment and the security situation, but because continuity was broken in the progress he was beginning to make at Haifa. However, the boredom of the troops was a compelling factor. They spent endless days on guard or stand-by duties, for ever surrounded by coils and coils of wire, and there were very few home comforts in their camps, no modern aids against the heat of summer and the winter winds and rain. It was a life of tedium and hardship haunted by a sense of bewilderment at the cold hatred displayed by so many Jews, a thing quite outside the experience of British soldiers. These were more pervasive influences than fear, which struck only rarely. It would arrive with a shudder and a bang and would lead, for the survivors, to that compound of sickness and anger sown by the sight of a comrade turned to human debris.

Excursions either for training, bathing, or operational duties provided the best antidote to brooding inside a wired-in camp, and there was full awareness of their need. Speed of turn-out was essential. Summonses for a search and cordon frequently came at short notice, keeping both staffs and troops alert, and it was not unknown for orders to be issued at 1 a.m., by a pyjama-clad brigadier, and for the troops to be deployed by dawn around a village 10 miles distant. The routine that followed was familiar enough, but the surroundings would probably be new, and there were usually fresh problems to be solved in the moving of the inhabitants to the screening cages prepared for them by the troops, with tentage provided for women and children. The outing would end with the troops themselves being searched in front of the village muktar, and they would then return to camp—with just time enough to prepare for evening guard mounting.

For the old wartime battalions of the 1st Division the routine was nearing its end. The 1st Duke of Wellington's and the 2nd King's Shropshire Light Infantry had left at the end of 1945; the 1/6th Queen's, 2/7th Middlesex, 6th Gordon Highlanders, and the 1st Hertfordshire—four territorial battalions—began to disperse in the autumn of 1946, and the 2nd Royal Scots left in December; the 2nd Sherwood Foresters, 1st Loyals, and 2nd North Staffordshire completed the dispersal in 1947. Of the arrivals from Europe, the 2nd Cheshire, 2nd East Surreys, and 1st Duke of Cornwall's Light Infantry left in the spring of 1947 after over a year in residence, and the 2nd East Yorkshire and 1st South Wales Borderers had earlier gone after shorter stays.

There was an adequate supply of armour. The 1st King's Dragoon Guards patrolled the northern and north-east frontiers from the end of the war until the early months of 1947, when they handed over to the 17th/21st Lancers; the 4th/7th Royal Dragoon Guards long provided tank support for the 1st Division and Jerusalem brigade; the 3rd Hussars provided tank support for the 6th Airborne and had two squadrons of armoured cars; the 12th Royal Lancers patrolled the centre of Palestine for a year between 1946 and 1947; the 9th Queen's Royal Lancers and the 8th Royal Tank Regiment filled a supporting role for shorter periods; and the 15th/19th King's Royal Hussars were in the southern sector until handing over to the Life Guards in April 1947. Thus harm seldom came to road convoys.

The British Government were at last coming round to the view, long held by every soldier, that sterner measures were needed in Palestine, and to provide the final push the Irgun kidnapped two British civilians on January 26. One of them was a judge, and they were held as hostages for a gangster, Dov Gruner, under sentence of death. They were in fact released, following the issue of a stay of execution to allow Gruner to appeal to the Privy Council, and in the meantime a step was taken that acknowledged that the whole of Palestine was a battle zone. British women and children were to be evacuated, together with anyone else not engaged on an essential task, and those civilians with jobs to be done were to be moved into 'fortresses', that is groups of houses segregated by requisition and afforded police or military guard. This involved the move of 1,500 civilians, of whom a few were army families, by road to Egypt: the great exodus in reverse. The task was entrusted to the army and completed without mishap by February 8, bringing many messages of appreciation which thrust a welcome shaft of good cheer across the sombre scene.

As the decks were now stripped for action, a new captain appeared on the bridge. Barker had become a special target for the hatred of the Jews, and its mainstream flowed from a letter he had sent his divisional commanders placing Jewish shops and suchlike out of bounds with the object of punishing the Jewish community as a whole for their failure to curb the terrorists 'by hitting them in the pocket'. The letter had a security grading, but there were Jewish civilians working as clerks at his headquarters and it was immediately released to the press. There was great outcry, not only from Jews in Palestine but also at Westminster, where M.P.s demanded Barker's dismissal. He was saved by Montgomery through use of that powerful political lever, the threat of his own resignation, and it was to promotion as G.O.C.-in-C. Eastern Command that Barker was returning home. He flew off to Egypt without announcement on February 12, and his last symbolic gesture of his feelings for Palestine was to urinate on its soil before stepping on his plane. The terrorists were to pursue him with their bombs by post, until long after the British had left their land.

His successor, the newly promoted Lieutenant-General G. H. A. MacMillan, late of the Argylls, met him at G.H.Q. Middle East, Fayid. A slim and soldierly figure, highly decorated in the First World War, he had commanded three divisions, in between wounds, in the advance through and beyond Normandy, one being the 49th, which he took over from Barker.

On February 14 Ernest Bevin virtually admitted defeat. He had had Arab and Jewish leaders in London for consultation and been unable to find point of contact between the two sides; they just did not respond to normal negotiating tactics. He therefore told the House of Commons that the Government had decided to refer the problem to the United Nations. It was as though the nurse, finding the child uncontrollable, had asked the step-parent—the United Nations in place of the dead League—for disposal instructions. The step-parent, in the fullness of time and with ponderous inevitability, appointed a fact-finding committee.

As if to show their contempt for the process of fact-finding, the Irgun struck another deadly blow in Jerusalem, blowing up the Goldsmith Officers' Club on March 1 and thus causing the death of thirteen people, with sixteen injured. In retaliation part of Jerusalem and the whole of Tel Aviv were placed under martial law, for which the softer term of 'controlled area' was introduced at governmental request. It was a punitive measure, bringing trade and even the postal and banking services to a standstill, and it naturally imposed an enormous administrative strain on the army. It lasted from March 2 to 17 and the soldiers were as glad as the inhabitants when it came to an end, particularly the brigades in residence: the 9th at Jerusalem, consisting of the 2nd Royal Lincolnshire, the 1st King's Own Scottish Borderers and the 2nd Royal Irish Fusiliers, and the 1st Guards at Tel Aviv, where the 3rd Coldstream were in permanent residence at Citrus House and the 3rd Grenadier and 1st Welsh Guards came in from Lydda and Sarafand. Practically every other unit of the 1st Division had a part to play, and certainly they impressed their commander, General Gale, with the patience, diligence, and humanity they displayed.

On April 16 Dov Gruner and three of the men captured by the paratroops after the floggings were hanged in Acre prison to become the first 'martyrs' of the Irgun, who in a broadcast declared the Army and Administration to be 'criminal organisations'. The Stern Gang forestalled them in reprisal by blowing up a Cairo-bound train, which caused thirty-five casualties, and by murdering the chief of Haifa's C.I.D. The turn of the Irgun came on May 4, and they could well be proud of the achievement. Midway through the afternoon they blew a hole in the mighty, ancient wall of Acre gaol and enabled 255 of its 623 inmates to escape, the great majority of them being Arabs.

The raiders came in British army vehicles and were dressed as British soldiers, and having done the deed they had bright prospect of making their escape, for there was no army camp within three miles. However, some men of the 1st Parachute Battalion were bathing nearby. They gave chase in their scout car and forced one gangster vehicle to crash near the beach, killing some of its load and scattering the rest. In the hunt for the latter Privates McCormack and Thorne saw some make off in another truck, and they at once commandeered a car from an Arab to give chase. They caught up with the truck. The gangsters turned off the road, leapt out amid some crops, and opened fire with a Bren gun. The privates stalked and slew the bren gunner, who was dressed as an R.A.S.C. captain, and turned his weapon on his comrades. They soon forced five of them into surrender with crippling fire and also re-captured three escaped Arab prisoners, and for this they each received the meagre award of the British Empire Medal. Although the troops were on active service, it was not yet the policy to grant martial awards.

In June the United Nations' fact-finders arrived. The Arabs boycotted them, the British troops were confined to their camps, and the Jewish gangster groups gave display of their devotion to death and destruction. An insight into the passion of the Jews was afforded the committeemen by the arrival at Haifa, on July 18, of a decrepit steamer laden with illegal immigrants, which had been intercepted and seized by the Royal Navy, with the death of three Jews in the boarding action. The army had to transfer these wretched waifs from their ship to three others and escort them back to Hamburg, a task assigned the 87th Airborne Field Regiment, whose main duties were concerned with illegal immigration. The aim of the Jews of course was to provoke the soldiers to brutality, and so hard did they try and so patiently was the attempt resisted that when at last the thwarted immigrants—some 4,500 in all—were delivered back on German soil a message for the troops arrived from the Foreign Secretary, Ernest Bevin, expressing his personal appreciation.

Meanwhile there was further furore over death sentences which had been passed on three Jews. Again the Irgun grabbed hostages, two sergeants of Field Security, Martin and Paice, neglecting to obey the rules for their personal security. The pleasant little town of Nathanya, where they were kidnapped, was invested by the 1st Division and for a fortnight the area was combed. But again the Irgun proved too skilled at the art of concealment. However, MacMillan was not deterred, and on July 29 the three Jews were executed. On the 31st the bodies of Martin and Paice were found hanging from an eucalyptus tree. There was a bang when an officer attempted the grim task of removal, and he fell seriously wounded by a booby trap. As culminating insult the Irgun placed notices claiming that the two sergeants had been tried and executed for being members of a 'criminal-terrorist organisation known as the British Army of Occupation, and not as a retaliatory act for the murder of Hebrew prisoners of war'.

There were the usual expressions of sympathy and disgust from officially recognised Jewish sources, and no doubt many were genuine. The British soldier knew their value, and he knew too that reprisal was the prerogative of the terrorist and that there could be no chance of fighting him at his own game. It is true that a handful of officers were employed on 'special duties', as they had been during the Arab rebellion, but that they had not the freedom to kill enjoyed within the gangster organisation was emphasised by a charge of murder against one of them, Captain Roy Farran. The charge had been made in June, on evidence of an abduction in May, and he was tried by court martial in Jerusalem, amid a glare of publicity, on October 1. His counsel gained him swift acquittal on the ground that no body had been found, but the mere fact of the court martial suggested that the army was turning to desperate methods in the attempt to counter the gangs, and this was not good. Farran left the country, and some months later his brother was killed by a bomb in a parcel addressed to him.

On September 26 came the first statement of the Government's intention, and it was a statement of unconditional surrender, made by the Colonial Secretary, Mr. Creech Jones, at the United Nations' debate on their committee's report, which advocated partition. Jones merely told the Assembly that his government would be giving up the Mandate and would not enforce any solution not acceptable to both Arabs and Jews. The bombs had done their work effectively, even if by the devious method of making the cost and political embarrassment of keeping order heavier than the Government were prepared to bear. There was general disbelief that the British really intended to act in this manner, and for the Jews, ironically, it was tinged with fear. The leaders of the Arab League had already pledged themselves to the extermination of any independent Jewish state.

IV—EVACUATION (1947-48)

The gangsters showed, only three days after the Colonial Secretary's statement, that they had no intention of allowing the British to depart in peace. Haifa police station was their target, and shattering damage was done by the release of an enormous bomb rolled down a ramp ingeniously fitted to a lorry. There were sixty-five police and civilian casualties, eleven of them mortal. Soon afterwards came reports that the Arab Liberation Army was beginning to assemble around the borders of Palestine. It was not going to be easy for the British to remove themselves with any dignity.

A sad, predictable result of the warning of surrender was a deterioration in the morale of the police. As Generals Barker and MacMillan both testify, it had until now been remarkably high, despite endemic recruiting problems and a costly tendency among the much enlarged British element to confuse bravery with bravado. Its Inspector-General, Colonel W. N. Gray, late the Royal Marines, had done much to improve its equipment and consequently its efficiency, and it provided the one exception to the rule that Jews and Arabs could not work together. But now that partition loomed the strain on loyalties became overpowering, and particularly in the case of the static Supplementary Police there would soon be desertions. Nevertheless an immense burden continued to be shouldered by the regular police, and with each withdrawal made by the soldiers, so did it increase in size and importance.

Among some widespread outbursts of gangsterism in November, the most disturbing smote Jerusalem on the 13th. Despite the Irgun's two great feats of destruction at the King David and the Goldsmith, Jerusalem had so far been comparatively quiet, and the swift fluctuation in the identity of its garrison—from the 7th Brigade to the 31st, the 9th, the 8th, and from the end of September the 2nd Brigade—was caused by the convulsions of an army in the throes of reduction, not by the heat of the task. Now at last its battalions were to remain until the end. The 2nd Royal Warwickshire, who had first come in November 1945 and had since had only one break from Palestine, shared the peripheral duties with the 1st Suffolk, and watch over the labyrinthal Old City, with its Arab and Jewish quarters side by side, was entrusted to the newly arrived 1st Highland Light Infantry, who were making their second visit, having served in 7 Brigade and since been in Egypt. They found Jerusalem a great improvement on the Canal Zone, while being

48

struck by the often observed contrast between the cheerful, cheeky, lazy friendliness encountered in the Arab quarter and the sullen, furtive tenseness found in the Jewish. Now on this grim November 13 the brooding erupted in a spate of bullets sprayed around a favourite haunt of the Jocks, the Ritz Café. One soldier of the H.L.I. was killed and fifteen wounded, and these were not the only casualties.

From now onwards Jerusalem resounded almost daily with the thud or crack of war. The Arabs became active participants after November 29, for it was on this day that the General Assembly of the United Nations, after much lobbying and postponment, passed a resolution in favour of partition, allotting over half Palestine to the Jews, although they comprised only a third of the population. This was a cause of great remorse and anger to the people of every Arab state, and in Palestine a three-day strike was called in protest. Inevitably the strike bubbled into violence, and it was at its fiercest in Jerusalem, where onslaughts were made on things and people Jewish and on the consulates of the nations that had voted for the partition plan. (Britain, in the manner of Pilate washing his hands, had abstained.)

The Jews, as was to be expected, retaliated three for one. Bomb explosions shook the Arab quarter in the Old City of Jerusalem and shots whistled from the gaunt houses of the Jewish quarter. The Arabs in turn slew such Jews as they could catch, and again the Jews retaliated three for one. The war of genocide had begun, and the troops would be kept at full stretch in keeping them apart.

Notice of the duration of this task came in a Government announcement in early December: the Mandate would be terminated on May 15, 1948, and the withdrawal of British troops completed by August 1. There could be no more disbelief, and this at least had the advantage for the British soldiers that the two rivals could now concentrate on their preparations for the war they had been licensed to wage without wasting their resources on attacks on peacekeepers who were scheduled to be leaving.

General MacMillan had of course been consulted about the withdrawal dates, and the reason such a late one had been fixed for the completion was that a vast residue of stores had accumulated, many of them through the frustrated intent of making Palestine a base. There were 210,000 tons of them, not counting unit equipment, and in addition 70,000 troops, 5,000 police, and a huge retinue of colonial administrators had to be evacuated either by land to Egypt or by sea from Haifa. The plan was to form an enclave at the latter port for the final evacuation and during the period of thinning out before the expiry of the mandate to concentrate on keeping the withdrawal routes open.

Both the divisions had new commanders for the final phase. That of the 6th Airborne was Major-General H. C. Stockwell, late of the Royal Welch Fusiliers, and he had held command since August. A lively, extrovert personality, he had already enlivened his division by going on a para jumping course, in company with some other senior officers who like him were not qualified to wear wings, and by making light of it on his return. More will be heard of him. The 1st Division passed at the end of the year to Major-General H. Murray, a Cameron High-lander by origin who, like his predecessor, Gale, and the two other generals in Palestine, would rise in due course to full rank.

Despite the tension, the most was made of the last Christmas to be spent by British troops in Palestine. Convoys hummed along the road to Bethlehem, and the carols boomed out from there and from every camp in the land. There was singing too, though perhaps rather more raucous, in the Goldsmith Officers' Club, which had recently celebrated a defiant gala reopening, following its destruction in March. Happily, the Jews and Arabs seemed briefly to enter the Christmas spirit, but for the Royal Lincolns in particular life resumed its spluttering course with a nasty crash on December 29, when raiders broke into the arms store, at their camp near Tel Aviv, after killing one man and wounding two. The gangster groups struck now only in quest of arms and—with the intelligence available to them, often from inside, and with their expertise in planning—they were hard to combat.

On January 9, 1948, the Arab Liberation Army began their vaunted invasion, led by Fawzi Kawukji, who had gained fame as the leader of the Arab rebellion in 1936. He responded with courtesy and charm when representations were made to him and halted his own advance on Jerusalem a few miles inside the frontier. But his army was widespread, and a column crossing the border from Syria into Gallilee showed no inclination to be stopped by verbal pressure. The mechanised regiment of the Transjordan Frontier Force were in this area, operating under 6th Airborne, and to their commanding officer, Lieutenant-Colonel Blackden, fell the delicate task of making them desist, by the use of minimum force, from an attack they were mounting against two Jewish villages, whose people they far outnumbered. He managed to do this by a combination of diplomacy and threat, the latter taking the form of mortar concentrations near the Arab irregulars, put down by some paratroops, and dummy attacks by Spitfires. The Jews were saved, and a few days later Blackden repelled another invasion in the same manner. However, these Arab colonial soldiers of the British represented everything the Jews hated, and the vilification they heaped on them— for saving their lives!—made it impossible to retain them and they had to be returned to Transjordan, which now stood on the threshold of expansion and independence as Jordan.

As replacement a scratch force was formed under the C.R.A. 6th Airborne, consisting of the 17th/21st Lancers, the 1st Irish Guards (who had been near Gaza), and the 1st Para. They covered a large area, harsh and hilly, dotted with settlements filled with fear and hatred of each other. On the night of February 15/16 an Arab column, 500 men strong, was reported to have crossed the frontier and attacked a Jewish village. The 1st Para could get only a platoon, with mortars and machine-guns, to the scene next morning. It was sufficient to bring the Arab commander to a parley, and the only condition he asked for the withdrawal of his force was that the paras should put down a mortar stonk nearby so that the Arabs could be seen to yield to overwhelming force. They had in fact suffered very heavily in the attack, and when the British officer agreed to the condition the commander of the Arab irregulars showed disarming relief and gratitude. Gay, courteous and endearingly incompetent, these men differed in every respect (except bravery) from their scowling foe, and it was hard for the British to conceal which side they preferred.

As the throb of violence quickened in the towns under dispute, most of all in Jerusalem and Haifa, and in the frontier districts, the roads and railways were under heavy pressure to sustain the flow of stores and troops out of the country. There was greater peril for trains than for road convoys, which had escorts of carriers or armoured cars, and there was consequently heavy drain on infantry battalions for the provision of train guards, as much against thieves as armed attackers. This was a dreary menial task, and its dangers received stark advertisement on February 29, when a mine claimed to have been detonated by the Stern Gang wrecked a train near Rehovoth, bringing death to twenty-eight soldiers and wounding a further thirty-five. It was the heaviest loss suffered by the troops. However, the line was soon patched up and kept open until the end of April.

Another activity undertaken by the battalions in between preparing themselves for the final move was showing the flag to the villages, both Arab and Jew, in hope of giving them reassurance and staying the urge to flee that was beginning to take hold of some Arabs living in the vicinity of Jewish strongholds. It was a task tinged with pathos, for it was a hollow form of reassurance that the troops brought, and the faith engendered in some Arab villages, after ponderous introductions and the ritualistic serving of mint-flavoured tea, sometimes made the visitors feel guilty of fraud. It was much harder to penetrate the cold suspicion encountered in the kibbutzes, but it was achieved from time to time. Not all these flag marches went entirely according to plan. A squadron of Life Guards put on a demonstration of weapons in a small Arab town near Gaza and scored great success giving children, old men, and veiled women rides in their scout cars, but when the fighters arrived overhead to provide some daring aerobatics as a grand climax there was panicked flight in all directions. It was left to the G.O.C., General MacMillan, to restore the situation. He landed all of a sudden in an Auster, as was quite a common occurrence, and the villagers gave him a great reception, their fears forgotten in delight at so brilliant a trick.

Meanwhile Haifa was rapidly coming to the boil as more and more Arab irregulars penetrated the gaps in the far stretched net provided by the C.R.A.'s force. The port was of crucial importance, and the fact that the Jews had not been so aggressive here in the past suggests that they appreciated the need to build up their strength. Although outnumbered by the Arabs, they had the tactical advantage in that their quarter was on the lower slopes of Mount Carmel and overlooked the Arabs' Old Town. The Wadi Rushmiya divided them, and overlooking both from the top of Mount Carmel was Stockwell's Headquarters 6th Airborne Division.

The blood was set flowing in earnest by a bomb thrown into a crowd of Arabs on December 30, whereupon some unfortunate Jewish employees at an oil refinery were at once throttled to death. The tempo had since been maintained, with steady graduation in the power of the weapons. The Arabs gained some successes when the Liberation Army men arrived with their machine-guns and rifles, but the Jews were never to be outdone and the explosions they produced rocked Haifa with harrowing monotony day after day, leaving listless clouds of dust and cordite to mark the spot for the rescue men. On February 20 the Arabs brought mortars into action and the Jews at once retaliated in kind. In fact the Jews always seemed to have the edge over their adversaries, and one of their assets, of which they made frequent use, was the possession of British Army vehicles and uniforms, complete with Airborne emblems. Consequently the Arabs were liable to assault the British, suspecting them to be Jews. They did this to a convoy near Acre, killing five soldiers, and the intelligence officer of the 1st Para Brigade was very nearly lynched in Haifa through a similar misunderstanding. He rushed to the scene of an explosion and its attendant carnage without of course realising that the bomb had been delivered by a person dressed as he was himself. He and his companions were saved from the clutches of the mob by a Liberation Army officer and had then to endure some most menacing questioning before their identities were accepted and profuse apologies made.

The 6th Airborne had been slimmed to one parachute brigade by the disbandment of the 3rd in January, and although the 2nd Middlesex and 40 Commando had been brought in to ease the great burden, so many points of communication needed to be guarded that only one battalion could be spared for the pacification of the war raging in the town: a duty borne, when at its fiercest, by Lieutenant-Colonel Birkbeck's 2/3rd Para. The policy was to hold strong points of tactical importance, usually with a platoon in each, and from there to bring fire down on anyone who fired. Patrols would then go and disarm the firers or at least disperse them. Peace was preserved by day in this manner, and for a time the adversaries were allowed to blaze away at night without hindrance. However, as their firepower increased tougher steps had to be taken. The tanks of the 3rd Hussars (with which one squadron was equipped) and the self-propelled guns of the Chestnut Troop, 1st R.H.A., entered the arena and patrolled the streets with infantry escort by day and night. Fired at point blank range to ensure accuracy, one round of gunfire was found to be sufficient to silence any fire-spouting strong point for many days.

April 6 was the day of the final redeployment before the withdrawal, and it also happened to be chosen by the Irgun for their final raid against the British. Ironically, spring had brought its touch of joy, and there was balm in the sunlight as the 12th Anti-Tank Regiment, R.A., began their early morning parade at their camp amid orange groves near Latrun. They were due to leave in a week's time and were cheerfully engaged on preparations for the move. Then came the shattering, sickening shots. Three army lorries had arrived at the camp's entrance, and as the sentry examined the documents held out by a man in the uniform of an R.A.S.C. major, he was shot dead, simultaneously with the bren gunner covering him from a sandbagged emplacement. Now an armoured car swept past from behind the lorries and opened fire with its machine-gun at targets all round it from the centre of the camp. The lorries came up behind it, and raiders rushed from them straight and unerringly for the battery armoury tents, where they shot or tied up the storemen and ran with loads of weapons back to their lorries. Others meanwhile had entered the guard tent, and there they lined up and shot dead its four occupants, all men of under 20.

The commanding officer, Lieutenant-Colonel Hildebrand, tried to rush the armoured car on his own and shoot its crew through the slits with his revolver. He was shot and mortally wounded. An armoured chassis, stripped of its anti-tank gun because of the impending move, now roared on the scene and bore down on the armoured car, tossing the raider's machine-gun bullets sky-high off its plating. There was a rush for the lorries and the Irgun were gone, their job half done. One lorry was pumped with sten gun bullets from close behind and must have lost some of its men. Otherwise the losses were all on the British side, and it is significant that they included a Jewish civilian employee, who was never seen again.

The redeployment on this day (April 6) consisted of the relief of the 1st Para Brigade at Haifa by the 1st Guards Brigade from the Tel Aviv–Natanya area. The latter were transferred to Stockwell's command, which was renamed North Sector, since the 6th Airborne dissolved with the departure of its last brigade.

The 1st Division was left with the 3rd Brigade deployed round its headquarter area at Sarafand, covering the road and rail confluence. The withdrawal from here was to be to the southwards, and the main problem was to prevent eruptions by the Jews from their great stronghold of Tel Aviv until the day of withdrawal, May 14. The 3rd Brigade's battalions were all veterans of the campaign: the 2nd Royal Lincolns, who came with the first reinforcement provided by the 3rd Division; the 2nd Royal Irish Fusiliers, who had come with 9th Brigade at the end of 1946; and the 1st Argylls, who had come with the 6th Airlanding in October 1945. The Life Guards and the 41st Field Regiment were there to support them.

At Jerusalem the 2nd Brigade, still independent, had not only to subdue mounting violence in the city but to keep the routes open both to Haifa and Egypt. War was fast spreading astride these routes, particularly to the north and west, and the 1st Para Battalion were consequently removed from their departing brigade to ease the task in the hills of Samaria. Tanks of the long resident 4th/7th Dragoon Guards and the guns of the 6th Field Regiment were also available to the hard pressed 2nd Brigade.

To keep the southwards routes open the 2nd King's Royal Rifle Corps, who had been eighteen months in Palestine, were placed under the 1st Division, and widespread in their half-tracked vehicles on either side of Gaza they quenched many conflagrations in this highly combustible area. Their colleagues of the 61st Lorried Infantry Brigade, the 1st Border and the 1st Royal Sussex, had departed in February, as also had the gunner regiments. Mention must also be made of the 2nd Royal Ulster Rifles, who had come in the spring of 1946 and served first with the 6th Airborne and then with the 1st, long outstaying the tour of their 1st Battalion; of the 2nd Royal Hampshire, who ended a year's service with the 1st Division in the autumn of 1947; and of the 1st South Lancashire, who had two short tours spread between 1945 and 1947.

There had also been changes in the 1st Guards Brigade. The 3rd Grenadiers and the 3rd Coldstream had been relieved in February by their 1st Battalions, and on their arrival at Haifa the Welsh Guards returned homewards after a tour of over two years. The brigade took over the paras' armoured support group, together with the 2nd Middlesex and 40 Commando, and certainly there was a need for every man that could be mustered in and around the town. Indeed, so difficult did the task of control become that the Guards withdrew from the most fiercely disputed area on the night of April 20-21, telling the leaders of both sides that they had done so. Next night the Jews attacked and utterly defeated the Arabs in a most raucous battle. The Arabs thereupon appealed to Stockwell to arrange a truce, and he succeeded in obtaining reasonable terms from the Jews. But instead of abiding by them the Arabs panicked and fled. There was an amazing massed flight, and it was left to the British, soldiers and police, to curb the inevitable looting, succour the wounded, and provide protection against constant sniping by the triumphant Jews. A dozen officers and men were hit in their efforts to guide and protect the pathetic, terror-stricken rabbles, and among them was Lieutenant-Colonel Chandos-Pole, of the 1st Coldstream, who was shot in the arm while leading forward a convoy of ambulances. Three officers of 40 Commando were wounded in similar circumstances.

The Jews next tried to exploit their victory by advancing beyond Haifa, but the British had retained firm control astride the exits and sent them back. The town had by now quietened. Out of an Arab population of 50,000, less than 10,000 remained.

On the eastern frontier of Stockwell's sector the C.R.A.'s meagre force was becoming increasingly overlapped by Arab incursions, and on April 16 it was authorised to make the first surrender of British occupied territory. This was the high-perched little town of Safad, which was at Palestine's extreme north-east corner and of no tactical importance to the British withdrawal. For three months its garrison—a half-company of the Irish Guards, a troop of the 17th/21st, and a section of police—had preserved a fragile balance of power, but now they were completely surrounded by Arab invaders and had to blast their way out by making a show of force. Tiberias, from which the Jews had put the Arabs to flight, was evacuated on April 28. The C.R.A. moved his headquarters to Nazareth, retaining only the 17th/21st, and the Irish Guards joined the Guards Brigade at Haifa.

In Jerusalem the tireless efforts of the High Commissioner had for long restrained the Jewish and Arab leaders from openly waging war. Nevertheless the situation deteriorated with each jerk of violence, a particularly savage one on February 22 setting the pace. The Jewish gangster organisation blamed the British for an explosion in their quarter that day and threatened to kill all British troops. They thereupon forced the police to evacuate a station by pumping it with automatic fire and laid a mine that blew up the truck of the H.L.I. platoon rushed to the scene. Although badly injured in the head, the platoon commander led an attack against the gangster fire, only to faint as he was in process of gathering his men for the assault. There were six killed and five wounded in this affair, and on the same day two men of the Suffolks were injured when their truck hit a mine. They were taken to a Jewish clinic and there shot by gangsters who burst in upon them, one being killed, the other making a miraculous recovery.

The H.L.I. tightened their hold over the Old City, making thump with a piat at any house from which there came crack of shot. They fought a fierce battle with the Jews near the end of March, from which five Jocks died and a string of wounded Jews passed safely through the Arab quarter. On April 18 an even bigger battle raged outside the city, when the Arabs ambushed a Jewish convoy and the H.L.I. had to go to the rescue of the side that had attacked them so often. They had to fight all day, with their 3-inch mortars crumping the Arab positions, to extricate these Hagana men. They brought out twenty-five wounded and recovered eighty bodies, at a loss to themselves of two killed and three wounded.

A week later the Jews openly carried the war to Jerusalem by seizing a house named Sheikh Jarrah, which belonged to an Arab doctor, and disregarding British warnings of the consequences. It was large and white and stood in a dominating position, overlooking the convoy route to the Mount of Olives. On the afternoon of April 26 the H.L.I. were ordered to attack it. They were allotted a troop of Cromwell tanks of the 4th/7th Dragoon Guards, two armoured car troops of the Life Guards, two 25-pounder troops of the 6th Field, and the machine-guns of the Suffolks. It was real war at last, and a surge of relief ran through the H.L.I. The attack went in at last light, with searchlights providing artificial moonlight to enable the tanks to strike target. They did so effectively enough, and the H.L.I. stormed the building to take thirty-seven prisoners and remove twenty wounded and dead. One of their men received a wound. Jerusalem, like Haifa, was restored to a sort of a peace.

Outside the city Jews and Arabs were increasingly coming to grips, and there was nothing the British could do about it, having only sufficient troops to keep the main centres and their own communications open. The worst example was the village of Beir Yassin, where in early April the Jews perpetrated a savage massacre. Much to the High Commissioner's regret, neither his soldiers nor his airmen were able to bring vengeance.

Jaffa, however, had to be protected. This ancient port, standing in desperately vulnerable proximity to Tel Aviv, was dear to Arab hearts, and rumours of a massacre there in mid-April caused sparks to fly between Bevin and Montgomery. The 3rd Brigade had in fact kept the Jews in check, by reinforcing two companies of the Royal Irish Fusiliers with a company of the Royal Lincolns, a troop of the 4th/7th, and a troop of Life Guards. But now the Irgun joined up with Hagana, and the Arabs were in real danger. The Argylls were brought in, leaving the Lydda area dangerously short of men, and from April 28 they probed and chivvied the Irgun commandos around gaunt and dusty buildings, with guns on call from land, sea, and air. Suddenly the Jews asked for a truce and agreed to make a radical withdrawal, which was swiftly enforced. The guns of the 41st Field Regiment had struck their headquarters and inflicted very heavy loss. Most Arabs used the respite gained for them to flock away to the south.

By a brief display of their full firepower the British had asserted their authority in the centres still of importance to them, and now came an announcement, on May 1, that 'owing to the unwarranted aggression of the Irgun in Jaffa' (which in fact ceased that day) 'considerable reinforcements had to be despatched'. They consisted of the 2nd King's from Cyprus, whence the 1st King's Shropshire Light Infantry had recently been brought, 42 and 45 Commandos from Malta, and the 4th Royal Tank Regiment by land from Egypt; although only 42 Commando, who came to Jerusalem, moved far into Palestine, their coming caused anxious speculation as to British intentions. Glubb Pasha and the Arab Legion, whose seconded British officers were about to be withdrawn, were meanwhile established on either side of Jerusalem, and there was fierce fighting at Katamon, just south of the city, which the Suffolks, having taken over from the H.L.I., managed to prevent spreading. Ben Gurion now surprised everyone by announcing that he would be willing to accept a cease-fire, and Cunningham succeeded in obtaining the agreement of the Arabs, after meeting Abdul Azzam, Secretary-General of the Arab League, at Jericho on May 6.

The British therefore had a welcome breathing space before the great withdrawal, which began at 8 a.m. on May 14 with the departure of the High Commissioner, Sir Alan Cunningham, from Government House. He had insisted on remaining in Jerusalem to the last, instead of moving the administration to Haifa, as the military would have preferred, and the soldiers were determined to accord him the honour they felt due both to the office and the man. The H.L.I., who had lost eighteen killed and sixty-one wounded in seven months' occupation of the city, saw him off with a guard of honour and their colours; a quarter guard of the Suffolks, also with colours flying, and of 42 Commando saluted him as he passed through Jerusalem with a Life Guards escort, as Jews and Arabs respectively scowled and grinned from sandbagged emplacements on either side; and as his Daimler armoured car (formerly used by King George VI) reached the airfield near Ramallah he was greeted by a guard of honour of the 1st (Guards) Para Battalion. At Haifa, King's Company, 1st Grenadiers, 40 Commando, and the Pipes of the Irish Guards provided the honours, and he was then piped aboard the cruiser H.M.S. *Euryalus*, which remained in harbour until the Mandate expired at midnight. Nominally, responsibility for Palestine was transferred to a United Nations commissioner, but he had no means of exercising authority.

For the troops, there was divergence from Jerusalem. Brigadier C. P. ('Splosh') Jones took the main body of his 2nd Infantry Brigade group southwards through Beersheba. Full tactical precautions were taken, and guns were deployed on instant call as the Suffolks evacuated Jerusalem. But opposition by either Jew or Arab was pointless, and although some shots caused near misses they were either let off singly out of sheer devilment or fired in greater volume (invariably by Arabs) through mistaken identity. After a night amid the stony hills by King Solomon's Pool, lying in hedgehog formations, the long column of fighting and soft vehicles entered Egypt. The troops hitherto attached to 2 Brigade, such as the 1st Para, 42 Commando, and a squadron of the 4th/7th, with the remnant of Headquarters British Troops Palestine, had meanwhile had an untroubled journey to Haifa, enlivened only by the sound of battle opening up behind them. The 17th/21st Lancers completed the withdrawal to the Haifa enclave by coming down from the hills around Nazareth.

The only movement made by the 3rd Brigade on the 14th was to draw in the troops on peacekeeping duties and form a defensive box around Latrun, Lydda, and Sarafand, into which the 3rd Hussars withdrew from the Samarian hills. They moved off next day along the road that skirts Gaza, with Main H.Q. 1st Division in the column. A symbolic glimpse of the true situation was afforded the last troops to leave the various camps, for they were engulfed by rabbles rushing to strip the few bare fixtures the British had been obliged to leave behind. Beyond Gaza, a very British looking column was seen approaching along the same road. It was in fact the Egyptian Army, starting its invasion, and there was an exchange of cheers or jeers. The shepherding role was entrusted to the Life Guards, the 2nd K.R.R.C., and the regiment that could claim longest residence of all in Palestine, the 3rd Hussars. The Rifles, sadly, came under attack by Egyptian aircraft, obviously in error, and lost one man killed and eight wounded. These would appear to be the only casualties of the withdrawal.

The rearguard spent the night near Rafah and entered Egypt on the 16th, leaving the full extent of the fine military roads the British had made in Palestine available for other armies.

General MacMillan was left to rule his Haifa enclave by proclamation, and on the 15th he read out its terms to the Jewish and Arab leaders outside the town hall, with behind him a powerful ceremonial escort of the Guards, who wherever they had been in Palestine had maintained the standards required for Buckingham Palace. They appear to have impressed the people, for during the next six weeks Haifa was the quietest place in Palestine, and there was no violent interference in the flow of stores and men on to the ships, for which the Royal Engineers built a road that could not be overlooked by outside snipers. The amount of stores evacuated exceeded the estimate, and it would have been larger but for some heavy stealing, for which Jews and Arabs could not claim full responsibility.

The final withdrawal was made on June 30, a month earlier than originally planned. It was made tactically by the 1st Grenadier and 1st Coldstream Guards, covered by the weapons of the 4th/7th Dragoon Guards, the 1st R.H.A., and 40 Commando from their ships. By 12.30 p.m. the tall, smart figure of the G.O.C. was the only military one left on shore. He stood at the salute while the Union Jack was lowered, then bade farewell to the British Consul-General and stepped aboard H.M.S. *Phoebe*. The ship's guns boomed in salute, and once outside the harbour aircraft both of the R.N. and R.A.F. paid their tribute to the General in immaculate style, and three fighting ships steamed past with their companies lined on deck giving him three cheers. At least the British knew how to leave in style.

223 officers and men died (since 1945) in the attempt to bring peace and stability to Palestine, and it is obvious that they died in vain. The troops had shown themselves quite capable of imposing the terms of any political settlement, and it is sad that they were denied the chance to try.

4

Europe

(1945-56)

THERE was understandable reluctance at the end of the war to
face up to the menace of Russian imperialism. It had long been
the declared aim of the Soviet Government to spread their dominion
across the world by the dissemination of Communism, and it soon
became clear that the countries liberated by Russia from Germany had
been converted into colonies, cynically advertised as 'people's demo-
cracies'. Yet neither Britain nor the United States wanted to quarrel
with Russia. They had won the war as her allies and now wanted to
give their full attention to the daunting domestic problems brought
with peace. The alliance was kept in being, with the more blatant of
Russia's predatory acts drawing little more than sighs of regret.

Governing Germany was the British Army's most absorbing task.
The country had been deprived of any form of national government by
the policy of unconditional surrender and was ruled instead by the
Supreme Commanders of the invading armies, American, British,
Russian and French. They formed the Central Control Council in
Berlin, of which the secretariat was the Control Commission, but very
little was agreed upon, apart from access routes to Berlin. From an
early stage the American, British and French Military Governors
realised that they would have to make their own arrangements for
governing their zones of occupation and sectors of Berlin, coordinating
their policy by consultation at the American headquarters, Frankfurt.

In the British zone there were twenty million civilians to be fed, a
million refugees from the Russian advance to be resettled or repatriated,
and two and a half million prisoners of war to be returned to civilian
life or charged with war crimes, and of all zones this had been hardest
hit by bombing. Civil divisions of the Control Commission worked in

conjunction with an enormous Military Government staff, all under the supervision of Field Marshal Montgomery's Deputy, Lieutenant-General Sir Ronald Weeks, who in July 1945 was forced by ill health to be superseded by Lieutenant-General Sir Brian Robertson, son of the C.I.G.S. of the First World War. The Director of Military Government was Major-General G. R. Templer, and among his many decisions was one that subsequently was to appear bizarre to those unacquainted with the circumstances, confirmation of the dismissal of Dr. Konrad Adenauer from the post of Ober-Burgermeister of Cologne.

For the troops, peace brought little merriment. In order to infuse a feeling of collective guilt into the German people, they were forbidden even to talk to them until the month of July, and not until September were they permitted to enter shops or houses. The winter was bleak, with the main military effort devoted to circulating sufficient food and coal to keep the Germans alive; with their rations down to 1,000 calories a day and the ban on fraternisation fresh in memory, the latter did not feel inclined to give thanks. The troops lived in a devastated land, amid sullen people, surrounded by the plainest countryside Germany possessed. They had good cause to envy their comrades in the other, sunnier parts of Europe, the slopes of southern Austria and the city of Vienna, the rich port of Trieste and its delectable coastline, the wild plain of Macedonia and the more sophisticated neighbourhood of Athens. In all these parts the troops had that comforting feeling of being welcome.

In 1946 the troops in Germany reverted to more conventional duties, and with Montgomery's elevation to C.I.G.S., on June 26, came a hardening of the division between the operational and governmental departments. Marshal of the R.A.F. Sir Sholto Douglas became Commander-in-Chief British Forces Germany, Military Governor of the British Zone, and British Member of the Central Control Council, in all three of which he was succeeded by his Deputy, General Robertson, on November 1, 1947. Lieutenant-General Sir Richard McCreery, the last commander of the Eighth Army, was appointed to a new and purely military command, that of the British Army of the Rhine, with headquarters at Bad Oeynhausen. In April 1948 one of McCreery's former corps commanders, the large cavalryman Sir Charles Keightley, was appointed to this command, following a brief tenure by Sir Brian Horrocks which was ended by ill health. Rhine Army had been reduced by now to two divisions, the 2nd Infantry and the 7th Armoured, both of which had the static functions of districts superimposed. It also had the newly formed 16th Parachute Brigade and a separate brigade in Berlin.

Meanwhile the surly belligerence of Soviet Russia began to take sharper shape. In June 1947 the American Government, in the person of General Marshall, the Secretary of State, made a massive contribution to European recovery by announcing the Marshall Aid Plan. Russia and her satellites were offered their share, but the Soviet Government gave revealing display of their outlook by turning it down for all. Their expenditure on their army meanwhile remained at wartime level, with 175 divisions fully operational and 25,000 tanks in service. In November 1947 a meeting of Foreign Ministers in London, come to discuss the future of Germany, ended in sad deadlock, and on his journey back to Russia M. Molotov visited Berlin and made a savage attack against his colleagues in alliance. In February 1948 Czechoslovakia was turned into a Russian satellite by coup d'état, the death of Jan Masaryk both signifying and symbolising the death of freedom.

These sombre happenings made the countries of Western Europe turn to thoughts of a defensive union, a thing into which they had never previously entered. They first found expression, though only in idealistic and economic terms, in the Brussels Treaty of March 1948, which embraced France, Britain, Belgium, Holland and Luxembourg. On May 10 a decision of great moment was taken in London, reversing the national policy of 400 years: at a meeting of the Chiefs of Staff under the Minister of Defence, Mr. A. V. Alexander, agreement was reached on a policy of tying their forces permanently to the defence of Western Europe. For Montgomery, according to his Memoirs, it brought to a triumphant end a prolonged battle of words he had been waging with his naval and air counterparts. As he saw it, there was little hope of an effective military alliance between the defeatist nations of North-West Europe unless Britain showed willingness to join and lead them. He was surely right.

The Russians were now beginning to apply pressure on the Western allies at the point where they were most vulnerable, in Berlin. Each sector was under a Commandant, and the British one, Major-General E. O. Herbert, still combined the dual responsibilities of military government and command of the troops that formed his meagre garrison. A former artilleryman, terse of manner and strong of nerve, he had become increasingly sceptical of the prevailing confidence in high places that the Russians would refrain from an attempt to prise the Allies out. From January 1948, when restrictions were placed on passenger traffic, signs steadily accumulated of the method to be used: blockade. In Herbert's words, 'With oriental deviousness and intricacy the pattern was gradually displayed. There was a cumulative series of innumerable moves like the small movements of a boa constrictor, each of which is barely noticeable and difficult to describe but is none the less important.' A few examples of these movements were the issue by the Soviet Deputy Military Governor, on March 31, of 'certain supplementary regulations' governing (and grievously impeding) the flow of freight traffic; the cessation of parcel mail on May 5; and the unsealing and examination of all military and civil freight from June 4.

Berlin had once been regarded as a holiday station for the two British battalions resident there. They had brief tours in which they did little more than gape at the grandeur and dereliction, taste the night spots, enjoy the splendour of the Reichskanzlerplatz—which was claimed to be the best N.A.A.F.I. in the world and was designed no doubt as a counter to less desirable attractions—rub shoulders with Russian, French and American soldiers, and mingle with a population that had had ten weeks' experience of Russian rape and pillage before the arrival of the others and was consequently better disposed towards the British than were the inhabitants of the British Zone. With the slow intrusion of the Russian menace a battalion's tour was extended to over a year's duration and a higher sense of responsibility infused. This eased the disciplinary duties of the Royal Military Police, but instead of being reduced their detachment was greatly enlarged, so that they could form a sort of outpost screen, obtaining information and acting as buffer in any disturbance before intervention by the fighting troops. Herbert also managed to strengthen his staff structure, notably in the spheres of intelligence and planning, thanks to a visit from the C.I.G.S.

General Robertson, although keeping his headquarters open in Berlin, was concerned primarily with his duties as Governor of the British Zone, over which he spent much time in Bonn, whither the British element of the Control Commission was in gradual process of transfer. This made it important to give the Berliners unobtrusive assurance that the British did not intend to desert them. It was hard to do this with only two battalions spread over a sector that formed a rough triangle of 15 miles each arm, and on February 4, 1948, a third was consequently sneaked in. The choice fell on the 2nd Royal Scots Fusiliers. They came on the night leave train, and since their destination had officially been kept secret from them, they had great fun on arrival in pretending that they did not know where they were. They joined the 1st Royal Norfolk and the 1st Worcestershire, and a squadron of those early inhabitants of Berlin, the 11th Hussars, who had armoured cars. There were no tanks, no artillery.

The need for an adequate garrison was grimly stressed on April 5, when a Russian Yak fighter, trying to intimidate, crashed into a British Viking transport plane about to land at Gatow airport, bringing them both down, with all killed, in the British sector. General Herbert found Russian soldiers confronting him when he went to investigate and had to remove the muzzle of a carbine from his chest. He was not freed from their menacing attentions until a company of Royal Norfolks rushed up, summoned by his A.D.C. On their approach the Russians returned to their own territory. They were playing the bully, and like most bullies, yielded when confronted with force.

One of the problems in the British sector was to prevent German hatred of the Russians overspilling into their sector; there was a grave risk of this when the Germans planned a May Day parade outside the Reichstag, which was 200 yards inside the British sector, near the Russian war memorial and the intersectional meeting point, the Brandenburg Gate. Yielding to political advocacy, British and German, Herbert allowed the parade to be held. Control of it was ostensibly left to the police, civil and military, and they successfully achieved the task without the appearance of a single infantry soldier on the scene. But some were very close at hand—the Royal Norfolks were lying up in strength inside the charred hulk of the Reichstag, having moved in at dead of night.

During June the Russians turned the screw as far as they dared. On the 15th they closed the autobahn bridge at Magdeburg, allegedly for repairs, thus blocking the only road to Berlin allotted their former allies. This did not deter the latter from announcing, on the 18th, measures of currency reform opposed by the Russians, who retaliated by suspending the passenger train service—which also brought the mail—and declaring the road formally closed. On the 21st barge traffic was stopped and on the 24th goods traffic; at the same time electricity was cut almost to nothing, because the three Western sectors relied for seven eighths of their supply on the Russian, the components of Berlin's main power station having been removed to Russia before the British could take occupation of their sector. Only one means of communication remained open—by air—and a situation that had long caused anxiety locally suddenly burst through, with all its terrifying implications, on the world.

In Berlin the situation on June 24 was even more critical than anyone outside Herbert's headquarters realised. Not content with cutting the land routes and electricity, the Russians made a deliberate attempt at intrusion into the British sector. At a meeting of Commandants, one of the last attended by the Russian, a demand was made for the evacuation by the British of a railway goods yard on the British side of the canal that formed the sector boundary. Herbert refused, whereupon the Russian general in charge of movement control displayed great truculence and said he would throw the British out. A swift summons was sent to the Worcesters, who were seven miles from the city centre and the furthest out. By the early afternoon they were fortifying positions covering nine bridges over the dividing canal. They had a troop of the 11th Hussars with them and a troop of sappers, who made necklaces of mines ready to pull across the roads, along which civilian traffic could pass without hindrance, a privilege by now denied the individual British soldier. At midnight the Worcesters were dragged, as it seemed, from the brink of war and ordered back to barracks. Herbert knew that the Russians would not move without orders from Moscow and, having thus exhibited his determination to resist trespass, he was not going to await the arrival of Russian troops opposite his and thus have one third of his force tied down.

Plans for an air lift, along the three air corridors allotted the Western allies, originally had only the needs of the garrison in mind, and this posed hectic enough a problem. The first move was the despatch by the R.A.F. of forty-eight Dakotas, which flew to Germany on June 25 and on the 26th brought a load into Gatow airport, the first drop in what was to become an ocean. The Americans showed equal vigour, and at an early stage a joint despatch headquarters was established at Frankfurt, based on the existing foundation of Bipartite Control, to which daily requirements were wired from Berlin. The Americans, as might be guessed, were better equipped with aircraft, but they needed airfields in the British Zone, which was nearer to Berlin, and the Royal Engineers performed prodigies in converting fighter stations or mere disused landing grounds into despatch centres each of the capacity of a London railway station. Marshalling yards, roads, runways, extensions of railway lines, lighting (for all-night loading from trains to runways), offices, and encampments all had to be constructed at great speed and a labour force of German civilians organised for the purpose. Wanstorf was developed first, then Fassberg, then Celle, followed by three other airfields and one flying-boat station. In the marshalling of the traffic and the unloading, sorting and reloading of their cargoes a great burden was shouldered by the Royal Army Service Corps.

One of the earliest complications stemmed from the coincidence that the Royal Scots Fusiliers were in process of being relieved in Berlin by the 2nd Queen's when the land routes were cut. Space therefore had to be made in the Dakotas for two companies of Queensmen. They were duly flown in and the remaining Scotsmen flown out, thus emphasising that the British were not to be shaken out of their routine by the minor inconvenience of having their land routes blocked. Smartness and calmness were the essentials, displaying neither bombast nor anxiety, and in exhibiting these qualities the British soldiers made a contribution of incalculable value to the allied cause as a whole.

Yet behind the appearance of normality, the troops had to be on their toes, as had already been shown; for the Russians held the initiative and it was impossible to know what they might do next. The one tactical relief afforded the British was that their sector was flanked by the French and American to north and south. This left them with a frontage of $2\frac{1}{2}$ miles against the Russian sector through the centre of Berlin and one of almost 20 miles against the Russian Zone, through the pine forests and village suburbs 15 miles west of the city. The military policemen provided the urban outpost line, and the Hussars patrolled the zonal border. Such of the infantry as were not committed to guard duties or airport fatigues were grouped in the centre, the Queen's and Royal Norfolks in Brooke and Wavell Barracks in the suburb of Spandau, a name notorious for the machine-gun its factory had produced and for the jail in which the war criminals languished, guarded by troops of the occupying powers in rotation. The Worcesters were in Montgomery Barracks, Kladow, further westwards.

Not until July 10 did each of the three Western Governments lodge formal protest against the blockade, and it drew a defiant admission from the Soviet Government that it had been deliberately imposed in retaliation against the currency reforms. It had become clear by now that not only the occupying forces but the very people of Berlin were under blockade and that the Russians aimed to force them into starvation in order to demonstrate that the Western powers were unable to protect them. There could be no hope of raising the blockade by force. The Russians had terrifying preponderance in troops over the three allies combined, and it was 100 miles to Berlin from the edge of the British Zone. Similarly the troops in Berlin were like fragile toys in a monster's hand, and the hand was twitching in expectation of being provoked into a clench. Yet the potential strength of the West was immeasurably superior to that of Soviet Russia, and the conclusion drawn by British Intelligence, which had firm historical foundation, was that behind all the bluster, ambition and sinister machinations of the Soviet Government lay an innate streak of caution that would always restrain them from open aggression. In Whitehall, Bad Oeyn-hausen, and Berlin the British command were determined to meet the crisis both firmly and coolly, and in this they were able to carry their allies with them. The temperature was lowered to the discussion of technicalities, desperately daunting technicalities though they were: those of supplying over two million people by air for an indefinite period.

It was of course an advantage that these people had had their taste of

Russian occupation and could therefore see the privations of blockade as the lesser evil. None the less their needs were depressingly comprehensive. 'Coal cannot be flown in,' pronounced a leading British newspaper. Yet coal was flown in, and every other essential with it, all through the remaining summer months, through the autumn, and through the winter, which by great fortune was much milder than the average. It was a tremendous team effort, with the tempo always at crisis level, never subsiding to routine. The resources of the R.A.F. were squeezed dry, with four-engined Avro Yorks, Lancasters and the new Handley Page Hastings joining the overworked Dakotas; civilian airlines also made a great contribution, eventually carrying as much as the R.A.F. and taking the most dangerous cargo, liquid fuel. The R.A.F. carried the dirtiest, coal. Even so, the Americans, with bigger and better transport planes, carried at least two-thirds of the total lift, which reached a daily average of around 4,000 tons by the end of August and, after a decline in November, made a steep ascent in March 1949 to 7,000 tons. This has to be compared with the figure of 12,000 tons, being the daily average before the blockade.

Selection of the 4,000 tons of supplies to have preference out of the 12,000 was the most teasing of all the many problems facing the staffs in Berlin. Second to it, less teasing perhaps but of greater complexity, was the organisation of the unloading and turn-around of the aircraft at Gatow, which was the regulating factor in the amount of supplies that could be brought in. A great feat of coordination was called for. Herbert's own departments were his Military Government staff (under Brigadier E. R. Benson), H.Q. British Troops Berlin (under Brigadier C. E. A. Firth), R.A.F. Gatow, and the improvised Headquarters Airlift, and these had to work very closely not only with each other but with the Control Commission and the staffs of the other two sectors, of which the French relied entirely on the British and American until the opening of an airfield at Tegel in the autumn. The British staffs excelled at improvisation, and their contribution was undoubtedly a great one. The Royal Engineers and the Royal Army Service Corps also made mammoth contributions with pigmy organisations, the former rapidly expanding Gatow's marshalling facilities with unskilled labour, and the latter raising the discharge rate from the airport to 1,500 lorry loads a day, using civilian labour for the loading and partly for the driving. The capacity of Gatow was doubled in a matter of weeks.

The 2nd Queen's staged a big parade on September 9 to celebrate their conversion to the 1st. It was held at that recreational gem of the British sector, the 1936 Olympic Stadium, and from each of the 84 masts around it fluttered a Union Jack. Yet the throb of aircraft gave constant reminder of the reality of the situation, and vehicles were waiting to whisk the Queen's away if emergency call arrived. During the party that followed the parade emergency did indeed flare, and it was extinguished without intervention by the infantry. There had been another demonstration outside the Reichstag, and this time the guard on the Russian memorial took fright, beat brief retreat, and knelt down to fire at the advancing crowd. Catastrophe was averted by a British civil police officer who calmly approached the Russians and told them in English, 'Now, now, we can't have any of that.' The message was absorbed.

From now onwards there was a slow but gradually discernible lowering of the tension, and although the intelligence staff were confronted with some alarming puzzles, it seemed as if the Russians were becoming aware of the dangers of playing with fire. The Berliners grimly settled down to endure the winter, knowing at least that the occupying troops and administrators were bearing a share of the hardship on their behalf. A spell of severe weather might have broken the people's will, but the weather remained reasonably mild. In January 1949 Herbert's tenure ended, and he handed over to another gunner of strong character, the ebullient, one-armed Major-General G. P. Bourne. The only adjustment made by Bourne was a small increase in the ration allowed the British element, bringing it nearer those of the Americans and French.

In March the Royal Norfolks were relieved by the 1st Royal Welch Fusiliers, who were flown in complete with regimental goat.

Supplies were now coming in greater quantity than ever to a population thinned by a steady trickle of emigration to the Western Zone. Indeed, the civilian food ration, although dull and dehydrated, was of higher calory content than before the blockade. Recognising that their gambit had failed, the Soviet Government reached agreement with the Western allies, under which all restrictions on overland transport were removed as from May 12, 1949. The great test of nerve, organisation and endurance had been passed at last, at a cost to the allies of sixty-eight airmen killed in accidents. Eighteen of them belonged to the R.A.F. and ten to British civilian lines.

By blockading Berlin Russia had come out in the open as an opponent, if not an enemy, of their former allies. The result was to sweep the latter into fresh military alliance. In September 1948 the five signatories of the Brussels Treaty set up their Western Union Defence Organisation, and at the same time discussions went ahead for its enlargement to include seven other powers, to the north, south and, beyond the

Atlantic, to the west. Recognising at last that their President Roosevelt had been duped by Chairman Stalin, the United States of America followed Britain's lead in reversing the strategy of generations. Involvement in the defence of Europe was accepted, and on April 4, 1949, the North Atlantic Treaty was signed.

The military organisation took rather longer to establish. The first move was the appointment of Field Marshal Montgomery as Chairman of the Commanders-in-Chief Committee of the Western Union as from November 1, 1948, and he thus became the first British soldier ever to preside over an international command in peacetime. He set up his headquarters in London, having handed over the post of C.I.G.S. to General Sir William Slim. Not until April 2, 1951, did N.A.T.O. set up its Supreme Headquarters, named SHAPE, in place of the Western Union organisation. General of the Army Eisenhower was Supreme Commander, with Montgomery his Deputy, and they opened business from the Hotel Astoria, Paris, pending a move to a permanent headquarters near Versailles. The French General Juin became C.-in-C. Allied Forces Central Europe and established headquarters at Fontainebleau.

The British Army of the Rhine was enlarged and strengthened by gradual stages to meet its new commitments, with the emphasis on armour and mobility in hope of slowly draining the momentum from the mighty blow the Russians could deliver. The first move was to free the 2nd Infantry and 7th Armoured Divisions—the 'Cross-Keys' and the 'Desert Rats'—from their static commitments by the formation of two separate district headquarters. A second armoured division was formed in the autumn of 1950, under the impetus of the belligerence displayed by Russia in Korea, and it took the name and bull badge of the 11th, which had accompanied the 7th through North-West Europe. A third came in early 1952, after rebirth in England, and this bore the mailed fist of the 6th Armoured, which in the war had journeyed to Austria via Tunis and Italy. Each armoured division had four regiments of armour (one of armoured cars) and four battalions of infantry (one motorised, the others lorried), and there was one armoured regiment among the nine battalions in the infantry division. With three extra armoured car regiments providing added fluidity and an independent brigade tied to Berlin, the total came to sixteen regiments (more than half the whole) and twenty-four battalions, and there was no shortage of guns to support them, with agras supplementing the divisional artillery. It was a powerful force, worthy of a leading defender of the democratic faith, and in the Centurion it had a tank that could at last be claimed worthy of the tank's founding nation.

The command structure of N.A.T.O. was never slow to provide a lead in the matter of expansion. Towards the close of 1951, the fighting troops of Rhine Army were formed into a corps, and for this purpose Headquarters 1st Corps made its first appearance in peacetime. It was indeed an enviable command, and appropriately the Commandant of the Staff College, Major-General A. D. Ward, was promoted to it. This was followed by the enlargement of the C.-in-C.'s command to include that of a Belgian corps and a Dutch corps, the whole taking the bloated title of Northern Army Group, which officially came to life on November 29, 1952, soon after General Sir Richard Gale had succeeded General Sir John Harding. Certainly N.A.T.O. had opened a wide panorama of prospect for the ambitious officer. With that of Northern Europe at Oslo included, there were four international headquarters needing British army officers, and there were eight subordinate general officers' commands (including Berlin) within Rhine Army. The only price to be paid for all this growth was a revision of staff duties throughout the Army, in the matter of drafting orders and suchlike, so that procedures could be standardised. It was also intended to standardise equipment, but this of course needed more time.

Bad Oeynhausen was not the best location for Headquarters Rhine Army now that new commitments had been superimposed upon it, and it was decided in due course that it should be moved nearer the Dutch border. A site near Munchen Gladbach was chosen. Here German workmen built a garden city at speed, and occupation of it was taken on October 4, 1954.

In May 1955 the Federal Republic of Germany joined the N.A.T.O. alliance, thus completing the haul, in exactly ten years, from the ignominy of being ruled by enemy soldiers to equal partnership with these same former enemies, whose duties had similarly changed from the punitive to the protective. It was political resurgence with strategic implications, for Germany had the right of a powerful contributor to demand a more forward defensive policy, designed to preserve a greater part of her land from the invading masses. This in turn had its effect on organisation, as also did the constant tactical search for the best solution to the awful problems of nuclear warfare. Infantry were needed now for the dogged, static, clinging role of old, and tanks had to be dispersed and decentralised to support them. The 11th Armoured Division was consequently converted, on April 1, 1956, into the 4th Infantry Division, which was restored with its old 10th, 11th, and 12th Infantry Brigades, each absorbing one armoured regiment as a fourth, integral unit. The extra infantry was provided by stripping the 6th and 7th Armoured, which thus became glorified brigades but remained in being as divisions for purposes of deployment.

The tactical experimenting that preceded and followed an organisational change such as this kept activity in Rhine Army at concert pitch, even though the prospect of an open clash with the Russians no longer seemed so real. Germany was the great arena which for British soldiers filled the void created by the evacuation of India and the emptying of the barracks of Aldershot. It was practically the only station that provided a period of stability for an infantry battalion in these troubled years. The barracks were good and the married quarters adequate, and the men could expect at least two and a half years in occupation, with excellent facilities for games. Yet life was very far from static. Training had always to go ahead at full throttle, and for many days on end the soldiers were far away from their barracks and families, carrying out field firing exercises on the great heaths of Luneburg or Sennelager, or advancing from a crossing of the Ems to that of the Weser. Returned to barracks, there would be little easing of the tempo, with cadres, ceremonial, specialist training, military and athletic competitions following each other fast, and the never ceasing turnover in personnel adding to the sense of rush. It was not so easy to keep morale high once the spur of the Russian menace became blunted, for Germany lacked the adventure and mysticism of India and the homeliness of Aldershot; it was neither one thing nor the other. Nowhere was it harder to persuade national-servicemen to become regulars.

The more popular stations in Europe had meanwhile been gradually closing down. Greece was the first to lose its British garrison, thanks largely to the bounteous aid offered by the United States. The British Army played no part in the second civil war against the Communists, other than to preserve calm by their presence and to help the training and equipping of the Greek Army through a military mission. During 1947 the troops were reduced from a division (the 4th Infantry) to a brigade, which after the evacuation of Palestine became the 2nd Infantry Brigade. By the end of 1949 only one battalion, the 1st Bedfordshire and Hertfordshire, remained, and they were stationed at Salonika. On January 22, 1950, they held a farewell parade in Aristotle Square and were cheered loudly as they marched through the streets. They embarked on February 4, being driven to the docks in Greek Army transport, and sailed next day.

Although rioting by Yugoslavia's adherents brought the troops out in the role of auxiliary policemen in the early days of the occupation, Trieste soon became a much coveted station and was for long enjoyed by the troops of the 24th Infantry Brigade, which had liberated the city as 24th Guards and achieved a unique tenure of occupation.

However, the Italians became suspicious of the intentions of the British Government, and there was some angry rioting in October 1953, as a result of which service families were sent home. It reached its peak in the first week of November, and both the 1st Suffolk and 1st Loyals were called out in aid of the police. By looking stern and being patient, they subdued the hot-heads without resort to fire. After a year's tension, a treaty was signed in London, returning Trieste to Italy, although not the whole of Venezia Giulia. On October 25, 1954, the Italian Army arrived and took the frontier posts over from the Loyals and Rozetti Barracks, Trieste, from the reborn 2nd Lancashire Fusiliers. The crowd raved hysterically as the Italian troops entered the barracks, and they treated the Lancashire Fusiliers to sullen silence, broken by the occasional jeer, as they marched to the docks to be embarked by the Royal Navy. A combined ceremonial parade had been planned for the following day, with the Italian, American, and British Armies represented, but the blast of the bora caused its cancellation and the British sailed away, not sorry to have missed it.

If a settlement of the Trieste problem seemed at one stage beyond hope, the one that followed bordered on the miraculous. Russia agreed to evacuate Austria, in exchange for a guarantee of her neutrality, under a treaty ratified on July 27, 1955. It fell to the 1st Middlesex to conduct the ceremonies of departure, which included the provision of a guard of honour for the Austrian Chancellor on ratification day. Although the British had come as enemy occupants, they received touchingly warm tribute from many sources, official and unofficial. Indeed, this had been the happiest of all tasks of occupation, and when on September 17 the Middlesex rearguard company lowered the Union Jack at Schonbrunn Barracks, Vienna, and saluted the flag of Austria run up in its place, they felt a sense of melancholy and pride.

There could be no similar scene in Germany. The Soviet Government under Khrushchev might appear more conciliatory, but as long as they held the states of Eastern Europe in bondage and kept 175 divisions operational, the N.A.T.O. allies had to remain alert, ever trying to keep abreast of the newest and most frightening methods of waging war. Europe remained the British Army's largest and most absorbing commitment. It absorbed the troops and it absorbed the attention of staff and instructors at the War Office, Imperial Defence College and Staff College. Methods of fighting guerrillas or of waging lightweight, rapier wars against weaker nations took second place, and this perhaps is exactly as the Russians intended.

5

Malaya

I—THE LONG GROPE (1948-50)

THE states of Malaya afforded one of the happier examples of British colonial rule. They consisted of three British possessions, acquired early in the nineteenth century, and nine principalities, brought separately under British protection between the years 1874 and 1919. The rulers of the latter—all Sultans, except for the Raja of Perlis and the Yang Di-Pertuan Besar of Negri Sembilan—sacrificed independence in their external affairs and accepted supervision in domestic matters in exchange for a guarantee of defence against aggression and help in building up their trade. By developing the growth of rubber and the mining of tin their British advisers made this the richest part of the Empire. Road and rail communications between the states were constructed, immigrants from China and India came pouring in, and shack towns were converted into miniature cities displaying the expanse, elegance and pomp of British India. The sultans had only to look around them to see the benefits of the treaties they had made. Then came the crash. The Japanese revealed the frailty of the British guarantee of protection, and misery fell on the states of Malaya.

The Malayan Communist Party came into being in 1930 and was soon outlawed. Composed almost entirely of Chinese, it was weak and ineffective until the war against Japan began. Now its penchant for the clandestine and its long sworn enmity to the Fascist powers enabled it to form a British sponsored guerrilla force, which in due course became the main resistance movement against Japanese occupation, with the title the Malayan People's Anti-Japanese Army. It survived, after almost being annihilated, by making survival its primary function. British officers of the clandestine Force 136 made jagged contact with it and brought it arms, ammunition, instructors and uniforms in mounting

73

number. The sudden surrender by Japan brought a surge of recruits to this widespread army, raising its strength to over 10,000, but the chance was missed to seize control of the country during the three weeks between the surrender and the arrival of the British, and the only gains were recognition for the Malayan Communist Party and the acquisition of a large supply of Japanese weapons. The Anti-Japanese Army was disbanded on December 1, 1945, after receiving handsome tribute from the British Military Administration. 6,000 of its men handed in their arms and received a bounty of £45 each. Some 4,000 took their weapons, mainly Japanese, into hiding.

The Communists turned to the conventional tactics of disrupting industry. They were thwarted by a tightening of the trade union legislation and by the favour gained for a new constitution introduced on February 1, 1948, which replaced the short-lived and highly unpopular Malaya Union. It brought a new Federation of Malaya into being, consisting of the nine Malay states and two of the British settlements, Penang and Malacca. Although joined to the mainland by a causeway, the island base of Singapore was kept separate as a colony.

February 1948 was also a month of destiny for the Communists. They staged a big jamboree at Calcutta, and it appears that the Malayan commissars received instructions or instigation here to go ahead with a campaign of violence aimed at the overthrow of British rule. The time was propitious. In Burma, India and Palestine the British had shown that they could quite easily be dislodged, and in China the greatest of all Communist warlords, Mao Tse-tung, was putting his teaching into practice by driving the superior forces of Nationalist China first to despair and then to defeat.

The Malayan Communists had a new young leader in the former resistance hero, Chin Peng, O.B.E. An ardent Maoist, Lau Yew, was made military commander and set about planning the four stages to victory—terrorisation, domination of certain areas, expansion and open battle—apparently confident of speedy success. Call-up notices went out to the 4,000 People's soldiers who had evaded discharge and most were obeyed, in some cases after forcible collection by 'blood and steel' units. Ten regiments were mobilised in different parts of Malaya, with the heaviest concentrations in Johore and Pahang, each of which had three. All but one of the regiments were entirely Chinese.

The rebel leaders had reason for confidence, since the people of Malaya had few unifying bonds and no warrior tradition. It was a thinly populated country, containing only 4,908,100 people on a peninsular 400 miles long and under 200 wide. 2,427,800 were Malays, a cheerful and lackadaisical people most of whom lived from the produce of the soil or sea, and in addition there were various aborigine tribes living nomadic lives in the jungle. 1,884,535 Chinese had been counted. Many of them earned good wages in the rubber plantations and the tin mines, and others eked a miserable existence from the jungle fringes, whither they had taken refuge from the Japanese. There were 530,600 Indians, proud that their fatherland had gained independence, and 12,000 Europeans, laden with complexes imbued by the Japanese occupation. There must have seemed bright prospect of driving these diverse peoples to confusion and despair.

The country itself was a guerrilla's paradise. Only one fifth of it had been fashioned by the hand of man, and most of this fifth lay adjacent to the south and west coastline, where rubber plantations abounded and tin was mined in smaller areas, notably around Ipoh and to the north of Kuala Lumpur. The remainder was covered by forest, commonly called jungle or 'ulu'. It was rucked by a spinal mountain range, running alongside the rich western strip, and sliced by innumerable rivers, some of which overflowed into vast, steaming, jungly swamps. From the air the jungle looked like an endless array of tight-packed cauliflowers, and at ground level it was night eternal, for the double canopy of treetop foliage reduced the power of the sun to that of a moon veiled by cloud, making melancholia a common affliction, sometimes lethal, among the jungle's human denizens. The undergrowth did not greatly impede movement when the trees grew thick and tall, sometimes to a height of 200 feet, but at higher altitudes dense and slippery bamboo entanglements formed wearisome obstacles, and in other parts former aborigine settlements had been overgrown by secondary jungle, which being exposed to the sun had rampaged into a much thicker and more prickly barrage than was to be found beneath the canopy. Lying at the very edge of the villages, plantations, roads, and railways, for which space had been carved out for them, these enormous expanses of jungle gave marauders as much freedom of movement as fish in an ocean, and they could not only move without risk of detection but keep themselves supplied through the fear that could so easily be injected into the village communities. This was the way of life known to the People's Anti-Japanese Army, and now some third of its members made sombre return to unearth the arms hidden in caches and submit once more to the hold of the jungle and to the savage discipline of the fanatics who led them. They now called themselves the People's Anti-British Army, a title later exchanged for the more predictable and more preposterous Malayan Races' Liberation Army.

The campaign began in April with acts of sabotage and with the intimidation, and in increasing number the killing, of the workers on

Gulf of
Siam

SOUTH
CHINA
SEA

PERLIS

Kangar

Alor Star

KEDAH

S.Patani

George
Town

PENANG

PROVINCE
WELLESLEY

Taiping

S.Siput

PERAK

Ipoh

CAMERON
HIGHLANDS

Telok
Anson

Kuala
Lipis

Fraser's
Hill

Raub

K.K.Bahru

B.Kali

Bentong

Batu Arang

SELANGOR

Kuala Lumpur

P.Swettenham

Kajang

Seremban

P.Dickson

NEGRI
SEMBILAN

Tampin

MALACCA

Malacca

Muar

Batu
Pahat

Pontian
Kechi

SINGAPORE

SUMATRA

Strait
of
Malacca

Tumpat
Kota Bharu

Pasir

KELANTAN

Gua Musang

TRENGGANU

Kuala
Trengganu

Kuantan

PAHANG

Mentakab

Pekan

P.Tioman

Endau

Mersing

Segamat

Kluang

JOHORE

Johore
Bahru

K.Tinggi

SIAM

Baling

MALAYA

0   40   100

Scale of Miles

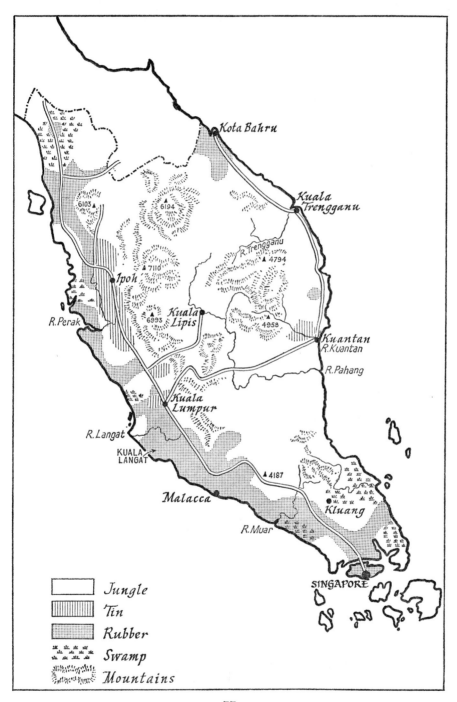

Kota Bahru

Kuala
Trengganu

6103▲ ▲6194

R.Trengganu
▲4794

▲7110

Ipoh

▲6993 Kuala
Lipis

▲4958

Kuantan
R.Kuantan

R.Perak

R.Pahang

Kuala
Lumpur

R.Langat

KUALA
LANGAT

▲4187

Malacca

Kluang

R.Muar

SINGAPORE

Jungle
Tin
Rubber
Swamp
Mountains

77

rubber estates and tin mines. Trusted foremen were the most common targets and could be felled with little difficulty, to become the first of many thousands of innocents slaughtered to satisfy the lust for power raging across Asia in the guise of political idealism. Vivid impact was made on a young army officer who saw the immediate result of one of these killings. The Chinese foreman was slumped in his chair on the verandah of his bungalow, a crimson patch down his vest, glowing in the fading light of evening. Sobbing could be heard but there was no one to be seen, until the eye fell on a ring of blank faces turned towards the corpse from the shadows outside. A police officer arrived and began questioning. No one had dared see it happen.

In June attacks on Europeans began. Three were killed on two rubber estates in Perak on the 16th; two of them, a manager and his assistant, were tied up and pumped with sten gun bullets in front of their petrified workers. The rebels had come out in the open, and on this same day a state of emergency was declared, which did not however impose any form of military control as had been the case in Palestine. It merely imposed restrictions on certain liberties and the death penalty on the unauthorised possession of arms. It also implied that the situation had passed beyond control by the police alone and that the military were being called to their aid.

The bulk of the British garrison was provided by the Brigade of Gurkhas, who had six battalions dotted up and down the mainland, along the western, cultivated belt, a seventh (the 1/2nd) on Singapore island, and the eighth (the 2/10th) at Hong Kong. Apart from the 1/6th, 1/7th, and 1/10th, who had come from Burma in January, the battalions were in a state of convalescence, for they had been drained of men and even of clothing in India and when they arrived in three shiploads, between March and April, many of the men marched bravely ashore without boots and without shirts, to receive a warm welcome into the British Army. There had since been a good flow of recruits, with plenty of re-enlisted veterans among them, but there were many on guard when the emergency broke holding weapons they had never fired. A project to reform the 17th Gurkha Division, complete with Gurkha arms and services, added complications, for the 7th Gurkhas were to form the artillery element and had begun to train for conversion. They swiftly reverted to an infantry role, but plans were to mature in due course for the raising of engineers, signallers, and a service column.

The only British unit on the mainland was the 26th Field Regiment, who were at Tampin, in Negri Sembilan, helping in the conversion of the 7th Gurkhas. They too were involved in the conversion in reverse, being required to take the field as infantry at shortest notice, a role in which they were greatly to prosper. There were also three British battalions available, all island-based. The 1st Devonshire and the 1st Seaforth Highlanders (who had been the first to taste civil war in Java) were at Singapore, and the 1st King's Own Yorkshire Light Infantry, who had begun their foreign tour, as the 2nd, in India in 1922, were at the north-west end on the island of Penang, which contained Malaya's largest town, George Town. Initially by companies, these three battalions were rapidly sucked on to the mainland.

The G.O.C. Malaya District was a distinguished Gurkha officer, Major-General C. H. Boucher, who also held the fatherly appointment, for which he was well suited, of Major General Brigade of Gurkhas. His headquarters was at the federal capital, Kuala Lumpur, whence he controlled three sub-districts each under a brigadier. The North Sub-District, centred on Taiping, had the K.O.Y.L.I., the 2/2nd and 1/6th Gurkhas, and the two regular battalions of the Malay Regiment, a colonial force led by British officers. The Central Sub-District, centred on Seremban, had the 26th Field and its intended converts, the 1/7th and 2/7th Gurkhas, together with the 2/6th Gurkhas, who were to have been going to Hong Kong. Johore Sub-District had the 1/10th Gurkhas in residence, the Devons and Seaforth on their way to join them and the 1/2nd Gurkhas destined to follow them from Singapore in August. Spitfires and Dakota transport aircraft were available, controlled by an Air headquarters established alongside Boucher's, and to assist in the puzzling task of finding targets, and in liaison duties, the army had its own air O.P. squadron, R.A., equipped with Austers.

The Malayan Police Force, to whose aid the battalions came, was poorly equipped, both mentally and materially, to combat rebellion. Its regular strength was only 10,000, and the morale of its men, who were nearly all Malay, still needed nursing after the poison injected by the Japanese occupation. The soldiers found a bewildering lack of information about the enemy and were swamped with requests, from both police and civil authorities, for guards, escorts and the means of improving a tenuous system of communication. Battalions had huge areas of responsibility, every corner of which needed reassurance if not more. It was hard to prevent the dissipation of reserves, and the immediate aim of the army was to instil sufficient confidence and self-reliance to enable troops to be freed for the offensive action into the jungle without which, it was realised from the start, the rebels could never be defeated. Any officer who had imagined the task was going to be simple was speedily disillusioned.

The most encouraging feature was the attitude of the people, most of all the European rubber planters, in whom the rebels' campaign of murder and sabotage had sown far more anger than terror. The battalions provided them with cadres for the raising of their own home guards, and backed often by the army experience of its manager, many an estate became an efficient armed camp. For the permanent provision of guards, as also for watch over the Siamese border, a Special Constabulary was formed, which was to free the army of many commitments. By the end of the year it had attained a strength of 28,700, by voluntary enlistment, and there was also a great surge of recruits into the Malay Regiment and into the part-time Auxiliary Police, which was a glorified home guard. It was a grievous blow to the calculations of the rebels that the people of Malaya should display such eagerness to defend themselves against liberation in communist form.

The most serious blow dealt at the British in these early days could only indirectly be attributed to the rebels. The High Commissioner of Malaya, Sir Edward Gent, was flown home for consultation on July 4 and killed in a mid-air crash when about to land through the fog over England. Three months were to elapse before his successor took office, and much might have been achieved in that period by some firm direction at government level.

The audacity of the rebels—or 'bandits' as the army called them—reached its peak in this month of July. On the 11th they took possession of a deserted tin mine, near Kuala Lumpur. Some raw, stocky soldiers of the 2/6th and 2/7th Gurkhas did battle with them for seven hours, killed four of them, and forced nineteen to surrender. The 2/6th lost a lance-corporal killed, the first soldier to die in the campaign, and a rifleman of the 2/7th slew a man with his kukri. The following day the rebels seized another mine nearby, the active one at Batu Arang and the only one in Malaya producing coal. They rounded up the pitmen and murdered the overseer and four others as the police began to put in an attack. They then withdrew.

On July 16, a party of policemen, under a British officer, gained a great and welcome success. In a dawn raid on a hut, also in the Kuala Lumpur area, they shot dead two of three people who ran away, and one turned out to be the rebel leader, Lau Yew, who was planning an attack on Kajang. A further six rebels were killed making a counter-attack, together with five of their women, who had been captured in the hut and tried to escape as the attack came in. The 26th Field Regiment now came as infantry to Batu Arang, two batteries strong, and they brought the month to a triumphant end by staging an operation with the police in which twenty-seven of the cocky gangsters in this area were killed.

Over 100 miles northwards, in the untamed and inaccessible state of

Kelantan, the rebels briefly enjoyed greater success. They established domination over two villages on a disused railway line, Bertam and Gua Musang, and declared it a liberated area. On July 19 they ambushed a party of the Malay Regiment, killing a British major and six men and inflicting a damaging blow to morale. On the 22nd the 2/6th Gurkhas were summoned from Selangor. It took them a week's travelling along jungle tracks to reach Gua Musang, and there they found that the Malay Regiment had driven the enemy back to the Pulai valley, an old, steep-sided pirate stronghold, covered in a mixture of crops and jungle. With Dakotas dropping them supplies and with Spitfires blasting the enemy positions with rockets, the young Gurkhas, who were so swiftly becoming veteran, put a speedy end to this second and last attempt at open defiance by the Anti-British Army. They had driven them all into hiding again by August 7, having lost one killed and two wounded in the fighting.

The Commander-in-Chief Far East Land Forces, with G.H.Q. at Singapore, was General Sir Neil Ritchie, who had savoured defeat as an army commander in the desert and victory as a corps commander in Europe. Sensing that the strong rebel concentrations in Johore needed separate treatment, he now transferred this sub-district, which was commanded by a highly experienced Gurkha, Brigadier R. C. O. Hedley, to Singapore Base District, under the newly arrived Major-General D. Dunlop, an artilleryman. He had made a fifth battalion available here by bringing down the 1st Royal Inniskilling Fusiliers from Hong Kong. They arrived by ship on August 4—seven weeks after the official start of the emergency.

A further reinforcement, with an offensive role in view, was Ferret Force. This had been formed in July by bringing veterans of Force 136 out of retirement, engaging British, Malay and Chinese civilians on short contract, and extracting volunteers from any battalion in the command. Its aim was to locate and harry the rebel bands in the jungle and to build up the techniques on which others might draw; the old hands swiftly regained their expertise. It was of course a strain on the battalions to provide the men; they had few enough in total and, whether Gurkha or British, very few with experience of jungle warfare. Compensation in kind came in August with the arrival from Borneo of forty-seven Dyak trackers, mainly of the Iban tribe. They were little men with long hair running down their backs like a horse's tail and with disarming smiles, which gleamed incongruously from beside their deadly blow pipes and their fearsome knives adorned with human hair. This was the start of a very fruitful partnership.

In mid-August the first reinforcement arrived from England in the shape of the 4th Queen's Own Hussars, 800 strong, They were to be employed partly as infantry and partly on road patrols and escorts, using soft-skinned vehicles because it was not thought that the bridges were strong enough for armour. Having examined them, the commanding officer successfully disputed this opinion, which came from a civilian source, and a request was made for the despatch first of scout and then armoured cars from England. Although their issue and shipment were put into train with all possible speed, the process was inevitably a long one.

The troops were by now coming to grips with the enormous problem of fighting the enemy in the vast, sombre expanse of his home ground. They had been issued with such items as jungle boots, neckerchiefs (or 'rags, sweat, J.G.'), the shorter rifle, pack rations and matchets (or 'parangs') and they were teaching themselves the art of penetrating the seemingly impenetrable silently and accurately, without fatigue and without sores, and with enough food to provide the range to catch the enemy in his lair, enough ammunition to fight against superior numbers, and enough clothing to withstand the habitual evening downpour and the chill of night. They were learning to live in silence, to cook in pitch darkness, of which there were twelve hours in every twenty-four, and to sleep on a sapling platform under mosquito net and poncho cape, with the pat of water above and its gurgle below. They were trying not to be depressed by the perpetual gloaming, worried by the uncanny silence during these hours of half-daylight, or frightened by the cacophony that arose at nightfall, as birds, insects, little animals, and vegetation began their rounds of shrieks, pops, hisses, and yowls; and then there were snakes, leeches, ants and hornets waiting to provide truer cause for fear. They had to be expert at first aid and able to make a stretcher from bamboos and a cape, and they had to be able to maintain touch with company headquarters. This last was the most baffling problem of all, since wireless sets probed in vain against the treetop canopy, except possibly in the early morning and late afternoon. It could be solved only by the issue of masts, whose erection at set times called for the skill of a steeplejack, or by the use of light aircraft, which could not conceal their presence from the enemy.

In September the troops in Johore began the army's first big offensive. Ferret Force brilliantly blazed the trail, Spitfires smote the targets obtained for them, and the Devons, Seaforth, Inniskillings (who made two sealandings), 1/2nd, and 1/10th Gurkhas plunged deep into the jungle in a phased programme of sweeps and cordons, cutting gaps in the canopy for supply by air. Twelve camps were found and burned, some with accommodation for 200, including lecture hut for the daily indoctrination lessons; ammunition was unearthed in huge quantities, as were Russian flags and communist literature; and twenty-seven rebels were claimed killed in some tough little actions. The announcement of such a haul provided a good advertisement for the security forces and emphasised both the size of the rebels' organisation and the confidence they must have entertained in the security of their hide-outs. On the other hand there could be no denying that the great bulk of them must have got away.

On October 6 Sir Henry Gurney was sworn in at Kuala Lumpur as High Commissioner, filling the chair that had been empty for three months. He had made his mark in Palestine, where he had been Chief Secretary to Sir Alan Cunningham, and he was not the only man to have been passed from the one emergency to the next, for Colonel Gray had arrived in August to take the appointment of Commissioner of Police, and of 500 British police sergeants come from England a large proportion had been in the Palestine Police. Gray's influence swiftly became apparent, particularly in the standard of communications within the police force and in the all-important, newly raised Special Branch.

Gurney similarly lost no time in implementing measures to restrict the rebels' freedom of movement, of which some had been initiated before his arrival. Starting in the north, where it was intended to seal off a 20-mile belt adjacent to Siam, the registration of the population began; it was a complicated task of daunting dimension, which the rebels tried their hardest to thwart by terrorising both the issuers and holders of identity cards. Then came powers to deport any unwanted person not a Malayan citizen, and this was followed by the notorious Regulation 17D, under which the inhabitants of complete villages could be placed in detention if the High Commissioner were satisfied that they had 'aided, abetted or consorted with the bandits'. These were tough measures, providing the rebels with desirable assets in the propaganda market, but fear was the most powerful weapon they wielded and it had to be countered in kind.

Simultaneously with Gurney's arrival came that of the most powerful reinforcement to be received, the newly formed 2nd Guards Brigade. It would appear that its choice was the result of much anxious deliberation at the War Office and the cause of consternation in Birdcage Walk, for although Shanghai had provided an exception between the two world wars, it had been the long accepted privilege of the Guards not to venture further eastwards than Egypt, even in wartime. Certainly the Army's 'parlous condition', as described by Montgomery, was shown up. The battalions chosen were performing their traditional functions for the King, newly reissued with their scarlet full dress: the 3rd

Grenadiers, after two and a half years in Palestine, at Windsor, the 2nd Coldstream and 2nd Scots Guards in London. They were not aware of their availability as a strategic reserve, were short of men, and had many young soldiers in their ranks, who were only barrack-trained. Yet at least these battalions could draw on others of their own regiments to bring them to strength, and this was more than could be said for the dozen Line battalions out of whom an operational brigade, the 27th, was in process of being raised. Germany, which had been the source of reinforcement for Palestine, was of course now in need of reinforcement itself.

There was little apparent urgency about the despatch of the brigade. Not until August 13—'Black Friday'—were the battalions warned and the formation of Brigade Headquarters authorised, under Brigadier M. D. Erskine, who until then had been Lieutenant-Colonel Commanding, Scots Guards. On September 5 the Coldstream and Scots Guards marched bravely to Waterloo Station, for embarkation from Southampton, and on October 4 they disembarked at Singapore, followed by the Grenadiers on the 7th. Their first task was to march through the sultry streets of Singapore with colours flying, salute the Governor, and duly impress a great crowd. They then exchanged their 'cheese-cutter' caps for the 'sloppy Joe' bush hats that could be squashed into a hundred shapes, providing rare opportunity for the expression of individuality, and for the remainder of October they were educated in jungle warfare in Johore, making friends with the Iban trackers, half their size, who joined them. They became operational at the start of November, taking over a sector in Selangor and Pahang, with the Coldstream in the wild mountainous district astride the inter-state boundary, the Scots in the troubled mining district around Batu Arang and the plantations north and west of Kuala Lumpur, and the Grenadiers further south, around Lau Yew's chosen objective, Kajang, and its nearby swamps.

The arrival of the Guards released the 2/6th Gurkhas for despatch to Hong Kong and brought the total of fighting units to seventeen, nine British, six Gurkha, and two Malay, of which less than a whole battalion was at Singapore. The figure does not include Ferret Force, which had been of great aid but was now in process of disbandment, partly because its civilians were under short contract, partly because its soldiers were needed back by their units. Some of the civilians joined battalions as liaison officers.

It is just possible that if the whole of this force had been available at the end of July the rebel organisation might have been smashed while reeling under the death blow delivered at Lau Yew. But Chin Peng, the political leader, was as determined as ruthless. He kept his army in being by concentrating on the first of Mao's principles for guerrilla warfare, self-preservation, and he strengthened their morale by providing them with jungle green uniform with a peaked khaki cap bearing a red star. He also stiffened his chains of committees and made them tighten their grip on the Min Yuen, or people's movement. This organisation passed orders, supplies and recruits on to the jungle troops and also conducted its own murder campaign, mainly of people who were slow to comply with demands for money. It was impossible to know how many active members it had or how many passive ones it held in thrall. The most important links in the chain were the branches, each of some fifteen members, whose job was to control the jungle fringes and maintain liaison between the district committees and units of the Liberation Army.

The British Army had at least proved that these fighters for Communism were no supermen and had forced them to be very much more wary, although some gangs still attempted to roam the jungle at company if not regimental strength. Both sides were still at the experimental stage, and with the arrival of 2nd Guards Brigade the British could achieve a greater degree of stability in which to work out their problems. They amounted in short to the domination of areas which in no brigadier's command measured less than 3,000 square miles per battalion.

Company commanders were the key figures in the day-to-day conduct of operations, and there was great scope for their resource and imagination. Their companies usually had tented camps near the jungle. They were sited near police stations, and there would always be a reserve ready to rush off to an S.O.S. call, for which purpose armoured vehicles were in gradual process of being issued. The remainder of the company might be on local police assistance, if for instance a cordon were required for a search, or on long range patrol, trying to trace the pattern of enemy movements and to ambush his supply routes. This could lead to a full scale company operation against an enemy camp. The larger pattern of rebel activity would meanwhile be crystallizing at battalion headquarters, and this might call for a redeployment just as companies were settling to their tasks. The brigadier obtained an even larger picture, and the prospect of making a big round-up by converging movements always appeared very tempting on the map. Consequently stability, which was so essential for 'framework' operations in partnership with the police, became a rare and valued asset.

The size of patrols was steadily whittled down from full company strength to a standard ten, plus two trackers. This was large enough to achieve all-round defence, and there was in fact little chance of more than three men ever coming into action, so fleeting were the contacts and restricting the tracks. Battle drills were evolved, designed for the instant production of maximum fire effect. Patrols were useless without good leaders, and this imposed heavy strain on subalterns, who seldom had time to heal the sores and skin irritations, which the humidity and prolonged exertion under a heavy load made unavoidable, between returning with one part of their platoon and setting off with another.

Five days' was adjudged the maximum supply of rations men could carry with them, and when added to weapon and ammunition, matchet, first aid kit, mosquito net, poncho cape, ground sheet, water bottle, and a change of underclothes, the load came to more than 60 lbs. If palm were the only obstruction—straggly attap palm, dangling down from the foliage canopy, or pandanus palm, with its vicious saw-toothed edge— or if a stream could be found with flat bottom and gentle gradient, the patrol might penetrate to within a radius of 20 miles on its five days' supply. But if there were hills to be climbed and they were littered with dense and slippery bamboo, it could be hard to travel a mile in a day, and in every steaming hour a bucket of sweat would be spilled that would give pang to the chill brought by the fall of darkness. It was not easy to lie still and alert on ambush duty after two such days of toil, particularly when tickled and tasted by ants, beetles and scorpions, and it is perhaps not surprising that an estimate made later in the campaign put the man-hours spent on patrol at 1,800 for every contact made. The need for silence greatly added to the tension, and the treetop canopy not only cast its perpetual gloom but gave some the panicky feeling of being caught in a sack. When a patrol returned across the demarcation line between operational zone and base, a torrent of conversation would burst forth like the roar of Niagara falls.

Patrols from almost every company in every battalion were daily engaged on these exhausting excursions, which the men insisted on calling 'ulu bashing', much to the despair of the erudite instructors at the jungle warfare school. Kills came in their ones and twos, at intervals of three or four days. This was just sufficient to provide incentive, and it seems also to have sown over-confidence in governmental circles, for it was stated in the Colonial Annual Report for 1948, 'The Communist-inspired military campaign had been reduced to the proportions of squalid guerrilla depredations by increasingly demoralised bandits, fighting for their lives against increasingly well-organised Security Forces.' It is certain that General Boucher did not take such an optimistic view.

The biggest problem was to distinguish friend from foe. The troops spent as much time laying cordons for screening purposes as on jungle patrol, and it was as a result of one these, conducted in a hotbed of rebel influence, that the Scots Guards received a shaft of publicity they did not want. A patrol led by a sergeant surrounded some huts on a rubber plantation near Batang Kali, north of Kuala Lumpur, on December 12. The male occupants were separated from the female, interrogated by the police, and confined to a single hut pending removal. One broke away and was shot dead, and subsequently the remaining twenty-five suffered a similar fate attempting a mass escape. The news caused such shock that the Attorney-General of Malaya, Sir Stafford Foster Sutton, personally carried out an investigation. He found no evidence that the sergeant or his men had exceeded their duties, which required that detained persons 'under no circumstances be allowed to escape'. The Batang Kali area became much quieter.

Further north, in Perak, the 2/2nd Gurkhas were trying to free squatter settlements from the grip of a powerful gang operating from Kelantan. This gang seems to have been the first to learn the art of laying a road ambush. The 2/2nd ran into one on Christmas Eve and lost four men killed and thirteen wounded. On New Year's Eve it was the turn of the 4th Hussars operating in this same area. They had received some armoured cars by now, but not enough to equip all troops, and the patrol involved consisted of two officers and sixteen men riding in two armour-plated trucks and, in the middle, an unarmoured 15-cwt. truck. They were caught on a road near Sungei Siput, and although well spaced were fully enveloped by fire from the hillside immediately above them. The troop commander backed his vehicle alongside the rear one, and the men leapt out and fought from the roadside, having no overhead protection in the trucks against the grenades showered upon them. The troop commander was killed and almost everyone else hit, including the young and newly commissioned 2nd Lieutenant Sutro. He ordered the men back in the two armoured trucks, lugging in the badly wounded, and the vehicles slowly reversed, flat-tyred, through the crash of grenades until reaching cover in a plantation. Six soldiers were dead, apart from the troop commander. Having grouped his remnant for defence, Sutro then took the better-running of the two trucks, and with the only unhurt man driving charged back through the ambush position and summoned help. There was an M.C. for him, the first of the campaign, and a D.C.M. for a Trooper Smith, who had left the road to fight his own battle with the ambushers.

A fortnight later the 1/6th Gurkhas lost two officers and six riflemen killed in a clash in northern Kedah, to which the rebels had easy access from across the Siamese border, and on January 19, 1949, twelve people, of whom four were soldiers, were callously killed in a bus on a road in Pahang. Only the K.O.Y.L.I., who had had some tough encounters in the northern sector, could provide bright success to offset these losses, killing five rebels in an action at Kulim on January 12.

The Guards were by now getting the feel of the jungle, and although the Grenadiers lost five killed and three wounded in an ambush near Kajang, they had a number of successes against the very tough gang in this area. The Coldstream in Pahang toiled endlessly with small return against some extremely wary rebels. Their Lance-Sergeant Gulston had an extraordinary adventure in their midst. Taking four men on a brief reconnaissance, without food or bedding, he found his return route to camp blocked by a large gang. He shot one with his sten, the only automatic available; but sensing they had him trapped, the rebels put down a widespread screen of fire, and for seven days—April 2–9—Gulston and his men roamed the jungle trying to find a way round, having beaten off the only serious attempt made to attack them. They lived on tapioca roots and huddled in improvised shelters to keep off the cold at night, for they were 4,000 feet up, and were in amazingly good spirits when at last found by a patrol. Gulston was awarded the Military Medal.

A combined attempt was now made to scour the wild and mountainous state of Pahang. Since Johore had become much quieter after the operations in conjunction with Ferret Force, the Devons were moved permanently into the south-west part of Pahang early in 1949, and in May the Inniskillings, Seaforth, and 1/10th Gurkhas, still under Hedley's command, came into the swampy and roadless eastern zone, while the Coldstream thumped the north-west of the state with the 2/2nd Gurkhas and 2nd Malay. Exertion was immense and contacts few and fleeting, with a notable exception near Mentakab, from which Captain Lucas, an officer of the Royal Berkshire with the Devons, won the first D.S.O. of the campaign. He was ambushed when using a railway jeep. He covered the withdrawal of his few men and sent them back in the jeep to summon the reserve platoon, while himself firing at the stubborn and large gang first from one position and then another, and shouting orders to imaginary troops. The platoon arrived by rail, but having held the rebels so long, Lucas found to his mortification that they had slipped away just as his attack came in.

In July the first relief took place. The 3rd Grenadiers handed their war against the Kajang gang—which was an independent company under the bearded Liew Kon Kim—to another battalion that had served in Palestine and now came from Greece, the 1st Suffolk; the Grenadiers could claim twenty-three rebels killed and fifty-one camps destroyed.

The Inniskillings, who had been due for home-posting the previous autumn, departed a month later, and in September the 1st Green Howards arrived from the Middle East to take their place. The Inniskillings had seen the opposition crumble before them. 'It is hard to see how the insurrection can last far into 1950,' reported their correspondent.

At the end of August the 2nd Guards Brigade began the most ambitious drive yet staged, with the Scots Guards in the main role, keeping three companies on air supply for eight weeks on end. The Dakotas also had a heavy commitment in dropping leaflets, offering an amnesty for all 'who had no blood on their hands'. It yielded a mere sixty-one surrenders in the course of ten weeks. The Scots Guards found the opposition as tough as the going. They lost two subalterns, a sergeant, and a guardsman killed in this operation, and could claim only three rebels in exchange. A further two officers and a sergeant had been killed in previous operations, although with heavier loss to the rebels.

Yet another officer of the Scots Guards to die—six were lost during their tour—was the brigade commander, Brigadier Erskine. Rugged and determined, he refused to be deterred from making a flight in his Auster by report of a common hazard, a thunder storm, and he and his gunner pilot were lost somewhere over Pahang on October 27. Endless search was made by air and ground patrol, but nothing was found, until a chance discovery of some relics ten years later. This was no surprise to those well acquainted with the vast expanse of the jungle and the enveloping power of its trees.

The rebels had by now sprung into the attack again, showing that they were much further from defeat than many people imagined. Police stations and, as always, underlings in authority were their special targets, and many a platoon went skeltering off to be faced with a scene of hideous execution and very few clues as to the whereabouts of its perpetrators. Soldiers were seldom deliberately molested, having armour now to protect their convoys, but chance encounters could lead to heavy fighting, as happened on November 12 when a company of Seaforth Highlanders were searching for clues outside the jungle near Segamat, Johore, in country rarely visited by troops. Automatics spat forth from a village, killing the officer with the leading platoon. The company commander came up and he too was killed, and a third officer was killed in attempting to locate the flanks of the enemy. They had bumped a very large gang indeed, and in a prolonged fire fight two more soldiers of the Seaforth were killed and another subaltern badly wounded. They themselves claimed seven rebels killed, after investigations following the occupation of the village after nightfall.

Two months later this same gang (supposedly) ambushed a small party of the 1/2nd Gurhkas. They were beaten off without loss to the Gurkhas, whereupon D Company of this battalion followed their trail and drove them out of a new camp that had accommodation for 1,000. B Company were summoned to cut off their retreat, and with some luck they intercepted them in a rubber plantation, close to the main trunk road, at dawn next morning, January 22, 1950. The company commander, Major Richardson, charged with one of his two platoons, shouting to C.S.M. Bhimbahadur that he was to cut off the retreat with the other. The latter acted with such agility that twenty-three rebels were mown down as they tried to escape through a paddy field and a further twelve were subsequently reported to have died of wounds. One Gurkha was killed, slashed by a parang in the initial charge. No single company action ever achieved greater success, and a D.S.O. and D.C.M. were awarded the two leaders.

There was little else to enlighten the gloom around this time. Both before and after this action there were arrogant and savage killings in this neighbourhood; sixteen civilians were killed in one road ambush, some by being thrown wounded on to the flames consuming their lorries, and nineteen policemen, two women, and two children were killed in an attack on a village police station. By the end of March 1950 the totals killed by the rebels since the start of the emergency were assessed at 863 civilians, 323 policemen, and 154 soldiers, and in the first two categories nearly half had been inflicted in the last six months. It is true that the rebels were reported to have lost 1,138 killed, 645 captured, and 359 surrendered over the same period, but replacements must have been arriving in larger numbers, and the strength of their jungle army was later proved to be far in excess of the 3,000 stated in the House of Commons in April 1950.

It was a depressing situation. The rebels' influence could be felt and their deeds of destruction seen; but there was little reliable information as to how many of them prowled the opaque fastness of the jungle as soldiers, how many villagers and townsmen owed allegiance to the Min Yuen, and how many reinforcements were trickling across the frontier from Siam, the effective sealing of which called for some 100,000 more police or troops than were available. Something needed to be done, wider in its embrace than the latest and biggest sweep the 2nd Guards Brigade were planning.

Since July of 1949 Far East Land Forces had had a new C.-in-C. in General Sir John Harding. Malaya was not his only source of anxiety, for Mao Tse-tung's army was closing on the frontier of the New Territories, Hong Kong, and there were plans afoot for the swift transfer of the 2nd Guards Brigade there to join the division already assembled. In the meantime the Guards carried on with their jungle operations, and to simplify problems of grouping Harding returned Johore to Boucher's command. Hedley had already moved his sub-district headquarters to Pahang, and in December it was redesignated H.Q. 48th Gurkha Infantry Brigade.

Boucher did not long enjoy his reorganised command. He had done his best—and as was to be recognised by knighthood, it was a good best—and in the process had fallen ill. Major-General R. E. Urquhart, who had gained fame at Arnhem in command of the 1st Airborne Division, succeeded him as from February 8, 1950. As G.O.C., however, he was responsible for only one aspect of the campaign, military operations, and the need of an overlord was increasingly being felt, to direct and coordinate the efforts of every department concerned in the struggle. Field Marshal Slim, the C.I.G.S., recognised this and turned to an Indian Army colleague who had served under him in Burma and been the last British commander there, Lieutenant-General Sir Harold Briggs. A quiet and modest man, with a high sense of duty and no illusions about the immensity of the problem, Briggs acceded to his former chief's wish and left the comfort of retirement in Cyprus. He arrived at Kuala Lumpur on April 5 to take up the government appointment of Director of Operations.

After a delicate appreciation of the risks, Harding had meanwhile ordered powerful reinforcements to come from Hong Kong. The 26th Gurkha Brigade, consisting of the 1st Cameronians, the 2/6th and the 2/10th Gurkhas—all Rifle regiments—arrived on April 7 and went to fill the vacuum now being felt in Johore. The 3rd Royal Marine Commando Brigade followed in May and June and went to the unruly wilds of Perak. A third reinforcement came from the Middle East, in the form of the 13th/18th Royal Hussars, who took over escort and support duties in the southern part of Malaya, leaving the 4th Hussars to concentrate on the northern. They were very welcome.

The air arm received reinforcement from Australia, the R.A.A.F. providing a squadron of Lincoln bombers in the hope of making life unbearable for the rebels in their jungle strongholds. Targets for the Spitfires had become increasingly scarce, and the new weapons could expect to achieve little more than wage a war of nerves. Dakotas and the faithful Austers remained the soldiers' best friends.

In early May the Suffolks, near Kajang, provided a fine example of what could be achieved by close cooperation with the police. The latter heard through a woman informer that a supply party of the Min Yuen would be lying up in an overgrown cemetery at a certain time. Putting full trust in the report, Lieutenant-Colonel Wight of the Suffolks sent a company there concealed, in stifling heat, beneath the tarpaulins of some rubber trucks, which were driven by Malay policemen in native clothing. After passing the cemetery, the trucks stopped behind some rubber trees, and the men leapt out and charged. They were fired at, but swiftly drove the rebels out of the jungle grass with flame throwers and phosphorous grenades. Four were killed and the remaining three captured, either by this company or a second one deployed as stops. A further five were netted as an immediate result of interrogation. But Liew Kon Kim's Kajang gang had only been chipped.

General Briggs was quick to grasp that something more radical was needed, however successful the occasional raid or jungle operation might be. The crucial need was to instil a sense of security into the population and thus deprive the rebels of their system of supply and communications, and if this could be achieved they would be forced to come out and attack the security forces on ground of the latter's choosing. The first requirement, which was aimed at the very vitals of the rebel nervous system, was to remove the squatters and isolated groups of workers from their sprawling shacks by the forest fringes and concentrate them in new villages. It was a tremendous project, involving great expense and running into political entanglement, since each state had separately to grant sites for the villages, and each grudged them the land. Yet as early as June this first, and in the long run decisive, feature of the Briggs Plan was under way.

Such speed of decision was the fruit of a new system of integrated committees, starting with a streamlined War Council at the top, whose authority however was by no means absolute, through Briggs's own Operations' Committee to War Executive committees at state and district level. Each committee had its civil government chairman, its police and military members—the latter being a brigadier at state level, a battalion or company commander at district—representatives of such organisations as Chinese Affairs and the local planters' association, and others who might be co-opted on occasions. It met never less frequently than weekly. Operational partnerships that had long been working

informally and in most cases harmoniously were thus enlarged and
regularised, and the ponderous machinery was set in motion for the
circulation of agenda, minutes and memoranda, and their passage
upwards, downwards, and sideways for query, action, or advice. There
was plenty of exasperation in store for soldiers eager to go ahead with
operational projects, but it would have been impossible to achieve the
wide degree of coordination required under the Briggs Plan without an
elaborate system of joint consultation, and the soldiers were after all
there to aid the civil power. Initially the committee system provided the
impetus needed: 410 new villages were occupied within two years of
Briggs's arrival. They were built to a tight schedule—rather too tight,
some thought—under the waves of urgency emitted through the new
combined chain of command.

To prevent interference by the rebels the move of each group of
squatters to a new village had to be kept secret from them, and this
called for close liaison between many departments, civil, police and
military. The civil authorities had first to get the village built without
disclosing who its occupants were intended to be. There would then be
a swoop at dawn. The army would throw a cordon and the district
commissioner or administrative officer would then break the news to the
squatters that they were to be moved. It was never well received, and the
soldiers had usually to assist the police in the unpleasant task of prying
the unwilling out of their squalid old homes, which would then be
burned to cinders. They had also to make the new villages defensible by
putting up wire and earthworks, by keeping watch on their surrounds,
and by trying to sow the seeds of responsibility that might blossom into
the formation of a home guard. This last was the hardest and most
important task of all. Some battalions were kept fully busy on these
duties for months, while others strove to counter the displays of
violence with which many gangs showed their disapproval of the
scheme.

The 2nd Coldstream Guards played a harmonious part in resettling
squatters as a final, contrasting task before their return homewards at
the end of July. They had spent months in laborious toil through the
jungle, often at no more than a mile a day, and could claim only eleven
rebels killed; and yet their Lieutenant-Colonel FitzGeorge-Balfour
earned a rare D.S.O., showing that kills were not all that mattered.
Nevertheless, they continued to be carefully substantiated by battalions
and avidly aggregated, for while the score of a good battalion might
remain low, that of a bad one could never be high. The 1st Worcestershire, from Germany and England, took over the sector astride the
Selangor-Pahang-Perak border, and since the Scots were the only

Guards left the 2nd Guards Brigade was redesignated the 18th Infantry.

Around the same time the two remaining sub-districts were converted into districts, North Malaya and South Malaya, each under a major-general, and a third Gurkha brigade, the 63rd, was formed in Negri Sembilan. Malaya as a whole was raised to the status of a command, but Urquhart remained a major-general, although he now had twenty-six fighting units under his command, fourteen British, eight Gurkha, and four Malay, two new battalions having been raised in 1949. Meanwhile war had broken out in Korea, increasing the anxieties of the C.-in-C. and boosting the morale of all who sought conquest in the name of Communism. There could be no dwindling of the garrison of Malaya.

Major-General Dunlop was the first commander of South Malaya District. Having set it on his feet, he handed it over to Hedley in October and returned to his Singapore Base District. This proved fortunate, for on December 11 he had suddenly to put into operation carefully prepared plans for internal security. The temper of the Moslem population had flared like ignited petrol in protest at a legal ruling declaring invalid the marriage to a Malay teacher of a 13-year-old Dutch girl, Berta Hertogh, who had been separated from her parents by the Japanese invasion. There was violent rioting outside and around the Supreme Court, Singapore, the extent of which was underestimated. By the time the military were called in night had fallen but the streets were lit by the blaze of burning cars and were full of wild mobsters. Nine Europeans had been beaten to death, three servicemen among them.

All fighting troops had been removed from Singapore to Malaya, in full realisation of the risk, and the base troops had been organised into two composite battalions and trained in internal security duties. The first of these battalions was fully assembled by 8.30 p.m., having converged from widely separated workshops and depots, and with notices displayed in the approved manner they successfully drove the still raving rioters away from government buildings and other places of importance.

Dunlop had been told, at the planning stage, that four days' notice would be required for the arrival of a battalion from the mainland, and it was with this knowledge that he applied to G.H.Q., at 7 p.m. this evening, for the despatch of two battalions and an armoured car squadron at once. To his delight, B Squadron, 13th/18th Hussars arrived complete during the night, and at daybreak they began a flag march round the main trouble centres. They dispersed a mob of Indonesians from the Cathedral precincts by the use of tear gas and handed thirty of them over to the police. But rioters began to assemble again in many parts of the sprawling city, their anger unquenched.

Lorries were by now streaming over the causeway from Johore, filled with Gurkhas carrying the mud of the jungle on them. The 2/6th were the first to arrive, followed by the 2/10th and elements of the 2/2nd and 1/2nd, and eventually by the Green Howards, who came from Negri Sembilan and were due for a period of retraining at Singapore anyway. There had been no time for the jungle fighters to consult the manual on 'duties in aid', and it was perhaps fortunate for all concerned that their mere arrival took the heart out of the rioters. By the evening of the 12th the city was quiet, with only a few sparks of defiance left to be extinguished next day, although there was still plenty of work for the troops in the enforcement of a curfew and the guarding of smashed shops and stores.

The base troops had nobly borne the brunt, and they deserved most of the praise bestowed upon the Army in the Colonial Office report on the affair. Six times the soldiers had had to open fire to quell the fury, and they had let off twenty rounds. It was a good example of economy of force, both in planning and execution. The fighting troops could now return to their jungle campaign.

Towards the end of 1950 a new unit began to operate in Malaya on the task of long range penetration that had been begun by the short-lived Ferret Force. It was known initially as the Malayan Scouts and consisted of a squadron and a headquarter group raised by voluntary enrolment from units in the Far East by Lieutenant-Colonel 'Mad Mike' Calvert. They were joined in 1951 by a squadron, originally intended for Korea, of 21 Special Air Service, who had made union with the Artists Rifles and were to carry the battle honours of the Long Range Desert Group. This territorial unit had kept the technique of special operations under study, and being part of the same family, the Malayan Scouts changed title to 22 S.A.S. A third squadron was provided by Rhodesia. The special skill acquired by the S.A.S. was to land by parachute attachment through the jungle's treetop canopy, and to avoid advertising their presence by air supply the men came down with rations for ten days instead of the normal five. They were to be of great service.

Their formation freed the Devons for the return homewards for which they were long overdue. They could claim seventy rebels killed and five captured and had themselves lost six killed and twenty-two wounded.

At the end of March 1951 the 2nd Scots Guards handed their expanse of jungle and plantations north of Kuala Lumpur over to the 1st

Queen's Own Royal West Kent Regiment. The Scots Guards ended with a flourish, for on Easter Day their Right Flank Company had achieved that rare thing, the complete envelopment of a rebel camp. A charge by a platoon drove its occupants on to a line of stops, who killed some and drove others back towards the attackers. Ten were killed, and of the only two to escape one was later picked up dead. This brought the battalion's score to over a hundred, although not without counting the twenty-six suspects killed at Batang Kali. However, the Scots Guards had proved themselves as jungle fighters, and they could also claim a tiger, shot with a rifle by a sergeant while menacingly barring the route, protecting his tigress and cubs.

The 26th Field Regiment were the next to go, and they could make undisputed claim to the hundred, putting the infantry to shame. They had of course made a flying start at Batu Arang in July 1948 and they had fewer moves than others, being always based on Tampin. The better training and equipment of their signallers could also have been a great aid; but it is obvious too that they excelled at the basic infantry skills of field craft, speed on the draw and markmanship. In overall terms they were replaced by a new, fifth battalion of the Malay Regiment, having handed the Tampin area over to the Green Howards. A battery of the 25th Field, from Hong Kong, maintained the Royal Artillery's representation, but they had come to use their guns on harrassing tasks.

In May the 1st Gordon Highlanders relieved the Seaforth in Johore. The latter had done fine work and narrowly missed their hundred, for the loss of ten killed, five on one day. The last of the original British troops to leave were the 1st K.O.Y.L.I. They had covered an enormous area from Penang, stretching into Kelantan and the Cameron Highlands, and had brought cheer to many an isolated planter as the men returned singing from patrol, their jungle green sweat-soaked and torn. They had had some tough encounters and had no great score to advertise; they had lost, either from battle, accident, or disease, thirty-five officers and men killed. They left in August, having handed over to the 1st Manchester, and in September the 4th Hussars, who had had a happier time since the full issue of scout and armoured cars, handed the northern district over to the 12th Royal Lancers.

These relieving units all came from Britain, although sometimes after only a staging visit from Germany. They had plenty of notice and brought most of the impedimenta of peacetime soldiering, a few wives and families, who would usually be quartered far from the zone of operations, and the knowledge that their tour would last three years. The post-war army was at last settling to a routine.

In June 1951 the second item on the Briggs Plan began. It was named after what it sought to impose on the rebels, Starvation, and it involved an immense amount of menial checking by troops and police. The troops had to wire off and watch all inhabited areas, search all workers who passed in and out, and provide guards on all food convoys. The police kept check on the sale of food and tried to enforce regulations affecting shopkeepers. It was an involved and wearisome business, from which results could not be expected for months, if not years,and there was little hope of success without the cooperation of the people, which from the Chinese in particular was in short supply.

The rebels struck back fiercely and angrily, taking advantage of the scarcity of troops in the jungle, enforced by the operation. During June 606 'incidents' were recorded, easily the highest monthly figure to date and one that was never exceeded. The unfortunate villagers were the worst sufferers, at times having their settlements sprayed with machine-gun fire, at others having their crops destroyed. There were occasional large scale clashes. The 1/2nd Gurkhas, for instance, lost a company commander and a soldier killed in a vain and prolonged attempt to dislodge a gang they found dug in on a hill at the jungle's edge, near Segamat, Johore. Another company gained vengeance a few days later, locating a gang of fourteen also in position on a hill and eliminating all but one of them.

The most devastating blow ever struck by the rebels fell on October 6. The High Commissioner, Sir Henry Gurney, was motoring northwards with his wife and secretary for a brief holiday at Fraser's Hill. He was 56 miles out of Kuala Lumpur when his Rolls was pumped with bullets, simultaneously with the police escort car ahead. He got out, shut the door, walked across the road, and was shot dead. An armoured car, following the Rolls, now came into action with its machine-gun and the rebel fire died. Great harm had been done to those in the escort car ahead, only slight injury to those that remained in the Rolls.

Gurney was admired for his sincerity, sense of duty and courage, but his death emphasised in the starkest manner possible the measure of his failure to quell the rebellion. It would appear that the rebels, whose number was established at thirty-eight, were waiting specifically for him, for they had let some tempting targets go by. They were just inside the area of the Royal West Kent, and this battalion, unlike their neighbours, had received no warning that the High Commissioner would be passing through. They at once organised a search and smote the jungle with bombs and 25-pounder shells in hope of driving the gang towards their stops. The explosive did no more than express the mood of enraged frustration; the gang got away. However, the 1/10th and 2/6th

Gurkhas brought it to battle a month later and killed five of its members. The Royal West Kent meanwhile had themselves suffered grievous loss, in an encounter on October 22, some 30 miles from the scene of Gurney's death.

A platoon had been picked up on completing a patrol and was being taken through a rubber estate in three vehicles when the bullets tore into them from some hillocks near at hand on their right. The company commander, who had brought the vehicles, was standing with three sentries just behind the cabin of the leading vehicle, an open 3-ton lorry, and all were killed at once. The platoon commander was in the back of the lorry. He was wounded as he jumped out, and having crawled under the lorry was hit again and knocked unconscious just as he was taking aim at a head in a red-star rebel cap that he observed wetting its lips. The platoon sergeant was killed, but a few managed to reach cover on the downward slope left of the road. A 100 yards in rear a 15-cwt. truck was also peppered and stopped; six of its occupants reached cover, in this case on the right of the road, at the foot of the hillock. The third vehicle was a battalion scout car, with two privates in it. It had a pair of bren guns mounted in the turret but received such volume of fire that the control equipment was wrecked, and the soldiers were left with their sten guns and a grievously restricted arc of fire through the slits.

The rebels were not content with this one lethal strike; a glorious supply of weapons and ammunition lay within their grasp and they were determined to seize it. They killed the men by the 15-cwt., since they had no protection, lying on the hillside, against the grenades showered on to the road behind them. There were five men left near the 3-tonner, and one was an N.C.O., Lance-Corporal Martin. Instead of withdrawing downhill in dead ground, he put his men in fire positions along the lip of bank by the side of the road. Five rebels tried to come round the right flank; Private Pannell, a regular soldier who had more than once held and lost a stripe, scrambled along the bank and caught them with a well thrown grenade. Another attack came in, under heavy covering fire, and this time Martin himself demolished it, using similar tactics and releasing the lever before throwing the grenade to achieve burst on impact. Soon afterwards he was sent spinning by a bullet through the shoulder, and to put him out of his pain Pannell gave him a morphia injection.

All four of these remaining privates had by now received wounds of sorts, and still they stuck it out, blazing back at the fire rained down on them from such close range. Pannell moved along the bank, shouting words of command to make it seem that he had plenty of men. At last a car approached. Stopped by the rebels' fire, it emitted a planter and four policemen, who joined the defenders; the driver remained inside, dead. The rebels made one more, less bold attempt at an attack and were then spotted bustling back towards the jungle. The six soldiers from lorry and scout car still able to walk could at last survey the gruesome scene. Eleven of their comrades and three Iban trackers lay dead in and around the smashed vehicles; a further five were badly wounded, one of them mortally; and almost on top of them lay four dead rebel soldiers, with their weapons beside them, so near the British ones that had been within their grasp.

There was a D.C.M. for Pannell and an M.M. for Martin. All battalions had their heroes, and most could boast from six to twelve decorations for gallantry (not counting mentions) in the course of a tour, but none surely will grudge the selection of this episode as a prime example of courage.

In the main the rebel attacks were directed against the police, not the army, and their mounting successes against them during this period were causing much concern. Equally worrying was a campaign started by the rebels in Negri Sembilan, in which they spread terror around the rubber plantations and tin mines by slashing the more trustworthy men and forcing the remainder to go on strike. Outwardly, the Briggs Plan seemed to be in ruins; the squatters had been resettled but seemed indifferent to their own security, and the rebels were more active than ever before. Its author, like Boucher before him, had fallen ill under the strain, and he retired in November, with less than a year to live. He was succeeded by another retired officer of the Indian Army, General Sir Rob Lockhart, who had been the first Commander-in-Chief of the new Indian Army. It was announced that he would be given wider powers. Briggs had been responsible only for directing operations and had suffered many exasperations in his attempts to make all sections of the community cooperate in the struggle.

Things in fact were not as black as they appeared, although it would have been hard to convince the people of Malaya of this, in particular the European planters. It is true that 381 policemen were killed in 1951, as against 222 in 1950, and 108 soldiers as against 72 in 1950. But civilian killings had declined, and the rebel casualties had risen from 369 killed and 294 captured (of whom 147 surrendered voluntarily) in 1950 to 1,025 killed and 322 captured (of whom 201 surrendered) in 1951. They were being forced to come out in the open, which was one of the main aims of the Briggs Plan, and in the process they had lost seven good leaders, among them Ting Fook, 'the Terror of Taiping', who fell to the Commandos. The depression was by no means one-sided.

Meanwhile there had been a change of government in Britain, and the first clue as to the sort of person who might be chosen to succeed Sir Hugh Gurney was provided by the new Colonial Secretary, Mr. Oliver Lyttelton, when he visited Malaya in December and spoke of the need for 'the overall direction of all forces, civil and military'. Not until January 15, 1952, did he announce the Government's solution. It was the unorthodox one of appointing a serving soldier as High Commissioner, one moreover who was unknown to the general public: General Sir Gerald Templer, the G.O.C.-in-C. Eastern Command. 'We are confident that we have the right man for the job,' said Lyttelton.

III—UNDER TEMPLER (1952–54)

Templer arrived at Kuala Lumpur on February 7, 1952, one day after an event that filled the whole of the British Army with grief and was the cause of many moving ceremonies, usually made all the more moving by their very remoteness: the death of King George VI. Thus the new High Commissioner swore allegiance to a new Sovereign, and this sharpened awareness that a new regime had begun. Templer had not previously been to Malaya. His name was known to even fewer people there than in Britain; yet it had made trenchant penetration through the army's manifold vines, and it was one to bring a flutter into even the most phlegmatic stomach at news of his approach.

Commissioned into the Royal Irish Fusiliers in 1916, he had become the youngest ever corps commander in 1942, but subsequently dropped rank to command a division in battle, first the 56th and then the 6th Armoured, both in Italy. A mine brought this phase to a close, tossing a piano on to him off the lorry it blew up. He recovered with a limp and a job at the War Office, and from there he became in turn Director of Military Government, Germany; Director of Military Intelligence; Vice-Chief of the Imperial General Staff; and then to Eastern Command, acquiring in the process the knowledge of politics and of communist strategems required for his new appointment. He had gained promotion to general just ahead of an earlier commander of 6th Armoured, General Keightley, who in 1951 had made an exchange with Harding, of Rhine Army for the Far East.

The Government had appointed a soldier as High Commissioner in token of their determination to stamp out the rebellion, and to achieve his mission Templer applied the military principles of man management on a nationwide scale. He dressed as a soldier, and in an utterly unpompous, uninhibited manner, he set about winning the cooperation of the people by impressing his own resolve and sincerity upon them. This involved much travelling, and to make certain the rebels were denied the chance of claiming a second High Commissioner, he moved in an armoured limousine or sometimes by armoured car, as part of a troop either of the 12th Lancers or 13th/18th Hussars, whose men waged competition in smartness, certain that it would draw comment from the red-hatted head that looked out from one of the turrets with hand waved in salutation at passers-by. The new villages were the objects of his greatest interest, and here he would meet headmen, district officers, planters, police, soldiers, and the villagers themselves. Sometimes he would explode and let fly rebuke in the language a sergeant might use when not in his officer's hearing, but he never failed to make manifest his sympathy for the common people and for the soldiers who protected them, nor to express appreciation of progress made. His enthusiasm was more than once described as boyish, his energy was staggering. 'I shall not spare myself,' he pledged at his installation, and only those nearest him could realise quite what this involved.

A disaster on March 25 provided one of the earliest displays of the Templer brand of leadership. A water pipeline at Tanjong Malim, on the notorious Selangor-Perak border, had been sabotaged for the sixth time and the repair party and police escort were ambushed, with twelve killed. Templer arrived two days later, addressed 350 of the town's inhabitants, and rebuked them for their cowardice in allowing such a crime. A curfew was imposed, during which a sheet of paper was delivered to each householder, with instructions to write down all he knew about the rebel organisation. The sheets were collected next day and put in sealed boxes, which were opened by Templer himself at Kuala Lumpur, in the presence of six witnesses from Tanjong Malim. On April 8 forty arrests were made as a result of the answers, and on the 10th the curfew was lifted with musical accompaniment by the band of the Royal West Kent. On the 26th the Suffolks trapped and killed a noted terror of the region, named Long Pin, and on the 28th Templer returned to Tanjong Malim, as he had said he would, and let the inhabitants know his pleasure.

The philosophy behind such methods was expressed by Templer in June with words that were to become guidelines for all future operations against the rebellious. When asked whether he had sufficient troops, he replied emphatically that he had, adding, 'The answer lies not in pouring more soldiers into the jungle but rests in the hearts and minds of the Malayan people'. He was echoing, as he was perfectly aware, a principle long preached by Chairman Mao, and indeed a directive had been issued by Chin Peng the previous August, containing rules for the observance of this principle. It was a long time before it had any noticeable effect, and by then the security forces had gained a decisive lead in the contest for the hearts and minds.

In the political field, the steps taken by Templer barely come within the scope of a military history. It is sufficient to mention two counts on which he took his potential critics by surprise. One was his remarkable width of interests, backed by knowledge of cultural and sociological subjects far beyond that expected in a soldier, and the other was his eagerness, demolishing forecasts of military control, to press wider responsibility on the not over-ambitious politicians of Malaya and to break down the barriers between the various communities, Malay, Chinese, Indian, and European. He was aided in this by a Colonial Office man, Mr. Donald MacGillivray, who came with him from England to fill the new appointment of Deputy High Commissioner.

In the number of its units the army Templer inherited had remained constant since 1950: twenty-four infantry battalions (including the 22 S.A.S.) and two armoured regiments, with a field battery added in 1951. It had recently become more multi-racial. The 1st (Nyasa) and 3rd (Kenya) King's African Rifles arrived at the close of 1951, and after jungle training they moved to Perak to take over from the 3rd Commando Brigade, whose three units had made 171 kills and forty-nine captures at a loss of nineteen killed themselves, this in under two years. The 1st Fijian Regiment came as the third battalion, full of men of tremendous physique and great warrior spirit, with a number of New Zealanders among the officers. At their request they went to Johore to join the Gurkhas, making bizarre contrast in size but not in performance. The representation in terms of major units was thus ten British, eight Gurkha, five Malay, two African, and one Fijian.

Templer's great project was to enlarge the Malayan contribution and further widen the multi-racial basis of his army by enlisting Malayan citizens other than Malays. To this end he raised the Federal Regiment. He also raised a sixth battalion of the Malay Regiment, and to provide the extra men he succeeded in steering through a bill introducing national service. Of even greater importance was his strengthening of the Malayan Home Guard. He appointed a local man, Major-General E. B. de Fonblanque, Inspector-General, and he gave proof of his trust by making a large issue of rifles and light automatics. The Home Guard was to soar to a strength of over 200,000, and some units, such as the all-Chinese Kinta Valley, were to become marvels of efficiency and fidelity. From the foundations built by Briggs, the crucial battle for the jungle fringes began at last to run against the rebels.

The police also received a boost. The force had risen, under Colonel Gray's direction, from a strength of 10,000 to one of 73,000, with jungle squads among its operational branches, and although its morale may have wilted at times under the physical and psychological assaults continually made upon it by the rebels, it still formed the front line of the resistance and the framework for military operations. But Gray had not been happy, being faced with conflicting requirements from his governmental and operational chiefs, and he had been succeeded, just before Templer's coming, by Colonel Arthur Young, from the City of London Police, whose principal aim was to improve the relationship with the public. Operationally, the police had suffered loss from a lack of armoured protection for their mobile squads. This was swiftly put right by Templer, by the supply of no less than 970 armoured vehicles, and each brought its own local rise in morale.

On the organisational side the committee system inherited from Briggs was maintained, except that the operational War Council at the top was converted into the wider embracing Federal Executive Council, for as Templer said, 'Government cannot have a split personality guided by two councils,' and Briggs and Gray would have heartily agreed with him. Templer himself took the appointment of Director of Operations, with Lockhart relegated to Deputy Director. At lower level the War Executive committees carried on—although not quite as usual, because of the new surge of energy pumped through them from above.

After all but two and a half years in command, during which his fighting instinct never sagged, Urquhart handed over in June to Major-General Sir Hugh Stockwell, as he had been made for his services at Haifa. Stockwell combined a foppish appearance with an absence of inhibition and, like Templer, he might erupt in anger at one moment, in laughter at the next. He had the knack of endearing himself to soldiers of all colour, and it was said of him that he was the only general who had ever been able to pat a man on the back without appearing patronising.

As from September 1, his command was placed on a more operational basis, bringing promotion for him to lieutenant-general. South Malaya District, which had been concerned primarily with administration, was converted into the 17th Gurkha Division. North Malaya remained a district for the time being, while advancing to a divisional organisation.

It was a great joy for the Gurkhas, whose commander was now Major-General L. E. C. M. Perowne, to have their old division of the Burma campaign reactivated, and at the same time the third brigade, the 99th, came back into being, alongside the 48th and 63rd. The 26th Gurkha Brigade, although not an integral part of the division, came under command, and all four were concentrated in the south, the 99th and 26th in Johore, the 48th in Pahang, and the 63rd mainly in Negri Sembilan. They had seven Gurkha battalions, three British—the Green Howards, Cameronians and Gordons—the bulk of 22 S.A.S. and the 1st Fijian. The 18th British Brigade remained independent in the centre, covering parts of Selangor, Pahang, and Perak with the Suffolks, Worcesters, Royal West Kent, and frequently the Manchesters, whose base at Penang was used as a general retraining area. In the northern sector the 1/6th Gurkhas and the two K.A.R. battalions were grouped with the six Malay battalions and one of the embryo Federal Regiment, which was also raising an armoured car squadron to ease the strain on the two British armoured regiments.

Tactically, the drudge continued with little alteration, but there was a marked intensifying of all the ancillary means of waging war. Even ships of the Royal Navy joined in the land battle, a bombardment by the frigate *Amethyst* of a camp 30 miles up the Sungei Perak being among thirty-nine made during 1952. Towards the end of the year the R.N. began their greatest contribution of all by manning a squadron of ten Sikorsky helicopters, supplied by the United States, and dropping troops in loads of five for enveloping operations in the jungle. Previously helicopters of the R.A.F. had been used for casualty evacuation, much to the benefit of morale, and in due course the R.A.F. would enter the tactical arena with their Whirlwinds, carrying eight men. But there would never be enough helicopters. Similarly, the firepower of the troops was much improved (and made safer) by the issue of the Patchet sub-machine-gun, of which the British version became the Sterling, but there would never be enough of them either.

On the psychological side, bombers, artillery and voice aircraft stepped up the war on the rebels' nerves, while the troops strove to win the hearts and minds of the people by aid to village communities and by assisting the police in training the home guards. The message was successfully put across that those who surrendered could be sure of lenient treatment, that a high price would be paid for good information, and that there was really nothing to be gained from enduring all the danger and discomfort of jungle soldiering. The deserters began to accumulate, and information with them.

The brazen willingness of most of these men to guide patrols to the lairs of their former comrades was a source of wonder to the simple British soldier and afforded a very profitable means of raising a battalion's score of kills; many of them remained with the troops they had surrendered to, enjoying the prestige (which surely would have been accorded in no other army) of mascots and providing useful lessons in the crafts employed by the men they had betrayed. The great problem was to draw in the many others who were inhibited by the fear of being shot in the attempt to surrender, either by one side or the other. The troops would therefore be withdrawn for certain periods, and the fact announced by leaflet and voice aircraft, accompanied by instructions as to how to surrender, pictures of happy deserters, and the oft boomed slogan, 'Templer keeps his word.' Full pressure had to be exerted in between appeals; the greater the torment, the more alluring the enticement.

Such was the army's philistine addiction to initial-naming that deserters were termed S.E.P.s, which meant surrendered enemy personnel and distinguished them from C.E.P.s, which meant captured enemy personnel. Templer's arrival brought an initial-name for the uncaptured ones. Previously they had always been called bandits. This may have belittled their status, but it gave them an undeserved tinge of romance and was liable to convey a false picture. They were therefore assigned the more exact label of communist terrorists, and this of course was at once transformed to C.T.s, as which they became universally known in military circles. Capture continued to bring with it the strange change of status to 'enemy personnel'.

The ultimate move in the process of turning enemies into friends was to come in May 1953, when the formation was announced of a renegade force known as the Special Operational Volunteers, who were graduates from rehabilitation centres. The risk of arming such men, of whom twelve small platoons were raised, proved fully justified, and they became deadly foes of their one-time comrades. They brought their instructors to despair on the barrack square, but this did not worry Templer in the least. 'To hell with drill,' he said. 'We want them to handle weapons and lay ambushes.' At this they were adept.

In October 1952, after a tour of three years and two months, the Green Howards departed, heavily laden with tribute, and in view of the swelling of the Federal forces, no British battalion relieved them. One of their officers, Major Oldfield, wrote a comprehensive account of the Green Howards' tour, and although no doubt they would blush to be singled out, it is worth providing some details as examples of the tribulations and triumphs experienced in varying degree by all battalions.

Tribulation packed the early stages. In their first six months the battalion lost six men killed, not all of them by the enemy, in exchange for six rebels, of whom five fell to a single platoon. They had been much on the move during this period and taken part in frustrating drives in Pahang and Selangor. A more static period in Negri Sembilan brought their score of kills and captures to sixteen at the end of their first fifteen months. They then had a two months' break for drill and retraining at Singapore.

On return to the jungle they spent two unfruitful months in Johore, and in April 1951 they took over from the 26th Field Regiment at Tampin. Now at last they had a period of fifteen months' stability, in which they could build on the good work done by their predecessors, notably in the matter of liaison with the police and civil administration. Their score mounted, and so too did the confidence of the locals, with the result that information became ever easier to accumulate, deserters ever more frequent. They had killed or captured (not counting deserters) sixty-six rebels in this area when the train pulled them out of Tampin station, leaving the skirl of Gurkha pipes and a flurry of waving hands behind them. Sharing the rearmost truck with the regimental police were the battalion 'pets', the dhobis, barbers, and S.E.P.s.

A subscription was raised for the Green Howards by the inhabitants of Tampin and district, and contributions poured in from rich and poor alike. Those who attended the resultant presentation ceremony were deeply moved by such a display of gratitude, which was not, it should be noted, by any means unique. The battalion had by now moved into the Cameron Highlands to spend their last two operational months as relief for a recuperation period by the Manchesters. A further twenty kills were added to their score, bringing it past the hundred mark, a feat that drew as much acclaim as a century in a test match.

If the Green Howards prospered from the confidence they built up among the locals, they infused it by the success they gained, and this in turn stemmed from a continual urge for self-improvement, which was evinced by the detailed post-mortems held at battalion headquarters after every contact, successful or not. But Yorkshire tenacity had to be harnessed to opportunism, and both were used in cohesion in a model operation that followed the surrender of a Min Yuen notability, Nam Fook, early on the morning of June 11, 1952. He was prepared, he said, to lead a patrol to a jungle camp, and Captain Bagnall, who was to win his second M.C. of the campaign, set off with him, accompanied by the only ten men of his Machine Gun Platoon in camp. The rebel camp was located on a cliff, surrounded by thick jungle, and the tops of three bashas could be seen, with sentries around them. Bagnall made a detailed reconnaissance and decided that they would have to remain out all night and make a dawn attack. He divided his patrol after dark, and both halves made use of two downpours of rain to creep up, unheard, to the fringe of the camp, where they lay at right angles to each other, having kept direction by a cook's fire lit in the rebel camp at 4 a.m.

The men edged forward to fire positions, peering at shrouded signs of stirring among the huts.

A sentry emerged through the pre-dawn gloaming. Bagnall shot him dead and set off the shattering roar of the five carbines, two brens, and four rifles of his patrol. Tracer bullets ricocheted and reared, and grenades crumped raucously. Then there was silence, complete and profound, before the men moved in to find seven dead sprawled about the camp and its exits. A bearer party, of storemen, clerks and cooks was despatched from the battalion camp to make the long, gruesome, and triumphant haul of the dead, slung on poles, back for identification.

The Green Howards' final score of rebels eliminated was 103, and their own losses were an officer and eight killed in action, with a further eleven dead from other causes. The ratio of killed, which may be slightly higher than average, reflects the British soldier's superiority over the rebel and is a balancing factor in considering the security forces' preponderance in material. Bombs and guns might play their part in shifting gangs and disturbing their peace, but the soldiers had no heavy weapons in support when contact was made and seldom enjoyed more than marginal superiority in automatic weapons or in numbers engaged. It was man against man in the jungle, and the rebels had the advantage of being the defenders, with intimate knowledge of the ground. That their losses were so hopelessly disproportionate may have been in part due to health causes, notably poor eyesight, and another grave drawback was their lack of shooting practice, resulting from reluctance to advertise their presence. But their defensive measures were often poor, however skilled their individual field craft. It was by virtue of better tactics and better weapon training that the British tilted the ratio of casualties so heavily in their favour.

This was achieved, within the British battalions, in the face of endemic fluctuations in manpower. There would be bound to be two complete change-overs of the national-service element during a three-year tour, and there was plenty of traffic among the regulars too, especially those on three-year engagements. Seventy-seven officers served with the Green Howards in Malaya and 1,646 soldiers, and of them a select one and seventy-five were on the strength throughout.

In January 1953 a battalion departed that had arrived before the Green Howards and had achieved a record in rebel destruction that dwarfed that of any other British battalion throughout the campaign: the 1st Suffolk. When they handed over their sector in southern Selangor to the 1st Somerset Light Infantry their score of kills and captures stood at 195, at a loss to themselves of twelve killed and twenty-four wounded. The headlines, 'The Suffolks do it again,' had many time cheered the people of Kuala Lumpur, and on their departure they marched through its streets and received, according to the *Malay Mail*, 'the most poignant and stirring adieu accorded any British Regiment in this country'.

Their greatest triumph, indeed the culmination of three years' endeavour, came in July 1952, when at last they slew the man against whom they had waged a personal war, 'the bearded wonder' Liew Kon Kim. If his beard was one of his unusual features, addiction to womanising was another—for although most gangs had their quota of girls, they were not there as recreational amenities and fornication was forbidden, in some gangs on pain of death. Kon Kim may have enforced this rule, but he did not observe it, and here lay the weak spot in the wall of intimidation he built round himself, for discards sought revenge in treachery. Information from one of them enabled the Special Branch to locate his camp somewhere in the Kuala Langat southern swamp. The water here was usually thigh-deep, and the undergrowth and mangrove were so thick that visibility seldom exceeded 10 yards and a distance of 2 miles was the maximum target for a day's march. The swamp measured some 10 miles by 8.

Two companies of the Royal West Kent came in to assist the Suffolks, and for three days and three nights the soldiers waded and floundered through the swamps, after police, home guardsmen, and other troops had been placed to seal the exits. Brief periods of rest were spent on improvised platforms, on mangrove roots, or else on islands where there was less water but always some. There were more contacts than kills, but enough evidence was gleaned to indicate that Liew Kon Kim had been flushed and taken refuge in a different part of the swamp. B Company of the Suffolks were withdrawn on the fourth day, by railway truck along a logging line, and put straight in to search this piece of swamp, led by an informer. They advanced on a frontage of nine patrols, but the informer failed them, losing his bearings amidst a morass of bomb holes. B Company persevered, and at 2 p.m. on the sixth day, a patrol under a national-service officer, 2nd Lieutenant Hands, flushed three rebels out of an island. Hands shot one dead with his Patchet gun and gave chase to the other two, guided by the sound of splashing. He caught up with the second, who was armed with a shotgun, and having hit target with another well aimed burst, he found he had killed a woman: thrilling clue to the identity of the third. He dashed on, and after splashing though 400 yards of water, he obtained view of the third. Again he scored lethal hit and ran panting on to recognise the face so often studied on posters, that of Liew Kon Kim.

This was a fine example of the tenacity that produced such a massive haul for the Suffolks. Stability was another aid. They spent nearly all their time in this area around Kajang, with the result that they felt intimately involved in the struggle here and were able to establish very close cooperation with the police and home guards. It may also be no coincidence that there was a high proportion of countrymen in their ranks—'swedes' they had been called for years—and, of even greater significance, that they won the Malaya Command shooting champion- ship in 1951. Yet their proportion of national-servicemen was as high as any, being 70 per cent on their return home. They had some out- standing leaders. Two commanding officers—Lieutenant-Colonels Wight and Morcombe—won the D.S.O. and nine officers the M.C., Hands, as might be guessed, among them. Such were the recent honours with which the Suffolks made their first homecoming since sailing for the assault landing on the Normandy beaches.

Next battalion to go, on relief by the 1st East Yorkshire in April 1953, were the 1st Cameronians. They too had built themselves a great reputation as rebel killers, particularly on their transfer from Muar to another part of Johore, Segamat, in December 1951, and in the sixteen months spent there they achieved over a hundred kills, which earned them a presentation from the locals. Close cooperation with the police and home guards was the familiar keynote of their success. They were never afraid to put small parties of two or three men in with the police and home guardsmen as a deterrent to intimidation or subversion, and as the confidence they inspired increased, so did the store of information accumulate. The large population of tappers and small holders in the area had made it a favourite hunting ground of the rebels, but it had lost favour with them by the time the East Yorks arrived.

With the Cameronians went a Captain Tedford who had an amazing story of survival to tell. In the early hours of July 8, 1952, he was return- ing from a night out in Johore Bahru with a planter, Charles Morgan. They were aware that the road ran through the domain of a notorious ambush setter, Goh Peng Tuan, but both had parades to attend and had to take the risk. The ambush was set and both were hit as they dashed from their demolished car in different directions. Tedford lay on his front, feigning death, when the rebels came to search for him. A foot sank into his back. Its owner yelled in fright and his comrades came up, shone torches at Tedford, yanked him over to examine him, jerked his head up by the forelock, and as a final horror, pressed the muzzle of a carbine against the corner of his eye. Tedford knew enough to keep his eyes open, and as his irises lolled and rolled they gave him a hideous close-up of his nearest tormentor, of 'the pore-pocked glistening skin, and his eyes, obliquely hawklike'. His pretence satisfied them, and they dropped his head and stripped him of everything except his blood-soaked shorts, causing intense agony as they ripped a garter and stocking off a bullet-pumped leg. They then lugged him to the car, kicked him under the petrol tank, lit a trail of stuffing, and ran for cover. Tedford rolled away in time to be merely winded and singed by the resultant explosion. He gained the cover of some scrub and at length realised, as he lay naked and sweating, feeling terribly conspicuous in the light of the blazing car, that the rebels were gone.

Morgan had also feigned death, but a kick in the face drew a groan from him, and he was thereupon bayonetted three times through the chest and once through the back, to be left lying face downwards in a pool of his own blood. Tedford heard him groan on the rebels' departure and hobbled over to him. Soon a car was heard approaching. It stopped short of the blaze, and for the next two minutes machine-gun bullets were pumped all around the anguished ex-revellers. However, they all missed and in due course their firers, Malay policemen, removed the men to hospital. Both were out within thirty days.

The Suffolks, Green Howards and Cameronians had joined the fight (in that order) during the second year of the rebellion and had been able to reap the benefit of the pioneering work done before their arrival. Others had been in it from the start and still had years of jungle operations ahead of them, namely the six Gurkha battalions (for two had been to Hong Kong) and the two senior battalions of the Malay Regiment. It seems almost superfluous to say that the Gurkhas had become masters at jungle fighting, although they were hillmen by birth. The recruits were coming in well and from 1951 onwards were trained centrally at Sungei Patani, in Kedah. The men revelled in the life of a soldier, and a battalion had far fewer changes in manpower than a British one, with the result that there was a massive accumulation of experience, which was saved from erosion by a rather more frequent period of retraining than the British received, two months every year. The senior battalion, the 1/2nd Gurkhas, appropriately became the first battalion (of all) to claim their hundredth rebel, which they did before the end of 1950, having operated exclusively in Johore. They reached 200 near the close of 1952, but were beaten to this target by the 1/10th Gurkhas, who added thirty-nine to their tally by making a swoop in assault craft on a part of the east coast hitherto unoccupied by troops, the Kuantan district of Pahang.

In the autumn of 1952 there was a marked slackening of rebel activity, showing that the gang leaders were at last beginning to pay heed to Chin Peng's directive of August 1951. October was the first month in which the security forces made more contacts than the rebels caused incidents. But contacts of course became harder to make as the rebels hid themselves deeper in the jungle. A number of food denial operations were staged, involving elaborate cordoning, the checking and searching of all workers crossing a demarcation line, a close watch on adjacent villages and their home guards, and a thorough combing of the area cordoned off. A further precaution, which was to become standard, was that food lorries were compelled to move in convoy, with armoured car escort, and were allowed to stop only at authorised halts. The hope was that the rebels would be forced to take rash action to obtain food supplies. It was sometimes fulfilled, but as in most operations on a large scale, the troops seldom saw the fruits of their labour.

One result of the blockade was that the rebels cultivated patches of jungle, which could be detected from the air. Some were sprayed with acid from helicopters, under cover of bombing attacks—although without much effect, it was discovered—and on other occasions patrols went out to burn the crops, just as they had burned so many camps in earlier days. Occasionally the discovery of a plot gave clue to the position of a camp, and one such deduction led to a bright success by a company of the 2/7th Gurkhas in Negri Sembilan on February 18, 1953.

The role of this company had originally been to provide stops for a dawn attack by the Gordon Highlanders, but on the previous afternoon a Gurkha lance-corporal, making a reconnaissance, spotted some bathers in a dammed-up pool and found their camp nearby. It contained seven bashas, with twenty rebel soldiers sitting around inside it, and was at a rather different location from that supposed. The lance-corporal sent the one man with him back to tell the company commander, Captain Thornton, and the latter, having seen for himself, obtained permission from the commanding officer of the Gordons to make the attack. In the early hours of the following morning the lance-corporal led the assault platoon to within two yards of the rebel sentry, and another platoon succeeded in making an enveloping movement undetected to take up position as stops. At the first glimmer of light the lance-corporal shot the sentry dead, and Thornton thereupon led the assault platoon into the camp, jumping a fence. They were met by fire from a bren, but killed the gunner without being hit themselves and sent the rest of the gang scuttling. A weird silence—an oft-noted phenomenon—followed the crash of the assault, then came the crackle of the brens of the stops and the crump of their grenades. 'We've got six, Sahib,' called the Gurkha officer when the shindy died (making eight in all). Such successes still sent their rays of jubilation far—in this instance after deflection round the Gordons.

In March 1953 the ten helicopters of 848 Naval Air Squadron were employed in their first large scale operation. Its object was to disrupt a meeting of rebel leaders scheduled to be held in the jungle depths by the Kelantan-Pahang border, and the troops involved were the 1st and 3rd K.A.R. and the 6th Malay. They were able to cast their net with impressive speed but could not spread it wide enough to make a catch of importance. The helicopters then flew southwards and lifted groups of the East Yorks, 2/6th, and 2/10th Gurkhas in a partially successful attempt to entrap the entire rebel committee for Johore. In June they were back in Pahang, providing the Manchesters and others with a lift into the jungle fastness west of Mentakab. These were experimental operations, and while the great flexibility afforded by the helicopter was emphasised, the need to find clearings on which to make a descent by rope imposed a restriction, and there was also an obvious requirement for more of them.

The 22 S.A.S., whose Abseil gear enabled them to descend from treetops 250 feet high, took part in most of these operations and were also engaged in another new project, the protection of the jungle-dwelling aborigines of the Semang and Sakai tribes. These scrawny little people had been completely at the mercy of the rebels and had been forced deeper into their service as the policy of food denial developed. Now the special airmen arrived by helicopter in groups of fifteen and began to win over these nomad tribesmen, staying with them thirteen weeks before relief. They built landing strips to enable them to market their supplies and brought them medical and engineering aid. Villages were turned into fortresses, in which police posts and even guns were established, the latter flown in by sections. Much depended on the few lone persons who stayed to sell them the idea of self-defence. It was all part of the battle for the hearts and minds.

In similar manner the terrestrial units provided as much domestic as defensive help for the new villages outside the jungle. A system of adoption tied each to its own company or squadron, and members of the latter made regular visits to play the villagers at football, take them on outings, construct playgrounds, or organise scout troops.

As the pressure was maintained against the rebels, with the emphasis always on strengthening the resistance of the Malayan people, the flow of organisational changes and reliefs continued its busy course. In March 1953 General Lockhart retired after seventeen months as Director of Operations or Deputy. His post was altered to that of Principal Staff Officer and filled by a serving officer, Major-General W. P. Oliver, who was Colonel of the Royal West Kent.

With Kenya now in turmoil, the 1st K.A.R. was withdrawn in April, leaving only one African representative, which in July became the 2nd K.A.R.

The Worcesters were relieved in July by a battalion from Egypt, the 1st West Yorkshire, exactly three years after they had themselves relieved the 2nd Coldstream. They had had little stability during their first eighteen months, and had then settled in the Ipoh district, where they had raised their score of kills and captures to fifty-two. But they had themselves lost an officer and eighteen men killed. The ubiquitous 13th/18th Hussars also left for home this month, having handed the southern part of Malaya into the keeping of the 11th Hussars.

One battalion of the Federal Regiment had by now been raised, filling the void created by the 1st K.A.R.'s departure, and in September the raising of the 7th Malay was ordered, enabling a Gurkha battalion, the 2/2nd, to return to Hong Kong. Thus for the first time Malaya became the largest contributor of infantry, with eight battalions against seven British (including the S.A.S.), seven Gurkha, one African, and one Fijian, and this gained recognition in October by the conversion of North Malaya District, still centred on Taiping, into the 1st Federal Division. It did not follow that the Malayan battalions were always to serve with their own division; there was to be considerable interchange.

Even the Iban trackers were involved in organisational change, being formed around this period into the Sarawak Rangers. This gave them the status of soldiers and brought them an issue of rifles to supplement their blow pipes. There was the drawback that, unlike a blow pipe, a rifle could not be fired silently, and it was not always possible to persuade these eager trackers to hold their fire. Some of them showed great bravery, as for instance Awang Anak Rawang, who was awarded the George Cross for a feat with the Worcesters in 1951. Although twice wounded himself, he saved the life of a wounded private and the weapons of the patrol, by fighting off a strong gang that had ambushed and inflicted heavy loss on the patrol.

At the end of January 1954 the Royal West Kent—or Queen's Own, as they were widely known—handed their area in western Pahang over to the 1st Royal Hampshire, having on New Year's Day become the sixth and last British unit to claim a hundred kills. They had gained many notable successes in some fairly stable campaigning and had more than avenged the fifteen men lost in that ambush in October 1951, which was the heaviest blow struck at any battalion. Their final score was 106, and they had buried twenty-four members of the battalion.

In March the Gordons were relieved by the 1st Queen's in the Tampin area of Negri Sembilan, and in April the Manchesters by the 1st Royal

Scots Fusiliers in Kedah, the most northerly area of operation for the British. Like the K.O.Y.L.I. before them, the Manchesters had not found this a very fruitful hunting ground, nor had the Gordons amassed a great score in peregrinations round the southern part of Malaya. It does not follow that others would have been able to do better.

The strain of non-stop exertion in the clammy humidity of Malaya had begun to take its customary toll on Templer's physique, and it was announced at the close of 1953 that he would be going. He left Kuala Lumpur on May 30, 1954, with touching display of gratitude from every section of the community, and the measure of his success in bringing the Federation over the hump of crisis was to be seen in the civilian dress worn by his successor as High Commissioner, his deputy Sir Donald MacGillivray. The office could again be separated from that of Director of Operations, and the latter appointment fell to the ebullient, one-armed gunner, Lieutenant-General G. K. Bourne, who was also G.O.C. Malaya, having taken over from Stockwell on April 7.

Casualty figures bespeak Templer's achievements. The killing of 532 civilians was recorded for 1951, 342 in 1952, and 84 in 1953. 381 policemen were killed in 1951, 207 in 1952, and 29 in 1953; 108 soldiers in 1951, 77 in 1952, and 34 in 1953. It is true that the rebel casualties, in killed and captured, had declined from 1,146 in 1951, and 1,217 in 1952, to 973 in 1953, but their desertion rate had advanced from 201 in 1951, to 256 in 1952, and 372 in 1953. These figures showed they had been quietened, not broken, and on occasions they still made fierce reprisal raids, mainly against the Home Guard, who lost fifty men in 1953. But on the roads and railways, where they had caused greatest torment, they had subsided into an inactivity that could hardly be believed. Only one bus was stopped and burned during the whole of 1953 and only one goods train derailed.

Of even greater significance to the people, part cause and part result, were the measures taken to free them from the bondage of emergency regulations. Early in 1953 the hated Regulation 17D, under which complete village communities could be placed in detention, was abolished, and in the spirit of trust that was the keynote of Templer's success the number of people in detention was reduced, during his regime, from 11,000 to under 2,000. On September 3, 1953, the first small part of Malaya was declared 'white', that is freed from the application of the emergency regulations. It consisted of 221 square miles of the British settlement, Malacca, and the declaration was made by the Resident Commissioner in the belief that a taste of freedom would inspire the people to expose any rebel who dared jeopardise it.

Between January and March 1954 three rulers of states followed his lead, parts of Trengganu, Kedah, and a coastal strip in Negri Sembilan being declared white. There could be no clearer way of saying that the rebellion was on the wane, and the danger now was that the new mood of confidence that had dispelled depression might in turn give way to complacence.

Templer emphasised at a farewell press conference that the rebels still had a large army. He said its strength was estimated at between 6,000 and 4,400 and that he himself believed the lower figure to be nearer the truth. The estimate had shown a remarkable capacity for increase, despite an annual loss of over 1,000. It was put at a maximum of 3,000 in April 1950, as reported in the House of Commons. Lyttelton placed it at between 3,000 and 5,000 when announcing Templer's appointment in January 1952. Now came Templer's assessment after two and a half years of victorious progress. There had in fact been over 8,000 armed guerrillas on his arrival, including the branch and district link men, and the number had now been cut by at least a third. The elimination of the remainder still posed teasing problems, for the jungle was large enough to devour many more troops than the 8,000 available after the deduction of battalions on retraining and the provision of specialists, which hardly ever left a battalion with more than 400 to pull the triggers of rifles and brens.

IV—MOPPING UP (1954–60)

The initiative had by now been wrested from the rebels, and indeed their aim was seldom seen to run higher than survival. In terms of news value, operations subsided to the level of routine, which for most British papers meant obscurity. The sense of crisis had expired which attended the despatch of the 2nd Guards Brigade and reached its grim climax three years later with the killing of the High Commissioner, and the success story that began with the arrival of Templer seemed to have reached its happy ending with the return of a civilian to the head of government. Yet there was no decline whatever in the tempo of operations. The new Director, General Bourne, was a man of vigour and imagination, and his zest was soon to be felt rippling through the chains of committees and military command of which he was joint fount. His Commander-in-Chief at Singapore was a fellow gunner of lively disposition, General Sir Charles Loewen, a Canadian who had spent all his service with the British Army.

With certain areas declared 'white' it was possible to make greater concentration of troops at others, and a series of long operations was planned, directed at the disruption of specific rebel organisations. This, up to a point, was a swing away from the standard 'framework' operations, which had most favour with commanding officers, to the more fluid tactics, involving drives by augmented brigades, of earlier days. The difference was that the helicopters, of which the R.A.F. now had a squadron as well as the R.N., gave the troops better prospect of ensnaring the rebels, and the home guards were available to cooperate in the strangulating process of severing them from their supplies. Bombers and artillery were liberally used, in hope of making the enemy feel perpetually hounded, and more antiquated aircraft were used to sustain the assault on his nerves with their messages of enticement. Bourne had great faith in the Psychological Warfare Section he inherited. One factor—of which use was made—was the prestige to be derived from ownership of a bicycle, and pictures of many a happy ex-comrade with gleaming machine beside him were showered upon the rebels.

Even so, mighty effort could still produce little apparent return. The largest army-air operation to date was staged from July to November 1954, with the object of smashing the rebel organisation east of Ipoh and liberating the aborigines from domination. It began with heavy bombing of the jungle by the R.A.F., followed immediately by a parachute descent by the 22 S.A.S. through the treetop canopy. Four battalions—the West Yorks, Royal Scots Fusiliers, 1/6th Gurkhas and 5th Malays—then cast their net, some being lifted in, some approaching on foot, and for long periods they were on air supply, through gaps hacked through the tree tops. Yet the bag of rebels came to only fifteen. The gain was in the conversion of the aborigines to allies.

Concurrently with this operation in Perak, others were launched on a smaller scale with the object of driving rebel leaders out of the fastnesses from which they had long conducted campaigns of terror. There were a number of notorious ones still at large, such as Teng Fook Loong in Negri Sembilan, Yeung Kwo in Selangor, and the one from whom Tedford of the Cameronians had escaped with a singeing, Goh Peng Tuan of Johore. Such men had from time to time been shifted by extensive patrol operations but had returned to their haunts. The plan now was to move them on, if not to kill them, by long term occupation of their jungle domains. But as the Queen's found, there could still be snags.

Lying on the border between Johore and Malacca and consequently posing special problems at committee level, Mount Ophir contained the lair of a rebel leader called Ho Lim Seng and was the area the

Queen's had to dominate. The plan was to keep a company on the mountain range for three weeks at a time, during which it was to send out patrols in all directions and at the end of which it would be relieved by a fresh company operating from a base in a different part of the mountain. The slopes were steep and slippery and the streams cascading down them provided the rebels with an excellent early warning system, for by a strange freak of nature any noise made by people alongside the roaring water was inaudible to them but travelled with remarkable clarity to ears far away. Surprise therefore was unlikely, and the most the Queen's hoped for was to conceal the location of their company by keeping it supplied by porter parties and making air drops elsewhere.

Within two days of the arrival of the first company huts were found which appeared to have been unoccupied for some days but had stores and rations inside them, suggesting that a return would be made. They stood in a ravine. An ambush was set, consisting of fifteen men who for two days lay still, without talking, smoking, or cooking, and were then relieved by another fifteen. Stringent measures of silence were meanwhile imposed at the company base. On the tenth day the rebels returned to their camp. After brief reconnaissance, they began the descent into the ravine, led by a man with rifle nestling in the crook of his arm like a sporting gun. The sergeant in charge of the ambush had his carbine ready, waiting to fire the shot that would act as signal for a general fusillade and finding it hard to believe his luck. Then there was a shot behind him and next moment the rebels were skeltering up the scrub-littered slope behind them, having come to within a few yards of the sandy bottom that formed the most perfect killing ground any patrol leader had ever contemplated. Every man fired into the scrub, but though two rebels were seen to be hit none was retrieved. It was a sad end to ten days' labour, and not surprisingly the soldier who fired the premature round would not own up. He had as much to fear from his mates as from his officers.

By the end of 1954 five major operations were in progress, each aimed at forcing specific rebel organisations into liquidation by constant harrying and food denial. Three of them were sustained all through 1955, with steady accumulation of captures and kills. Another, which was named Apollo and had been started in June, ended in June 1955, after sixty-nine rebels had been eliminated and 3,464 square miles in the very centre of Malaya, around Kuala Lipis, Pahang, had been so thoroughly cleansed that they could be declared white. The fifth, which was named Nassau, cleared the swampy southern part of Selangor of the evil attention of a formidable independent platoon that had the backing of a ruthless district organisation.

Before the start of this last operation the Somerset Light Infantry, who had taken the swamps over from the Suffolks, made an exchange with the Royal Hampshires for the densely covered but more salubrious hills of Pahang. Both battalions gained distinction from the move. The Somersets rapidly chipped away at the rebel organisation already dwindled by operation Apollo. Their best bag was six killed and one captured in a clash just before Christmas, but an action a month later is of greater interest because it afforded one of those rare occasions when the rebels stood and fought. The commander of C Company, Major Haigh, bumped their camp on the fourth day of a reconnaissance in which he was accompanied only by two soldiers and two Iban trackers. A prolonged fire fight developed, with Haigh and his men yelling curses to give the impression of a large force. They appeared to be outnumbered by twenty to one, for it was a huge concentration by the standards of those days, but drove them off in the end, having killed three and captured one. One more was killed by a platoon sent by helicopter into virgin jungle to cut them off.

For seven months the Royal Hampshires laboured on operation Nassau, waist-deep in the sombre, debilitating, and demoralising swamp. They began in December 1954, combining food denial with deep patrolling, and after months of apparently fruitless toil, their kills and captures began to gush forth like oil. Companies of the 1st Fiji had now come in to help them, and in July the Hampshires handed over to the 7th Malay, who completed the elimination of the eleven rebels left out of thirty-seven starters. Ships of the Royal Navy, bombers of the R.A.F. and guns, not only of the 25th Field Regiment but of the Singapore Regiment, had meanwhile kept up a continual pounding of likely hide-outs, complementing the harrying by the infantry and the blockade maintained by soldiers, police and home guardsmen. It was a triumph of inter-service and inter-allied cooperation, and it enabled one more area to be declared white.

On August 18, 1955, the 1/10th Gurkhas became the first battalion— and indeed the only battalion—to claim their 300th rebel. When the rebellion began they were the only battalion stationed in Johore, and apart from their raid on Kuantan in the autumn of 1953, they had spent all their operational service in this constant magnet of rebel activity. Like the Suffolks before them, they were able to point to the part played by markmanship by winning the Malaya Command championship in 1955. They also gained distinction as cross-country runners—though the quality of patience, which cannot be measured by competitive event, must have played just as large a part towards their success in the field.

For a combination of shooting and running, it would be hard to excel the feat that had won the D.C.M. for Rifleman Birbahadur Rai of the 1/10th. His platoon flushed some rebels in an oil palm plantation just as it was beginning to get dark, and the order 'Charge!' was given. Armed with his new Patchet carbine, Birbahadur ran the fastest and after 200 yards was well ahead of the others. He saw a rebel firing a sten, paused, and shot him dead. He ran on to reach a camp and came under fire from the last two rebels to flee from it. He shot them both dead as they raced off into some swamp grass. Changing his magazine as he ran, Birbahadur himself raced into the swamp grass. He followed a track and came face to face with a rebel who fired at him from 20 yards; he ducked, returned the fire, and shot the rebel dead. Jumping over his victim, he ran on, gasping for breath, and got view of one more rebel, whom he felled at long range, bringing his score to five in half as many minutes.

Another important event in 1955 emphasised that military and political progress run side by side. The first general elections in Malaya were held at the end of July and resulted in an overwhelming victory for the Triple Alliance led by Tungku Abdul Rahman, who thus became Chief Minister. Among the first measures he introduced, by announcement on August 23, was the offer of an amnesty to the rebels. The tempo of military operations was relaxed, except of course by the Psychological Warfare Section and the aircraft that transmitted their messages. Battalions still sent patrols out, but they could not act offensively, and indeed fire could not be opened until its intended recipient had first been called upon to surrender. This was tantamount to inviting him to fire the first round, and the risk had to be taken. Sergeant Ramsor Rai of the 1/6th Gurkhas, for instance, discovered a rebel camp near his platoon base east of Ipoh and spent an hour observing it while some men were summoned and stealthily put in position. He now stood up, waved his hat, and dutifully shouted 'Ty-say' (being Chinese for surrender). He produced a scurry and a clatter of shots, which fortunately missed him. Only now did his men open up, and instead of all eight of the camp's inmates, they shot only three. The others were saved by the conscience of Ramsor.

Elsewhere the rebels used the amnesty as an opportunity to revert to the offensive. In Johore lorries were set alight, rubber trees were slashed, and three British planters were attacked and badly wounded; in Negri Sembilan ambushes were laid and telephone lines cut; and in the Cameron Highlands a large scale attack was made on a new village, with the loss of two lives and a depressing quantity of arms, ammunition, and food. There was no curtailment of the amnesty offer, but the military were permitted to take off the brake, General Bourne announcing that full scale operations would be resumed as from December 1, 1955.

The Royal Hampshires had been flown down from Selangor to thicken the drive against marauders in Johore. They spent a frustrating, mosquito-plagued two months toiling through the jungle around Kluang without success. Then at the start of December they returned to Selangor and almost at once achieved a success that brought them over fifty congratulatory telegrams. Its source lay in the information obtained by the Special Branch from a deserter, to the effect that some rebel leaders were attending a course of political instruction in a camp just inside the jungle a few miles from Ulu Langat.

A full company, under Major Symes, set off after dark on December 10, guided by the deserter, who was named George after the automatic pilot. The 11th was spent in some exhausting climbing and in untangling errors of navigation, at the end of which confidence in George was fast declining. However, at 9 a.m. on the morning of the 12th he was able to show Symes the camp, and it was only 300 yards from where the company had spent the night. For the next four hours the platoons crawled into enveloping positions, being assisted by the rustle of a rainstorm. Symes then led in the assault group. They had a difficult approach and succeeded only in flushing the rebels. A tense silence followed. Then came the bark of a bren, a long pause, and the bark of another. The rebels were trying to crawl to safety, but those four hours had not been wasted; every escape route was covered. Eleven dead were eventually picked up, together with a girl prisoner who had been wounded. The most wanted man, who was secretary of the Ulu Langat branch, was missing, but not for long. Captured a few days later, he said that he was the only survivor of the attack on the 12th. It was the most fruitful company action since that by A Company, 1/2nd Gurkhas in January 1950.

Tungku Abdul Rahman had a meeting with Chin Peng at the end of December 1955, at Baling, 20 miles from the Siamese border. The two men found no ground for agreement, and the talks broke down. The Tungku announced on his return that the amnesty would be ended and gave it as his conviction 'that no half-measures would ever bring to an end this struggle which has been going on for the past eight years'. He then flew to London and returned with an assurance from Her Majesty's Government that Malaya would be granted full independence within the Commonwealth, provisionally by August 1957. This deprived the Liberation Army of the last vestige of pretence.

The Director of Operations could add a stimulating tit-bit to follow this thrilling news for the Malayan people, and again it was brought about by a combined effort by various branches of the security forces. The recently arrived 1st South Wales Borderers made the initial, vital discovery, that of an unoccupied but efficiently established rebel camp on an island amid a swamp near Kluang, Johore. The Special Branch obtained the information that it was the lair of the dreaded Goh Peng Tuan and would be inhabited on February 21, 1956. The kill was entrusted to a squadron of Lincoln bombers of the R.A.A.F., followed in by Canberras of the R.A.F., all of which were to fly straight in without preliminary circling. Never before had the bombers had the chance to attack such a clearly defined target. They did a thorough job. A hundred bombs were dropped, and not until the second day of searching the slimy dereliction around the craters did patrols of the Welsh discover the dead. There were thirteen of them, Goh Peng Tuan included. Seven are said to have escaped, wounded and shocked.

On May 19, 1956, Bourne handed over the appointments of Director of Operations and G.O.C. Malaya to Lieutenant-General R. H. Bower, an officer of the K.O.Y.L.I. newly promoted from being Chief of Staff, Allied Forces Northern Europe. Bourne could claim, with justification, that the rebels were 'at their last gasp'; their killings had subsided to about five a month, civilians, soldiers, police, and home guard included. Yet it had to be admitted that there were still over 2,000 armed rebel fighters, of whom the great majority were now the branch men, the supply and political operators working in and out of the jungle fringes. The task of rounding up these crafty die-hards remained a daunting problem, and Bower had soon to give warning that it was wrong to regard the terrorists as no more than a nuisance while the hard core of their organisation was still in being.

Certainly he was better equipped with men and material than any of his predecessors, bearing in mind that one third of the country had by now been declared white. There were still twenty-four infantry battalions on call, except that a British one was now permanently based on Singapore and provided only two companies for operations. Counting this battalion, the British contribution had been restored to eight, thanks to the reduction of commitments in Korea and Kenya, and a second Gurkha battalion—the 2/7th—had consequently been returned to Hong Kong, leaving six. There had been no further increase in the eight Malayan battalions available, recruiting into the Federal Regiment having fallen below expectations, although an armoured car squadron had been raised. Australia provided one of the other two battalions. The 2nd Royal Australian had arrived in October, together with a field battery, to form the nucleus of the 28th Commonwealth Brigade, a title made famous in Korea. The brigade became operational in 1956, taking over an area in Perak. There was a New Zealand squadron working with 22 S.A.S., in place of the Rhodesian one, and an additional (fourth) squadron had been provided from the Parachute Regiment. This great gain was offset at the end of May 1956 by the departure of the Fijians, who had done magnificent work. However, African representation was maintained. The 2nd K.A.R., who had distinguished themselves in northern Perak, were relieved by the 1st North Rhodesians, who also gained distinction, and they in turn by the 1st Rhodesian African Rifles in April 1956.

Of the British battalions, the Royal Scots Fusiliers, based on Penang, were the most northerly, and like their predecessors they toiled far for a few successes, one company making an 80-mile trek through virgin jungle into Kelantan, which lasted five weeks. They now joined the Commonwealth Brigade. The West Yorks had toiled in adjacent jungle and had gained a notable success in the Cameron Highlands, but they had left Malaya in March 1955, and the only other British battalion north of Kuala Lumpur was now the 1st Royal Lincolnshire, who had relieved the Somersets in September 1955, after the latter had raised their score of rebels killed or captured to sixty-one. The 2nd Royal Welch Fusiliers—one of eight second battalions reformed—were in Negri Sembilan, where they had been rebel hunting since September 1954, having been diverted from Korea by the armistice there.

Since December 1955 Wales had been doubly represented, for the 1st South Wales Borderers arrived and took over from the East Yorks in the Kluang district of Johore, where they achieved, as already recorded, the destruction of Goh Peng Tuan. The East Yorks had not found this part very fruitful and although they had made a few good kills, they had had longer experience of being soaked, torn, tired and frustrated. There was also a second Lowland battalion in Johore. The 1st King's Own Scottish Borderers came to Singapore in September 1955, and first with two companies and subsequently as a whole battalion they joined operations around Batu Pahat. Uniquely among battalions engaged in Malaya, they had had battle experience in Korea, which they had followed with two and a half years at home.

The Royal Hampshires, as has been related, were in the notorious Ulu Langat area of south Selangor. Typically, their sensational success in December was followed by months of dreary toil on a large scale strangulation operation named Bonanza. The searching of workers—2,000 passed one check point each day, and rice was just as likely to be found inside the tubes of their bicycles as on their persons—and the constant watch for rebels, either in the jungle or amidst the tappers, kept the battalion at full stretch for seven months, and not until August 1956, after they had handed over to the 1st Rifle Brigade, was reward displayed in the body of Yeung Kwo, who as vice-secretary general of the Malayan Communist Party ranked as Chin Peng's second-in-command. His was the first kill made by the Rifle Brigade, and it was made in darkness so thick that the shot was aimed by sound, as the men were in process of taking up an ambush position. Yet if it were a lucky way of unearthing the fruit of another's spadework, the Rifle Brigade were no novices to rebel hunting, having come straight from Kenya, where they had been rounding up Mau Mau, and they brought with them the new self-loading rifle, of which they had, in the best historical tradition, been the first to make operational use. Nevertheless the Royal Hampshires had sixty-seven scalps to their credit, for the loss of two officers and seven soldiers killed.

The Queen's had, from April 1956, been based on Singapore, where the throb of political agitation was quickened by the promise of independence for the rest of Malaya. They maintained a three-company detachment in Johore, and a routine patrol from it, consisting of Sergeant Isaac and five men, had a notable success in July. Bumping a gang of the elusive Pontian Road branch in an oil palm plantation, they charged and fought a running battle with them through the trees and grass. Five rebels and one Queensman were killed.

Near the end of October 1956 the Queen's had to recall their companies from Johore at speed. Rioting had again broken out in Singapore, caused this time by the closure of two schools, and the Queen's had to clear the streets. One round fired at a ringleader was sufficient to disperse the most unruly mob, and order was soon restored, thanks largely to the speed with which troops were again brought in from the mainland. The Royal Welch Fusiliers, South Wales Borderers, and King's Own Scottish Borderers were among those switched in a matter of hours from jungle and village operations—the last-named came first and were the most heavily involved—providing a rare gathering, which was celebrated by a massing of the bands, that of the 23rd, 24th, and 25th of Foot. They were soon returned to Johore, and by December the Queen's had returned their companies as well, where they were to bring the battalion's score to a final forty-six, for the loss of an officer and six soldiers killed. The Queen's departed in February 1957, having handed Selarang Barracks, Singapore, over to the Royal Welch Fusiliers. The Suez Canal being blocked, they journeyed homewards round the Cape and roused the streets of Capetown with the beat of their band and drums.

The 1st Loyals had meanwhile arrived in Malaya to keep the Line represented at seven battalions. The eighth British infantry unit was of course the 22 S.A.S., who were now making a great offensive effort, having made the aborigines secure in their forts and being reinforced by the Parachute Squadron. Their influence was widespread and great.

The Royal Armoured Corps still had two regiments farflung on unspectacular duties of escort and road patrol, which they supplemented with foot patrols and the occasional shoot in support of an operation. Since August 1954 the 15th/19th King's Royal Hussars had been in circulation along the northern routes in place of the 12th Lancers, a task now shared with the armoured car squadron of the Federal Regiment. In the southern sector the 1st King's Dragoon Guards relieved the 11th Hussars in June 1956.

Since May 1956 the 48th Field Regiment (complete) had been the Royal Artillery's representative in place of the 25th Field. Australia and Singapore contributed extra batteries, and Malaya a troop, and the shells fell on the rebel hideouts in an endless, nagging stream, at three times the density they had endured in Templer's time.

Surprisingly little use had been made in the early years of the engineering arm. Indeed the Royal Engineers' contribution had amounted to no more than the provision of a staff to supervise local works, and not until 1953 did the 50th Gurkha Field Engineer Regiment become operational, after spending their formative years in Hong Kong. In 1956 they embarked on an extensive programme of road building in company with the 75th Malayan Field Squadron. They built roads in Pahang and Negri Sembilan, and in 1957 extended the project into Kedah, near the frontier, joined now by the 11th Independent Field Squadron, R.E. The object, particularly in the latter stages, was more to help the civil population than the military, and both by their presence and the physical aid they gave, the Sappers did much to boost the morale of the people.

The services had from the campaign's start been quietly performing duties which involved great exertion and considerable risk on their part and formed the very stuffing around which the morale of the fighting troops was built. R.A.M.C. parties often ventured deep into the jungle to meet an infantry group engaged on the long, anguished haul of bringing back a casualty, and although helicopters had greatly speeded the process of evacuation ever since 1950, journeys still had to be made by foot from the landing clearings and there was no reduction of the risk. R.E.M.E. men also performed hazardous tasks of evacuation, and their workshops were often established on the jungle fringes to reduce the delay between repair and return.

In the field of supply, an immense burden, for ever astir with danger, was shouldered by 55 Company R.A.S.C. (Air Despatch). Prodigious work was done by its men in pushing rations and ammunition through the hatches of Dakotas and Valettas down to the men around the tiny jungle clearings that had been hacked through the trees and were hard enough to spot, let alone to hit, with the loads that had to be delivered on to them either by free drop or parachute. During 1956 alone 3,000 tons of supplies were delivered in this manner, and in the crashes that resulted from flying, so often at low altitude and in poor visibility, forty-three men of the company were killed during the whole campaign.

General Bower had his sights set on Independence, or 'Merdeka', day, which was scheduled for the end of August 1957, and to this end he intensified operations along the vitals of Malaya, stretching north and south of Kuala Lumpur, and brought more Malayan troops south-wards. The Commonwealth Brigade took over operations in Perak, the 1/6th Gurkhas and 1st Malay joining the Royal Scots Fusiliers and 2nd Royal Australian, with the S.A.S. operating among the aborigines on the Kelantan border. The 7th Malay joined the Rifle Brigade on the protracted operation Bonanza in Selangor, and the Royal Lincolns came down from Pahang to join the Royal Welch, the 2/2nd and 2/6th Gurkhas in Negri Sembilan. The remaining British and Gurkha battalions were concentrated in Johore with the Rhodesian African Rifles and the 5th Malay.

Results, as usual, came at the rate of coins tossed into a beggar's hat at time of slump. The S.A.S. reported a success in July 1956, with four killed out of five who had the temerity to attack them, and in September a company of the Royal Welch killed all six occupants of a camp after being lifted to its vicinity by helicopter. A rebel leader of importance was killed in Johore in November, but there was a setback in December when a party of Malay soldiers were caught in a road ambush in Pahang and suffered seven killed, a British sergeant among them.

After the dislocation caused by the rioting in Singapore in November 1956, the Rifle Brigade and the Royal Welch were both brought to Johore, and the Royal Lincolns, after some good hunting in Negri Sembilan, went to Perak to join the Commonwealth Brigade in place of the 1/6th Gurkhas, who were due for a spell in Hong Kong. Their places in Selangor and Negri Sembilan were taken by a further influx from the Federal Division, as was appropriate with Merdeka approaching. By building on the foundations laid, these Malayan troops were able to claim two great triumphs: the elimination of the Kuala Langat gang and the organisation behind it, and the death of the terror of

Negri Sembilan, Teng Fook Loong, or 'Ten Foot Long' as the troops had always called him. They both came in May, and at the end of this month there was a symbolic but unobtrusive occurrence, the disbandment of those old inhabitants of Selangor, Headquarters 18th British Brigade.

There were now more British battalions in Johore than ever before, some of them under the 1st Federal Brigade, and the jungles, plantations and villages were being sieved for rebels as never before. The South Wales Borderers, now in the Segamat area, brought a typical operation to a happy ending just before leaving for Singapore in June 1957. Their quarry was one Ming Lee, who for years had kept the local tappers and small holders trembling. The operation began with food denial measures applied so thoroughly and impartially that the planters were on the verge of rebellion before at last Ming Lee's men began to display the strain on them by giving themselves up or by blundering into ambushes as they came out of the jungle in search of food. Ming Lee himself seemed to be protected by a charm, the reality of which was amazing agility, but no sooner had he dodged the bullets for the umpteenth time, as ambush was sprung, than he suddenly decided that the risk and hunger were just not worth it. A good meal and cigarette at the nearest police station rapidly dispelled the ignominy of surrendering and turned him, as so often, to hatred of the organisation for which he had suffered so much. He was pictured, all smiles, sitting among his captors as if he were their captain, and there were smiles too on the faces of all the working people in the neighbourhood, whereas previously they had been sullenly turned away on the approach of a soldier. This was the best reward of victory.

This was by no means the end of the Segamat district organisation, and the long scrutiny continued, making occasional chips of success. It was established, by prolonged observation, that food was collected at regular intervals from a house in a certain village, and one night in July six men of the 2/10th Gurkhas sneaked into a chicken coop six feet away from this house. Despite the chickens inside and the five adults, six children, and their dogs in and around the house, the Gurkhas not only squeezed themselves in undetected but stayed there all day. At the hour of readiness, after darkness had fallen, the door of the coop was pushed open and Corporal Jitbahadur Gurung found the muzzle of a shotgun within an inch of his navel. He was the quicker to react, and within three seconds three rebels had fallen to his Patchet gun. A cordon had meanwhile been thrown round the village, and two hours later a highly experienced district committee member was shot dead trying to creep through it.

This July of 1957 was the first month to pass since the emergency's start without a single killing by the rebels, either of a civilian or member of the security forces. It augured well for Merdeka, and with a week to go Kuala Lumpur was declared white, as part of a belt stretching right across Malaya. Independence was duly granted on August 31 and warmly celebrated.

With it came changes of appointment in the posts of British High Commissioner, who now of course had no executive powers, and of Director of Operations. Lieutenant-General Sir James Cassels filled the latter. Since commanding the 6th Airborne in Palestine, he had gained great success with the Commonwealth Division in Korea, where he had charmed soldiers of many nations, and he now came from being Director-General of Training. As Director of Operations, he was responsible to the Emergency Operations Council, whose chairman was the Minister for Internal Defence. This system had been in force for over a year.

The Tungku announced another general amnesty for the rebels during his inaugural address as Prime Minister. Its terms, dropped in leaflets by the million, were generous, but it was made clear that there was to be no suspension of operations. There was relaxation in their tempo nevertheless, with the main effort directed towards giving the rebels confidence in their chance of surrender.

In October the first great breakthrough began. The rebels' political commissar for South Perak turned up at a police station and offered to obtain the surrender of every branch in his district, for which it was agreed he would receive the reward on offer of 20,000 Malayan dollars for every ten men brought in. His surrender was kept secret, and during the next six months he made good his promise, watched with wondrous eyes by soldiers of the Commonwealth Brigade, patrols of whom kept watch from hiding on the long and elaborate process.

In Johore operations were resumed in December with a naval and air bombardment of likely strongholds in the jungle. The 17th Gurkha Division then applied full pressure, and at the same time the 1st Federal Division fell on northern Perak with the Commonwealth Brigade, effecting the heaviest concentration of troops of the whole campaign. The breakthrough in Johore, which had spluttered with rebel activity more persistently than any other state, came in April 1958, when Hor Lung, who was head of the whole organisation for Southern Malaya, gave himself up to a recently arrived battalion, the 1st Cheshire. His surrender was announced and he rapidly made himself a rich man by bringing in 160 of his underlings, providing the first public instance of a surrender widespread enough to warrant the term 'mass'. By the end of August the north and centre of Johore were declared white, and the estimate of the rebel strength in the southern part could be pinpointed at seventy-three, such was the welter of information that had at last accrued in the files of the operational committees. It had taken ten years to achieve this result, and there was one battalion of the British Army that had been in it all the time, the former artillerymen designate, the 1/7th Gurkhas. No battalion ever spent a longer period on active service.

The British element of the garrison had meanwhile been steadily dwindling. The Royal Scots Fusiliers left Perak at the end of April 1957 to sail home from Penang; the 2nd Royal Welch Fusiliers sailed from Singapore in June, having been based on the island for four months; the Rifle Brigade left in October, having made the most of a few opportunities to display their marksmanship in Johore; and the South Wales Borderers completed a protracted withdrawal to Singapore in December and sailed two months later, with the satisfying record of thirty-six kills or captures without mortal loss to themselves either by the enemy, accident, or disease. The Royal Lincolns left the Commonwealth Brigade in February 1958 and came to Johore, where they staged one very successful ambush, before departing for Aden in May; and the King's Own Scottish Borderers sailed homewards from Singapore in September, having been resident there since March. The most significant mark of the waning of the rebellion came in November 1958, when the 22 S.A.S. began their first journey to England, two squadrons finding an assignment in Oman en route.

Only three British battalions were left after these moves. The Loyals had joined the Commonwealth Brigade in Perak in place of the Royal Scots Fusiliers; the Cheshires had been combing Johore for rebels since October 1957; and since June 1958 the 1st Sherwood Foresters had been based on Singapore with companies deployed in Johore. Similarly, the K.D.G. had been the only British armoured regiment resident since the departure of the 15th/19th in mid-1957, and in August 1958 the 13th/18th Hussars made the return journey to Malaya—the only British unit to do so during the emergency—to take over familiar duties from the K.D.G.

In January 1959 Cassels was succeeded by the newly promoted Lieutenant-General F. H. Brooke, a man who had made a great contribution to the growth of the Federal Army, having been its G.O.C. since 1957 and the original commander of the 1st Malay Infantry Brigade. There had been further dwindling of the task. The whole of Johore had by now been declared white, the whole of Negri Sembilan, and a large part of Perak. The Cameron Highlands, scene of such breathless exertion, followed on March 8. It remained to chivvy the remnant in northern Perak, estimated at 350, and to isolate them from the 480 die-hards adjacent to the border, who formed the rearguard of Chin Peng's army.

In chipping away at the Perak remnant, the Loyals struck a clarion note of Nemesis on March 9, soon after their return from a three-months break in Hong Kong, for which the Foresters had provided their relief. In an ambush set by the Loyals two typical scarecrows, as the starving rebel soldiers had become, were netted when on their way to obtain food from a rendezvous near Ipoh. They were willing enough to turn traitor and led a patrol to their leader's lair, where he was shot dead by a corporal. He turned out to be Siu Mah, leader of the gang that had killed Sir Henry Gurney.

The Loyals, who were the only British battalion still operational, finished their tour with the Commonwealth Brigade in December 1959 and received a compliment that emphasises the lack of opportunity, as also the continued preoccupation with scorekeeping. It came from General Sir Richard Hull, the tall cavalryman who had become C.-in-C. Far East in succession to a large infantryman, General Sir Francis Festing, who had made his mark in the Burmese jungle and whom Hull was to follow to the summit. His message to the Loyals was, 'Your record of seventeen C.T.s killed and two captured during your first two years of operations is one that has not been equalled in your brigade or elsewhere in recent times.' It was also a sign of the times that the Loyals should be relieved by a battalion with the unfamiliar name of the 1st/3rd East Anglian, which was an amalgam of the Bedfordshire and Hertfordshire and the Essex. Much had happened in the world at large since the outbreak of the Malayan rebellion.

With January 1960 came yet another change in command, Brooke being succeeded by Lieutenant-General Sir Rodney Moore, who had commanded the 1st Guards Brigade before the final phase of the Palestine campaign. He now became the eighth and last Director of Operations, and the eighth G.O.C. since the emergency began. He exerted the final squeeze, and on July 31, 1960, as already promised in April, the State of Emergency was declared to be ended.

It had been a victory, most of all, for perseverance. The jungle, so far from being neutral, provided wonderful opportunities for the waging of guerrilla warfare, and it would never have been possible to liquidate the stoic and endlessly patient rebels without the determination to prise them out of their huge, unfathomable fastnesses and to sustain the offensive against them by every possible means. It was fortunate for the British Army that the Brigade of Gurkhas had become available in the nick of time. In raw and delicate condition at the onset, its battalions had built up an immense fund of knowledge and skill and had provided the continuity necessary to maintain cohesion. For the British troops there had been a challenging problem of adaptability. Most of the men were young, town-dwelling conscripts, used to comfortable living conditions, and they had responded wonderfully well to the demands made upon them. Their enthusiasm never sagged, and this reflects credit on the leadership running all the way along the vine from generals to corporals. Mention has been made of some of the generals. Among others who deserve it are L. H. O. Pugh, who brought the 26th Gurkha Brigade from Hong Kong and rose to become Chief of Staff Far East; R. N. Anderson, who commanded the 17th Gurkha Division between 1955–57; J. A. R. Robertson, who began as G.S.O.1 to Boucher and ended in command of the 17th; and an officer of the 6th Gurkhas, W. C. Walker, who was a major when the campaign started and about to become a major-general when it closed.

Yet the military effort could never have been sufficient on its own. It brought success in the end because it was harnessed to the vision and determination of Briggs in regimenting the people, the inspiration of Templer in making them believe in victory, the network of information built up by the police, the clemency shown to prisoners, and the political advance to independence. The key was cooperation between a wide variety of agencies, and it had not been easy to find the correct combination.

Some 2,473 civilians had lost their lives in the struggle, together with a further 810 reported missing and unlikely to have survived. 1,346 Malayan policemen had been killed and 128 Malayan soldiers. The British Army had lost 70 British officers and 280 men killed, and 159 Gurkhas. The rebel dead numbered 6,710, not counting the inestimable horde that perished in the jungle from starvation, melancholia, disease, bomb blast, or execution by their comrades; 1,287 had been captured and 2,702 surrendered. A further 500 terrorists, it was reckoned, still roamed the jungle bordering Siam, a fair proportion of whom were the ordinary career bandits that had long infested Malaya. The rebel leader, Chin Peng, was among those still at large. Hopeless though his situation was, politically as much as militarily, he remained defiant to the end, refusing to capitulate as long as recognition of his party was withheld.

On August 1, the day following the official ending of the emergency, a victory parade was held in Kuala Lumpur. It was the measure of Britain's achievement that Malaya's own soldiers should have pride of place and should earn the cheers, fully deserved by their appearance, of their own people; the army still had British officers at its head, but they were becoming fewer. There were also British, Gurkha, Australian and New Zealand contingents, and aircraft of the four Commonwealth partners flew overhead. Among the British representatives, appropriately, were the 13th/18th Hussars, who had spent five years on active service during the emergency, and those doughty ex-infantry substitutes, the 26th Field Regiment, who had returned to join the Commonwealth Brigade, which was to remain as a strategic reserve. The British infantry representatives were the 3rd East Anglians, the thirtieth and last British battalion to take part. They had had little chance to distinguish themselves as jungle fighters; yet in seven months of patrolling they had worn out 4,000 pairs of jungle boots. It had been a tiring campaign.

6

Korea

THE departure of the Royal Inniskilling Fusiliers to Malaya at the end of July 1948 reduced the garrison of Hong Kong to two battalions of infantry—the 2nd (soon to be 1st) Buffs and the 2/10th Gurkhas—and the 25th Field Regiment. It had soon to be increased. Civil war was raging on the mainland of China, and by December the Red army of Mao Tse-tung had not only captured Peking but presented such threat to Shanghai that the Buffs were embarked to go there to protect the evacuation of British subjects. The latter preferred to stay, and in May 1949 Shanghai fell without intervention by British troops, although with loss to the Royal Navy in the River Yangtse. Plans were by now under way for the despatch of substantial reinforcements to Hong Kong. The British Army was heavily taxed with its commitments in Europe and Malaya, but the only sure way of deterring Mao from an attempt to add Hong Kong to his conquests was to scrape together more troops for its defence.

The despatch of the 2/6th Gurkhas in December 1948 brought the 26th Gurkha Brigade to full strength. In June 1949 the 1st Royal Leicestershire arrived from England as a newly enlisted member of the 27th Infantry Brigade, which had been formed the previous July as the first of the 'fire brigades' but had always had a floating, disjointed population. Its other battalions soon followed, being the 1st Middlesex—who had been released eighteen months previously from their long-held machine-gun role and had spent six of the intervening months on public duties as a result of the Guards' removal to Malaya—and the 1st Argyll and Sutherland Highlanders. Tanks also came, manned by the 3rd R.T.R., and sufficient artillery and ancillary units to equip a division that was numbered the 40th and placed under command of a man of sturdy stature and great vigour who had gained distinction in the jungle of Burma: Major-General G. C. Evans. The 3rd Commando Brigade came from Malta, and finally the 28th Infantry from England, consisting of the 1st King's Own Scottish Borderers, the 1st South Staffordshire, and the 1st King's Shropshire Light Infantry, whose arrival in October straddled that of Mao's soldiers along the frontier of the New Territories. The rugged hills on the British side now bristled with defences, and no spark of aggression was directed at them.

While these British troops were being hurried by sea towards the mainland of eastern Asia, others of powerful nations were being brought away. 1,300 miles to the north of Hong Kong lies the peninsular of Korea, which in 1910 had been annexed by Japan and was now to be made free, with its people masters of their own destiny. The Americans and Russians had shared the task of ejecting the Japanese and of temporarily administering this backward, mountainous land, with the line of the 38th Parallel arbitrarily settled as the boundary between their zones. A United Nations' commission arrived in January 1948 to supervise free elections. The Soviet Government refused to allow the commission entry into the northern zone. None the less they removed their troops from Korea by the end of 1948, after establishing a communist government at Pyongyang. Six months later the American troops were also withdrawn, leaving a government elected by crude democratic process at Seoul, the old capital of Korea, 40 miles south of the 38th Parallel. There was one difference. Whereas the Russians equipped their North Korean protégés with T.34 tanks, aircraft and powerful artillery, together with a liberal supply of instructors, the Americans provided the South Korean army with nothing more lethal than bazookas and field artillery. It had no tanks, no aeroplanes, and its numerical strength of 50,000 was barely half that of the North Korean army.

The United Nations commission remained, charged now with the forlorn task of finding some way of uniting the country, although denied passage across the 38th Parallel. There was in fact only one way of imposing unity—by invasion—and the commissioners had to report to their dismay that the North Koreans had had resort to this drastic step in the early hours of Sunday, June 25, 1950. The choice of a Sunday was well in keeping with the tone of the enterprise. It was such an astounding and brazen act of aggression that, despite all their experience of the mood called communism, the democratic governments were taken completely by surprise.

Russia happened to be indulging in a boycott of the United Nations Security Council, because Nationalist China retained a permanent seat

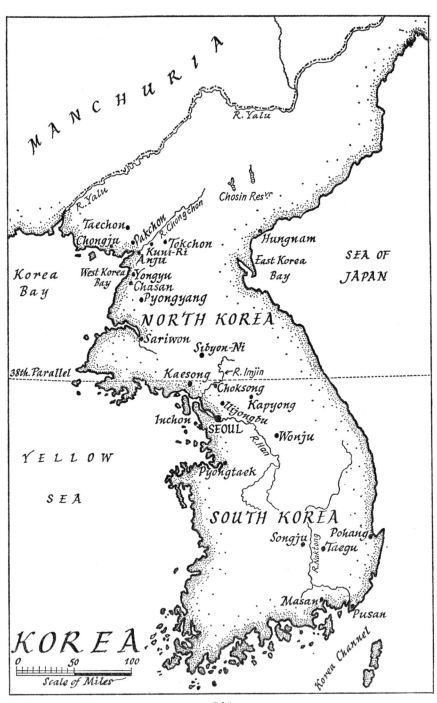

MANCHURIA

R. Yalu

R. Yalu

Chosin Res.ʳ

Taechon

Chongju

Pakchon

R. Chongchon

Tokchon

Kuni-Ri

Anju

Hungnam

East Korea
Bay

SEA OF
JAPAN

Korea
Bay

West Korea
Bay

Yongyu

Chasan

Pyongyang

NORTH KOREA

Sariwon

Sibyon-Ni

38th. Parallel

Kaesong

R. Imjin

Choksong

Kapyong

Iuchon

Uijongbu

SEOUL

Wonju

YELLOW

SEA

R. Han

Pyongtaek

SOUTH KOREA

Songju

Pohang

Taegu

R. Naktong

Masan

Pusan

Korea Channel

KOREA

0   50   100

Scale of Miles

upon it, and there was consequently no veto on a resolution condemning North Korea for an act of aggression that 'openly flouts the authority of the United Nations'. When put to the General Assembly, forty-one nations voted in favour of intervention, and only the serf nations of the Soviet opposed it. This was a wonderful expression of the world's determination, fulfilling every idealist's hopes in the U.N., but something more than mere expression was needed. The South Korean army was outnumbered, outgunned, and defenceless against the Russian tanks, off which the only anti-tank missiles available rebounded. Seoul fell on June 28, only three days after the invasion's start, and even America had as yet offered no more than support by sea and air. The United Nations were in danger of being made to look as feeble and foolish as their predecessors, the League of Nations.

They were saved by the courage of President Truman, backed by the iron nerve of his Supreme Allied Commander in Japan, General of the Army Douglas MacArthur. The latter had four divisions of the United States Army in this country 120 miles from Korea. They were at half strength and employed on occupational duties, enjoying comforts and delights such as no commander would have permitted if he had been training them for war. There was great risk in launching such troops into battle, and indeed there could be no guarantee that they would not be swept straight into the sea by the North Korean onslaught, which seemed to be gaining in strength and irresistibility with every report that came in. The risk was accepted and the divisions sent, their spearhead entering the battle as early as July 5. Already bombs from American aircraft were slowing down the enemy advance, and seventeen warships from the navies of the British Commonwealth were among those performing a similar task from the sea. An Australian squadron of Mustang fighters also joined the battle, making impact at once.

On July 20 MacArthur announced the successful fulfilment of what he called 'the desperate decision to throw in piecemeal American elements as they arrived'. The enemy, he said, had had a great opportunity, but had lost it 'through the extraordinary speed with which the Eighth Army has been deployed. . . . I do not believe that history records a comparable operation. . . . We are now in Korea in force and we are there to stay.' From their newspaper correspondents the American public received less reassuring news. Never prone to toning down a good story, they told of 'American boys' streaming back 'with panic in their bellies' and although such reports were intermixed with ones of great heroism, it was clear enough that the situation was still fluid to say the least. The North Koreans had reached the south coastline, 240 miles in a beeline from the 38th Parallel, and hemmed the combined South

Korean and American forces into a shallow arc around the port of Pusan on the south-east corner. Although two divisions arrived from America at the start of August, the fall of Masan, some 30 miles west of Pusan, was reported on the 6th. Masan was recaptured on the 16th, but further north the North Koreans made a crossing of the River Naktong, and both Taegu and the port of Pohang, on the east coast, were in peril. There was also a report from a survivor that twenty-six of his comrades of the 1st U.S. Cavalry Division had been bound and shot by their North Korean captors.

Such were the news items reaching Hong Kong when orders arrived on Friday, August 18, for the despatch of the 27th Brigade less one battalion. It had been announced as early as July 26, by Mr. Shinwell, Minister of Defence, that 'a self-contained British force' was to be sent out, and orders had gone out for the mustering of one more brigade of infantry in England and for its preparation for the five-week sea journey to Korea. But the Americans wanted aid more quickly than that. They had already put elements of five divisions into the battle, of which three had been badly mauled, and the strain of holding the fort on their own weighed so heavily upon them that MacArthur made public appeal for speedy contributions in troops from all consenting members of the United Nations. Where America led Britain had to be the first to follow. There had been recent withdrawals of troops from Hong Kong to Malaya, slimming the garrison there to the minimum within the bounds of calculable risk, but there could be no other source of swift succour to the hard pressed Americans. Hence the signal, and hence too a new nickname for the brigade that had once been called the Fire Brigade: 'The Something for God's sake Brigade.'

The Middlesex and the Argylls were the two battalions chosen and the senior member of the brigade, the Royal Leicesters, the one omitted. It was mortifying for the latter to be left out, and it could only be explained to them that two battalions were all that could be spared and that the choice had been made by the War Office on grounds of the availability of reinforcements.

Although the instruction arrived on the Friday, August 18, it was kept secret from the men until the Monday the 21st. There was great hub-bub throughout the Colony, and soon every battalion was astir with the realisation that the men of the Middlesex and Argylls were not the only ones affected. For the two chosen battalions were suffering from that endemic complaint in the British Army, shortage of manpower, and were further weakened by an order preventing any soldier under the age of 19 accompanying them. There was no other battalion of their brigade groups at Hong Kong, and reinforcements for them had consequently to

136

be levied by the traditional ritual of calling for volunteers. The response, all accounts agree, was remarkable, and just as remarkable was the eagerness within the two battalions not to miss the boat. Some 250 men were required to bring these two to strength, and many more than that number stepped forward when the question was put to the four battalions remaining, the Royal Leicesters, the K.O.S.B., the South Staffords, and the K.S.L.I.; indeed the 'Kosbies' responded on a battalion parade as if they had received word of command.

Yet even so, the two battalions were brought to a strength of only 600 soldiers to fill an establishment specially ordered of three rifle companies and a headquarter company which took over the mortar platoon (of six 3-inch mortars), the machine-gun platoon, each with four Vickers that had been brought back from retirement for the defence of Hong Kong, and the assault pioneer platoon. There was a lack of anti-tank weapons, even of the piat with which each platoon should have been armed, and to redress it the Americans sent a supply of bazookas, with instructors, by air from Korea. A brigade anti-tank platoon was also raised and equipped with the cumbersome 17-pounder.

Hong Kong was no longer gripped by the sense of crisis that had prompted the despatch of reinforcements. The Gurkha Brigade and the Commando Brigade had both gone to Malaya, and the first families of the battalions that had come post-haste from England were nearing the end of their journey to Hong Kong, where some would arrive to find their menfolk gone. There had, however, been no slackening in the tempo of training across the hills that would have to be held against overwhelming odds if Red China opted for invasion. Much sweat had been spilt in climbing them and much discomfort had been endured during the many nights spent on them in the open, with the result that the six battalions that had arrived from England soft and green had become tough and confident. Evans had driven them hard, and they had better cause to be grateful to him than anyone could have anticipated. Now he was left with no more than an enlarged brigade group, and over him as G.O.C.-in-C. of all land forces, both regular and local, was a lieutenant-general, Sir Robert Mansergh. As their garrison dwindled, so did their anxieties increase. Success for North Korea might easily lure Mao Tse-tung over the brink.

The Commander-in-Chief Far East, General Sir John Harding, shouldered an even heavier share of the new burden of anxiety. Although the troops sent to Korea would come under United Nations' command for operations, he retained moral and administrative responsibility for them, and of course the outcome of the war there would have its effect not only on the threat to Hong Kong, which was external and problematic, but on the civil war in Malaya, in which the challenge of the rebel Communists would wax all the stronger and from which Harding was determined to resist the temptation to return the three battalions and three commandos taken from Hong Kong in the spring. The only personal contribution he could make to the Korean war was an infusion of his own resolve into the two battalions, and he made it on Thursday, August 24, by giving a short informal talk to each in turn near their old battle stations in the New Territories. He told them to expect tough fighting and a chaotic situation, and there was something about this slight, finely moulded, war-scarred man that put the 'Die-Hards' and the Argylls in the right frame of mind to meet it.

They embarked next day, Friday the 25th, Brigade Headquarters and the Middlesex in the maintenance carrier H.M.S. *Unicorn*, the Argylls in the cruiser H.M.S. *Ceylon*. Not since the reign of Queen Victoria had British soldiers received such a send-off as these. Proceedings began with another pep talk, delivered this time by the British High Commissioner for South-East Asia, Mr. Malcolm MacDonald, from ship's deck to the troops on the quayside of Kowloon harbour. The men then filed up the gangways, in their olive green drill and full service marching order, while the band of the Royal Leicesters and the pipe band of the K.O.S.B. provided alternate, weirdly contrasting musical accompaniment. A great crowd gathered, and during the long wait to cast-off there was singing, cheering, ribald exchanges, and a flurry of waving hands from both decks and quayside—or in the words of an Argylls officer, 'bags of ballyhoo'. Darkness had fallen when at last the ships departed, leaving a galaxy of twinkling lights behind them and the fading skirl of the pipes. The well-wishers on the quayside dropped their hands with a sigh, and the infantry soldiers among them pondered on when their turn would come.

On Tuesday, August 29, the ships reached the coast of Korea with the two regimental flags flying below their White Ensigns. They entered the port of Pusan, South Korea's one remaining link with the outside world, which the Americans called 'Poos'n' and reviled for its squalor and stinks. *Ceylon* was the first to berth, and the Argylls consequently bore the brunt of a welcome that outstripped the fervour of the farewell from Hong Kong. Cheers, sirens, songs, yells and whistles pierced the air, and it was some time before the pandemonium had sufficiently subsided for the music of a Korean naval band to be heard. Just before the disembarkation began, a girls' choir gave a shrill rendering of God Save The King, and for Major Muir, who led the Argylls ashore, there was a bouquet from the hand of a fair maiden, followed by a round of handshakes with gold braided officials and drab clad representatives of the United States. Cheering and flag waving meanwhile raged unabated, and as final tribute to the men who had come in response to the despairing plea 'Send something quick', an American Negro military band gave a highly original and spirited version, with music and rag-time marching combined, of Colonel Bogey.

The commander of 27 Brigade was Brigadier B. A. Coad, an officer of the Wiltshires, who had won the D.S.O. during the war as a battalion commander and a bar as a brigade commander. He was well imbued with the phlegmatic virtues that characterise the British officer in the eyes of the world, and never was the need for them stronger, for there was a world of difference between American staff methods and British, and Coad found it just as hard to obtain firm instruction as to how his brigade was to be employed, administered and supported as to penetrate the veil of vernacular that enshrouded military talk. He had been flown in with his battalion commanders, Lieutenant-Colonels Man of the Middlesex and Neilson of the Argylls, while the troops were at sea, and at least was able to arrange for the swift removal of his brigade from Pusan to a reserve area close behind and near the centre of the front line. He had originally been told that the Americans would provide all—transport, artillery and rations—but transport had been removed from the list, and the brigade's vehicles were coming from Hong Kong by sea. The first move was by train, and after the sailors had helped the soldiers to carry all their equipment on to it, the men set off on a journey of raw discomfort, which would have lasted longer had not officers taken it in turn to shake the Korean engine driver out of slumber whenever there was a halt.

The American Eighth Army had taken control of all land forces, under command of a man of rugged determination, Lieutenant-General Walton Walker. Although pressed uncomfortably close to the sea, it had a frontage to hold far larger than the accepted capacity of the troops available, nine battered divisions being spread across some 150 miles. Four of these were American, and they were on the left, from the south coast, where a Marine regiment held the line, to the river defences in front of Taegu, the central pivot of the system. The other five, stretching to the east coast, were the reorganised remnant of the South Korean Army, other parts of which were dotted here and there among the Americans, some even forming parts of American units. The Republic of Korea was the self-conferred title of South Korea and her soldiers were consequently known as Roks. Those of North Korea, for more obscure reasons, were called Gooks, and one of the problems was to distinguish Rok from Gook. It could not be solved by asking him.

Both sides were by now under heavy strain, for the American Air

Force had gained complete ascendancy over the meagre North Korean one and had wrought havoc along the supply lines of the invading army. It thus happened that the arrival of 27 Brigade coincided with a lull in the fighting, and its officers and men gratefully made use of it to receive further training in the use of the bazooka and to become acquainted with such strange things as the required procedure for artillery support and the digestion of rich American rations.

The lull was brief. It was broken on September 1, when the North Koreans crossed the wide River Naktong at many points and advanced on Taegu, 10 miles beyond the river. To relieve an American regiment (i.e. brigade) for a counter stroke, 27 Brigade were put into the line on September 5, having just been joined by their own, already hard-used transport. They held a frontage of 10 miles, covering a curve of the Naktong south-west of Taegu, and had two batteries of American artillery and some Sherman tanks in support. There were pimply hills to be held, very similar to those in the New Territories, Hong Kong, except that most had undergrowth and fir trees on the southern, sheltered side. There was similarity in the frontage too, which was five times as large as that considered reasonable for a full three-battalion brigade under European conditions.

Plenty of patrolling was called for, particularly in the $3\frac{1}{2}$-mile void between the Argylls' left and the next American sector, and on the very morrow of their arrival the Argylls lost a gallant officer, Captain Buchanan, who in locating the enemy was hit by their fire, with six others of his patrol. He insisted on being left with his wounded batman to give the remainder a reluctantly accepted chance of escape. Their two graves were discovered when an opportunity to search for them was taken six months later.

At the first glimmer of dawn on September 15 a mighty bombardment fell on the port of Inchon, 20 miles west of Seoul, and landing craft steamed shorewards, bringing in the 1st U.S. Marine Division. There were many hazards, but none too big to obstruct the genius of MacArthur; the Marines soon captured their objectives, allowing the remainder of the amphibious X Corps to sprout forth to east, south-east, and north-east. On the 16th the Eighth Army began to sprout forth from Taegu. It was the North Koreans' turn to be hopelessly outgunned now, and the hard fought Americans began to penetrate their defences with gradually increasing momentum. The 27th Brigade were ordered to chime in on the 21st, in order to secure the left flank for an advance by the 24th U.S. Infantry Division, who had been the first to arrive and had already had more casualties than the British would suffer during the entire campaign.

The brigade had to come a few miles northwards to cross the Naktong and advance along a minor road on the town of Songju, some 7 miles beyond the river. An American reconnaissance company had gained the far bank, established a rickety footbridge, 300 yards long, and brought some light tanks over on a raft, which broke down soon after the arrival of the British. At 4 p.m. on September 21 the Middlesex led the way across the bridge with Colonel Man at their head. As the men filed over a self-propelled gun took shots at them, first from one place and then another, and mortar bombs fell too. Although the aim was erratic, it was a harsh test of nerve, and indeed some casualties were incurred. There were few below the rank of sergeant in the Middlesex with any battle experience and more than half were national-servicemen. Yet Coad, in his own words, 'gulped with pride' as he watched the young Die-Hards march unfaltering to their first taste of battle. The Argylls followed as calmly. They had rather more regulars in their ranks, and of the majority who had missed the war, a number had heard plenty of explosive burst around them in Palestine.

There were some big hills astride the road, 3 to 5 miles beyond the river, and Coad divided them between his two battalions as their objectives. The attack did not begin until daylight on the 22nd, after a night spent in manhandling mortars and machine-guns forward—for the raft's engine defied all attempts to repair it, leaving the British without any transport for three days—and in listening to the sounds of digging from the enemy lines. A platoon of B Company, 1st Middlesex, made the opening move, an attack on a hill named Pudding just to the right of the road; it was the first time the Middlesex had made a set attack as infantrymen since 1918. There were two light tanks in support, with the battalion mortars and machine-guns, but no artillery. Carried out with great verve, the attack gained swift success and an M.C. for the platoon commander, the newly joined 2nd Lieutenant Lawrence, who was as brisk in bringing fire down on the Gooks after capturing his objective as in leading forward his men. It was a bright start.

Further to the right there was a larger hill, 1,000 feet high, and D Company now made a wide movement to attack it from the right flank, while every available supporting weapon blazed away from the front. After a stiff climb, a fierce fight developed for the hitherto invisible summit. A platoon commander was killed, while advancing intrepidly, and his platoon sergeant was badly wounded. The situation was grim, until an American artillery officer arrived out of the blue and brought down an accurate and fearsome stonk from his 155-mm. guns. The Gooks fled, leaving forty dead behind them and four medium machine-guns. The Middlesex had played their part, at a cost of fourteen casualties.

It was the Argylls' turn now. Their objective was a hill called 282 (its height in metres) about a mile to the left of the road. Again, there was no great sense of urgency, and all that was attempted and achieved before darkness was the establishment of A Company in a supporting position. As dawn broke on the 23rd, B Company followed by C, began the climb through scrub and over rock, and an hour later B Company surprised the Gooks at their breakfast on the hilltop, having unwittingly bypassed their leading elements. There were some sharp exchanges at both ends of the company, in the course of which the two leading platoon commanders were struck down wounded. However, they cheered their men on from where they lay, and the Jocks charged with shrill vocal accompaniment, drove out the Gooks, and bowled several over as they fled downhill. Both companies were soon digging in, speeded in their exertions by the sombre aspect of another, higher feature on their left, Point 388, on to which C Company were due to advance.

With the carriers still stranded on the other side of the river, the mortars could not be brought within range of this ridge, and now, deaf to all pleas, the American artillery officer departed, having other work to do; it was with wry pride and good cause that the 27th called themselves the Cinderella brigade. Mortar bombs and shells began to fall among the men on Hill 282, and the casualties mounted, causing further frittering of manpower on the long and laborious task of evacuation down the steep slope. A counterattack from the left began to develop in a nagging, debilitating manner, with the Gooks making good use of the bountiful scrub and firing bursts from their 'burp' guns, now from here, now from there. The two platoons furthest on the left suffered heavily and were pulled back to a tighter perimeter.

Such was the problem of casualty evacuation that the second-in-command, Major Muir, mustered a party of stretcher bearers and led them up the hill. He saw at once that there was a need to reorganise the two companies into a single defensive entity, and he stayed to do this. He tried to get the light tanks to fire on this troublesome ridge on the left, but their observation was sadly restricted, and arrangements were made instead for an air strike to be brought down upon it. Recognition panels were put out.

Muir, according to eyewitnesses, 'was literally everywhere', helping the wounded, distributing ammunition, directing fire, and the presence of this short, square-shouldered smiling man in the balmoral put such heart into the dwindling garrison that there was fresh confidence that the position could be held. The sound of aircraft overhead turned confidence to conviction. They were three Mustangs, displaying the

star of the United States Air Force. They zoomed low over the Argylls'
hill—and each emitted a yellow cylinder that burst on landing into a
hideous, spewing sheet of flame. Napalm! Argylls, their ammunition,
and indeed the whole hilltop were ablaze, and to complete the torment
of the survivors, the Mustangs returned and pumped machine-gun
bullets at them. It was impossible to stay. Even Muir was forced to
leave the furnace and take shelter on a lower ridge, where he set about
rallying his singed, dishevelled, stark-eyed men. Many had plunged
through the flames down the shortest and most precipitous route to
the bottom.

Yet not everyone had left. Firing could be heard from the hilltop,
and it was from the rifle of Private Watts, who was wounded too badly
to move but not to defend himself. It was enough for Muir. There were
three other officers still standing and about thirty men, and with hastily
arranged covering fire he led a party back on to the black and smoking
hill through the bullets of Gooks, who had been slow to accept the
chance to take possession. Watts was safely evacuated, with one or two
others who had escaped a roasting. But ammunition was now desperately
short, and the Gooks were closing in on three sides, fiendishly persist-
ent. Muir again spread inspiration around him, filling every post with
his own matchless spirit. He fired bursts from a sten until he ran out of
ammunition, and he then manned a 2-inch mortar, with the commander of B Company, Major Gordon-Ingram, as his number two, and
sent its bombs crashing upon the enemy. Two bursts from a 'burp'
gun smote him as he fired. As he was lugged to shelter he summoned
strength to say, 'The Gooks will never get the Argylls off this ridge,'
and died.

It was not to be. Gordon-Ingram had only ten men left and scarcely
enough ammunition to fill one magazine for each of his three brens.
With the commanding officer's permission, he withdrew his men to the
foot of the hill, leaving no wounded behind and taking most of the
surplus weapons. The absence of artillery support and the attack by
the Mustangs had been too deadly a combination. Bitterness was felt
at the time but it did not endure.

Kenneth Muir was to win the Victoria Cross for his valour, and there
was also an award of the American Silver Star both for him and for
2nd Lieutenant M. D. W. Buchanan, who had nobly borne the brunt
of the Gooks' counterattack before being killed by the aircraft; he was
a cousin of the Buchanan killed earlier. The Argylls' losses, which
included all platoon commanders and their sergeants in the two companies, were seventeen killed and seventy-six wounded, the majority
being inflicted by the enemy, not the aircraft, especially in the case of

the wounded. Their fight made a great impression, most of all on the Americans, and rightly filled the Highlands with pride. Yet only the Middlesex gained the battle honour NAKTONG BRIDGEHEAD: an anomaly explained by the peculiarities of regimental preference.

II—ON THE MOVE (1950)

The next two days, September 24 and 25, were spent by 27 Brigade in recuperating, in gathering in their transport from the erratic ferry, and patrolling. The Americans meanwhile crossed the Naktong further north and came up round the right of the Middlesex. The Argylls prepared to resume the attack on Hill 282 on the 28th, with stronger surety of artillery support, but the enemy was found to be gone, and both battalions advanced to Songju, 3 miles on. They found evidence enough here that the Gooks had been demoralised by the convergent drives from Inchon and Taegu. Men surrendered without a fight, and some were rounded up having exchanged their uniform for the white garb of a peasant—and since local peasants had been impressed into their ranks, this was not so surprising. The Americans drove on, leaving 27 Brigade to clear the primitive little town of Songju at leisure.

There were some important arrivals for the brigade here. Each battalion received a company of reinforcements drawn from Germany and flown out by the R.A.F., that for the Middlesex being provided complete by the 1st Queen's. This gave them four rifle companies, while the Argylls were able to resurrect their third one. Then on October 1 the brigade altered its title to the 27th British Commonwealth Brigade, being now joined by the 3rd Battalion The Royal Australian Regiment. It was a happy day for Coad, and likewise for his two British battalions, and since they were all volunteers, many of them re-enlisted war veterans, and were all itching to get into battle, it was a happy day for the Australians too. But the battalions had still to rely on the Americans for fire support, supplies and, when necessary, transport to lift them.

The first taste of American transportation came on October 4, when without a single written instruction, trucks arrived—the powerful 2½-ton six-wheel driven trucks—to take the three battalions to Taegu airfield, whence they were flown without a hitch to Kimpo airfield, Seoul, while their transport laboured along 200 miles of bumpy road to join them. There was high excitement. The United Nations forces had by now completed the task of driving back the invaders, and on

October 7 MacArthur received the authority of the General Assembly to pursue them into their own territory and thus bring about the unification of Korea. Chou-en-Lai had already given warning of the consequences on behalf of Red China, but no one cared. The hunt was on.

The 27th Brigade had a preliminary pause at Kaesong, just short of the 38th Parallel, and they took the chance to change into battle dress, with the woollen 'cap comforter' as the most favoured head-dress, or else a floppy jungle hat—steel helmets were worn by the Americans but seldom by the British. The Middlesex were the first to cross the Parallel, on October 11, only to spend four days in jostling for position with other columns and in rounding up prisoners from localities bypassed by the Americans in the great surge to get forward. Not until October 16 were the Commonwealth Brigade able to forge ahead, now forming the advanced guard of the 1st U.S. Cavalry Division (which was in fact an infantry division). There was heavy rain this day, giving foretaste of the chill to come.

On the 17th the Argylls took the lead with the garrison town of Sariwon, 30 miles distant, as their objective. The leading company rode on tanks and in trucks, interwoven with many vying journalists and roaming generals. There was no reckonable opposition until 4 miles short of the town, where an enemy force was in position with anti-tank guns and machine-guns. An attack was briskly mounted by the vanguard company, and such execution was done by the tanks and mortars that the Gooks fled, leaving behind fifty dead, with ten machine-guns. The other two companies then passed through to occupy Sariwon, which had been turned to grim wreckage by American bombers, and to clear the northern approaches. The Australians then came through to enlarge the brigade's holding beyond the town.

There were two roads into Sariwon, one from the south, which was the brigade axis, and one from the south-west, down which Colonel Neilson of the Argylls was belatedly ordered to put a company in a blocking position. He set off on a reconnaissance, having narrowly evaded the cross-fire between his own men and a stray lorry load of enemy soldiers in Sariwon. His party was in two jeeps and included his second-in-command and a Captain Mitchell (who will reappear in the Aden chapter) representing the company due to take up the block position. It was getting dark, and the jeeps were upon the troops marching towards them on both sides of the road before there was a chance to identify them. They were met with shots, but drove on fast, and the firing stopped as they whizzed past the head of the column. For 4 miles Neilson and his party drove with pounding hearts past file

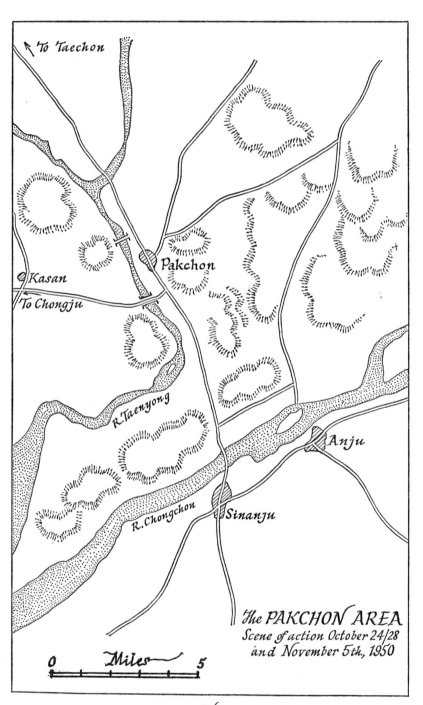

To Taechon

Kasan

To Chongju

Pakchon

R. Taenyong

Anju

R. Chongchon

Sinanju

The PAKCHON AREA
Scene of action October 24/28
and November 5th, 1950

0   Miles   5

upon file of enemy soldiers. Then at last they had the chance to turn off the road unnoticed and lie-up for the night.

Meanwhile the head of the column entered Sariwon unchallenged and unsuspecting. The mortar officer of the Argylls, standing by the roadside, did not realise who it was until asked the question, 'Russky?' He replied with guttural noises of assent and was rewarded with the gift of a comforts girl, with whom he exchanged headwear. The Russians were adept at giving their allies expectation of their coming, and it was easy for an Argyll, in his eccentric hat, to turn expectation to illusion. But a stray American gave an outraged, 'Hell, no!' when the question was put to him, and the firing started. A night of pandemonium and fantasy followed, with the losses all incurred by one side. Some 165 Gooks were killed either in Sariwon or on its northern exits, where the Australians obtained plenty of shooting practice. Between 1,200 and 2,000 surrendered (versions differ), many of them driven to wailing despair. The total loss to 27 Brigade was one Argyll wounded in the brief fight for entry into Sariwon.

It was now on to Pyongyang. There was much jostling. The Middlesex took the lead, but lost the race to a South Korean division who rushed in from the east to enter the enemy capital on the morning of October 20. A pause was expected here but did not materialise. Thirty miles north of Pyongyang an American regiment made a parachute descent on this same day, and on the 21st 27 Brigade led the advance to join up with them, transferred now back to the command of the 24th Division. They spent the night in close proximity to the sound of furious firing, and early on the 22nd the Argylls drove some snipers out of the town of Yongyu. The Australians then went bald-headed at some dug-in positions and in the course of an hour or two killed 270 Gooks for a loss to themselves of seven wounded. The Middlesex then passed through to join up with the paratroops, who had had a much tougher fight than expected but done great execution. Next day, the 23rd, the Argylls advanced against light opposition and reached the estuary of the River Chongchon, where they encountered a broken bridge and shell fire. They had come 65 miles along the road from Pyongyang in three days.

It was still 'on, on!'—or in Americanese, 'Barrel-on!' Assault boats were brought up during the night, and at 8 a.m. on October 24 the Middlesex launched them at a point 4 miles downstream from the main axis, where the river was less wide, although 800 yards, and opposition less likely. It was particularly fortunate for them that there was nothing to meet them on the far bank except a civilian committee of welcome, for the leading boats were swept far off course by the tide, which then abruptly subsided, leaving the last two companies stuck on slimy black mud. They waded ashore, lugging their boats, and after hours of toil spent a dank, chill night without blankets or rations. However, a bridge was constructed on the other side of the main axis, at Anju, and next day the Australians pushed on almost to Pakchon, 7 miles beyond the Chongchon, passing many highly defensible but abandoned positions.

From here 27 Brigade had to change direction from north to west. Their objective was Chongju, 20 miles on, and even on October 25 the Australians made the first move westwards by crossing the River Taenyong. Now, with the men tired but exhilarated by the flush of victory, came an ominous hardening of the opposition. A fierce counter-attack with tanks was launched against the Australians' bridgehead during the night, and they had such difficulty in beating it off that the Argylls were ordered to make a subsidiary crossing further right next morning (the 26th) having come through Pakchon. The Jocks crossed this firm-bedded river riding on tanks under heavy covering fire from artillery and gained their bridgehead without loss. The two battalions then joined up and the Middlesex passed through. They were 4 miles beyond the river by nightfall.

Retaining the lead on the 27th, the Middlesex encountered T.34 tanks and dug-in infantry on a hill beyond the cross-roads at Kasan, and not until they brought down an air strike and fire from the 155-mm. guns did they gain their objective by an enveloping movement. Ten tanks were knocked out by the aircraft, and five were added next day, when the Argylls warily carried the advance to the foot of the hill feature in front of Chongju, their faith in the air arm fully restored.

On October 29 the Australians attacked this rugged, shaggy hill, liberally supported by tanks, guns and aircraft. They had a hard fight for its summit and an equally hard one to ward off two counterattacks, in one of which a Private Simpson knocked out two tanks with his bazooka. The hill was won, at a cost to the Australians of thirty-eight casualties—and there was one more that night, when their inspiring commanding officer, Lieutenant-Colonel Green, received mortal wound from a chance shell. On the 30th the Middlesex came round the right flank to occupy some densely wooded hills overlooking Chongju, and the Argylls then took possession of the heaps of rubble into which the town had been turned. Here they were treated to an unfamiliar sight, the passage of an American regimental combat team, sent through to relieve them.

In the course of fifteen days the 27th Commonwealth Brigade had advanced about 185 miles, always in the lead. In most of these miles opposition had been encountered, sometimes from coordinated groups of troops, sometimes only from snipers, and the enemy had seldom missed the chance to blow up the bridges over the many rivers running across the main axis into the sea. The troops had performed a remarkable feat of sustained activity, vivid trace of which was to be seen in their bronzed complexion, their pink-rimmed yet happy eyes, the torn and filthy state of their battle dress, and the palpable dereliction of their vehicles. Yet once again expectations of rest proved brittle. The Middlesex were ordered to Taechon, 20 miles north of Pakchon and 40 south of the River Yalu, and here they were to be in reserve to the 1st Cavalry, who had gone on to the Yalu intending to complete the destruction of the North Korean Army. Two days were needed to lift the Middlesex, since they no longer had a tied allotment of troop carriers, and scarcely had they settled into their new area and begun the urgent task of mend and clean than disturbing rumours arrived, pricking flat the buoyancy inspired by victory and the prospect of Christmas in Hong Kong. Chinese 'volunteers' were streaming across the Yalu!

Rumour was confirmed as grim truth on Thursday, November 2. Troops of the 1st Cavalry passed glumly southwards through Taechon, and word quickly spread that they and a Rok division had been surprised and badly mauled. In the afternoon the Argylls arrived, sent up to join the Middlesex as rearguard for a general retreat, and that evening a warning order arrived giving its extent as far away as the Chongchon, 30 miles to the south. American emotion had taken a mighty plunge from exultation to gloom. 'Coad, the Chinese are in—the Third World War has started!' was the greeting received by the Brigadier when he reported to the G.O.C. 1st Cavalry for orders.

The two British battalions were out on a limb, a good 15 miles ahead of their Australian colleagues and even further ahead of the nearest Americans. The first harbingers of Mao's army came in the form of three smiling deserters, dressed in quilted uniform and fur boots, but there was nothing more during the night, which was cold, crisp, moonlit and quiet. In the morning air reports showed troops north, north-east, and even south-east of Taechon, and around noon Coad decided to extricate his battalions and bring them back to the neighbourhood of Pakchon. Tanks, which providentially had remained attached to the battalions, and artillery vehicles helped to ease the shortage of troop-carrying trucks, but some troops had to march all the same. They left Taechon forty minutes before the Chinese arrived and withdrew without bumping any. This was converted in the newspapers to 'fighting their way out'.

Instead of falling back beyond the Chongchon, 27 Brigade were now required to hold a bridgehead well north of the river. They were based on Pakchon and had an American regiment on their right, divided from them by a 6-mile gap. The Middlesex took up position north-east of the town, the Australians on its west side, ahead of a sand-bagged bridge over the River Taenyong, and the Argylls, less one company, also west of the Taenyong, in front of another damaged bridge a mile to the left of the Australians. The third company of the Argylls were held back near the Chongchon to cover the gap, 7 miles wide, between the Middlesex and the river. Between this company and Pakchon were some 155-mm. guns and a battery of field artillery.

November 4 passed still without sight of any Chinese, but during the night firing could be heard from the right flank and it was reported that the Americans were in trouble. Sure enough it was from this direction that the Chinese came, and the first troops they encountered, around 8 a.m., were C Battery, 61st U.S. Field Artillery Regiment. Brigadier Coad was diverted from attending early service at his headquarters behind the Argylls, for it was a Sunday. He could see that the Chinese were swarming around his right rear as they came down a long, dominating ridge that gently descended towards the road, and he could see the American guns being formed into half circle to meet the onslaught, and he thought it 'a stirring sight ... up to the very highest traditions of any artillery regiment'. Some of the men of the battery fought as infantrymen, some as gunners, and every so often a gunner fell, hit by mortar bomb or by the burping, industrious small arms fire directed at them, and a man would leap from an infantry post to take his place. Shells from the guns smote the teeming hillside at ever decreasing range, and the wide overall sweep of the slope was meanwhile thumped by the heavier shells of the 155s, by mortar bombs, by napalm and cannon from aircraft, and by streams of bullets from the faithful old Vickers, fired at extreme range by those machine-gun experts, the Middlesex, and bringing the Chinese their first taste of what they termed 'the silent death'.

The Argylls were the first to be switched from west to east. The bridge behind them was rickety and under fire, and not until 10 a.m. were the leading companies assembled east of the river with their tanks and able to attack southwards to release the guns from the enemy's grasp. They drove the Chinese back, finding some of them dead only 30 yards from the guns and capturing some bren guns, 1943 pattern. The smoking guns were towed away, their wagons laden with dead and wounded and dauntless survivors, and passed a hill on the east side of the road which had just been captured by the backstop company— A Company of the Argylls—who had been rushed up from near the Chongchon on tanks and in a few spare vehicles. They took heavy toll on the weaving, khaki forms still spilling down the slope, but running short of ammunition, they were driven off this little hill before they had linked up with their B and C Companies, who were still advancing southwards. However, a tenuous junction was soon effected.

Coad now brought the Australians back across the Taenyong and filtered them through behind the Argylls to launch an attack round their right flank to enlarge the funnel of escape from Pakchon. Put in during the afternoon, the attack gained full success, and first the Middlesex and then the Argylls were pulled back to form a tighter bridgehead in front of the Chongchon. Some Chinese had penetrated to the very banks of the river and were driven out by the Middlesex with aid from some well aimed airburst shells. It was the end of a hectic day for 27 Brigade. They had extricated themselves from a situation of great peril and uncertainty at surprisingly light cost, especially to the Argylls, who had only eleven casualties.

Twice during the night the Australians repelled attacks; but next morning patrols probed to a depth of 5 miles without finding trace of any Chinaman. In the manner of the guerrillas from whom they had evolved, the Chinese were wont to remove themselves from any battlefield of which they could not gain full possession, taking their dead with them.

Cautiously and with lengthy pause between each step, 27 Brigade returned to Pakchon, and as they did so they came under sudden, violent assault from the weather. On the night of November 14 the temperature plunged without warning to 22 degrees below freezing point (Fahrenheit), and the wind swept from Siberia with terrible bite. The elementary tasks of keeping vehicles, weapons, cookers, rations and the men themselves in functional order became all-consuming, and there was much suffering, most of all among the Australians, many of whom were too old to combat the rigours. Shaving caused agony, but still had to be done, and it was as easy to incur frost bite in the process of changing socks as through failure to enact it daily. American bounty soon asserted itself. There was an issue of windproof jackets and fur hats, of 'drawers woollen long' (which the Argylls accepted unashamedly!) and of string under-shirts. The campaign went on.

On November 24 the 24th U.S. and 1st Rok Divisions set out on another attempt to reach the Yalu, leaving 27 Brigade in reserve around Pakchon, where the men had the luxury of hot shower baths. Reports soon indicated that the advancing troops were in grave difficulties, but instead of staying to form a bridgehead over the Chongchon 27 Brigade were withdrawn behind the river to form a reserve for the American

IX Corps at Kuni-Ri, 20 miles back from the Chongchon and further inland than the former axis of advance.

This brief respite for the 27th coincided with a stern ordeal for an even smaller force of British troops 100 miles to the north-east. Among the first gestures of support for the American initiative was the raising of a fourth commando of Royal Marines, which took an old number, 41. Its men were flown out to Japan in civilian clothes in August, and on September 12 it made its first seaborne raid, near Inchon on the west coast. Two more were made, on the east coast, in October, and all inflicted much damage on the enemy's communications. On November 20 the commando joined the corps that had made the assault landing at Inchon, X Corps. The latter had since made another long journey by sea and was now installed around Chosin Reservoir, 50 miles inland from the east coast and the most northerly point held by United Nations troops.

The first task assigned 41 Commando was to open the route to the Reservoir force, since it had been cut by an attack launched on November 27. They did this in two days, having fierce fighting and making an advance of 10 miles. For six days battle raged around two towns by the Reservoir, and the commando twice retrieved ugly situations, once with a sterling counterattack and once by a daring advance to destroy some abandoned guns. The withdrawal from the Reservoir began on December 6. Having played a crucial part in the extrication of the rearguard, the Royal Marines were evacuated from Hungnam a few days before Christmas, just ahead of the last elements of X Corps. They had had seventy-nine casualties—of whom thirteen were killed and twenty were victims of the cold—out of a strength of only 250. Their exploits won them an American Presidential Citation, with the right to fly a streamer from their colour.

These were isolated operations on the east coast. The Eighth Army's main axis was near the west coast, and there was very little to impede Chinese progress down the wild centre of Korea, except for the newly arrived Turkish Brigade, who gave first display of their prowess and devotion at Tokchon but were far too few in number to do more than delay. The Americans had by now become seriously rattled. So badly had their divisions fared that the Chinese strength was put at a million by the intelligence branch, IX Corps. This was certainly five times the real number, probably more, although in terms of overall strengths there would be as many infantrymen with bayonets among 200,000 Chinese as among a million Americans. The disconcerting thing about the Chinese was that they relied mainly on mule transport, paid great heed to camouflage, and hardly used the roads at all, with the result that the Americans' supremacy in the air paid a much reduced dividend and their positions on the ground were constantly being enveloped by seemingly overwhelming numbers, usually at night. The right flank of the Eighth Army was in this manner prised wide open.

Coad was consequently summoned by the G.O.C. IX Corps, as his brigade were settling into primitive billets at Kuni-Ri, and told that there was to be a swift and radical withdrawal. It was agreed that his task should be to keep the main supply route open through Sunchon and Chasan, and since no transport turned up, the battalions set off on their feet in the early afternoon of November 28. The men marched in single file on either side of the road, with yellow ice dust thrown into their faces by the vehicles that streamed past them from behind. Then the traffic ceased, and an uneasy quiet fell on the columns, broken in the case of the Argylls by the wail of the pipes spread singly among the platoons.

After the Middlesex had marched 18 miles, trucks arrived to take them on to Chasan, 12 miles further on. They reached it well after midnight and dossed down huddled together on a frozen paddy field. Next morning, as they watched the jostling throng of vehicles continue the retreat, they were told to return to an awesome mountain pass, where they had halted briefly the previous evening, in order to keep it open for the retreat of the 2nd U.S. Division. After motoring a few miles they found the road empty—except for a jeep lurched in the drain ditch with an American colonel and soldier dangling from it dead. Eerily conscious of their isolation, the companies began to take occupation of the features at the start of the pass, with higher features menacingly close on either side. American fighters swept in and strafed the wooded slopes ahead, and as their crash echoed and re-echoed across the valley the Chinese came to life. First rifle shots, then mortar bombs, then the harsh stabbing beat of a Russian machine-gun fell on the Middlesex, as the leading company pressed on dismounted. The Vickers gave swift reply. Ahead a jeep was seen racing down the pass from the north, amid a crackle of fire; it disappeared round a spur and was seen no more. Now fire spouted forth from the stark slopes on either side of the Middlesex. Their peril was great.

Making lusty use of his own support weapons, Lieutenant-Colonel Man began to extricate his forward companies, and as he did so wireless communication with brigade, which had been broken, was restored, bringing instructions for the occupation of a block position at a village 8 miles back. Although the rearguard company had to fight their way out with bayonets and grenades, the withdrawal was accomplished without disaster as darkness was falling. After a night spent at the village without molestation, Man was ordered to take his battalion back to the southern end of the pass, aided this time by some tanks and a battery of 105-mm. guns. Much to his surprise, he achieved this unopposed, but when some American vehicles were seen coming down the pass from the north, darting in and out of view as they zig-zagged round the bends, the Chinese revealed that they had not gone far. Their fire could not stop a group of tanks and jeeps, though they killed plenty of those riding on and in them. A convoy that followed nose to tail was turned into a hideous, piled up wreckage, and all the Middlesex could do was to direct the fire of the guns and give succour to the wounded and the distraught who broke through to their positions. 250 of them received treatment at the regimental aid post. By 4 p.m. the forlorn stream had ended and the Middlesex again withdrew. Chivvied from both sides by machine-gun fire, to which the guns and tanks gave spirited reply, they made their escape, with the loss in killed of only an officer and a private over the two days. They were lumbered back to Chasan in vehicles overladen with the flotsam of the oncoming red tide.

The retreat continued to the outskirts of Pyongyang, where preparations were made for a stand, which involved the Argylls in some extraordinary marching, climbing, and counter-marching, all to no ultimate purpose. Then on the morning of December 4 the brigade were again pulled back, and now they had trucks to carry them far out of the line to just south of the 38th Parallel. And as the soldiers rode back, gaunt and set-faced, they had the chance to wave at other British soldiers who, although pinched by the cold, had the eager, expectant look of new arrivals and had a lavish supply of new, British equipment.

III—THE RICH AND THE POOR (1950–51)

The 27th's role as rearguard in front of Pyongyang had been taken over by the brigade that would, under happier operational circumstances, have replaced them as the British representatives in Korea: the 29th Infantry Brigade Group. This was the 'self-contained force' promised by Mr. Shinwell on July 26, and it had taken over four months for it to reach the front line. Its commander was Brigadier Tom Brodie, late of the Cheshires and the Chindits, a man with a cheerful and friendly nature well attuned to keeping morale at the buoyant state required.

His battalions were the 1st Royal Northumberland Fusiliers, who liked
to be called the Fifth Fusiliers and had followed garrison duty at
Gibraltar with a year as demonstration battalion at the School of
Infantry, Warminster; the 1st Gloucestershire, who had returned the
previous winter from that sybarite of stations, Jamaica, and been
welcomed into 29 Brigade with despatch to London docks to offload
strike-encrusted ships; and the 1st Royal Ulster Rifles, who had gone
to Palestine with 6th Airborne in the autumn of 1945 and had since
served as brigade depot battalion before joining 29 Brigade at Colchester in 1949. Each of these battalions had been brought to full
strength by the receipt of around 400 reservists, provided by a selective
recall of the Regular Army Reserve, and consequently the average age
was considerably higher than in 27 Brigade. There was an understandable absence among the reservists of fervour for the cause. Many
had produced compassionate reasons for their return to civilian life, and
investigation of their problems had placed added strain on overworked
administrative machines.

There was to be no cause for the 29th Brigade to beg supplies or
support weapons from the Americans. Indeed, whereas the 27th could
still claim to be the Cinderella brigade, the 29th might have been
termed the millionaire's brigade. Heading a formidable array of supporting arms were the 8th King's Royal Irish Hussars, late of 7th Armoured
Division, newly equipped with the tank, weighing 52 tons and mounting
a 20-pounder gun, which was to restore the prestige of British designers,
the Centurion. For closer infantry support Churchill tanks were
available, mounting petards, flails, and flamethrowers and manned by
C Squadron, 7th Royal Tank Regiment. The Royal Artillery was
represented by the 45th Field Regiment, the 11th (Sphinx) L.A.A.
Battery, and the 170th (4·2-inch) Mortar Battery, the latter undertaking
a role previously assigned to infantry support battalions. The Royal
Engineers provided the 55th Field Squadron, the R.A.S.C. the 57th
Company, the R.A.M.C. the 26th Field Ambulance, the R.A.O.C. the
Brigade Ordnance Field Park, and the R.E.M.E. the 10th Infantry
Workshops. The C.R.M.P. and the R.A.P.C. also had their representa-
tive detachments, and the Royal Signals of course held the force together.

After more than two months of preparation the brigade group had
set sail in four 'Empire' ships, in each of which the War Minister,
Mr. John Strachey, bade the troops farewell. They disembarked at
Pusan between November 3 and 18, to be greeted with a welcome
similar in procedure if not in fervour to that accorded 27 Brigade and to
be chilled not only by the freezing wind but by alarming rumours in
conflict with official optimism. Their first taste of hardship was a

journey in a windowless train, during which they acted as magnet at every halt to a flock of wailing, pitifully begging refugees, whose plight left deep furrows in many memories and made the men conscious of their own bounty. They had been issued with string vests, heavy pullovers and underwear, oiled socks, ski-type boots, and a camouflaged windproof suit for overall wear.

After concentrating south of Seoul, the brigade moved forward to Kaesong on November 19, and from here they were sent off in pursuit of the guerrilla bands into which various remnants of the North Korean Army had turned themselves. The Gloucesters were the first in action. Operating to the north-east of Kaesong, they unearthed an arsenal of weapons and on November 25 had a clash with a band in which they lost two men killed. On the 29th they handed a pinnacle named Sibyon-Ni over to a two-company group of the Fifth Fusiliers, under Major Pratt, who had a troop of the 45th Field in support. At 3 a.m. next morning the North Koreans attacked the hill in mass from all sides. After some desperate fighting, in which one company position was dented, the attackers gave up and vanished. Five Fusiliers had been killed, and three were missing.

The Ulsters meanwhile had moved northwards beyond Pyongyang, and only now did realisation dawn, in starkest manner, that the Eighth Army were in retreat. On December 2 they came back and joined the Gloucesters in a rearguard position in front of Pyongyang, and on the night of the 4th/5th they withdrew without interference from the enemy and motored back through the wreckage of the North Korean capital, along streets strewn with abandoned equipment and lit by the blazes into which bounteous supply depots had been turned. After occupying further rearguard positions without molestation by the enemy, the brigade were relieved by a Rok division and went into reserve.

The Chinese were not advancing at any great speed, but they had made the Eighth Army extremely sensitive to outflanking movements and had hustled them back to the rough line of the 38th Parallel, where the frontage to be held was narrower. Falling snow, the bleakness of the countryside, and a numb sense of depression evoked thoughts of Napoleon's retreat from Moscow. The difference was that the retiring troops could achieve much greater mobility than the enemy and, subject to the solution of defreezing problems, suffered no shortage of supplies. Yet morale had taken a severe shaking, especially in the Rok divisions, and no sooner was the line established along the 38th Parallel than it began to recede beyond it.

Ironically, this was the first period of stability for 27 Brigade—and it was needed, most of all by the creaking transport. They had been taken back to a wretched village named Uijongbu, some 15 miles south of the Parallel, and here they had the fortune to be joined by the 60th Indian Field Ambulance, who by commandeering an abandoned train at Pyongyang and cutting wood as fuel for it had saved their stores from joining the great blaze the Americans had made of theirs. A white Christmas was spent at Uijongbu, with dinner eaten out in the snow. Two days previously the Middlesex and Argylls had been getting on parade for the ceremonial presentation of citations by the Army Commander, General Walker, when the news arrived that he had had an accident and been killed.

Lieutenant-General Matthew B. Ridgway was nominated to succeed him and took over command without delay. He clipped two grenades to the front of his windcheater and rapidly made his fighting instinct felt.

Throughout December 29 Brigade saw plenty to gasp at but no one to fight. They had joined a headlong retreat without being allowed the chance to stop it and without believing that it could be really necessary. They had suffered agonies from the cold and seen agonising things around them, in terms both of human suffering and of military demoralisation. The 8th Hussars had to bear the greatest exasperations. Having brought two squadrons of their precious Centurions by train to Pyongyang, they had then to drive them back along ice-packed roads not just across the Parallel but through Seoul and far to the south, for it was considered that they would only encumber the withdrawal. For two days without pause the monsters lumbered southwards on what by rights was their running-in journey, leaving one behind broken down and demolished. Then, unbelievably, they were ordered to Pusan, where these two squadrons (but not the third) embarked for Japan, vehicles and crews in separate ships, before recall orders reached them. It was a bewildering and humiliating start to a campaign, and it is a marvel that morale remained high.

On the evening of January 1, 1951, 29 Brigade occupied positions they had originally dug for the 1st Rok Division, who were in process of disintegration under enemy attack further ahead. These positions were about 10 miles north of Seoul, which was to give its name to the coming battle. They covered a frontage of 5 miles, which seemed enormous to these fledglings from England, and a mile beyond their left extremity ran the main north-south road, which was covered by the 25th U.S. Division. Brodie happened to have his senior battalion, the Fifth Fusiliers, on the right, the Gloucesters in the centre, and the Royal Ulsters on the left, as if aligned for a battle of old.

Throughout January 2 the troops fortified their positions while convoys, stragglers, and refugees streamed back, probably interspersed with enemy agents sent to examine the posts. Just before dawn on the 3rd the two left platoons of the Ulsters came under sudden attack, after men had appeared waving white flags and shouting, 'South Koreans— we surrender!' Obviously these platoons had been carefully located and a skilled approach had been made through scrub. The Ulsters' positions stood astride a valley, known ludicrously as Happy Valley, and these platoons belonged to different companies, B in front and D behind, on an all-important ridge that formed the left flank. They were overwhelmed after a hectic fight, some being captured, some falling back. The coming of dawn revealed a Chinese soldier standing on the skyline and blowing a bugle from the summit of B Company's part of the ridge.

By prompt and forceful action Major Gaffikin, commanding D Company, restored the situation on his part of the ridge. The Chinese infesting the rest of it were now pounded by fire from artillery, mortars, aircraft and a force of six Cromwell tanks of the 8th Hussars Recce Troop, reinforced by a further six provided for artillery observation officers of the 45th Field. The Chinese wilted under the battering, and soon after 1 p.m. B Company were able to regain their positions without aid from a reserve company brought up to counterattack. The Ulsters' front was again intact and they had lost only twenty men.

Meanwhile a fierce battle was raging 4 miles to the north-east, where the Fifth Fusiliers held three steep hills forming a triangle round the village of Chungdung Dong. The hills stood too far apart to prevent the Chinese coming between them at night, and by daybreak they had overwhelmed the men of Support and H.Q. Companies defending the village and had killed the signallers in the telephone exchange. After this bewildering start the battle swung in the Fusiliers' favour, with the Chinese caught on the low ground by artillery and machine-gun fire and felled in droves in their attempts to gain the summits held by the three rifle companies. The reserve company, previously held back under brigade control, launched a counterattack at 2.15 p.m. supported by Churchill tanks of the 7th R.T.R. They routed the infiltrators, and by 5 p.m. Lieutenant-Colonel Foster, commanding, was also able to report that his front was intact. He had lost some fifty officers and men, of whom two and fourteen respectively were killed.

Gloomy orders reached the battalions at about 6.30: the withdrawal was to continue, back beyond Seoul, and was to begin in two hours time. The Gloucesters, who had not come under attack, and the Fusiliers were able to carry them out without interference. The Ulsters had no such luck. They ran into a death trap, and it was sprung from the rear portion of the left flank ridge, nearly a mile behind D Company and another mile from the American position on the left, which had in any case already been evacuated. There was an inviting gap here, and being masters of infiltration tactics, the Chinese found it.

The ridge here rose precipitately above a track by a river, and it is odd that the Ulsters apparently made no attempt to hold it with a rearguard, for the track was their withdrawal route. As if to advertise their passing the scene was brightly illuminated by flares from an American aircraft as the leading company, B, made their withdrawal soon after 9 p.m. B passed unmolested, followed by the wheeled transport (but not the carriers) and most of C Company. Then mortar bombs and grenades crashed down from this overlooking ledge, machine-guns chattered, with greater volume than accuracy, and Chinese soldiers came whizzing down in person. The Ulsters fought back, with pandemonium and confusion all round them.

Major Blake, commanding in place of a sick colonel, tried his hardest to keep men and vehicles moving on, but the carriers skidded to an interlocked halt on the ice and could do no more than retaliate with machine-gun fire. Blake was killed, probably by an enemy machine-gun firing straight down the track. It was wiped out by a spirited attack mounted by the Battle Patrol, which had recently been formed out of the Anti-Tank and Pioneer Platoons, and now the Cromwell tanks, which were to have formed the rearguard, made an attempt to break through across the frozen river. It almost succeeded. The leading one tore past the ledge and through a blazing village half a mile further on, but it then skewed round, after losing its commander killed by a mortar bomb, and blocked the one behind. Others tried a wider sweep through paddy fields, with all guns blazing and a rapidly diminishing party of infantry riding on them, as the Chinese plastered them with grenades. All were brought to halts, usually with broken tracks, and among those killed, after baling out, was the troop commander, Captain Astley Cooper, who had wrought great destruction on the enemy that morning and shown great dash that night.

Meanwhile Major Shaw of the Ulsters was gathering together all those that could walk, and with sixty such he led a charge that successfully penetrated the blazing village and the route beyond. Painfully and slowly, the men toiled southwards all through the night, and having evaded the fire of an American rearguard, they clambered into the two lorries left for them and were bumped through the streets of Seoul as dawn began to lighten the bleak, freezing scene. Shaw won the D.S.O., as also did Gaffikin, for his counterattack with D Company in the opening hour of the battle.

The Ulsters lost 208 officers and men during the night. Some were to be recovered, as were seven wounded (not all Ulsters) who were coolly collected by an American helicopter a mile or so away from the battle-field. They had managed to disentangle themselves from the freezing, shivering carnage around the carriers and to drag themselves past the Chinese who were exultantly examining the dereliction. It was a grim night.

Inevitably 27 Brigade were also sucked into the retreat, and just as inevitably they were assigned rearguard duties. They took them over when the front line receded to their billeting area on January 1, and on the same day they moved back to positions on the right of those held by 29 Brigade, the Australians having two extrication clashes. Ridgway was determined to hold this line, but it could not be done, and on January 3 the 27th were ordered to cover the retreat through Seoul; 'We're pullin', Coad,' were the words with which the G.O.C. IX Corps broke the news. The Argylls provided the rearguard on the two bridges over the River Han, which loops the southern outskirts of the large and hilly capital city. They saw the trucks with the sad remnant of the Ulsters pass and were then on their own in the eerie, deserted streets. Two things broke the silence: the crack of fires burning in many parts and the screech of a siren on a jeep. It belonged to the Army Commander, General Ridgway, and having toured the city he gave the order for the bridges to be blown.

The retreat continued, with the troops huddled in lorries and the lorries huddled in tight-packed convoys, to Pyongtaek, 45 miles south of Seoul, to Wonju, 45 miles to its south-east, and thence to a point on the east coast, about 20 miles south of the 38th Parallel. Here Ridgway called a halt and made it known that there was to be no more 'bugging-out', to use the colloquial term. His force was approaching a strength of 365,000. It included seven American divisions, five Rok ones in process of further reorganisation, a British, a Commonwealth, a Turkish, and a Philippino brigade, and battalions from France, Holland, Belgium, Greece and Thailand, with others yet to come. It was large enough to hold its own, even if the enemy forces were rising to 400,000, a strength they are said to have attained by March. They were confronted now by troops inspired with fresh resolve. The Chinese were held at Wonju after some desperate fighting around January 20. Ridgway thereupon took the offensive, but without the impetuosity that had characterised previous operations, whether forwards or backwards. The war at last was settling to a more stable pattern.

Neither of the British brigades played a part of great importance either in stopping the Chinese advance or in launching the Eighth

Army's counter offensive. The 27th took over a defensive sector near the centre, in front of Changhowon-Ni, and the most important thing that happened here was that they were joined by their own artillery, the specially raised 16th Field Regiment, Royal New Zealand Artillery, equipped with 25-pounders. The 29th held the extreme left of the United Nations' line at Pyongtaek, where the Gloucesters helped an endless, heartbreaking stream of refugees across a plank bridge over the river. The frost reached a fresh nadir of ferocity, plunging to 48 degrees below freezing point (Fahrenheit) in mid-January, with the result that an officer of the 8th Hussars left the skin of his lips on his flask. For a few lucky members of 27 Brigade five days' respite was available, either to the flesh pots of Japan or their families at Hong Kong, under a newly introduced leave scheme.

As Ridgway's offensive steadily gained momentum, both the British brigades were brought into it. Relieved from the extreme left of the line on January 31, the 29th were moved forward to Suwon, 25 miles south of Seoul, on February 11 and on the 12th relieved the 1st Cavalry after being switched north-eastwards. They were to advance across bleak, windswept hills and crush the enemy against the River Han in conjunction with a converging sweep by the 25th U.S. Division from their right. Centurion tanks were at last available to help them—the eighteen of C Squadron, 8th Hussars—and on February 11 the chance was taken to fire their first shot at the enemy, one of the captured Cromwells being spotted in action at a range of 3,800 yards. A miss by the first shot was redeemed by the second, which crumpled the Cromwell.

The 29th Brigade advanced with the Gloucesters right and the Ulsters left, the former on the only thing in the district that could be called a road. Three days were spent in probing slowly forward and in trying to solve problems of supply across the jagged, icy wastes. It was established that the Chinese were strongly entrenched opposite the Gloucesters—and with the previous battle in mind, this was fair—on a glaring, almost vertical feature named Hill 327. A deliberate attack was launched on February 16, after postponement caused by a counterattack against the Americans. Two battalions of a Negro regiment of the 25th Division first attacked two outlying features, and the Gloucesters then attacked the main one, on a frontage of two companies. They had a stiff climb and a stiff fight for the summit, where the Chinese had to be blasted out bunker by bunker. C Company, on the right, were in trouble, with the company commander wounded, but an enveloping movement round the left flank by D Company helped to keep the assault moving. After a pause caused by a snowstorm, the position was prised open by some deadly fire from the 20-pounders of the Centurions, controlled by a dismounted forward observation officer, and the Gloucesters gained their hilltop, finding thirty-three Chinese dead and taking five prisoner. They lost an officer and eight soldiers killed, and thirty wounded. It had been a test both of fitness and ardour, and as Lieutenant-Colonel Carne, commanding, wrote, 'Our rather middle-aged and sometimes unenthusiastic reservists were splendid.'

Two further features adjoining Hill 327 were found to have been abandoned, and on February 18 a strong patrol of Gloucesters and 8th Hussars penetrated as far as the wide and placid River Han, encountering plenty of snow but no enemy. However, some peaks further westwards were still held, the highest of which, dauntingly jagged, was Hill 630. This hill was allotted the Americans, who approached it along a ridge from the right, and in supporting them the Ulsters, who previously had encountered North Koreans eager enough to retreat, spent the 20th in raw exposure to machine-guns that defied repeated attempts against their positions in the rocks. At an altitude of over 2,000 feet the frost bit cruelly that night, and loss of route by the porter party deprived the men of greatcoats, blankets and rations. But the Americans had by now gained their objective, and next day there were no enemy to be found west of the Han. On the 23rd relief arrived for the frozen men of 29 Brigade.

Meanwhile 27 Brigade had been striking out north-eastwards from the other bank of the Han. The task allotted them was to go to the relief of a regiment of the 2nd Division (which included the French battalion) cut off by a Chinese counterattack at Chipyong-Ni in the central sector. Their advance began on February 14 from the ruins of Yoju, just across the River Han.

There had been an American reconnaissance company on a hill 6 miles ahead, but stragglers said they had been driven off it, and it was hard for the Middlesex, leading 27 Brigade, to tell friend from foe. They found this hill was held by the enemy and they also found that beyond the humpy, apparent crest of the hill stretched a spine, half a mile long, with deep ravines at its sides. By a series of outflanking movements, A Company won the ridge at no great cost. But at 5 next morning in came a counterattack, heralded by the sound of mortars, machine-guns and tinny bugles. After breathless grappling the right platoon of A Company were eventually forced into retreat, having exhausted their ammunition, and one section were captured. The Chinese kept coming on and had twice to be repelled at bayonet point, and then suddenly they gave up and made off, leaving the Middlesex in possession of their ridge with cheeks flushed and weapons hot; as the New Zealand gunners fired the final salvoes of a successful initiation, the section of A Company came panting back, having evaded their captors. Twelve Chinese had been taken prisoner and forty-eight of them lay dead, against seven of the Middlesex.

This action, which took the name of Chuam-Ni, secured the right flank for a successful advance by the Americans, which on the evening of February 17 linked up with the besieged regiment at Chipyong-Ni. On the 18th there was a happy event within 27 Brigade, for they were joined this day by a fourth battalion, the 2nd Princess Patricia's Canadian Light Infantry, who had been in Korea since December. There were now seven units of seven different peoples, English, Scots, Australian, Canadian, New Zealander, Indian and American, the last in the form of the 2nd U.S. Mortar (4·2-inch) Battalion, who had been a permanent part of the brigade since December and were as admired as admiring. It was a happy blend, producing a rugged cheerfulness that defied the most chilling hardships and amazed not only American officers who had temporary dealings with the brigade but even their British commander. Noting that 'this great spirit was apparent always,' Coad confessed, 'I never quite understood this, but it was a considerable source of strength and inspiration to me, their commander.'

There was no pause in which to absorb the Canadians; 27 Brigade had to drive on as right flank guard for the 2nd Division, through a wild and roadless range of hills that gradually became higher and steeper, with the final peaks rising to some 2,000 feet 25 miles beyond Yoju. The weather imposed greater torment than the enemy, whose opposition at this stage was spasmodic. There had in early February been a few exhilarating shafts of spring, but on the 18th the battalions were swept by blizzards as they toiled up a fresh line of peaks, with the staccato, echoing crash of shells on the rocks ahead making demoniac cacophony with the howl of the wind. Rain followed snow and then gave way to snow again, and still the brigade plodded on, step by step, battalion by battalion, with Korean porters taking their share of a supply problem that called unavailingly for the employment of mules. The resistance stiffened, giving 'Princess Pat's' the chance to show their mettle. Then on March 13, with the Argylls installed on a hill measured at 752 metres, the brigade were relieved.

The Chinese had by now been pushed back almost to the 38th Parallel. On March 14 Seoul was recaptured for the second time, and a fortnight later the left wing of Ridgway's army reached the village of Choksong 40 miles further on. This lies on the 20-mile stretch of the River Imjin between its curve from south to west and its emergence into estuary and is a few miles short of the famous Parallel. 29 Brigade were brought up to take over this sector defensively, under command of the 3rd U.S. Division. They carried out the relief on March 30.

With his left standing firm, Ridgway pressed steadily on in the centre, aiming to form a triangular wedge to a depth of some 20 miles across the 38th Parallel. After twelve days at rest 27 Brigade were brought forward again, coming under their old partners, the 24th Division. Since March 23 the brigade had had a new commander, Brigadier B. A. Burke, who had come out as Deputy Commander 29 Brigade. Coad had been relieved, with promise of promotion, after a tenure of command that can seldom have been exceeded for the mixture of exasperation, exhilaration and sheer wonderment it afforded. His men had been fortunate in having a commander who could retain his calm and sense of humour in any set of circumstances.

They had now to carve another passage across the mountains, up the very centre of Korea, with the town of Kapyong on their right rear. A wild and jagged ridge had first to be crossed, then the valley of the River Kapyong, and they had then to plunge into even more mountainous country beyond. They set off on March 28, meeting only light opposition at first. As the country became more precipitous the opposition stiffened. On the 31st the Middlesex had to gain a crag along a spine too narrow to afford deployment even for a section and were held up until next morning, when an air strike cleared the way. The Australians also ran into trouble, but they nearly always did, being very hard to restrain. On April 4 the Argylls had two officers killed in driving some Chinese off a ridge, and these were their first mortal casualties since the action at Pakchon on November 5. Next day, after some delay for mine clearance, they crossed the 38th Parallel, having come 15 miles since the advance started, with the River Kapyong intervening.

The next peaks to be captured, rising to a height of almost 3,000 feet, lay at the end of the valley of the Kapyong-Chon. The Royal Australians and Princess Pat's made the initial advance, on left and right of the valley, and on April 11 the Middlesex passed through, leaving the Argylls in reserve. Heavy snow fell as the Middlesex set off, and visibility was so bad that they had to advance by compass. They took one peak that day, gaining a foothold on a long and narrow ridge, along which they sustained their bleak advance for four days more on a one-company frontage. At times the task seemed hopeless, so steep and restricted was the approach and so hot the mortar and machine-gun fire encountered. But by perseverance and skilful use of all supporting weapons, aircraft included, they advanced two miles and were almost on the final objective when, at midday on the 15th, a misdirected stonk by some 155-mm. guns badly wounded the leading company commander and disorganised two of his platoons. The Australians came through to complete the job, and on the 19th the brigade were relieved by the 6th Rok Division.

While the battle for these last peaks was raging—that is on April 11—news arrived that made every man in the United Nations Force gasp: their Supreme Commander, General MacArthur, was dismissed. He had wanted to bomb the Chinese supply lines in Manchuria, believing this the only way to complete victory, but his request had been refused by the United Nations, and he had thereupon switched his verbal attack from council room to the public press. This was insubordination to his political chiefs, and great and well deserved though his fame was, he met his match in President Truman, who struck a brave blow for the Free World by asserting his authority as elected leader. General Ridgway was appointed to the Supreme Command and Lieutenant-General J. A. Van Fleet to the command of Eighth Army.

The dismissal of MacArthur could be interpreted as a gesture of peace to the Chinese and once again expectation of an early end percolated through the tents, holes, and shacks that housed the United Nations' soldiers. Only for the Middlesex and the Argylls was there firm foundation for hope, for battalions from Hong Kong were under orders to relieve them, and now at last the Argylls received definite instruction: they were to leave the brigade on April 24, for embarkation from Inchon. But the 23rd dawned with the distant boom of gunfire, and the Argylls had to unpack their equipment and prepare positions near their rest area 35 miles north-east of Seoul. Then, after a night spent in listening to the approach of the firing, even to the sound of small arms fire from the Australians' sector, they received orders letting them go. True to the traditions of the Korean campaign, a recall order reached brigade headquarters just as they were moving off, and as the Middlesex began to move the other way. The Brigadier sent it no further. Passing the 1st King's Own Scottish Borderers *en route*, the Argylls reached Inchon, embarked on a ship named after an old tribal foe, U.S.S. *Montrose*, and still not quite believing it was true, set sail for Hong Kong.

Certainly the luck of the Argylls had taken a sharp turn for the good after the tragedy of Hill 282. Of their thirty-one killed in action, twenty were lost on or before September 23, whereas the Middlesex had suffered in opposite ratio and had still more losses to come. Yet there is no doubt that the luck of the Argylls was well deserved. They had become very canny at capturing objectives at minimum cost.

The firing that so nearly delayed the departure of the Argylls announced the start of a mighty attempt by Red China to defy the world. Not content with rescuing the North Korean Government from the consequences of a brash military adventure, Mao's generals now renewed the attempt at conquest, undaunted by the fact that representatives of seventeen nations were lined against them. They attacked over an 80-mile frontage. Seoul was the primary objective, and the 63rd Chinese Communist Army the main instrument, employing three divisions in a thrust along the most direct and oldest route midway between the roads running to Seoul from north-east and north-west. This was the sector held by Brodie's 29th Brigade.

Some adjustments had been made to the positions on the River Imjin taken over by 29 Brigade on March 30, the most important of which was a crossing of the river, conforming with an advance by the 3rd U.S. Division on the right, under whose command the brigade came. The crossing had been made by the Ulsters on April 10. It had not been easy, for the river was 300 yards wide, fast flowing, overlapped by steep banks, and fordable only in a few places. However, a way was found round the corner, where the river changes course from south to west, by first crossing its tributary, the Hantan, and then getting over the Imjin itself. The Ulsters made the dual crossing riding on tanks and occupied a hill feature unopposed. On the 20th they handed over to the Belgian Battalion, which temporarily joined the brigade as a fourth battalion. Its men were all volunteers, and there was a hardened bearded look about them reminiscent of the French Foreign Legion.

Immediately behind the Belgians, south of the river, were the Fifth Fusiliers. They held various pimply hills on the left of the main supply route, which was a rough road with hills on either side of it, and they also had two companies thrown almost 2 miles westwards on features overlooking, but not very closely, the winding Imjin. Just behind the Fusiliers were the gun lines of the 45th Field and the harbour area of C Squadron, 8th Hussars, whose tanks were the only ones available to the four battalions since the terrain offered no scope for the employment of more. Brigade Headquarters was a little further back along the main axis, and further back still, some 6 miles from the river, the Ulsters were in reserve in the village of Hwangbang-Ni, behind a pass.

The Gloucesters were on the left astride another rough road, which wound a hilly course southwards, involving a 12-mile journey between

Battalion and Brigade H.Q. through the village of Kwangsuwon. This was the ancient road to Seoul and it crossed the one recognised ford over the Imjin, which had been rechristened Gloucester Crossing. The battalion's battle positions were 2 miles behind the ford, on some hills around the village of Choksong. To the right rear of the Gloucesters' positions, rather more than a mile away, rose the mountainous slab of Kamak-San, which had been left unoccupied because there were insufficient troops to hold it and at the same time cover the two axis routes. On the Gloucesters' left, with a substantial gap intervening, were the 1st Rok Division, holding the left of the Eighth Army line.

The brigade frontage measured nearly 10 miles—almost double that of January 3—but because a further advance was envisaged the positions had not been fortified by mines or extensive wiring. Patrols penetrated far in search of the enemy. On April 20 a squadron of the 8th Hussars, with Gloucesters riding, drove 18 miles beyond the Imjin and found only a few enemy posts to shoot up. Yet Intelligence said the Chinese were massing. Spring had arrived, putting balm into the valley bed, along which the big river idled so serenely, and conveying a mocking sense of unreality. On Sunday, April 22, there was a church parade within the Fifth Fusiliers' perimeter in dedication for the morrow, St. George's and the Regiment's Day, to celebrate which red and white cloth roses were issued for display in the men's caps. In the afternoon came further, more precise reports of enemy movement. Parties were observed from the brigade's posts.

Lieutenant-Colonel Carne, commanding the Gloucesters, sent half a platoon, under Lieutenant Temple, down to the ford at the fall of darkness. As its men took up position a full moon arose and soon it gave them a clear view of the first party of Chinese to wade across. The Gloucesters waited until they were at muzzle point and despatched them all. More followed and suffered the same fate, and then a drove of them came across, yelling, screaming and wildly firing their burp guns, and they too were sent splashing and swept downstream. Having turned a fourth attempt to bloody chaos, these sixteen Gloucesters were compelled to withdraw by lack of ammunition, and there was nothing more to smite the Chinese at their point of greatest vulnerability except some chance crumps from the 25-pounders, which were already in demand elsewhere. Great though Temple's achievement was, it was one that begged repetition both there and further up the river.

The Belgians were now under attack—in a reckless, insidious manner, reminiscent of German onslaughts in March 1918, which was to be sustained for the next three days. First came the attempt at surprise, then the yelling and blaring of trumpets, then the feeling for the flanks

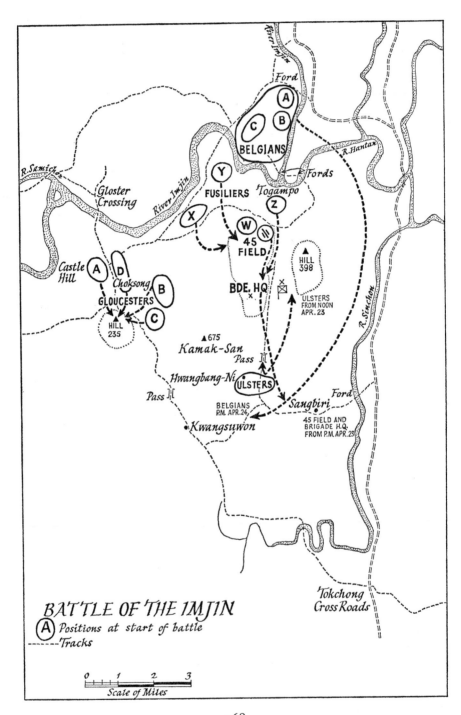

R. Imjin

Ford

A
C B
BELGIANS

R. Hantan

R. Samichon

Gloster Crossing

River Imjin

Fords

Y
FUSILIERS
Togampo
Z

X

W
45
FIELD

HILL
398

Castle Hill

A D
Choksong
GLOUCESTERS
B

BDE. HQ

C

ULSTERS
FROM NOON
APR. 23

HILL
235

R. Sinchon

▲675
Kamak-San
Pass

Hwangbang-Ni
Pass

ULSTERS

Ford

BELGIANS
P.M. APR. 24
Sangbiri

45 FIELD AND
BRIGADE H.Q.
FROM P.M. APR. 23

• Kwangsuwon

Tokchong
Cross Roads

BATTLE OF THE IMJIN

(A) Positions at start of battle
------Tracks

0   1   2   3
Scale of Miles

and encirclement, and finally concentration at one particular point, and all the time men would be falling and others running forward to take their place. Stick grenades and burp guns were the assault weapons, with light mortars and heavier machine-guns in continual, nagging support, and persistence—sheer demon persistence regardless of cost—the means. The Chinese showed great devotion and suffered horrifying casualties.

Soon after the Belgians came under attack the Ulsters were ordered to send a carrier patrol to cover the crossing place they had pioneered. Just before reaching it, the vehicles were ambushed and every man of the patrol was lost. The Chinese had crossed the river, leaving the Belgians unsubdued behind them, and from around midnight the Fifth Fusiliers were under attack. The most telling one came in against a platoon of Z Company—it is an eccentricity of the battalion that rifle companies bear letter W, X, Y, and Z—on a double-pronged peak numbered 257 that formed the very apex of the position, immediately above Battalion Headquarters. For four hours the platoon grappled with this sudden onslaught but as dawn broke they were forced off their hill and Battalion H.Q. had to make a speedy evacuation.

Y Company, far to the left of Z, had been undisturbed, but X Company, who were stretched along a ridge a mile to the left of Y, had been forced out of one platoon position and been brought back to a hill nearer the axis in accordance with prearranged plan. The problem now was to regain Hill 257 and to extricate Y Company from dangerous exposure. Z and W Companies between them attempted the first, reached the summit, but could not retain it against the swarms around them. The second, however, was successfully achieved by Centurions of the 8th Hussars, and after a swift ride back Y Company were put in position on a peak blocking advance from 257.

One further service performed by this tank squadron was to probe towards the Gloucesters, whose positions had been under heavy attack all night. They soon reported that the lateral route was cut, that the enemy in other words was established in strength in the soft centre of the brigade locality. To Brodie it must have seemed that they were everywhere, and he had to pierce the smoke and decide where the menace was greatest. He opted for the right flank, where strength was essential for the extrication of the Belgians, who were still bravely holding out north of the river. He therefore brought the Ulsters up to grab Hill 398, a dominant feature on the right of the road over a mile to the rear of Hill 257 and the key to the valley along which the main brigade axis ran. But he providently left one company of the Ulsters back at the pass near Hwangbang-Ni.

The guns had supplied the three battalions under attack with an unflagging stream of shells all through the night and in the morning had fired over open sights at the enemy on Hill 257. Lieutenant-Colonel Young, commanding 45th Field, knew they were too far forward, but did not order any back until after midday, after the Ulsters had fought their way on to Hill 398 and the tempo had subsided. He then moved one battery at a time back to Sangbiri, whence the Gloucesters' forward positions were just in range, but not the Belgians'. The departing guns drew plenty of mortar fire, which caused some casualties. Brigade Headquarters later withdrew to the same area, under more distant and less effective fire.

By committing his reserve to the right on this hectic Monday morning, Brodie had been forced to set the pattern at an early stage. The Gloucesters had to fight on their own, with C Troop 170 Mortar Battery as their only companions; they had been fighting desperately hard since midnight, when—being free to cross the Imjin—the Chinese had swarmed upon the two forward companies on hills astride Choksong, A on the Gloucesters' left and D on the right and slightly in rear.

After six hours of bustling, raucous pressure, unsubdued by the splinters and bullets that crashed, crumped and sta-ta-tabbed in among them, the Chinese drove the six surviving, officerless defenders from the top of Castle Hill, the foremost and highest of A Company's positions. It was now dawn. A counterattack was launched by a platoon commanded by Lieutenant Curtis, whose parent regiment was the Duke of Cornwall's Light Infantry. After mounting half the hill, his men were stopped by machine-gun fire and grenades, and he had to reorganise. With half his platoon giving covering fire, he leapt up to lead the assault but fell wounded within a few yards. His men dragged him back to cover and examined his wound. He freed himself from their attention and, refusing to be restrained, went forward again, pistol in one hand, grenade in the other, quite on his own. Up, up he went, pausing every now and then to hurl a grenade, until almost at the summit. He threw one grenade more and was crumpled by the full force of a burst from point blank range. His grenade exploded with a deep, muffled crunch, and whether or not it caused much destruction, there was a marked slackening of enemy activity from the top of Castle Hill. It was an act deserving a Victoria Cross and when at last witnesses were free to give evidence, Curtis was posthumously awarded one.

Soon afterwards the commander of A Company was killed. D Company were also under heavy pressure and forced to tighten their perimeter despite the continuous toll taken on the enemy. At about 8.30 on this Monday morning Colonel Carne ordered the remnant of these two companies back to a steep, scrub-covered hill, numbered 235, on the left of the axis track and a mile or so in rear. The withdrawal was carried out tenderly and well. The Chinese, inevitably, had their own problems of recuperation and were still being pounded by the 25-pounders. Nevertheless the second-in-command, Major Grist, found them astride the supply route and in occupation of Rear Battalion H.Q. when he returned from the main position during the afternoon. He dashed through in his Land Rover, past captured vehicles, and escaped with a smashed windscreen and a slashed wrist.

Some Americans had now arrived to counterattack, not in relief of the Gloucesters but to regain the hill lost by the Fusiliers at first light, 257. The attempt fizzled out as darkness was falling, but perhaps it eased the pressure on the Belgians, for the latter triumphantly fought their way back over the Imjin, making a wide sweep round the Ulsters' right flank. Next day they were brought to a block position between the two separated halves of the sector, some 3 miles behind the Ulster's back stop company and 5 behind the Gloucesters.

The Chinese, predictably, resumed their attack in earnest by the light of the moon, again showing amazing persistence in the face of appalling losses. At 3.30 a.m. the mass exertions of these little men gained them the forward peak held by Y Company, Fifth Fusiliers. Although a counter-attack was mounted without success, its loss was not vital, for other companies held firm on the ridge behind it, and on the right side of the valley the Ulsters repulsed many attempts on their dominant Hill 398, which now became the brigade's foremost bastion.

Also at or near 3.30 on this Tuesday morning, the 24th, the Glouces-ters lost a peak of greater importance. It was that held by C Company, opposite the one on which A and D Companies had taken refuge, and in the narrow valley between them were Battalion H.Q., the regimental aid post, reserves of food and ammunition, and the mortars. There was a scramble to remove the wounded and the more important stores, followed by laboured toiling up the slopes of Hill 235. The remnant of C Company, under command of Lieutenant Temple, held on long enough to cover this evacuation and then joined the others on this shaggy feature that included a ridge running southwards from the summit to a subsidiary, flat-topped feature and was quite large enough to absorb the resources of the whole battalion in its weakened state. Hill 235 had become Gloucester Hill.

Not everyone was on it yet. B Company were deployed on the right flank and had been pulled back, after the withdrawal of A and D, to a position with their backs to the massive Kamak-San, over a mile from Gloucester Hill. They were surrounded during the night but were still fighting hard in the morning. They were in view from Gloucester Hill, and as the Chinese brought up more troops and deployed over-whelming strength against B Company, the Vickers opened up from Gloucester Hill and shells churned the attackers—but not mortar bombs, for the mortarmen, both Gloucesters and Royal Artillery, had been unable to lug their baseplates up the hill and now fought as infantry. Still the Chinese came on, and one platoon disintegrated under the weight of their numbers. Then the remnant of the company made a sudden dash, well coordinated with an artillery stonk, and with their Major Harding at their head twenty of them broke through and safely achieved the long, perilous haul, through scrub and pine, to Gloucester Hill.

The Gloucesters were now immersed by the enemy to a depth of 4 miles. It was a situation well in keeping with an heroic past, for the Gloucesters wore a second, replica badge at the back of their berets, as reward for a feat of all-round defence near Alexandria in 1801, and their regimental colour bore more battle honours than that of any other regiment. Probably such things meant nothing to the majority of the men wearily manning makeshift defences on that hill; but they meant a great deal to the men who provided the leadership, in particular the senior officers and sergeant-majors. Tradition demanded that the 'Slashers' stuck it out.

Lieutenant-Colonel Carne had been in the regiment since 1926, although without chance of gaining distinction prior to his battalion's attack in February, for which there was a D.S.O. in the pipeline for him. Lean of face and sparse of speech, he was not naturally communi-cative, but now he spread inspiration around him as he strolled about with pipe in mouth and rifle slung over his shoulder. Twice he led some regimental policemen and drivers against infiltrators and drove them off with grenades, or in his own words 'shooed them away'. Brigade Headquarters found inspiration too from his calm assurance over the wireless, never minimising the danger but always confident his battalion could hold out.

There was a good example of his judgement soon after B Company's return. Food, water, wireless batteries, medical supplies for the poor wounded lying in a mounting row on the open hilltop, and ammunition —ammunition most of all—were all sorely needed, and all were available down below in the valley beneath the hill, which had been evacuated early that morning. Carne arranged a fire programme with his battery commander, in which smoke played an important part, and under cover of it R.S.M. Hobbs led a sortie to the abandoned trucks and dumps. His party returned unharmed, sweating under enormous loads, and heaviest laden of all were some stalwart native porters who were besieged with the battalion they served. The food problem remained serious, being aggravated by the fact that ordinary bulk rations had been issued. In the hand-out to individuals, one might get a tin of peaches, another a loaf of bread, a third a tin of salmon.

An attempt was made by a Philippino battalion, with aid from the C Squadron, 8th Hussars, to force a route through to the Gloucesters during the day. They received news of the situation from some Gloucesters who had been taken prisoner but made their escape when their guards were set on fire by napalm dropped on Kamak-San, which was now teeming with Chinese. It was of little avail. The Philippino infantry met hot opposition in the foothills of Kamak-San and their leading tank was knocked out in a jagged defile and could neither be bypassed nor removed, thwarting the further use of armour. Although themselves hard pressed on the right, the 3rd U.S. Division promised to make a further attempt next morning, and expectation of it at least helped to keep despair at bay on Gloucester Hill.

On each of the two previous nights the Chinese had made important gains against the two wings of 29 Brigade. On the third (April 24/25,) against hastily organised defences and men sagging under tremendous strain, they made none at all. For the Fifth Fusiliers Z Company triumphantly redeemed their loss of Hill 257 on the opening night. They now held a steep and narrow ridge, guarding the battalion's rear on the left side of the valley, and it was from the left rear that the Chinese attacked. There was some desperate, bloody fighting, in the course of which a pinnacle was lost but swiftly regained. Thirty-three members of the company fell dead or wounded—around half their strength—and this figure does not include the company commander, Major Winn, who was hit three times in the course of hurling sixty-eight grenades, but remained with his men until fainting during the evacuation. There was a D.S.O. for him, and, for prodigies performed with his bren, the D.C.M. was won by Fusilier Crooks, a veteran of the Durham Light Infantry, who served with the Fusiliers grudgingly.

On the right the Chinese resumed their attempts, already counted as sixteen, on the Ulsters' Hill 398. They made little variation in their method of approach and once again they crumpled beneath the lead and steel hammered into them by the 'Irish Giants' and their supporting artillery. B Company alone were under heavy pressure with the coming of dawn—and they held the Hwangbang-Ni pass 4 miles in rear.

Some 450 thirsty and haggard men were left on Gloucester Hill to fight from shallow slits among rocks and scrub, and a high proportion of them were specialists of Support or H.Q. Company or of 170 Mortar

Battery, manipulators in the normal course of duty of radar equipment (for locating mortars), drumsticks, kitchen knives, and typewriters. A further fifty plus were on stretchers, some of them dying. The Chinese began their attacks at about 10 p.m., here, there and everywhere, in a nagging, uncoordinated manner, and at no point did they make penetration. There was much shrilling of trumpets, mark perhaps of dwindling morale and a source of irritation to the Gloucesters. 'Haven't we got a bugle?' asked Carne as dawn was approaching. Drum-Major Buss had one. Standing up out of his slit trench, he sent the clear brassy notes of Reveille echoing across the valley, first the long Reveille, then the short, then the full repertoire of barrack calls, leaving out (wisely enough) only Retreat and Last Post. There was silence as his last note died away. Then the Gloucesters gave final echo to this clarion of defiance with a lusty cheer. No more trumpeting came from the enemy lines.

At last, after daybreak, the Chinese made a concentrated attack on the peak point, 235 itself, from the north-west, where it adjoined the perimeter. The thirty survivors of A Company holding it suffered grievously from a mortar stonk, and soon a remnant of them came down the hill, helping or carrying the wounded, among whom were the two remaining officers, one being the assistant-adjutant. Something had to be done at once. The adjutant, Captain Farrar-Hockley, rallied these tattered, slashed, battle-worn men, led them back up the hill, and drove out the enemy. He then brought artillery fire down on the Chinese crowding the immediate proximity of the hilltop, knowing some of the 'unders' would be bound to fall among his own shallow trenches. The shells smote the Chinese with deadly effect and did no more than cover the Gloucesters with dirt. Gloucester Hill was secure again, with only a subsidiary pimple in enemy hands.

At 6.5 a.m. Carne was notified over the wireless that there could be no hope of relief; the Americans had been unable to make any progress in their counterattack. He was to fight his way out if he could. He asked for an air strike, together with a supply drop, and the request was relayed to airfields in Korea and Japan. The Gloucesters meanwhile held on against their ever-nagging assailants, making parsimonious use of their dwindling supply of men, weapons and ammunition. Only the gunner wireless link now remained open, and at 7.30 a message was sent to Brigade Headquarters to say the battery had half an hour's life left. When it was brought to him on the log, Brodie wrote against it, 'No one but the Gloucesters could have done it.' These words, in which so much emotion was packed, were transmitted to the Gloucesters during the battery's dying minutes.

The planes came over at around 9 a.m. and, guided in by a single puff of violet smoke from a grenade, first scared and then delighted the Gloucesters by the devastation they wrought on the crowded slopes below point 235. Seven runs were made, and to within a few yards of the Gloucesters the hillside was turned to flame by napalm and pounded by cannon. The supply aircraft that followed, however, flew far from target.

Carne used the lull forced on the enemy to summon his company commanders and order them to break out independently along a route he pointed out to the south-west. The wounded of course would have to stay, and the doctor and padré, Captain Hickey and the Reverend S. J. Davies, elected to stay with them. The withdrawal was to begin at 10. 'Good luck, and God bless you all,' Carne ended, unflurried as ever, and then as an afterthought, 'Any of you chaps happen to have a spare twist of tobacco?' The words may be apocryphal, but not the impression he made.

With one exception, the Gloucester groups had no luck. The Chinese barred practically every variation of route and soon made most of the surviving Gloucesters prisoner, showing an unexpected desire to capture them when they could easily have killed them before their hands went up. The Colonel, with his headquarter group, appears to have evaded the enemy longest but fell into their hands early on the morning of the 26th.

The exception was D Company, which was the strongest company and consequently assigned the duty of rearguard with the Machine Gun Platoon. Its commander, Captain Harvey, a reservist from the Royal Hampshire Regiment, chose to move north-west instead of south-west and for the first 3 miles met no opposition. Veering round left-handed, his men drove off the first party of Chinese they encountered, and he then led them through a gorge that eventually opened out into a wide valley devoid of cover except for a ditch. Now they came under machine-gun fire, and some were hit and others dispersed as they dived for the ditch and crawled along it for over a mile, with pounding hearts, aching limbs and hardly any ammunition left to hold off the Chinese who kept closing in on them from flanks and rear. One soldier, Private Cleveland, rescued his wounded sergeant and carried him all the way back. Aircraft helped by strafing the hillsides, and at last an American tank was seen ahead. Sickeningly, it opened fire and added a few last names—the most tragic—to the Gloucester dead, before an air-dropped message rectified the error. The tanks thereupon played the role of shepherd with passionate devotion, and by soon after noon Harvey, four other officers, and forty-one men were safe, out of some ninety who set out with him.

A further thirty-four of the Gloucesters had been evacuated wounded in the early stage of the battle. Of the remainder, seven officers and fifty-one men were eventually listed as killed or missing, assumed dead, and nineteen and 505 as prisoners of war. Four officers of the 45th O.P. party and the mortar troop were also taken, with about forty gunners and signallers. There is no exact record of how many of the prisoners were wounded, but nineteen Gloucesters died in captivity and probably three times as many had been hit and survived.

As proof that the Gloucesters carried their fighting spirit with them into captivity there were many attempts at escape and an act of supreme devotion by Lieutenant Waters, from the West Yorks, who had been wounded in the head and arm, when the last surviving officer of A Company. Realising that it was the only hope for the wounded men who lay languishing with him in the squalid horror of the water-logged tunnel to which they had been taken, he issued an order that they were to consent to be enrolled as 'peace fighters', as which they had prospect of treatment. He himself refused, and consequently died alone.

When at last the fighting ended and the captives were released, Waters was posthumously awarded the George Cross. The Victoria Cross was won by Carne for 'powers of leadership which can seldom have been surpassed in the history of our Army' and also, as already mentioned, by the late Lieutenant Curtis. There were D.S.O.s for Harding of B Company and for Farrar-Hockley, M.B.E.s for the Padre and the R.S.M., and M.C.s for Temple and for Dr. Hickey, while a third had already been awarded to Harvey. Two D.C.M.s were won, eight M.M.s and one B.E.M.

Collectively the Gloucesters received an American Presidental Citation, in company with C Troop, 170 Mortar Battery. The award was made to the rump of survivors, with humble tribute, by General Van Fleet, and permission was given by the King for a commemorative emblem, of dark blue silk, to be worn by all men of the battalion and troop. Both British and American journalists coined their own award in the sobriquet 'Glorious Glosters'. Not since the stand of 'the Noble 24th' at Rorke's Drift had any battalion action so touched the public imagination. The two were similar in being feats of forlorn heroism performed in wars in which the British people felt only remotely involved, and this very remoteness made them all the more poignant. The difference was that whereas the Zulus presented menace to no one outside their own country, the Chinese were seeking to overthrow the newly established world order, as vested in the United Nations, and terrifying consequences could have followed any swift submission to their profligate expenditure of manpower.

The Gloucesters may have been alone on their hill, but they would claim no monopoly of the glory, for the whole brigade had been under unrelenting attack and were together faced with a desperate crisis of survival. Throughout the night of the 24th/25th expectation of a counter thrust by the 3rd U.S. Division still ran high. Their 165th Regiment had come up on the Belgians' left and at dawn they struck out for the Gloucesters, 5 miles distant. But they could make very little headway against the tide that had come swirling in between the rocks of Gloucester and Northumberland, and the divisional commander, General Soule, who had been busy fighting a hard battle on the right of 29 Brigade, realised at last that the main enemy effort had been directed along this route from Gloucester Crossing and that despite the terrifying toll taken by infantry, guns and aircraft there were far too few troops to contain it. He ordered Brodie to pull out as best he could and make a radical withdrawal. This was at about 6 a.m. The Gloucesters were sent the forlorn instruction already described. Lieutenant-Colonel Foster, of the Fifth Fusiliers, was ordered to coordinate the withdrawal of the other two British battalions down the southward and then eastward route of the main axis, covered on the south-west flank by the Belgians. Brodie gave the orders by wireless from his headquarters near Sangbiri, and scarcely had he finished than some 25-pounders in the nearby gun lines opened direct fire on enemy machine-gunners 200 yards away. It was going to be a hazardous withdrawal.

C Squadron, 8th Hussars, on whom so much depended, were early in trouble. Half of them, under Captain Ormrod, set out at dawn from their leaguer by Hwangbang-Ni to join the forward battalions, dropping off valuable reinforcements for B Company, 1st Ulsters, on the pass, in the form of a troop of the 55th Field Squadron, R.E. There was a shroud of early mist along the valley bed, and it clotted periscope vision, with the result that two Centurions lost direction and were bogged. The Chinese swarmed upon them like angry wasps, and the two tanks sprayed each other with fire to free themselves. Other tanks joined in and scattered Chinese in all directions with point blank salvoes from their 20-pounders. The mist lifted, to the advantage of the tanks, and the valley temporarily quietened. One tank was eventually recovered under fire; the other had to be demolished.

Under the guns of the tanks, the Fusiliers were able to move back in good order, having first sent off their carriers and soft-skinned vehicles with the wounded from the night's fighting. Few of the men had had more than the odd doze during the last three nights and days, and there was a wooden look of exhaustion on their face. But they had not lost their pride, and the rose of St. George was still to be seen in some berets and cap comforters.

The Ulsters, as in the previous withdrawal, were the unlucky ones. So far their three companies on Hill 398 had between them had only one man killed in repulsing the multiple attacks. Some rare 'shorts' from the artillery caused their first misfortune on this fateful Wednesday morning, inflicting four casualties; to evacuate them the medical officer remained behind, waiting in vain for an ambulance. However, by midday the battalion had evacuated their positions without further loss and were ready to follow the Fusiliers up the familiar track along the valley bed. They could of course have avoided the valley by striking out south-eastwards along a rough and precipitous but more direct route to the final rendezvous—and this is what most were forced eventually to do. They had been marching in ominous quiet for some ten minutes when heavy fire burst upon them from the west wall of the valley. They were caught amid paddy fields, with no cover except the occasional bund, and among the first casualties was the rear link wireless set to brigade. The leading company plugged bravely on by platoon rushes towards the pass held by B Company over 2 miles away, while the battalion mortars and the Centurions smote the fire-spouting hillside as hard as they could. The remainder of the battalion, after several minutes of confusion, took to the hills now on their left, out of the valley they could have avoided from the start. They had no means of notifying their change of route, except by sight.

B Company of the Ulsters, and the tanks and sappers helping them, were now under great torment from the little demons plaguing them with their burp guns, mortar bombs, and insidious little rushes down the scrub-covered hillside from Kamak-San. A Centurion did much to hold them at bay, standing like a chamois on the pinnacle over the pass. After the Fusiliers had passed, Colonel Foster had a few last words with the Ulsters' B Company commander and set off in a gunner Land Rover. He was ambushed within a mile and a half and killed at the wheel crossing a ford, as reported by a lance-bombardier who escaped. He had seen his men uphold the traditions of 'the Fighting Fifth', in which his father had also held command, and he had such concern for them that he had written 400 letters about their private affairs in between conducting operations ably enough to gain the D.S.O.

The withdrawal degenerated into a schemozzle as awareness dawned that the bulk of the Ulsters had been diverted. The half-squadron of 8th Hussars made a dash for the head of the pass, some squelching perilously across paddy fields, crushing and spitting fire at fanatical Chinese. Two were knocked out by sticky bombs and one pitched on to its gun crossing a ditch. B Company, 1st Ulsters, and the sappers who had so ably assisted them split into groups, their task completed, to make best speed rearwards. Some went across country on their feet, others loaded the tanks with wounded and leapt on them themselves. An awful journey lay ahead. The Chinese were by now astride the route in mass, and they plastered the tanks' passengers with bullets and grenades, sending them flopping off their hulks and rewounding the wounded. Although restricted by their burdens in their arcs of fire, the tanks blazed away as long as they had ammunition, and they left rows of crushed, shelled, and machine-gunned Chinese behind them. Yet still they were pestered. One sergeant ran his tank through a house to rid it of a grenadier trying to lever open the hatch. Along both its southwards and eastwards courses the valley was turned to a mad inferno of fire-belching, lurching, roaring monsters beset by a myriad of crackling, clinging, collapsing midgets.

The infantry were now spread over a wide area, heading south-eastwards in general and fighting where necessary in stubborn but un-coordinated groups. The 45th Field withdrew by batteries without great loss, after some robust bouts over open sights in which they were joined by some Bofors of the 11th (Sphinx) Battery. The 25-pounders had fired around 1,000 rounds each and given the infantry faithful and unflagging service, for which the call had declined as the confusion grew. Brigade Headquarters extricated themselves successfully, with plenty of bullets flying around them, but the aid post of the Hussars alongside them failed to do so and a third medical officer fell stoically into enemy hands.

The Belgians formed the rearguard along the route to the east, having pulled out 'firing over their shoulders' as a heavy attack came in against them. A number of Americans and British joined them, and they were shepherded along by a troop of tanks, which lost two of its members through an unlucky accident, bringing to six the losses in Centurions sustained by the 8th, together with five other armoured vehicles.

As the Belgians approached the main road, where Americans were in position, it was realised that they were ahead of a column of Ulsters, who were wearily toiling down an escarpment from further north, carrying a stretcher case and propping up other wounded. The com-mander of C Squadron, 8th Hussars, Major Huth, who had rushed back from leave when battle started, had personally been shepherding the Belgians back with his own Centurion and one other. Warned by air-dropped message that a mass of Chinese were fast coming in between him and the Ulsters, he moved back to confront them. A tense fight followed, with the Chinese going down in scores, but always coming on behind the paddy bunds on the valley's bottom. Slowly the two tanks gave ground, peppered and stalked from every piece of cover and yet giving protection with their turrets to some wounded they carried. Their speed was regulated to that of the troops trying to dodge the fire as they headed for safety, and although the power traverse in Huth's tank jammed, the Chinese were held at bay until the last soldiers, British and Belgian, had hobbled past the Americans' positions. The Ulsters then stumped 4 miles further down the main road to Tokchong, where they dug themselves positions in failing light and had their first meal since early morning. Just before midnight they were relieved by an American regiment. The Battle of the Imjin was over.

29 Brigade had been torn apart, suffering over 1,000 casualties, but without being driven by direct assault off any of the key features held. The Royal Northumberland Fusiliers lost 142 officers and men, the Gloucesters 626, and the Royal Ulster Rifles 186, of whom the great majority fell during the withdrawal with among them, never to be traced, the Major Shaw who had so gallantly brought the remnant out of the trap sprung by the Chinese in the battle of Seoul. The Belgian Battalion, the 8th Hussars, Royal Artillery and Royal Engineers had at least 400 casualties between them. Only the roughest guess can be made of the casualties they all inflicted. Farrar-Hockley of the Gloucesters counted 216 dead Chinese on one part of Gloucester Hill when awaiting removal as a prisoner. There were twenty other places on the brigade front at which attacks of comparable density were made and many other areas of assembly swept by the guns, and for every 200 killed a further 400 must have been wounded.

The 27th Commonwealth Brigade also had a battle. They had handed over their gains north of Kapyong to the 6th Rok Division, and unlike the 1st Rok Division, who had fallen back slowly on the left of 29 Brigade, the 6th broke when attacked on the night of April 22. The 16th New Zealand Field Regiment, who had been left in the line to support the 6th Rok, were in some peril. They withdrew during the night, but were required to go back next morning as the situation seemed to be stabilising, and the Middlesex went with them in light American transport. They moved forward 7 miles against a stream of refugees and retreating troops, and took up a commanding position in bleak isolation. They were pulled back at dusk, forestalling the Chinese and were moved to a stop position astride the road to Kapyong, with the River Kapyong enveloping their right flank. The 3rd Royal Australian were ahead of them on their right, on the other side of the Kapyong, and on the left, also ahead of the Middlesex, were the 2nd P.P.C.L.I.

A heavy attack was made this night (23rd/24th) on the Australians. Around 4 a.m. D Company, 1st Middlesex, were despatched to their aid. The Australians' commanding officer, undismayed by having his headquarters overrun, put them on a ridge covering his left flank. These Middlesex swiftly repelled a hot attack, but in the morning the road behind them was cut and they were ordered to fight their way out. This they succeeded in doing by making a long, mountainous detour across the enemy front, bringing their wounded with them. The Australians meanwhile were being forced into ever closer confinement, while felling Chinese fast. That evening they carved a passage for themselves over the river and by midnight had withdrawn behind the Middlesex. Industrious as ever, the Chinese followed up their attack, but the Middlesex had no difficulty in holding them off.

A big effort was now being made against the Canadians on the massive Hill 677. By dawn on the 25th they were surrounded, and arrangements were made for a supply drop, which gained very much more success than the one attempted on Gloucester Hill. The Chinese swarmed in vain around Princess Pat's unshakable Canadians, and in the afternoon they cut their losses and fell back with such dead as they could carry away. A Presidential Citation was awarded both the Australian and Canadian battalions, together with the American tank battalion supporting them, for their stands on the Kapyong.

V—COME TO ROOST (1951)

The Kapyong was the last battle fought by 27 Brigade as such. As from the first minute of Thursday, April 26, its number was changed to 28, for Brigadier G. Taylor, an officer with a reputation for pugnacity in battle, had arrived from Hong Kong to take command, bringing with him his Headquarters 28th Infantry Brigade, which from the same moment proudly added 'Commonwealth' to its style. The flag of the 27th was presented to the 3rd Royal Australian, those old faithfuls who were to serve as long with their new master as with their old.

The first of Taylor's two battalions from Hong Kong, the 1st King's Own Scottish Borderers, had become operational on April 25, after a rush from Inchon, and on the 26th they took up a rearguard position south of Kapyong to cover the withdrawal of the brigade as part of a general one by the whole Eighth Army, enforced by the eruption of the Chinese beyond the Imjin. Having seen the others fall back through them, the Borderers themselves withdrew at some speed on the 28th, saturated by rain and confused by mist. It was the same depressing start as experienced by 29 Brigade—and made all the gloomier for the Borderers by the sound of their dumped baggage, much regimental property among it, being blown up by its caretakers.

Determined to keep his withdrawal within the bounds of necessity, General Van Fleet called a halt on a line that denied Seoul to the enemy, although only by 4 or 5 miles. The 29th British Brigade, after only one day's rest, were put in on the extreme left, where they had the mouth of the River Han between them and the enemy and were not molested. Reinforcements were rushed in from Japan to bring the Gloucesters to a strength of three companies, and on May 3 the former second-in-command, now Lieutenant-Colonel Grist, was able to report, 'We are operational again.'

The 28th Commonwealth Brigade, with scarcely a pause, were allotted some pinnacles north-east of Seoul, ahead of the confluence of the Rivers Han and Pukhan. They rapidly set about fortifying them, and having first prepared to repel attack and then to make one more advance, the Middlesex were, on May 14, relieved by the 1st King's Shropshire Light Infantry, who had had to await the arrival of the Argylls before being released from the defence of Hong Kong and had been further delayed by a typhoon. After their last and fastest journey in the familiar 2½-ton trucks, with Negroes as always at the wheel, the Middlesex sailed back to Hong Kong with memories of actions more numerous and more varied than would be experienced by any other British battalion. Six of them were to win them battle honours, together with a seventh for the campaign. Their cost in killed was six officers and thirty-four men, with a further hundred wounded. Only by the soundest management could so much have been achieved at so small a price.

With their momentum drained by their appalling losses, the Chinese could not rush Van Fleet's new line and their attack flopped when it did come, without active participation by 28 or 29 Brigade. They then switched their effort to the east coast and launched an attack on May 15. They gained initial success and then suffered slaughter egregious even by their standards. One American division claimed to have inflicted 37,000 casualties for the loss of 134 killed themselves.

This was the signal for the Eighth Army to leap up and regain the ground lost. The advance became general on May 21, and the Chinese, true to form, disputed it only with rearguards. The two new British battalions consequently had the sort of initiation that might have been specially arranged for them, were such a thing possible. The K.S.L.I. were the first to make a set attack, as the brigade set off in conjunction with their old partners, the 24th U.S. Division. A and D Companies stormed twin hill features and A then passed on to a higher one beyond, scotching a counterattack with aid from the Australians on their right. All objectives had to be fought for, and some casualties were suffered. On May 22 the Borderers ran into trouble in an ambitious advance on a hill that rose to 432 metres. Early objectives were taken after some stiff fighting here and there, but a minefield caused delay and the elimination of three tanks. Not until the 23rd could D Company assault Hill 432 itself, and not until dawn next morning was it gained; the Chinese had gone, leaving twenty-five dead behind them. The Borderers suffered fourteen casualties in this their first grim offensive toiling up the precipitous, heartbreaking slopes.

Relieved after carrying the advance into higher hills yet, with rain the main enemy now, the 28th were transferred to the command of the 1st U.S. Corps and taken on a long truck ride that brought them to the hills that five weeks earlier had been held by the Northumberlands and Ulsters and were still littered with the wreckage, human and material, of battle. On May 30 they took over positions by the Imjin, with two battalions forward and only one back, since the 2nd P.P.C.L.I. had departed two days previously to join their own 25th Canadian Brigade. Alongside them on their left, undismayed by the sombre outline of Kamak-San over their shoulders and the remaining, poignant signs of their own sacrifices, were the 29th Brigade, who had also been brought forward by truck to relieve other units. Most of them were ahead of Gloucester Hill, with four battalions where one had stood, since the Belgians were still with them. The two wanderers had been brought to roost at last. Soon they would be fused into formal partnership, and to ensure that there could be no splitting asunder on this fateful stretch of ground great exertions were made to strengthen the riverside positions with wire and minefields and to turn the tracks connecting them into wearable roads.

By June 2 all the Eighth Army's April positions had been regained, running from 20 miles south of the 38th Parallel on the west coast to 20 miles north of it on the east. Now came a statement from Van Fleet that had been prompted by his political masters and indicated their wish (but not his) to avoid another venture towards the Yalu. His army, said Van Fleet, would continue to 'stop the enemy's unwarranted aggression against South Korea and will, when necessary, meet such threats within North Korea'. This was an unmistakable feeler for peace and it was grasped, with a sneering twist, by the Soviet Government, with the result that 'peace talks' began on July 10, with garish publicity, at a town south of the Parallel but in North Korean hands, Kaesong. They soon degenerated into the prolonged haggling that the North Koreans, Chinese and Russians had surely envisaged all along.

It was a weird, make-believe life for the men in the front line. Both 28 and 29 Brigade had pushed the enemy back from close proximity by a series of sweeps beyond the Imjin, which were at times hazardous but rarely costly, and by lavish shelling of positions located. The result was that their own positions became free from disturbance by the enemy. Companies built bashas as canteens and dining rooms, and at a short walking distance from the front line such unwarlike events were held as concert parties by professional entertainers (of whom Jack Warner was among the first to appear), athletic meetings, cricket matches, rifle meetings and cocktail parties. The weather was hot, making tropical kit welcome, and the opening of the peace talks produced almost a sense of hubris, making the operational side seem rather pointless. Yet the Chinese were quite capable of preparing another big offensive under cover of the talks, and the men were made to realise that the pressure had to be maintained.

Meanwhile the 1st Commonwealth Division was emerging from embryo, recreating in closer integration the one first formed for the occupation of Japan. Much of the pioneering work had been done by an Australian, Lieutenant-General Sir Horace Robertson, who for some months had held the appointment of Commander-in-Chief, British Commonwealth Forces in Korea, as which he was responsible for matters of reinforcement and supply. The final stage of chrysalis was the arrival of the 25th Canadian Infantry Brigade Group in a reserve position behind the other two on July 26. Two days later, on the 28th, there was ceremonial flag hoisting at Tokchong, site of Divisional Headquarters. The 1st Commonwealth Division had come formally into being.

The brigades kept their infantry: three Canadian battalions in the lowest numbered and therefore the senior, the 25th Canadian, two British and one Australian in the 28th Commonwealth, three British in the 29th British. Their arms and services were pooled, although remaining affiliated wherever possible. They consisted of one Canadian squadron of armour and one British regiment, with C Squadron, 7th R.T.R. detached to an American regiment; one Canadian regiment of field artillery, one New Zealand, and one British, and two British mortar batteries, the 11th (Sphinx) having been converted from light anti-aircraft; one Canadian field engineering squadron and one British, the 28th having never had one; one Canadian supply and transport company, one mixed, predominantly New Zealand, and one British; one Canadian field ambulance, one Indian and one British; and one

Canadian infantry workshops and two British. Only the headquarters was new, and such adjuncts as a British field squadron and field park squadron to form a full field engineering regiment, the 28th, signallers to complete a divisional signal regiment, a Canadian field dressing station, an ordnance depot, and an international provost company. It was of course a great advantage that the five national armies represented were all organised on similar lines, having matured under the aegis of Lord Haldane's creation, the Imperial General Staff. A sixth, the South African, was soon to be represented by individual officers, and like Australia, South Africa was also well represented in the sky.

Apart from the G.S.O.1, who was Canadian, all the heads of arms, staff, and services were British, with integrated staffs under them. The G.O.C. was Major-General A. J. H. Cassels, who has already appeared briefly in this book as G.O.C. 6th Airborne in Palestine and (subsequent to Korea) Director of Operations Malaya. A Seaforth Highlander by origin, as witness of which he still wore a balmoral, he had commanded the 51st Highland Division in battle at the age of 38. He was tall, courteous and gay, and was admirably equipped to channel the ardour, of which there was a large and varied supply, into harmony. It had already been proved within what had been 27 Brigade that the blends mixed remarkably well, and Jim Cassels, as he was known throughout the division, was to prove as skilful at the larger task of team management as Coad had been at the smaller.

Particularly within 29 Brigade, where there was tremendous team spirit undimmed as yet by any change of unit since mobilisation a year previously, there was some regret at the passing of those days of adventurous independence. Certainly there was little adventure ahead. A new phase was in process of opening, a phase of static warfare and elaborate defences, of long and intimate acquaintance with the same few acres of ground, of monotony and hardship. The division was to show great powers of endurance and consequently shoulder a wearisome burden, and there was to be little distraction for its members other than that derived from the wide range of internal contacts.

One more advance had first to be made, nearer to the Parallel, and as a preliminary to it increasingly aggressive sorties were conducted across the Imjin. On August 4 two battalions of 28 Brigade, the Shropshires and the Australians, and two of 29, the Ulsters and the Belgians, probed to a depth of 6,500 yards without arousing strong reaction, and while they did so the monsoon rain poured down in earnest, calling for great feats by the Sappers and their intrepid commander, Lieutenant-Colonel Moore. Streams became foaming brown torrents, and the Imjin rose with such fury that the rafts were sunk by debris swirling

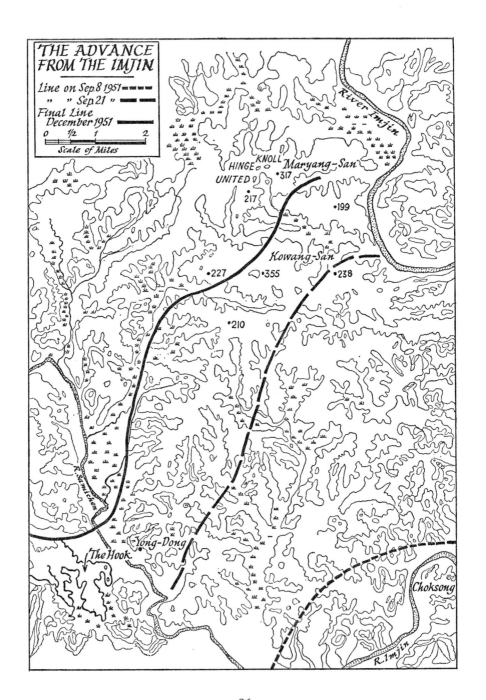

THE ADVANCE
FROM THE IMJIN

Line on Sep. 8 1951 ━ ━ ━
  "   " Sep. 21 "   ━━━━
Final Line
  December 1951 ━━━━
0   ½   1   2
Scale of Miles

River Imjin

HINGE KNOLL Maryang-San
UNITED ○ ○ •317
    •217
        •199

Kowang-San
•227   ○•355   •238

•210

R. Samichon

The Hook   •Yong-Dong

Choksong

R. Imjin

186

downstream, leaving some troops marooned for two nights on the far bank, unprepared for exposure to torrential rain. This was followed by two deep penetrations, each made by the Canadian Brigade at battalion strength, and in between them 29 Brigade sadly bade farewell to the Belgian Battalion, their comrades for the past five months.

The first permanent lodgement beyond the Imjin began on September 6, when the 3rd Royal Australian were ferried over the Gloucesters' old crossing, on 29 Brigade's front, to be joined two days later by the other two battalions of 28 Brigade, who sufficiently enlarged the bridge-head for a Class 50 pontoon bridge to be built by American engineers. On the 12th 29 Brigade passed through to carry the advance a further 2 miles into a maze of choppy hills, so characteristic of Korea. On the same day 25 Canadian Brigade also crossed, using a second bridge, and came up on the right of 29 Brigade. The Chinese did not seriously dispute the advance. None the less their artillery fire became more intense than anything they had previously produced, and patrols encountered sufficient opposition to indicate that the next line of hills was strongly defended. There was edgy expectation that a counterattack might be coming in, supported by tanks, and much digging, mining and wiring took place in consequence. The attack did not materialise, and on September 21 the Commonwealth Division received orders for an attack on this next line of hills, named Operation Commando.

The attack was part of a limited offensive by the whole of the Eighth Army, designed to disrupt the Chinese potential for attack, dominate the routes across the Parallel and extend the diplomatic pressure beyond the conference table. The 1st U.S. Corps were to advance some 4 miles with the 1st Rok Division on the left, the 1st Commonwealth in the centre between the Rivers Samichon and Imjin, and the 1st Cavalry on the right. On the Commonwealth's sector, 28 Brigade were to make the main assault by delivering a right hook against some dominant hill features.

Flanked on their right by a bend in the Imjin, 28 Brigade's objectives stretched to a depth of 4 miles and consisted of rocky, rugged peaks, with sides covered in scrub and pine. The highest was Hill 355, or Kowang-San, a bare slab of a hill towering over its neighbours. It stood left of centre, $2\frac{1}{2}$ miles from the start line, and was the objective of the Borderers. Beyond it, further left, was Hill 227, and this was the objective of the K.S.L.I. To the right, nearly 4 miles from the start line, with centre curved away from the attacking troops, was a ridge of which the highest point stood on the extreme right and rose up like the horn of a rhinoceros; it was numbered 317 and named Maryang-San. This was the objective of the Australians. The approach to each was up a ridge littered with subsidiary pimples, either from east or south-east, and each presented its own problems. The Borderers, for instance, were confronted with dense pinewoods in the early stages, and the tanks of the 8th Hussars were consequently allotted the flanking battalions, A Squadron to the K.S.L.I., B to the Australians. Care was taken to bring the tanks forward unheard and unseen. The Fifth Fusiliers also came forward, lent by the 29th British Brigade as reserve for the 28th Commonwealth.

The attack began at daybreak on October 3. The valleys were clogged with mist and lined with mud, as a result of which the tanks could at first do little more than slither and grope. The K.S.L.I. were hardest hit by this misfortune. However, B and C Companies battled their way on to two preliminary objectives by early afternoon, in each case after some raucous exchanges of grenades and sub-machine-gun fire. The arrival of four tanks, laden with provisions, cheered them. Only these four succeeded in ascending the steep and slimy slopes, and each happened to be the troop commander's tank. Plans were made for a continuation of the assault next morning.

For the Borderers it was a day of tense grappling up the pine-clad slopes against an enemy who fought with vigour from well chosen positions of great natural strength. Using Hill 238 as firm base, C and B Companies set off together, left and right, and while B Company had a comparatively easy passage to their objective, C had to fight with grenades, bayonets and stens for post after post, often renewing the fight on an objective to liquidate snipers who had lain low in the undergrowth. A Company came up and joined C in a fresh effort, which at last won them their objective at 3.30 p.m., with aid from some tanks of B Squadron. A Company pressed on and gained a feature called Kidney after further mixing of grenades and bayonets. The gaunt slopes of Kowang-San, bare and stark amid their ligneous surroundings, were now close at hand and seemed to be staring menacingly at the Borderers as they hacked themselves holes in the sandstone, laboriously carted back their wounded, awaited the long line of faithful Korean porters, and listened to the crash of shells from friend and foe.

The Australians on the right made best progress of all. Taking full advantage of the early mist, they sped across the valley north of Hill 238 and gained the important Hill 199. From here fire could be brought down on the far side of Kowang-San, and it was agreed that the Australians should await, and assist in, its fall before continuing the advance on Maryang-San.

October 4 began with a well executed attack on one further intermediary objective—Hill 210—by D Company of the K.S.L.I., under

Major Cottle, and the four troop commanders' tanks of A Squadron, 8th Hussars. The divisional artillery, thickened by American heavies and mediums, put down its full weight of crump, while the Centurions crashed forward through pine and scrub to churn the position with their 20-pounders. The K.S.L.I.'s charge caught the enemy in dazement. Forty-one of them lay dead, and the unusually high number of eleven were made prisoner.

The Borderers now began the assault on the great Kowang-San. D Company had the main task, and boldly led by Major Robertson-Macleod, the men scaled the heights and drove the Chinese off the spacious summit with great spirit. Its capture was complete by 1 p.m., causing great rejoicing at Divisional Headquarters and bringing an immediate D.S.O. for Lieutenant-Colonel MacDonald, commanding the Borderers. The fighting of the previous day must have broken the back of the opposition. The cost to the battalion was seven killed and thirty-four wounded over the two days, while in exchange they found twenty-four enemy corpses and took seventy-four wounded and fourteen sound prisoners.

This success greatly facilitated the K.S.L.I.'s advance on Hill 227, which lay at the end of a ridge from Kowang-San, and after a brisk, brave fight A Company gained possession of this final objective by 4.30 p.m., finding labyrinthal defences to be explored.

Next morning, October 5, the Australians began their attack on Hill 317, Maryang-San, and the Fifth Fusiliers attacked a hill on the other end of the ridge, 217, a mile to the left. The Fusiliers were the first to reach their objective. Advancing under mist that did not lift until midday, Z Company gained possession unopposed at about 3 p.m. and rounded up a number of Chinese taken by surprise. Now came a violent reaction. The Chinese emerged in great numbers from behind the ledge of a narrow ridge, where they were immune from shellfire, and brought a deluge of grenades, machine-gun bullets and mortar bombs down on the Fusiliers. Ninety minutes later Z Company had thrown all their grenades, used up all their .303 ammunition, and lost thirty out of their original sixty attackers, including the officers and sergeants of the two assault platoons. There was no scope for an outflanking movement up the narrow spur to the objective. Z Company were pulled back.

The Australians gained a preliminary objective in the mist and had then lost direction. Not until nearly 5 p.m., as the Fusiliers were yielding to the pressure, did their assault go in on the steepling Maryang-San. B Squadron, 8th Hussars, had sixteen tanks perched on peaks already captured, and from here they provided the final carpet of fire after aircraft and artillery had rocked the enemy positions on either side of the hill. The tankmen gasped in admiration at the calm deliberation with which the Australians, often on hands and knees, clambered up the steeps 'seemingly immune from the enemy fire and mortars which were raining down on them'. By nightfall they were masters of Maryang-San.

Next day, October 6, W Company of the Fifth Fusiliers made an attempt on Hill 217, coming up the ridge from the south-west as opposed to the spur from the south-east used by Z Company. There was desperately little room for manoeuvre along the rocky hump to the summit, and the attack disintegrated within 20 yards of the objective beneath a welter of grenades, thrown in clusters of four. Now X Company tried the direct approach from the south-east, only to run into heavier fire than ever and to enlarge the row of wounded perilously lugged back to the pine trees below the jagged, blasted wastes around the summit. All told, the Fusiliers suffered 113 casualties in their attempts against this bastion, of whom sixteen were killed and three were missing. Nine of the 113 were officers. They also had two of their Korean porters killed and twenty wounded in the crucial and daunting task of ammunition replenishment. The devotion shown by these men was the cause of surprise and admiration.

On the 7th the Australians attacked along the ridge running first north-west and then south-west from Maryang-San. There were three intervening peaks or pimples between them and 217, and they could capture only the first in the teeth of determined counterattacks and hot artillery fire. It was planned that the Borderers should come round to continue the attack from this direction on the 9th. However, massive toll had been taken on the Chinese—although not without hurt to the attackers!—by the great concert of supporting weapons fired by infantrymen, tankmen, artillerymen and airmen, and it was found during the afternoon of the 8th that the defenders were gone from the remainder of the ridge. The Borderers duly passed through the Australians and linked up with the men from the Northumbrian side of the border, who in the persons of the Pioneer Platoon at last took possession of Hill 217.

On the second day of this gruelling attack by 28 Brigade, that is on October 4, 25 Canadian Brigade swept forward on their left. The hills here were lower and the opposition lighter, and apart from one stronghold, which gave the P.P.C.L.I. some trouble, all objectives were speedily taken.

The Royal Ulster Rifles played a subsidiary part in this attack, coming up on the left of the 2nd Royal Canadian to complete the occupation of a ridge. It was accomplished without loss or difficulty, and this gave particular cause for joy, for the Ulsters knew it was their last battle, after eleven months' service in Korea. Their relieving battalion, the 1st Royal Norfolk, had already arrived from England, highly stocked with national-servicemen, and on October 8 the Ulsters set off for Pusan, bound for Hong Kong. It was just that they should be the first battalion of 29 Brigade to go, for they had twice been caught in situations of great peril and no less than ninety-five members of the battalion lost their lives, thirty-three being missing assumed dead and eight dying in captivity.

Simultaneously with this first dissolution of his well tried team came the departure of Brigadier Brodie, who like Coad had much endeared himself to his men and earned eventual promotion. His successor was Brigadier A. H. G. Ricketts, late of the Durham Light Infantry.

The Royal Northumberland Fusiliers were the next to go (also to Hong Kong), being relieved by the 1st Royal Leicestershire on October 19. They had lost five officers and fifty-five soldiers killed in action and a further twenty-nine were missing, assumed dead, almost as many as the Ulsters. For the Leicesters it was belated redemption of their humiliation at being left behind when the remainder of 27 Brigade went to war with much trumpeting. They were the fifth and last battalion to reach Korea of the six that were rushed to Hong Kong in 1949. Only the South Staffords went no further.

The Gloucesters were a new battalion, practically undamaged since reforming after their epic stand, and consequently they had to wait until November 11 for relief by the 1st Welch, who were coming from Britain after being stationed there four years. A voyage home was in store for the Gloucesters, and they could await it in reserve position, for only 25 and 28 Brigades were in the line.

However, both these brigades had frontages of over 5 miles and relied on components of 29 Brigade to block gaps between localities. Cassels was sensitive to the danger. The Chinese had shown none of their usual inclination to pull back from ground they had lost, and the volume of the artillery fire they emitted presented a new and ominous threat. At no point did the Commonwealth troops have the required density in defence to meet an attack, and it seemed clear that one was in the offing.

It fell, predictably enough, against the Maryang-San ridge, which had since October 9 been in the full possession of the Borderers, who had handed Kowang-San over to the K.S.L.I. The ridge formed an arrowhead piercing the enemy lines, with each shoulder just under a mile long, and there were three companies distributed among the five peaks, organised into five self-contained localities, on which much work was done. The Chinese had with their guns, mortars and patrols made supply of these localities perilous and revealed their concern about this hill, but no one imagined that they were capable of the sustained fury of shellfire that rose to a crescendo in the afternoon of Sunday, November 4, some of it from tanks or self-propelled guns close below the ridge. It was beyond anything experienced by veterans of the Second World War, and so stifling was its effect that communications were among the earliest casualties and some good targets escaped the guns. A testing situation confronted Major Tadman, who had been left in command of the Borderers on the sudden departure of MacDonald to take command of the brigade in place of Taylor. Both were to be substantiated in their temporary posts.

Defying expectations by attacking in daylight, the Chinese came on at about 4 p.m., lurching up the ridge in their hundreds in among their own shells. It was established that a complete division was employed, numbering 6,000 infantrymen. The apex of the arrowhead was a feature called Hinge, held by C Company less one platoon, and it was here that the attackers were thickest. Blinded by the dust of shell burst, one platoon were soon overrun by the leading wave of picked, determined men. Company Headquarters and the other platoon, with a section of Vickers machine-guns, held out for two hours, ceaselessly ripping the attackers, yet always being confronted with more. By the fall of darkness hardly a man was left unwounded. By a final flurry of grenades they gained respite for the evacuation of some of the worst hit, and the company commander thereupon brought the remnant off the ridge, helping to carry a stretcher with his New Zealand gunnery officer upon it.

Left of C Company, B Company held a peak called United, with a platoon further left on the notorious Hill 217. By accurate use of their self-propelled guns, the Chinese blew in the slits of the forward positions and carved large holes in the wire. B Company were early forced back to the crest, and there they met the attackers with a barrage of grenades and with brens fired from shoulder and hip. It was here that Private Bill Speakman, an amiable giant who was attached from the Black Watch and employed as company runner, revealed amazing powers of leadership and valour. Seeing that the Chinese were all over the left shoulder of the position, he decided to drive them out. He quickly collected a large store of grenades and persuaded six men to come with him. The Chinese broke under the impact of their onslaught. Speakman restocked with grenades and led another assault, utterly indifferent to the burp-bullets and explosive with which the teeming Chinese incessantly sprayed the Borderers. Ten times he sent enemy groups flopping and scuttling and then was wounded in the leg. He carried on with his charges, the inspiration now of the whole company, and only paused to have his wound dressed under constraint of a direct order.

Still the enemy came on. The platoon on 217 ceased to emit sound of resistance from around 5.30 p.m., and with the fall of darkness the main position became immersed by the non-stop flow of the little khaki-clad men. The company commander, Major Harrison, who had always been to the forefront, brought artillery fire down all round him. This effectively earned respite at slight cost. But by 8.30 the Chinese were coming on again in spate, and Harrison was ordered to bring his men back to a lower slope held by the Battle Patrol. Contemptuous of his wound, Speakman led one last charge, which threw more Chinese into contortions and enabled him to hold the crest while an orderly withdrawal was made.

On the right arm of the ridge a feature called Knoll lay ahead of the towering Maryang-San and was held by a platoon of C Company and a platoon of D. The commander of the former was a 19-year-old national-service officer, 2nd Lieutenant Purves, and when the other officer was wounded he took command of the position. The Knoll held out against all attempts, Purves making particularly effective use of his 2-inch mortar, and meanwhile a ferocious battle developed for 317, Maryang itself. The remainder of D Company, under Major Robertson-Macleod, held this feature and for long defied the Chinese swarms that soon penetrated the wire round this jagged hilltop. There was a desperate exchange of grenades, back and forth from 20 yards, until at last the Borderers' stock was exhausted and they were reduced to throwing pieces of rock, beer bottles, and even the company commander's haversack. The Chinese gained the summit, and just before 10 p.m. Robertson-Macleod brought his men back to his reserve platoon position, close below Maryang-San.

There was still firing to be heard from the Knoll: Purves and his two-platoon group were turning every attack into a heap of bodies. At 2 a.m. orders reached him by wireless that he was to withdraw. Purves surveyed the destruction he had wrought and carefully arranged to cover the withdrawal of his wounded and of all his stores. All were safely brought out, under the noses of the enemy gazing down from Maryang-San, and when Purves reported to Battalion Headquarters for further instructions he was sent at once to the aid post. Blood was streaming down his shoulder from a wound that had long been undressed.

The evacuation of the ridge was now complete. The Borderers had made the Chinese division pay a lavish price for it, at a cost to themselves of seven killed, eighty-seven wounded, and forty-four missing. Some indication of the intensity of the fighting is provided by the fact that the Mortar Platoon fired 4,500 rounds during the battle and had to use their own beer ration to keep their six tubes cool. A remarkable crop of decorations was gleaned. Speakman won the V.C. and Harrison, his company commander, an immediate D.S.O. Purves also won the D.S.O.—a unique, indeed phenomenal feat for a national-service officer—and in due course there were also D.S.O.s for Tadman and Robertson-Macleod. There were two immediate awards of the M.C., one of the D.C.M., and four of the M.M.

The Royal Leicesters, who so far had done no more than occupy reserve positions, were called upon to counterattack and regain the whole of this ridge that had absorbed three battalions in its initial capture and a division in its recapture by the Chinese. It was a daunting task for a newly arrived battalion, lent by its own brigade to another, by 29 to 28. The attack began at 2 p.m. on the 5th with two companies forward, D on the left being directed on Hill 217 and A on the adjacent peak, United, each moving from the south-east on either side of a spur made bare by shelling. The other two rifle companies were to pass through to occupy the remainder of the ridge, Maryang-San included.

Accurate shellfire, undeterred by widespread concentrations from the Commonwealth guns, took an early toll on the assault companies as they strode across the 1,200 yards of rock, brier, and tree stumps between start line and objective. Even so, a platoon of D Company fought their way on to Hill 217 with a spirited charge, and with aid from two Centurions, skilfully and daringly manoeuvred up the slope, some men of A Company reached the top of their peak too. But the Chinese could still rain grenades and bullets upon them and pour shells on the approaches. Like the Fifth Fusiliers before them, the Leicesters could not sustain their attack, and the dwindling remnants were called back as darkness began to fall. Their withdrawal was facilitated by some deadly strikes on would-be assailants by the Centurions. The Leicesters had lost seven officers and ninety-eight soldiers killed, wounded or missing: a bitter initiation. Reprieved from renewing the attempt, they instead relieved the Borderers in their positions under the brow of the bloody Maryang-San. Making free use of the guns they had surreptitiously assembled in such number, the Chinese made life hard for them.

Hill 227, held by D Company, 1st King's Shropshire, had also come under attack on the night of November 4, as the Borderers fought for their lives and Maryang-San. It had been beaten off even without penetration of the wire, of which there were three double apron fences and 50 yards of 'spider' wire, not to mention a minefield. D Company subsequently handed 227 back to its captors, A Company, and at 4.30 p.m. on November 17 the latter had the misfortune to become the target of the concentrated weight of the Chinese artillery, wheeled and self-propelled. Twenty-nine batteries were employed, according to a counter-bombardment estimate, and everything disintegrated under the blast of their shells, wire, mines, sandbagged positions, trees and scrub. By 7 p.m. it was deduced from survivors, who included an officer party of eight escaped from capture, that resistance was at an end, and the Commonwealth guns, which were already overheated, were turned on 227. D Company meanwhile were alerted for a counter-attack. They put it in at 7 a.m. and regained the dishevelled hill unopposed. Some men of A Company were unearthed still alive beneath collapsed entrenchments and dead Chinese. There were enough left to form a composite platoon.

D Company endured plenty of shelling on Hill 227, and that night (November 18) they came under heavy attack, despite the massive curtain of defensive fire put down around them. The Chinese gained the summit, forcing D Company to make a limited withdrawal, in which they suffered some loss. Again the hill was plastered by the Commonwealth guns and mortars, and again it was devoid of living Chinese next morning. Its slopes were in fact too exposed to shellfire to be tenable by either side, and the K.S.L.I. decided to keep no more than an observation post upon it. They claimed to have killed 300 Chinese in these pounding matches, and a subsidiary battle developed over the removal of the dead; no trace was found of a woman in black who was said to have led the first attack. The K.S.L.I.'s casualties came to ninety-one, of whom twenty-one were killed and six missing. They had forestalled attack on Kowang-San.

The Royal Leicesters also came under attack during the night of November 17/18. Their B Company held a ridge below Hill 217, with one platoon further right astride the spur. This latter platoon received the worst of the shelling and were crunched and overwhelmed. The Chinese did not stay and, accepting the hint, the Leicesters left only a patrol when they reoccupied the spur, where the body of the platoon commander lay among others. The Chinese kept up their shelling, causing damage enough to enforce the relief of B Company by D during daylight on the 19th. The Chinese arrived on the ridge in among their shells soon after nightfall and were driven out after some hand-to-hand fighting, leaving piles of dead on the wire and among the trenches. They came again at 3 a.m., this time making a silent attack, and forced D Company's two weakened platoons off the ridge. A signaller, Private Webster, remained behind and kept Battalion H.Q. informed of events. Having survived the full weight of a stonk from his own divisional artillery, he reported the departure of the Chinese. The Leicesters again accepted the hint and reoccupied the ridge with only a standing patrol. The latter withdrew when another attack came in next night and on returning in the morning counted a fresh 118 corpses, the yield of half an hour's rapid fire by guns, mortars, and machine-guns.

The Chinese kept up their fury, both with guns and infantry, and a chill mixture of mist and sleet added to the misery, although without serious impact on the indomitable morale of the Commonwealth troops. However, relief was at hand for the 28th Brigade and their assistants from the 29th, who in addition to the Royal Leicesters included companies of the Royal Norfolks filling various gaps. The G.O.C. I Corps, Lieutenant-General J. W. ('Iron Mike') O'Daniel, had accepted Cassels' submission that his division was overstretched and had ordered the 3rd U.S. Division to take over the right of his two brigade sectors. The relief was completed in daylight and under heavy shellfire on November 23, and no sooner had darkness fallen than the Chinese gained possession of the key feature, Hill 355 or Kowang-San. The Americans set about regaining it with great vigour, and although the sleet, now thickening to snow, had turned every track into a quagmire, they succeeded as darkness was falling on the 24th. This was particularly welcome to the Canadians, who were much imperilled by the loss of Kowang-San and had already withstood heavy attack.

The Chinese made no further attempt on Kowang-San now that winter had arrived. It would have been a useful bargaining counter for their negotiators now moved to Panmunjon, only a short distance south-west of the sector held by the Commonwealth Division. One point had so far been agreed, namely that the truce line be the front line at the time of signing, not necessarily that of the 38th Parallel, and this of course greatly increased the value, in terms of lives to be paid, of every hill that could be gained. For Maryang-San the Chinese may have paid 1,000, and no doubt they thought it cheap. It was up to the United Nations troops to deter them from further bartering by keeping the price high and their own costs low.

For the 8th Hussars the end had now come. The 5th Royal Inniskilling Dragoon Guards had arrived to take over their tanks and in December took their place in the line. Despite the restrictions imposed by precipitous slopes, woods, and soggy paddy fields, the 8th had raised the art of close support of infantry to a new pitch of efficacy and had not only pleased their clients but were themselves bubbling with enthusiasm for the Centurion. Five of their officers (including a doctor) and thirteen soldiers had been killed, the majority when cut off in the Cromwells in their first battle. They were the last of the fire support units of what had been 29 Brigade Group to depart. C Squadron, 7th R.T.R. had left in October, and the 45th Field Regiment had been relieved by the 14th Field in November. The two light batteries, whose 4·2-inch mortars had wrought deadly destruction, had been relieved by elements of what was to become the 61st Light Regiment, consisting of three mortar and one light anti-aircraft batteries.

VI—TRENCH WARFARE (1952–53)

The cold was the main enemy in the months of December, January and February; it was a new one for all the British troops. The challenge was met in the belief that 'any fool can be uncomfortable' and with determination not to be a fool. It was found that there was greater warmth beneath the ground than above it, and that a front line dug-out, in which three or four could huddle round a fire, could be made quite as cosy as any slit and 'pup' tent in the rear area. Fires of course called for close vigilance, and so did weapons, to ensure the oil on them did not freeze up. Once again the temperature sank far below zero Fahrenheit after Christmas, with the result that blankets could be stood upright each morning and digging was a near impossibility. But the winter clothing, which included some white ski suits and special clothing for sentries, drew the approval of the troops. 'How pleased we were with it!' was the comment in the Royal Norfolk's journal, *The Britannia*.

The thaw that came at the end of February 1952 caused the tracks to develop 'thaw-boils' and 'frost-heaves', requiring all the skill and exertion of the Royal Engineers to keep them usable. There was no revival of a hostile offensive, and the Commonwealth Division carried on with a defensive routine that suffered no serious operational interference for almost a year. In exchange for the relief of the right brigade an extra 2 miles had been taken over on the left from the 1st Rok Division; they included the hills west of the River Samichon, of which one was known, from its outline and mark on the map, as The Hook. The valley of the Samichon was held by one brigade, with two battalions forward west of the river and one east of it, covering a frontage of some 4 miles, and the brigade on the right had nearly as large a frontage, also necessitating the forward deployment of all three battalions. The third brigade was in reserve and relieved one of the other two every six or seven weeks.

Thus the 28th Commonwealth Brigade relieved the 25th Canadian in the right sector on January 19, 1952, and the 25th in turn relieved the 29th British in the left sector on March 10. In mid-April the division's frontage was shifted back north eastwards. The 1st U.S.

Marine Division took over the territory west of the Samichon and 25 Brigade sidestepped to relieve two battalions of 28, while the third was relieved by 29 Brigade, who at the same time took over Kowang-San and Hill 238 from the 3rd U.S. Division. Although not quite as long as in November, the divisional frontage was again extended, but there were now ten infantry battalions available, for the 1st Royal Australian had arrived to join their colleagues, the veteran 3rd, in 28 Brigade. The latter remained in reserve until the end of June, when they relieved 25. The next relief was on August 8–10, when 25 relieved 29 in the right sector.

Not since the Great War had British troops had a static defensive role like this, and even in that war no division ever remained continuously in the line for over a year. The Commonwealth Division were able to do this partly because morale was high and the organisation efficient, partly because the Chinese lapsed into spasmodic activity. Sometimes their artillery burst forth in full blast—as against the Borderers on April 5, followed by an attack that was punishingly repulsed—but often battalions spent a full tour in the line without reporting fall of shell. No-man's-land was wide, over a mile in most places, with both sides holding their own hill features without dispute. Yet patrol activity was intense, and as in all wars demands for the capture of a prisoner kept the telephone lines alive from Army Headquarters downwards. Apart from standing patrols and routine protective patrols, each battalion in the line sent out upwards of four patrols each week. Most were reconnaissance patrols, four or five strong, and the others were fighting patrols, of a strength of twelve to fifteen, intent either on ambushing an enemy party or raiding an outpost. Almost always a subaltern was in command.

Much thought, training and rehearsal went into these patrols, and the standard of individual proficiency must have been high. There were many acts of bravery on the paddy fields and hillocks between the two front lines, and many, many more tense hours of crawling and waiting under the stars, often in camouflage suits soaked by the water that abounded in the valleys. Plenty of Chinese were killed in encounters, but they were amazingly hard to capture; even if trapped in one of their deep shelters they preferred to die inside rather than come out captive and alive. It was perhaps no coincidence that prisoners were uppermost in the minds not only of the generals but of the negotiators at Panmunjon, where the most stubbornly contested debating point was whether a prisoner should have the right to choose his land of domicile on release.

Usually, when there was a clash, Chinese reinforcements would be close at hand. This meant among other things that every patrol had to have its own wireless set, which encumbered both movement and silence, and that rescue operations had often to be staged to extricate a patrol surrounded in No-man's-land. The return was invariably the most perilous part of the journey, at the time when caution begins to yield to the thumping urge for haste. And even if the enemy were absent, a fractional error in navigation could cause a drift away from the narrow gaps in the minefields that had been spread, by spasmodic development, in front of the Commonwealth defences. In the early days unsuspected mines greatly added to the peril, for more zeal had been shown in their laying than recording.

On occasions something more ambitious than a mere patrol was attempted. On June 17 the Inniskilling Dragoon Guards sent out the equivalent of a squadron to shoot up enemy positions from almost a mile ahead of the front line. Bad going halted them after half a mile and they had a struggle to extricate their Centurions under shellfire, but they had plenty of shooting. This was followed by four raids on consecutive nights, specially ordered by Corps Headquarters in the despairing quest for prisoners. The first two were carried out by Canadian battalions, and both resulted in heavy losses without capture of the objectives.

The third, on June 22/23, was assigned to the Welch and carried out by their B Company under Major Jackson. The objective was the battered Hill 227, which had been abandoned even as a patrol base since soon after the K.S.L.I. had handed it over. The company gained the hill and were then subjected, predictably enough, to strong counterattack, in which the commanders and sergeants of the two assault platoons all became casualties. The problem was to hold on long enough for the evacuation of the wounded, and Jackson staunchly did this, bringing back twenty-three of his men wounded and three dead, including his gunner officer. None was left in No-man's-land.

Next night it was the turn of the third Canadian battalion—of the Royal Vingt-Deuxième Regiment—and they too gained no success, at a cost of ten casualties which brought the total for the four fruitless ventures to eighty.

The two Australian battalions, having relieved the Canadians in the left sector, kept up the costly belligerence, and although the 1st Battalion caused considerable slaughter in a daylight raid with heavy fire support, neither could make a capture in the process of suffering a further forty-five casualties between them. Such results were depressing, and despite pressure from above, Cassels put a stop to further impetuous bull charge assaults.

Something more subtle was attempted by the Royal Norfolks, combined with the nightly laying of four ambushes by parties of nine. Having lost a subaltern who died a gallant death on an outpost, Hill 118, the Norfolks decided to leave this hill untenanted by night and to strike when next the Chinese occupied it. For three nights a force of four platoons lay up in No-man's-land, with an artillery programme ready for the firing, and on the night of August 2 the flare went up and the attack went in. One of the platoons, with protective duties on the flank, was already hotly engaged, and this caused some confusion and the diversion of one of the assault platoons. But the objective was gained, with heavy destruction of the Chinese. Twenty were counted dead— and six wounded were brought back. They did not live, even one whose wound appeared quite slight when examined at the regimental aid post, and the promised reward for a prisoner, a bottle of whisky, continued to dangle out of reach. It seems that the prisoners willed themselves to give up the ghost. The Norfolks lost three killed and twenty-one wounded, most of them slightly.

There was at all times a steady trickle of casualties, and it grew stronger after the return to Kowang-San and vicinity, where the Chinese were more active with their mortars and guns. Meanwhile the arguing continued at Panmunjon, and the searchlights marking out the neutralised zone sent out their nightly reminder of the absurdity of continuing the fighting. Yet morale within the Commonwealth Division, all accounts agree, remained remarkably high. The comradeship that grew so fast between its various elements was an undoubted aid to this. The continual round of visits paid by leading national figures, whether in government, church, or the world of entertainment, may have been another; soldiers of course came too, the most important of whom from a British viewpoint were Field Marshal Lord Alexander, who in fact came as Minister of Defence but dressed and spoke as the soldier he always remained, and General Keightley who came as C.-in-C. Far East and Colonel of the Inniskilling Dragoon Guards. Another factor was the countryside, which abounded with leaf and bird life once spring arrived, and yet one more the prospect of the five-day jaunt to Japan that fell to every soldier once and left him, so it was said, in greater need of recuperation than before. There was also a good supply of beer, and the engineers and services ensured between them that it always reached the troops, whatever the strain on the tracks and roads.

Knowledge that his tour of duty was of fixed and limited duration also played its part in keeping a soldier's morale high, even though it inevitably made a battalion rather too risk conscious during the final two or three weeks. Although a year was the prescribed ration for a battalion from England, it did not apply to all. Thus the Royal Leicesters were relieved in 29 Brigade by the 1st Black Watch in June 1952, which was only eight months after their arrival but a month after they had completed three years overseas. They had lost fifty-five killed, the great majority during their hectic start.

The King's Own Scottish Borderers and the King's Shropshire Light Infantry, alone of British battalions, exceeded the year, having had lusty shares of mobile warfare and static, of attack and defence. The Borderers were just over fifteen months on active service, never far from the front line, and lost sixty killed; the K.S.L.I. completed sixteen months and lost fifty-two. Their places in 28 Brigade were taken respectively by the 1st Royal Fusiliers in early August and by the 1st Durham Light Infantry in mid-September.

The Royal Norfolks were the first battalion to complete a tour without launching or repelling a full scale attack, and yet they had lost thirty-nine killed or missing in action, either in raids, patrols, or from shelling, when they sailed for Hong Kong at the end of September, having handed over to the 1st King's (Liverpool), who came direct from England, as did all battalions now, except for one or two that staged at Hong Kong. The Norfolks' comrades in 29 Brigade, the Welch, were also relieved just inside a year of becoming operational, by the 1st Duke of Wellington's on October 31. The Welch had lost thirty killed.

The commanders also maintained a regular, slightly less frequent cycle of reliefs. In February 1952 General Maxwell Taylor relieved Van Fleet in command of Eighth Army, and in May General Mark Clark became Supremo on Ridgway's elevation to S.H.A.P.E. On September 7 the founding G.O.C. of the Commonwealth Division, General Cassels, handed over to Major-General M. M. A. R. West, late of the Ox and Bucks and the Chindits. Cassels was responsible more than anyone else for the wonderful spirit in the division, of which comment appears in the record of practically every regiment, and it was important that his successor should also be a man of engaging personality, devoid of 'side' or pretentiousness. Mike West—again the abbreviated christian name came swiftly into circulation—proved himself to be well chosen. His team had gained greater width of internationalism with the appointment at the end of June of an Australian, Brigadier T. J. Daly, to the command of the four-battalion 28 Brigade in place of MacDonald.

In the second half of October the Chinese sprang to life again. They started with an attack on Kowang-San, launched on the afternoon of the 23rd, and not until early next morning had the 1st Royal Canadian restored a critical situation. This was followed by an attack on the Hook, which was held by the 1st U.S. Marine Division but was due to be returned to the Commonwealth Division, with reciprocal trimming of their right flank. The Marines fought a desperate battle, in which they managed to retain precarious possession of the Hook, and on October 28 the Black Watch took over some much battered and primitive defences from them, 29 Brigade having relieved 28 in the left sector. This was now the only battalion position held by the division west of the Sami-chon, and it was a large one of crucial importance.

Unlike most hills in the neighbourhood, the Hook was bare. Its shape was that of a camel's hump jutting into the enemy's lines. It was the highest point of a ridge running from south to north, and only on the south-east side, where the ground descended in a series of lower humps, did the Black Watch have adjoining positions. From both north and west subsidiary ridges rose towards the Hook, and both were available to the enemy for assembly and assault. A Company of the Black Watch held the Hook itself, and the company commander, Major Irwin, made his men dig hard and deep. Extensive wiring and tunnelling were also carried out.

From early on November 16 the Hook came under heavy and continuous shellfire, but so industriously had the Black Watch dug themselves in that they suffered no casualties until a standing patrol forward of the Hook found themselves surrounded at about 7 p.m. on the 18th. The shelling now became intense, and around 9 p.m. flares revealed a mass of attackers struggling through the wire and dodging their own shells. A great weight of fire was brought down on them. Battalions now had Browning machine-guns to supplement their Vickers, and from both sides of the Samichon they belched forth in concert with the mortars. A troop of the Inniskillings' Centurions joined in from the flanking ridge in rear of A Company's positions, finding targets with their searchlights until blinded by the smoke, and to the crash of the divisional artillery's seventy-two 25-pounders was added heavier crumps from American medium and heavy guns and 'howling ripples' emitted by the rockets of the 1st Marine Division.

The Chinese came on with great fanaticism, reckless of loss. Although only one battalion strong, or at the most two, they attacked on a narrow frontage and soon spilled into A Company's trenches, completely overrunning the forward platoon commanded by 2nd Lieutenant Black. But the Jocks fought on. They went at them in the trenches with bayonets, grenades and fists, and the Hook was torn by the barb of savage, intimate grappling throughout its length, with grenades slung from trench to trench as in battles of old on the Western Front.

A company of the divisional reserve, the 3rd P.P.C.L.I., were brought up to free B Company, 1st Black Watch, for a counterattack. Two platoons of the latter were placed under command of Major Irwin, who despite the stress of the onslaught prepared a carefully coordinated plan of attack. It went in at 1.30 a.m., an hour after the enemy had made further gains by bringing in a fresh wave, and it was preceded by the vicious crack of airburst shells, which Irwin brought down above his own positions. A tank, which had been brought by the Inniskilling troop commander almost to the summit, gave very close support and maintained it until it was holed by a grenade almost two hours later. The platoons of B Company went in with great spirit, drawing several leaderless men of A Company along with them. Two platoons of D Company followed them, and as dawn broke Black's platoon at last had friends around them, and the only Chinese left on the Hook were dead, to the number of a hundred. Soon afterwards C Company of the P.P.C.L.I. arrived, and tattered, drawn and triumphant, the Highlanders left the churned wastes of their hilltop.

The losses of the Black Watch during the night were sixteen killed, seventy-six wounded, and fifteen captured. Irwin won an immediate D.S.O., and Lieutenant-Colonel Rose, commanding, in due course won a bar to his D.S.O. There were two M.C.s (one of them for Black), one D.C.M., and three M.M.s.

The Chinese quietened down after their repulse and during the next two months little disturbed the routine of trench life except for the occasional raid by a Commonwealth battalion; even the weather was much less ferocious than expected. Although the Canadians and Australians made most of these raids, three carried out by British battalions deserve mention. The first two were launched by the Royal Fusiliers in the last week of November, both at night. In the first a platoon attacked and captured a hill, on which they counted fifteen dead Chinese before returning with thirteen of their own men wounded and three missing. The second was a joint effort by two platoons, the first of whom themselves came under heavy attack when trying to establish a firm base for the other. Both pressed on and suffered heavily, despite the bullet-proof vests the men were wearing. Fourteen Fusiliers were killed and eight lost missing, with one platoon commander in each category, and twenty-one were brought back wounded.

The Duke of Wellington's opted for a raid at dawn, with the sun rising behind the two small officer parties that made deep penetration over frozen paddy near the east banks of the Samichon, under extensive covering fire from guns, mortars and tanks. This variation in tactics proved highly successful. The Duke's caught the enemy cowering in a deeply tunnelled outpost position and killed many of them before hauling back a dead officer for examination. They themselves suffered no loss at all.

This was on January 24, 1953, and on the 27th an unique experience began for the Commonwealth Division: they were relieved by the 2nd U.S. Division, having continuously confronted the enemy for a period of exactly eighteen months. After two months of rehabilitation and graduated training they returned to take over the same sector on April 8. Apart from the arrival of the 74th (Battleaxe Company) Medium Battery, R.A., from Hong Kong, the only change in the British element had occurred the previous December, when the Inniskilling Dragoon Guards were relieved by the 1st Royal Tank Regiment and the 14th Field Regiment by the 20th Field. The infantry, however, were slightly changed in appearance. Steel helmets had become obligatory, reflecting the changed character of the war, and each section had its Oriental members in the form of a pair of South Korean soldiers, dressed and equipped like the others. These 'Katcoms', as they were called, proved useful additions and were distinct from the team of civilian porters that served each battalion.

General West had since December had all three of his brigades in the line, leaving it to them to hold one battalion in reserve in rotation, while the tenth battalion formed a divisional reserve. The 29th British Brigade returned to the left sector astride the Samichon, the 25th Canadian to the centre, and the 28th Commonwealth to the right, which extended as far as Kowang-San (or 'Little Gibraltar'), whence the Durham Light Infantry fought some sharp and successful actions against enemy patrols. The Black Watch were again on the Hook, and they celebrated their return by netting a prisoner on April 23, the first capture made since October. There had been a new commander of 29 Brigade since December, when Brigadier D. A. ('Joe') Kendrew took over from Ricketts. Formerly of the Leicestershire Regiment, Kendrew had gained fame as a rugger player before the war and as a fighting soldier during it, with a D.S.O. and two bars won.

There had been a sudden and dramatic change of attitude by the North Korean negotiating team at Panmunjon, evinced by their concession that prisoners should choose their own domicile and resulting in the first exchange of prisoners, which took place near the end of April. It soon became clear, however, that the Chinese had not abandoned their military ambitions and that the Hook was still at the top of their shopping list. A raiding party attacked it in the early hours of May 8, to find the Black Watch as firmly ensconced as ever and able to send a platoon to intercept the raiders' withdrawal and return with three wounded prisoners. This was followed by a strong attack a week later against the Turkish Brigade on the feature left of the Hook. Staunch as ever, the Turks repulsed it.

From now on the Chinese made preparations for a renewal of the attack as blatant and blustering as those that preceded the British attack by the Somme in 1916. A great number of guns were assembled, some of much heavier calibre than anything used before, and during the night of May 20/21, 4,000 shells and mortar bombs were counted down on the Hook. Since May 16 the Duke of Wellington's—famous rugger players, like their brigade commander—had held the feature, and on the 23rd the Black Watch were brought back to take over the adjacent right-hand ridge, thus enabling the Duke's to concentrate at greater density on the Hook itself. The King's were on the other side of the Samichon, holding the prominent Yong Dong, and the Royal Fusiliers were released from 28 Brigade to form Kendrew's reserve. On the night of May 24 the King's made a raid across the river, designed to disrupt the attack that all knew would be coming in. It disintegrated on an undetected mine-field, and as so often before the heroism had to be directed to the evacuation of the wounded, fifteen in number, from perilous exposure.

On May 27, with tension high and the shells still falling fast, evoking massive response from the Commonwealth guns, the King's exchanged positions with the Black Watch and took over the hills protecting the right flank of the Duke's. Next day, the 28th, the Duke's left forward platoon on the Hook came under concentrated shellfire, which caved in a number of posts, and at 7.35 p.m. the Hook was rent by a mighty stonk, heavier than anything yet experienced. The first wave of attackers came in through the splash of their shells, still in daylight, and slowly overwhelmed this left forward platoon, its subaltern dying in some desperate hand-to-hand fighting amid the ruins of his sand-bagged positions. The commander of Support Company, Major Kershaw, was also with this forward platoon. He had been organising the wiring of the battalion position and had supervised the erection of a massive apron of wire under constant fire. He now led some men to a tunnel entrance and from here took heavy toll on the Chinese with a sten. His leg was shattered by a grenade, but he fought on, even throwing grenades as he lay in the tunnel, until the Chinese blew it up at both ends, trapping the men inside it.

D Company held the Hook, and in anticipation of the attack Lieu-tenant-Colonel Bunbury of the Duke's (who was to win a bar to his D.S.O.) had brought platoons of the reserve company, A, up to the edge of D's position for swift reinforcement. This proved a sound policy, and the Chinese were prevented from exploiting their early gain.

Two fresh waves coming up the ridge from the north-west were struck and shattered by the full weight of the divisional artillery's shells. An attack next came in from the north-east, at about 8.45 p.m., with the enemy shelling still intense, and this gained a section post of D Company's right forward platoon, but was thereupon halted by a hail of fire from the battered positions beyond. B Company, holding the left flank, received the next attack, launched from due west at about 10, and so deadly was the defensive fire that it was turned to carnage on the wire. It was now the turn of the King's, holding the ridge on the right flank with their A and D Companies. A complete battalion, it transpired, were caught by the artillery as they tried to form up and were blown to smithereens, machine-guns joining in the slaughter from both sides of the Samichon. An hour later, at 12.30 a.m., one more attempt was made, this time on the left rear of the Hook from the west. It was smashed by the combined fire of Duke's and Kingsmen, the latter arriving as timely reinforcements, and by a Centurion of the 1st R.T.R., which made good use of its searchlight.

The enemy's effort, which had been made by eight specially selected companies of three battalions, was at last expended, and it was left to Captain Emett, commanding D Company of the Duke's, to regain the lost ground with two methodical trench clearance movements by platoons fed forward to him. By 4.30 a.m. they reported the task complete. The Hook was clear once more yet, as daylight revealed, it was in a horrifying state of devastation. Trenches and dug-outs had been turned to mere slides of earth, and there were many wounded still to be evacuated, among them Major Kershaw, who gained a D.S.O. and lost a leg, and the ten men with him in the collapsed tunnel. The Chinese were sprawled everywhere in macabre contortions. 250 of them, it was estimated, had been killed. The British losses came to twenty-four killed, 105 wounded, and twenty missing, a total of 149, of which the Duke's share was 126.

Brigadier Kendrew, who gained his fourth D.S.O. for his conduct of the battle, rated the attack 'the worst in all my experience'. The Duke's had been under tremendous strain. They had endured a week's heavy shelling, which had risen to some 10,000 rounds on the night of the attack, and they had then fought with such spirit that five men won the Military Medal for great feats of close quarter combat in the few positions that the Chinese were able to reach. Once again—and for the last time in Korea—the British infantry had displayed that 'stubborn grandeur' which Winston Churchill noted in the Nile campaign of 1884-5, and it was from proud, although desperately weary, men that the Royal Fusiliers took over the Hook on the afternoon of May 29.

VII—THE END (1953)

June 2 was a day of fireworks. The Commonwealth guns put down concentrations of red, white and blue smoke, the tanks fired a ceremonial royal salute with live ammunition, and at night a 'feu de joie' fired with tracer rippled all along the infantry positions. 6,000 miles away Queen Elizabeth II was being crowned.

On the night of June 4 the King's performed the epilogue to the Battle of the Hook. They made a raid to demolish caves used by the Chinese at the foot of the ridge ahead. Again a minefield inflicted grievous loss during the approach, and only one officer, 2nd Lieutenant Williams, and three men were able to reach and blow up one of the caves, after a fierce grenade fight. Three were killed and twenty-four wounded, five sappers among them, in this venture.

There was now a lull, with expectation of a truce running high. It subsided on the night of July 24, when a fierce attack came in on the 1st U.S. Marine Division, who had returned to the line in the sector next the Hook, which was itself now held by 28 Brigade. Plenty of shells came down on the Commonwealth positions, and they were returned by the divisional artillery at multiple interest rate. The battle reached a crescendo of fury on the 26th and then suddenly died. On the 27th a truce was signed at Panmunjon, and at 10 p.m. the firing ceased.

Next morning the troops stood on their positions in brilliant sunlight and waved at the Chinese, who replied with a lavish display of banners and the blaring forth of music and propaganda messages. The Commonwealth Division then withdrew to either side of the Imjin, 29 Brigade returning to their old haunts around Gloucester Hill. Here defensive positions were prepared and tented camps were pitched, with comforts provided by the dismantling of the timber that had propped up the dug-outs (or 'hoochies') in the front line. A brigade of Indian troops took over the duties of custodian along the demilitarised front line.

Near Panmunjon stood a hutted camp, entered from the north through an archway bearing the words 'Welcome to Freedom'. It was for the reception of returned prisoners. Thirty-seven British officers and 950 men passed through it, the majority not until the end of August. Three-quarters of them had belonged to 29 Brigade, taken at the Battles of Seoul or the Imjin, and nearly all had stood up staunchly to over two years of privation, disease and indoctrination. Of the Gloucesters, Colonel Carne had endured nineteen months' solitary confinement with unruffled stoicism and Major Harding, who had also been tortured,

207

fourteen months; Captain Farrar-Hockley had had four doses of the water torture after his third escape; and other officers and N.C.O.s had been kept handcuffed in cells too small to lie down in. The Ulsters also had their heroes, and the Fifth Fusiliers had an outstanding one in Fusilier Kinne, whose determination to escape and open contempt for his captors remained unbroken by brutish punishments which included eighty-one days in handcuffs and frequent beatings past the point of consciousness. He was awarded the George Cross. As for the British prisoners in general, the best tribute came from a Chinese officer guard, who had been so often driven to exasperation in his attempts at indoctrination and finally confessed to a private of the Gloucesters: 'I shall be as pleased to get rid of you as you are to be repatriated.'

The total British losses were eighty-six officers and 779 soldiers killed, and 185 and 2,404 wounded; nearly half were incurred after the opening of the peace talks, when the only issue of importance was the right of the prisoners to change sides, a matter affecting half the 132,000 North Koreans and Chinese taken, twenty-one Americans, and one Briton. The United Nations total in killed was 447,697, of whom the great majority were South Korean and 25,550 American. Losses on the other side must have brought the combined total to around two million.

The 1st Commonwealth Division remained in being until November 1954, during its final year under the command of Major-General H. Murray. There was a full relief of the British element before the close of 1953. The Black Watch were relieved by the 1st Royal Scots, in 29 Brigade, just before the cease-fire, and in the autumn the King's and the Duke's were relieved by the 1st North Staffordshire and the 1st King's Own. In 28 Brigade the Royal Fusiliers were relieved by the 1st Essex in August, and the D.L.I. by the 1st Royal Warwickshire in September. December brought the relief of the 1st R.T.R. by the 5th, and of the 20th Field Regiment by the 42nd.

All these units had gone by the end of 1954 and there were only two replacements, the 1st Royal Irish Fusiliers and the 1st Northamptonshire, who in turn were relieved in 1955 by the 1st Dorset and the 1st Queen's Own Cameron Highlanders. By March 1956 only the Camerons remained together with the 55th Field Squadron, representing a hardworked arm for which the need had at last subsided. The Camerons said good-bye in this month to the last of the Australian, New Zealand and Canadian troops, and in August they handed over their spruce and well equipped camp by the banks of the Imjin to the 1st Royal Sussex. The latter remained until July 1957, when they sailed from Inchon, after an exchange of ceremonial compliments with American and South Korean troops, and the Commonwealth Contingent, as it had been renamed, closed down. Its last commander was Brigadier V. W. Barlow, who wore a bar on his D.S.O. for commanding the King's Shropshire Light Infantry during their tour.

A small British presence remained, consisting of a subaltern and a section of men detached from a battalion in Hong Kong. With French, Turks and Greeks, they formed—and indeed in 1970 still form—what must be the smallest international contingent ever, a single platoon, and as such perform ceremonial guard duties at Panmunjon. They are there to remind the quarrelsome negotiators from the North that their countries once made sacrifice to redress aggression, and it is to be hoped that this may dissuade the North Koreans from violating an armistice that seems unlikely ever to be translated into peace.

7

Regimental Revival

(1950–52)

I T will have been observed that the British Army had to rise from its 'parlous state' of 1948 to bear a heavy and unexpected burden. Between 1948 and 1950 twelve extra infantry battalions, four armoured regiments, and five artillery regiments, together with four commandos, were despatched to the Far East to combat aggression or the threat of it, raising the force out there to forty fighting units. A divisional headquarters and five brigade headquarters had been raised for the control of their operations. The British Army of the Rhine was also in process of expansion, to the extent of one armoured division, with another to come.

Nor was this all. The crises in Malaya, Hong Kong and Korea had each in turn revealed the inadequacy of the reserves available in Britain, and with the Korean war tautening the tension throughout the world, the British Government at last decided, as announced in a White Paper of August 31, 1950, that a powerful strategic reserve would have to be built up at home, consisting of an infantry division, an armoured division, and an infantry brigade. To provide the men to make this reserve effective, and likewise fill the gaps in the ranks of units overseas, this same White Paper asked for an extension of full-time service under the National Service Act from eighteen months to two years. Parliament was recalled to give sanction to this measure. It was regretfully accepted on the Government benches and drew from Winston Churchill, as Leader of the Opposition, an expression of satisfaction that, 'In giving faithful and fearless support to the United Nations Organisation, in confronting totalitarian tyranny, whether it was in the garb of Communism, Nazism, Fascism, or Russian Imperialism, on these supreme issues Britain could indeed present a united front.'

As a result of this display of resolve the 3rd Infantry Division was reborn on April 1, 1951, under Sir Hugh Stockwell's command. It consisted of three recently raised brigades, the 32nd Guards, 19th and 39th Infantry. A month later the 6th Armoured Division was brought back to life, consisting of the 20th Armoured and 61st Lorried Infantry Brigades, but at the end of the year it was assigned to Rhine Army, leaving a scarcity of armour in reserve that would be painfully felt five years later. The 16th Parachute Brigade formed the third component of the Strategic Reserve, briefly making it large enough to deserve capital letters.

The extension of national service brought the Regular Army to a strength of around 420,000, excluding Gurkhas and the W.R.A.C., and even this was insufficient to bring the 176 units of infantry, armour, and artillery to full fighting strength, such were the demands of the ancillaries and of training, staff and welfare duties. The provision of battalions also posed a problem, for the only saving to offset the heavy commitments newly undertaken was the release of five battalions from Somaliland and Eritrea, caused by the return of the one to Italy in April 1950 and the accession of the other to Abyssinia at the end of the same year. There had also been release from Greece, but the brigade there was required in Cyprus to rebuild a reserve in the Middle East.

The most obvious way of providing the battalions for the new strategic reserve was to release the fourteen employed as basic training battalions for their brigades or groups. This arrangement, which worked well enough among armoured regiments, was highly unpopular in the infantry, most of all with the battalion saddled with the depot role, and there was also much discontent over the working of the Group System as a whole. Very little attempt appeared to be made to allow either officers or men to serve with their own regiments, and when a battalion moved from one command to another it invariably suffered an upheaval in its manpower. The system screamed for reform.

The C.I.G.S. was Field Marshal Sir William Slim, as he had been promoted within a month of taking office in December 1948. His had been an unconventional route to the top and it had provided him with experiences far outside those normally acquired by a regular officer, such as employment as a lumberjack, battle experience in the ranks (of the Royal Warwickshire Regiment), demotion from lance-corporal to private, and more recently the management of the newly founded British Railways. It was fortunate for the British Army that a man of such broad and rugged outlook was available to undertake the great task of reconstruction. Yet as a former officer of the Gurkhas—and the first since Wellington to rise from Indian service to the head of the British

Army—he had to tread warily on the delicate issue of infantry reform. One can be sure that his own inclination was to strengthen brigade ties, as was being done in his own brigade. The Gurkhas had never before had a central depot and training centre until the one at Sungei Patani was opened in August 1951, after three years in germination.

The framework for the development of a similar system within the British brigades had already been provided by the depot battalions, and it would have been easy enough to release these battalions for active roles while converting the depots they ran to separate organisations. But the old regimental system had a staunch advocate in the Adjutant-General, General Sir James Steele, Colonel of the Royal Ulster Rifles. He was aware of the strength regiments had derived from being served by their own regimental depots in their own county homes, and he was aware of the yearning within the regiments for a return to this system. For once the proponents of centralisation, in the cause of economy and progress, were defeated. It was agreed that the regimental depots, which had remained in being for caretaking duties, should be reactivated for recruit training, thus releasing the fourteen basic training battalions. Only the Guards retained a centralised system.

This did not mean that the brigade organisation was abandoned. On the contrary, it received strength and lubrication from the formation of brigade headquarters, each under a brigade colonel, who was responsible for matters requiring coordination between the regiments, most of all in the distribution of officers and men. His function was to keep battalions happy, and few had inkling that the formation of these brigade headquarters presaged the shape of less acceptable things to come.

An important corollary to these reforms was designed to reduce the amount of cross-posting and thus make battalions homogeneous. Although the pairing of battalions for home and overseas tours had been discarded with the Cardwell System, those overseas still did long tours and with the individual's obligation reduced to a tour of three years there were consequently perpetual shifts in manpower. Now a battalion's tour was to be reduced to the three years prescribed for the individual. Thus a much greater degree of stability was achieved, and the Group System ceased to be a target for abuse.

The period that followed might well be described as the evening glory of the regimental system. The depots sprang joyfully to life again between the spring and autumn of 1951, and since this was the first time in peacetime that County and Regiment had mutual obligations, the one to provide recruits under the National Service Act, the other to look after them, the relationship between the two became closer than ever. Depot commanders gave much thought to public relations, and it was common practice for parents of recruits to be invited to the depot and be shown their boy's living accommodation. Passing-out parades became family occasions, and great local interest was taken in the doings of the regular battalion. On return from a three-year tour the latter was usually afforded the chance to visit its county and could be sure of a great welcome if it had been fighting, for instance, in Malaya. Thus the Suffolks were accorded official receptions in Bury St. Edmund's, Ipswich, and Sudbury, and the streets of these towns rocked with applause; the Queen's Own Royal West Kent were similarly received and welcomed by both Maidstone and Tonbridge; and the Somerset Light Infantry, touring the towns of the county, were greeted with banners bearing the slogan 'Set 'em alight, Sets,' and roars of delight from the crowd. Many a Freedom was conferred, in every part of Britain, and many a presentation made of silver drums or bugles.

It was natural that battalions returning from Korea should receive heroes' welcomes, and it was appropriate too, for regimental spirit burned higher out there than anywhere, as should have been made apparent in the chapter on that campaign. No one appreciated this more than American officers and journalists, who were quick to absorb the significance of such things as the Gloucesters' back badge, the Middlesex's nickname of 'Die-Hards', and the Argylls' pride in the words 'thin red line'. Yet a great miscellany of men served in the ranks of the battalions in Korea, some having volunteered from regiments with no territorial or military connection, others posted from a regiment of the same brigade, and on the relief of one battalion by another those men would also be handed over who had served there less than six months and were not regulars serving with their parent regiment. Because the need for such exchanges was accepted, these 'foreigners' were quickly made to feel at home and became proud of the new colours under which they served. Here lay the strength of the regimental system. Similarly, the brigade system was beginning to show its strength, for when a battalion was posted overseas it had invariably to rely on drafts from other regiments to bring it up to strength and was glad to have familiar friends on whom to call.

By April 1952 the post-war Army had reached its peak of 440,000, of whom just over half were national-servicemen. The introduction of a three-year short service engagement contributed to this result. It had come soon after the change of Government in October 1951, when Mr. Antony Head became War Minister in place of Mr. John Strachey, who had approved the infantry reorganisation leading to the regimental revival. The strain on the Army was now at its heaviest, for the whole of the strategic reserve had been committed to the Middle East as a result of an eruption in Egypt. It was up to the Conservative Government now to show their determination to shoulder the ever increasing burden of defence, and they did so by raising new battalions—or more accurately, by resurrecting old ones.

The King's Royal Rifle Corps had already, in March 1951, reformed their 2nd Battalion as motorised infantry for the 6th Armoured Division, and since there were only two regiments in the Motorised Brigade it was an obvious choice for expansion. Seven more 2nd Battalions were brought back into being in April 1952, and they belonged to regiments from seven different brigades, whose homes were in the northern part of the British Isles: the Green Howards, Lancashire Fusiliers, Royal Welch Fusiliers, Royal Inniskilling Fusiliers, Black Watch, Sherwood Foresters and the Durham Light Infantry. Great was the pride and joy within these regiments. Yet great also was their reliance on their brigades, for however successful each was in raising recruits none had enough officers and men for two battalions.

8

Egypt

I—THE PROTRACTED DEPARTURE
(1945-56)

BRITISH troops came to Egypt in 1882 in order to suppress a nationalist, military rising against the viceroy of the Turkish Sultan, the Khedive. Contrary to original intention, they remained, until at length Egypt gained full independence, nominally at any rate, under the Treaty of 1936. It was signed in London by Nahas Pasha, Prime Minister of Egypt, and Mr. Anthony Eden, the Foreign Secretary, and allowed for the retention of a British force in the Canal Zone, limited to 10,000 troops and 400 airmen and charged with the task of 'ensuring in cooperation with the Egyptian forces the defence of the Canal'.

Although the British had freed Egypt from thrall to Turkey and regained her a half-share of her lost province, The Sudan, the occupation had been the cause of much bitterness, with one eruption into savage violence in 1919. Now, in 1936, all was joy, and in Alexandria British troops were even cheered. Disillusion soon followed. The Egyptian Government had undertaken to build the necessary roads and barracks by the Canal, and since no urgency was displayed in this task the British troops stayed on in the big cities with their customary, easy air of owner occupants. With the outbreak of war they could claim the right of full occupation under the Treaty. Egypt was both battle area and base and accommodated hundreds of thousands of wartime troops, who almost without exception despised the Egyptian people and made no attempt to conceal the fact. It was not explained to them that it was to Britain's advantage that Egypt should remain neutral when used as a base.

By the end of the war Egypt had become a gigantic staging centre

215

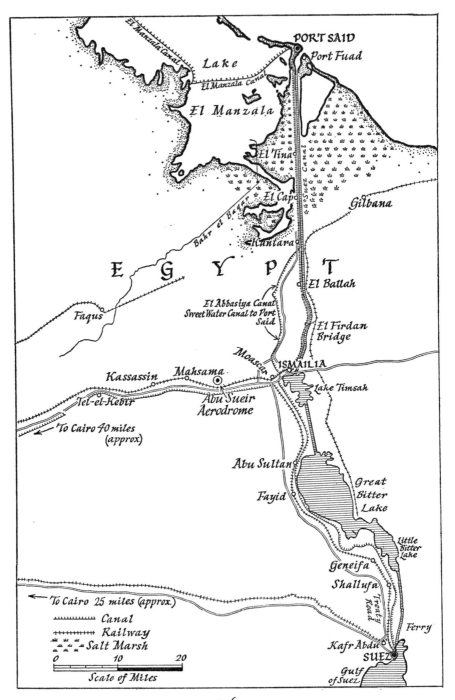

PORT SAID

Port Fuad

Lake

El Manzala Canal

El Manzala Canal

El Manzala

El Tina

El Capo

Gilbana

Bahr el Bakar

Kantara

E G Y P T

El Ballah

Faqus

El Abbasiya Canal
Sweet Water Canal to Port
Said

El Firdan
Bridge

Moascar

ISMAILIA

Kassassin   Mahsama

Lake Timsah

Tel-el-Kebir

Abu Sueir
Aerodrome

To Cairo 40 miles
(approx)

Abu Sultan

Great
Bitter
Lake

Fayid

Little
Bitter
Lake

Geneifa

Shallufa

Treaty Road

To Cairo 25 miles (approx.)

Ferry

.... Canal
++++++++ Railway
⚊⚊⚊ Salt Marsh

Kafr Abdu

SUEZ

0   10   20

Gulf
of Suez

Scale of Miles

216

and depository for all things naval, military and airpowered. G.H.Q. Middle East and Headquarters British Troops Egypt were both lodged in Cairo, occupying requisitioned buildings, and both had immense problems on their hands, which were aggravated by the emergency in Palestine and the prospect of evacuating India. There was understandable reluctance to disrupt this great centre of command from which so much had been achieved and around which there were so many installations, depots and facilities, not least the permanent married quarters and hired flats. The obligation to move to the wastes of the Canal Zone could conveniently be left to rust beneath Egypt's failure to provide the barracks, and when Mr. Attlee, trying to soothe the Egyptian Government, pressed for the move to begin, he found (in his own words), 'One was constantly up against the military capacity for delay'.

The Egyptian people meanwhile gave alarming display of their temper. Near the end of December 1945 Egypt's Prime Minister, Nokrashy Pasha, made formal request for a revision of the 1936 Treaty with words that reach the roots of Britain's problem in the Middle East but rarely received full appreciation: 'The presence of foreign troops on our soil, even if stationed in a distant area, is wounding to the national dignity'. The reply took five weeks in arriving and was damping in tone, offering no more than 'preliminary conversations'. Rioting broke out, reaching its peak on February 21, 1946, with violent attacks on British service clubs and other property in Cairo. Kasr-el-Nil Barracks, the prominent Nileside stronghold which contained District Headquarters as well as a quota of troops, came under heavy siege, and in relieving it the Egyptian police made free use of their weapons and inflicted a high proportion of the 140 casualties of the day's total. In the outskirts of Cairo two lorries were blocked and burned out of seven in an army convoy, and their drivers only just escaped with their lives. At Alexandria on March 4, during a further outbreak in commemoration of the 'martyrs' killed by the police, two British military policemen manning a control post had less luck. They were overwhelmed by a mass onslaught and thumped to death. The severed head of one was displayed in triumph.

The British Government swiftly showed a more conciliatory attitude. Negotiations were opened, and on May 7 Attlee announced a plan for the complete evacuation of Egypt, drawing a famous growl from Winston Churchill: 'Things are built up with great labour and cast away with great shame and folly'. The plan, which was only vaguely divulged in the Commons, envisaged the use of Palestine as a base and command centre, with mobilisation facilities retained in Egypt, and to show the Government's sincerity Field Marshal Montgomery came to

Cairo on June 10 and applied his own special brand of ginger to achieve a swift withdrawal to the Canal Zone as a start. There was great commotion at the various headquarters.

The Citadel was the first fortress to be handed over, and both because of its name, its position, and the fact that British troops had made their entry into Cairo here, it was an event of symbolic importance. It took place on July 4. The 1st Highland Light Infantry ceremoniously handed the gaunt bastion over to an Egyptian battalion and marched away with pomp and elegance. Other transfers followed, and by the end of September the G.O.C. British Troops Egypt, Lieutenant-General Sir Charles Allfrey, had moved his headquarters into barracks at Moascar, a suburb of Ismailia.

In October the Egyptian hopes for the complete removal of the British were dashed. On returning from talks in London, the Prime Minister, Sidky Pasha, felt constrained to announce that he had obtained Egypt full possession of the Sudan, and on this being strongly denied in London negotiations collapsed. The people yelled their rage, and the British barricaded themselves in their barracks until it subsided.

Work had meanwhile fast been going ahead on a camp for G.H.Q., which had at first been regarded as temporary but now seemed likely to become permanent. The site was next the village of Fayid, on the western shore of the Great Bitter Lake, and nearly all the builders were prisoners of war, German, Italian and Austrian. Occupation, as promised, was taken before the end of the year, and such were the deficiencies still to be remedied that the only officer with a lavatory chain to pull was the Commander-in-Chief, General Sir Miles Dempsey, who had succeeded General Paget at the end of June. The families had communal, Butlin-style centres, serviced under protest by N.A.A.F.I. It was primitive living, far removed from the luxury of Cairo and the haunts that officers and men had long regarded as their own.

There was still a remnant in the big cities. The final evacuation from Alexandria came on February 9, 1947, when the 2nd Royal Fusiliers handed Mustapha Barracks over to the Egyptian Army. This was done with imposing ceremony, and the Fusiliers then marched off towards the station to be deluged by spittle from the expert, jet-spraying mouths of the mob waiting for them. They marched on. It remained for the Life Guards to leave the barracks so well known to the Household Brigade, Kasr-el-Nil, Cairo. They gave a large farewell party, attended by all nationalities, but issued no invitations to the act of departure. C Squadron formed the rearguard, and at 5 a.m. on March 28 their armoured cars purred quietly out of the palatial barracks, watched through the grey dawn by a large and passive crowd. A few miles east of Cairo they met B Squadron, come to cover their withdrawal to the Canal. The Egyptians made no attempt to impede or insult them. The zealots had all gone to Kasr-el-Nil, where the newly arrived Egyptian soldiers spent the day waving at them through the windows, celebrating an occupation that had been promised almost eleven years previously.

After various fluctuations culminating with the passing of troops withdrawn from Palestine, the Canal Zone was divided militarily into two brigade districts. The 3rd Infantry Brigade formed the northern one, while still being part of the 1st Division (headquarters at Tripoli) and available as strategic reserve, in which role it sent a battalion to Akaba in January 1949 and thereafter had only two in Egypt, together with a regiment of field artillery. The 17th Infantry Brigade in the south had only one infantry battalion, which was at Suez, and a field regiment. Split between the two for administrative purposes were two armoured regiments, one of tanks and one of armoured cars, and an artillery group of medium and anti-aircraft regiments.

The Egyptian Army, which had rid itself of its British advisers at the close of 1947, met defeat in what had been Palestine and was forced to follow the British example of withdrawal, causing some sniggers of mirth among the exiles from civilisation in the Canal Zone and a further souring of the Anglo-Egyptian relationship. For a time the Egyptian Government were fully occupied in holding down the malcontents, who could count the murder of Nokrashy, when again Prime Minister, among their achievements. In 1950 Nahas Pasha returned to power and tried his hand at social reform. Encountering difficulties, he reverted to that old standby of Egyptian politicians, the removal of the British. He received encouragement in August 1951 from the summary manner in which Dr. Mossadeq of Persia seized the Anglo-Iranian Oil Company and expelled its British employees. Although battalions stood by to fly-in at Moascar and Akaba, they were not despatched and Mossadeq was left to rant his defiance with impunity and be hailed as a hero throughout the Middle East. It was a lead that could not be ignored. On October 8, 1951, Nahas tabled decrees abrogating the 1936 Treaty and the Sudan Condominium agreement of 1899. They were made law on October 15, amid scenes of great emotion in Parliament, after a combined Western proposal for the conversion of the Canal Zone into a N.A.T.O. base had been rejected with disdain.

In celebration of 'Abrogation Day' rioting broke out next day in the Canal towns. It was at its worst in Ismailia, where a mob arrived on the early morning train from Cairo. It was not for the British to restrain them, unless British life and property were endangered, and it soon became apparent that the lives in greatest danger were the most vulnerable, those of service families. A company from the battalion at Moascar, the 1st Lancashire Fusiliers, took occupation of French Square, and despatched a platoon to the N.A.A.F.I. grocery shop in the town's centre, where four military policemen were protecting some thirty women and children from the clutches of a raving crowd of hooligans, who had broken into the stores, helped themselves to whisky, and set part of the building on fire. The platoon had to leave their lorries over 100 yards from the building, such was the density of the crowd, and carve a passage by the display of bayonets and a burst into the air from the subaltern's sten. They put their own steel helmets on the heads of the besieged ones and escorted them back to their lorries, into which they bundled them under tarpaulins. They made their departure under a hail of bottles and stones, after a corporal had fired two rounds to hold the ruffians at bay.

The whole of Ismailia was now in furore. Cars had been set ablaze, and a mob were trying to storm the imposing block of quarters known as Army Mansions. The Lancashire Fusiliers were ordered to clear the streets and seal off the exits from the Arab quarter. The task was done with calm deliberation, mainly by young soldiers under young officers, and with aid from a few shots deliberately aimed and some bursts from stens fired into the ground to ricochet over the heads of the rioters, who often could not retreat because of the pressure from behind. The town was pacified and garrisoned until the 18th, when it was handed back to the police.

In Port Said trouble did not break out until the afternoon, when a mob attacked a camp that contained the headquarters of the Royal Military Police. A few shots had to be fired to subdue them, and key points in the town were then occupied by a motley of military police, sappers, troops in transit, and a few spare details from the 1st Loyals and 42nd Field Regiment, who were at El Ballah. The 1st Royal Lincolnshire, who were at Akaba, were flown in next day, leaving one company behind, and restored a measure of quiet to Port Said, having helped to bring the families living in hired quarters into garrison perimeters.

The order to bring in the families was issued on October 16, as Ismailia erupted, and it was the cause of most of the commotion at Suez, where the 1st Royal Sussex were the resident battalion. The order reached them at 1 p.m. and after some frantic packing and the mustering of every available vehicle and man, all were gathered in soon after nightfall and installed in some hastily prepared huts and tents in the camp 2 miles out of town. For some, abrogation brought exclusion. The *Empress of Australia* reached Port Said as the trouble started with many service families aboard. Most had to return to England after the briefest glimpse of their menfolk, accompanied by evacuee families from the camps. One third were eventually returned, the remainder being concentrated in seven 'protected areas'.

If the need to take such drastic action had not been foreseen, at least the British Army as a whole was not caught off balance. The 2nd Infantry Brigade—1st Cheshire, 1st Oxfordshire and Buckinghamshire Light Infantry, and 1st Royal Berkshire—and the 16th Para Brigade were both in Cyprus, the latter having arrived in June. By October 22 they had both been ferried by air and sea to Egypt, leaving only the 1st Para to follow; the 2nd Brigade relieved the 3rd in Port Said and other places north of Ismailia, and the 16th Para went to Fayid. In the first week of November Headquarters 1st Division flew in from Tripoli with the 1st Guards Brigade—3rd Grenadiers, 3rd Coldstream, and 1st Queen's Own Cameron Highlanders—a squadron of the 4th/7th Royal Dragoon Guards and the 26th Field Regiment, who were learning to be gunners again after their campaigning in Malaya and had now to revert to infantry duties. Divisional Headquarters went to Moascar and the Guards to Tel-el-Kebir, a name emblazoned on the colours of all three battalions. There was a move within the 1st Division on November 10, when the 1st East Lancashire were flown in from Khartoum to relieve the Loyals in 3 Brigade.

The 3rd Division were also astir, answering their first emergency summons since reconstitution. The 19th Infantry Brigade were airborne in Hastings aircraft within a week of ending the biggest post-war exercise on Salisbury Plain, which appropriately had the name of Surprise Packet, and by October 31 they had relieved the 1st Guards Brigade in Libya, who were flown on in the same aircraft. The 39th Brigade came by sea, sailing to Cyprus in two aircraft carriers during November 4–11, and on the 14th they were summoned to Egypt, for duty in the south, at a strength of two battalions, the 1st Buffs and the 1st Royal Inniskilling Fusiliers. The 1st Border followed a month later, bringing the British garrison to a total of sixteen infantry battalions, two and a half regiments of armour, and seven of artillery.

It was the swiftest build-up ever achieved by the British Army in peacetime, and it included the air despatch of 6,000 men, 170 tons of stores, and 330 vehicles in a matter of ten days. The message was clear enough: happen what might in Persia, the British were not going to be bullied out of Egypt. It is of interest that all the main troop movements were put in train while Parliament was in recess for a general election, a factor that no doubt prompted Nahas in his timing. Held on October 25, the election resulted in the Conservatives' return to power, with Churchill as Prime Minister and Eden as Foreign Secretary. Thus by strange coincidence Nahas was confronted, within ten days of abrogating the Treaty, by the man with whom he had signed it. Eden showed that his Government were determined to be firm without being provocative. He was willing to negotiate a fresh treaty, he told Nahas, but in the meantime the old one remained effective and the Egyptian Government would be held responsible for 'any damage to life and property that may result from their purported abrogation'. At the same time the War Office were informed that the principle of the minimum use of force must be rigidly applied. Churchill had been hurt by smears of 'war-monger' during the election and was determined that they should be thoroughly disproved.

It was as well that the C.-in-C. Middle East was a man with plenty of experience against browbeating tactics, gained in Berlin: General Sir Brian Robertson. The G.O.C. British Troops Egypt, in office since January 1949, was Lieutenant-General Sir George Erskine, late the K.R.R.C. A forthright, beefy character, fully restored to favour after his controversial dismissal from command of the 7th Armoured Division in Normandy, he had made a notable comeback. He knew Egypt well, having served with the Eighth Army from its earliest days as such.

The British were in the position of guests summarily ordered to move out, and the first problem was to ensure that the servants of their hosts, the Egyptian Army, were not involuntarily drawn into conflict with them. It was a situation of some delicacy, for half the Egyptian Army were east of the Canal, making elaborate preparations to redeem themselves in the next round of the war with Israel, and the other half were around Cairo. The British stood between the two, but with no agreed demarcation line. Erskine therefore drew a line around his localities and made it known to the Egyptian Army, as soon as abrogation was declared, that any movement inside it would be regarded as hostile. Only one point was disputed, the all-important railway bridge over the Canal at El Firdan, north of Ismailia. Egyptian troops guarded it on both banks and were not removed. The battalions were so overburdened with guard commitments that the Defence Platoon of Headquarters 3rd Brigade were summoned from Ferry Point, and on the night of October 17 they attacked and drove out the Egyptians, capturing the bridge without loss. Two Egyptian soldiers were killed in this affair, after which there was no further intrusion across the Erskine Line. A careful watch was kept on it, both for Egyptian troops and for arms smugglers, and this caused heavy expenditure of men.

The most powerful weapon available to Nahas, as to the Russians at

Berlin, was blockade, and he had the advantage, denied to the Russians, of being able to intimidate the enormous civilian labour force, 66,000 strong, on which the British forces relied for the rudimentary requirements of living. Intimidation was an art in which the Minister of the Interior, Fuad Serag El Din, was highly skilled, and in the weeks that followed 'Abrogation Day' he enforced a pathetic exodus of families, with handcarts croaking under enormous loads, away from the Canal Zone, the former bakers, butchers, grocers, hairdressers, electricians, drivers, domestic staff, sweepers, storemen and clerks to His Britannic Majesty's forces, now unemployed and soon destitute. Only a very few of the very brave stayed, to be granted refuge with the army families inside the fortresses into which camps had been turned. And it was not only the services of their direct employees of which the British were deprived. An intricate railway service, which kept the life-blood flowing in and out of the supply and ordnance depots, was brought to a halt, and dock labour was withdrawn at Port Said.

Erskine spoke the language troops appreciate. 'We shall be neither shoved out, starved out, nor knocked out,' he told his men in a special broadcast, and they set to with a will on the vast assortment of chores and guard duties they had to undertake. Powerhouses, water filtration plants, and even sewage works were among the installations they had to operate and protect. Almost every battalion, the Guards included, did turns of duty as dockers, and the circulation of supplies absorbed a great number of troops, either as escorts or porters. As counter to the disruption of his railway system, Erskine was tempted to retaliate by stopping the flow of oil along the pipeline from Suez to Cairo. This measure would probably have been less effective than the British command imagined, but it would have caused great fury and might have led the Egyptians to try out their ultimate weapon, the blocking of the Sweetwater Canal. Calmer counsels prevailed, aided by the arrival of reinforcements to relieve the domestic crisis. Some 4,000 pioneer troops came from Mauritius; a civilian labour force of 3,500 was enlisted from Cyprus and Malta; and the R.A.F. sent out 5,000 technicians from England.

For a month following the initial riots there was comparative peace in the Canal towns; the pedlars of violence were engaged on the removal of the civilian employees and indulged only in some spasmodic sniping against the troops, combined with the murder of the odd soldier or two caught in isolation. On November 17 a new, more sombre phase began. That evening a patrol in Ismailia disturbed an Egyptian auxiliary policeman asleep on the pavement. The man fired his rifle and ran, whereupon sixty of his comrades ran from their barracks and wildly opened fire, wounding a civilian. An officer of the Royal Signals, Major McDowall, tried to arrange a parley and was shot dead by a policeman on a roof behind him. The patrol opened fire on the police and forced them back to their barracks.

This was the first appearance of the Bulak Nizam, as these auxiliary police were called; most of its members had been specially enlisted by El Din and given battle training at Zagazig before despatch to the front. They were in action in Ismailia again next day, shooting up service families in a new suburban estate. Two officers of the R.A.F. were killed, and so too was an officer of the Royal Military Police, Captain Kelsey, who was shot dead at close quarters while bravely trying to persuade the auxiliaries to desist. Troops of the 3rd Brigade soon drove them away and patrolled the town in strength, finding in the Sweetwater Canal the bodies of a bombardier and a lance-corporal, both with bullet wounds, the fifth and sixth victims of murder in the course of twenty-four hours.

Agreement was reached with the Governor, who appeared genuinely to deplore the assault, that the auxiliaries should be disarmed and returned to Cairo, and in exchange Ismailia was placed out of bounds to troops and the remaining families were removed. The policemen were acclaimed as great heroes in Cairo and awarded decorations, while a note of protest to the British Embassy described the measures taken to impede them as 'criminal acts of aggression which surpass in horror and savagery all those previously committed'. Such things at least provided a crumb of mirth for the troops, who themselves were not even eligible for martial decorations, not being rated as being on active service. This was part of the policy of playing the crisis down.

The Bulak Nizam made their next appearance at Suez, and it led to as weird a mixture of farce and tragedy as any enacted in these mad post-war years. The Buffs had come here to ease the pressure on the Royal Sussex, and the policemen's target was a guard of two N.C.O.s and six privates of the Buffs in occupation of a hut that had been a petrol station but was no longer. The policemen arrived by lorry on the morning of December 3, dressed in black uniform and berets and carrying rifles. They calmly took up fire positions, and there was nothing the guard could do to disturb them until they opened up, which they did with far greater volume than accuracy. Some galabiya-clad supporters stood cheering them on, and others made advance with home-made bombs. The Buffs fired back from their unfortified hut and dropped a few of the more intrepid.

Lieutenant-Colonel Connolly, commanding, was a light-hearted officer with D.S.O. and bar, and on hearing the firing he drove to the scene with his second-in-command and intelligence officer. Their Land Rover was met by a wild hail of bullets, which forced them to take refuge in a second, smaller hut. They had one rifle with which to return the fire, and Connolly shared it with his I.O., claiming six kills between them from fourteen shots fired. The shindy lasted until well into the afternoon, when the command party made a getaway, covered by the Vickers of the Royal Sussex, which had been brought into the compound in their carriers. Permission was obtained to remove the guard, and they too got away unscathed, with the Egyptians still blazing their wild but unquenchable defiance. The finale came when fire was opened from a scrap heap close to their barracks on a company of the Royal Sussex returning from playing a supporting part. A platoon returned the fire and charged, killing four armed policemen and capturing three wounded. Twenty-five of their supporters thereupon emerged from hiding and gave themselves up.

One machine-gunner of the Royal Sussex wounded was the only man hit by the Egyptians with their prolonged and intense rifle fire. Yet within a mile of the petrol station, on the Suez side, there was a different story to tell. A party of garrison engineers, in two vehicles, had been ambushed here, and five Mauritian pioneers were lying dead by the burnt-out vehicles. The mutilated bodies of a captain, a sapper, and three more Mauritians were discovered some days later, and there was only one survivor, a sapper who escaped his captors. It was with good reason that the term chosen by Erskine for Egypt's 'Heroes of the Liberation' was thugs.

The Buffs also had a guard on a filtration plant on the northern out-skirts of Suez. The normal approach to it was through the village of Kafr Abdu from the west, but it had become infested with snipers who could fire downwards into the supply vehicles, and on December 4 the convoy (of six carriers provided by the Royal Sussex) therefore made a wide detour and came in from the north along the Treaty road. They were met by shots from a great crowd of Egyptians blocking the bridge over the Sweetwater Canal. The major in command blasted his way through by a burst from a Vickers gun and delivered the supplies. On the way back he had to run the gauntlet of a fusillade from some high buildings beside the road and, having recrossed the bridge, was himself shot through the head just after a soldier in the same carrier had been shot through the face. Both made miraculous recoveries.

The filtration plant could not be abandoned, since it provided the garrison with drinking water, and in his determination to reduce the risk in keeping its guard supplied, General Erskine now took a step of dire consequence. He ordered a large part of the village of Kafr Abdu to be demolished, thus opening the route from the west. It was explained at a press conference that 'several mudhouses' had to be destroyed. When work began, the houses were seen to be of brick and mortar, some two storeys high, and eighty such were sent crashing by bulldozer, under protection by the 1st Para. In contrast with Kafr Abdu itself, where there was little trouble, Cairo flared with outraged indignation. Nahas had at last won dividend from baiting the British. 'As a protest against aggression' he recalled his Ambassador from London, dismissed the 176 British subjects still employed by the Egyptian Government, mainly as school teachers, authorised the carrying of arms without licence, and generally made life difficult for the British community in Cairo.

There was a feeling among the latter, who could see the results of the demolition more clearly than the need for it, that the Army had blundered. Equally, there was a feeling at Erskine's headquarters that some firm words to King Farouk, as in 1942, could bring the crisis to a swift end. It did not help the relationship between Embassy and Headquarters that each had a separate line to London, nor that along the military one came a personal message for Erskine, conveying the Prime Minister's congratulations on his firm action.

The campaign of 'non-cooperation', as the Egyptians had termed it, now became really venomous, as witness the murder of two men of the Royal Berkshire caught by a mob in Ismailia, followed by the death of another officer of the R.M.P. in Ismailia, slain by a fusillade from the police station as he drove past. The Egyptian press poured forth their hatred and one paper offered a reward of £E1,000 for the killing of Erskine, of £E100 for that of any British officer. Students and mere schoolboys were enlisted into 'youth commandos' with heroes' fanfares. Erskine's response, under prompting from the Embassy, was to give warning of 'the powerful weapons at my disposal which have not yet been brought into action' and to appeal to parents to 'stop this criminal waste'.

The Suez filtration plant was again the objective of the Bulak Nizam on January 3, 1952. There were now one officer and sixteen men of the Buffs guarding it, and for over twenty-four hours they were subjected to continuous sniping from every side, to which they replied from behind sand-bagged posts and an irregular wall. Some of the fire came from the remaining buildings of Kafr Abdu, and these were soon cleared by sortie, but no sortie was feasible against the maze of alleyways, doorways, and windows that concealed the snipers on the south and east sides. At 4.30 p.m. on the 4th an Egyptian marksman brought to six the number of Buffs felled, of whom four were officers, including the padre; none was mortally hit. A troop of the 4th R.T.R. was ordered to the scene, and each of its four Centurions sent one shell, as personally allotted by the G.O.C., into the labyrinth where the snipers lurked. At last there was silence, broken only by a final crackle at nightfall, upon which the Bulak Nizam departed for their next engagement. A full company came in to take permanent occupation of the remains of Kafr Abdu and to pose the question as to whether such a course might not have served as substitute for the demolition in the first place.

The youth commandos had now arrived. Operating in groups of twenty from nearby villages, they made life perilous for the drivers of vehicles using the Cairo road west of Moascar. Units of 3 Brigade had a number of little skirmishes, to and fro across the Sweetwater Canal, and they rounded up a number of the galabiya-clad youngsters and transferred them to prison cages, whither their schoolbooks were sent from Cairo. The 2nd Para helped by clearing two villages near Abu Sueir aerodrome, after which the youths' activities veered further westwards, where they were closer to the refuge that was theirs beyond the Erskine Line.

On January 12 a large gang ambushed a military train approaching Tel-el-Kebir, in the area of 1st Guards Brigade. A patrol of Cameron Highlanders, sent to investigate, lost two men badly wounded by a mine laid across their path. The train meanwhile had made a retreat, and the 3rd Coldstream were summoned to remove the marauders. They found them in a wood and attacked under covering fire from mortars and Cromwell tanks of the 4th/7th Dragoon Guards. Having cleared the wood, they went into the village of El Hammada and winkled out parties of firers here and there, after crumps from their 3-inch mortars. It was a harsh end to the youths' adventures. Twelve were killed, fifteen wounded, and twenty-one others captured, and of the hundreds of rounds fired by them only one hit target, killing a sergeant.

Next day an infantry patrol of the 26th Field Regiment had a brisk battle with some native-clad Egyptians near the village of Tel-el-Kebir, which is 2 miles south of the triple artery of railway, road and Sweetwater canal, and of the military depots. The gunners had the better of the fight, with a claim of five hits to none, but on the following day (the 14th) a recce patrol of Camerons lost first a private and then the major in command shot dead in this area, with one other private wounded. A carrier was ferried over the canal on a raft and, with bren blazing, recovered the dead and wounded and enabled the patrol to withdraw. Six of the enemy were claimed killed.

The 3rd Grenadiers were brought in, and they shot dead a desperado who leapt from a bus and ran firing a pistol at the brigade commander,

Brigadier W. L. Steele. There was much firing from Tel-el-Kebir and the adjacent El Hammada, and the 26th Field hastily borrowed some 25-pounders and formed a composite troop for the heaviest punishment yet administered. Their shells crashed down when a fusillade broke out from the villages at last light, and again next day, January 15, they engaged targets that revealed themselves, in conjunction with the Camerons' mortars. The Coldstream meanwhile were brought back from the docks of Port Said, where they had just relieved the Grenadiers on stevedore duty. During the night the Grenadiers laid a cordon round the two villages, and at dawn on the 16th the Coldstream went in with aircraft flying overhead and a formidable array of weapons on call. They flushed two armed youths, who were killed by the Grenadiers, and captured 160 auxiliary policemen, under an indignant major-general, without a fight. Such was the second Battle of Tel-el-Kebir.

Always the most explosive town, Ismailia was the scene of the finale. The prelude came on the afternoon of January 19, when a barrow laden with oranges erupted with a bang that in turn set off some anti-tank mines by a post alongside the Sweetwater Canal. It was manned by the Royal Lincolns, and they lost two men killed and six wounded. A far flung crackle of fire now broke out, some of it from a convent, which had been entered by gangsters. A much beloved nun, Sister Anthony, was shot dead in its grounds as she tried to shepherd children to safety. The Lincolns went in grimly, covered by fire from posts already established. The armoured cars of the 1st Royal Dragoons escorted them up the Avenue Sultan Hussein, pumping bullets at windows and rooftops whenever fire was opened at them. Next day the houses overlooking the Sweetwater Canal were cleared of their inhabitants, except for the old and the sick, to safeguard the passage of military traffic, and on the 21st the 2nd Para undertook a search of the Moslem cemetery. They had to fight their way in, killing four armed gangsters and losing an officer badly wounded, and they then unearthed a great haul of ammunition, the largest item of which was 6,000 40-mm. Bofors shells. El Din shrieked his anger at these blows against his commandos. He accused the British of flogging their prisoners and turning savage dogs on women and children, and he promised fearsome reprisals.

Erskine had ample evidence that the Bulak Nizam formed the backbone of the resistance and were in fact being used as an instrument of war. He therefore decided to disarm all the Ismailia police and to expel the Bulak Nizam, a move that had for long been considered and eschewed in the face of much provocation. The task was entrusted to the commander of the 3rd Brigade, Brigadier R. K. Exham. By dawn on

Friday, January 25, he had thrown cordons round the main police station, or Caracol, and the buildings used as barracks by the auxiliaries, the Bureau Sanitaire, using the Lancashire Fusiliers, with two troops of the 4th R.T.R. (Centurions) and four of the Royals (armoured cars). His other battalions formed an outer cordon round the town. At 6 a.m. the Governor of Ismailia and the Major-General of Police were awoken at their houses and handed letters asking them to order the police to lay down their arms. The only reply was that they had orders from Cairo to resist.

The Bureau Sanitaire lay in wooded grounds and consisted of two double-storey main buildings, with flat roofs on which the police had sand-bagged positions, and five single storey barrack blocks scattered around them. At 6.20 a.m. an appeal was made by loudspeaker, calling on the occupants to come out unarmed. It produced a general stand-to and the emergence only of a veterinary officer and his family. After a second unsuccessful appeal, a tank entered the grounds, knocking part of the entrance down. It fired one round of blank from its 20-pounder and drew a vibrant volley in response, from stens, rifles and shotguns. Six rounds of high explosive were now fired at one of the buildings, interspersed by further broadcast appeals and long pauses for digestion. Still the Egyptians blazed forth their defiance.

It was now 8.30 and time for the next, much grimmer move, an infantry assault on the widespread fortified buildings. It was made by C Company of the Lancashire Fusiliers, under cover of a ration of two shells each from the three tanks that fanned out ahead of them and a smokescreen put down by the armoured cars. They were met by a hot fusillade, and among the first casualties was the company commander, who was brought down with a multiple pellet wound in the thigh. Undaunted by this upset, one platoon made good progress round the right flank and, after silencing adjacent snipers with some piat bombs and lobbing grenades through the upper windows, they gained possession of the smaller of the two main buildings. They lost one killed and two wounded in the process. The platoon on the left flank also made progress, although as often as the crump of grenade and burst of sten heralded their entry into a building, they ran into fire from other buildings, which each time sent one or two of them spinning. The Centurions were allowed a further ration of shells, which brought masonry down with crash and dust cloud, and the Royals joined in with their 2-pounders. The Corps of Drums of the Lancashire Fusiliers took up position in a higher building, from which they brought deadly fire down on the policemen's rooftop positions. C Company fought their way into the ground floor of the final citadel, but still the Egyptians held out on the first floor, even hurling petrol bombs at the tanks. The stairways up to them were on the outside and vulnerable of access.

C Company were now withdrawn under a smoke screen to allow the Centurions greater freedom of action, and they suffered further loss in coming out. One sharp crash was followed by one more broadcast appeal, and now at last the policemen began to emerge, their faces grey and set, their black trousers and jerseys caked in dust and flecked with blood. But on the back stairway one last defiant rump of an officer and six men still held out. The Drums were given the task of winkling them out, and they achieved it by dint of an accurately thrown grenade. A sickening sight awaited the victorious but far from jubilant soldiers. Dead and wounded littered the barrack rooms and rooftop, and around them was a pathetic jumble of blood-soaked blankets, private knick-knacks, and a lavish strewing of ammunition. All told, there were forty dead and sixty-five wounded. It was a horrifying price to pay for compliance with El Din's orders.

The British command were shocked and distressed. It was such a different story from the Guards' easy win at Tel-el-Kebir—but not so different from a forgotten affair in 1924, when the Argylls encountered furious resistance from some Egyptian mutineers in Khartoum. Yet it was hard to see an alternative, short of keeping an escape route open, which would have enabled the policemen to continue the fight as guerrillas, and the casualties among the Lancashire Fusiliers afford justification of the fire support employed. Four were killed and ten wounded, of whom one died. One George Medal, one British Empire Medal, and one Queen's Commendation were won for acts of gallantry.

This battle was over soon after 10 a.m. Brigadier Exham meanwhile had personally been conducting a prolonged parley at the main police station, the Caracol. While he spoke outside to a police captain, policemen manned positions on the roof and opened desultory fire, which was not returned by the Lancashire Fusiliers' cordon company. Not until 9.30 a.m., after many broadcast appeals and the return of the captain, did the troops return the policemen's fire. At this the captain reappeared, displaying blood on his arm, and asked for an Egyptian ambulance. A British one was sent and turned away. After further appeals and further defiance, a more intensive burst of fire at the rooftop positions produced the required surrender just after 12 noon. One policeman had been killed and three wounded. The regulars were less ardent for the cause than the auxiliaries, and many were found in the cells, where they had taken refuge with their prisoners.

Next day, Saturday January 26, came the counterattack. It was directed initially at British property in Cairo and launched by professional ruffians, with in support a mob swollen by the workless thousands from the Canal Zone. The Turf Club, being the most prominent British stronghold left, was the first to go up in flames, and eleven of its members were done to death inside it. This was the worst of the killings, but only the start of the burnings. Soon shops, offices, restaurants, and cinemas joined the target list, whether owned by Englishman, Frenchman, Greek, or Jew and among the contributors to the massive pall of black smoke was Shepheard's Hotel, from the flames of which guests cowered in the courtyard or leapt from upper storeys into the jaws of the baying mob. Only near the British Embassy, which the military attaché had organised for defence, did the Egyptian police make any attempt to intervene. A crowd approached it in the afternoon and was scattered by three shots.

There was a plan for the despatch of British troops by direct call from the Ambassador if he considered that British lives and property were sufficiently endangered, and the G.O.C. 1st Division, Major-General F. R. G. Matthews, was ready to advance along the road from Suez with a mixed infantry and armoured force built round the 2nd Brigade and 16th Para. Despite the presence of two Egyptian brigade groups dug in astride the Suez road, there was ample confidence that the task could be speedily done and not a little enthusiasm for it after all the slaps the troops had taken during the past three months. However, the occupation of Cairo posed mammoth problems, administrative as much as operational, and a message from Erskine's headquarters, which was brought to Eden in London, expressed concern about the project, quoting the new sample of Egyptian resistance. Eden replied that the troops must go if required by the Ambassador, Sir Ralph Stevenson, and it may perhaps have been as well that the latter was not of the headstrong type.

In the event King Farouk at length bestirred himself, after making anxious enquiries about the movement of the British Army, and gave orders for the summons of Egyptian soldiers, who cleared the rumpled streets of their arsonists and looters as night was falling. Next day Farouk again bestirred himself and dismissed Nahas for his failure to keep order. His successor turned to other, less dangerous ways of ridding his country of the foreign troops whose presence placed such a stain on the national pride. The 'Heroes of the Liberation' were called off. They had killed at least forty British soldiers since the abrogation, and of these thirty-three, together with sixty-nine wounded, belonged to the 3rd Brigade and units under its command in the Ismailia area. Never can a brigade have suffered heavier casualties when not on active service.

The sudden easing of the tension brought only slight improvement to the lot of the British soldier in the Canal Zone. The people remained surly, and only a few dared return to alleviate the domestic situation in the camps. Conditions in most of these camps were primitive, since some three-quarters of them had no permanent fixtures, other than relics of wartime occupation. Yet it was on facilities inside the camps that the troops had to rely for their recreation. Outside, in the majority of cases, there was nothing but sand.

There was no diminishment of the garrison. Indeed, it became even larger in February, when a second brigade of the 3rd Division, the 32nd Guards, came over from Cyprus as part of a redeployment under which the 1st Division moved to the southern part of the zone and the 3rd took over the northern commitment. Training became all-important, to keep the men fit and occupied, yet guard duties, construction work, and domestic chores continued to impose a very heavy strain, making large scale exercises as rare as green pastures. Thieves were the new heroes in the struggle against the British Army. Particularly at the great ordnance depot at Tel-el-Kebir, with its 17-mile perimeter, they showed remarkable skill at penetration through wire entanglements, minefields, and searchlight beams, and kept many a battalion fully stretched and often exasperated.

In July 1952 King Farouk was neatly deposed by the junta of Free Officers, and their nominee, Major-General Mohammed Neguib, was made Prime Minister. British troops, now under the command of Lieutenant-General Sir Francis Festing, were alerted but made no move, much to the glee of the Junta, who attributed this to weakness. In fact the relationship between Britain and Egypt took a turn for the better. Neguib, who was half Sudanese, gave up the Egyptian claim to full sovereignty over the Sudan and acknowledged that its problem was separate from that of the Canal Zone, thus removing an absurd and long lasting obstruction to negotiation. In February 1953 he reached agreement with the British Government for the advance of the Sudan to independence. It was completed, after some stormy interludes, on August 16, 1955, and having performed various ceremonial rites, the 1st Royal Leicestershire left Khartoum on October 10, bringing an end to a British occupation begun in 1898.

In July 1953 negotiations were again opened for the evacuation of the Canal Zone. General Harding had been C.I.G.S. since the previous November. Like his predecessor, Field Marshal Slim, he did not have a conventional military upbringing, having gone to war as a territorial in 1914, and he could bring an alert mind to the many problems on hand, unimpeded by prejudice. He did not believe that it was feasible to maintain troops in the Canal Zone without cooperation from the government in Cairo, which could always tie them down to self-defence, and he therefore proposed that only an administrative base should be maintained in Egypt and that Cyprus, which was under British rule, should be used as command centre and as base for an air portable reserve within easy reach of the countries through which threat to the Suez Canal might develop. This plan promised not only to free reserves but to rid the whole Army of a commitment that had a detrimental effect on recruiting, for there were upwards of 70,000 troops in the Canal Zone, and none enjoyed being there.

The logic of the proposition was accepted with a sigh by Winston Churchill, who was acting as his own foreign minister at that time, and reckoning that a soldier could best deal with Egypt's soldier rulers, he turned to General Robertson, who was freed from his duties as C.-in-C. Middle East in April 1953. It was at a house in Cairo still owned by the British Army that negotiations began in July. Colonel Nasser headed the Egyptian delegation, and agreement was very nearly reached. The breakdown, which came in October, hinged on the touchy issue of identity. The Egyptians conceded that the British might retain a base for maintenance purposes and reoccupy it with fighting troops if Egypt or an Arab country were attacked, but they would allow no flag to be flown or uniform to be worn by any of its staff. This condition Churchill could not accept.

Although negotiations were kept open informally, the Egyptians now had recourse to more primitive methods of gaining the concessions they required. At the end of November a ban was placed on the entry of foodstuffs into the Canal Zone, and there was an ominous slump in the protection afforded by the police against thugs and thieves. The situation blackened in March 1954. Fire was opened on British soldiers at least five times in four days, resulting in the deaths of a medical officer and two soldiers. There was some burning of lorries and at Port Said of a transport store. All the tedious trappings of security had to be fastened down, and to such effect that in fifty-two attacks made against British troops between April 2 and May 13, only one was killed.

Meanwhile tense grappling for power was going on in Cairo. On April 17 Nasser emerged triumphant and took the post of Prime Minister, with Neguib relegated to a puppet role as President. At the end of May Nasser called a halt to the campaign of violence in the Canal Zone, and soon afterwards detailed negotiations for its evacuation began, with another soldier, Major-General E. R. ('Lofty') Benson, who had been Herbert's chief of Military Government during the Berlin crisis and was now Chief of Staff, Middle East, playing a prominent part on the British side. There was anger in London's clubland at this brazen appeasement in the face of bullying tactics. Yet if the British command wanted the same thing as the Egyptian Government, it was foolish to be deterred by pride, and the crucial concession had now been made by the British Government: the base need bear no mark of being British and would in fact be manned entirely by civilians. Nasser conceded that Turkey be included among the countries against which an attack would provide cause for the reoccupation of the Canal Zone. Junction point had been reached at last. As token of the military significance of the occasion, the War Minister, Mr. Antony Head, came to Cairo and on July 27 initialled the Heads of Agreement on behalf of the British Government. The gangster war, which since its start in October 1951 had cost fifty-four British servicemen their lives, came to an end.

There was just time to obtain the consent of Parliament before the summer recess, and again the military played their part, by providing the implement with which to thwart the 'Suez rebels', the twenty-eight Tories who had declared their resolve to oppose the treaty. It took the form of a secret report by the Chiefs of Staff Committee, the gist of which was that the Canal was so vulnerable to attack by a hydrogen bomb as to be not worth defending, and it was brandished by both Head and Churchill to keep the rebels in isolation. The argument could have been used ten years earlier, since it applied equally to the less pretentious atom bomb, and it made the clauses for reoccupation in the event of an attack appear somewhat ridiculous.

Many details of the Agreement remained to be settled, and not until October 19 did the negotiating teams in Cairo finish their work, with the British now under Mr. Anthony Nutting, Minister of State for Foreign Affairs. He signed in company with Nasser, whereupon Egypt erupted in glee. The departure of the British forces was to be phased over a period of twenty months. They were to retain the workshops at Tel-el-Kebir, which would remain the chief repair centre for the Middle East, and various depots both there and around Ismailia and Fayid, containing petrol, ammunition and stores. Up to 800 civilians could be brought in to run these depots and a further 400 technicians enrolled locally. Accommodation was the toughest boulder of dispute. The Egyptians conceded in the end that the top executives would be allowed villas at Moascar, where their headquarters was, and the remainder took over Kensington Village, Fayid, and quarters at Tel-el-Kebir.

General Keightley was now C.-in-C., and by December 1 he had transferred G.H.Q. to Cyprus, opening up at the barracks previously occupied by District Headquarters pending a move to another new township, that of Episkopi. By the end of 1954 both the 3rd Division and the 16th Para Brigade had returned to England to rebuild the strategic reserve. There could be no clearer indication of Britain's desire to comply with the new treaty, both in spirit and word.

During 1955 there was a steady deterioration in the political relationship between the two countries, caused largely by Nasser's opposition to Eden's product, the Baghdad Pact. Fears that the rage voiced against Britain over Cairo radio might be translated to acts of terrorism against the departing troops proved groundless. The British and Egyptian military staffs remained on the good terms established during the negotiations, and everything was done on the Egyptian side to help the British keep to their programme. The 1st Division returned to England at the end of the year, leaving the 1st Guards Brigade in occupation of Moascar and Port Said, and the R.A.F. had by now handed over all but one of their nine aerodromes.

The last fighting troops to leave were the 2nd Grenadier Guards, who were in Golfcourse Camp, Port Said, and they went as inconspicuously as possible and not without a touch of comedy. The main body slipped away by ship on the night of March 24, 1956, and for the whole of the next day, which was Easter Sunday, 1 Company, as rear party, had to simulate a larger presence and dash from point to point on the camp's perimeter, expelling intruders. They thankfully handed the camp over at dawn next morning and made their departure from the R.A.F.'s last stronghold, Abu Sueir. The tall cavalryman, Lieutenant-General Sir Richard Hull, followed two days later, the last G.O.C. British Troops Egypt. A small administrative rearguard, under Brigadier J. H. S. Lacey, remained.

Seven hundred British civilians, who as the employees of ten firms forming the Suez Canal Contractors' Company were misleadingly termed the 'contractors', had by now taken over the depot installations. They had handbooks with them telling them to respect Egyptian customs, be liberal with their tips, and avoid wearing khaki drill 'so as to emphasise your civilian status'; they found the Egyptians willing enough to cooperate with them. The thieving, which had caused the troops such exasperation, dropped almost to nil.

The rearguard performed their final duties of disposal from Navy House, Port Said. The authorities of this town, in particular Governor Riad, had always been cooperative, within the limits imposed by pressure from governmental intimidators, and with the pressure off the end was harmonious. At sunrise on Wednesday, June 13—three days before the promised date—Brigadier Lacey handed Navy House over to an Egyptian colonel, and after a cheerful farewell he stepped on to a launch, preceded by the table G.S. on which the last British foothold had been signed away. He was taken to a chartered tank transport ship, named *Evan Gibb*, where he joined his seventy-eight officers and men, the remnant of an army that had been in occupation for seventy-four years. The ship had sailed quietly away when at 8 a.m. the green flag of Egypt, with the three stars known to British troops as Maleesh, Mafish, and Baksheesh, went up over the imposing Navy House to announce the fall of the last bastion. The people leapt with joy.

II—THE STRANGE RETURN (1956)

On July 27, 1956—just over six weeks after the final evacuation—the Chiefs of Staff were summoned by the Prime Minister, Sir Anthony Eden, and told to prepare plans for the reoccupation of the Canal Zone. President Nasser had, on the previous day, taken over the Suez Canal Company in melodramatic style, in retaliation for the abrupt withdrawal of the offer of a loan by the American Government. For a day or two the world was shocked, and in the Commons Nasser was likened to Hitler and Mussolini by party leaders on both sides.

No plans for the reconquest of Egypt had been made at the War Office, where General Templer had been C.I.G.S. since September 1955, forming the third of a distinguished trio who entered the Army during the Great War and gained early experience of soldiering at its most gruesome and foul. He has been criticised for this lack of readiness, but the critics did not have to bear the responsibility, and unless wild risks were to be run the invasion of a country of the size of Egypt was not an undertaking the British Army could be expected to accomplish at the drop of a hat. Eden emphasised that he did not wish risks to be run. The use of force was to be regarded as a last resort, to be employed only with the backing of the Canal user nations if they could obtain no satisfaction from the combined demands they had yet to make. There is little doubt that great hopes were entertained in the mere threat of force, just as they had been in the tank that opened up with a blank round outside the Bureau Sanitaire, Ismailia. Yet to be effective the threat had to be real and substantial. To this end the French were invited to cooperate, and a selective recall of the Regular Reserve and Army Emergency Reserve was proclaimed, which was to bring in as many as 23,000 officers and men, some to bring units to strength, others for the mobilisation of specialised units.

Within a few days officers were summoned from here and there and ushered into the warren beneath the Thames, which had been constructed for the War Cabinet, and there in an aura of great secrecy they made the first 'appreciation of the situation' in the approved military style. They were joined on August 5 by their appointed commander, Lieutenant-General Stockwell, who came with some of his staff from I Corps, Rhine Army, and was now to form II Corps. He had been to Egypt as G.O.C. 3rd Division in 1951–2, and the commander of the 16th Para Brigade at that time, Brigadier K. T. Darling was appointed B.G.S. The Brigadier A/Q had the greatest and most recent knowledge of Egypt, being Brigadier Lacey.

With both the 1st and 3rd Infantry Divisions recently returned to England from Egypt there was for once no shortage of infantry. The 3rd were mobilised during the first fortnight of August, prepared for embarkation and given concentrated training, while the 3rd Brigade, of 1st Division, were flown out to Malta, four battalions strong, as one of the 'precautionary measures of a military nature' announced by Eden in the House. It was intended that they should relieve the newly formed 10th Armoured Division in Libya. The 16th Para and the 3rd Commando Brigades were obvious choices for an assault landing role, and orders for their preparation and assembly were sent to Cyprus, much to the detriment of the anti-terrorist operations on which they were engaged.

The selection of armour was more difficult. Honour forbade the removal of any of the regiments serving N.A.T.O. in Germany, and the six in Britain were in no state of readiness, being employed either on Territorial Army assistance or basic training. The 10th Armoured Division in Libya was not so perfectly placed as it appeared to be and consisted of no more than a mixed brigade. A lack of tank transporters put the overland route out of reckoning, and there was in any case doubt as to the attitude of the Libyan Government, with whom Britain had recently signed a treaty of friendship which entitled her to station troops in the country but only to use them for purposes of which Libya approved. After various permutations had been considered, including the mustering of a territorial regiment, two of those on territorial assistance, the 1st R.T.R. and the 6th R.T.R., were chosen for infantry support and the 10th Armoured Division was also made part of the force, with greater optimism than would prove to be warranted. The mobilisation of the 1st and 6th R.T.R., the issue of Centurions and training of reservists in their use, the zeroing of guns, and the provision of special ammunition for use against Egypt's latest acquisition, the mighty Joseph Stalin tank—these caused the greatest delay, among purely military factors, in bringing the force to readiness for action. The Life Guards, at Windsor, were also mobilised, as armoured car regiment.

The French were eager enough to participate, being almost at war with Egypt because of Nasser's open championing of the rebel cause in Algeria. Showing less inhibition about touching their allotment to N.A.T.O., they made available a powerful amphibious and airborne division, the 10th Aéroportée, and a mechanised one, the 7th Mécanique Rapide, which had AMX tanks, capable of 50 m.p.h. Thus the allies had the equivalent of almost five divisions to put in the field against an Egyptian maximum of ten infantry and three armoured brigades, a large part of which was deployed along the Israeli frontier. Accepting the need for an integrated command and their status as junior partners, the French submitted to subordination to the British, a decision they were to regret. Stockwell became Commander Allied Land Forces and General André Beaufre his Deputy. Large naval and air task forces were placed under British commanders in like manner, with continual increase in the number of staff officers, of all three services, congregating in civilian clothes beneath the Thames.

One of the first discoveries of the planners was that the realm of combined operations, once Britain's pride, had become badly impoverished. Defence expenditure had rocketed to meet the cost of containing aggression, and apart from such rare rashes of profligacy as the short-lived substitution of the Land Rover by the Rolls-Royce-engined 'submarine' the Champ, the Army's needs had been cut to the bare essentials for the many tasks on hand, with the result that the easing of the military burden had been celebrated in 1955 by a marked descent in the estimates, much to the Government's joy. The danger of slimming was now emphasised. There were sufficient landing craft only for two battalions and a squadron of tanks, and most of them had been stowed away in mothballs since the end of the war. The largest command ship available was designed for a brigade headquarters, and the tank landing ships were slow and old, with only eighteen available. There was a shortage of transport aircraft, and the Valettas allotted the 16th Para were old-fashioned compared to those used by the French, being side-loaded as opposed to back. Furthermore, the para battalions had been so busy on anti-terrorist operations that they were very short of dropping practice and had to be flown home from Cyprus, one at a time, to gain it.

Undaunted, Stockwell swiftly formulated his plan and on August 10 he presented it for the approval, which was duly accorded, by the Prime Minister. It was as dashing as its codename, Musketeer. The landing was to be made at Alexandria, with the object of obtaining the best port facilities in the shortest possible time, and there was then to be an armoured thrust up the desert road to Cairo, combined with an air drop to gain the bridge over the Nile. Without pausing to mop up, columns were then to speed for Suez, Ismailia and Port Said. It was to be an eight-day wonder: two for the preliminary air operation, one to establish lodgement ashore, two for the build-up and defeat of the Egyptian counter thrust, and three more to reach the Canal. The agreed target date was September 15, which meant that the main body from England, due to land on day four, had to sail on the 8th. Cyprus, which had poor port facilities, a hostile population, and was within easy range of enemy aircraft, was to be used only for air and airborne operations. The sea assault, by commandos with tanks and some infantry in support, was to come from Malta and Algiers. There was a cover plan, aimed at persuading the Egyptians that the attack would come through Port Said.

There was no single overall commander, the idea being to switch this duty between the air, naval and land task force commanders for the phases in which their arms dominated. This arrangement was short-lived, for on August 11 General Keightley was appointed Supreme Commander: an exacting climax to eight strenuous years in which he had successively held command of Rhine Army during the Berlin crisis, of the Far East with war raging in Malaya and Korea, and of the Middle East when Egypt had to be evacuated and a rising was being staged in Cyprus. Unlike Stockwell, he did not discard his existing duties, which would in any case have been closely concerned with the mounting of the operation. He came to London to establish a headquarters, with Major-General R. G. S. Hobbs his Chief of Staff, and then returned to Cyprus, whence to keep touch by liaison officer with the farflung outstations of his command at London, Paris, Toulon, Malta and Algiers. As Deputy he had the lively and diminutive Vice-Admiral Pierre Barjot.

Inevitably the technique of planning an invasion lacked the well oiled proficiency of 1944, and furthermore there were obstacles to be overcome such as never bothered the wartime planners. Information was scarce as to the hold capacities of ships and even as to their availability, since they were chartered, not requisitioned; peacetime regulations, differing from port to port, imposed maddening restrictions on loading; and of course dockers and civilian staffs of mobilisation depots worked to trade union hours. Consequently officers and men of the 3rd Division had to endure many exasperations in the process of drawing stores for war, painting their vehicles sand-coloured, and despatching them, with groaning springs, first to one port and then to another in search of a berth, in some instances covering the length of Britain and back again. An overlapping of the two chains of command, of the operational through division and brigade and of the static through command and district, caused further confusion. It is hard to see how there could have been swift deployment on landing, and most vehicles, surprisingly, were loaded with no such thought in mind.

The tanks caused the greatest anxiety. The 1st R.T.R. were to have joined the assault group at Malta, but Movement Control chose to route the 6th ahead of them, and so meagre were the Army's resources that Pickford transporters had to be hired to take their Centurions from Tidworth to Plymouth. Although the trip took ten days, as ordained by union rules, the 6th were away by the end of August and would just have had time to marry up with the commandos. The 1st R.T.R. were not fully embarked until September 8 and they too could have caught their convoy with perhaps a minute to spare—but on the 4th came the first postponment. It was followed by another, and finally by orders to prepare a new plan, Musketeer Revise.

The truth appears to be that the user nations, most of all the United States, showed none of the enthusiasm for the use of force which Eden had anticipated from the initial reactions. By summoning the users, he made the invasion conditional on their backing, and as the prospect of obtaining it receded so did the strain on the military instrument increase, until on October 6 instructions arrived for the preparation of a winter plan, capable of implementation at ten days' notice. It had already been decreed that only the Canal was to be taken. This meant that Port Said had to be the first objective, as which it had originally been dismissed because of the difficulty of egress along the 26-mile causeway linking it with the mainland proper, the lack of berthing space, and the likelihood that the Egyptians would block the Canal as soon as the attack came in. Two different plans for mounting this difficult operation had been prepared, and now a third, more flexible one, had to be devised. The strain was beginning to tell on the men in the tunnel.

There was no release for the vehicles and stores crammed aboard the transports that creaked at their moorings in estuaries and bays around the British coast, nor for the reservists, of whom each battalion of the 3rd Division had upwards of 300. Both posed problems. There was much insidious pilfering and erosion aboard the ships, calling for bleak and dreary guard duties, an elaborate system of maintenance for the recharging of batteries, and in some cases complete reloading. As for the reservists, only by the highest standard of man management could they be kept content. This was achieved almost everywhere, the exceptions springing from too demanding a standard of discipline within a Guards battalion at Malta and from the difficulty to keep interest alive within specialised service units.

As October advanced noises of war grew louder along the frontiers of Israel. A reprisal raid launched by the latter against Jordan on October

10 caused Keightley to put troops and aircraft at readiness to go to Jordan's aid, but Jordan wanted no help from her old mentor and ally, and on October 25 General Hakim Amer of Egypt received a delirious welcome in Amman to be declared Commander-in-Chief of a unified command whose purpose was 'to launch the assault for Israel's destruction'. Next day, Friday the 26th, Eden told his Cabinet that he had information of Israel's intention to launch a spoiling attack and that in order to keep the Suez Canal out of the zone of the fighting he had decided, in conjunction with his French colleagues, to put in motion their plan for reoccupying it. This was Musketeer Revise, and on October 15 the commanders had been instructed to bring it from their files and prepare it in detail for mounting. No date had as yet been given them.

The plan placed heavy reliance on the air arm, first to neutralise the Egyptian Air Force and then to disrupt and demoralise the ground forces, aided by a verbal bombardment by a Psychological Warfare team from Cyprus; in some quarters there was high expectation that this last would be sufficient to 'make the wogs pack in'—although certainly neither Keightley nor Stockwell belonged to this school of thinking. The assault was then to be made by the 3rd Commando Brigade on Port Said and by French commandos on Port Fuad, the joint township on the east bank of the Canal, and parachute landings were to be made simultaneously, by a British battalion on the coastal Gamil Airport, just to the west of Port Said, and by a French one astride the causeway south of the town, controlling the exit. The remainder of the 16th Para Brigade, coming seaborne from Cyprus, were then to advance down the causeway to take Ismailia and Abu Sueir aerodrome and prepare for exploitation by the French AMX tanks. The 3rd Division were to come in for the final phase, the occupation of the whole Canal, and the 10th Armoured were to be held in reserve. The capture of Ismailia within three days of landing and of Suez within six was the aim.

The timetable hinged on the departure of the commandos from Algiers and Malta, six days' sailing being required by the ancient barks leaving the latter. By coincidence—so Stockwell testifies—a loading and signal exercise, named Boathook, had been planned to start at Malta on the Monday, October 29, and over the week-end the headquarter staffs left their dungeon, not knowing that it was for ever, and flew in to board the command ship, H.M.S. *Tyne*, which had been converted from use as a submarine depot ship. Stockwell himself arrived on the Saturday evening, having visited General Beaufre in Paris and sensed from him that more was afoot than he (Stockwell) realised. 'From the urgency he expressed for us,' Stockwell wrote ten years later,' it was clear that the

French knew what was cooking.' Stockwell had merely to guess, and as a result the pleasures of a Maltese Sunday were rudely disturbed for officers of the Commando Brigade and the 6th R.T.R. They were ordered to stast Boathook at once.

The Israelis struck as the sun was setting on the Monday evening. A parachute battalion landed at the Mitla Pass, 40 miles from Suez, and two mechanised columns crossed the frontier and began the charge across the Sinai Desert. A communiqué issued that night claimed that the paratroops were only 15 miles from the Canal, and this meant of course that it was already almost in the fighting zone. At 4.15 p.m. on the Tuesday, October 30, Eden announced the terms of 'urgent communications to Egypt and Israel'. They were to stop fighting and pull back to no nearer than 10 miles of the Canal on either side. Egypt was to allow an Anglo-French force to move temporarily into position along the Canal. Failing consent, 'British and French forces will intervene in whatever strength may be necessary to secure compliance'.

Eden knew, as he startled some and thrilled other Members of the House with this announcement, that the land forces could not intervene until November 6, for the embarkation at Malta was only then nearing completion, the most taxing preliminary being the waterproofing of the tanks of C Squadron, 6th R.T.R. Seventeen transports were loaded, or in many cases overloaded, and they cast off that night, October 30. Aboard them were the 3rd Commando Brigade—less 45 Commando— and their comrades in support, the 6th R.T.R., the anti-tank platoons of the 1st Somerset Light Infantry and the 1st Royal Berkshire, of 3 Brigade at Malta, and the transport of a battalion of 3 Division, the 1st Queen's Own Royal West Kent, who in the original plan were to have accompanied the commandos in the assault on Alexandria but were now preparing for a ceremonial parade at Maidstone and were not due to embark with 3 Division until November 2. As for 45 Commando, they were to go in by helicopter and were still considering plans and practising offloading drills. Not until the late afternoon of Saturday, November 3, were they under way in two carriers, *Ocean* and *Theseus*, both capable of 24 knots.

Nasser's reply to Eden's 'urgent communication' was announced early next morning, Wednesday the 31st, and it was an uncompromising refusal. The world waited for hostilities to open, but there were two reasons why they did not do so just yet: the air operations had all along been geared to start at night, when most confusion could be caused, and fresh evidence was at hand of the danger of running risks. It had been obtained by the crew of a Canberra bomber that at dawn on the Tuesday was carrying out a photographic reconnaissance of the Egyptian coast at great height. It had been intercepted and badly damaged by Mig fighters with skill that belied their Egyptian insignia. Khrushchev, the Russian leader, had given warning in September that 'if there is an attack on Egypt there will be volunteers'—they could be drawn from the legion of Russian instructors already in Egypt. If this was a sample of their capability, Keightley's men might have a tough task ahead of them.

There was tense activity in Cyprus. Three anti-aircraft regiments, who had come in August, took up action stations, and alerted by the message, 'A state of war with Egypt exists', all units turned eyes to the sky. Lorries climbed into the mountains to bring the grimy men of the 16th Para Brigade back from operations against Eoka, while their aircraft received urgent recall from flying supplies to Vienna for the benefit of Hungarians fighting for freedom. At their speedily constructed aerodrome at Tymbou hardy French paras, who had so often given display of their skill, eagerly made preparations for the real thing, and as the light faded at Nicosia on this Wednesday evening Canberra bombers climbed into the sky to send out the message that at last fantasy had become truth, the war against the despised Egyptian had really begun. They were joined by Valiants from Malta.

Warning of the approach of the bombers was broadcast to Egypt so that the people could take cover, but no fighters came up to intercept and the only anti-aircraft shells seen burst far away. The bombs fell on two aerodromes in the outskirts of Cairo, a third gaining last minute reprieve to avoid danger to a column of American refugees. Leaflets were also dropped, compiled in Cyprus by the Psychological Warfare team. 'We are obliged to bomb you wherever you are,' they untruthfully told the Egyptians, for only those on military establishments were in danger. 'You have committed a sin . . . this is, you have placed your confidence in Abdul Nasser.'

At daybreak next morning the air assault opened in earnest. Every airfield in Egypt was struck by a continual stream of lead and explosive from four hundred fighters and bombers, British and French, land-based and carrier-borne. It was a grand example of how to achieve the first requirement for a successful invasion, the destruction of the enemy air force, and it gained complete success, almost without loss. Yet it had to last five days before the assault was due to go in, with the effort turning to the disruption of troop movement. Every material blow suffered by Nasser could be turned to psychological gain; a barrage of words fell on the British and French Governments from all over the world. In London the House of Commons was in uproar and at New York the United Nations, having passed a resolution calling on all sides to desist, were considering means of raising their own special peacekeeping force. Eden told the House that he would be delighted to hand over to it. 'But police action there must be to separate the combatants.' The plan was for military action, and as the soldiers were discovering, the word 'police' merely implied restraint on fire support.

Nasser had by now ordered all troops that could be extricated from Sinai to fall back on Cairo, and he had also ordered the blocking of the Canal, which began on Thursday night and made substantial increase on every subsequent night. The need to advance the date of the landing was as obvious as urgent, but this was a naval matter, regulated by movement tables forming a book as large as a telephone directory and based on the knowledge that the transports were old, heavily laden, and liable to encounter sudden storms. The navy was not to be bustled. The ships from Malta chugged on at a steady 6 knots, and as the loading of follow-up and support units began at Cyprus, by lighter off Limassol and by derrick at the old and confined port of Famagusta, the difficulty of eking acceleration out of inadequate facilities became all too obvious.

Instructions from London were still concerned with the avoidance of risk, in particular the risk to civilian life and property, to preserve which a veto was placed on many tempting targets, Cairo radio station among them. The French, on the other hand, thought delay the greatest risk, and while Keightley was peppered with signals from London restraining his bombing offensive, he was under constant agitation from his Deputy, Admiral Barjot, for daring action by the paratroops, all of whom, French and British, came under command of that restless warhorse, General Massu, commander of the 10th Aéroportée. Inaction was humiliating when the Israelis had already put the enemy to rout and could have reached the Canal on the Friday, November 2, if they had not agreed to halt 10 miles short as required. Yet the Egyptians still had a substantial force of tanks intact, including some Joseph Stalins, on which a close watch was kept, and some T.34s both in Port Said and covering the exits from the causeway 26 miles further south. If they had Russian 'volunteers' inside them, they could make life perilous for the paratroops, and the further along the Canal they were landed the more fleeting would be the air support they could expect. Barjot's earlier projects were courteously turned down.

However, the pressure for action became more compelling, and at 4 a.m. on the Sunday morning, November 4, a plane screeched down at Akrotiri aerodrome, and out of it stepped Mr. Antony Head, newly promoted to Defence Minister after five years at the War Office, and the C.I.G.S., General Templer. Air reports showed that even the T.34 tanks from Port Said were now on their way back to Cairo, leaving a garrison there that was known to include a fresh brigade, part regular, part National Guard, and still to have some tanks or self-propelled guns. It was agreed that the paratroops should go in on the Monday, a day ahead of the seaborne landing. They were to seal off the town of Port Said—thus trapping the garrison, as the police had been trapped at the Bureau Sanitaire, Ismailia. The British 3rd Parachute Battalion were to take Gamil airport, 2 miles west of Port Said, and a French battalion, of the 2nd Colonial Regiment, were to cut the causeway immediately south of the town and seize the water works. A second battalion of the Colonial were to be flown in on the return of the aircraft and dropped on Port Fuad.

Brigadier M. A. H. Butler, of the 16th Para, was to take command of the operation, instead of going in by sea with the remainder of his brigade, and he had now to disembark his tactical headquarters, adding complications to loading operations that were lagging behind schedule. No other adjustment was made to the agreed plan of assault, except that the 3rd Para, according to Keightley's despatch 'was to advance into the town and occupy it if resistance was slight but if unable to do so it would wait for the seaborne assault on the following day'. It seems strange that nothing more was done to press home the capture of an airfield with a runway almost a mile long. The 3rd Brigade in Malta were within comfortable flying distance, and two regiments of French paratroops were being left behind in Cyprus, longing for action, while 45 Commando, aboard their carriers, could have been within range of helicopter by midday and were in fact within view of Port Said before nightfall (on the 5th). Here were three means of speeding the fall of Port Said and of obviating the bombardment for the sea assault, but none was attempted. There had been so many changes of plan that the British commanders appear to have developed inbuilt resistance to more.

After much toil, exasperation and confusion, the loading at Famagusta and Limassol was completed and the ships sailed in the evening gloaming of this busy Sunday, November 4. Stockwell had with him in *Tyne* the naval and air task force commanders, Vice-Admiral D. F. Durnford-Slater and Air Marshal D. H. F. Barnett, while General Beaufre had his own command ship, *Gustave Zede*. The Supreme Commander remained in Cyprus. Other ships contained two battalions of the 16th Para Brigade, the 33rd Para Field Regiment less a battery, the 9th Independent Para Field Squadron, most of the 37th Field Engineer Regiment, which had been removed from its work in Cyprus and issued with some belatedly ordered bridging equipment, a port operating company full of hardened reservists of the Royal Engineers and Royal Pioneer Corps, medical units, supply units, provost units, and many smaller adjuncts of the great headquarters, including the vanguard of a Civil Affairs department originally designed for the administration of the whole of Egypt. Surrounded by a powerful naval escort topped by the French battleship, *Jean Bart*, the convoy linked up with its fellows from Malta and Algiers. A fourth was approaching the straits of Gibraltar, consisting of speedy troopships with on board the 3rd Division, less their newly joined brigade and the last to occupy Egypt, the 1st Guards; a day's sailing ahead of them, but travelling more slowly, were the transports carrying the divisional vehicles and the 1st R.T.R. Back in England two more armoured regiments were in process of being earmarked to join the expedition. It had been finally established that the 10th Armoured could not be made available for political reasons and Keightley had been offered the 3rd Brigade instead. After discussing the matter with Stockwell he had replied that he had sufficient infantry but wanted more armour as a reserve. Such was the tempo of military expectation.

The 3rd Para had meanwhile stacked their equipment on their planes at Nicosia and were attempting to get some sleep before rising for breakfast at 2 a.m. If sleep was elusive, at least they had fewer disturbances than the men at sea. The first one came at around 8 p.m., when the lights went out and there was urgent clanging of the action-station bells. It proved not to be Russian submarines, but a brush with the American Sixth Fleet, and soon the men were back on the troop decks and laughing at the message that had been sent to the Americans and relayed down to them: 'Why don't you come and join us?' Later that night they listened to a political broadcast by Mr. Gaitskell, Leader of the Opposition, in which he called on Parliament to repudiate the policy that had made the Prime Minister 'utterly, utterly discredited in the eyes of the world'. This indeed was most extraordinary fare for troops about to go into battle, yet all accounts agree that if it had any effect on morale it was to strengthen it, for the men were pleased that the months of frustrated waiting were over and were angry at this attempt to split the nation when they were about to go into action.

A message reaching General Keightley that night showed that even at this hour the Government were fussing and uncertain. The plan to despatch the United Nations' force was crystallising, and the Cabinet had met to consider whether or not to leave the whole task to it. Keightley was required to state how much notice he would need to postpone the assault. He replied that he must know by 1 a.m. (11 in London) which in fact was four hours before the paratroops were due to take off. The hour arrived without further word from London. The plan was firm at last.

A ball of fire blazing out at sea heralded the return of the British on Guy Fawkes' Day, Monday, November 5. It had been dropped by a Canberra bomber as guide for the transport planes, eighteen Valettas and fourteen Hastings, flying towards the Egyptian coast in pairs at low altitude. It was about 7 a.m. The sky was blue and the sun was bright.

The objective, Gamil airport, lay on a strip of land half a mile wide which tapered to less than a quarter nearer Port Said. It was bordered on the north by the gleaming Mediterranean and on the south by the murky Lake El Manzala, on the edge of which the feluccas could be seen sailing. Weapon pits, two pill boxes, and gun emplacements had been identified around the runway and on features on the 2-mile strip between it and the town, and there was thought to be a battalion group in occupation of them. It was a direct drop on known enemy defences, a thing eschewed as too hazardous during the wartime operations of the Parachute Regiment.

Seahawk fighters of the Royal Navy swooped down and sent their rockets hurtling at the enemy's defences and at the airport control tower, which was soon ablaze, while Hunters of the R.A.F. strafed anti-aircraft guns nearer Port Said. The transport planes lumbered in from west to east, their pilots trying to shield their eyes from dazzlement by the sun and at the same time hold their craft steady against shudders from airburst shells. Out streamed their loads, jerking to apparent stagnation as their parachutes took the strain. For the honoured men of the 3rd Para and their supporting detachments there was a violent rush of air, a tug, the sound of tearing as the parachute opened, and then a sublime silence, which was rudely shattered by a crackle that shook the very sky, as a myriad of bullets crashed the sound barrier. The men could see the Egyptians firing at them, but could not fire back as they made their agonisingly slow journey to the ground. Once there they had a desperate struggle to free themselves from their parachutes, grab weapons from containers, and join up in 'ad hoc' groups to attack the nearest post. Some landed right among the enemy. One paratrooper heard a cry of, 'No, Johnny, no, Johnny, no!' as he floated towards a trench, on which he first hurled his container and then lashed out with boots and jack knife as he followed. The Egyptians ran from here, and from many another post too, as the automatic fire and burst of grenade brought down upon them mounted in volume. The road to Port Said was soon dotted with their diminishing forms.

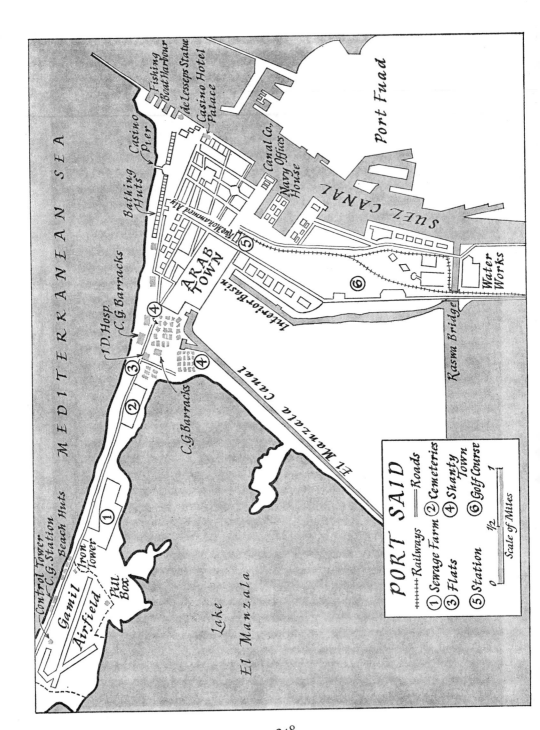

PORT SAID

MEDITERRANEAN SEA

Port Fuad

SUEZ CANAL

Control Tower
C.G. Station
Gamil Beach Huts
Airfield
Iron Tower
Pill Box

I.D. Hosp.
C.G. Barracks

C.G. Barracks

Bathing Huts
Casino Pier

Fishing Boat Harbour
The Lesseps Statue
Casino Hotel
Palace

Canal Co.
Offices
Navy House

Rue Mohammed Ali

ARAB TOWN

Interior Basin

El Manzala Canal

Lake El Manzala

Raswa Bridge

Water Works

PORT SAID

+++++ Railways ———— Roads
① Sewage Farm ② Cemeteries
③ Flats ④ Shanty Town
⑤ Station ⑥ Golf Course

0 ½ 1
Scale of Miles

248

It was on the western extremities, on the side away from the town, that the resistance was strongest. This was A Company's objective, and they encountered hot fire from one of the two pill boxes, which caused some breathless dashes across the expanse of sand next the concrete runway. A rocket launcher was brought into action, after a skilful approach covered by fire from a flank, and blasted the machine-gunner to extinction with a direct hit through a slit.

Of the 668 who landed, together with seven jeeps and six 106-mm. recoilless anti-tank guns, the only one killed as yet had been blown on to the beach coming down and had exploded a mine; two landed in the sea but escaped drowning. But while the men were still ridding the airfield of its last defenders or looking around for their comrades, high velocity shells and mortar bombs shrieked and crashed among them, passing the message that so far from being over the danger had only just begun. Some were hit, and others escaped because of the boggy state of the ground, which much restricted blast. Brigadier Butler, a man with a trim and spritely figure and the nickname of 'Tubby', had set up his headquarters in the reception centre, and its walls, bearing tatty posters of welcome to Egypt, were pierced at regular intervals by solid shot from a self-propelled gun. A Seahawk soon put an end to that nuisance, setting the pattern for a day's service that was to make the paras' hearts overflow with gratitude, but there was another aggravation that could not be so easily overcome. Butler's rear link wireless set, a number 52, was a casualty of the descent, and so too were the spare parts dropped as insurance. This left him with an old 19-set that could make only sporadic and distorted communication with *Tyne*.

Within half an hour of landing the 3rd Para had cleared the airfield, grouped themselves in tactical order, and were fast digging in, with A Company holding the west side, B clearing some houses by the coast road as a prelude to advancing eastwards, and C in reserve. Three 3-inch mortars had come into action from pits still being excavated and the anti-tank guns were in position to fire. A troop of the 9th Squadron, R.E. had begun the search for mines on runway and beach, and around Battalion H.Q. at the reception building a command party of the 33rd Field Regiment were trying vainly to make link with the guns of a destroyer, the 13th Air Contact Team were having more success with a link to pilots, a detachment of the 23rd Para Field Ambulance were already treating wounded, both British and Egyptian, and members of the 63rd Company, R.A.S.C. were assembling supplies and preparing to receive more. Lieutenant-Colonel Crook, large and calm, now ordered the advance on Port Said to begin.

Fifteen minutes after the arrival of the planes with the British paratroops, aircraft carrying their French colleagues of the 2nd Colonial Regiment flew in from the north-east and circled right-handed to approach Port Said from the south, flying over the causeway at an altitude 100 feet lower than that permitted for training drops. The men had had much more practice at dropping than the British and better equipment, too; they needed all their skill, for the causeway was only 150 yards wide, including the two roads, railway, and the Sweetwater Canal. They came down under cover of smoke, dropped by canister, and with weapons in hand as they landed, they went straight into a brisk battle, with the enemy all round them. They had three objectives of great importance: the waterworks, which was Port Said's most southerly building, and two bridges over a wide canal just to the north of it, one being a swing bridge carrying Treaty road and railway, the other a pontoon bridge linking the Canal road.

Two small parties of British paratroopers dropped with them, of which one was of Royal Engineers charged with the task of stripping the bridges of demolition material. Having seen the pontoon bridge disintegrate before the French gained it, they joined the fight for the other, more important bridge, and their officer, Captain Owen, played a key part with his Sterling automatic in enabling the French to capture it intact after a stiff little fight. The detonators for its destruction were found in a shed nearby. The waterworks was also captured undamaged, after a brisk fire fight, and there was nothing more for these tough Frenchmen to do but to hold on to their possessions and bar the route into and out of Port Said. They had suffered a dozen casualties.

The other British party was from the Guards Parachute Company, nine strong under Captain de Klee. Their task was to reconnoitre southwards along the causeway. Leaving two behind wounded, de Klee marched 10 kilometres with the remainder and had then to stop because this was where the bomb-line ran. He returned to report that he had seen no one.

B Company, 3rd Para had meanwhile begun the advance on Port Said, wearing their camouflage smocks and nozzle-shaped helmets. The objective, standing on a slight prominence, was a group of buildings and concrete emplacements that formed a sewage farm half a mile beyond the airfield's end, and the approach was across boggy ground through reeds. There was some shelling and mortar fire, and the company commander, Major Stevens, who had previously been hit in the hand, was hit in the leg. An anti-tank gun, thought at first to be a tank, also caused trouble, until knocked out by one of the paras' anti-tank guns. At this the enemy abandoned the farm, although it was of daunting defensive potential, and there was no further trouble until the leading platoon debouched on the far side, having climbed across some irrigation ditches. Now they met an inaccurate hail of bullets from a cemetery, 600 yards away, where many Egyptian soldiers were seen prancing around, and mortar bombs and high velocity shells also crashed down, rather less inaccurately. The platoon commander decided to pull his men back, and before they had gone far in zoomed two French fighters and spattered bullets all round them. There was a rush for some concrete sewage troughs, which previously (as the platoon commander put it) 'had seemed the last word in nauseating filth', but now afforded every man protection through ten minutes of terror.

The enactment of this miracle of survival caused delay, and a co-ordinated attack on the cemetery, which was a far flung maze of Christian, Jewish, and Moslem tomb stones, could not be delivered until 12.30. It was carried out by C Company, under cover of a devastating strike by the Seahawks, and the men moved with such gusto that they silenced the Egyptian fire without loss to themselves and drove out a company that left thirty dead sprawled among the gravestones. An arsenal of weapons, some crumpled, others usable, fell into the paras' hands, including three Russian self-propelled guns, two 3.7-inch anti-aircraft guns, mortars, machine-guns and a bren carrier.

This success called for swift exploitation, and two ways of achieving it had already been demonstrated. At 11.30 the first helicopters had come in from the three air support carriers, which were under separate command from the two others that were steaming into range with 45 Commando. They brought gifts of cigarettes and beer and carried away British casualties, leaving the 23rd Field Ambulance to concentrate on the Egyptian wounded. While the paratroopers waved their thanks to the naval pilots, Vice-Admiral Power, the carrier strike force commander, was mustering his marines, at a strength of more than a company, to send them to Butler's aid. He called *Tyne* by radio to ask if they would be acceptable and was told that Butler was confident that he could handle the situation. While this was true, it was also true that he would willingly have used them to free A Company from defensive duties and thus speed the advance. Soon afterwards a Dakota landed on Gamil's runway, bringing a liaison officer from Admiral Barjot, come to enquire how the battle was going and to take some wounded away. It could easily have brought more troops.

Reinforcements did arrive at 3.15 p.m. They parachuted down from planes making their second trip, some of them bearing scars from anti-aircraft fire incurred in the first. They consisted of the residue of the 3rd Para—a mere fifty-six men—together with more, much-needed ammunition, blankets, and stores. The French Nord-Atlases also returned. They brought another battalion of the Colonial Regiment, 460 men strong, and dropped them on the outskirts of Port Fuad, from which they gained full possession of the town by nightfall with a fine display of *élan* and vigorous fire power.

Port Said was ripe for similar treatment. Beyond the cemetery C Company, 3rd Para were met with fire from a coastguard barrack building and a nearby block of flats, both from machine-guns and a self-propelled gun. Again the Seahawks were brought in; the self-propelled gun was silenced and the barracks turned to a smouldering heap. It was not permissible to give the block of flats such rough treatment, and the situation was further complicated by the first indications that the Egyptian soldiers were discarding their uniform in favour of galabiyas. However, C Company, as Crook has stated, could easily have made an attack on these buildings, which formed the final objective allotted the battalion in the original plan, and A Company, having been relieved of their protective duties on the west flank by the newly dropped re-inforcements, could have gone on to secure the docks for the slowly approaching ships. All that was needed was urgent direction from above. This was lacking, and instead of attacking buildings that would have to be evacuated for next morning's bombardment, Crook obtained Butler's permission to withdraw from the cemetery, which was uncomfortably overlooked, back to the unsalubrious, mosquito infested sewage farm. He cannot be blamed for not risking further casualties when it appeared to be ordained that the battle should run its predetermined course. They already amounted to thirty.

Reports from Europeans, many of whom took refuge in the Italian Consulate, tell of the defeatism that overcame the Egyptians when the first landings were made. But they are a mercurial people, as easily elated as depressed, and under the stimulus of some skilful propaganda initiated by the secret police, combined with a free-for-all issue of arms, a mood of exuberant defiance was germinated from the apparent repulse of the advance from Gamil. The military commander, however, had already decided that the situation was hopeless, and soon after the second fly-in he sent a message to the French at the waterworks asking for a cease-fire. News of its arrival reached Butler just as he was stepping into a helicopter to visit the waterworks after agreeing to the withdrawal of the 3rd Para back to the sewage farm. Having banned his own troops from firing, except in self-defence, and signalled *Tyne* for instructions, he duly visited the French para commander, Colonel Chateau-Jobert, and after receiving agreement on the terms he notified the Egyptian command, over the civil telephone system, that he was willing to receive a delegation at the waterworks.

It arrived in two large American cars, bedecked with white flags, soon after dark. A stiff meeting took place between Butler and Chateau-Jobert on the one side and on the other the Commanding General in person, El Moguy, and various officers, one of whom turned out to be the Chief of Special Police, Colonel Rouchdi. Butler's terms were that the Egyptians should lay down their arms and march to two concentration areas. El Moguy seemed inclined to accept, but Rouchdi intervened with some defiant talk, brushing his general aside. The latter could do no more than ask time to consider his reply and he despondently took his delegation away, with the provisional cease-fire still in force.

The reply came over the telephone around 10.30 p.m. and was a dismal negative, delivered by El Moguy. A line to Cairo was unfortunately still intact, and over it President Nasser had ordered the garrison to fight to the last, adding as incentive the news that Russia had intervened and was that night smashing London and Paris with atom bombs. Broadcast vans at once toured the streets of Port Said, passing on this joyful news to the people together with a further hand-out of weapons, most of them still encased in packing grease. Butler's 19-set, always at its least penetrative after dark, managed with difficulty to pass El Moguy's refusal on to *Tyne*.

The Russian bombing amounted to no more than a threatening note, which they broadcast to the world before delivery to the British and French Governments. It did not stop the invasion fleet from plodding on to its destination, but it may have had its influence on the despatch of orders that first reduced the weight of the bombardment and then cancelled it altogether. There was exasperation on board *Tyne* and her subordinate ships. Hours of work had gone into the preparation of the fire plan, and now it had to be scrapped and a substitute hastily improvised, which was termed 'naval gunfire support' and naturally lacked the sting of the original but at least would give the troops some cover in their assault across the open beaches. The A/Q staff meanwhile were busily drawing up a document of surrender.

The first assault wave consisted of fifteen elderly amphibians named Buffaloes. They were driven by men of the 7th R.T.R. and each contained thirty tight-packed men, in most cases a half-troop, either of 40 or 42 Commando or of a Royal Artillery fire control team in link with naval guns. They debouched from the transport ships $2\frac{1}{2}$ miles out at sea, by the flooding of their holds, and set off landwards with only their rims visible above the waterline. Dawn had broken in mist, but now the sun was coming through and the guns of destroyers and frigates (but not of cruisers as originally planned) were shelling beach huts and houses by the sea front just to the right of the harbour entrance and de Lesseps' statue. Soon the beach huts were ablaze, providing an effective smoke screen both for the soldiers running out of them and the oncoming amphibians. Fighters took over the task of covering fire as the craft drew closer to the beach, zooming down to rip the huts 200 yards ahead of them, while to the right, about a mile distant, the machine-guns of Crook's paratroopers stuttered.

The square hulks of the Buffaloes rose out of the water and roared up the beach at close on 20 m.p.h., gaining extra speed from the absence of the armour plating that should have been, but was not, provided for them. With brens blazing from them to silence machine-gunners on either flank, they careered past the blazing huts, where ammunition was exploding amid newly abandoned equipment and accoutrements, and jerked to a halt after slewing round against the doors of various buildings by the sea front. The men jumped out at commando speed, their green berets bobbing, and quickly forced an entry into the Casino Palace Hotel on the left, a block of flats further right, and a motley assortment of well-to-do houses in between. The reserve troops came by assault craft and lost two or three men from machine-gun fire as they ran across the beach: the only casualties of the landing. The Centurions of C Squadron, 6th R.T.R. soon followed, waddling ashore through the 4 feet of water in which their craft had run aground. Having rid themselves of their waterproof clothing, to do which crewmen had to get out, they took up fire positions covering the streets.

The men of 40 Commando on the left had the task of clearing the harbour and 42 on the right that of advancing through the town to seize the gas works and power station and to join up with the French at the waterworks. It rapidly became clear that they were confronted with a task of daunting complexity, demanding as much forbearance as courage. Darting figures were to be seen up every alleyway and through every window. Some belonged to women, old and young, many to children, terrified or belligerent, and many more to men in night shirts who might or might not be soldiers in disguise; apart from the occasional black uniform of a policeman, nothing but civilian garb, native more often than European, was glimpsed. Bullets were cracking and fizzing from every angle, singly and in bursts, and only when the firer could be seen was it permissible to shoot back. Fever had smitten the Egyptians, turning some to panic, others to daring beyond the point of foolhardiness. With useful aid from snipers dropped off at vantage points, the commandos sorted them out house by house, bringing fury down on the desperadoes and succour to the wounded and petrified. The Centurions gave them diligent support. They fired belt after belt from their Brownings at located strong points, put down smoke canisters to cover street crossings, and shepherded men across open spaces by use of their hulks.

Initially, 40 Commando made the swifter progress. They captured the main police station under the shelter of a tank and advanced up the road flanking the harbour towards the original bone of contention, the Canal Company's palatial office. The 42nd met tough opposition in the main governorate building, from which a great number of men were ejected without any slackening of the resistance inside. The brigade commander, Bragadier R. W. Madoc, decided to bring in 45 Commando to start the task of clearing the streets in between the axis of the 40th and 42nd. They taxied in with a mighty roar made by their assorted fleet of twenty-two helicopters and landed near the Casino Palace; a more daring landing on the golf course had been considered, but in the end the helicopters merely acted as substitutes for non-existent assault craft. Their commanding officer, Lieutenant-Colonel Tailyour, had been diverted by the smoke of battle and had escaped hit from many bullets when he landed on a sports stadium not yet captured, but was less lucky when a British naval plane, misdirected by control, swept down on his men soon after they had begun their task of house clearing. He was one of nineteen casualties it inflicted.

There were also a few losses to 42 Commando from this strike but they had no complaints about a very accurate one that smote the troublesome governorate building and enabled them to gain possession of it. This was about 9 a.m., and Lieutenant-Colonel Norcock, commanding, now re-embarked two troops in the Buffaloes and with tank escort ahead and behind led them full tilt up the rue Mohammed Aly, a spacious boulevard flanked by high houses. There was a tremendous shindy as the Egyptians opened up from windows and side roads, at some points with women and children all round them, and the tanks blazed back with their Brownings and the Commandos with brens from the tops of their tin-sided conveyances. Two anti-tank guns were blasted out by the tanks and more were overrun as they emerged into more open territory at the end of the thoroughfare. The Buffaloes followed, with some dead and wounded inside them, a sergeant of the 7th R.T.R. driving team being among the former. The gas works were captured, and there was then a fight near the prison, from which the inmates had been let loose. Egyptian troops were seen here, in considerable numbers, but were soon dispersed by an air strike. The route was clear now past the golf course through to the French at the waterworks, and it was flanked by a massive pall of black smoke. Egyptian self-propelled guns had made an attempt to break out along the causeway, and in knocking them out the aircraft had also hit and set light to an oil tank.

Another great cloud of smoke was rising from the shanty town on the west side of Port Said, where C Company, 3rd Para had resumed their advance. A self-propelled gun had been spotted here and engaged by a destroyer, which had set fire to the shacks that housed the overspill from the adjacent Arab quarter. C Company had subsequently gained the block of flats and the coastguard barracks without great difficulty, but a patrol probing forward towards a hospital came under machine-gun and mortar fire and had four men hit, including its officer and sergeant. The fire came from the Arab quarter, and while the paras brought up an anti-tank gun to quieten it, Captain McElliott, of the field ambulance, made a cool and daring evacuation of the wounded. The paras consolidated in the buildings they held and kept close watch over the Arab quarter and the still burning shanty town. They could see refugees streaming away along a bund across Lake El Manzala, and although many were recognisable as soldiers, they let them go through fear of hitting others.

Conscious of the danger of air attack, Admiral Durnford-Slater kept his ships far out at sea while a reconnaissance was made of the harbour entrance, headed by minesweepers carrying machine-gunners of the 3rd Grenadier Guards, from Malta, for their protection. Although the harbour was littered with the masts of ships sunk to cause obstruction, the entrance had not been blocked and it was possible to bring the first transports into the fishing harbour, just inside the harbour wall, without great delay. Engineering equipment and the remainder of the 6th R.T.R. headed the list for unloading, and once a wall had been demolished to give them egress the tanks began to trundle to their assembly area just inside the town. They came in four tank landing ships that could be berthed two at a time.

By 10 a.m. the Italian Consulate was within the Commandos' gains, and an officer of the 6th R.T.R. was hailed and welcomed inside to learn from the Consul, Count Mareri, that the Governor of Port Said was eager to arrange a cease-fire. A message was passed to *Tyne* and a rendezvous made: 11 a.m. at the Consulate. Stockwell set out in the Admiral's launch, accompanied by the Admiral himself, Air Marshal Barnett, and Brigadier Lacey, who was armed with the document of surrender he had spent the night preparing. The launch chugged sedately past the forlorn mastheads by the harbour entrance and on towards the Canal Company building, which stood out white and magnificent against the black backcloth of smoke billowing from the oil tanks beyond. Bullets were flying around, to the obvious alarm of all except the General and the Admiral. One crashed into the woodwork behind Stockwell a hair's breadth from his ear without producing a flicker. However, Durnford-Slater grasped its message. 'I don't think they're quite ready for us, General,' he observed and altered course for the Casino quay. Having landed there, Stockwell went to the Italian Consulate, but no further contact with the Governor could be made. The battle went on.

The Canal Company Office was taken by 40 Commando, but they ran into heavy fire from the warehouses between it and what had been Navy House at the other side of the next berthing bay. The 20-pounders of the Centurions were brought into use and let loose their shells for ten minutes; even then the 40th lost two officers killed and three marines wounded before they were inside the warehouses. It was slow plugging along this route by the harbour, and to reach the French at the water-works A Squadron, 6th R.T.R. made a detour round the station to come in along the road first penetrated by 42 Commando. The leading troop became the third victim of attack by supposedly friendly aircraft, and although only one human casualty was suffered, the tanks became badly bogged in trying to take evasive action. A second troop tried the golf course and also got bogged, but a third managed to reach the water-works, and Stockwell gave permission for it to advance down the causeway as far as El Tina, 10 miles on. Setting off at around 4 p.m. and mounting some Algerian paratroops as escort, the tanks made the journey unopposed, passing *en route*, though without noticing them, the party of guardsmen parachutists who had again set out southwards and had this time rounded up a motley of people on the move, most carrying arms beneath their galabiyas and lavish with offers of servitude for the sparing of their lives.

Brigadier Butler meanwhile was champing for the release of his seaborne troops who were to lead the advance down the causeway. They were to have disembarked at a berth beyond Navy House, but with the latter still held by the enemy it was inaccessible. Their ships therefore had to await berthing space at the fishing harbour. The Guards Para Company and a battery of the 33rd Field were disembarked with their vehicles during the afternoon, but the sun was going down by the time the 2nd Para began to file off their steamer and there was now thick congestion around the harbour exits, with support vehicles for the commandos' attack on Navy House caught up with those trying to join the follow through. Butler's D.A.A. & Q.M.G.—Major Farrar-Hockley of Gloucester Hill fame—was meanwhile bustling round the town commandeering every vehicle he could to provide a lift for 2nd Para.

The Egyptians in Navy House were cornered and, as had happened before in such a situation, they fought desperately. 40 Commando called for an air strike, by naval aircraft on the Navy's old home, and it went in at around 5.45, just as darkness was falling, with superb accuracy. Weird, wild figures were seen to be blasted out window by window, caught grotesquely by the light of the inevitable flames that gushed forth from the adjacent warehouse. Rather than make one more attack at the end of this long, long day, the 40th sealed the area off and next morning recovered thirty dead and twenty prisoners from the battered building. The 2nd Para began to filter through in section groups, uncertain whether the bangs that periodically rang out were caused by enemy fire or by ignition from one of the blazes that cast their flickering light on the ghostly forms of roaming cattle and horses, corpses, and the distorted barrels of crumpled self-propelled guns.

At 6 Stockwell gave out orders for the next day's operations: the 16th Para were to break out from the causeway and capture Abu Sueir aerodrome, and General Massu, who had been much exasperated on landing at Fuad by the lack of anyone to fight, was to launch a combined airborne and waterborne assault on Ismailia. Having arranged all necessary details, Stockwell looked round for a lift back to *Tyne*, since the Admiral had returned in his launch. A Royal Marine coxswain offered his assault landing craft with all the eagerness of a cabby in search of a fare, and Stockwell set off with Lacey, his G.S.O. 2 Major Worsley, and his A.D.C. Having taken a short cut by crashing over the breakwater, the craft ran into a heavy sea and suffered damage to its pumps and steering gear. It was pitch dark, and there was no means of finding *Tyne*, which was 4 miles out, other than by hope of response to the message, 'S.O.S. G.O.C.,' flashed on an Aldis lamp by Worsley, straining his knowledge of Morse. After being lost and buffeted for a horribly long time and having decided to return to Port Said, they suddenly saw a light above them and heard a miraculous voice calling, 'This is *Tyne*.' Hoisted aboard, they were confronted by an unamused Durnford-Slater, who had received a message telling him to expect the Russians to intervene with force. Very soon afterwards Brigadier Darling appeared with another one, ordering a cease-fire as from midnight, G.M.T. Stockwell was cold, wet and weary, and yet exhilarated by having seen his men fight so splendidly and successfully in their very difficult battle of the streets. In his own words, 'It was difficult at that moment for me to take in the words, let alone grasp the full impact of that brief signal.'

The time must have been around 7.15, which was 5.15 in England and 5.15 by the watches of the invasion force, since they had all been retarded to G.M.T., as if to emphasise the tight control exerted from

London and to put a touch of fantasy to the advent of dawn and dusk. The signal reached Keightley's headquarters at 5 p.m., G.M.T., and it caused as much amazement there as when it arrived at *Tyne*. No one had imagined that a time limit would suddenly be imposed, although warning could have been sent at 9.45 that morning, when the Cabinet met to discuss the matter. In the event Keightley received warning about an hour ahead of the world, for it was soon after 6 that Eden broke the news to the House of Commons.

Butler probably suffered the heaviest shock of all. He had for two days been in the forefront of complicated and difficult operations and was issuing orders at the waterworks for the advance that would pluck the fruits of victory when the message arrived that 'Sunray' wanted him on the wireless set. He sent someone else at first and had to be summoned again to hear the dire news. He agreed with Stockwell that the only feasible objective within the time limit was the railway halt at El Cap, where there is a bulge in the causeway, making it more suitable for defence. This was 8 miles ahead of the troop of tanks at El Tina and 5 short of the end of the causeway.

A patrol could, it seems certain, have been sitting on the end of the causeway for the past twenty-four hours, and the failure to put one there, which appears to have caused no retrospective blushes, affords in its way a fitting epitome of the entire operation. It is made all the stranger by the haunting influence the causeway had on planning, based on fear of the blocking power it offered to a single Egyptian gun or section of men, and it was to locate the nearest blockage that the party of Guards' parachutists were dropped with the French. Although restricted by the self-imposed limitation of the bomb-line, they obtained revealing information, which they had to come back to deliver and of which no advantage was taken. When the tanks arrived they were ordered to go no further than halfway down the causeway, accompanied though they were by a protective party of infantry. This was well in keeping with the policy, enunciated at highest level from the very start, that risk must be eschewed, and its corollary was the assumption that the Egyptians were as formidable fighters as the Russians, if not of the Germans in their prime.

There were still six hours left before the cease-fire when news of it reached Butler. If the order full steam ahead had now been given to the tanks at El Tina, they might have reached Ismailia, which was 38 miles distant, and men of the Guards Para Company could swiftly have joined them in vehicles they had brought, after a skirmish or two, through Port Said. But again overwhelming force had to be assembled, and not until 11.20 G.M.T. did the advance from El Tina begin, when after being badly held up by a road obstruction the remainder of A Squadron, 6th R.T.R. arrived with the 2nd Para, who were riding in the comical assortment of trade vehicles acquired by Farrar-Hockley. Now at last the Centurions could show their paces, and with two troops forward, just visible to each other on Canal and Treaty roads, they hummed along at 20 m.p.h. They reached El Cap a few minutes before midnight in England, confirming the amazing truth that the Egyptians had made no attempt to block the road.

Butler was sorely tempted to go on, and so too were Lieutenant-Colonels Bredin, commanding 2nd Para, and the one-armed Gibbon, commanding 6th R.T.R. All three had Irish blood in their veins, tingling with impetuosity. But high-powered journalists had tacked themselves on to the column and would be bound to reveal any violation of the cease-fire. From Bredin they obtained a quote that aptly expresses the soldier's futile sense of exasperation at this culmination to the months of planning and change of plan, of order and counter-order: 'War is really a pretty simple thing. It only becomes complicated when the politicians take a hand.'

The political object, as proclaimed, had in fact been achieved. Egypt and Israel had been separated and the entry ensured of a United Nations force that was to keep them apart for ten years. At the time of the cease-fire Eden was applauded by his supporters, and not until President Nasser was seen to emerge as the political winner was anger expressed at the stopping of the troops. His fall was the simple cause for which the troops were imbued with the will to fight, and it has since been widely assumed, in the remorse of lost prestige, that it would automatically have followed the capture of the final military objective. This is a debatable hypothesis, which would surely have been put to the test if the brilliant daring of the initial airborne assaults had only been boldly exploited, instead of awaiting ponderous adherence to a plan that commanders and staffs had grown weary of altering at political behest. The soldiers therefore had no right to feel deprived. Equally they had no cause for remorse. They did what they set out to do, as far as time allowed, and what their political masters expected of them.

The battle cost the 3rd Para three killed and thirty-two wounded and the 3rd Commando Brigade eight killed and sixty wounded, figures that indicate a high standard of life-saving by medical teams. The French lost ten killed and thirty-three wounded, and the Egyptian casualties, as estimated by a British Official investigator, were 650 killed and 900 wounded in Port Said alone.

IV—FAREWELL AGAIN (1956)

There was no clear cut ending to the battle in Port Said. Cracks and bangs echoed from street to street in desultory fashion all through the night, emanating as a rule from the Arab quarter, where there were plenty of gunmen at large, or from fires still burning, one of which set off an explosion of terrifying volume. When daylight came the 3rd Para had one final fire fight before entering the Arab quarter and linking up with 42 Commando. Although resistance had now been stifled, there were weapons in every shack and every household, calling for an immense and urgent task of search. The Arab quarter alone yielded fifty-seven 3-ton lorry loads in the course of a single day.

Other tasks of equal urgency required more specialised skills, and as fast as berthing space could be cleared for them the specialists came in. Among the first were officers of the Civil Affairs section, of whom a vanguard of fourteen came with the convoy from Cyprus. Governor Riad, elusive on the 6th, was located on the 7th and brought by tank to the Canal Company Office, where Stockwell was in process of transferring his headquarters from *Tyne*. After a sad meeting with Brigadier Lacey, with whom he had been on such good terms during the evacuation, the Governor was installed in a temporary office, since his own had been a centre of resistance and was now a wreckage. The Civil Affairs officers eked a measure of uneasy cooperation from the hapless man. The police had all vanished, as had the convicts from the jail, and about a quarter were retrieved and persuaded to return sullenly to duty. However, the magistrates were more reticent, and looters ran risk only of temporary custody by the Royal Military Police, since Stockwell was not going to add the cactus of justice to his many other thorny problems of control. Measures to feed and accommodate the homeless were also briskly instituted, with happier results.

The R.M.P. had many parts to play, among the most grisly of which was the marshalling of prisoners of war for the collection of the Egyptian dead and for their disposal, where possible after identification by a relative. The Royal Engineers, in the persons of 323 Electrical and Mechanical Squadron, set about restoring public utilities to full usage, finding everything repairable except for a sewage drain, which had been broken by an air strike and remained the cause of much anxiety. The R.A.M.C. brought swift succour to the hospitals, two of which had been badly damaged, and the R.A.S.C. speeded the unloading of the ships, manning Z craft and working in close cooperation with the naval

261

Beachmaster, with much manual aid provided by the Royal Pioneer Corps. The fighting troops meanwhile were kept busy on tidying up the streets, when not engaged on the search for arms.

Shops were opened, on Stockwell's orders, on Saturday, November 10, in the hope that the tension would be lowered by the lubricating power of Egyptian currency, of which a limited supply was available for issue to the troops, being a legacy of the hoarding forced on British Troops Egypt during the days of the occupation. The response was disappointing. The people, not unnaturally, were wary and were frightened of being seen to cooperate with the enemy occupants. Most shops remained closed.

Further customers were now close at hand, for on this same morning, November 10, the troopships arrived off Port Said carrying the 3rd Division (less 1st Guards Brigade) and a powerful increment for port and clearance work in the 35th Corps Engineer Regiment. The 29th Brigade, which was a conversion of the 32nd Guards and had no direct link with the 29th of Korea fame, came ashore first, led by the 1st Queen's Own Royal West Kent, whose transport had accompanied the convoy from Malta. The bulk of the divisional transport was still being tossed about on the sea. It would arrive on the 13th, having dropped the 1st R.T.R. off at Malta, and would exact a mighty effort from the R.E.M.E. port workshops in the revival of dead batteries and the driving of 2,000 vehicles ashore. The first to be landed, so it was reliably reported, to the great glee of the whole force, was the officers' mess truck of the Life Guards, who had been removed from the order of battle six weeks earlier, when Musketeer was switched from Alexandria to Port Said.

Intended originally as reinforcements, the 3rd Division now had the task of relieving the Parachute and Commando Brigades, thus freeing them for further operations in Cyprus. The Royal West Kent took over the El Cap position from 2nd Para in daylight on Sunday the 11th. It was a cramped position, affording deployment for only one company forward, and all along the causeway behind it, motley and colourful in their variegated berets and camouflage smocks, were the frustrated warriors, more French than British, whose march on Suez had ended in a hole or hovel only a few miles outside Port Said. The Egyptian Army had arrived on the 8th and taken up position half a mile from the forward British troops. They fired many bullets at them, as if to prove they they had stopped the advance, and when two distinguished journalists, French and American, drove through to visit them, they shot their vehicle into the Canal and killed them inside it. This was the sum of their killings, and on the arrival of the Royal West Kent they were quieter, although always prone to sporadic outburst. The main problem from now on was to control the flow from behind, the flow of generals, admirals, staff officers, journalists from almost every country of the world, United Nations officers, and mere unauthorised, unrepentant sightseers.

The 3rd Division completed the relief on November 14, with the 29th Brigade responsible for the causeway and the southern outskirts of Port Said and the 19th the main part of the town, the French still being in possession of Port Fuad. Suddenly the town sprang to life. Vendors came out in force and did good business with the troops, some undoubtedly earning extra duty pay as spies; a few shopkeepers pulled down their shutters and some were even seen to smile; and urchins scampered around delightedly, drawing ample bounty in sweets from officers and men from the G.O.C. downwards. However, a curfew was still imposed, running from 6 to 6, and for none was the task of enforcement harder than for the 1st Royal Scots, who controlled Arab Town (as they called the quarter) and every evening cleared its narrow, teeming streets by jeep patrols, which with horns blaring and look-outs alert chivvied the people into their houses, firmly, patiently and with good humour. Of the other battalions of 19 Brigade, the 1st West Yorkshire were allotted the waterfront, docks and business quarter, and the 1st Argyll and Sutherland Highlanders had Shanty Town, the Manzala Canal and the sandy islands by the edge of the lake, including the village of El Kabuti. Searching the feluccas that streamed in from the south was among their most important tasks and involved the construction of a home-made boom to channel the boats to the required point.

The honeymoon ended as abruptly as it had begun. A general strike was declared, with murder displayed as the penalty for blacklegs. The shops shut down and the street vendors vanished, never again to plague a British soldier in uniform. It was another trick to the Secret Police, whose leader, Colonel Rouchdi, had been arrested on Stockwell's orders and subsequently released in the cause of promoting harmony. Never was cause worse served.

The United Nations force was by now under way, drawn from ten nations that in some cases had never before sent their soldiers overseas. The advanced party arrived by sea on November 13, preceded by the commander, the Canadian Lieutenant-General Burns, who flew direct to Cairo, and on the 21st the first contingent reached Port Said by train, having flown to Abu Sueir the day before. Its men were Norwegians, wearing the sky-blue helmets that were to earn the U.N. troops the nickname of 'Blue-Bells'. The people accorded them an hysterical welcome. Indeed, such was the furore that the villains of the piece, as represented by the West Yorks, had to rush to the rescue of Egypt's new saviours, just as their R.M.P. escorts were on the point of being overwhelmed. With bayonets fixed the Yorkshiremen carved a passage for the bemused Norwegians to their camp in the Governorate gardens, while the Royal Scots neatly shepherded the mob on to Arab Town.

The withdrawal of the 3rd Division began on November 24, exactly a fortnight after its arrival, with the departure of the Royal West Kent, who had handed El Cap over to the 1st Royal Fusiliers. Divisional Headquarters left on December 5, two days after the Foreign Secretary, Mr. Selwyn Lloyd, had told downcast friends and derisive opponents in the House of Commons that the British and French Governments had agreed to 'withdraw forthwith', as urged by the United Nations. On the 7th the last remaining battalion of 29 Brigade, the 1st York and Lancaster, handed El Cap over to Indian troops. As if eager to make amends for their Government's indignant condemnation of Britain, the Indian officers gave an effusive greeting to their old comrades-in-arms.

Only 19 Brigade now remained, placed directly under Stockwell's command, and already the Egyptian underground army had advertised their intention to do all in their power to slay and upset the departing troops. The first grenade was thrown on November 28. Its target, which it missed, was a Champ of the Royal Scots leading a patrol through Arab Town. The officer in charge, Lieutenant Addison, saw a man in a doorway, chased him into a house, ran into the muzzle of a sten, pressed the trigger of his own sten without response, and leapt upon a shadowy, pliant figure whose own weapon was found also to have jammed. Two days earlier Arab Town had reverberated with cheers for a British soldier. C.S.M. McMahon of the R.M.P. had entered a burning building and, by his coolness and strength of arm, rescued seven people of all ages trapped in an upper storey. There was to be no more cheering, although there would be more acts of mercy, in particular by the medical officer of the Royal Scots, who was the only doctor willing to visit Arab Town after dark and frequently journeyed forth to deliver child or abate fever.

On the night of December 9, when it was clear enough to every Egyptian that the British had begun the process of evacuation, the guerrillas stepped up their offensive with a heavier attack on a Royal Scots' vehicle patrol, but though a clutch of grenades was thrown and at least three automatics opened up, only one minor casualty was suffered. A sombre sullenness could be felt next day in every street in town, presaging further assaults on the so vulnerable targets the soldiers presented every time they made street patrol, either in vehicles or on foot, deployed to cover every direction, the rear included. It was as well that their morale was high, boosted by the knowledge that at last they had a crucial part to play after the months of preparation and, for the reservists in particular, frustration. Much had already been accomplished by individual acts of alertness. Because a lance-corporal of the West Yorks thought the absence of a padlock from a shop shutter seemed odd, a printing press was discovered from which leaflets of hate and ghoulish vengeance had been flowing under the signature of 'the Black Hand'. Because a corporal of the Argylls noticed some baskets being offloaded from a rowing boat, he went to investigate and ended up by unearthing a huge dump of ammunition and explosive in the village of El Kabuti.

On the evening of December 10 a national-service subaltern of the West Yorks, 2nd Lieutenant Moorhouse, led a raid on a flat owned by a doctor and arrested six 'fedayin' officers, of the guerrilla movement, together with the doctor himself. A guard remained in the house and next morning netted another man, whom Moorhouse took in his Champ, with escort, to Battalion H.Q. He then dropped escort and driver off to have their breakfast, and hearing that the guard on the house had been relieved, he drove off on his own to visit the fresh one, disregarding in his enthusiasm the standing order forbidding unaccompanied movement. On seeing a youth stick up a subversive poster, he stopped his Champ and got out presumably to arrest him. Men gathered round him arguing. He lost his pistol and was bundled into a black car which was later found abandoned in Arab Town.

Every means of retrieving Moorhouse was attempted, through the Governor, through the United Nations commander and finally by direct appeal to Nasser himself, and meanwhile the crash of grenade became ever more frequent in Port Said, showing that the guerrillas were in no mood to hand over their acquisition. A full scale search by 19 Brigade was carried out on December 15. Arab Town and other parts were sealed off segment by segment and thoroughly combed. But the friend proved as hard to find as foes had been in Tel Aviv and Limassol, and the men probed, felt and knocked in vain, although they were said to have come within a board's width of success, for Moorhouse's captors subsequently claimed that they had left him trussed in a cupboard when the search parties came and that he had died of suffocation by the time they returned.

The violence rose to its peak this day, the 15th. All battalions suffered casualties from grenades, and the Centurions even had rockets fired at them. In the West Yorks' sector the driver of a French journalist caught the full blast of a grenade, and the regimental stretcher team come to retrieve him would also have been blasted but for the prompt action of a well placed picquet in shooting two grenadiers as they came up for the hurl. In Arab Town, which had been vibrant all day with the bark of explosive, a patrol of the Royal Scots came under heavy automatic fire at 10.30 p.m. and its leader, the commander of B Company, fell mortally wounded. A volley of shots simultaneously smote B Company's base, on the edge of Arab Town. The tanks were brought in, together with more Royal Scots, and whenever grenade was thrown or automatic fired it would draw a long, thumping burst from a Browning or the ja-ja-ja-jab of a bren, followed on occasions by a thud as a body fell from window on to street. Until 2.30 a.m. the narrow streets shook with the din of battle and the tracer reared high from ricochet. Then the guerrillas were quelled into what turned out to be a lasting silence, at least as long as there were British troops around. The latter quietly withdrew to an inner perimeter a night later, the Royal Scots from Arab Town and the Argylls from Shanty Town and the reaches of the Manzala Canal. The inhabitants of these districts were now free to fire their weapons as they pleased, and they could nightly be heard enjoying this liberty.

One last task remained, and this was to retrieve the 472 employees of the Suez Canal Contractors' Company, whose brief spell in charge of the demilitarised base had ended in incarceration in a school in Cairo, where they endured much hardship until their lot was improved through the intervention of the Swiss *chargé d'affaires*. The bargaining counter was 230 prisoners of war held by the British and a further hundred odd by the French, and arrangements were made for an exchange to take place on December 20. However, there was a breakdown, caused by the reluctance of the French to give up a certain officer, and a day went by before it was dissolved. By now the main building containing the Egyptian prisoners was in the front line, so contracted had the British perimeter become, and a full company of Royal Scots were employed to guard them overnight and escort them on the morning of the 21st to the Sherif Quay, where they embarked with their various chattels on a train with silver engine, which was driven by Canadian engineers and carried an escort of Finnish troops. Just after 5 p.m. the train returned with the stoic 'contractors'. After a cup of tea on the quay and the exchange of badinage with officers and men, they were taken by lighter to a troopship to follow home the 448 British subjects already evacuated from Port Said.

The Argylls had by now embarked and that night two companies of the Royal Scots followed, leaving docks and warehouses that seemed strangely bare after their encumberment by all manner of military paraphernalia during the past six weeks. The final positions were in buildings covering the Casino quay and fishing harbour, where landing craft waited with bow doors open. There was an outer and an inner cordon, and just before dark on Saturday, December 22, the companies of Royal Scots and West Yorks left the outer and filed aboard the craft, the former led by silent pipers. There was one staccato burst of fire. Its bullets spattered a wall a few feet above a platoon of West Yorks. Sky-blue helmets bobbed about on rooftops just taken over from the British, trying anxiously to spot the delinquent. Though disinclined to suppress the Egyptian urge to shoot, the United Nations troops earned the gratitude of the British by their cooperative spirit.

General Stockwell watched these penultimate companies go aboard and then took launch for the minelayer *Manxman*, whence he supervised the final act of allied cooperation, the simultaneous evacuation of Ports Said and Fuad. At ten minutes to 7, in full darkness now, the last tank of the 6th R.T.R. reversed through the gaping doors of its landing ship, while tracer bullets soared sky-high from Arab Town as part of the nightly carnival. The last platoon of the rearguard, B Company, 1st West Yorkshire, then marched on to an adjacent landing craft with that alert yet unhurrying gait with which they had patrolled the streets.

Only the commander of 19 Brigade, Brigadier E. H. W. Grimshaw, remained on the jetty, together with the naval beachmaster and a United Nations liaison officer. A report had arrived through United Nations channels that Moorhouse would be delivered up at the hour of departure. It proved to be a mockery; he was already dead. After five minutes of waiting, with ears strained for the sound of vehicle, the Brigadier bade farewell to his United Nations friend and jumped on a landing craft to complete the second act of evacuation in the course of just over six months. Brigadier Lacey, enactor of the first, had returned by air this time with a load that grimly emphasised the melancholy of the ending, eleven British corpses, brought home to avert their desecration.

The British left one memento behind them: a Union Jack nailed to a mast that had been greased throughout its length by an agile and daring sailor from *Tyne*. All through the night Egyptians scuffled frantically to climb the mast, so the story goes, and every effort failing, it had in the end to be sawn down. Some thought it wrong that the flag of Britain should be offered for debasement in this manner—as also was the Tricolour on de Lesseps' statue. Yet if there was ever true symbolism in a farewell gesture this surely was it.

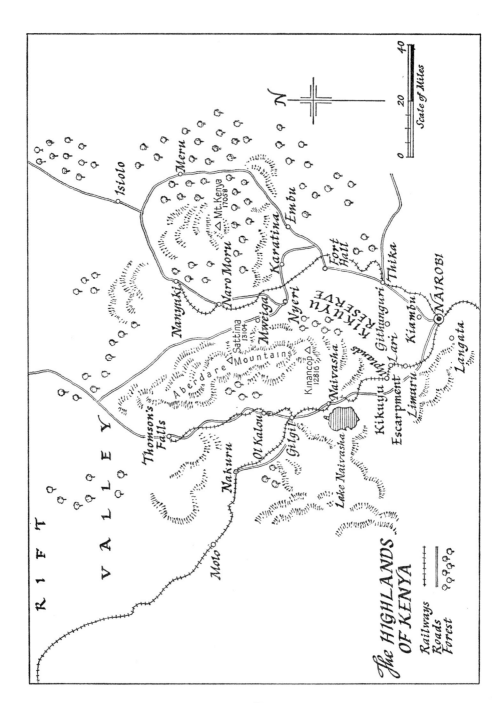

The HIGHLANDS OF KENYA

Railways
Roads
Forest

Scale of Miles

N

RIFT VALLEY

Isiolo
Meru
△ Mt. Kenya 17058
Naro Moru
Narynki
Embu
Karatina
Fort Hall
Thika
Nyeri
Mweiga
△ Sattima 13104
Aberdare Mountains
△ Kinancop 12816
Githunguri
Lari
KIKUYU RESERVE
Kiambu
NAIROBI
Langata
Thomson's Falls
Naivasha
Kikuyu
Escarpment
Limuru
Ol Kalou
Gilgil
Lake Naivasha
Nakuru
Moto

9

Kenya

(1952-56)

THE Government of Kenya had never, in fifty years' rule, been much impressed by the threat of rebellion. The Member for Law and Order also happened to be Attorney-General, and like his colleagues in government he took a complacent view of the reports that the mysterious society named Mau Mau, which had been proscribed in 1950, was active again, stirring the Kikuyu people to lawlessness and revolt. One of the favourite ploys of the Mau Mau was to set fire to the homes of African loyalists, and they were to be seen blazing even when Queen Elizabeth made her sad, hurried departure from Kenya on her first day as such, February 6, 1952. In the months that followed evidence of their evil influence steadily grew. Oaths were being administered, it was correctly said. They graduated in importance from mere vows of obedience and secrecy to those of death to European settlers, and there was similar graduation in the obscenity of the attendant ceremony. The words 'May this vow kill me if I fail', formed part of every one, and the trembling initiate had stronger cause than his own innate superstition to comprehend the reality of this alternative.

The Mau Mau stepped up their campaign of intimidation in mid-September 1952. They slew fourteen of their compatriots in under a week and provided a grisly sample of their power and outlook by setting five farm buildings alight and mutilating, by hamstringing and partial disembowelment, 500 cattle and sheep in a single night. On the 29th Sir Evelyn Baring arrived to assume the appointment of Governor, three months after the departure of his predecessor on retirement leave. A nine-day tour of the colony was sufficient to persuade him that a state of emergency had to be declared and that the political leaders suspected of involvement in Mau Mau had to be arrested. This was a task stretching the Kenya Police to the limits of its resources, and it was clear that the Army would have to play a supporting role.

Although East Africa Command had a senior officer as G.O.C.-in-C., Lieutenant-General Sir Alexander Cameron, it was an outstation of G.H.Q. Middle East and until this month of September 1952 far the most drowsy one, indeed the only drowsy one. It had no higher staff officer than colonel, and its only regular troops were Colonial. Since the abandonment of the Mackinnon Road project, its main preoccupation had been preparing battalions of the King's African Rifles for service in Malaya, two of which had been despatched in January 1952.

Kenya formed only a small part of the command, and likewise the Mau Mau affected area formed only a small part of Kenya, measuring little more than a hundred miles by a hundred. But being highlands blessed with rich red soil, it was the most thickly populated part of all East Africa. Up its centre, stretching northwards from Nairobi, the hub of administration and command, runs the great spine of the Aberdares, rising to 13,000 feet and covered in dense forest. North-east of the Aberdares and connected with it by a carpet of forest is the mighty Mount Kenya, 17,000 feet high. The rest of the highlands was farmed by European settlers, either with livestock or a wide variety of crops, apart from a few other areas of forest and a cultivated stretch running along the east side of the Aberdares for 50 miles. This was the Kikuyu Reserve, on which Europeans were forbidden to encroach, although many covetous eyes had been cast on its empty acres. As the Kikuyu tribe expanded from 300,000 to over a million in the fifty years of British occupation they were persuaded that so far from being protected against the settlers they were victims of land theft. This formed the grievance from which the Mau Mau drew their strength.

It was fortunate that not being a warrior tribe few Kikuyu enlisted in the K.A.R. and the latter's ranks therefore were free from infection by the Mau Mau canker. Indeed, only two of its eight battalions—the 3rd and 2nd/3rd or 23rd—were enlisted in Kenya. Even so, its troops could not provide that reassuring sense of comfort so needed in the settled areas, and a request was therefore made to G.H.Q. Middle East for a British battalion to be sent in to reinforce the three battalions of the K.A.R. resident in the White Highlands and the elements of a further three being brought in from Uganda, Tanganyika and Mauritius. Crisis had fortunately subsided in Egypt, and the battalion that had borne ten brunt of it was made available, the 1st Lancashire Fusiliers. After ten days at readiness to move, Battalion Headquarters and A Company arrived in Valetta aircraft at 7.30 p.m. on Sunday, October 19. They were accommodated by the R.A.F. at Eastleigh aerodrome. Around midnight the police began the arrest of eighty-three suspected Mau Mau leaders, Jomo Kenyatta among them, and encountered no resistance.

From dawn onwards on this Monday morning Lancashire Fusiliers were to be seen in all parts of Nairobi and its suburbs, sitting upright in open trucks, engaged on that familiar ritual of imperial policing, a flag march. But it was not familiar to the people of Nairobi, and there was a touch of the miraculous about this sudden appearance of British troops, literally out of the blue. They were the first, anyway of fighting troops, to be seen in Nairobi since Tanganyika had been wrested from Germany, and with their bright primrose hackles in their berets and bayonets fixed on the rifles between their knees they succeeded in looking both stern and debonair. Certainly it was an impressive performance in ubiquity by a single company. Although the Africans merely gazed at them with that blank, inscrutable stare which was to become such a characteristic feature of the emergency, the Europeans felt a relaxing of the tension and did not conceal their joy on seeing the troops. To the men who had confronted the fanatics in Ismailia, it seemed more like pantomime than emergency.

Not until 8 p.m. on that night, October 20, did the Governor sign the declaration of a State of Emergency, and next morning he explained its reason and effect in a broadcast to the people. On the 23rd the last company of Lancashire Fusiliers arrived, bringing the battalion strength to a meagre but fairly typical 450. Of the three rifle companies A remained in Nairobi until November 15 when it moved with Battalion Headquarters to Naivasha in the midst of the settled area west of the Aberdares; D went to Nyeri, the important centre midway between the Aberdares and Mount Kenya; and C to the Kikuyu Reserve, where law and order, being the responsibility of the Tribal Police as opposed to the regular force, had virtually collapsed. From these widespread bases they carried on with the task of showing themselves to the people, first by formal flag marches on foot or on wheels and then by patrol visits to farms and police stations. They also laid cordons to assist in the arrest of suspects. Theirs was still a supporting role.

It looked at first as if the Mau Mau had been quelled merely by the raising of the stick. Then on January 1, 1953, two Englishmen were disturbed while supping in their farmhouse at the foot of the Aberdares and hacked to pieces. Next day two European ladies were disturbed in similar circumstances, but bravely repulsed their assailants with pistol and shotgun. However, by murdering a Kikuyu district chief as he lay in a hospital bed and by their ghastly slaying of the Rucks, a family well known for its devotion to the humble and the sick, the Mau Mau made swift amends for their one reverse. The settlers were tough, many of them having carved their own farmland out of forest, and were determined to stay. They could also be truculent, in the manner of most men fired with the pioneering spirit, and their traditional contempt for the Government now turned to rage, of which they gave massed display by a demonstration in Nairobi.

The Government had in fact already decided to form an emergency committee, on the Malayan model, and had secured the appointment of a military adviser, who would coordinate the activities of administration, police and army, and would in due course be styled Director of Operations. The choice fell on Brigadier W. R. N. Hinde, an unassuming and quietly individualistic cavalryman who had acquired the typically daft and undeserved nickname of 'Loony'. His career as a fighting commander had ended simultaneously with Erskine's and over the same issue, the feasibility of a task set 7th Armoured Division in Normandy, in which he commanded the armoured brigade. He had since gained the high opinion of Robertson when Deputy Director of Military Government in Germany, and it was Robertson, as C.-in-C. Middle East, who now took him from his present command, that of Cyrenaica District, just as he was on the point of retiring. *The Times* touched the crux of the matter in mentioning his 'unusual gift for getting on with difficult people'. Never was he in greater need of this gift than when he set out to visit the settlers following his arrival at Nairobi on February 1, showing the rank of major-general.

Hinde developed the 'trinity' system of command, down to the level of district officer—company commander—assistant inspector of police in each division of a district, and he also attempted to strengthen the Kikuyu Home Guard, whose formation had been authorised before his arrival and on whose loyalty the fate of the campaign hinged. But it fast became apparent that he was up against an enormous clandestine organisation, about which there was pathetically little information available, other than that three-quarters of the whole Kikuyu tribe—this proved an underestimate—had been forced into taking the Mau Mau oath and if not members of fighting gangs had a part to play in the vast Passive Wing that kept the gangs supplied both with provisions and orders from the Central Committee in Nairobi. More police were needed to penetrate the organisation—most of all Special Branch men—and more battalions to track down the armed gangs. Fortunately the C.I.G.S., General Harding, paid a visit towards the end of February, and Hinde was able to persuade him of the need for more battalions.

A year before, following the big exodus to Egypt, it is hard to see how any could have been found, but in October a brigade of the 3rd Division

—the 39th—had been returned to England to rebuild the strategic reserve and, at a strength of two battalions, it was now warned for embarkation, with three weeks in which to prepare. One of these battalions, the 1st Buffs, had accompanied it to Egypt, and the other, the 1st Devonshire, had been in the brigade of the 3rd Division flown out to Libya and had joined 39 Brigade on return to England in October. This battalion, it will be remembered, had been in the Malayan rebellion from its start until the end of 1950 and had not yet dried up its store of experience of jungle fighting.

While these battalions were preparing to move, the Mau Mau provided lurid and terrible evidence of the need for them. March 26 was the night of the Lari massacre, during which they slashed eighty-four of their Kikuyu compatriots to death with sadistic relish, taking delight in carving up babies before they set to work on their mothers, and left a further thirty-one survivors in a gruesome state of mutilation. This was only 25 miles from Nairobi, and on this same night at Naivasha a gang of eighty Mau Mau made a brilliant surprise attack on its fortified police station, put to death or flight all its men, and released 173 prisoners. Four platoons of Lancashire Fusiliers were in camp nearby, but they could do no more than head for the sound of firing and draw what clues they could from the horrifying scene they found, a common enough experience for the security forces. However, they were able to round up half the prisoners in a search next day.

There was therefore an eager if nervy welcome awaiting the Buffs and the Devons when they arrived, in that order, during the first week in April, having come for the most part in chartered aircraft and staged overnight at Malta and Khartoum, with a number of unscheduled halts enforced by engine failure. It was the longest troop movement by air yet made. Both battalions went to the tawny, wide acres of the Rift Valley, the Buffs to an improvised camp near Thomson's Falls, where a fire burnt many of their tents as they were arriving, and the Devons even further westwards to Molo, leaving two companies on internal security duties in Nairobi. These static duties hampered the task of acclimatisation and training, and the Buffs in particular were heavily committed in bolstering the morale and fortifications of the police and in visiting farms merely for the sake of reassurance.

There were now eight and a half regular battalions of infantry, together with the East African Independent Armoured Car Squadron and the 156th Heavy Anti-Aircraft Battery, East African Artillery, which like the K.A.R. had British officers and senior N.C.O.s, all eager to play their part, if needs be as infantry. There was also the territorial, all-European, officer-producing Kenya Regiment, which had been embodied for the emergency. Its members were to be of immense value dispersed on specialist duties of various rugged types.

Obviously these troops could not stamp out the Mau Mau movement merely by performing protective duties for the police and settlers, and with the arrival of 39 Brigade plans were at once studied for penetration into the Mau Mau's great forest domain, the Aberdares. The commander of this brigade was Brigadier J. W. Tweedie, a Scotsman with the drive and anger to make things move, and taking the Lancashire Fusiliers also under command, he made the first probing inroads into the Aberdares, while the battalions of the K.A.R.—the 4th, 5th, 6th (less two companies), 7th, 23rd, and 26th (less two companies)—carried on with their duties of supporting the police in other parts of the Highlands, grouped into a single brigade, the 70th East African.

After initiation into the art of forest warfare at a battle school near Nyeri, the company commanders of the newly arrived battalions led their men out on the first patrols. They dressed in jungle green, with floppy hats and rubber boots (which were not very popular), and had African trackers with them to detect the normally indistinguishable trail of man. For general guidance and interrogation of natives, an officer and some N.C.O.s of the Kenya Regiment were attached to each battalion, and rare characters many of them were. For wireless communication with patrols, for supply, information, and even for offensive action with grenade, bullet, and later light bomb, the battalions had American Piper Pacer aircraft, piloted by specially enrolled members of the Kenya Police Reserve. Most were ex-R.A.F. pilots and were men of skill and courage, both of which were much needed, for they had to manoeuvre their hardy little two-seater craft off and on strips little larger than required for a helicopter and through air which, because of the altitude, was too thin and feckless for the floatation of any helicopter then in service. From an initial allotment of one aircraft to each battalion, the system was to expand and be of immense benefit, morally as much as materially.

Another arrangement of great advantage, which followed the arrival of 39 Brigade, was the classification of areas. The Aberdares and Mount Kenya, being all forest, were declared Prohibited Areas, which meant that they were authorised battlefields, where the troops had the right to open fire on sight and, since they were traditionally the place of refuge for the Kikuyu from Masai raiders, they were the obvious habitat of the armed gangs, members of which were in any case liable to be hanged if caught. Nearly all the rest of the Highlands was declared a Special Area, and here the troops had the right to halt and question, to open fire if a challenge were defied, and to open fire on sight during the hours of curfew. They had a much better chance now of sifting the lawbreakers from the peaceful, although of course their custody, charging and prosecution remained the responsibility of the civil power, and the military did not wish it to be otherwise.

The range of the Aberdares is over 60 miles long, and the forest begins at heights varying between 7 to 9,000 feet, covering 10 to 15 miles of slope on the east side and 5 to 10 miles on the west. Along the lower slopes the podo, wild fig, and cedar trees stretch to a height of 60 to 80 feet, usually branchless for the first 20 and then extending in such profusion that hardly a ray of light can penetrate, and it is cold, dark, damp and eerie down below. The undergrowth varies in density, sometimes forming massive entanglements, to cut a path through which calls for hours of hacking; although there are plenty of animal tracks, these wind inconsequential courses and the twigs and dead wood on them make stealth of approach a high skill. Above the trees, covering most of the slope, is the bamboo belt. There are great tall bamboos and thinner, densely packed bamboos, and the rotting, slippery hulks of bamboos litter the ground, bringing labour and peril to every stride; again animal tracks offer the best prospect of silent approach, but plenty of hazards too. At about 11,000 feet the bamboo gives way to moorland, which is interspersed with 12-foot tall tufts of heather, lobelia and jungle grass, and with the springs of the many streams and rivers that roar down the mountainside. It lies on a plateau between the great peaks of Sattima (13,104 feet) in the north and Kinangop (12,816) in the south. It is breezy up here and the glare of the sun is sharpened by contrast with the murkiness down below. But mist is apt to descend at night, giving the Equator the bite of the Pole.

It was a fortress of daunting and confusing dimensions for penetration by the three weak battalions that also had their commitments in the settled areas. There were baffling problems to be solved of navigation, map reading, supply, instant readiness—for the target inevitably would be only a fleeting one—and above all of silent movement. There was also the problem of avoiding self-inflicted casualties, and of all problems this caused the greatest distress. The soldier had first to overcome his own clumsiness; against an enemy much higher endowed with the animal senses of hearing, smell and stealth than he was himself, he inevitably became an easy target in those early days for the scorn of those settlers who always knew best anyway and had a genuine fund of knowledge on questions of forest lore.

The problems were of course very similar to those in Malaya, and the experience gained there had its influence in the organisation of patrols at a strength of a dozen and the carriage of a maximum of five days' rations. Altitude imposed an extra hardship. This made men breathless and unduly short-tempered to start with, and enormously added to the fatigue of a climb over slippery bamboo. Animals gave extra cause for fear. Rhinoceros were the most common, the most belligerent, and the cause of many alarms that usually ended in retrospective laughter—but were no joke at the time; buffaloes were the most dangerous, and elephants the most alarming for the silence with which they could approach and the thunderous noise of their eating. Hyena, monkeys, frogs, nightjar, and the diminutive hyrax all contributed to the scarifying night time chorus, as also did the hiss and pop of bamboo. But the insects were less deadly than the leeches and hornets that infested the Malayan swamps, and the stinging red ants appear to have been less populous in the Kenyan bamboo. The snakes were fewer, too. Indeed, the climate and whole atmosphere were very much more salubrious. Although awe-inspiring enough, the forest did not have the clinging, depressing effect of the dark and damp of the jungle.

The first blood in these tentative probings into the Aberdares was drawn by the Devons. On May 11 two of their patrols simultaneously claimed the £5 offered by the commanding officer for the first kill. One, operating on the west slopes, tracked a gang to its lair and burst into it at dusk, killing two of its occupants and capturing a home-made rifle, primitive in its design and crude in its workmanship. Another patrol, on the east slopes, came under fire from one such rifle, and in the ensuing battle made a kill without loss to itself.

This gang on the eastern slopes showed much more aggression than was later to be displayed, for two subsequent patrols of the Devons were ambushed and one man was wounded in the bottom. The Devons struck back and by the end of May could claim eight killed and two taken prisoner, after exchanges as hot as any that were to take place during the whole campaign. It seems that some of the service rifles captured in the attack on Naivasha police station may have been in use here.

The other battalions found the enemy more elusive, and not until Hinde mounted his first coordinated operation at the start of June did they make their first kills in the forest. They acted in conjunction with another type of reinforcement, Harvard bombers of the Royal Air Force, whose normal role was merely a training one. In the first phase of the operation, which with wistful thoughts of the scene at home was named Epsom, patrols went out to locate enemy hide-outs, operating from company bases in the forest. They then withdrew to the forest fringes and laid ambushes on the Mau Mau supply routes while the bombers plastered the hides, guided very often by smoke dropped from a Piper Pacer. Whether or not any Mau Mau were killed by the bombing it certainly stirred them up, and fifty-seven of them were killed or captured by the three battalions during this operation, some food carriers, some genuine gangsters. The soldiers were not impressed now that they at last had a close-up of their foe. They were unkempt and scruffily clad, with hair and clothes covered in red murram, and those that had homemade rifles seemed pathetically inept at handling them. It was hard to believe that they could be formidable killers. Yet the documents found in their neatly made bamboo huts showed that they took themselves seriously enough and were organised in platoons, battalions and army corps under grandiosely styled leaders, and there were in fact many more men in these formations than anyone yet realised. Retrospective estimates vary between 12 and 15,000, and they were backed by almost a million sworn supporters.

At least the British Government had been impressed by their power of destruction, as revealed by the Lari massacre, and the decision had been taken to upgrade East Africa to a separate command, directly responsible to the War Office. Having spent a year at Eastern Command on return from Egypt, General Sir George Erskine was a fairly obvious choice for the appointment of Commander-in-Chief. He was instructed to take all military measures required to end the emergency, with full control over all security forces, and was to be accorded such help as he needed by the Governor, who remained in administrative control of the colony, of which only one-sixteenth part was affected by the emergency regulations.

Erskine arrived in Nairobi on June 7, and his ample form was soon to be seen hurtling by jeep around the countryside, with police escort ahead and red dust cloud behind, bringing cheer to the troops and at least making the settlers aware that here was a man who meant business. Among other things he produced was a swelling of the huts in Waterworks Camp, on the city's edge, where Command Headquarters was housed. General Cameron became his Deputy, with special responsibility for territories outside the emergency area. General Hinde was moved from Police to Army headquarters, but carried on with the same duties, although nominally only Deputy Director of Operations now. He was in the position of field commander, freeing his chief for the political problems that entangled his job. It was a good partnership between two men very different in temperament who knew each other well. Not only had they shared misfortune in Normandy; Hinde had been with Erskine in Egypt, ready to take charge of Civil Affairs if military control had to be imposed.

Erskine saw the need to step up the tempo of offensive operations and decided to use 39 Brigade for shock action, while the remainder of his troops took firmer grip on the Mau Mau in their allotted areas, aided by a mobile column formed by the Independent Armoured Car Squadron and 156 A.A. Battery. The first task he gave the two battalions of the 39th was to descend on the Kikuyu Reserve, which had become virtually a Mau Mau reserve, with the Kikuyu Guard in danger of complete collapse. The Lancashire Fusiliers remained in the Rift Valley and on the western slopes of the Aberdares, under command of the 39th, and the Buffs and Devons still had a company apiece in the Rift Valley. It was hard to eradicate the blight of dispersion.

The Buffs motored to the area of Fort Hall on June 20 and 21, arriving to find fires blazing from three Kikuyu guard posts that had just been overrun and destroyed. The Devons meanwhile combed the approaches to the Aberdares and intercepted carrying parties supplying the forest gangs. Sorting the good from the bad was an almost impossible problem. The circular thatched huts of the Kikuyu were spread inconsequentially all over the reserve and between them ran little gorges affording unlimited cover for the lawless. There were no villages, apart from a few groups of shops that had been abandoned, unlocked, by their Asian owners and posed unanticipated problems of security. The population had been swollen by evictions from the settled areas, and the police could not tell resident from stranger. But by ambushing parties moving after curfew, when the good Kikuyu huddled in their huts, the two battalions eased the clutch of the Mau Mau and laid the foundations for further operations by the K.A.R. and hard-pressed police. Of equal importance was the boost they gave the Kikuyu Guard, who although due to receive a quota of service rifles were armed with spears, pangas and a few shotguns; they were surprisingly jovial despite the losses they had sustained. One further task in a brisk fortnight's work was the clearing, marking and wiring of a one-mile belt beside the forest, thus enlarging the prohibited area and jeopardising the prospect of unlawful entry into it.

In mid-July the Buffs came up on the right of the Devons and both began a series of operations into the Aberdares, which were fused into each other, providing the first period of continuity since the brigade's arrival. The Devons early had a notable success, which might so easily have been greater. Some cattle had been driven by four Mau Mau through a patrol base established by A Company in the forest, and in the ensuing fight one of the drivers was captured. Most unusually he was prepared to talk and, through a sergeant of the Kenya Regiment, explained the position of a large forest camp, on which sentries were posted by day but not by night, as was the Mau Mau habit. The company commander decided to make a night advance and dawn attack, but although the distance to be covered was only four miles the slope was so steep and slippery, the darkness so pitch, and silent movement so essential that the march had to be spread over three nights instead of the one intended. At last the assault group recognised the outline of a bamboo hut close ahead and after huddling together to keep out the cold, they took up position, still in pitch darkness. Then there was the sound of movement from behind, and rather than be led into a fight with some stray food carriers, the patrol let fly at the camp with their five brens and five rifles. There was utter pandemonium.

When it was light enough to see, the Devons counted twenty bashas— they had brought the word from Malaya—and they had all been pierced by their bullets, and all bore signs of recent hastily abandoned habitation. They picked up sixty pangas, yet found only eight Mau Mau, all dead. There can be no doubt that many others were hit as they made their desperate, jabbering exit in all directions, and indeed prisoners captured later said thirty of this gang had died of their wounds. It was to be a source of constant amazement how hard a wretched Mau Mau could be hit without being felled.

The Buffs had been slower starters than the Devons. Fewer of them were countrymen and none had jungle experience in Malaya, and in any case luck played an enormous part in the amount of contacts made if not of kills. Now the luck turned from the Devons, who found their forest area increasingly bare of Mau Mau, and swung towards the Buffs. From mid-August the latter were at last fully concentrated, albeit on a frontage covering twenty miles of forest fringe, which was divided between the Reserve and settled area to the north and controlled from a headquarters next Nyeri. Three months later they had raised their score of kills to well over a hundred in the most productive period of Mau Mau hunting enjoyed by any British battalion. They were aided by the issue of the short rifle, as had been used in Burma, and of the Patchet machine carbine in place of the sten, and of even greater importance by tracks bulldozed into the forest. Five such tracks had been cut by mid-August to a depth of some 6,000 yards. The work was undertaken by the Public Works Department, using prisoner labour, the guarding and protecting of whom was a commitment willingly taken on by the battalions. Later the 39th Corps Engineer Regiment, Royal Engineers, would continue this crucial task of forest penetration. But to take full advantage of it the troops had to know their allotted area of forest and to work in concert to an overall plan.

The best results for the Buffs were obtained by a company—B— organised in permanently allotted six-men patrols. They were employed as a rule in conjunction with each other, either to surround and assault a

Mau Mau hide, to hound down gangs disturbed, or to lay a network of ambushes on the supply routes. The principle was to deny the enemy any chance of respite and to keep harrying him by all means available, bombs from aircraft and mortars included. The sphere of operations was threefold, the forest itself, its fringes and its bare, one-mile belt of access, and the legally populated areas, either by Kikuyu or European farmers. In this latter zone a proportion of each company would be employed on building up the home guard and on tightening security and thus easing the flow of information, which was also being scooped up by specially formed field intelligence teams, composed of officers of the British Army and Kenya Regiment, working with police and special branch men. A typical product of this organisation enabled the Buffs to make a sweep through a northern part of the Reserve in mid-November, with the Kikuyu Guard cooperating under the Buffs' N.C.O.s, and to corner a gang of twenty, all of whom were killed or captured. Control of the operation was exercised from a spotter plane, which thus assumed one further task to add to those of communication with forest patrols, supply, and offensive action.

The first inter-battalion relief took place in August. Having been relieved in Korea on July 8, the 1st Black Watch reached Kenya by troopship on August 1. They took the Rift Valley over from the Lancashire Fusiliers, enabling the latter to make the return homewards for which they were four months overdue. On August 28 the Black Watch moved to take over a section of the Aberdares and Kikuyu Reserve on the left of the Devons. Operating from Thika, they carried out the same threefold tasks of forest penetration, watch on the forest fringe, and boosting the home guard.

Erskine had asked for yet more battalions, and near the end of September two arrived by air from England, under Brigadier G. Taylor and his Headquarters 49th Infantry Brigade. They were the 1st Royal Northumberland Fusiliers, who had spent a year in England after returning from Korea via Hong Kong, and the 1st Royal Inniskilling Fusiliers, who had returned from Egypt with 39 Brigade the previous October and, like the Devons, had formerly seen service in Malaya. After acclimatisation in the settled areas and, for the Inniskillings, a brief sojourn in Nairobi to assist in a round-up of thugs, the brigade journeyed eastwards to the lower reaches of Mount Kenya, where the battalions set about ridding two newly affected tribes of the Mau Mau canker, the Inniskillings the Meru and the Fifth Fusiliers the Embu.

Of all the accumulated experiences of the five British battalions, in Malaya, Korea and Egypt, none could rival the present for the sheer exhilaration it afforded. The men lived rough and they lived hard, often clambering up and down the prickly, densely strewn slopes of the forest for ten days on end, enduring heat by day, cold by night, constant murkiness, self-imposed silence, and the lurking danger of sudden attack, by beast if not man. But the air was good and from the cosy company camps by the forest edge sensational views were obtainable, giving a sense of uplift and serenity. Furthermore, however critical the settlers might be of the conduct of the campaign, they certainly made the soldiers feel they were wanted and extended hospitality towards them which in most regimental accounts receives the grading 'staggering'. It must also be admitted that the enemy was far less lethal than any encountered in the previous campaigns, Indeed, evasion appeared to be his one ambition against the army, although he was still committing sufficient murder of the civilian population to make the task of hunting him seem thoroughly worthwhile. Kenya in short was the best recruiting agent the army ever had. In the words of Brigadier Tweedie, commander of 39 Brigade, 'The keenness was tremendous and in spite of very isolated conditions and lack of the things that everyone believed young soldiers *must* have, they were entirely happy.'

One of the means of sustaining this keenness was to encourage competition between battalions and companies in the number of Mau Mau killed, and since they had come there in order to kill Mau Mau this seemed a reasonable enough thing to do. Far away in England it did not seem so reasonable. The trouble started when a copy of the Devons' magazine, in which mention was made of the £5 offered by the C.O. for the first kill, reached a Labour M.P. He asked a question in the Commons, and the *Daily Herald* reported it under a front page headline asking IS YOUR SON A MURDERER? Snide mention was also made of the Devons' nickname, 'Bloody Eleventh', without explanation of its honourable origin. Other papers pursued the same theme, although some counterattacked. It was infuriating for the troops to read the attacks made on them at home by people who displayed their ignorance of the situation, and wisely the War Office convened a court of enquiry under Lieutenant-General Sir Kenneth McLean. Its findings fully exonerated all British battalions from charges of indiscriminate firing, and a Parliamentary delegation that arrived in Kenya in the New Year made a point of stressing that 'we were all impressed with the high state of discipline and cheerfulness of the troops.' But there was no longer any public recording of kills and captures, no 'league table' between companies. Although obfuscating the task of a historian, this was perhaps not such a bad thing.

Certainly the British soldiers were in a difficult position, for there was much brutality around them and, despite a stern warning from Erskine at an early stage, their colleagues of the K.A.R. and the police were not so blameless in their treatment of Mau Mau suspects, being more susceptible to the hatred that was ripping their country apart. The demand for tougher measures of reprisal persisted, and there were many outside the British Army who wanted martial law enforced. As an example of the need for it they could point to the experiences of a sub-altern of the Buffs. He had wounded and captured a woman gangster high in the Aberdares, given her morphia, tea and chocolate, and spent twenty-four hours in conducting her laboured evacuation to hospital. His reward at her trial in Nyeri was to be spat at, accused of raping her, and of carrying her off into the prohibited forest. Although her evidence was palpably false, she was acquitted because of technical irregularities. The Mau Mau had clever friends to advise them and had learned that in legal matters attack was the best form of defence. Every accusation they made had to be carefully investigated.

An officer of the British Army might wryly smile at such proceedings, but in those more intimately concerned with the fate of Kenya they engendered rage and disgust. Yet perversely such feelings were accompanied by the determination to preserve the normal peacetime flow of life. The strength of it was conveyed to the battalions toiling to tighten their grasp on the Mau Mau by the following message from GHQ, dated October 30: 'The wartime habit of officers attending civilian functions in uniform is against local dress regulations stop. This specially refers to Limuru Hunt Ball being held to-morrow stop. Any officers attending will wear tails or dinner jackets stop.' The one exception 'on this occasion' was made of the Black Watch, since they had come straight from Korea.

Laughable though this message was the War Office itself acknowledged that the emergency had drifted into a state of routine by authorising the despatch of families around this time and the grant of an allowance for their living at hotels. This brought its problems and the favour was not granted to battalions that came later. But the War Office also showed awareness of the complexity of the problem still to be solved by sending in late November Major-General G. D. G. Heyman to be Erskine's Chief of Staff in place of Colonel G. A. Rimbault. Like General Cameron, the latter remained as a deputy, and Erskine appreciated the loyalty with which both accepted their relegation.

On Christmas Eve a tragedy within the Black Watch emphasised that hunting Mau Mau was not without its dangers. Major the Earl Wavell, only son of the late Field Marshal and Colonel of the Regiment, was shot dead by a sudden, unexpected bullet when following the trail of a gang with a few soldiers and policemen close to the main road to Thika. This turned out to be a tough gang. It was surrounded that night, but a police officer was shot dead by the light of a fire kindled to flush the gangsters. The gang then broke out through a point held by police gendarmerie, shooting two in the process.

The battalions had certainly made life hard for the Mau Mau and driven many gangs out of the forests, where 1,000-pound bombs from four-engined Lincolns had been adding to their discomfort. By skilfully exploiting the pressure through the contacts he had established, Superintendent Ian Henderson, of the Special Branch, obtained the surrender, which was disguised as a capture, of General China, a young man holding command in the Mount Kenya area and ranking as deputy to the Commander-in-Chief, Field Marshal Dedan Kimathi. After some sympathetic interrogation, he offered to negotiate the surrender of all Mau Mau leaders, and the troops were consequently withdrawn from the forests for the elaborate, intricate, and delicate operation named (with China in mind!) Wedgwood. China's two lieutenants surrendered, and there were reports of a gathering in the Aberdares of 2,000 Mau Mau eager to accept the terms offered by Erskine before their expiry on April 10, 1954. Then on the 7th a battalion of the K.A.R. on routine operations cornered a large gang in the Reserve, where the cease-fire did not apply, and destroyed it. In itself it was the most successful coup by a battalion to date, but its result was to smash the fragile Wedgwood, and it was never clearly established whether this gang intended to join the prospective deserters or deter them. In any case they were deterred now, and not only did the 2,000 disperse but China's lieutenants escaped. As for China himself, his life was spared, much to the rage of most Kenyans. He had done his best to halt the rebellion.

Erskine had been faced with a difficult decision, for while wishing to extract full value from the cooperation inveigled out of China, he was also planning a great purging of the pervasive and truculent Mau Mau element in Nairobi. This operation was named Anvil, and the duration of Wedgwood had been tailored for the closest fit between the conflicting demands of the two. The military share of Anvil consisted of laying a cordon round the entire city, the close cordoning of sectors in turn, and escorting suspects to reception and detention centres. It was entrusted to 49 Brigade with the Buffs, Black Watch and 6th K.A.R. also under command. The police, who included twenty-six special combat platoons, were responsible for marshalling of the population, searching of their houses, and interrogation. After clandestine reconnaissance, the cordon was laid before dawn on April 24, and despite the extensive preparations that had to be made the population were taken by surprise.

For twelve days the soldiers blocked roads, searched more occult lines of exit, endured abuse from unthinking Europeans and Asians, bundled suspects on to buses, with possessions packed and labelled, for the journey to the reception camp at Langata, 5 miles from the city centre, and escorted them thence in trainloads of 1,000 to detention camps at Mackinnon Road and Manyani, where Y Company of the Fifth Fusiliers performed guard duties, 250 miles from their comrades in Nairobi. The surrounds of Nairobi were then similarly combed and relieved of those elements that could not pass police scrutiny as lawful inhabitants. It was wearisome toil for the troops, and they derived no joy from their herdsmen's duties. But the 16,538 men and women they removed to the detention camps cut a gaping hole in the Mau Mau organisation. Their departure caused a dramatic drop in the crime rate in Nairobi and, of greater military importance, a steady crumbling set in of the strongest of the Mau Mau defences, secrecy. Informers were the most important fragments cast by the hammer upon the Anvil.

Keeping a battalion of 49 Brigade in Nairobi—first the Northumberlands then the Inniskillings—Erskine now assigned his British troops the task of organising the Reserve and settled areas for their own self-defence, in particular the territory north and east of Nairobi. Much diplomacy had to be exercised to persuade farmers to concentrate their labour and much chivvying to re-settle the inhabitants of the Reserve in villages. But the Kikuyu enjoyed being turned into soldiers and great enthusiasm was displayed at the culmination to a period of training, a *baraza*. The steady build-up of the Kikuyu Guard, and likewise of the combat units of the police, provided the strongest evidence that the Mau Mau were losing the battle. No longer could they roam the countryside with impunity. Information about them had at last begun to circulate, and the great combination of forces ranged against them were killing them off at almost a hundred a week.

In August 1954 39 Brigade, with the Inniskillings under command, left the Thika-Fort Hall area for that of Meru and Embu, there to combine the strengthening of the home guard organisation with Mau Mau hunting up the slopes of Mount Kenya. Very soon after their arrival at Embu, the Devons encountered that rare phenomenon, a gang prepared to stand and fight. Indeed, a patrol returned with the news that it had used all its ammunition in a fight against it, whereupon the company commander, Major Hastings, took nine of his men after it, together with a home guard patrol under an European officer. Hastings located the enemy in the forest below the bamboo belt and led a charge, with Patchet blazing from the hip, only to be sent spinning by a bullet fired by a Mau Mau from ten yards. 'Kill the bastard!' he cried, firing his Patchet from the ground. His men killed two, who turned out to be brothers holding high rank and armed with service rifles. This was at 3.30 p.m. and not until 11.30 next morning did Hastings, who had been shot through the chest, at last reach the airstrip for evacuation after a carry of 8 miles through thick forest on an improvised bamboo stretcher.

There was to be a D.S.O. for Hastings and for the troops in Kenya a Sycamore helicopter, following a plea to the House of Lords made by Brigadier Lord Thurlow, who had been commanding 39 Brigade since February. Requests for one had been made before, but the altitude and the scarcity of casualties had caused Kenya to lag far behind Malaya in this respect. The former still posed its problems; the Piper Pacer remained the soldier's best friend.

In November a scratch party of Devons arrived in the lorry of a mobile bath section to complete the destruction of a large gang forced into the River Tana by a motley collection of highly excited policemen and home guardsmen, directed from above by a Pacer. This was one of the more successful of many similar adventures, which generally were not very productive in this area, the Mau Mau having vast room for manoeuvre on the slopes of Mount Kenya. The greatest achievement made by this brigade here lay in the conversion of sullen and suspicious tribesmen into enthusiastic home guardsmen.

Elephants liked this district. A section of Buffs were put to flight naked by an inquisitive bull while under the showers of a mobile bath. A fusilier of the Inniskillings found the only way to evade a charging herd was to charge back through them. Having safely done this, he shot up a party of Mau Mau and spent three days alone in the forest before rejoining his patrol.

There was a pause for the relief, as the year ended, of the two British battalions that saw most action in Kenya, the Buffs and the Devons. They left respectively in December and January, having each made a ceremonial march through Nairobi in a manner that belied their lack of practice. The Buffs could claim 290 Mau Mau killed and 194 taken prisoner, usually wounded, and had themselves lost only one man killed by a Mau Mau, whose rifle was one of two service rifles out of 114 assorted and in most cases absurdly crude firearms they had captured. These figures could neither be published nor publicised. The Devons had encountered tougher opposition. They had inflicted rather fewer kills and themselves lost five killed on operations and six wounded, although not in all cases by the enemy. Whereas the Buffs gained no decoration higher than a mention or Queen's Commendation, the Devons won five.

The relieving battalions, who joined 39 Brigade after a month's acclimatisation, were the 1st King's Own Yorkshire Light Infantry, who had been in Germany since their return from Malaya in August 1951, and the 1st Rifle Brigade, released from the role of motorised infantry in which they had fought their way into Germany.

Still faithful to the principle of concentration of force, Erskine now staged a divisional operation, named Hammer, on the Aberdares, where according to the intelligence estimate, which was usually short of the mark, there were now 1,700 Mau Mau. The northern part was allotted to 39 Brigade, with the Northumberland Fusiliers, K.O.Y.L.I. and Rifle Brigade; the centre to 70 Brigade, with the 3rd, 5th, and 7th K.A.R. and a company of the Inniskillings; and the southern to 49 Brigade, with the Black Watch, 4th and 26th K.A.R. They were controlled by Hinde from Nyeri. It was possible to deploy such a force deep inside the range because of the tracks made by the 39th Corps Engineer Regiment and the battalions themselves. Even so, there was room enough in this area for a further nine battalions, and the task of search was made the harder by heavy, sustained rain—this began to fall, ahead of seasonal schedule, on January 6, 1955, just as the battalions began to comb the moorland summit, having completed the preliminaries of barring the fringes and putting the stops in position. Such was the cold that two of the Rifle Brigade's pack ponies died of exposure, and the men would no doubt have done likewise but for their two blankets and nightly issue of rum.

This operation ended on February 11, after companies had made a coordinated sweep down to the stops, which included home guardsmen, lining the fringes. It produced a mere 161 kills and captures. There was then a switch to Mount Kenya for a similar dusting by 39 Brigade, reinforced by companies of the Black Watch and Inniskillings, and by 70 Brigade. Gangs of Meru panga men were employed to cut jeep tracks right up to the snowline. Hinde called this operation First Flute (after a racehorse) and it differed from Hammer in that each battalion attempted to scour and dominate its allotted area rather than sweep the enemy out of it. Valettas joined the lighter craft to achieve a mammoth supply drop. But more animals were stirred up than Mau Mau, including a herd of elephants at 14,000 feet, and when the operation ended on April 7 eliminations again amounted to no more than ten per cent of the estimated total—277 out of 2,800. The Rifle Brigade obtained a good share of these when, having found that they had 'rented a bad moor' on the western part of the range, they switched to the east to make a combined swoop from below and above without reconnaissance or other hint of their intention.

The forests were now handed over for the Special Branch men to mix, unarmed, with the Mau Mau and make another brave but vain attempt to negotiate a surrender. The battalions setttled to the humdrum task of food denial operations, 39 Brigade around Nanyuki, 49 Brigade in the Rift Valley. They had enormous areas to watch and control, countless eyes upon them from huts and gorges, and many touchy farmers sceptical of the need and feasibility of bringing their stock in nightly for its custody behind bomas. Meanwhile the watch on the forest fringes continued, and for penetration beyond it each battalion selected a company for specialised 'tracker-combat' duties, complete with dogs and trackers. The idea was that now that the forest Mau Mau had become fewer in number and greater in skill, only the highest standard of bushcraft and marksmanship could prevail.

It was a time of change. At the end of January 1955 the 1st Royal Irish Fusiliers arrived from garrison duty in Korea to join 49 Brigade and take over a part of the Rift Valley from the Black Watch, who were due for a tumultuous welcome from Scotland on return from their two exacting but so dissimilar campaigns. The 1st Gloucestershire arrived from England at the start of April, with seventy officers and men left who had fought on the Imjin and, tiring of the aura of 'Glorious', were eager to embark on a new campaign. Thus for the first time there were six British battalions available for operations; with the customary six of the K.A.R., Erskine handed them over at the start of May to a new and younger C.-in-C., Lieutenant-General G. W. Lathbury, formerly of the Ox and Bucks Light Infantry and the Airborne.

Erskine by his bludgeon blows had reduced the Mau Mau to an irregular maze of disjointed, dispirited groups, whose ambitions ran no higher than to lie low until the storm seemed over and the forces dispersed. About 8,400 of them had been killed, 889 captured, and 22,502 placed in detention. Their own killings had been cut down from almost 100 a month at the time of Erskine's arrival to twenty, and almost all of their victims were their own Kikuyu compatriots. The Kikuyu Guard had been merged with the Tribal Police and was a real force to be reckoned with. The Reserve had been organised into villages, and district officers were to be seen with happy faces, a thing that amazed the Black Watch on their return for operation Hammer. Indeed, Fort Hall and Thika Districts and a large part of the Rift Valley had been handed back as the full responsibility of the civil administration.

Yet there were still fifty-one gang leaders at large, according to intelligence reckoning, and it was clear that they still exerted powerful influence, particularly on the Kikuyu who tended the crops and stock of European farmers around Naivasha to the west and Nanyuki to the north. Furthermore these men were as cunning as they were ruthless, experts at the art of survival. Lathbury was quick to realise that military measures on their own could never squeeze these last hardy, evanescent gangs into extinction, and that the most effective means of hounding them down, gang by gang, would be by use of ex-gangsters. The system had been introduced some eighteen months previously by one of the young field intelligence officers Erskine had brought in, Major Kitson of the Rifle Brigade. He had stumbled on the idea while questioning a captive who changed sides, so to speak, in the midst of his interrogation and subsequently performed prodigies as a spy. With Erskine's blessing 'pseudo' gangs were formed, consisting of both loyalists and ex-Mau Mau, and they made deep penetration into the Mau Mau organisation, disguised as real gangs and working under white officers daubed black, in most cases of the Kenya Regiment. Lathbury planned to expand this system and to allow the pseudo gangs to operate under their own Kikuyu leaders.

He still intended to use his troops for offensive action in conjunction with the pseudo gangs and in order to free them from their tedious protective duties preventing thefts of wheat and cattle, he addressed farmers on the need to establish their own farm guards. Lathbury records that 'the response to my appeal was most satisfactory', and this must have been pleasing, since it was not the first to have been made. He was able, for the first time in the campaign, to allot his battalions periods of intensive training, concentrating on bushcraft, tracking, and swift marksmanship.

Around this time, in the month of June, the 1st King's Shropshire Light Infantry, having spent two years in Germany after return from Korea, came to Muthaiga Camp, Nairobi, and took over from the Inniskillings. The latter had been there since December and taken part in many swift search and cordon operations in conjunction with the police. They were awarded the Freedom of the City and celebrated the honour with a ceremonial march prior to their return home.

On July 15, 1955, the last great trouncing of the Aberdares began, under the guise of Operation Dante. The Gloucesters, Irish Fusiliers and K.S.L.I., all of 49 Brigade, entered the forest before dawn, together with the 26th K.A.R., and in that order from the left formed a network of ambushes inside the southern end of the range. Then down came the bombs, from Lincolns and Harvards, and shells from the 3.7-inch guns of 156 A.A. Battery. This lasted a week, at the end of which the ambush cordons patrolled inwards to comb the moorland roof and examine the effects of the bombardment. Certainly the Mau Mau were shaken up, but a disappointingly high number escaped. This may have been partly because the battalions were short of experience of forest warfare, which could only be gained by wearisome trial and disappointment and was less evenly distributed under the new system of forming specialised tracker-combat teams. It was a sad iniatioitn for the K.S.L.I. Their commanding officer, Lieutenant-Colonel Brooke-Smith, was accidentally shot dead, to become the highest-ranking, but far from only, British soldier to lose his life this way.

Outside the Aberdares A Company of the Irish made a successful sortie to kill one Njathi Kigiri, who was ranked third in the Mau Mau hierarchy. Information about his hide was obtained from a prisoner, and its location was thought to be established after prolonged questioning. The company commander did not move his platoons from their farm areas until after dark, and they then made a long ride to take up cordon positions in thick bush by use of map and shrouded torch. The assault group attacked at dawn, after a difficult and uncertain approach. They found the supposed hide empty—but soon afterwards a gangster was flushed from a shelter near by and shot dead with three of his lieutenants. He was the wanted man.

Another important leader, Waruingi Kurier, the top Mau Mau of all Nairobi, was killed early in August, having probably been forced into motion by Operation Dante. He was tracked down by Kitson's pseudo gang and met his end in the Lari forest, the undergrowth of which was systematically hacked down by an enormous line of panga-wielding Kikuyu women, as eager for blood as any pack of hounds. It was the Mau Mau who risked massacre at Lari now.

The people of Kenya could take over the offensive. Lathbury pulled his battalions back to the forest edge, from there to lay blockade and patrol certain zones only, leaving the rest to pseudo gangs bearing the imposing title Special Force.

The withdrawal of British troops could begin, and 39 Brigade in the Nanyuki area were the first to thin out. The Royal Northumberland Fusiliers departed homewards on August 14, having completed almost two years in Kenya and spent a great deal of energy without much to show for it in their private scorebook. The K.O.Y.L.I. left in the second half of October, being required in Aden. They too had had to work desperately hard for a few successes, and their score of thirty kills was well below their expectations on their arrival a year earlier. Most of them had been gained by their combat-tracker company, who had been continually on operations in the Aberdares and Mount Kenya since the last week in May. The Rifle Brigade had similarly been employed and had split many gangs into fragments, making good use of the new self-loading rifle, with which they had been issued, as by birthright, for the first operational trials. In late November they completed the disintegration of 39 Brigade by moving to the Rift Valley and relieving the Royal Irish Fusiliers in Naivasha, which was now the only district not yet restored to the peace system of administration. The Irish had been very successful in organising their widespread farmlands against the depredations of the Mau Mau, and when they left for home just before Christmas, after a stay of eleven months, they took with them a presentation from the settlers of Naivasha and the warm congratulations of the C.-in-C.

The only part of the huge battalion area that had not been scoured by the Irish was Lake Naivasha itself. There were thought to be seventy Mau Mau sheltering within this great reed-enclustered swamp of 400 square miles, and a great round-up of them began on December 30, under the name of Operation Bullrush. It was the last, and perhaps greatest, combined effort by all branches of the security forces. The Rifle Brigade and three companies each of the Gloucesters and K.S.L.I. formed the main search force; the East African Recce Squadron provided mobility for the cordon; the Royal Engineers built rafts (which did not prove too seaworthy) and tracks; the Kenya Police deployed nine special combat platoons, or general service units, and four tracker teams; the Kikuyu Guard was represented by a striking force of tribal police: and 300 prisoners were employed on cutting rides into the interior. The R.A.F. had by now lost both its Lincolns and Harvards, but was able to wage propaganda warfare by bombarding the Mau Mau with broadcast appeals.

For twenty-four days the wading, boating and beating continued across the misty, insect-plagued swamps, and the meagre yield was twenty-four Mau Mau, killed, captured or surrendered. But they included a field marshal, and at least the remainder had been deprived of a secure base. Twenty-four at this stage of the campaign was the equivalent of 200 in the days when Mau Mau were easier game. This was the last operation launched by General Hinde and he left for England, to receive a well-deserved knighthood.

In April 1956 there were more departures. The Rifle Brigade sailed off to Malaya to try out against a more formidable foe the techniques they had perfected. The Gloucesters went by air to Aden, having spent almost a year based on Gilgil and done endless, patient patrolling into the Aberdares around Kipipiri. 'We were loath to say farewell,' wrote their correspondent to *Back Badge*, the regimental magazine. He spoke for all battalions.

Directed now by Superintendent Henderson, the pseudo gangs were swinging into their stride. The renegades were allowed to carry on with the exact pattern of life of a Mau Mau gangster and there could of course be no more deadly foe for their former comrades, most of whom showed equal willingness to change sides on being captured. Not one case was reported of desertion from a pseudo gang. By June the fighting strength of the Mau Mau was down to 900, a drop of over 2,000 since Lathbury assumed command, and the location of nearly all the gangs was known. The most important of these was that of Dedan Kimathi, the self-styled Field Marshal Commanding-in-Chief the Kenya Land and Freedom Armies, Knight Commander of the African Empire, Popular Prime Minister of the Southern Hemisphere. On October 7 the pseudo gangs concentrated in the Aberdares for a special drive against this gang. It ended at dawn on October 21, when a tribal policeman or Kikuyu Guardsman fired three shots at a man in a leopard skin coat lurking at the forest edge near Nyeri. The third one brought him down, and as a result the legendary Kimathi was captured, tried, and hanged.

Within a fortnight—that is on November 2 1956—the King's Shropshire Light Infantry, who had been doing plenty of patrol and picquet work from Nairobi, were flown off to the Persian Gulf at two days' notice. Thus the last British battalion to fight the Mau Mau departed as abruptly as the first had arrived four years, plus a fortnight, earlier. Although the State of Emergency was not officially declared at an end until January 12, 1960, its only function now was to keep suspects in detention. The country was safe again, for Kikuyu and Europeans, and the military garrison in the White Highlands was reduced to four battalions of the King's African Rifles. The askaris of the latter had won a great reputation as forest fighters and had made an immense contribution to the Mau Mau's defeat.

Yet the Kikuyu had themselves won the war in the end. It is to the credit of the British generals, both Erskine and Lathbury, that they appreciated from the start that this was the only way it could be won, and the contribution of the British Army was in showing the Kikuyu how to win it. Some 1,817 loyal Africans were killed in the struggle, 32 Europeans and 26 Asians, against 11,503 Mau Mau. The security forces lost 590 killed, according to the official Colonial Office return, and of them 63 were European. But the War Office listed only five British officers and seven soldiers killed in action, which means by the Mau Mau. They were not the only soldiers killed.

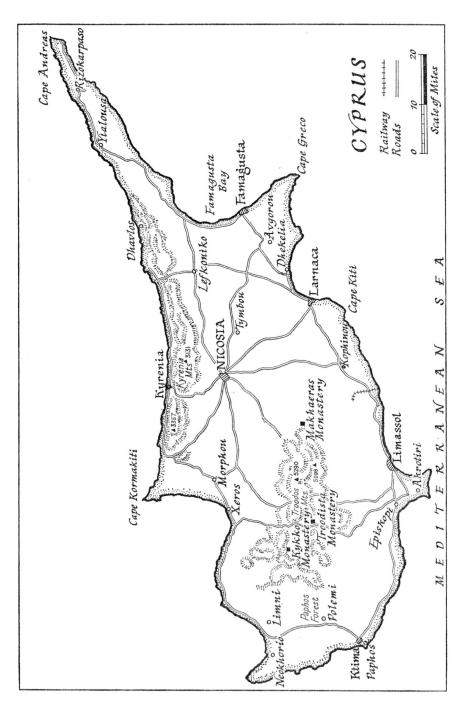

CYPRUS

Railway +++++
Roads ———

Scale of Miles
0 10 20

Cape Andreas

Rizokarpaso

Yialousa

Dhavlos

Famagusta Bay

Lefkoniko

Famagusta

Cape Greco

Avgorou

Dhekelia

Kyrenia

Kyrenia Mts. 3131

Tymbou

Larnaca

Cape Kiti

3357

NICOSIA

Kophinou

Morphou

Makhaeras Monastery

Xeros

Troodos Mts. 5290

Limassol

Kykko Monastery

Troodista Monastery 5098

Akrotiri

Limni

Paphos Forest

Polemi

Episkopi

Neokhorio

Ktima

Paphos

MEDITERRANEAN SEA

Cape Kormakiti

10

Cyprus

1—THE GANGS SUBDUED (1954-57)

I T was a great moment for the old Lord Beaconsfield when he returned from the Congress of Berlin of 1878 with the news that Turkey had ceded Britain the island of Cyprus in exchange for concessions wrung from Russia. 'High and low, the whole country is delighted,' wrote Queen Victoria.

For the romantic Beaconsfield Cyprus was the collector's gem of all colonial possessions, being the Isle of Venus, a conquest of Richard Coeur de Lion on behalf of the Crusaders, and a land with the climate and scenery to match its historical enchantment. His Foreign Secretary, Lord Salisbury, was more concerned about its value as a 'place d'armes' from which to intervene if the route to India was endangered. It proved very useful for this purpose as early as 1882, when a brigade was hurried across to Alexandria to free it from the clutches of Arabi's soldiers, but once the whole of Egypt was occupied that country proved a better base than Cyprus and the latter reverted to the role of a somnolent resort.

When the question of leaving Egypt arose Cyprus again came into the reckoning as a base. Britain had treaty obligations to Jordan and Iraq; she was in alliance with both Greece and Turkey; and she had made an undertaking to keep the peace between Israel and her neighbours. Cyprus was quite as well placed for the fulfilment of these commitments as Egypt, and on June 24, 1954, while negotiations for the evacuation of Egypt were reaching their final stage, it was announced that the Middle East headquarters, both Land and Air, was going to be moved to Cyprus. Britain's experience in the Middle East suggested that this was akin to placing a curse on a hitherto blessed land. Wherever her soldiers tried to find refuge for the discharge of their obligations towards other states, the pervasive fervour of nationalism seemed bound to turn its normally amiable and easy-going inhabitants into scorpions.

In this instance the timing was particularly unfortunate. Of the inhabitants of Cyprus, which is about half the size of Wales, 419,000 were Greeks and 105,000 were Turks, and among the Greeks there was a long established movement for union with their own country, called Enosis. Just before the British Government decided on the move of the Middle East Command, Enosis made far the biggest advance in its history. Its leader was Archbishop Makarios, an ambitious young churchman who in a manner familiar enough in Greece combined the duties of political and religious head of his people. Early in 1954 he made a long visit to Athens and near the end of it announced in a sermon that he had obtained the support of the Greek Government— who being in difficulties on the domestic front were in need of diversion —for the cause of Enosis. It was obvious enough that Britain's strategic plans for Cyprus were quite incompatible with those of Enosis, and Makarios promised a hostile reception for the Middle East Command when its move was announced.

The reaction of the Colonial Office, which hitherto had paid little heed to the aspirations either of Greeks or Turks in Cyprus, was to promise a new constitution conferring a high degree of internal self-government, while ruling out even contemplation of any change of sovereignty. A statement to this effect was made in the Commons by the Minister of State on July 26 and drew caustic comment from Mr. Aneurin Bevan on the folly of establishing Middle East Command 'in the midst of a hostile population'. Next month the population gave their first big display of hostility. Defying newly passed laws against seditious behaviour, the Greek Cypriots paraded in their thousands in Nicosia and were assured by Makarios, who had expressed contempt for the offer of internal self-government: 'We shall remain faithful to our national claim'.

Militarily, Cyprus had become a vacuum after fulfilling the function, as in 1882, of a springboard for the despatch of troops to quell nationalist stirrings in Egypt in 1951–52. It formed a district under a brigadier, whose headquarters was at the capital, Nicosia, and whose troops consisted of no more than a company of infantry on detachment from Egypt, a regiment of artillery, and one of engineers, whose main function was to convert the village of Episkopi, near the south coast port of Limassol, into a township for the accommodation of G.H.Q. It was now thought desirable to bring more troops in, and on August 30, 1954, the 2nd Green Howards arrived from Egypt by the unconventional method of practising an assault landing. The 2nd Royal Inniskilling

Fusiliers, who already provided the detached company, followed on September 22.

Neither of these battalions encountered hostility. Indeed, there is comment in the *Green Howards Gazette* on the warmth of the welcome accorded them by the people of Larnaca, near which they were encamped. The Inniskillings went to Waynes Keep Camp, Nicosia, and impressed the people with a show of pageantry by making a ceremonial flag march round the walls of the old city, which they reported as 'very popular'. On December 1 General Sir Charles Keightley officially transferred G.H.Q. from Fayid to Wolseley Barracks, just outside Nicosia, pending the completion of the work at Episkopi, which true to the tempo of Cypriot life was not expected for another five years. H.Q. Cyprus District had to move to a temporary camp.

In mid-December the United Nations General Assembly refused even to consider the Greek claim to Cyprus, and with vitriolic incitement from Athens radio the youth of Nicosia and Limassol gave volatile outburst to their anger. The police just managed to subdue them in Nicosia, by resort to baton and tear gas, but in Limassol the military had to intervene. The task fell to a squadron of the 35th Field Engineer Regiment, who had studied their procedure. Having obtained the District Commissioner's authority on the back of a bill note, they hoisted their warning banners and eventually fired three shots. The first went high and had no effect; the second and third felled prominent stone hurlers and promptly cleared the street. However, the crowd soon regathered and swelled, without throwing stones. Youngsters were in the forefront, yelling their rage. Another dose of the traditional 'duties in aid' treatment was obviously inadvisable and at the District Commissioner's suggestion the troops withdrew at dusk, drawing a shower of stones as they got in their vehicles under police protection. At 9 p.m. a rainstorm conveniently effected the required dispersal.

It was a worrying situation, of which the most alarming aspect was the fanatical hatred that had been imbued into mere schoolchildren, calling for a revision of long accepted principles of the military role. Now came evidence of an even more sinister influence. An army of guerrillas was being formed to fight for the cause of annexation by Greece, and an oath was being administered to the youths recruited into it: 'I swear by the Holy Trinity to work with all my power for the liberation of Cyprus from the British yoke, sacrificing even my life.' Its name was Eoka, and with the consent of Makarios it had been skilfully built up since the previous October by its founder, Colonel George Grivas, late the Greek Army, whose messages would soon be floating around the island under the signature of Dighenis, a legendary hero.

Known already to be utterly ruthless, he was to prove himself a man of resource and determination, of immense courage, immense ambition, and immense conceit.

In early January 1955 the 40th Field Regiment (from Egypt) became the resident gunner regiment, taking over a camp outside the ancient port of Famagusta with one battery detached at the other end of the island, guarding the radar station near Paphos, on the wild south-west corner. Here, on January 25, they played a leading part in the capture of a party of men making a nocturnal landing in a caique that was found to be laden with arms and explosives. A dramatic trial at Paphos followed, which brought the 40th Field out on crowd control duties.

Despite this blow to their ambitions, Eoka were able to open their campaign, as intended, with a series of explosions that shook G.H.Q. and other places in the early hours of April 1, 1955: an ironic date presaging four years devoid of laughter. As at the start of every colonial emergency, precious little information was available about the marauders and there was nothing much the Government could do other than conceal their perplexity and deploy troops on the protection of important installations, which imposed a heavy strain and wide dispersal of the three gunner and infantry units. Elements of them combined for a search operation on the long and narrow Kyrenian range, which runs parallel to the northern coastline. It did little more than emphasise the enormity of the problems. There would be bigger ones on the higher, thicker clad, and very much more extensive Troodos range, which makes the west centre of the island a bandit's haven.

There was a further spasm of explosions in mid-June, one of which did damage to Keightley's house at Kyrenia, but much greater worry was caused by attacks on police stations and individual policemen, both in the towns and country districts. The Greek element of the Cyprus Police was being systematically undermined, and the morale of the whole country with it. Frightening rioting in Nicosia on August 2 showed the hold Eoka had over both the masses and individuals, but still the Government seemed content to regard it as a passing phase, putting faith in the talks with representatives of Greece and Turkey that were being held in London at the end of the month. They resulted, predictably enough, in deadlock, and meanwhile in Nicosia Eoka struck a deadly blow at the police force by shooting dead a Greek member of the Special Branch in broad daylight. The days of contented, complacent colonial rule were gone; Cyprus was a land of fear.

The first sign of any military girding for action came in August with the promotion of the district commander, Brigadier Ricketts (whom we last met in command of 29 Brigade in Korea), to major-general and his appointment as Director of Public Security, although without the much needed increment of a joint intelligence staff. Headquarters 50th and 51st Infantry Brigades, both formed in Egypt in 1952, were brought respectively to Nicosia and Famagusta, and the 1st South Staffordshire and the 1st Royal Scots came with them (in that order). The 3rd Commando Brigade, consisting of 40 and 45 Commandos, came from Malta and established its headquarters at Limassol, freeing the engineers for constructional duties.

These moves were completed by mid-September, and as if to prove that they were necessary Greek rioters burned and destroyed the British Institute at Nicosia. At the same time there was a mass escape by people detained under an emergency law. The British Government retaliated by announcing, on September 25, that 'in view of the import-ance of the island as a base for the discharge of treaty obligations and having regard for the need for concerted action by all security forces', a serving soldier, Field Marshal Sir John Harding, had been appointed Governor and Commander-in-Chief in place of the luckless servant of the Colonial Office, Sir Robert Armitage.

Harding was due to hand over the duties of C.I.G.S. to the soldier who had already performed a task of rescue for the Colonial Office, General Templer. The date was advanced by over a month, and on October 3 Harding landed at Nicosia aerodrome to get to grips with the slippery, many-headed vipers let loose by Eoka. His was a more delicate task than had faced Templer in Malaya, for whereas the latter had to galvanise the population to action against a self-evident menace, Harding had to subdue the belligerent members of a movement that had the support of three-quarters of the people and it had to be done with the minimum combustion of animosity amid highly inflammable material. There was a certain grim justice in the chance that it should have fallen to him to clean up the mess, for he had been influential in saddling Cyprus with its strategic commitments and thus restricting the concessions that could be made to nationalist aspirations. Yet from the very start he showed himself more than equal to the daunting task he had inherited.

None was more impressed than the writer Laurence Durrell, who was press adviser to the Cyprus Government and noted in Harding 'the deftness and dispatch of a francolin . . . the keen clear bird-mind of one trained to decisions based in a trained power of the will . . . the graces of a courtier combined with the repose and mildness of a family sage.' Makarios was also impressed and was heard to echo the oft-heard lament, 'Why did they not send us such a man a long time ago?' But he could not accept any of the proposals Harding was empowered to put forward, however tactful and friendly the approach, and there was nothing for it but to counter force with force. Dressed as a civilian for the performance of his political duties and as a soldier for his many visits to his troops, the Field Marshal was swift to clarify the duties of the latter. 'Courtesy and firmness' were the watchwords he gave them, and he had the knack of inspiring confidence.

A further influx of troops followed his arrival. The 1st Royal Norfolk and the 1st Gordon Highlanders arrived by air from England and the 1st Royal Leicestershire from Khartoum, and on October 28 the 1st Middlesex disembarked at Famagusta for a three-year tour complete with families, who had to wait for rioters to be cleared from the streets of Larnaca before they could take possession of their hired quarters. Meanwhile the command set-up was being thoroughly overhauled. General Ricketts reverted to the role of administrative district commander, and the coordination of every type of activity concerned with security was entrusted to a Chief of Staff, an appointment for which an artilleryman, Brigadier G. F. Baker, was chosen and arrived from the Imperial Defence College in early November. In a wired-in compound containing requisitioned houses and huts outside the Old City of Nicosia, he presided over a network of departments, some controlling things of substance, such as Maritime, Army, Air and Police, and others concerned with intangible matters just as important to the fate of the campaign, Intelligence, Information, Immigration Control and Public Relations. A slogan was circulated: 'Cooperation is not enough: there must be integration.'

Command was exercised through District Security Committees, the familiar trinities of district commissioner, brigade or battalion commander, and superintendent of police, and there were seven of them within the larger administrative areas of the three brigades. At Nicosia 50 Brigade had direct command either of the South Staffords or the Royal Norfolks, with the other acting as island reserve; to the north-west the Gordons controlled a large area from Xeros; and further west the Royal Scots had taken over the Paphos area, with base at Coral Bay camp. From Limassol the 3rd Commando Brigade extended as far as the inscrutable steeps of the Troodos range. At Famagusta 51 Brigade had the Inniskillings and 40th Field directly under command; the Royal Leicesters were spread eastwards from Kyrenia along the sharp and narrow range running into the Karpas Peninsula or Panhandle; and the Middlesex controlled Larnaca, based on Dhekelia and helped by the Green Howards, until their departure in December.

Thus the troops were spread all round the island, and each battalion was itself far spread. Again to quote Durrell, their 'splendid professional bearing and brown faces—still smiling and kindly—brought a fresh atmosphere to dusty purlieus of the five towns.' Yet the hearts and minds of the people, most of all of the young, were too far estranged to be swayed by smiles and kindness, and the very nature of the soldiers' duties militated against the friendliness that in normal times would have been reciprocal. For their foremost duty was to bolster a police force on the verge of collapse, and the fact that it had been necessary to bring them to Cyprus for this purpose signalled a victory for Eoka in itself and made these foreign soldiers of an invading imperialist army the principal target for the venom that was still being spread unimpeded by Athens radio and could also be circulated by an only mildly censored press.

It was a cardinal principle of 'duties in aid' that soldiers and police should stick to the methods and equipment in which they were trained, but the weakness of the police and the vulnerability of even one shot to adverse propaganda turned the principle topsy turvy. Battalions were therefore ordered to form their own riot squads to 'underpin' the police. Wearing steel helmets and face shields and with gasmasks at the ready, the members of these squads carried a baton in one hand and in in the other a shield, as which a dustbin lid served initially. Two sections of each internal security platoon were equipped in this manner, and behind them came the platoon commander with bugler (who also carried a megaphone), recorder, and his two projectile firers armed with tear-gas gun and dye sprayer. The latter was expected to be particularly effective against women and girls but had limitations in range; unlike flame-throwing, for which the equipment had been designed, there were plenty of volunteers for this job. The third section came behind, with dannert wire, stretchers, wireless, and a reserve of fire power for use only if life was endangered.

In the early months the riot squads seldom came to close quarters. The troops would be greeted with stones and bottles as they jumped out of their trucks to quell a disturbance, and there would then be a dust cloud through which fleeting forms would be visible darting up back streets. But there were exceptions, one of which was encountered by the Royal Scots early in October in the remote village of Neokhorio, close to the Baths of Aphrodite on the island's north-west tip. The police went in first, in an attempt to disperse a crowd waving Greek flags after dark. They were set upon by women, backed by a barrage of stones from behind, and unwisely threw tear-gas grenades at their assailants. The wind blew the gas into their own unmasked faces, and they were routed by the time two sections of the Royal Scots arrived to 'underpin' them. The latter were obliged to withdraw to the police station, and retaliatory action had to await the imposition of a two-day curfew from dawn the day after.

A steady increase in the bang of amateur bomb and sterner crump of professionally manufactured grenade gave warning that black comedy could so easily lapse into tragedy. Lance-Corporal Milne of the Royal Scots was the first soldier to lose his life, when driving a vehicle into which a grenade was tossed near Paphos, giving this district notoriety that it was to maintain. This was on October 27, and on the following day three Gordon Highlanders were wounded by a grenade while engaged in clearing the streets of Morphou of rioters.

In the larger towns schoolchildren rampaged and pestered, undeterred by two broadcast rebukes from Harding. The Middlesex had a sample of their sting as their first taste of action in Larnaca. Having laid out a British police officer with their stones, a swarm of boys and girls bolted on the approach of a Middlesex platoon and took refuge in St. Lazarus Church and its churchyard, whence they deluged the troops with pieces of rubble and catapulted marbles. Rather than turn the churchyard into a battlefield, the young platoon commander laid siege to the gaggle of would-be heroes. Parents were persuaded to extract some of the less defiant and more infant ones, and at length, after the mayor had done his best to raise the siege by diplomatic means, the sight of food arriving for the troops was too much for the sixty boys and girls still defending the unattacked church, and they laid down their catapults and came out in subdued little groups.

In mid-November Eoka stepped up the momentum of their attacks, compelling Harding to declare a State of Emergency on November 26, although the detaining of suspects, the outlawing of Eoka, and the banning of assemblies had already been authorised. Scarcely a day passed now without an incident being reported from some part of the island, either of the ambush of a vehicle by grenade throwers or sten gunners, a bomb explosion in camp or cafe, or the murder of a soldier, policeman, or uncooperative Cypriot, shot at close quarters in the back. While bombs could cause the biggest sensations, such as the one at Kykko Camp, Nicosia, in which a staff-sergeant was killed and a warrant officer badly wounded and the one at the Caledonian Ball in which five people were wounded by a bomb intended for the absent Harding, the street shootings were the most unsettling and deadly form of attack. A sergeant was shot dead in Nicosia on November 24, four soldiers were wounded when walking out in mufti in the city on December 7, shot from behind with a sten gun, two more were shot on December 14, and so it continued, never with any witness of the attack available.

On December 15 Major Brian Coombe of the Royal Engineers had the rare experience of coming face to face with the foe. He had command of a field squadron sent out to improve facilities at the hastily pitched camps of the new battalions. One detachment was on Mount Olympus, the highest peak of the Troodos range, and the squadron lost two men killed in this excellent ambush country and would have lost two more, including an officer, if the gangsters had not muffed the chance of adding them to their bag as they rolled downhill out of their wrecked jeep. Coombe, however, was returning from Troodos and had reached supposedly safe country, with himself at the wheel of his Land Rover. Then came the shots from an automatic, and Coombe's passenger (his appointed driver) flopped, mortally wounded. He pulled up round the other side of a spur and climbed it armed with a sten, to find the gunmen just below him. There was an exchange of fire at short range, but to his annoyance Coombe could not score a hit, and neither could his opponents, who were firing wildly from behind a bank. Out of ammunition, Coombe returned to the jeep to get his driver's and, going back where the spur was higher, caught the gunmen where they had less cover. Three came out with their hands up, but then a machine-gun opened up and, reacting to the trick, Coombe shot the three men coming towards him and emptied the last magazine of his sten at the machine-gun. This produced a cry of 'Don't shoot, I surrender,' and a man emerged with his hands up, moving very unsteadily. However, he suddenly made off and escaped hit from the bullets Coombe had left in his revolver. Of the three that had previously surrendered, one was dead, one badly wounded, and the third full of defiant chat about British Nazis. Luckily a patrol of the Gordons arrived before he had time to realise that Coombe was out of ammunition.

The dead gunman was accorded a hero's funeral in Nicosia and the South Staffords had to intervene to disperse the frenzied crowd that illegally assembled for it, while the dead sapper was buried with full ceremony in the privacy of Nicosia's military cemetery at Waynes Keep. Coombe, who was awarded the George Medal, was persuaded to submit to interview by press correspondents and somewhat surprised them by begging them not to make him a hero for killing 'a frightened young Cypriot' who had murdered his driver. 'Do not deepen the rift between the Cypriots and the British. Do not encourage the Cypriots to build up a hero by producing a British hero; do not force them to make a hero of a murderer. I ask that there should be no jubilation, no exulting over this affair.' It was a wise, indeed noble, plea for sanity, and if nothing more, it did something to reduce Eoka's lead in propaganda, both in Cyprus itself and in the outer world.

On the day after Coombe's feat by Troodos, the 40th Field lost a subaltern killed when on bolster duty at a police station at Yialousa in the Panhandle. He was shot dead while throwing a grenade at the attackers. Within six hours a patrol of the 40th Field gained revenge by netting six heavily armed Eoka men caught in ambush near Dhavlos, on the eastern end of the Kyrenian range. This was more than had been achieved in a drive by elements of five units here the previous month, with Auster aircraft and helicopters to aid them, and showed what could be achieved by perseverance.

In the Troodos range, where peaks such as Mount Olympus and others standing well over 5,000 feet were now covered by snow, the Commandos were slowly coming to grips with the immense problems facing them. The flower of Grivas's army, the mountain guerrilla gangs, lived up here, and they had wonderful facilities for concealment in the pine forests, monasteries, myriad of caves, and the well-cellared villages that were liberally sprinkled both around the summit and the foothills. Police tracker dogs, sent out from London, proved a valuable aid, especially when the weather was not too hot for them, and helped the Commandos to make some arrests in a combined drive with the Royal Scots and Gordons. But the army was still at the groping stage, having to build up its own information as it went along, and there was a strong need for more troops yet.

It could for once be met, with the evacuation of Egypt almost complete and the back broken of the Mau Mau rebellion. Troop movements in January 1956 brought an overall increase of three battalions. The 16th Parachute Brigade, with the 1st and 3rd Battalions, came to form the island reserve, encamping near Nicosia; this freed the Royal Norfolks, who took Limassol over from 40 Commando, who in turn relieved the Royal Scots at Paphos, enabling them to return home. The 1st Highland Light Infantry came next, also by air from England, and after a brief initiation they took over the Panhandle, with headquarters at Dhavlos. The Nicosia garrison was strengthened by the arrival from Egypt of the 1st Royal Warwickshire, who opened yet another new camp, a bleak performance in the gales and mud of winter. Then came the 1st Wiltshire, ready for a three-year tour on disembarkation by lighter at Famagusta off the ancient *Lancashire*. They took over the Kyrenia district from the Royal Leicesters, with tactical headquarters in a roadside cutting in the hills. The latter moved to Famagusta, to patrol its oft shaken streets in place of the 2nd Royal Inniskillings, who like the already departed 2nd Green Howards and the remainder of the resurrected 2nd battalions were due for disbandment.

One of the aims of Eoka was to tie as many troops as possible to maintaining order in the towns, and to this end full use was made of the hatred poured so industriously into the schoolchildren by Athens radio and their teachers. The South Staffords endured a pelting in Nicosia from hundreds of children egged on by two priests, and such was the turbulence that Harding ordered the closing of the city's largest school on January 19. On February 10 there were demonstrations by school-children throughout the island, whipped to fresh rage by the fact that a youth had been killed in Famagusta while aggressively defending a barricade the Royal Leicesters had been ordered to dismantle. The Royal Norfolks at Limassol had to contend with the liveliest foray during these demonstrations. They were pelted with stones by girls who had the Greek flag illegally hoisted in their midst. It was grim, beastly work for the 'swede-bashers' to have to close on the hell-kittens, be spat upon and scratched, and eventually win a tug-of-war for possession of the flag. Yet the job was done without the thing most wanted by their adversaries, a display of anger to match their own.

The example of the schoolgirls inspired youths in neighbouring villages to stage similar demonstrations, and on at least one occasion the Norfolks retaliated in a manner of their own devising. A mob of thirty or so persistently refused to disperse, until at last a line of Norfolks came up from behind them with bayonets fixed and a grim look on their normally patient faces. The youths were herded into a lorry that had been backed into position behind the baton men facing the crowd. It was driven off with two bren guns trained on it from an escort vehicle just behind, leaving the elders of the village with gaping mouths and popping eyes. For four miles the vehicles bumped and whined their way up into the foothills of the Troodos range. Then they halted and the captives were ordered out. Some obviously imagined that the great moment of martyrdom was at hand and some had lost the urge to be heroes. But none had an inkling of the awful fate in store. 'Don' lookt so anxious, bor,' said the officer. 'It's a lovely afternoon for a walk. Cheerio.' The soldiers drove off, waving farewell to some flabbergasted faces. There was no more trouble in that village.

For many soldiers life seemed an incessant drudgery of guard or stand-by duties, broken only by the strain and indignities of mob dis-persal or the scarcely more uplifting task of patrolling the streets with shouts of 'Mesa, Mesa!' (Inside) in order to enforce the curfew that was invariably clamped down on the bang of bomb or shot and was in turn followed by a search. But as in Malaya and Kenya the importance of combining offensive with defensive action was appreciated from the start, and as often as a party left camp to counter a threat from their adversaries another sallied forth to make some surprise swoop, guided either by word from an informer, an officer's hunch, or the mere hope with which a hand is plunged into the sawdust at the church fete's lucky dip. There was a perpetual search for information, and the greater the shortage the more haphazard had to be the means.

There were three different kinds of swoop. The smallest in scope and most frequent was the 'whirlwind', which involved a sudden descent by a small party that might travel incognito in the back of a civilian lorry to make a search of a particular house or might erect a road block and search and question all passers-by. On a larger scale there was the village search, so familiar to those who had served in Palestine. This posed the problem of an unheralded dawn occupation, which would be followed by loudspeaker announcement that curfew had been imposed, a house by house search by police with soldier escort, and the marshalling of the inhabitants for screening. There was a touch of adventure in such an operation for those inured to routine security duties. Laying a cordon at night in unreconnoitred country is an art of some delicacy, and the sense of occasion was usually sharpened for the assembling troops by the sight of a masked informer come to make identifications and girls of the W.R.A.C. who were serving with the R.M.P. and had the task of searching women suspects. Sunrise was the crucial time, for any fugitive seen sneaking away would be sure to have a price on his head, especially if he offered a sentry bribe to let him pass.

The third was the large scale swoop, involving large numbers of troops and calling for a high degree of coordination and security. One such was the island-wide search of monasteries, carried out on December 8, 1955. It was conducted with conscientious decorum, with battalion padres playing the role of mediators, and both arms and ammunition were unearthed. Predictably there was outraged protest, led by Makarios himself, against the violation of the sanctity of holy places by 'British barbarians'.

It was obvious enough that Makarios was in unholy alliance with Eoka; indeed a search of his house revealed a store of bombs and letters signed 'Dighenis' indicating his approval of the 'execution' of faint-hearts who failed to carry out the terrorist activities assigned to them. On March 9, 1956, Makarios was arrested and deported to the Seychelles. The deed was done by the police as he arrived at Nicosia aerodrome to go to Athens and was consequently at the right place for the R.A.F. to convey him to a different destination. The army played no part, except for a company of South Staffords that stood by in the belief that they were to act as a guard of honour and a company of Wiltshires who cordoned the palace of the Bishop of Kyrenia so that he could be deported with Makarios. There were strikes and rioting in protest, and in Nicosia a single company of the Royal Warwicks made twenty baton charges during March alone. Eoka planned some ambitious and callous attacks in revenge, and in the next three months there would be an average of nearly two members of the security forces killed each week, by bomb, mine, or more rarely bullet, with more injured and many innocents, in one case the United States Vice-Consul, falling dead or wounded in the wilder attacks. The army had to concentrate on defence, both of Government property and employees, and neglect operations against guerrillas to keep order in the towns. Curfew enforcement became a monotonous part of a soldier's life, imposed either for a search or as collective punishment combined very often with the imposition of a fine.

One of the more successful Eoka attacks was the shooting of a British police sergeant dead and a Turkish policeman wounded in a street adjacent to Ledra Street, Nicosia, on March 14. This was the tenth murder in this part and the twentieth attempt, and in no instance had information been supplied by a spectator, although the deed was invariably done in daylight and in a crowd, and just as regularly from behind. In most cases the victim had been a serviceman disobeying the regulations requiring him to walk out only if a member of two pairs, one in front, one behind, all armed. By observing these regulations members of the garrison battalions had avoided casualties, but others had been more casual, not reckoning that the danger was as great as portrayed by British newspaper correspondents, who were to dub the narrow, curving Ledra Street 'Murder Mile'.

Now at last drastic action to purge the area of its killers was taken. While the Royal Warwicks cordoned it off and posted rooftop sentries to watch the network of alleys running off the streets, the 1st and 3rd Para carried out a search and handed paper and envelopes to all inhabitants, with a request for anonymous information in the manner employed by Templer in Malaya. It did not work. Ten houses were therefore permamently emptied of their 120 inhabitants. The Paras subsequently carried out a series of whirlwind searches, while the South Staffords and the Royal Warwicks provided patrols and stand-by companies. They established an efficient partnership, and next time there was a shooting, the area was sealed within six minutes and the murderer identified among the 4,000 screened. A watchful eye was also kept on the innumerable alleyways, and there was further discouragement for Eoka when one of their grenadiers was shot dead in the act of throwing by a bren gunner of the Royal Warwicks concealed in ambush position.

On Sunday March 18 two Eoka gunmen showed their respect for the Greek Orthodox Church by entering the one at Kythrea during a service, lining up the congregation, and shooting dead a chorister. Two days later a bomb was placed in Harding's bed, by a member of his house staff in league with Eoka. Having not disturbed him during the night, it was discovered next morning by his batman and removed by the commander of the guard platoon, a subaltern of the Royal Norfolk, who calmly carried it out on a shovel and exploded it in a trench, for which he was awarded the M.B.E. If nothing else, this incident caused realisation that Eoka had made deeper penetration than imagined, and from now on no Cypriots were employed at Government House.

By including Turkish policemen among their targets, Eoka ignited fresh powder that had frightening power of combustion and was to add a new dimension to the peacekeeping duties thrust on the British troops. The first clash between the Greek and Turkish communities occurred in March, in a remote village near the northern coast; the first at Nicosia followed in April. Near the end of May three Turks were battered to death at Aphania, 12 miles from Nicosia, and a half-platoon of Royal Warwicks had to open fire, killing one man, before a sort of quiet was restored to the village. This set off the Turks in Nicosia on a rampage of reprisal, and again the Royal Warwicks had to bear the brunt, forcing frenzied Turks and Greeks from each other's throats and erecting a wire barricade between their two quarters.

Yet more troops had by now arrived. The Royal Horse Guards came in March to relieve the squadron of Life Guards resident until then and give the island the benefit of a complete regiment of armoured cars, with squadrons based on Nicosia, Limassol and Famagusta. In mid-April the 1st King's Own Yorkshire Light Infantry arrived by air from Aden, to achieve the unique triple event of Malaya, Kenya and Cyprus and to raise the garrison to a strength of fifteen fighting units. The K.O.Y.L.I. pitched camp at Limni, in the island's extreme north-west.

The army could now revert to the offensive, and in mid-May the biggest operation yet staged began. It was aimed at the elimination of Grivas himself, whose description had been issued early that month, with the offer of £10,000 for information leading to his capture, which put him at twice the price of any of his lieutenants. He was known to be lurking in the Troodos range, and the first half of the operation, named Pepperpot, was a comb of the northern part of it, and the second half, named Lucky Alphonse, a comb of the southern part. The Para Brigade, as island reserve, had the conducting role and after feint moves to deceive Grivas's pervasive agents, they moved on Troodos in cooperation with 40 and 45 Commandos, companies of the Gordons from Xeros, of the K.O.Y.L.I. from Limni, and in the latter stage of the Royal Norfolk from Limassol. Helicopters, Auster aircraft, police dogs and searchlights were available to increase the troops' powers of detection, and the Blues provided mobile fire support.

The plan was to make converging searches of villages and thus build up information from which to seal and make detailed searches of the forest sector by sector. Grivas tells us in his Memoirs that he heard that the operation was to be mounted and moved out of his headquarters by Kykko Monastery—not to be confused with the place of similar name outside Nicosia—to a hiding place deeper in the Paphos Forest, west of Troodos. Even so, he could not prevent three of his small mountain groups—he had only four in the Kykko area—from being rounded up as the panting blobs of men in green, red, or blue berets, or balmorals, closed through the thickets upon them, and he himself had to make a hazardous night march across precipitous rock to avoid the net closing in on him. This first part of the operation was a success. The troops had made some important captures without encountering opposition and would have suffered no casualties if they had not shot each other up or been tipped out of lorries down mountainsides.

In the second phase, which lasted from June 8–23, Grivas was again set in motion, and as the sun was setting on June 10 he and his five men were filling their water bottles in a stream when a patrol of the 3rd Para came up the winding stream bed and bumped into them at close range. There was a flurry of darting figures and flying bullets, but no human prize fell to the paras, although they picked up a shotgun and Grivas's beret, Sam Browne belt, and some documents. Grivas says the shots went high and that his group hid in pairs in the dense undergrowth that rose beneath oak trees on either side of the stream. They listened to the search mounted all around them and to helicopters flying overhead and after dark made their escape in stockinged feet, 'wondering at the majestic clumsiness of the enemy.' Grivas found refuge at Troodista Monastery, by the main road through the mountains, and a few days later went by road to Limassol.

While the troops still strove to redeem the misfortune of Grivas's disappearance, disaster struck them as awful as any in these post-war years. On June 17 a fire started, by means attributed to Grivas, and made hideous ascent up the dry, parched foliage on the slopes, being swept up re-entrants at something like 30 m.p.h. as by giant bellows up a chimney. Twenty-one officers and men died in or as a result of this awful blaze, most of them Gordon Highlanders who lost one and twelve and Norfolks who lost five. A further sixteen were injured, while a million pounds worth of vehicles and equipment was lost. With another seven deaths caused by shooting mistakes and road mishaps, it was a high price to pay for the capture of a dozen armed gangsters. Depressingly bad markmanship allowed many to escape, Grivas of course being among them, and this was undoubtedly due in part to the great variety of tasks that had been heaped on the soldiers right up to the start of their excursion into the mountains. Guard duties, baton charges, village searches, road block checks—these were hardly the ideal preparation for an exacting test of fitness, forest craft and skill at arms.

But whatever the defects, a stunning blow had been delivered at the mountain guerrillas, on whom the Eoka movement depended for inspiration and cohesion. The prospect of further blows at them was brightened by the despatch of the 2nd Parachute and the Guards Independent Parachute Company, whose arrival was complete by July 21, although without much increase to the overall strength, since the Royal Warwicks went homewards on completion of their foreign tour, being replaced at Nicosia by the K.O.Y.L.I., who handed Limni over to 2nd Para.

Confidence ran high at Harding's headquarters, and with good reason, for every component of the diverse and complicated machinery directed against Eoka was producing better results. All departments of the Police Force had been strongly reinforced by voluntary enlistment from England, with a new chief, Lieutenant-Colonel G. C. White, also imported, and information was at last mounting satisfactorily, thanks in part to better liaison between police and army intelligence agencies, which now included a 'Q' unit consisting of renegade Eoka men and Cypriot loyalists working under a British leader (usually a young officer) like the counter-gangs in Kenya. The navy and air force had between them enormously tightened their hold on arms' smugglers, and the army cooperated at times with interceptions on the coast, by radar watch, and by the provision of three Field Security sections for the scrutiny of immigrants and imported goods. The Royal Corps of Signals formed a special troop to effect the jamming of Athens radio, which had been belatedly ordered in March, and no doubt helped lower the fever. Certainly there was slackening of the Eoka offensive. The army had to devote less strength to police support, and with techniques in the use of helicopters and tracker dogs showing great improvement, prospects for a decisive offensive were good.

Now, at the end of July, President Nasser intervened by seizing the Suez Canal, and Harding's operational plans were jammed by the rebounding tremors. The 3rd Commando Brigade, who had done so much to turn the guerrillas on the Troodos range from hunters to fugitives, had to be returned to Malta and the 16th Para prepared for real war, which involved the despatch of the 1st and 3rd Battalions to England for brief refresher courses in jumping. Replacements came but needed time to settle into their stride, the 1st Oxfordshire and Buckinghamshire Light Infantry being pitched into the heat outside Nicosia and the 1st Suffolk coming to Xeros, there to relieve the Gordons so that they might take over from 45 Commando, who had done some fine work on the summit. The 1st Agra (artillery group) took over command responsibilities, and the 21st and 50th Medium Regiments, both of whom had been training in internal security duties at home, relieved 40 Commando and 2 Para respectively at Paphos and Limni. There was also an influx of anti-aircraft gunners—the 16th and 43rd L.A.A. and the 57th H.A.A. Regiments—for defence against Egyptian planes, and the 33rd Para Field Regiment came to provide operational support for their brigade.

Meanwhile the execution of the two men Major Coombe had captured had been confirmed. Two had already been executed in May, for the murder of a policeman and a civilian, and Grivas announced the reprisal killing of two soldiers known to be missing; but lacking the flair for the macabre displayed of old by the Irgun he did not produce the bodies and it was never established whether his claim was true, even though one of the bodies, that of a lance-corporal of the Royal Leicesters, was later found. Being unable to catch any more soldiers, he now grabbed an old English civilian as hostage but released him when one of the condemned, echoing his captor, made noble appeal. It did not prevent the execution of the men amid high tension from Nicosia to London, and they were hanged in the early hours of August 9. The unpleasant duty of prison guard and burial of the dead fell, like so many others, to the South Staffords.

On August 16 Grivas publicly ordered the suspension of operations, but obtaining no concession he soon resumed hostilities starting with a raid on Nicosia hospital in which one policeman, two members of the staff, and two terrorists were killed, and one prisoner-patient escaped. On September 28 two vehicles of the Wiltshire Regiment were ambushed after dark at a hairpin bend above Kyrenia on the main Nicosia road. A soldier and a lady of the W.V.S. were killed. Revenge came swiftly. The whole of 16th Para Brigade were again in the island, and with Wiltshires, H.L.I., K.O.Y.L.I., and 40th Field Regiment in support they scoured the Kyrenian hills. The 2nd Para found the gang leader who had sprung the ambush hiding in a farmhouse with five of his men; they rounded them up without a fight and unearthed three machine-guns of various types and a number of other arms. It was exhilarating on the narrow hilltop. To the north was the blue Mediterranean, and to the south the torrid plain of Nicosia, on which the activities of the French paras could be seen as they flew their planes on and off their airfields at Tymbou, in readiness for the battle which no one believed would happen.

The British paras had returned to the Troodos range and were taking part in a search operation which yielded (to the Gordons) the Grivas diaries for April and May, when on October 30 the message arrived, 'A state of war with Egypt exists. Return to camp.' There were a few other disruptions for the invasion of Egypt: air sentries had to be posted on all headquarter buildings, causing more laughter than anxiety; some units had to perform dock labour; and the anti-aircraft gunners, who were giving valuable internal security aid, had to man their guns; and guards had to be strengthened on those favourite targets of Eoka, the Nicosia and Akrotiri aerodromes, on the latter of which an explosion shortly before the ultimatum to Egypt did some damage but far less than claimed by Grivas. There was a week's excitement as the bombers and fighters streamed to and fro and the armada sailed from Limassol and Famagusta. Eoka did nothing to impede its progress, but by a sustained effort throughout November they made this the month of greatest woe for their adversaries, killing thirty-nine persons and doing injury to seventy-one. A new device encountered was the bomb laid in a bank or tree to give maximum effect to its blast through being above ground, and one such made a ghastly mess of a truckload of Royal Norfolks passing through a village at night. Two were killed and fourteen flung out in various stages of laceration. There were other ambushes of a similar nature, but most of the casualties were inflicted by gun or grenade attacks in towns, and it was in Limassol, near Grivas's hiding place, that most were made. At Episkopi, near Limassol, the house being built for the C.-in-C. was set alight and largely destroyed.

The cease-fire in Port Said brought reinforcements for Cyprus. The 3rd Infantry Brigade, which had been sent from England to Malta in the early days of the Suez crisis, came to fill the reserve role in place of 16th Para. It had four battalions, of which the 1st Royal Berkshire had already come over in company detachments. The 1st Duke of Wellington's came next, being followed in an aircraft carrier shuttle service by the 1st Somerset Light Infantry—who, although Field Marshal Harding's own, had only a brief stay and were relieved in January 1957 by the 1st Gloucestershire from Aden. Then came the 3rd Grenadier Guards, to join the others in scantily equipped camps outside Nicosia, from which the Ox and Bucks were glad to move to Limassol and enable the Royal Norfolks to return home in early December, fourteen months after their emergency despatch.

Of the invaders of Egypt, the 1st and 3rd Para were back within a week of the landing, and in early December the 3rd, who had made the assault, led the return of the brigade to England. The 1st followed just before Christmas, having carried out one more search operation. The 2nd Para and Guards Independent Company also made a swift return from Egypt but stayed in Cyprus rather longer, moving into the Troodos range in late December and relieving the Gordon Highlanders, who like the Norfolks had become overdue for return home. The H.L.I. completed a year's duty in January 1957 and were more punctually relieved in the Panhandle by the 1st Queen's Own Royal West Kent Regiment, who had led the 3rd Division into Egypt and were the one battalion of this division to be diverted from the journey home.

The only mortal casualties suffered by the H.L.I. had been two soldiers killed by a mine detonated on a football field at Lefkoniko as a game ended. As happened after almost every search, heated complaints of barbarism followed the one made by the H.L.I. Harding investigated the charges, repudiated them, and passed a law making false allegations punishable. He had court-martialled two officers for the ill treatment of a prisoner and was determined that there should be no undermining of confidence by irresponsible accusers. The H.L.I. went happily homewards, heartened as were many others by a congratulatory message of farewell delivered personally by the indefatigable Governor and Commander-in-Chief.

Meanwhile the gunners were showing themselves worthy substitutes for the commandos and paratroops they had relieved. The 50th Medium in the extreme north-west displayed superb swiftness on the draw and on four occasions their patrols inflicted heavy loss on gangsters who tried to ambush them. In ambushes they laid themselves three important Eoka leaders were captured, bringing a rare D.S.O. for their Lieutenant-Colonel King-Martin, a former Indian Army infantryman. The 21st Medium were less fortunate. They had two commanding officers badly wounded by bombs detonated by their vehicles, and suffered dreadful loss from a bomb that had been hidden in a chair in their N.A.A.F.I. and went off during tombola, killing three men and wounding fifteen.

The anti-aircraft gunners also did excellent work when stood down from their guns in December. The 43rd L.A.A. became a permanent part of the Nicosia garrison: the 16th L.A.A. took over duties at Episkopi and Dhekelia; and the 57th H.A.A. took a share of the patrolling around Limassol until departing in February.

With January 1957 came a change of command. Major-General Kendrew had relieved Ricketts as district commander at the end of October, just as had happened in Korea. He now assumed operational command as well, on the departure of the Chief of Staff, Brigadier Baker. Kendrew was formally made what Baker had in fact been, Director of Operations. His Chief of Staff was Brigadier FitzGeorge-Balfour, who had commanded the 2nd Coldstream in Malaya.

A tighter grip was now taken on the guerrillas in the Troodos range, on the top of which the snow lay thick. Special winter clothing was issued to the paratroopers and companies of the Suffolk resident up there, and as a further aid helicopters, of which the R.A.F. had a squadron of twelve Sycamores at Nicosia, were now being used for troop conveyance, although carrying only three men each. They were used for the swift occupation of observation points, of which there were many good ones in the hills, the men usually having to make a descent by rope in between trees. It could be an effective means of speeding the casting of a net, but it had its limitations, one of them being the atmosphere, which restricted its use to the foothills of the Troodos range.

The Suffolks used helicopters in this manner and from the information gleaned these old masters of the jungle were able to score the most important success of the campaign to date. On the night of January 19, 1957, Grivas's most trusted lieutenant, Markos Drakos, walked into an ambush laid by a corporal and was shot dead, going down with sten blazing. Meanwhile the 2nd Para had been acquiring information which brought down the guerrilla organisation to the east of Troodos like a house of cards. First one wanted man was caught in his hide, then another, and then a gang of eight, found in a hide beneath a fireplace, details of which were cooperatively provided by a former comrade. Many of these men were high on the Eoka order of battle drawn up by Intelligence and three were priced at £5,000. The 2nd Para claimed the elimination of twenty-one 'hard core terrorists' during January and the capture of 46 weapons, two rocket launchers among them, and all with scarcely the discharge of a shot, except at one gang leader who was felled as he tried to break cordon on a motor bike. Much of the credit was due to the Special Branch use of agents and to the 'Q' men, in a brief role as which a Para subaltern had recently made a neat little haul of five captives and fourteen weapons. It had been found that, being career criminals, a number of Eoka's members were willing enough to transfer their loyalty.

In early February the remnant of the 16th Para Brigade were relieved by 40 Commando. At the same time the 1st Lancashire Fusiliers arrived from England and pitched camp in thick yellow mud at Polemi, north of Paphos, as reinforcement for 1 Agra. An all-out effort was now made against the mountain guerrillas, of which the hub was a nine-week watch and curfew on the austere village of Milikouri, sprawled on the steeps below Kykko Monastery. It was conducted by 3 Brigade. The Duke of Wellington's, Royal Berkshires, Ox and Bucks, Lancashire Fusiliers all had parts to play, and so too did the South Staffords, released at last from their long and tiring duties at Nicosia for a final fling before a well deserved trip home. The Duke's brought off an important coup on March 3. On vague guidance from an informer a platoon made a pre-dawn approach to the alleged lair of another of Grivas's dearest lieutenants, Gregoris Axfentiou. It was in a hillside near Makhaeras Monastery at the east end of the range, and it was only because a corporal noticed a certain hollowness underfoot that the hide was found. Four men were flushed from it and captured, but a burst from inside hit a soldier and showed that Axfentiou was still very much alive. He was killed in the end, by the grim bludgeon tactic of bringing up 50 gallons of petrol, igniting it after interruptions from showers, and burning him to death still inside his hide.

Other disasters befell Eoka in all parts of the island. Near Famagusta a corporal and three men of the Royal Leicesters came under fire from a farmyard and in the ensuing fight killed one gangster and forced five others out from well fortified positions, which they abandoned with words that showed their faith in British humanity, 'All right, Johnny, you win.' From Dhekelia the Middlesex made a lightning swoop to a hide radioed them from Troodos, said to contain the Eoka leader of Larnaca, Rossides, for whom they had long been searching. Briefed at 1 a.m. a company travelled over 12 miles on wheels and foot to lay cordon as dawn was breaking at 5, and the first person apprehended trying to sneak through turned out to be Rossides.

Grivas himself was not in the mountains, as had been believed, but in a specially built cellar beneath a bank clerk's house in a suburb of Limassol. He admits in his Memoirs that by the end of February 'Harding had rounded up the majority of our guerrilla bands in the mountains'—and this was before the death of Axfentiou and other misfortunes. On March 14, following a call for peaceful negotiations from the United Nations, he issued a proclamation declaring his willingness 'to order the suspension of operations as soon as the Ethnarch Makarios is released.' The British Government responded on March 28 by announcing that Makarios was to be released, with freedom to go anywhere but Cyprus, and towns that had lain in gloom and darkness erupted in joy. As the Royal Leicesters reported from Famagusta, 'No force on earth would have stopped the Cypriots celebrating on that night.' But finding the mobs getting even wilder next morning they had to disperse them with their batons.

Grivas himself was offered a safe-conduct back to Greece. He haughtily spurned it and was enraged to learn from the Greek Government that they regarded the struggle as over—in other words, they had given up his cause as lost. Sulkily he set about quietly rebuilding his shattered forces, while the hunt for him continued. He could at least claim to have drawn an army of 20,000 to the island and caused it plenty of aggravation with what he states to have been 273 front-line fighters, sharing a hundred guns, backed by 750 villagers armed with shotguns. Yet amid a friendly population and with mountains and caves for concealment, other guerrilla armies have caused greater aggravation for longer periods at comparable odds.

One of the most crippling restrictions suffered by Grivas was the blockade, which as has been mentioned was a combined effort with navy and air predominating. Yet ultimately all depended on the observation of individuals. There was, for instance, the corporal of Field Security on immigration control who refused to be bullied by outraged protests from scrutinising some little clay Madonnas, imported as 'religious symbols', and chanced to find that they contained pencil bombs; and there was the gunner sergeant on road block duty who found two messages wrapped inside a cigarette lighter, one of them being an order for the execution of a supposed traitor. On such shreds hung the balance of the campaign, and they formed an essential complement to the determination of the British command to go out in search of information and to hound the gangs regardless of the difficulties of the terrain.

II—TEMPEST AND CALM (1957-59)

The troops were freed from many of the restrictions on off-duty movement and could enjoy some of the tourist delights of the island. Yet their camps had still to be heavily wired and guarded, and many tedious duties had to be done in the unrelenting search for Grivas and his men. There was a certain surly tension in the air. Eoka had merely gone to ground, and its leaders were engaged in repairing the cracks in security that had so nearly caused its complete collapse. Fear was their cement, and they spread it by murdering the untrustworthy and threatening others.

In June 1957 Grivas was nearly caught, according to his memoirs. Some soldiers on a search operation entered the house at Limassol under which he had his hide. He heard them open the door into the cupboard where a sink masked his trap-door, and then he heard the exchange of greetings and clink of glasses. His protector had offered the soldiers a drink, and being good at English, and the possessor of a pleasant wife and baby, had been able to allay their suspicions. There is a certain symbolism in this escape, for Grivas owed it to realisation of the simple truth that friendliness is the strongest form of defence against the British soldier.

It was aggravating for Harding to be denied this one capture that would have completed his task of restoring order and saved much of the bloodshed yet to come. However, the Government decided that sufficient strength had been established for a switch to diplomacy and in October they announced Harding's succession by a Colonial servant with a high reputation for liberalism, Sir Hugh Foot. It was an ominous coincidence that in the same month a fracas between gangsters put the police in possession of a document listing 200 Greek-Cypriots for 'execution' by Eoka as traitors.

Harding departed on November 3, proudly and appropriately escorted to Nicosia aerodrome by armoured cars of the faithful Blues. Foot did not arrive until exactly a month later, and during it—on November 26—Eoka achieved their most startling coup of all, the complete destruction by pencil bomb of a Canberra bomber at Akrotiri aerodrome, with others badly damaged. There was still plenty of work for the Director of Operations, General Kendrew, who inherited wider responsibilities with Harding's departure. But the Governor, as was normal, still held the appointment of Commander-in-Chief, and he was to sustain the morale of his troops almost as ably as his predecessor.

Within three weeks of his arrival Foot had walked unescorted through the Old City of Nicosia, waving to the people, and announced the release of a hundred detainees. One result of his friendliness was to make the Turks fearful of a British deal with Greece, and near the end of January 1958 they gave a foretaste of the ferocity in store by a rampage in Nicosia, in which six people were killed, fifty injured, and many vehicles burned. The Suffolks, the Gloucesters, and the 43rd L.A.A. (who had come, it will be remembered, to provide air defence for the Suez operation) bore the brunt of their quelling, making repeated baton charges in the face of stoning and close-quarter blows such as they had never encountered from the Greeks. For the Gloucesters it was a breath-taking finale to a three-year tour begun in Kenya and continued stormily in Aden and Bahrain. They now handed over to the Lancashire Fusiliers, from 1 Agra's area, and later the Royal Berkshires also joined 50 Brigade to share the either tedious, distasteful, or nerve-racking duties in Nicosia.

Grivas was just as suspicious of Foot's intentions, and in March he began an insidious campaign of boycott and sabotage against the British. Inevitably it degenerated to murder, first of a British policeman and on May 4 of two soldiers of that long-suffering corps, the Royal Military Police, shot dead in Famagusta. The freedom to walk-out unarmed and unescorted had already been withdrawn. It was back to the knife-edge of perpetual alertness.

On May 14 yet another big search for Grivas began, named Operation Kingfisher and conducted by the Ox and Bucks from Limassol, with aid from 40 Commando, who were still in the Troodos hills, the 39th Heavy Regiment R.A. from Episkopi, and from the 1st Argyll and Sutherland Highlanders, who had arrived the previous February and were based on Limni, next the 46th H.A.A. at Paphos. Later in the month the operation was taken over by the 3rd Infantry Brigade, which had the role of mobile striking force and consisted of the 3rd Grenadiers and 1st Royal West Kent. It was no good; the search passed through the hills to the north of Grivas's hide, and troops, helicopters, armoured cars and patrol dogs had eventually to return to their camps with little to show for their labour.

Of the other troops on the island, the Middlesex were still at Dhekelia, near Larnaca, and were in occupation of splendid new barracks, Alexander Camp; the 1st Royal Ulster Rifles, having already sampled Xeros, Platres and the Panhandle since their arrival the previous May, had now taken over from the departing Royal Leicesters—who had suffered twelve killed—outside that ancient powder barrel, Famagusta, where their partners, the 40th Field Regiment, had been relieved by the 29th Field; the 1st Welch were patrolling the Panhandle from their base at Dhavlos, having arrived the previous October, and the Wiltshires were still encamped above Kyrenia; and at Xeros, patrolling into the Troodos range, were the most recent arrivals, the 1st Royal Welch Fusiliers. The Blues were still ubiquitous in their armoured cars, bringing the total to eighteen fighting units.

On the night of June 7 Nicosia flared up literally, with a blaze that brought all available troops of 50 Brigade in from the frying pan of their sweltering quarters. It was started by Turks, who set upon all people and things Greek with terrifying, hooligan rage. The Greeks of course were swift to retaliate and for the next two months the whole land was rent by orgies of inter-racial savagery, undiminished by the publication of Britain's new plan for Cyprus, which was ironically styled A Great Adventure in Partnership. Time and again the troops had to prise raving combatants apart, sometimes by baton charges, sometimes by a round or two of rifle fire, and as often they had to act as escorts for small parties of refugees, usually Turkish, who were forced out of their homes by the hatred of their neighbours and had to be resettled in other villages. It was bewildering, exhausting work, well expressed by the cartoon in a British paper captioned, 'Who are we fighting today, sarge?' which caused many wry smiles in Cyprus. By the end of July fifty-six Greeks and fifty-three Turks were reported to have been killed, many in a spine-chilling manner. But there would have been many more if it had not been for the efforts of the troops, and this was acknowledged at times by cheers from the people they protected.

In the midst of the heat and madness a patrol of four armoured cars of those widespread peacekeepers, the Blues, visited the village of Avgorou, not far from Famagusta. The subaltern in command ordered the arrest of a youth who kept taunting the troops with Eoka symbols. Seven troopers dismounted and grabbed him but were set upon by a group of villagers, men and women, who freed the boy and took him to a house. The officer called for reinforcements and three more cars arrived with twenty-four men. They tried to enter the house, only to be forced back by a deluge of bricks and stones. The villagers then charged in mass, some 250 of them, and forced the troopers back into their cars. One man hit the officer in the face with a brick and leapt on to his armoured car. The officer carefully elevated his machine-gun so as to hit no one else and killed the man with a short burst. The Blues then withdrew, leaving one other dead behind them, a woman who was proved by post mortem to have been killed by a stone. While one may admire the audacity of the unarmed attackers in the face of so lethal array of weapons, they gave revealing display of their faith in the forebearance of the British troops. It was a case of faith fulfilled, except where stretched to absurdity, and of course the Greeks made the most of the two killings, blaming that of the woman on the 'British murderers' as well. Two soldiers were murdered in Famagusta, as reprisal for what Grivas termed 'the outrage of Avgorou'.

During all this tumult, anxieties about the aggressive intent of the newly formed United Arab Republic (Egypt and Syria) added to the burden of the C.-in-C. Middle East, who was installed at last at Episkopi in the person of Lieutenant-General Sir Roger Bower. To meet the threat to the Arab kingdoms, Cyprus had to fulfil its almost forgotten function of a base, and in mid-June the whole of the 16th Para Brigade Group arrived by air from England, followed by the 1st Guards Brigade with the 26th Field Regiment, who borrowed guns from the 29th. A Squadron of the 6th R.T.R. also came, and so too did Headquarters 3rd Infantry Division. The Para Brigade again encamped near Nicosia and concentrated on training, but the Guards were split, the 2nd Grenadiers to Limassol, the 1st Irish to Nicosia, and the 1st Royal Scots Fusiliers to Famagusta, and were allowed to take a share of security duties in between training. There were now twenty-six fighting units in Cyprus.

On July 17 the summons arrived and the 16th Para were catapulted, somewhat jerkily, to Jordan, as will be described in greater detail in Chapter 12. Only the 1st Para remained in Cyprus. As replacement the

19th Infantry Brigade were flown out, and so short were reserves becoming that the 20th Field and 34th L.A.A. Regiments came as the infantry colleagues of the 1st East Surreys. For two months they bore a share of the internal security duties, the Surreys with 50 Brigade at Nicosia, where there was a rotation of reliefs between the torrid city and areas outside; the 20th Field at Famagusta, and the 34th L.A.A. at Limassol. By mid-September the tension in Arabia had subsided sufficiently for 19 Brigade to return homewards, except for the Surreys, who went instead to Libya as stimulant to King Idris's resistance to Egyptian intrigue.

There was also a routine relief in July. The 1st Durham Light Infantry came by sea and took the Paphos area over from the 46th H.A.A., bringing two years of gunner occupation here to an end.

On July 21 the troops made an island-wide swoop, as a result of which 1,200 Greeks and fifty Turks were arrested and detained. By taking this sad, repressive measure, Foot dealt Eoka an unexpected blow, and the Prime Minister, Mr. Harold Macmillan, followed it up with an impassioned plea, which drew echoes of agreement from the Prime Ministers of both Turkey and Greece: 'Humanity demands that violence in Cyprus must stop.' Eoka gunmen shot dead a lieutenant-colonel in Limassol and a sergeant in Nicosia, the latter being left to die with his 2-year-old son sobbing beside him while people passed unconcernedly by, sending currents of anger through the cordoning troops stronger than any that had so far stirred them. Having brought the cauldron to the boil, Grivas announced next day—August 4—that he was suspending attacks on both British and Turks. The Turkish organisation made reciprocal announcement. A strange, unnatural calm fell on the land.

Searching incessantly for a compromise solution the British Government put forward a new one on August 12, which was announced in Cyprus by Macmillan himself. It satisfied the Turks but not the Greeks, and Eoka now began a widescale campaign of blowing up vehicles, either by pressure mines or electrically detonated ones, of which the latter were more selective but less popular since it needed the presence of a firer in concealment near by. Activity was at its most intense in the Panhandle, where the Welch bumped twenty-seven such ambushes during August and September. They cost them only one man killed and seven badly injured, thanks mainly to the work of clearance parties that set off each morning at a speed of 2 m.p.h.

The Royal Ulster Rifles had some successes outside Famagusta in August. They captured a number of Eoka couriers by night ambushes and had a fight with a party of four who were pushing bikes that were found to be heavily laden with arms after three of the men had been

killed. Then on September 2 they were directed by an informer to a barn
near Liopetri and drew a burst from inside when they began to remove
the chaff in it. Grenades were thrown without effect, followed by
eleven rockets from a 3·5-inch rocket-launcher. An officer and sixteen
men then made an assault. Three fell wounded but the others made
a lodgement and tried desperately to prise their enemies out of their
emplacement. At last one came rushing out with sten blazing, hitting
the platoon commander and mortally wounding a rifleman. Out of
ammunition, a Corporal Shaugnessy hurled a piece of masonry, which
knocked the gunman sideways, and next moment he was dead, shot by a
rifleman. Still the other two defied all attempts to winkle them out, and
after the platoon commander had been dragged clear and his men
evacuated under heavy covering fire, the Colonel and two lance-
corporals climbed the roof, set fire to it, and thus ejected the two Eoka
die-hards, who were shot dead as they ran.

At the other end of the island the Argylls lost a soldier killed and
three wounded in ambush on the hilly road between Polemi and Limni
on the night of September 13. A search was briskly mounted, in the
course of which two Argylls were almost killed by a knife-man before he
was himself killed. Once again heated, outraged complaints followed the
search, and a visiting M.P., Mrs. Barbara Castle, did nothing to reduce
the heat by joining the Greek chorus. Foot investigated the charges and
repudiated them, saying of the Argylls, 'I am not surprised they were
rough with those who resisted arrest. Nor am I surprised some damage
was done in the searches. It is impossible to search for arms in cleverly
concealed hides without doing damage, but I am satisfied from the
report of the special investigation team that, although they were
extensive, damage and injuries were minor.' It is significant that
Mr. Gaitskell, Leader of the Opposition, swiftly dissociated himself from Mrs. Castle's criticism and made a statement expressing
appreciation of the behaviour of the troops under 'almost intolerable
provocation'.

While willing to admit that Eoka men did on rare occasions display
great bravery, the troops were sickened by the glorification of those that
did not deserve it. The D.L.I., for instance, were sharp enough to
kill a man as he detonated a mine from a supposedly concealed position.
His funeral had to be supervised, and a party of young mourners, who
came in three carloads from far away and were observed singing and
smiling, were to their disgust turned back. However, a number of
women from the village attended and put on a horrifying display of
hysteria, rolling on the ground, foaming at the mouth and screaming.
As the coffin was lowered into the grave, they turned on the unfortunate

soldiers on escort duty near by, cursed and spat upon them, and screamed, 'Eoka! EOKA! EOKA-AA!'

On the other hand, utter indifference to the sufferings of the dying, whether or not it was a British soldier, was often observed in the towns. It struck a young private of the Ox and Bucks on his first emergency summons in Limassol. He doubled with his patrol past a blur of faces until they came to a small crowd gathered round a man lying with a bullet through his chest (probably for supposed treachery to Eoka) coughing up blood in his death agony. While he was being removed in an army truck, the crowd were told to line up against the wall. 'Many excuses and some reasons are voiced to get away. Most of them do not give a moment's thought to the victim. They laugh and joke, complaining how they will be late for work. This attitude seems to be commonplace in Cyprus.'

Just as revealing are the soldier's feelings on his first acquaintance with the delicate duties of crowd control. 'Strangely,' he recorded 'I found myself carrying out all the things I should do, keeping the crowd back and so on, just as if it was a parade. This may be the result of military training or of apathy, I don't know.'

On September 26 an attempt on Kendrew's life failed by a hairbreadth. He was being driven into Nicosia in broad daylight, to visit Government House, when a mine was exploded just behind his car, making a big crater and overturning a R.M.P. Land Rover behind him with the death of one soldier.

A week later, on October 3, the troops were at last driven beyond their stoically maintained self-restraint. Mrs. Mary Cutliffe, wife of a sergeant of the 29th Field Regiment and the mother of five, was shopping in Famagusta with another sergeant's wife when both were shot in the back, Mrs. Cutliffe dropping dead, the other badly wounded. The 29th Field and their good neighbours, the Ulsters, were quickly brought into the town to turn out the entire Greek male population and search their houses. They were, in the words of *The Times* correspondent, 'in the grip of sheer cold rage. No pretence was made that kid-glove methods were used.' And the *Daily Telegraph* correspondent reported, 'I was shocked when I saw rows of bloody and bandaged Greek-Cypriots lying on floors in Famagusta hospital.' Foot and Kendrew flew by helicopter from Nicosia. Neither made comment.

Grivas simultaneously disclaimed responsibility for the attack on the ladies and ordered an all-out offensive, although caution was urged on him by the Greek Foreign Minister. During the next six weeks more damage was done than in any period since November 1956. Mine explosions were at their heaviest along the Kyrenian range and in the

Panhandle; in the towns arson was widely used to supplement bomb explosions; and in the Troodos range the guerrillas resumed their ambushes, bringing death to an officer and two men of 45 Commando, who had relieved the 40th, and to two men of the Royal Welch Fusiliers, but more frequently being worsted in some fierce encounters with these two units. Most serious of all were the attacks at R.A.F. stations. Another Canberra was wrecked at Akrotiri, ten servicemen were injured by a bomb intended for a Comet at Nicosia, and on November 8 two airmen were killed and seven wounded by a bomb explosion in the N.A.A.F.I. canteen there. This latter cost 3,000 Cypriots employed by the N.A.A.F.I. their jobs, and it is expressive of the sympathy felt in Britain for the servicemen that 17,000 people answered the first appeal for volunteers to replace them.

In the midst of these happenings, that is on October 11, the burly, reserved Kendrew completed his tenure as Director of Operations and was succeeded by the lively extrovert Major-General Darling, who last figured in these pages when B.G.S. to Stockwell for the invasion of Egypt. His Chief of Staff, inherited from Kendrew, was Brigadier P. Gleadell, who had commanded the Devons in Kenya.

Darling at once made clear his determination to strike at Eoka hard, not least by psychological means. He laid great stress on marksmanship, insisted that it was the duty of every soldier, whether cook, clerk, or storeman to kill the Eoka murderers, and at a demonstration to press correspondents made a remark that might have caused outrage under the regime of a soldier Governor: 'The only Eoka terrorists I am interested in are dead ones.' Following the separate murders of three British civilians, he authorised the issue of revolvers to such people, and he encouraged his troops to strike hard enough at Eoka for Athens radio to describe them as 'wild cannibals' and to elevate Hitler to 'a saint in comparison'. Allowed shorter licence than in 1956, 'the daily dose of muck' from Athens was switched off by jamming.

Darling overhauled his intelligence system, bringing in Mr. John Prendergast from Kenya with good results. He had also to reshape his forces as a result of a round of routine reliefs. They began in mid-October with the 25th Field Regiment taking the Panhandle over from the Welch and losing a driver killed and nineteen badly injured when a vehicle was blown up by a particularly destructive mine. At the end of the month the Middlesex went home, having completed three years on active service, which only the Wiltshires and the Royal Horse Guards would emulate and which made the Larnaca area the least turbulent in the island at a cost to the Middlesex of no mortal casualties. The Argylls took their place at Dhekelia, after brief occupation by the departing

Welch, when the 1st Black Watch arrived in December and took over the Limni area. At Episkopi the newly amalgamated 1st Devonshire and Dorset relieved the 39th Heavy Regiment.

Astride November and December the 1st Guards Brigade and the 26th Field Regiment returned home. The situation was calmer in Arabia now, and in Cyprus at least the inter-communal fighting, which was the greatest consumer of troops, had subsided. Darling was left with eleven battalions, one commando and three gunner regiments on area control, the Blues on mobile patrol, and 3 Brigade, with 1st Para forming its third battalion, as his main striking force.

At the start of November the brigade moved overnight into the troublesome Kyrenian range for a drive in which companies of the Royal Berks joined from Nicosia, working with the resident battalion, the Wiltshires, with whom they would soon be amalgamated. It led to a satisfactory build-up of information, and on November 16 the Wiltshires were able to track down the man for whom they had been searching for almost three years, Kyriakos Matsis. He had a hide beneath a house, similar to Grivas's, and the soldiers would never have discovered the trap-door to it without detailed information from an informer. Two men came out, but Matsis stayed inside on his own, calmly awaiting death, and was destroyed by a grenade.

Ruses were now being added to the offensive repertoire of the troops, in particular by the Commandos in the Troodos mountains. A guerrilla might see a soldier, apparently dead and covered in blood, lying with weapon beside him, and find himself ambushed as he attempted to retrieve it; another might see a soldier lackadaisically riding a donkey and find himself held up at close quarters as he followed the trail of this tempting quarry; and in the towns and villages there would be no tramp of foot at night, nor whine of military vehicle, but the soldiers would be there, out of sight and out of hearing. Indeed, vehicles were forbidden to move at night, and this much reduced the prospects of the ambush layers. They switched to setting fire to isolated vehicles, more often civilian than military, and burned forty between November 25 and December 4, while Cyprus was the subject of another U.N. debate, which produced nothing but an appeal for good will.

The Paphos area was thoroughly combed at the end of November, with the 3rd Grenadiers and the Blues assisting the D.L.I. and Argylls. The yield was ninety members of Eoka arrested. There was then a concentration in the Panhandle, with infantrymen disguised as resident gunners to conceal their arrival, and a fruitful haul of arms and ammunition was made. Grivas had been driven back to the defensive.

The first great political breakthrough came on December 18. On the initiative of M. Paul-Henri Spaak, Secretary-General of N.A.T.O., the Foreign Secretaries of Britain, Greece and Turkey met in Paris, and here Mr. Selwyn Lloyd set Cyprus on the road to independence by announcing Britain's agreement to grant it in exchange for the retention of two small base areas around Episkopi and Dhekelia. Political pressure from Athens was added to the military pressure exerted on Grivas, and on December 24 he issued one more pontifical declaration: 'We shall now halt our activity for as long as the other side does so as well.' Foot responded by releasing 350 Cypriots from detention and commuting eight death sentences to life imprisonment.

Search operations continued and in January there was a large drive through the snow-capped Troodos range, where the 1st Para had now taken over on the departure of 45 Commando just before Christmas. It ended in early February with the capture of the last of the known guerrillas without the discharge of a shot. There was no retaliation by Eoka, although tension was still high. On February 11 a conference opened in London, which progressed with dramatic ups and downs to a meeting of Prime Ministers in consultation with Foot, Makarios, and the Turkish Cypriot leader, Dr. Kutchuk. On the 19th Macmillan announced that agreement had been reached for the grant of independence to Cyprus within the British Commonwealth, with the retention of British sovereignty over the two small base areas.

There was wild joy in Cyprus, of which the climax came with the return of Makarios on March 1, full of praise for 'General' Grivas and 'the gallant fighters of Eoka'. The hero emerged from hiding, although his whereabouts were not disclosed, and told reporters of his narrow escapes and of the hazards of fighting 'a mighty empire'. Conscious of the self-imposed restraints by which they had always been hampered, the British command arranged symbolic, although secret farewell. A Greek air force plane came over to take Grivas to Athens, and a staff officer, a lieutenant-colonel of the Coldstream Guards, was deputed to see him off. Grivas arrived in full battle regalia, garbed with pistol, light automatic, binoculars, and trench boots: the guards officer was unarmed and unadorned. Grivas saluted with great ceremony: the guards officer stood rigidly to attention and made no other move. It was not that he intended any insult, merely that he had no right arm.

Grivas in fact was an embittered man. Union with Greece, for which he had been fighting, had not been achieved, and his men had been duped, as he saw it, into handing in their arms. However, he could claim to have advanced the date of independence for Cyprus, even if largely by stirring the Turks to such rage. He could also claim to have held the British Army to a draw and to have killed seven of its officers and seventy-two men, out of a total death roll of 393 (of whom 218 were Greek), not counting the victims of the intercommunal fighting. The army for their part could claim to have prevented Cyprus from disintegrating in violence and to have provided the opportunity for a settlement to be reached which satisfied the fair aspirations of the Cypriot people and the strategic needs of the British Government. Furthermore they had achieved this without arousing lasting bitterness against themselves, and considering all the efforts made to stir up hatred against them this was no mean achievement.

III—AFTERMATH (1959–67)

There was no immediate return to the easy-going relationship between the troops and the inhabitants of this once somnolent island. Indeed in Nicosia the luxury of walking-out unarmed brought an increase of duty on town patrol to prevent fights with belligerent youths. However, it was easier in the country districts, and by providing agricultural aid and playing the villagers at football the soldiers healed the sores, and life resumed its sunny, ambling, or more often lounging course. There was a flurry of excitement on August 16, 1960, when Cyprus formally gained her promised independence and contingents of both Greek and Turkish troops arrived to take up residence. The British troops were quartered by now in their two sovereign areas, but were free to roam the island and had special facilities, for which troops made visits from England and Germany, for training on the Troodos slopes.

Strategically, a ban on air space over Israel and the Arab countries much reduced the value of Cyprus as a base for troops and virtually split Middle East Command in two. Kenya was therefore developed as an alternative, a process begun well before the Cyprus emergency ended, and on March 1, 1961, the Middle East Command (now a fusion of all services) was divided. The name was transferred to the H.Q. at Aden, and the territory left under control from Episkopi was renamed the Near East Command. As an air base, with N.A.T.O. commitments in mind, Cyprus retained its value, but militarily its decline was marked by the disbandment in 1963 of the one brigade that had remained in occupation, the 3rd. Two battalions remained on garrison duty for the security of the aerodrome.

Over Christmas 1963 these battalions had suddenly to spring to arms. Greeks and Turks were at each other's throats again, both in Nicosia and in Larnaca, where some families of the battalion at Dhekelia, the 1st/3rd

Green Jackets, the Rifle Brigade, were quartered. A company went in on Christmas Day to protect their evacuation, and a soldier was shot dead by one of the many bullets flying around. On Boxing Day the 1st Gloucestershire, from Episkopi, motored to Nicosia aerodrome with the 3rd Wing, R.A.F. Regiment. President Makarios had called on the British for aid, and the delicate task of providing it was entrusted to the G.O.C. Cyprus District, Major-General P. G. F. Young, late the Ox and Bucks. On the 27th the Gloucesters sent patrols into the city, but could as yet do little more than assess the problem and provide protection for service families.

After intervention by Mr. Duncan Sandys, the Commonwealth Secretary, the leaders of both communities were brought together, and at 4 a.m. on the 29th General Young obtained agreement on a demarcation line through Nicosia, named the Green Line from the colour of the talc with which he traced and retraced it over his map. A few hours later the Gloucesters and R.A.F. Regiment began to erect barriers along it and to chivvy the deadly rivals back 100 yards on either side of it by the display of Union Jacks, good nature, and the glint of their bayonets. The Rifle Brigade also arrived this day and were assigned a suburb that bore gruesome evidence of the recent fury. The soldiers were both interlopers and saviours, exercising no authority except through the confidence they could inspire, and at this stage, while fear still reigned, they were hailed as saviours.

Between December 29 and January 5, 1964, three units arrived by air from England. The 1st Sherwood Foresters took the Rifle Brigade's place at Dhekelia; the 2nd Regiment R.A. (formerly Field and soon to be Light) then took the Gloucesters' at Episkopi and were at once drawn to Nicosia, leaving a battery behind; and the 1st Parachute, together with the Guards Independent Company, also came to Episkopi, to patrol the adjacent countryside. The island was divided into three zones: the Eastern under control of Dhekelia Garrison, the Western under R.A.F. Akrotiri, and the Northern, including Nicosia, under Headquarters 16th Para Brigade, flown out from England. A squadron of armoured cars for the latter was sent from Libya by the 14th/20th King's Hussars and relieved by one of the Life Guards near the end of January, and the Guards Para Company manned some scout cars for the Western Zone, until replaced in early February by a squadron of the Royal Dragoons, who had recently had their first issue of tanks in England.

Although the Greek national contingent had been persuaded to return to their barracks and the Turkish one was lying low within Turkish domains, there were many armed irregulars at large, operating in connivance with their compatriot police. The problem was to obtain warning of likely clashes, for which purpose units were spread far in sections and even pairs of men, and the aim was to intervene, from dominant ground, before the fighting began. Once it had started, separation had to be achieved without resort to firing, and as the paratroops showed at Paphos this could be done by the insertion of armoured cars, with infantry coming in by helicopter to stabilise the wedge. But it was proved at Limassol on February 13, when the Greeks set savagely upon the Turks, that there could be no stopping determined attackers without the prior deployment of posts, and the force available was absurdly inadequate for the prevention of such attacks.

The 1st Duke of Edinburgh's had just arrived from Malta and been assigned to Nicosia. Now, in the second half of February, the remainder of the Life Guards, a second squadron of Royals, the 1st Royal Inniskilling Fusiliers, and the 26th Medium Regiment R.A. (who had gained distinction as infantry substitutes when the 26th Field) arrived from England, and ahead of them came the G.O.C. 3rd Division, Major-General R. M. P. Carver. Having laid the foundations for a much longer task of peacekeeping than he can ever have envisaged, Young handed command of the Truce Force to Carver and returned to his District Headquarters.

Increasing truculence was being displayed against the British, particularly by frustrated Greeks, and the troops' forbearance was being tested as sternly as their alertness. It was therefore a relief to learn that the United Nations had agreed, on March 2, to take over the duty. The Greeks greeted the announcement with fresh assaults. A few men of the 26th Medium, reinforced by helicopter, deflected fearsome exchanges between a Turkish minaret and a Greek stronghold at Ktima, thus preventing the slaughter both of contestants and hostages, while nearby the Royals thwarted the advance of armoured bulldozers. At Mallia, also in the south-west, a few members of the Gloucesters, who had exchanged areas with the 1st Para, were threatened with a mass attack on the school they occupied and averted it largely by ignoring the threat and turning to other topics. Up in the Kyrenian hills a troop of Life Guards rescued some school children under heavy fire from the Turks, only to be stoned by these same children when passing the school a fortnight later.

There was swift response from the consenting members of U.N.O. By the end of March the areas around Ktima and Famagusta had been handed over respectively to Swedes and Finns, enabling the resident battalions to return to their base areas and the Duke of Edinburgh's to Malta. March 27 was the official day of transfer. The British troops still operational donned, for the first time, the light blue berets, scarves and brassards of the 'bluebells', and the Indian General Gyani, who had been on the island nearly three months as observer, took over command from

Carver, who remained as his deputy until July, when he handed the job over for permanent possession by a British brigadier. In April the Canadians began to take over the Nicosia area, amid mounting conflict in the Kyrenian range. The 1st Para, who had a company based on Kyrenia holding key features of dispute, were relieved under siege conditions near the end of April, and a month later they were followed out by their Brigade Headquarters and by the Sherwood Foresters, who had spent two months of sharp-edged duty on the Green Line or in mobile reserve. The 26th Medium, who had relieved the 2nd Light in April, completed the British withdrawal from the capital in early June, under the gloom cast by the disappearance of a U.N. liaison officer, Major Macey of the R.A.O.C., who was lost without trace with his vehicle and driver and presumed dead.

Not until August was the British contingent slimmed to its final size, which was still to be the largest of any national contingent. The area allotted was that around Limassol, and after handing Larnaca over to fellow Irishmen from across the border with much emotion and camaraderie, the Royal Inniskilling Fusiliers took over this lasting U.N. commitment from the Life Guards, who left behind a squadron as the complement of armoured cars. The departure of the main body of Life Guards was delayed by the appointment of General Grivas to the command of the newly formed Cypriot National Guard and the retaliatory appearance of Turkish aircraft overhead. Although this particular crisis subsided, it was inevitable now that the Security Council should extend the lifespan of their creation at six monthly intervals.

A six months' tour was prescribed for the British contingent, and the battalion came initially from Rhine Army. It faced an exacting test of patience and of presenting the other cheek to be smacked by people who seemed to have no aim in life other than to humiliate the British representatives of the United Nations. The men manned sandbagged posts or patrolled the streets knowing they could not return the fire that they had to pretend was not aimed at them, and for the officers, particularly subalterns, there were hours of parleying, and hundreds of cups of coffee to be drunk as they nudged at the complex obstacles impeding cease-fires.

Violence flared spasmodically, and all the time the Greek and Turkish communities steadily built up their rival armies, the Greeks being backed by a massive swelling of the Greek national contingent far, far above its size of 950 ordained by treaty. The tension reached breaking point in November 1967, and its point of breaking was the village of Kophinou, in the British zone, for which the battalion responsible was the 1st Royal Green Jackets, who had gained close acquaintance of the

Limassol district as the Ox and Bucks. The village was Turkish and it dominated the main Nicosia road. For several months routine police patrols had been denied entry, and now Grivas decided to end such insubordination by launching an attack on this and an adjacent village. It was delivered on November 15 by a battalion of the National Guard with artillery support. The Turks were overwhelmed with heavy loss, and four scattered posts, manned by sections of the Green Jackets, were overrun. The function of these was observation, not defence, and the men hugged their slit trenches as the shells fell, making no attempt to resist. Greek officers demanded the arms of two of the sections, but were denied them by the soldiers, except at one two-man post where overwhelming numbers told. The Greeks consolidated beyond the villages, leaving the Green Jackets to remove the Turkish human wreckage, dead and living, and tidy up their own looted tents.

Turkish reconnaissance planes were now seen over the island and there were reports of the assembly of a powerful invasion force. Cyprus's slide to disaster seemed to have reached the bloody depths. Then on November 19 Grivas was recalled to Athens, ostensibly for consultation, and he did not return. The Greek thousands in excess of the 950 were withdrawn and that strange lethargic, uncertain calm embraced Cyprus once again.

11

The New Model

(1956–65)

O N November 27, 1956, the Queen and other members of the
Royal Family were the guests of the Army and the Army Council
to a dinner at the Great Hall, Royal Hospital, Chelsea, celebrating the
fiftieth birthday of the General Staff, whose Chief Imperial, Sir Gerald
Templer, was promoted Field Marshal that very day. It was a stately
occasion, made poignant by recent happenings, for the pride of the
Army had been bruised by the halting of the advance up the Suez Canal
and the debating at the United Nations presaged deeper humiliations to
come. Nostalgia lay as thick as the post-prandial cigar smoke, and Her
Majesty's speech gave it a stirring, while being tinged with sufficient
optimism to inspire the belief that the grand old days were not gone
beyond recall.

Her theme was the strength of the regimental system, and since all
available Colonels of Regiments were present there could have been no
more welcome one. 'The British Army,' she said, 'more than any in the
world has always lived through the regiment and regimental tradition,'
and she probed the essence of the system by stressing that all were of
equal military status, unburdened by the complexes derived from being
storm troops or second line. 'There is no first among the regiments and
corps of my army.'

She went on to quote a letter from a private to his colonel, as evidence
of the strength of the regimental bond. This man had been posted away
from his regiment and described his feelings thus: 'You will see from
the above address that disaster has overtaken me. I feel something like a
man awakened from an operation to find himself minus a limb. They
have taken my cap badge away and with it the great love of my life. The
traditions of my county regiment are in my blood, and to be known as a

329

Forester was an estate of which I was deeply proud.' It was of course known by every infantryman present that a soldier was liable for posting to any regiment in his brigade. Surely, the thought now occurred, the Queen would not have been briefed to bring lumps to throats on this thorny issue unless some adjustment to the system was in mind?

Within two months Britain had a new Prime Minister, Mr. Harold Macmillan—'Unflappable Mac'—and on taking office he put in a new Minister of Defence in place of Mr. Antony Head, who had held the post barely three months after five years as War Minister, the longest tenure since Haldane's famous one. The new Defence Minister was Mr. Duncan Sandys and he was selected to carry out a special task made expedient by the financial strain the Suez adventure had imposed and made feasible by the obvious political impracticality of attempting any further return journeys. He was to 'formulate policies to secure substantial reductions in expenditure and manpower'.

He announced his plans to Parliament on April 5, 1957. National Service was to be progressively reduced, tailing off completely in 1960, after which year there would be no more calls-up. Thus from January 1, 1963, Britain's armed forces would consist entirely of volunteers and she would once again be standing alone, among the powers of the world, in this respect. Rhine Army was to be slimmed from 77,000 men to 64,000, and the N.A.T.O. allies were to be placated by the formidable nuclear effort Sandys promised them, including the use of nuclear artillery. Garrisons further afield would also have to be slimmed, as had happened under Cardwell's reforms, and it was intended to redress the reduction by strengthening the strategic reserve. To make the latter mobile the provision of more transport aircraft was pronounced an essential, as had been apparent for some time. Indeed, not since the airlift to Egypt in 1951 had the army been moved with any speed at any strength.

From the national viewpoint, particularly for its effect on youth, there were many who deplored the curtailment of national service. In the army itself it was an event long awaited, most of all by those who had to cope with the swift turnover of manpower which made life in the average unit akin to that in a transit camp and tied an undue proportion of seasoned N.C.O.s to basic training duties. Nevertheless the national-servicemen had made an immense contribution, as would be acknowledged by every commanding officer who took a battalion on active service, and now that they were due to go there was sudden realisation that drastic reorganisation would have to accompany their departure. In fact they had alone propped up the infantry structure erected by Cardwell in 1873 and redecorated by Childers in 1881. Emergency repair work had prevented its collapse during the removals after the

Second World War, but now there must inevitably be widespread demolitions. There were some anxious months of waiting for news of the blows to fall, and a spate of rumours and speculation to keep the anxiety high.

Thought had been given at the War Office to the problem of reorganising on a voluntary basis, as was suggested by the Queen's speech at the Royal Hospital. A committee had been formed under Lieutenant-General Hull, following his return from Egypt in the spring of 1956, and they had put a strength of 220,000 as the 'absolute minimum' at which the Army could meet the complicated commitments still to be undertaken. (The report was issued after the Suez operation.) Under governmental pressure, which it was the duty of Mr. J. H. Hare to exert as War Minister, this minimum was now compressed to 165,000, although it was found in the event that a strength of 180,000 had to be maintained. This needs to be compared with the 373,000 (not counting Gurkhas) to which the Army's strength had declined by 1957.

The axe was to fall at its heaviest on depot staffs, of whom far fewer were needed in a force of long term regulars, on services, whose soldiers were to be reduced from a percentage of 42 to 35 of the whole, on static headquarters, and on the domestic duties at schools and base camps which had made soldiering so uninspiring for a large number of national-servicemen. Hare intended, with some optimism, to make a saving of 100,000 men in these spheres, largely by the substitution of civilians. He was thus able to enlarge the proportion of fighting men, particularly of infantrymen, who rose again to over a quarter of the whole, with a planned 45,800 out of the 165,000. This figure was intended, again optimistically, to prevent any battalion falling below 490 or below 635 if actively employed.

In terms of battalions the infantry was cut from seventy-seven to sixty, and in addition all eight Gurkha battalions were kept in being, as also was 22 S.A.S. The eight 2nd battalions raised in 1951–52 are not included in these figures, six having already been returned to their graves and the other two being about to join them. With the great troop-consuming tasks in Korea, Egypt and Kenya completed, with victory almost won in Malaya, with Cyprus quiescent, and with hope running eternal, the apparent adequacy of sixty-eight battalions in that summer of 1957 is understandable. The garrison of the Far East was already in process of reduction to fourteen; the Middle East could manage with nine once Cyprus settled down, and this would include a brigade in reserve; Gibraltar and the Caribbean required two between them; and Rhine Army was to be reduced from twenty-four to twenty. This would leave twenty-three for a strategic reserve and for garrison, training, and recuperative duties in the British Isles.

As further infantry reserve, there were always the commandos, and with speed of deployment assuming increasing importance, not to mention the recruiting appeal of the commandos, the Royal Marines made a saucy advance while all other services were in retreat. 41 Commando was reformed in 1960 and 43 in 1961, bringing the commando strength to five. The role of the new ones was to act as home reserve and keep 40, 42, and 45 supplied with men, in the manner of the Cardwell System, thus enabling them to maintain station overseas indefinitely, with the men under obligation to stay only a year. The commandos had two carriers, *Albion* and *Bulwark*, specially made for them to provide them with their own independent mobility by sea and air.

The armour was condemned to reduction from thirty regiments to twenty-three, a slightly larger proportional cut than inflicted on the infantry. With fourteen regiments still allotted to Rhine Army, this left only nine available for other roles, but in the familiar escort duties by armoured cars, which was the usual task in overseas campaigns, a single regiment could cover a great deal of ground.

The Royal Artillery suffered the heaviest mauling of all, being slashed by twenty regiments and the equivalent of one more in minor units, and this was on top of the disbandment of Anti-Aircraft Command, which had been ordered in 1954 and involved the disbandment of fourteen regular regiments, leaving the Gunners with responsibility only for the air defence of field units. All that remained after these two assaults were thirty-four regiments and a battery, barely a third of the total in 1949. This was the price to be paid for the increase in striking power vested in the nuclear-hurling Honest John and in the even more powerful Corporal. It was an ironic fate after so many artillery regiments had proved their value as infantry in Cyprus.

The Royal Engineers on the other hand received the comparatively light sentence of reduction by four regiments. For them, nuclear warfare meant increase, for mobility on the battlefields called for immense structural effort, which was to raise the allotment of field squadrons from one to two for each brigade. Awareness of the immense contribution that the Sappers could make to the welfare and content of backward peoples was also beginning to dawn. As for the Royal Signals, they had to keep communications open and suffered loss only by the closing down of a few headquarters in Germany and by the transfer of jobs to civilians here and there. This latter expedient caused greatest reduction in the services.

In those arms whose members all wore the same cap badge disbandment of units was the practice, and their choice was an internal matter of little interest outside the corps concerned. But in the Royal Armoured

Corps and Infantry the problem was charged with emotion and was of great public—and therefore political—interest, being concerned with the future of institutions that had played their individualistic parts in building up the national pride, which had been nourished by three victory celebrations that century and was now in need of further nourishment. It was agreed that amalgamations would cause less hurt than disbandments, and committees were formed to decide on the awful choice of those to be spliced together.

The first problem for the R.A.C. committee was to decide how the seven amalgamations were to be split between the two Household Cavalry regiments, the twenty late Cavalry of the Line, and the eight of the Royal Tank Regiment. In the event the Householders were preserved unscathed and the R.T.R. heavily pummelled, being saddled with three of the amalgamations. The pairings ordained were the 3rd and 6th, 4th and 7th, and 5th and 8th, leaving only the old founder-members of the Tank Corps, the 1st and 2nd, unblemished. Nominally, if not in spirit, the 6th, 7th, and 8th R.T.R. disappeared.

Eight pairs of cavalry regiments had endured the ordeal of amalgamation in 1922, and it was agreed that they should be spared further upheaval, partly as a matter of fairness and perhaps partly through horror of creating some such title as the 13th/14th/18th/20th King's Royal Hussars (Queen Mary's Own). Apart from the Dragoon Guards, who had been badly slashed, the junior regiments had borne the brunt of the 1922 reductions, but there was the complication now that both the 11th Hussars and the 12th Lancers, the two most junior survivors, had added great lustre to their reputations in the Second World War and that the 9th Lancers and the 10th Hussars were regiments of fame and influence and were in any case naturals for linking with the 12th and 11th respectively. They were given preference over four more senior regiments, all of Hussars, 3rd The King's being linked with the 7th Queen's Own, and the 4th Queen's Own—which was Winston Churchill's—with the 8th King's Royal Irish. The Dragoon Guards were squeezed dry to provide a third pair, the 1st King's Dragoon Guards and the Queen's Bays (2nd Dragoon Guards), both partners at the Battle of the Boyne, being forced into union. The fourth amalgamation was scheduled for the second phase, to take place between 1960–62, and a decision on it was reserved for the time being. The choice fell eventually on the 9th and 12th Lancers, the 9th Queen's Royal and the 12th Prince of Wales's Royal, leaving only four cavalry regiments still untouched.

Most cavalry regiments had only tenuous territorial connections, which had yet to be stabilised by the allotment of home headquarters;

the cavalry spirit was in any case almost as strong as the regimental and the interchange of officers and men was readily accepted as a fact of life. All this made the process of amalgamation less painful. In the infantry there were no such palliatives, and the situation was very much more complex. As the Queen had so recently pointed out, the good soldier felt tense loyalty to his county regiment and no greater disaster could befall him than to be forced to change his cap badge. None felt any sense of loyalty to the infantry as a whole and only a few to the brigade.

The members of the infantry committee might have been specially chosen for their understanding of regimental sentiment. Its chairman was General Whistler, Colonel of the Royal Sussex and the beau ideal of a regimental soldier, unsullied by attendance at Staff College; it was nine years since he had evacuated India and he was now on retirement leave, newly promoted general. His vice-chairman was the Seaforth Highlander Lieutenant-General Cassels, fresh from successes as a field commander in Korea and Malaya, where he had had close acquaintance with the quality and problems of modern infantry. Two major-generals, of whom one was C. L. Firbank, Director of Infantry, two colonels, and a major completed the committee.

Their first problem, similar to that in the sphere of armour, was to decide what share of the sacrifice should be borne by the stronger brethren flanking the Line on right and left, the Foot Guards and the Parachute Regiment. The latter had proved its value as the thing most needed in the future, an adaptable and mobile striking force, and all three of its battalions were kept in being. The Guards were less fortunate. The 3rd Grenadiers—who were as old as their other two battalions—and the not-so-old 3rd Coldstream, were ordered into abeyance in phases II and I respectively, the 3rd Grenadiers being the last battalion to go under these reforms. Eight battalions of the Guards survived, the Scots keeping two.

This left fifteen pairs of regiments to be selected for amalgamation from the Infantry of the Line, but this was not the only task. The whole structure had to be reviewed in the light of a recommendation, made by the committee appointed in 1956, that brigades should be reduced to a strength of three or four regiments, sharing common depot and promotion rolls and bound together by the strongest bond of all, a common cap badge. Whistler and his men accepted the need for this radical measure and furthermore saw it as a transitory stage towards the evolution of larger regiments, like the reforms introduced by Cardwell in 1873. They realised that depots would have to be centralised, with the much slower flow of only regular recruits, and that with manpower always in short supply and further reductions to be anticipated as

Britain's commitments dwindled, a single-battalion regiment could no longer survive, without gross overstrain on its nerves. However, the immediate conversion of the brigades into large regiments was considered too large a pill to be swallowed at one gulp—although in fact the patient would never again be in so tractable a state—and the commitee merely expressed the hope that it would follow the reorganisation as a natural process of evolution.

This was the grand design into which the selection of the fifteen pairs had to be fitted, and the recruiting potential of the revised brigade area as a whole was picked as the most important factor, followed in order of priority by the territorial affiliations of the existing regiments, their standard of officers, recruiting potential and, lastly, their seniority. In short, the fate of a regiment depended most of all on the fertility of the recruiting area allotted it by Cardwell, and obviously those few that shared counties were the most vulnerable. Thus the most predictable of all amalgamations was that of the South and the North Staffordshires, both of whom wore in their caps versions of the Staffordshire Knot with which to tie themselves together. With them the strong regiments of Cheshire and of Worcestershire formed a small brigade, the Mercian, which could be left without further spoliation in the oak heart of England.

The only counties divided regimentally further south were Surrey and Kent, and they were the homes of England's oldest Line regiments, the Queen's and the Buffs, 2nd and 3rd of Foot. Age could not save them from fusion with their county colleagues, the East Surreys, who like the Queen's were proud of their naval connections, and the Queen's Own Royal West Kent, the 50th of Foot. The Royal Sussex and the Middlesex were preserved, and to slim the Home Counties Brigade to four the Royal Fusiliers was removed to form a new brigade corresponding to the Light Infantry, the Fusilier. This was a popular move among the strong Fusilier regiments of England, of whom the other two were the Royal Northumberland and the Lancashire.

The removal of these two eased the overloading of the two biggest brigades, the Lancastrian and the Yorkshire, and it is of interest to note that although Lancashire is the smaller county, with half a million fewer inhabitants today, it was allotted seven regiments by Cardwell against Yorkshire's six. Since the Lancastrian Brigade also embraced the Border Regiment, it still had seven regiments after the transfer of the Lancashire Fusiliers, and the only one to remain intact was the most junior, the Loyal (North Lancashire), which was so named because its junior founder, the 81st Foot, had been formed by the voluntary enlistment of a complete regiment of Militia. Of the others the King's Own—the 'Old

Lions' or 4th Foot—was linked with the men of John Peel's country, the Border; the King's (Liverpool)—another old regiment, numbered 8th—made an inter-city union with the Manchester; and the East Lancashire was joined to the South, the 'Lily Whites' to the Prince of Wales's Volunteers, the 30th to the 40th (or XLth, the 'Excellers').

Yorkshire came off lightly, the only amalgamation being of the senior pair, of the West Yorkshire and the East, the 14th and 15th, the Prince of Wales's Own and the Duke of York's Own. The Green Howards, the Duke's, and the York and Lancaster (whose home, strangely, was at Sheffield) completed the Yorkshire Brigade, and the K.O.Y.L.I. brought the county total to a proud five.

Elsewhere it was a case of joining counties together and the less pock-marked they were by industry the smaller their population and the stronger the case for military surgery. East Anglia was totally dismembered. The swede-bashers of Norfolk and Suffolk—the Royal 9th or 'Holy Boys' and the 'Old Dozen'—found themselves in predictable union; the Bedfordshire and Hertfordshire made a three-county fusion with the Essex, bringing 16th and 44th, the 'Old Bucks' and the 'Pompadours' together; and the Royal Lincolnshire, although covering a vast area, was removed from the Midland Brigade into a merger with the Northamptonshire. This made the East Anglian a brigade of three amalgamating pairs, and next to it, in the Midlands, lay one of three regiments untouched, the Royal Warwicks, Royal Leicesters, and Sherwood Foresters.

The West Country similarly was ripe for the scythe. Devonshire and Dorset formed as natural a partnership as Norfolk and Suffolk, regimentally and geographically, and Berkshire and Wiltshire could also be joined without regimental discord, containing the Royal Princess Charlotte of Wales's and (by happy inheritance from the 99th) the Duke of Edinburgh's, a title that had again become fact. The Gloucestershire, well protected by its coat of post-war glory, and the Royal Hampshire completed the far spread Wessex Brigade.

The Somerset Light Infantry and the Duke of Cornwall's formed another West Country union, and although wounding to Light Infantry pride, it was a convenient way to reduce the size of its brigade, which retained strongholds in Yorkshire, Shropshire, and Durham. Its sixth member, the Oxfordshire and Buckinghamshire, was transferred to what had been the Motorised Brigade and became the Green Jacket on the release of its two members from their motorised role. The Ox and Bucks intruded with the precedence of senior and in 1958 changed title to 1st Green Jackets, 43rd and 52nd, bringing pride to every heart on which one or other of these numbers was carved and leading the King's Royal or 60th Rifles and the always green-jacketed Rifle Brigade along the road towards the large regiment with a similar change of style.

Two more pairs had to be sentenced to splicing, and they were not to be found in Wales or Northern Ireland, both of which supported strong brigades of three. Scotland also had a good record for recruiting, but there would be outrage if the entire sacrifice fell on English regiments, and the Highland Brigade had in any case to be slimmed from six to four regiments in adherence to the guiding principle. Cassels' regiment, the Seaforth, and the Queen's Own Cameron Highlanders, joint inhabitants of Inverness-shire and the even more remote north, were picked for one of the pairings. The other was achieved by banishing the Highland Light Infantry from the Highland Brigade, which meant that they would lose their treasured right to wear the kilt, and tying them up with one of the four regiments of the Lowland Brigade, the Royal Scots Fusiliers. This was bound to be a high combustible bundle. Being Glaswegians, the H.L.I. were renowned as tough fighters, whether in the front line or at base, and had in fact gained the status of Highlanders as a special reward for their prowess in battle, which set them apart from the native Highlanders. It seemed unlikely that as both Highlanders and Light Infantrymen they would lie quietly down with the proud Lowland Fusiliers from Ayrshire.

In the event they did not, and they were alone in this respect. The plans were announced by Hare in the Commons on July 24, and at the same moment commanding officers everywhere opened the sealed envelopes containing news of the fate of their regiments—unless of course they had disobeyed the instructions on it and opened it earlier for a secret peep. The initial reaction, when the news was bad, was one of shock. When it wore off there was realisation almost everywhere that the decision was unalterable, and this was backed by the determination to present a brave face to the prospect openly and to strike the best bargain obtainable in private negotiation with the partner in amalgamation. The War Office was keen to help but not to interfere, hoping that all such details as title, badges, and the location of regimental headquarters would be mutually agreed by the two partners. Only from Glasgow and Ayr was there a sustained bombardment. Members of Parliament laid counter proposals before the Prime Minister without avail, and in Glasgow there was a large protest march. The two Colonels, Major-Generals Hakewill-Smith and Urquhart (of Arnhem and Malaya), eventually agreed on a solution, that the kilt should be worn with the Fusiliers' tartan. This was not acceptable for a Lowland regiment, and Hare had to call on the two Colonels, who had both retired from the active list, to resign. They were replaced by two serving officers who had reluctantly to 'accept the necessity of amalgamating, with all that this entails'. A thriving, happy battalion was to emerge from this acid germination.

It was fortunate that in Field Marshal Templer the army had at its head an infantryman of considerable fame. He personally forewarned Colonels of Regiments of the grim decisions that were to be announced, and he was moved by the loyalty with which they were received, in particular by serving officers and men. Naturally members of older generations made their dismay known with some force, in one instance breaking the barrier usually imposed by death. This occurred when Templer was explaining the reason for the H.L.I. and Fusilier amalgamation by going through the alternatives. He mentioned the Gordon Highlanders, and at this there was a crash. One of the pictures of his predecessors, on the wall behind him, had fallen to the ground. It was of Sir Archibald Murray, C.I.G.S. in 1914 and Colonel of the Gordons, and the glass was cracked diagonally from corner to corner.

A great palliative to regimental morale, showing the reformers' appreciation of the need for gradualism, was the exemption of the Territorial Army from the infantry reorganisation, both in the matter of the amalgamations and the new brigade bondage. Thus the regiments still had their representatives to display their badges and carry the old traditions aloft. The new responsibility cast on them spurred the territorial officers on to meet the challenge posed by the ending of national service, which had been announced so abruptly that their conscripts were gone before they could appeal to them to become volunteers. There had already been an adjustment of the ambitious role envisaged for the Territorial Army by Montgomery. Since the end of 1955 only two divisions had been earmarked for reinforcement of N.A.T.O., the airborne element had been reduced from a division to a brigade, and the remaining six divisions had been organised for home defence, with the armour converted to infantry. Now all were assigned to home defence, with support of the Civil Defence Corps among their duties. Pride in regiment and in voluntary service could not burn quite brightly enough to sustain the strength of most battalions for these menial-sounding, though gravely important duties, and in November 1960 the axe was wielded, cutting down eighteen infantry battalions and a proportionate number of support units. Now for the first time amalgamation spread to the Territorial Army.

In the Regular Army the amalgamations lasted from April 25, 1958, when the West and the East Yorks became The Prince of Wales's Own Regiment of Yorkshire during the course of a symbolic parade at Dover, to March 1, 1961, when the Buffs and the Royal West Kent pledged union as The Queen's Own Buffs, The Royal Kent Regiment in a similar brave little ceremony at Shorncliffe. By now all the regimental depots had closed down and every infantryman (but not guardsman) had changed his cap badge to that devised for his brigade, thus regaining his ancient right to wear the same one throughout his service. Naturally it smacked of a confidence trick. However ardent the evangelism of a brigade colonel and the support given him by colonels of regiments, it was hard to make a convincing case for the intrusion of this unfamiliar symbol in place of the old and well beloved. Particularly in the sergeants' mess, that citadel of a battalion's morale, there was apt to be a feeling of sullen, cynical perplexity, and it ran deepest in those regiments that had escaped amalgamation. The new ones were fully occupied in building up the new *esprit*, showing that the 'hybrid vigour' sought by stock-breeders could be generated equally well by human material. But only in the East Anglian Brigade, where all three regiments were new, and in the Green Jacket was there any apparent inclination to follow the finger Whistler had pointed towards the large regiment. The Army Council remained willing enough to point but not to coerce.

It is easy enough to see in retrospect that the anxieties that were to make such a neurosis of regimental life for the remainder of the 1960s could have been avoided by one sharp rap, an order for the conversion of the brigades to regiments, similar to that issued by Childers in 1881. But it needed a politician to make it, and the Tories were no keener to interfere than they had been in the 1870s. Recruiting was the main, perennial problem, and it could only be aggravated by further organisational changes. Pay had been raised, by the end of 1960, to £6. 9s. 6d. a week for a recruit enlisting on the six-year engagement that in most arms was now the shortest open to him. This needs to be compared to the 28/– a week paid a regular recruit eleven years earlier, and still the lure was not strong enough. It was in his desire to sell the army to the public that the Prime Minister brought in a comparatively junior man as War Minister—Mr. John Profumo—who had shown flair in the technique of publicity and was eventually to release a spate of it upon himself. The army had in the meantime acquired more recruits, keeping its strength to 185,000.

The first modification to the new organisation was made on May 1, 1963, and although it attracted little notice it was a disruptive affair, being the result of second thoughts on the ideal size of a brigade or large regiment. Operationally, the preceding years had been unusually quiet, with the result that further cuts were under consideration, to the tune of ten infantry battalions. This meant that some brigades would have to be reduced to two battalions, and although regiments had flourished at this strength during the Cardwell era it was considered that the new ones, into which the brigades were intended to transform themselves, needed to be bigger. One brigade had therefore to be scrapped: an ironic sequence to the formation of a new one, the Fusilier. The choice fell on what had been the Midland Brigade and was now the Forester Brigade; it was a happy little brigade, consisting of three untouched regiments that all had animals of the forest as their emblems and were making good and dutiful progress along the path to the large regiment. They were now removed from their forest to bring others up to a strength of four. The Royal Warwickshire, of which Montgomery was still Colonel, elevated itself to Fusiliers by a piece of historical acrobatics, based on the fact that it was raised jointly with the 5th (which itself had belatedly become a Fusilier regiment in 1836). There was no such joy for the others. The Sherwood Foresters joined the Mercian Brigade, being forced to wear a badge they had had no part in choosing, and the poor Tigers of Leicestershire were swallowed up as junior members of the East Anglian, which was poised for conversion to the Royal Anglian Regiment. Thus was the Forester Brigade sold for a ducat.

Other changes happened to coincide with the organisational ones, as if to make a thorough job of the new face-lift. In terms both of appearance and tactics none had greater impact than the issue of the self-loading rifle, which as the F.N.L. (Fabrique des Nations Libres) represented N.A.T.O.'s first big achievement at standardisation. First issued for experimental purposes in 1955 (to the Rifle Brigade in Kenya), it was in general circulation throughout the regular infantry by 1959. It was the first time there had been radical alteration to the infantryman's basic weapon for over sixty years, and it gave a boost to the ordinary rifleman, making him once again a real force on the battlefield. It also meant that he had to be taught a new arms drill, for the rifle would not rest comfortably on the left shoulder and instead had to be propped upright inside the right arm, bringing the old command 'Shoulder Arms', which was still heard in Rifle regiments, back into general usage. With a new badge in his cap, a new weapon in a new position, and in blue number-one uniform (which had not previously been seen on parade because of its issue to regulars only), the modern soldier stood transformed in three aspects, much to the wonder of old regimental loyalists. Soon he would be back in khaki again for ceremonial, wearing an officer-style service dress with buttons that did not need cleaning.

Inevitably the staunch old Vickers machine-gun, so often discarded and as often brought back, and the younger but just as faithful bren gun had to leave the stage in the train of the Lee-Enfield, being succeeded at a later date by the General Purpose machine-gun. The infantry's carriers also departed in favour of the swifter Land Rover, mobility being preferable to armour plating that could not withstand the higher velocity of modern weapons.

Standardisation also brought changes in artillery, although not until 1966 were the 25-pounders—for so long the pride of the Royal Regiment—replaced by the 105-mm. self-propelled Abbots as the divisional field weapon. The Italian 105-mm. pack-howitzer came into use earlier, bringing its users change of title to Light Regiment, with the result that a change of station frequently brought change of style, only the number remaining constant. The 5·5-inch medium gun, with its horn-like recoil springs, gave way by a slow process of transfer to the venomous 155-mm. gun.

The armour also changed from 'pounders' to metric measurement, mounting 105-mm. guns in Centurions and obtaining a bigger tank, the Conqueror, which soon gave way to the less cumbersome Chieftain. In armoured car regiments, the powerful Saladins were introduced, mounting 76-mm. guns, to provide support for the Ferret scout cars.

In Rhine Army the eerie, mind-taxing expectation of nuclear attack brought organisational changes to comply with tactical demands. Decentralisation became the cry, such was the vulnerability of communications. Divisions dropped the Infantry or Armoured from their titles and were organised into brigade groups, each of a three-to-one ratio of infantry and armour, or vice versa, and with its own integral regiment of artillery and squadron of engineers. They had immense power of strike. Each brigade commander had a mixed regiment of medium and field, and a nuclear regiment, of both howitzers and rocket firing Honest Johns, became part of the divisional artillery and provided the only pool of fire power under the G.O.C.'s direct control, with the even more horrific Corporal available on application to Army H.Q. Cross-country mobility was of greatest importance, and to achieve it armoured troop carriers, named Saracens, were provided and manned initially by armoured regiments, in similar manner to the sawn-off tanks used for this purpose towards the end of the Second World War. Their issue expanded from armoured to infantry brigade groups, until every battalion in Rhine Army received its own allotment and provided the drivers for them. This widened the skills required of the infantryman and the attractions sought by the army's advertising agency. It also brought the Saracens the insult of being branded A.P.C.s which stands for armoured personnel carriers.

The combined effect on Rhine Army of the evolutionary changes and the overall reduction was to slim it from a strength of two infantry divisions, the 2nd and the 4th, containing their own armoured elements, and of two armoured divisions, the 6th and the 7th, which were no more than glorified brigades, to one of three divisions, containing a total of two armoured and five infantry brigade groups. The Berlin Brigade and three armoured car regiments brought the total of units to twenty of infantry and fourteen of armour, which was still a fair force, particularly when reinforced by the 4th Canadian Infantry Brigade Group, which became part of the 4th Division and subsequently of the 2nd; between 1961 and 1963 the 4th had a Canadian G.O.C., Major-General J. V. Allard. The first big change was the conversion in April 1958 of the 7th Armoured Division into the 5th Division, to redress which the former's 7th Armoured Brigade Group was granted permission to retain its badge of the jerboa or desert rat. In June of that year the 6th Armoured Division was disbanded, having despatched its 20th Armoured Brigade Group to 4 Division. The next change came on June 30, 1960, when the 1st Division, having been put out of business in England by the shortage of troops, exercised the predatory privilege of a senior and dispossessed the 5th, later taking over both armoured brigade groups as part of a reshuffle.

Although tension throughout Germany was tightened by the building of the Berlin Wall in August 1961, Rhine Army suffered further reduction when a surge of crises—in Borneo, Cyprus, Kenya and Aden—made their sudden demands on the British Army in the early days of 1964. The 5th Infantry Brigade Group was released to re-equip the strategic reserve, leaving the 4th Guards, the 6th, 11th, and 12th Infantry, and the 7th and 20th Armoured Brigades for redistribution between the three divisions. A reaction against decentralisation enabled the latter to regain their proprietary rights of command, with the result that the word Group was removed from the brigades' titles in November 1965, but it was less easy to retain battalions now that the principle had been accepted that Rhine Army could be tapped as a reserve and usually one, and sometimes two, would be absent, with the remainder under strength.

The air played an increasingly important part in soldiers' lives. On September 1, 1957, the Army Air Corps was formed, to perform a service that had been casting heavy strain on the Air O.P. wing of the Royal Artillery. A reconnaissance flight formed part of the establishment of the brigade group, being equipped with Sioux helicopters and the wonderfully adaptable and manoeuvrable Beaver. And of course air movement became a common experience for all soldiers, whether tactically by helicopter or strategically as the passengers of the R.A.F. or a civil line. From 1962 even routine changes of station were carried out by air, and the old, nostalgic ritual of 'trooping', with all its discomforts and leisurely joys, came to an end. The last battalion to make its homecoming in this manner was that offspring of controversy and anguish, the 1st Royal Highland Fusiliers, and its men reached Southampton on December 19, 1962, aboard the T.T. *Oxfordshire*, which had picked them up at Malta, having left Singapore on October 26.

The time spent on such a journey was more than could be afforded with battalions in such short supply. The new army had to be mobile, and even when operational demands were not heavy, as between 1960–62, there would be flights to other continents merely for training and for the variety and excitement they afforded, in compensation for the reduction in permanent overseas stations. In the mid-1960s there would be plenty of operational calls, keeping battalions away on unaccompanied tours usually of nine months' duration. Family separation again became the blight of service, and it presented bigger problems than ever before, for the soldiers married much younger than of old and could claim marriage allowance at the age of 21.

Just as the slimming of the army increased the need for mobility, it also increased that for closer cooperation between the services. Indeed Sandys saw that economy as well as efficiency could be achieved this way and made integration of the services one of his primary aims. He started well enough by appointing a Chief of Defence Staff soon after he took office in January 1957, thus for the first time giving the service chiefs a service overlord, such as had long been recognised as an essential for any operation of war. Unfortunately he could not shed his service identity, and the first to be appointed was Marshal of the R.A.F. Sir William Dickson, on the understanding that the turn of the other services would come.

Although many boulders were encountered, progress was made at the integration of staffs, and on April 1, 1958, Field Marshal Templer opened the first inter-service headquarters, that at the former R.A.F. preserve, Aden, which was renamed Headquarters British Forces Arabian Peninsula. The Middle East followed in May 1960 and the Far East, lagging somewhat, in November 1962, and on April 1—the favourite day of reformers—on April 1, 1964, integration was at last achieved at the summit, with Mr. Peter Thorneycroft now the Minister of Defence. His Ministry absorbed its hitherto constitutional equals, and sailors, soldiers and airmen were interwoven in a great new network of command, there to do battle in private for the very survival of their services. The Army Council became the Army Board, and the Secretary of State for War, Mr. J. E. Ramsden, changed his title to that of Minister of Defence for the Army. The C.I.G.S. was General Hull, who was late of the 17th/21st Lancers and had a formidable fund of mechanical knowledge. He was the first cavalryman to hold the post since Sir 'Wully' Robertson and had succeeded the fifth successive infantryman in office, Field Marshal Festing, late Rifle Brigade, who was the first to have been born too late for service in the First World War. Hull now moved across the Horse Guards Avenue from the stately slab of Victoriana that had ceased to be the War Office into the twentieth-century slab built for the Air Ministry, and as he passed between the massive stone amazons guarding his new home he dropped the Imperial from his title.

One more piece of reorganisation needs to be recorded. It was in the matter of supply that there was strongest call for integration, and in the absence of any enthusiasm for a neutral Forces Supply Corps, it was up to the services to overhaul their organisations for the benefit of all. The R.A.S.C. therefore concentrated entirely on transportation and passed their responsibilities for providing ammunition, petrol, and foodstuff on to those hardware experts, the R.A.O.C., together with such miscellaneous duties as barrack accounting and the training of clerks. From the R.E. they took over railway movement, waterways and port operating, so that every form of army transportation, by land, sea, air, on wheels or on mules, was in their hands. On July 15, 1965, they changed their title, dropping the word Army, and became the Royal Corps of Transport.

12

Arabia

(1949-70)

RITAIN's earliest interest in the great untrammelled wastes of the Arabian Peninsula lay around its north-east border. Here ran the principal trading route from Europe to Asia, along the rivers of Mesopotamia, along the Persian Gulf, and onwards to India, and the British were not slow in blowing the tang of their influence upon it. From the Ottoman Empire concessions were obtained granting navigational rights through Mesopotamia, and treaties were made with the sheikhs whose tribes inhabited the southern coast of the Gulf, establishing a loose form of British overlordship in exchange for the protecting arm of the Royal Navy against some hitherto prosperous pirates. The opening of the Suez Canal reduced the traffic through the Gulf, but it regained importance in the early 1900s when oil was discovered in the mountains of Persia (predictably, by a Briton) and run by pipeline to Abadan, from there to feed His Majesty's newest ships.

It was partly to protect this oil supply and partly to retain the allegiance of the sheikhs that Britain invaded Mesopotamia in 1914. When at last she had completed its conquest it formed a convenient compensation prize for the new King of Hejaz's son, Faisal, who had been cheated by the French of Syria, his expected reward for rebelling against the Turks. Another of the King's sons, Abdulla, was awarded a smaller, less fertile part of the old Ottoman Empire, which was named Trans-Jordan and bordered the third of the territories mandated to Britain, Palestine. All were wild, roadless lands, containing great potential for turbulence, the curbing of which would have imposed a heavy commitment on the British Army if Sir Hugh Trenchard, the founding Marshal of the Royal Air Force, had not offered to place them on air control, which meant cowing the rebellious merely by the display of the

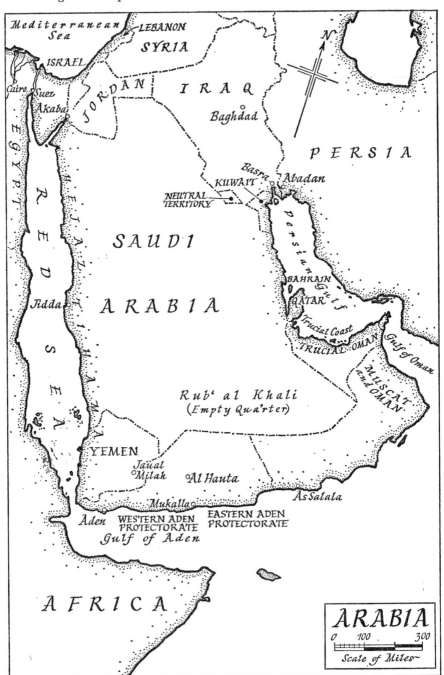

miraculous and irresistible, at a miraculously low cost in manpower. The offer was accepted, and the system worked so well that it was extended to Britain's one Arabian colony, Aden, and its adjacent protectorate, which are the subject of a separate, subsequent chapter of this book. The only British troops left in Arabia were two battalions in Palestine, which were there to help the R.A.F. This force, as we have seen, had to be enlarged.

On the evacuation of Palestine in May 1948 the British Army had no footholds left on the territory from which it had expelled the Turks, although the R.A.F. still maintained bases, by treaty right, in the former mandates of Iraq and Jordan; both these relied on their old guardian for military aid. This aid proved insufficient to extract them from defeat in the war against the new-born state of Israel, in which the British officers seconded to Jordan's Arab Legion were withdrawn from participation on orders from London. By the closing days of 1948 the Israelis were free to advance to the Gulf of Akaba and seize the port of that name, which the British had built during their mandate. King Abdulla made appeal for direct and immediate aid, and as a result the 1st Royal Lincolnshire (until recently the 2nd) were gathered up at El Ballah, by the Suez Canal, and shipped off by two frigates with full supporting arms including some tanks of the 4th R.T.R. They arrived on January 5, 1949, and had to wait until March before the Israelis reached the head of the gulf and took occupation of the fishing harbour of Eilat, which was 4 miles from Akaba and suffered from a water shortage. The Israelis made no attempt to molest the British, who had built themselves strong positions protecting the port.

Christened 'O' Force, after the Lincolns' Lieutenant-Colonel Oulton, the battalion group stayed on at Akaba, being changed every six months by relief from Egypt. Although devoid of accommodation for families, it was not an unpopular station. The gulf looked a gorgeous blue from the tented camp, and to the north rocky mountains rose serene. Watch was kept on the Israelis across the Wadi Araba, and a wide expanse of desert was patrolled for spies and marauders. King Abdulla made visits to show his appreciation of the British presence, but on July 20, 1951, he was assassinated in Jerusalem by a Palestinian extremist and the tension that perpetually grasped Jordan tightened its hold.

In the years that followed Jordan was slowly pulled from Britain's embrace, through leverage by the nationalist fervour raging from Cairo to Tehran. Templer, when C.I.G.S., was assigned a diplomatic role in the attempt to stop the rot, being despatched on a mission in December 1955 with the object of persuading the Jordanian Government to join the Baghdad Pact, which linked Iraq to N.A.T.O. and roused Nasser to

347

venomous hostility, broadcast daily from Cairo. The mission did not succeed; Jordan was not to be wooed.

The most wounding blow to British ambitions and pride came on March 1, 1956, and it was struck by King Hussein, grandson of Abdulla, as counter to the agents of subservion whose most deadly weapon against the King was the taunt 'imperialists' stooge'. Hussein summarily dismissed his family's faithful servant, General Glubb Pasha, from command of his army, the former Arab Legion, and he thus broke a brotherhood in arms of fifty years standing, which had stirred the hearts of many Britons; for the officers seconded from the British Army, including three brigade commanders, had to go too, leaving only technicians. It was with great sadness that these officers bade a brief farewell to their endearing men and discarded their shermaghs, the flowing headdress kept in place by a coloured cord. It was the end of a romance, and the 'deep shock' officially expressed by a Foreign Office spokesman was felt by the whole nation. Here lay the seeds of the Suez intervention.

The slide reached its nadir on October 22, when an election in Jordan was won by the party dedicated to the abrogation of the treaty with Britain, to military union with Egypt and Syria, and to all-out attack against Israel. A week later the Israelis forestalled them, setting off the sequence of events that brought British troops back to Egypt. And still 'O' Force stood at Akaba, uncertain from whom to expect an attack. Armour had predominated since the 1951 crisis in Egypt, which had sucked most of the infantry away, and the 10th Royal Hussars formed the main component, with a company of the 1st Middlesex from Cyprus, 187 L.A.A. Battery, and a troop of the 40th Field Regiment, hastily flown over from Cyprus on October 30. They could hear the Israelis attack the Egyptian line near Eilat and for eight weeks manned their positions, quietly performing the task claimed for the invasion force, that of preventing the fire from spreading.

In March 1957 the Jordanian Government duly snapped the treaty ties with Britain, and for the next three months the stores were removed from Akaba and the two R.A.F. bases, in the course of which an air crash cost forty soldiers their lives, mainly men of the R.E.M.E. attached to the 10th Hussars. Past services were not forgotten at the parting. King Hussein personally bade farewell to the R.A.F., and on July 6, 1957, guards of the 10th Hussars and Middlesex exchanged ceremonial compliments with some fine representatives of the Jordan Arab Army. The British then embarked in lighters and chugged out to the cruiser *Devonshire*, to the strains of 'Colonel Bogey' played with impish gusto by the band of the 10th. For the Middlesex men a month's journey round the Cape was in store before reunion with their battalion in Cyprus.

One year and eleven days after this departure, the British returned to Jordan. Remarkably, the United States Government had become as keen as the British to curb the expansionist ambition of Egypt, which made its greatest advance by union with Syria in February 1958, and both made preparations for intervention if requested by any government of Western Arabia, the British contribution being the despatch of the 16th Para Brigade and much of the 3rd Division to troubled Cyprus. The blow fell on July 14, too swiftly even for the sending of an S.O.S. King Faisal II of Iraq was shot down with his family in sickening manner, power was seized by a brigadier, and the British Embassy was sacked. There was, however, no attack on the R.A.F. base at Habbaniya, notice merely being served to quit. As ever, a wider plot under Nasser's inspiration was suspected, and calls for help came from Beirut and from the last survivor of the Hashemite kings in Amman.

On July 15 marines of the Sixth U.S. Fleet streamed ashore on Lebanese soil, and at 3.50 p.m. on the 16th orders reached the 16th Para Brigade, warning them for a flight to Amman. The brigade commander, Brigadier T. C. H. Pearson, left early next morning with a single 'chalk' —a mere handful of men—of the 2nd Parachute, touching down at Amman at 6.30 a.m., July 17. The news here was that the Israeli Government had forbidden further flights over their territory, and nine hours elapsed before they relented, with Pearson and his men wondering whether the officers who had welcomed them so warmly might not suddenly declare for the revolutionary cause. It was a great relief for them to see a flight of Hunter fighters swoop in to land at 5.30 p.m. and an hour later Beverleys arrived with the bulk of the 2nd Para and some 75-mm. guns of the 33rd Para Field Regiment. They were joined next day by the 3rd Para, the Guards Company, the whole of the 33rd Field less a battery, and the 9th Field Squadron, leaving only the 1st Para behind.

The task was to defend the barren hills overlooking the long and torrid runway of Amman's aerodrome, and as the men stepped out of the planes they were at once removed to the hills in a ramshackle assortment of commandeered transport, having brought only light transport with them. The blistering toil of digging-in went on night and day, and meanwhile bivouacs, beds and beer were produced, with eager cooperation from the Jordan Army, and a motley array of tentage sprang up, of white, khaki, red and blue, shimmering in the dust haze with the black tents of the Bedouin beside them, adding flavour to the scene. Visits to Amman were soon arranged, and the troops gasped at the antiquity of the scene in its dusty streets and at the contrasting garishness of American cars and advertisements. They found the people friendly

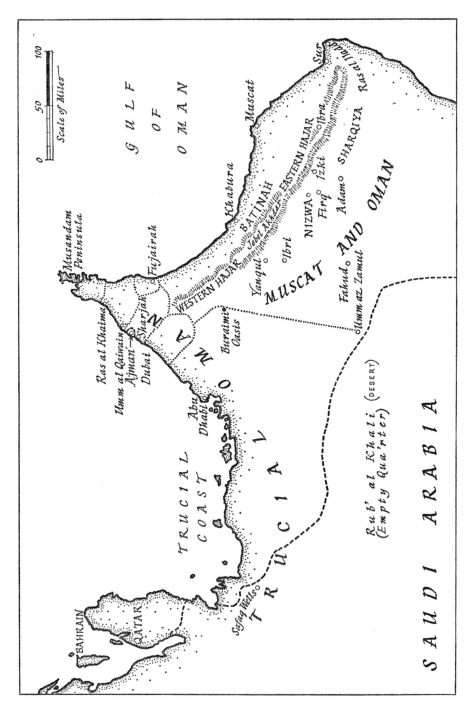

enough and amazed them by telling them that they had fought at Port Said, since it had been announced by the Jordanian Government that they had all been wiped out.

On August 7 the 16th Para Brigade received a third battalion. This was the 1st Cameronians, who were based on Kenya and had been flown to Aden in July. They had come thence in the commando carrier, *Bulwark*, landed by helicopter at Akaba, and been taken by plane to Amman. They too were taken straight to the hills to dig in, and it was three days before they were joined by their vehicles, which being painted for the jungle added a further note of eccentricity to the brigade column.

By mid-October the outlook was settled enough for the British to go, and as a preliminary the two armies staged a combined beating of the Retreat before King Hussein. The paratroops then flew off to Cyprus, for onward routing to England, and the Cameronians made the return journey through Akaba, whence they departed by cruiser on November 2. The King came to bid them farewell and to take the salute at a combined parade. It was a happier ending than had once seemed likely.

While their responsibilities in Western Arabia, acquired through defeating the Turks in 1918, were being wrested from them, the British had been showing increased activity in their much older sphere of influence further east. This was the territory lying to the east of the great heart of Arabia conquered by King Saud, and it was a part untouched by any modern invention except that of the rifle. Now there was prospect of oil, and with appetite whetted by the sniff of it, King Saud sent an armed column 600 miles in American vehicles across the desert known as the Empty Quarter to seize the Buraimi oases. This was in 1952, and since frontiers were fluid and perforce unmarked on the ground it was not uncommon for a ruler to make claim to territory, however slender its basis. The oases in fact lie 100 miles beyond the acknowledged frontier of Saudi Arabia. Six of them were claimed by the Sheikh of Abu Dhabi as his property and the three to the south-east by the Sultan of Muscat and Oman. Both had protective treaties with British and both were restrained from resort to force by the British preference for diplomacy and patience. This was particularly aggravating for the Sultan, a short, square berobed figure of a man, with an even squarer beard and an air of great authority, who had a bodyguard of slaves and a pugnacious little army mainly of Baluchis, officered by Britons and Pakistanis under contract. His territory bordered 1,000 miles of coastline, from the Eastern Aden Protectorate to the entrance into the Persian Gulf.

Abu Dhabi was more closely tied to Britain. It was the most southerly and far the largest of the seven sheikhdoms bordering the old pirate coast, which because of the truces that bound them were named the Trucial States. Further northwards Dubai, Sharjah, Ajman, Umm al Qaiwain and Ras al Khaima lie close-packed inside the Persian Gulf, and Fujairah is on the other side of the elbow, off the Gulf of Oman. British troops had not been employed here since 1819, when the 65th (1st York and Lancaster) opened a two-year campaign against the Arabs with an assault landing at Ras al Khaima, but typically the R.A.F. maintained a station, controlled from Bahrain, the island to the north of the Trucial States which had for years been the centre of British influence. This station was at Sharjah, a town described by an officer posted there as 'a huddle of little grey hovels, made of dried palm-leaves woven into shaggy mats. . . . Lurking in the midst of this shanty town was the Sheikh's palace, a crumbling structure painted blue and white like Gorgonzola cheese, with a cannon outside it used for public floggings'.

To preserve peace inside the Trucial States a gendarmerie had been started under British aegis in 1951, known as the Trucial Oman Levies, with headquarters at Sharjah. This had been expanded to contain the Saudi invasion of Buraimi, mainly by the enlistment of discharged soldiers of the Aden Levies, but a mutiny, in which the British commander was shot dead, had thrown the process into confusion, and in 1953 a fresh start was made, with the enlistment of local Arabs, awkward, weedy, yet keen, and the secondment of British officers on a scale of two per squadron and of a larger cadre of N.C.O.s. By 1955 four squadrons were operational and fully mobile, and in October of that year they were ordered to eject the Saudis from Buraimi, the Saudi delegate having displayed childish chicanery before an arbitration tribunal.

The Saudis were in occupation of a village and also had a police camp, which was their nerve centre, 3 miles from it, and both were some 18 miles from the nearest Levies' fort, which was held by a squadron. The latter was due for relief on October 25/26, and Lieutenant-Colonel Eric Johnson, commanding the Levies, therefore chose that night for his attack. One squadron motored straight for the police station, driving in with lights blazing an hour before dawn and swiftly rounding up all the Saudis without a fight, although the latter were standing to. They were at once flown to Sharjah. The other squadron attacked the village and, delayed until daybreak by loss of route, had to fight for it. The battle lasted all day, from mud wall to mud wall, until at nightfall the defenders surrendered, having lost six or seven killed and themselves killed two Levies.

British troops returned to the Trucial States to provide a sedative after this affair. C Company, 1st King's Royal Rifle Corps were the nearest that could be spared, and they came from Tobruk, in Libya, arriving at Sharjah in the early hours of October 27, 1955, having been flown in six aircraft with halts in their 2,000-mile journey at the R.A.F. stations in Jordan and Iraq. It was a pleasant surprise for them to find cool accommodation awaiting them in the storage rooms cleared by the R.A.F., whence they soon journeyed forth to tour the harsh and jagged countryside in Land Rovers or to visit islands in dhows. As a Christmas speciality the company formed a dhow-borne party of carol singers, bringing wonder and delight to water-bound Sharjah town.

On March 11, 1956, this same company of the 60th made a second pioneering journey as soldiers. They were flown at an hour's notice to Bahrain, where fierce rioting had broken out under instigation from Cairo and Tehran. Commanded by Major Gibbs, who by strange coincidence was to become the first G.O.C. Persian Gulf, the company found the rioting had been largely quelled and did little more than secure the causeway connecting the main island, which contained the naval base, and the smaller one possessing the civil and military air bases and Bahrain's largest town, Muharrek. With Persia laying claim to Bahrain, it was decided that there should be a permanent army presence, and a second company of the K.R.R.C. were brought in. Both were relieved, between April and June, by companies of the 1st Gloucestershire from Kenya, and by the end of August the Gloucesters were assembled astride the Gulf complete, with companies at Sharjah and Dubai. They had to contend with another rash of rioting in Bahrain when the Suez crisis reached its climax. Condemned to inactivity by political considerations while the B.O.A.C. block of flats was burned down before them, D Company were at last let loose to clear the streets of Muharrek, advancing in box squares against a hail of bottles and stones. The rioters had dug a precipitous ditch and built a great barricade, but neither obstacle stopped the Gloucesters, and the task was accomplished after the discharge of fifty gas bombs and a single round of ·303.

The 1st King's Shropshire Light Infantry were hurried out from Kenya to join the Gloucesters, but in January 1957 the garrison at Bahrain was reduced to the elements of a single battalion, the newly arrived 1st Cameronians, who kept a company at Sharjah and sent another two to Kenya because of the shortage of air-conditioned accommodation at Bahrain, the original billet in the old royal palace being primitive in the extreme. Such were their dispositions when they were suddenly called upon to eject rebels from the Oman half of the Sultanate of Muscat and Oman.

There had been revolt here in 1955, led by one Ghalib, who claimed independence as the elected Imam of Oman. The Sultan swiftly re-established his authority, making a triumphant entry into Nizwa, capital of Oman, to the booming and bursting of cannons fired in salute. Ghalib was consigned to retirement, but soon his brother Talib arrived by sea with sixty men of his 'Oman Liberation Army'. He succeeded in joining up with Ghalib, and with the aid of a renegade sheikh, Suleiman, and some blunders by some raw levies of the Sultan, they regained control of Nizwa and the villages around it on the craggy Hajar range 50 miles inland. They were well supplied with machine-guns, mortars and anti-tank mines, some of Russian make, some of American.

The Sultan acknowledged the defeat of his troops by appealing to Britain for aid on July 17, 1957, and Air Marshal Sinclair, A.O.C. Persian Gulf, was next day ordered to mount an operation. To command the land forces Brigadier J. A. R. Robertson, late 6th Gurkhas, was jerked away from command of 51 Brigade in Cyprus. He formed a head-quarters by enrolment of the staff officer at Bahrain and the N.C.O. caretaker of the garrison church. The Sultan of Muscat's troops, the Trucial Oman Scouts (as the Levies had been renamed) and the Cameronians all came under his command.

Airfields were in loyalist hands at Ibri, 60 miles north-west of Nizwa, and at Fahud, 70 miles south-west of it, where an oil development centre had been established in a saucer amid some conical hills, giving clue to the British concern over the rebellion. It was from here that the main advance was to be made, with diversionary pressure from a column of the Sultan's men from Muscat, directly opposite, and by the establish-ment of A Company, 1st Cameronians at Ibri, whither they were flown from Bahrain on August 3. Venom aircraft had meanwhile been buzzing over the rebel strongholds of Nizwa, Tanuf and Izki, first with messages giving warning of the punishment to come and, two days later, with the punishment. This they administered with cannon and rocket, making dummy runs first to make sure all took cover and leaving some forts untouched through mistaking the white flag of the Iman for one of surrender.

The build-up at Fahud, where Robertson established his headquar-ters, was by land and air, and the main component took the long, rough and parched land route, consisting of three squadrons of the Trucial Oman Scouts, whose Lieutenant-Colonel Carter, a dashing and flam-boyant figure, was to be force commander. As suggested by the change of title, the Scouts had had a considerable face-lift since 1955, and once again British soldiers were to be seen in shermaghs, of red and white, with black cords keeping them in place on the head. A squadron of the

Sultan's Northern Frontier Regiment also arrived overland, while the Cameronians flew in their D and Support Companies from Bahrain, the latter having started in Kenya; from Aden came a troop of five Ferret scout cars of the 15th/19th Hussars, and some Royal Engineers. Beverleys brought the heavier vehicles, although suffering stoppages from the heat. Hastings and Valettas brought troops and Land Rovers. Some 20,000 water cans were assembled and filled with eager aid from the oil company, for there was a dearth of information about the water supply in the hills.

The advance began on August 6, with the 15th/19th still to arrive, and it rapidly became apparent as the men bumped across the desert in their open trucks that the heat was going to be the worst enemy, at any rate of the British. They were in motion most of the night and were subjected to sandstorms next day. The ascent to higher, rather more fertile country brought some slight relief. The village of Izz fell on the 7th, after no more than a parley, and the column was now within 6 miles of a known stronghold just to the south of Nizwa, which was named—the troops could hardly believe it—Firq. On the 8th the Scouts attempted a wide left-flanking movement past Firq. They encountered heavy, although inaccurate, fire from some caves, and although some progress was made, the fire persisted, undiminished by a raucous lashing from the Venoms and from the Cameronians' 3-inch mortars and Vickers machine-guns. The troops were withdrawn to recuperate, while the R.A.F. delivered further venom on the rebels.

The heat had by now caused the collapse of ten Cameronians, of whom seven had to be evacuated, by 3-tonner to Fahud, thence by air to Bahrain. Most were men from Kenya, who had had nine days under the harsher glare of Arabia and had proudly been wearing their balmorals—until bush hats were flown out for them, adding further strain on the commissariat. Water had run low at times, through difficulties of distribution, and the men had been inclined to gulp it down with great speed when it arrived. The principles of water discipline, as practised of old by infantry soldiers, had become obscured beneath the medical insistence that fluid lost must be replaced.

The troop of the 15th/19th had by now arrived, and on the night of the 10th they obtained some useful information about the defences around Firq. The village was dominated by a precipitous ridge named Crown Hill, on the right of it as viewed by the British. D Company of of the Cameronians, by great endeavour, scaled it during the night of the 11th, sending their mortar bombs crashing on a few snipers who tried to interfere. Most of the rebels had repaired to the village for the night and, realising their peril, they rushed away before daybreak, leaving seven bren guns behind. There was no further opposition. By midday the Scouts were inside the great old walls of Nizwa, marvelling at the might of its fortress, which had been scarred but far from crumpled by the R.A.F. One Scout killed and four wounded comprised the sum of the enemy-inflicted casualties paid for its capture.

On the 12th Carter's column linked up with the British led one from Muscat, which had advanced as far as Izki, swollen by many irregulars come to back the winning side. Harried constantly by the R.A.F., the rebels had retreated to the highest feature of the Hajar range, the mighty Jebel Akhdar or 'Green Mountain', a stronghold that had its own fertile plateau and had gained the reputation over the centuries of being quite impregnable. It was not within Robertson's brief to invest the rebels there, and he was in any case under pressure to bring the operation to a speedy end, since the United Nations were in process of assembling. Having restocked from forward airstrips and seen his sappers blow up some forts and other rebel property, he withdrew his troops through Muscat, the capital and port, leaving behind only the 15th/19th troop, which was relieved by the end of October by one from the 13th/18th Hussars, and two squadrons of the Scouts.

The main function of the armoured cars was to escort oil convoys across the ruffled wastes of Oman. There were many adventures for their crews and commanders as they bumped over rock and sand in their red-hot Ferrets. Mines were struck in ever growing number, and while the Sultan's men might wave friendly greeting from one hill top, a burst of fire might come from the next. Among the strange sights seen was a batch of prisoners in leg-irons, brought out for an exchange of hostages.

In November 1957 the Sultan's troops, with support from the 13th/18th, launched an unsuccessful attack on the Jebel, and since the mines laid by the guerrillas were by now threatening the flow of oil, the British Government decided in January 1958 to give the Sultan further aid. Twenty-three army officers, with eight Royal Marine sergeants and certain specialists, were seconded to his army, and at their head was an officer of the Blues, Colonel D. de C. Smiley, who was appointed Chief of Staff and applied himself to the delicate task of fusing the seconded officers in with those under contract to the Sultan and preparing them to endure the furnace heat of the interior. He also received five aircraft and pilots on secondment from the R.A.F. and had his own artillery troop, together with the residue of the Nizwa expedition and a field force of about 450 men, most of them Baluchis. But he did not consider his army strong enough to eject the rebels from the great Jebel, and by pressing the War Minister, Captain Christopher Soames, when he made a visit, he eventually obtained the promise of more British troops.

The first arrivals were the Life Guards, who relieved the 13th/18th (who had been increased to two troops) with a full squadron, operating from Sharjah by the end of September. In this same month a subaltern of the R.A.S.C. was sent from England with four N.C.O.s in order to raise a donkey train. He bought two hundred in Somaliland after some crafty haggling and brought them to Oman, where they were dispersed to units, ill prepared for the toil ahead. Near the end of November the first assault troops 'tiptoed in'—D Squadron, 22 Special Air Service, numbering less than eighty men divided into four troops, armed on a scale that made the eyes of the seconded officers bulge with envy. The S.A.S. were on their way home from Malaya, and it was convenient that they should have been available for a task for which ordinary infantry would have needed at least a month's special training.

Smiley's force had already made good progress in enveloping the rebels' stronghold and just before the arrival of the S.A.S. a patrol of the Muscat Regiment, under a contract officer, scaled a path up the north side of the Jebel which gained them a foothold on the plateau unopposed. The S.A.S. were quick to exploit this gain by a series of patrol bounds, provoking some counterattacks that were broken up by the variegated ring of Life Guards, who had brought their Brownings forward dismounted, Trucial Scouts, the S.A.S. themselves, and of the Sultan's two regiments, the Muscat and the North Frontier, whose officers wore balmorals, turbans, or shermaghs and whose men were determined to prove their mettle in such distinguished company. Near the end of December the S.A.S. made a night attack on a pinnacle commanding the western approach to the 17-mile long plateau. By scaling a precipice with the use of ropes, they gained surprise and inflicted casualties, but the rebels fought stubbornly—'Come and fight, Johnny' they shouted—and were not to be shifted from their crags and caves.

It was now numbingly cold on the mountain, with hail and even snow adding their bite, and yet only three months remained before the heat would be too intense to make operations feasible. A Squadron of the S.A.S. arrived and relieved D astride the western approach on January 13, 1959. For the next ten days continual probing attacks were made from either side of the plateau's western slopes. Supply was an exhausting task, calling for a seven-hour haul by donkeys, for which a scratch team of Life Guardsmen acted as 'wallopers', carrying man-packs themselves and labouring so hard and often, with mortar bombs frequently crashing around them, that they were permitted to grow beards.

The *coup de grâce* was delivered on the moonlit night of January 26/27, following diversionary attacks by the North Frontier Regiment

357

and the spreading of deceptive rumours. Lieutenant-Colonel Deane-Drummond, commanding 22 S.A.S., had selected a spur on the south side during an air reconnaissance. It rose sheer and contained no track, the goats preferring the re-entrants, and after being brought to its foot by transport after dark, D Squadron, with part of A, began the climb. A few shots were fired at them, one of which hit a grenade in a soldier's pack, mortally wounding him and the next man and hitting a third. A heavy machine-gun, firing from a cave, caused some obstruction, until knocked out by a neatly placed grenade. For eleven-and-a-half hours the men toiled onwards, and soon after dawn they were on the highest peak.

Practically the entire rebel force had been drawn westwards to meet the diversionary attacks, and now, as realisation came that the enemy had gained the summit behind them, parachutes came floating down upon it. They in fact held supplies, but the rebel leaders took them to be troops and made all speed for Saudi Arabia, successfully breaking through Smiley's cordon next night, and thence onwards to Cairo. Cairo radio reported that 120,000 British troops had been employed in the attack, and Moscow added the tit-bit that 13,000 paratroopers had been dropped. Such was the honour accorded the 1,100, of whom barely 250 can have been British (including seconded officers and N.C.O.s), who broke the myth of the Jebel's impregnability. The cost over the whole operation was fifteen killed and fifty-seven wounded, seven and eight of them British. Mines caused the most casualties.

This was a famous victory for 22 S.A.S. in particular, for their reward was that most coveted of things, survival. They had previously been faced with dissolution on completion of the tasks for which they had been raised in Malaya. It was acknowledged now that they could be of lasting value, and the men in the beige berets thus took permanent post in the Regular Army.

Ludicrous though the blarings of the frustrated dictators were, they were correct in supposing that Britain was prepared to bring such might as she still possessed to the aid of her old protégés, especially now that the importance of their lands had been so immensely raised by the discovery of oil. Indeed, the reorganisation of the Middle East Command in March 1961 showed new sensitivity to the threat to the Gulf States, for it connected them, within the single corridor of command, with the reserves available from Nairobi, 1,200 miles from Aden and a further 1,000 from Bahrain by direct air route. The chance to demonstrate the efficacy of the planning, and likewise Britain's resolve, came in June 1961 just after a new agreement had been made with Kuwait, at the head of the Gulf, replacing the old and unrealistic overlord relationship. It provoked President Kassem of Iraq to claim, on June 25, that Kuwait was part of his country and to announce that he was going to annex it. On the 27th the Amir of Kuwait appealed to both Britain and Saudi Arabia for aid, and Air Marshal Sir Charles Elworthy, as C.-in-C. Middle East, made ready to send it, with the loan of spearhead units from neighbouring commands, the Far East and the Near. Intelligence reports indicated that Kassem was in earnest and was assembling an armoured brigade for a swift coup, as a result of which Elworthy was instructed to go ahead.

42 Commando were already *en route* from the Far East in their carrier *Bulwark*, being very conveniently and appropriately scheduled to carry out some hot weather trials, for briefing on which the commanding officer flew to Bahrain, leaving his men to have some shore leave at Karachi. He was briefed instead about the coming operation, from the mouth of Major-General Robertson, the same as had led the Nizwa expedition and who was now in charge of the army side as G.O.C. Land Forces Middle East. *Bulwark* set off from Karachi on the morning of June 29, making 24 knots, and was off Kuwait on the morning of Saturday, July 1. Undaunted by the sand swirling above Kuwait's new, as yet uncompleted aerodrome, C Troop spiralled down in their helicopters soon after 11.30 a.m. and were followed almost at once by a squadron of Hunters, of the R.A.F. The Kuwaitis, who had some tanks deployed round the aerodrome, gave them eager welcome.

The 2nd Parachute, from Cyprus and the Near East, were to have joined 42 Commando, but exactly as had happened to this very battalion three years earlier, they were delayed from flying by a refusal to grant air space, in this case by Turkey. 45 Commando were therefore summoned from Aden, and this involved a fine piece of transportation by the R.A.S.C. in bringing in their frontier detachment from Dhala, a journey normally filling two days now compressed into less than one. The men were ready by Saturday morning, but no planes were available until the late afternoon and only two reached Kuwait before nightfall, carrying fifty men. However, other troops had arrived. Two companies of the 2nd Coldstream Guards, on detachment at Bahrain from Kenya, were removed at shortest notice from the porterage duties assigned to them at docks and airport and flown to Kuwait during the afternoon to make the aerodrome secure against attack. One other very important element suffered less disturbance. A half-squadron of the 3rd Dragoon Guards or Carabiniers were already afloat with their Centurions in H.M.S. *Striker*, in readiness for such an emergency. The tanks were disgorged at a landing place found by 42 Commando, whose own vehicles made slower emittance from *Bulwark*.

359

More than half a brigade group, with powerful air support, was therefore ready for action by the night of July 1, and in command of it, rushed in by plane ahead of his staff, was Brigadier D. G. T. Horsford, who in his time had been both a Gurkha and a Gunner and now held command of the reserve from Kenya, 24th Infantry Brigade Group, in which capacity he was to command all British troops in Kuwait.

The key feature to be held was the Mutla Ridge, 25 miles from the aerodrome and 5 short of the Iraqi frontier, and because companies of the Kuwait Army, which could muster 1,200 men, were somewhere on it the helicopter lift had extended no further than the aerodrome, through fear of starting a battle between friends. The first move to the ridge was made during the night. Using a variety of commandeered vehicles, A Troop, 42 Commando took possession of a part of the ridge near the road; 45 Commando were alloted a feature 15 miles to their left, the approach to which a recce party just had time to examine in daylight under the effusive guidance of a village sheikh. As each planeload of men arrived, staggered throughout the night, they were rushed off in an assortment of vans and lorries and were usually turned from passengers to pushers by the sand on their rough route. Nevertheless the position was occupied well before daylight, with some holes dug through the rock and sand. With dawn came a lashing from a sandstorm that smote the face with the sting of a whip. The temperature rose to 125 degrees Fahrenheit. It was a scorching and exhausting trip for the remainder of 42 Commando and the crews of the Centurions who moved out to the ridge that morning.

The build-up progressed. Nearly all 45 Commando had arrived by the evening of July 2, together with a battery of the 33rd Para Field Regiment and, also from Aden, A Squadron, 11th Hussars with Ferret scout cars. Sandstorms delayed the fly-in of the latter, and they were not operational on frontier patrol until the 3rd. They could see no sign of the enemy. Also on the 3rd the other half of the Carabiniers' squadron became ready for battle in Centurions stored in Kuwait for this very purpose, and the 2nd Para began to arrive, freed from the ban on flying over Turkey.

Prospects of an attack were receding and need in any case no longer be regarded with alarm. But a stern battle was being waged against the old enemy, heat, which was of course at its most savage in July. There was no shade whatever on the Mutla Ridge, except for the blankets erected over slit trenches, and even men from Aden and Singapore, who showed stronger resistance than those from slightly cooler Cyprus, were beginning to go down, although not in the number reported in some newspapers, which drew the scorn of the men; one said that 42 Commando had lost 30 per cent of its strength, whereas its total treated for heat exhaustion in a stay of three weeks was twenty-nine. Horsford was disarmingly frank. 'Morale is terrific,' he told reporters, 'but there is a limit. Chaps are passing out quite a lot from heat exhaustion. We get them back to an air-conditioned place and usually they are able to return the same day.'

Water supply, initially, was a frightening problem, for the town of Kuwait was the only source and a limited one at that. Horsford bought every bottle of soft drink that could be obtained, running up a bill of £400 without knowing whether he would have to pay it himself. The men were kept alive by these means, until the strain was greatly eased by the resources of the Kuwait Oil Company at Ahmadi, whence helicopters flew a constant stream of ice and water to the front line. The 2nd Para reported an average consumption of twenty pints a day per man, and there were some who still collapsed, an R.A.M.C. major who had come to study the problem being among the casualties. 'Your eggs arrive hard boiled,' ran the report in *Pegasus*, 'and you can make Nescafé with water out of a jerrican.'

On July 4 the 1st Royal Inniskilling Fusiliers and the 34th Field Squadron began to arrive from Kenya, and on the night of the 6th the Inniskillings took over from 42 Commando. Next day the 1st King's (Manchester and Liverpool) relieved 45 Commando, being the second and last battalion of 24 Brigade to come from Kenya, since the 2nd Coldstream provided only their detachment from Bahrain. The troops from Kenya were even more vulnerable to heat exhaustion, not being sufficiently acclimatised, but there were a few comforts in the front line by now, including a canvas water tank for each company, which was used as a swimming pool, and 'liberty' runs were made to the oil company's recreation centre. Further reinforcements came from England, including the remainder of the Carabiniers and most of the 7th Para Field Regiment, and ten per cent of them were out of action within five days. The total casualties from heat exhaustion reported for the whole period of occupation, requiring admission to the R.A.M.C.'s field hospital, came to 137.

The enthusiasm with which the first troops had been welcomed slowly turned to sourness, which was not sweetened by the misfortune of three sappers who lost direction in a scout car and were consigned to captivity in Iraq until sufficient diplomatic pressure was mounted to secure their release. Fortunately the Arab League at length mustered sufficient forces to take over the protection of 'fraternal Kuwait' and, starting with the 2nd Para, the relief began in September. By October 19 the British withdrawal was complete, leaving analysts to discuss the feasibility of a repetition, both in terms of the financial cost and the availability of men acclimatised to take the strain. But at least there could be no complaints about the speed of the response.

By 1965 the Middle East reserve had become fully committed to the defence of Aden, and by the end of 1967 the Middle East Command itself had disappeared, with the evacuation of Aden. A combined head-quarters was left at Bahrain, controlling British Forces Persian Gulf, and the Army's contribution was raised to two battalions, one in Bahrain and one based on Sharjah, with an armoured squadron in support. No sooner had this increase been made than the sheikhs were informed that, contrary to recent assurances, the British military presence would evaporate in three years time. It was unusual for the initiative to come from the occupying power, and the tidings were not well received at all. For the British troops the news would normally have been welcome. Their short stay in the Persian Gulf had brought little but boredom and discomfort, most of all for the battalion at Bahrain, which had been put into a camp in the desert so that it should not be too conspicuous and offend nationalist sensibilities. However, it had become one of the very few foreign stations remaining, and the most was made of good facilities for amphibious training, which brought the troops in contact with the colourful little warriors of the various private Trucial armies and opened their eyes in wonder at many things, at the harshness and antiquity of the surroundings, and the contrasting display of wealth derived from oil.

The Conservatives' return to power in Britain gave the sheikhs the chance to retain a modified British military presence, but they no longer appear to want such a thing, feeling perhaps that it is sufficient that British troops are to remain in Singapore, whence the Persian Gulf is more readily accessible, via the air staging posts on Gan and Masirah islands, than from the west. Yet whether or not the sheikhs continue to regard Britain as their protector, they would surely be wise to preserve that fine British creation, the Trucial Oman Scouts, rather than let it collapse beneath their ambitions for their individual armies. Forty-seven British officers and 120 soldiers were, and may still be, seconded to the Scouts. They have been proud to maintain the traditions of Lawrence and Glubb.

13

The Caribbean

(1948–69)

THE gaining of no portion of empire cost the British Army more suffering than the multiple islands of the West Indies. Scattered around the Caribbean Sea and linked with possessions on the mainland of America, they were spread over an area more than 2,000 miles long from east to west and 1,000 from north to south and had been the scene of fighting during the eighteenth century, when the Government's one standard ploy on the outbreak of war with France was to cram the soldiers into ships and send them off to this tropical zone to do battle in uniform designed for war in Europe, heavy red coats, breeches, leggings, waistcoats, and cravats. The voyage was almost as beastly and debilitating as for the slaves bound for the same destination from Africa, and on arrival there were plenty of lethal diseases waiting to be caught, headed by the dreaded yellow fever. Few of those early soldiers can have associated these lovely islands with calypso gaiety.

The conquest over disease and the adoption of tropical uniform brought about a dramatic transformation. The Caribbean became the army's holiday station, and there was envy for the single battalion that enjoyed its delights, usually as its first station of an overseas tour. The battalion was based on Jamaica, which was centrally placed and the largest and oldest island possession, and one company was detached far away in the Atlantic Ocean at Bermuda, where its function, so the officers believed, was to act as a tourist lure for American millionaires and their womenfolk.

Inevitably the eruption of nationalist and other ambitions spread to this part in the post-war years, but although they gave the Colonial Office plenty of anxiety and brought furrows to the brows of staff officers at Headquarters Caribbean Area (a brigadier's command) at

Kingston, Jamaica, they rarely caused the troops more trouble than firecrackers and if anything enhanced the holiday mood. The first scare was typical of many to come. The state of Guatemala, on the isthmus connecting the North and South Americas, laid claim to its smaller neighbour, British Honduras, and threatened to gobble it up. This occurred in late February 1948, and the resident battalion at Jamaica was the 2nd Gloucestershire, soon to be redesignated the 1st. After twenty-four hours of hectic naval and military preparation, two companies of Gloucesters were embarked in the training cruiser, H.M.S. *Devonshire*, on the night of February 27 and by dawn on March 2 they had covered the 770 miles to Belize, Honduras's diminutive capital and port, which had once been a pirate's stronghold. It was a great novelty for the 'Baymen of Belize' to see the soldiers come ashore by lighter, although not until well after midday, and the whole town turned out to gaze, laugh and wave. While some Gloucesters stayed as token of Britain's resolve to protect her people, others squeezed into an assembly of buses and grimly set out for the frontier. They found no sign of any invader. There were, however, serious consequences. As a permanent dampener on Guatemalan ambition, it was decided to keep a company in British Honduras, and this meant that the company at Bermuda had to be withdrawn, so that a reserve would be available in Jamaica, where the battalion was split between Kingston and a company hill station at Newcastle, 19 miles away.

The Gloucesters were followed by the 1st Royal Inniskilling Fusiliers and they, after a brief tour, by the 1st Royal Welch Fusiliers, for whom the first excitement among many was a hurricane in August 1951. This caused great devastation in Jamaica, and the Royal Welch turned out every man on relief work, clearing roads, circulating food, and making camps for the homeless. Later in this year they had to despatch a company first to Grenada and then to Antigua to subdue troublemakers, but as was apt to happen trouble dissolved during their approach and the company returned, having enjoyed the outing. The next call came in October 1953, and this time they made the army's debut in a very much more taxing and enduring involvement. It was in British Guiana, on the mainland of South America, and was presaged by a Colonial Office announcement expressing concern about the 'disappointing and anxious conditions' (following the introduction of a new constitution) and 'the intrigues of Communists'. Dr. Jagan, leader of the People's Progressive Party, had in fact been publicly praising the Mau Mau for killing not only 'white men who took away their land' but 'their own people who turn stooges'.

Two companies of the Royal Welch were already at sea when the

Colonial Office announcement was made. They sailed into Georgetown, the capital of Guiana, at sunrise on October 8, having been at sea three days, and they were in two frigates, ready to open up with all they had. The commanding officer was met by 'a very sam-browned and official party' at the quayside and was assured there was no cause for immediate alarm. Having changed from battle to parade order, his men received a big welcome as they marched ashore, where they were billeted in two hotels and four sports clubs. Dr. Jagan meanwhile expressed his amazement at the intrusion of the military when the situation was 'normal and peaceful'. The British Government thought otherwise. Guiana's constitution was suspended and a separate battalion was brought from Britain for garrison duty. Arriving in the carrier H.M.S. *Implacable*, the 1st Argyll and Sutherland Highlanders had relieved the Royal Welch by the end of October, enabling the latter to send a detachment twice to Bermuda, in order to add pageantry, with the mascot goat Billy ceremonially clad, to visits of their Colonel-in-Chief and Queen and of allied heads of state.

The situation in Guiana remained sultry yet outwardly quiet, with the troops making little contribution except by their presence. Politically the climate made temporary improvement and when the Argylls' successors in the colony—the 2nd Black Watch—left in March 1956 they were relieved by a company of the battalion in Jamaica, now the 1st Worcestershire, who had relieved the 1st Duke of Cornwall's Light Infantry at Jamaica and British Honduras. In December 1957 the Worcesters had to rush a second company to Honduras, where there was danger of a political coup by Guatemala, but on its arrival in the frigate H.M.S. *Ulster* the situation made a characteristic shift of emphasis and the men had to be kept out of sight below decks or on the seaward side of the ship, until at last being admitted to carry out some training.

Only a month later this same company made just as urgent a journey to the Bahamas, where the capital, Nassau, was in the grip of strikers and its one industry, the tourist trade, was at a standstill. This conveniently made the Royal Victoria Hotel available as the company's billet, and soon after taking occupation the Worcesters found the strike had ended and all was joy. 'The female population literally opened their arms to the company,' reported the correspondent to the regimental magazine, *Firm*, and on the return to Jamaica after five weeks at Nassau: 'It was like starting a new term at school.' However, a further rash of unrest brought about the resumption of the holiday and its conversion to a permanent duty. Thus when the 1st Royal Hampshire arrived in February 1960 there were three company detachments to be taken over, in British Guiana, British Honduras and the Bahamas, as well as garrison duty in Jamaica. In terms of mileage and direction it was the equivalent of having battalion headquarters at Berlin with detachments at Ankara, Land's End and Oslo.

No sooner had the Royal Hampshires settled comfortably to the tempo of Caribbean soldiering and surmounted the summit of the year's activities, the Queen's Birthday parade, than there was a sudden, chastening call to arms in Jamaica itself. A fanatical sect, the Ras Tafarians, sought to win Jamaica for the Emperor of Ethiopia, undoubtedly without his approval, and reinforced by various Negro gangsters from the United States, they had been indulging in banditry. The police knew that they operated from the Red Hills, above Kingston, and before dawn on June 21, 1960, B Company of the Hampshires laid a cordon round them for a search. One group of gangsters broke through the cordon, shooting two privates dead and wounding a third, and a runner with a written message for a platoon was shot through the chest. He feigned death and had his rifle removed, but completed his journey as soon as the gangsters had gone, and delivered his message before admitting to his wound. Although it was too late now for the Hampshires to round up these men, the police and West Indies Regiment did so a few days later, and among them was the Ras Tafarian leader.

To strengthen the garrison in Jamaica and to search the coastal islands for arms, using *Ulster* and two R.A.S.C. launches, Y Company of the Hampshires was replaced at Nassau by a company of the 1st Duke of Edinburgh's Royal Regiment from England. Jamaica quietened down swiftly, only to be roused and battered by another hurricane. A year's calm followed, in which the Bahamas garrison was again withdrawn, and then in the early hours of October 31, 1961, it was the turn of British Honduras to endure a hurricane, more terrible than any of the previous ones. Some 400 people were killed and 65,000 made homeless in this great destroyer with the cosy code name of Hattie.

Z Company, 1st Royal Hampshire, had their camp a few miles out of Belize and by bringing in all families and battening everything down they avoided human loss during the terrible night of destruction, in which most houses either had their roofs ripped off or were lifted *in toto* many yards and usually overturned, while every window was smashed and torrents of rain water flung horizontally through it. Parties of Hampshires set out when the fury subsided in the morning. They found the airfield usable, and after brave and adventurous journeys, wading, swimming and using a wonderfully tough launch that had been presented by Lord Nuffield, they reached Belize as night was falling, a feat which earned the company commander, Major Matthews, an immediate M.B.E. The devastation was horrifying and the people had succumbed either to despair or to the temptation to loot. These little groups of Hampshires set about quenching the looting and performing the most urgent of the welter of tasks overwhelming the colonial administrators. Among them was the unloading of an American destroyer, the first to bring relief to Belize, and controlling food queues, which involved standing waist deep in water for hour after hour and day after day.

Next morning, November 1, the Recce Platoon under Lieutenant Tillard (who also won the M.B.E.) set out for Stann Creek, over 50 miles distant. They found the bridge over the River Sibun had collapsed and therefore split in three, one section swimming, one repairing the damage under an R.E. corporal, and the third making a crossing and continuing clearance work along the road. They linked up at Stann Creek at 4.30 next morning.

The area commander, Brigadier D. W. Lister, flew in on November 1 and put in motion a swift build-up of troops and the establishment of a joint headquarters with his naval counterpart. On the 3rd B Company of the Royal Hampshires arrived by air from Jamaica, and on the 5th the main body of the battalion came in H.M.S. *Troubridge*. The Hampshires took over the administration of Belize, which had no drinking water, no telephone system, over 10,000 homeless, hundreds of rotting corpses to be buried, and medical needs reaching a peak 'sick parade' of 600 casualties and 4,500 innoculations a day, administered by the battalion team. The navies, both of the United States and Britain, provided stalwart aid.

The battalion in England with closest knowledge of Honduras, the 1st Worcestershire, had meanwhile been alerted. They flew out from Worcester, arriving between the 6th and 15th, to find ruin and stink in place of the pleasant scene they had known. They took over relief work at Stann Creek, where the foremost task was to 'inject into terror stricken people the will to take up life again'. The 12th Field Squadron, R.E., also flew out from England, and using 'Marsh Buggies' loaned by an American oil company they speeded the work of clearance begun by the Royal Hampshires. In a month of stupendous exertion they also repaired the electricity and water supplies, re-roofed houses by the hundred, and erected temporary accommodation for thousands. By the end of November the Worcesters had done enough in Stann Creek to relieve the Hampshires at Belize, and by December 20 they had themselves returned to England, leaving a company of Hampshires in sole occupation once again. It had been decided now that Belize would have to be completely rebuilt on a different site, and the sappers had done planning work on the project before their departure.

Strangely, the daunting project of building a new city appeared to have no effect on Guatemalan ambition, and on January 21, 1962, news reached the resident company of Royal Hampshires—now Y Company —that twenty troops had crossed the frontier in a remote jungly district and put up the flag of Central America in place of the Union Jack, which they ceremoniously burned. A platoon was rushed off by boat, and after various excitements a corporal and three men bumped the invaders on a jungle-covered hill on the 23rd. There was a brief exchange of shots, followed by a search. Two men were found, one of whom claimed to be leader of the 'Belize Liberation Army'. All but one of his nineteen followers were soon rounded up. It transpired that they were not Guatemalan soldiers. Nonetheless the great 'invasion trial' that followed caused almost as big a sensation as had the invasion itself.

Crisis next switched its spotlight back on to British Guiana. There had been mounting conflict here, and the struggle was not so much for independence as for racial domination between those of Indian origin led by the Prime Minister, Dr. Jagan, and those of African origin led by Mr. Burnham. It erupted into violence in February 1962 when a general strike was called in protest against Jagan's budget. On the 14th the threat of mass disorders in Georgetown set orders and appeals for more troops flying. There was swift response. Once again Battalion Headquarters and B Company, 1st Royal Hampshire prepared to leave Kingston, and at 4 a.m. on the 15th the 1st/1st East Anglian (Royal Norfolk and Suffolk) were alerted at Ogbourne St. George, Wiltshire, whence they were due to fly to Northern Ireland for an exercise. At 8 that same night two companies of East Anglians were airborne from Stansted, Essex.

The police in Georgetown retained control until 1.25 p.m. on the 16th, when a summons arrived for the garrison company—A of the Royal Hampshires—who were waiting at Atkinson, the camp on the old American air base camp 28 miles inland. The sky was thick with the smoke of blazes as they drove into Georgetown, and all around them was pandemonium. Two platoons were rushed off to guard Jagan's house and public installations, leaving the third to undertake a gigantic task of street clearance. By steady advance in square formation they sent looters scuttling from the smashed shops of the main street and enabled the police to procure a great flock of them, who were lined up face to face in the main square, adding to the company's guard commitments. At 4 p.m. the detachment from Jamaica arrived in *Troubridge*, and thus there were two companies of Hampshires, under their C.O., to continue the task of rounding up looters all through the night, with the occasional shot fired at the more brazen act of hooliganism.

The two companies of East Anglians flew in next morning, the 17th, to be followed by the remainder of the battalion and a company of the Duke of Edinburgh's. The men were sent off to patrol trouble spots still dressed for winter training in Britain. Suddenly, characteristically, passions subsided, and to their surprise and delight the East Anglians found themselves among 'the most friendly people imaginable; a complete mixture of every race and colour, they extended the open hand of friendship and showed a most gratifying liking and respect for the British soldier.' By the end of March the East Anglians had assumed full responsibility for the garrison of the colony, keeping only the resident company of Hampshires until the latter's departure in June.

Jamaica meanwhile was moving towards independence. It was scheduled for August 1962, and on June 2 the Royal Hampshires performed the British Army's farewell rites. Dressed in white drill, they trooped their colours through the ranks of the 1st West Indies Regiment and on the same day they handed over the King's House guard to them. Their departure was spread over the next three weeks and made by air, the first such for a routine change of station with families. On July 1 Headquarters Caribbean Area closed down, to be reopened at Nassau as part of a combined inter-service headquarters. Thus ended the longest occupation in British history, begun in 1655, when the island had been wrested from the Spaniards.

In British Honduras the company garrison became the responsibility of a battalion in England, initially the 1st Duke of Wellington's and then the 1st King's Shropshire Light Infantry. A platoon of the latter made an excursion to El Salvador in May 1965 following an earthquake in that country. They opened a refugee camp intended for 500 but occupied by 1,700, whose feeding was undertaken by the one A.C.C. private on strength without the aid of a tin opener, which swiftly broke under the strain. The 1,700 were nevertheless fed, housed and comforted, and in appreciation the President of El Salvador shook every man of the platoon by the hand on its departure and the El Salvador Army made ceremonial presentation of a cane. During 1966 the resident company, now provided by the 1st Staffordshire, had to support the police in quelling rioters within the colony, and the commitment remains, providing employment for a colonel and pleasant diversion for a company from England.

British Guiana remained outwardly quiet for over a year, and then, in April 1963, another general strike was started in protest against Jagan's government. The 1st Coldstream Guards were now the garrison batta-lion, having relieved the East Anglian the previous October for the eight-month unaccompanied tour that had become routine for this station. For the most part they merely stood by, while police riot squads dispersed gangs of rioters by copious use of gas, some of which invaded the Coldstreamers' premises, on one occasion forcing a mess waiter to serve champagne wearing his gas mask. A more serious hardship was the absence of mail, caused by the strike.

Famine set in, and rioting gave way to wider dispersed roamings of groups bent on murder and intimidation. The Coldstream were soon stretched to the limit in providing escorts and patrolling the villages that lay beyond the jungle wastes off the one metalled road that ran through Guiana, alongside the Demerera. The barber, cinema projectionist, equipment repairer, and cobbler—all guardsmen—formed a party under a subaltern that released one village from the grip of a terror raid. Another of six men and an officer encountered a mob that uniquely showed no inclination whatever to disperse at their approach. A shot had to be fired, and it killed three people and wounded one. Such was the use of minimum force, as applied by the high velocity self-loading rifle. Old principles had to be reconsidered.

More troops had to be summoned, and the call fell on the 1st/2nd Green Jackets, K.R.R.C. at new barracks built for speed of discharge at Colchester. Warned on July 3, they arrived on the 8th and took over the coastal sector from the Coldstream, who were themselves in process of being relieved by the 2nd Grenadiers. The 60th found their task reward-ing. They fanned out to east and west along the coast road, which was lined endlessly with ribbon-developed houses, and everywhere they were eagerly welcomed by inhabitants who had hair-raising stories of murderers armed with cutlasses. No spark of defiance was displayed against them, and the talks given by company commanders to village elders on the need for racial peace were well received. Within a month the tension had again subsided.

After a spell at Atkinson, whence like others before them they made thrilling adventure journeys by raft and vehicle through the jungle to the great Kaieteur Falls, the 60th returned to England in January 1964, together with Headquarters 2nd Brigade which had come out with them. The pattern this year followed that of its predecessors, if anything more jaggedly because of the extra animosity aroused by the Colonial Office's decision to change the electoral system. Arson was the latest policy of the marauders, and once again there was an alarming increase in activity as summer approached, not that there is noticeable change of season in this equatorial zone. A strike of sugar workers produced an unprecedented crop of murders and burnings, setting taxing problems of mobility and readiness for the 1st Queen's Own Buffs, who had relieved the Grenadiers in March 1964. On May 22 a state of emergency was declared, and on the same day the 1st Devonshire and Dorset received 24 hours notice to move from Northern Ireland. The first company of Devons and Dorsets flew in on the 24th and were rushed by helicopter to the remote town of Mackenzie, where they joined a scratch company of Queen's Own Buffs in staying the terrible vengeance wreaked by the Negro population on outnumbered Asians. The rescue, guarding, evacuation and rehabilitation of the latter, and the protection of their abandoned property kept the troops at full stretch for ten days, with sleep rationed to three hours in twenty-four, and it was achieved without the firing of a shot. The Asians sought retribution in Georgetown, where the colony's senior civil servant was burned to death in his house with seven of his children. Wide scale searches and arrests were made, with the troops using helicopters, Land Rovers and launches to make swift swoops, interspersed with more conventional cordoning, road block duties, border patrols for gun-runners, and the raising of a home guard. In July the 43rd (Lloyds Company) Medium Battery R.A. was brought in to ease the strain on the two battalions. The military exerted a firm but sympathetic hold over the colony, and again violence receded. On December 5 the great hurdle of the general election was leaped without hurt. It resulted in the removal of Jagan's party from office in favour of a coalition dedicated to multi-racial consultation.

For over a year the garrison remained at a strength of two battalions, both with headquarters at Georgetown under a colonel. The Queen's Own Buffs were relieved by the 1st King's Own Royal Border Regiment immediately after the elections, and in January 1965 the Devon and Dorset by the 1st Lancashire Fusiliers. These two were in turn relieved after tours of eight and nine months by the 1st King's and the 3rd Parachute, having kept the peace merely by their presence. In March 1966 the garrison was reduced to one battalion, in the persons of the 1st Middlesex.

The Middlesex plucked the fruit of their predecessors' labours. There were smiles all around them, friendly welcomes wherever they went. On May 26, 1966, the colony celebrated its independence, taking the name of Guyana, and still the Middlesex stayed quietly on. They were required to train the Guyana Defence Force, and not until October, after providing a farewell, and loudly applauded, Beating of the Retreat, did they fly home to Northern Ireland, honoured at the aerodrome by a contingent of the army they had raised.

Only Honduras was left with a garrison, and there was no reserve

373

available for swift intervention when next one of Britian's diminutive island dependencies spluttered its discontent. The island in question was Anguilla, and it showed both discontent and defiance by driving a British minister come to discuss its problems out of the island by force in early March 1969. The British Government decided, after due deliberation, that this tiny island barely 16 miles long and 3 wide, with a population of less than 6,000 would have to be occupied. The task was entrusted to the 2nd Parachute from Aldershot, but secrecy was unobtainable and as the paras emplaned at Lyneham on March 18 the press was ablaze with sarcastic references to the unfolding of Britain's might, which had of course been so much reduced that an operation of this size seemed in keeping with its capacity. 'President' Webster, the rebel leader of Anguilla, was meanwhile promising resistance to the death, hinting at hidden stocks of arms and simultaneously appealing to the United Nations.

The most the paras could aim at was to uphold the British Army's tradition in this region for creating anti-climax. This they achieved. They landed at first light on March 19, in battle order. They had been brought from Nassau in two frigates and were discharged on to the pure white sand of Anguilla's beaches by motor launches, while two helicopters landed a half-platoon on the island's airstrip. They then raced for the principal road junctions in commandeered vehicles. There was no firing, no resistance, but some spat and raved at the British soldiers, a thing that everyone the world over knew it was safe to do. In reply the men issued leaflets explaining why they had come. Soon they were pictured with children on their knees.

Close behind the 2nd Para came half the 33rd Field Squadron, R.E., and from mid-September they formed the entire garrison. They had come to turn peace into prosperity, and at the moment of writing are engaged on a long list of work projects prepared by Mr. Webster on his conversion from rebel to recognised leader. The only thing that would now seem likely to resurrect his defiance would be a threat to withdraw his British troops.

14

Borneo

I—REVOLT (1962–63)

BRITAIN had three dependencies bordering the northern coast of the wild and enormous island of Borneo. On the north-east was the colony of North Borneo, with a coastline of intricate bends and a mountainous interior; in the centre was the little oil-rich sultanate of Brunei, under British protection; and to the south-west, spread along 500 miles of coastline was the colony of Sarawak, a land idyllic in the memory of middle-aged Britons for its association with its former owner, Rajah Brooke, and his lovely daughters. Borneo was off the peacetime beat of the British Army, and indeed very few Europeans had ventured inland into the roadless sprawl of jungle and rivers that covered almost the entire island. However, some of its inhabitants—the diminutive Dyaks, mainly of the Iban tribe—had emerged from obscurity to help Britain quell the Malayan rebellion and had endeared themselves to the troops both by their skill as trackers and their sunny nature. They had even been formed into a regiment, the Sarawak Rangers, and it was still in existence on a reduced scale, although most of its veterans had returned to their private pursuits, which everyone knew to be head-hunting. What was less well known was that the crime rate in their countries was minuscule. The police forces were consequently weak and the special branch almost non-existent: classic setting for the outbreak of rebellion.

The rest of Borneo, three times as large as the British part, belonged to Indonesia, whose President Soekarno was hungry for territory, especially at the expense of an 'imperialist'. Vibrations from his ambition could be felt in Sarawak, where there were restless stirrings among the Chinese population, and in North Borneo there was an alarming outbreak of murderous piracy, with the result that troops went there for

375

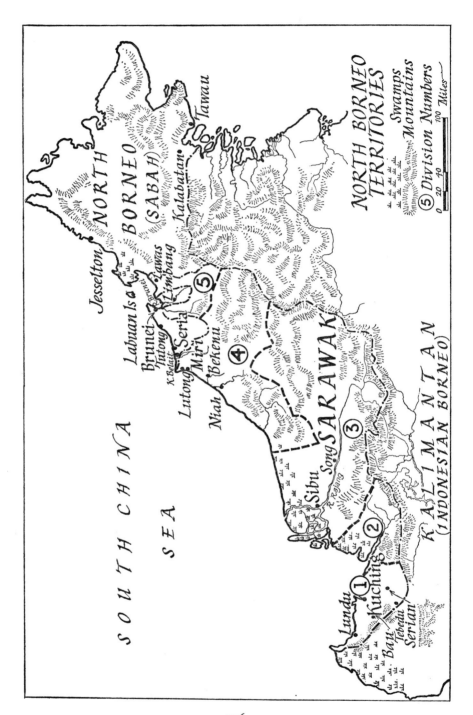

SOUTH CHINA SEA

NORTH

BORNEO (SABAH)

Jesselton

Labuan Is.
Brunei
Tutong
K.Belait
Lutong
Miri
Niah
Bekenu
Seria
Limbang
Lawas
Kalabatan
Tawau

SARAWAK

Sibu
Song
R.Rajang

KALIMANTAN
(INDONESIAN BORNEO)

Lundu
Kuching
Bau
Tebedu
Serian

① ② ③ ④ ⑤

NORTH BORNEO
TERRITORIES

Swamps
Mountains
⑤ Division Numbers
0 20 40   100 Miles

376

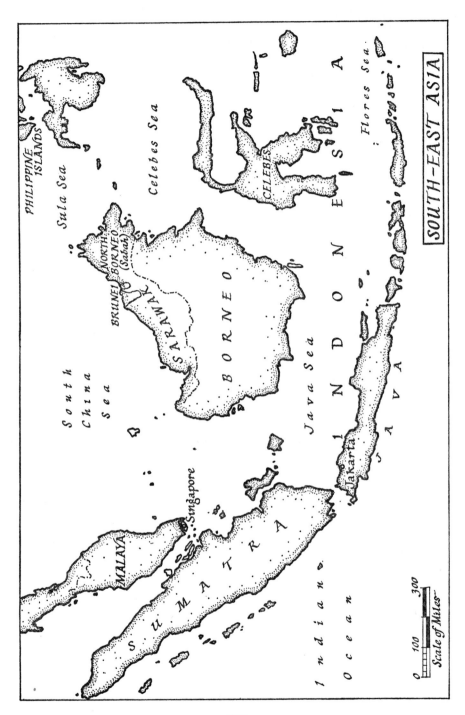

SOUTH-EAST ASIA

PHILIPPINE ISLANDS

Sula Sea

Celebes Sea

CELEBES

Flores Sea

South China Sea

NORTH BORNEO (Sabah)

BRUNEI

SARAWAK

BORNEO

I N D O N E S I A

Java Sea

MALAYA

Singapore

S U M A T R A

Jakarta

J A V A

Indian

Ocean

Scale of Miles

0   100   300

377

training and left a company permanently in residence to keep watch along the coast. But it was Brunei that flared suddenly in revolt. Its instigator was an absentee politician, A. M. Azahari, who claimed the leadership of all the British territories and was known to be in league with Soekarno. His field commander was Yasin Affandy.

It started at 2 a.m. on December 8, 1962, with a crash of shots at the Sultan's palace in Brunei town, at the police station and power station, and at similar targets in all of Brunei's towns. Warning had been received from sources in Sarawak, and the Sultan's guards stood firm in Brunei town, except at the power station whose capture by Affandy's men was notified by the extinction of all the lights. They also entered the British Residency and captured the A.D.C. In other parts of the Sultanate the rebels had even greater success, and with daylight came alarming boasts of the captures they had made and of the hostages they held.

Thanks to commitments under S.E.A.T.O., the British Army was still strongly represented in the Far East, and its units were at greater readiness and enjoyed better facilities, both militarily and domestically, than in 1948. In Malaya there were two British infantry battalions, of which one belonged to the 28th Commonwealth Brigade, two Gurkha battalions, an armoured car regiment, and a gunner regiment. The 99th Gurkha Infantry Brigade Group, consisting of one British and two Gurkha battalions, was at Singapore, which champed restlessly on the threshold of independence, and the 3rd Commando Brigade was also there, although one of its two commandos was usually itinerant on exercise in the carrier *Albion*, as was now the case. Hong Kong had a British battalion and the three Gurkha ones of the 48th Gurkha Brigade. The eighth Gurkha battalion—the 1/6th—had made a pioneering journey to England, where its own brigade, the 51st Gurkha (which was an amalgamation of the 51st British and the 63rd Gurkha), formed the spearhead of the strategic reserve, having brought with it detachments of the Gurkha Engineers, Signals and Service Corps. The 17th Gurkha Division was therefore far spread.

The need for inter-service cooperation was nowhere higher than in the Far East, and there had been a good example of its application in August 1959, when a company of the 1st Cheshire was flown at short notice from Singapore to one of the Maldive Islands, a distance of 2,300 miles, in order to help the R.A.F. Regiment quell rioting at this important staging post. Even so, this was the last major command to be integrated, and not until November 28, 1962, only ten days before the outbreak of revolt in Brunei, was a small combined headquarters established, with Admiral Sir David Luce as Commander-in-Chief. The

G.O.C.-in-C. Land Forces was Lieutenant-General Sir Nigel Poett (who was shortly to be succeeded by Sir Reginald Hewetson, and he in 1964 by Sir Alan Jolly). Poett was in the Philippines, attending a demonstration, on this night of December 7/8, having left his Chief of Staff, Major-General W. Odling, in charge.

Under contingency planning, 99 Gurkha Brigade in Singapore were to provide a two-company group for intervention, and at 5 a.m. on December 8 C and D Companies, 1/2nd Gurkhas, were alerted for air despatch to Brunei under the second-in-command, Major Lloyd-Williams. They reached the aerodrome at 12.30 p.m. but here had an aggravating wait before emplaning in three Beverleys and a Britannia, all of which had only recently arrived in the Far East. They were not airborne until 3 p.m., after the brigade commander, Brigadier A. G. Patterson, had put a stop to such formalities as the recording of each man's name on entering the plane—an elaborate procedure with Gurkhas. It was over two years since the Malayan emergency had ended, and peace had as usual stiffened the works.

The result was that darkness had fallen when the planes touched down at Brunei's main but far from large airport near Brunei town, at around 8 p.m., and the arrival of the Gurkhas did not have the moral impact that it might have had in daylight, nor were they able to assess the tactical importance of buildings and features. It was due only to brisk and courageous work by the airport staff that the landing ground had been cleared of obstructions and a police squad brought in from North Borneo to guard it. In the town the Commissioner of Police, Mr. Outram, had personally rescued the A.D.C. from the British Residency and had mounted a spirited attack to recapture the power station, killing eleven rebels and taking over a hundred prisoner. The spacious and well-to-do town, dominated by its enormous mosque, was therefore quiet as the Gurkhas marched in wearing full battle order to help the police enforce a curfew in the town and to prepare for operations against more successful rebel groups in other parts of the state.

The most urgent task was to reach Seria, 50 miles distant, the coastal town around which the Shell Petroleum Company had all the sprawling paraphernalia necessary for the despatch of four million tons of oil a year. The rebels were in command here, had captured the police station and rounded up men, women and children as hostages—and just after midnight the ominous news reached Brunei by telephone that these hostages were to be used as a screen for an attack on the police station at Panaga, west of Seria. C Company of the Gurkhas set off at once, two platoons strong, in four requisitioned lorries and a Land Rover. They had hot exchanges of fire with various rebel groups, swirled round two road blocks, and sped past two rebel-held police stations with bullets flying to and fro. At Tutong, 30 miles short of Seria, the company commander's Land Rover crashed into a monsoon drain, with its driver hit, and its occupants took refuge in a verandah, through the ceiling of which they fired at rebels above. The remainder of the company careered on and captured a bridge before realising the Land Rover was missing. They did not link up until daybreak and could do no more now than clear Tutong of its rebels. They had lost an officer and seven wounded.

Meanwhile D Company had been in trouble in Brunei. Fire had been opened from the government offices on a curfew patrol, mortally wounding an officer and a lance-corporal, and there was confused and prolonged fighting by both Gurkhas and police before the main buildings of the town were cleared and consolidated around 9 a.m. Twenty-four rebels were killed in this fight, most of them armed with the No. 5 (jungle) rifle, and as a further five hundred were reported to be advancing from the south, C Company were called back for the defence of Brunei. They brought 106 captives with them.

It was obvious by now that very much more than two companies were needed, and the remainder of the 1/2nd Gurkhas were promptly despatched by air and sea to make Brunei town thoroughly secure. The 1st Queen's Own Highlanders (Seaforth and Camerons) were also alerted, but General Odling did not care to release Headquarters 99 Brigade from its internal security commitments at Singapore, and consequently a small 'ad hoc' headquarters was formed under his B.G.S., Brigadier J. B. A. Glennie, who wore a D.S.O. won for commanding the 1st Royal Sussex on the blasted slopes of Cassino. Drawn from Singapore Base District and G.H.Q., his officers and a single corporal clerk assembled to meet him at 10.30 a.m. (December 9) and at 8 p.m. they opened business at Labuan, an island in the Bay of Brunei possessing a good civil airport, whence this little group of strangers to each other took control of the most delicate situation with which the British Army had been faced since peace came to Cyprus in 1959. Glennie had with him a brief and lucid mandate from the C.-in-C. ordering him to restore Brunei to the rule of the Sultan and placing him in command of all services. It was clear from the start that his naval and air subordinates would need no urging; gone were the defensive attitudes that encrust a more formal headquarters.

At 2.20 a.m. (December 10) Lieutenant-Colonel McHardy of the Queen's Own Highlanders arrived from Singapore with his A Company. There was grim news from Seria, where the hostages had been used as threatened in an unsuccessful rebel attack on Panaga police station, in which one hostage had been killed and five wounded. McHardy was told to take his men on to Brunei and mount an operation for the release of the hostages with all speed. Forebears of this battalion had made the first entry into what was to become Indonesia in 1945 and been among the first to fight the Malayan rebels in 1948; further back their bagpipes had brought the sweet message of relief to the besieged in Lucknow. The situation was not so dissimilar now.

Soon after dawn the Highlanders arrived at Brunei airport, where the R.A.F. were fast achieving a considerable build-up, with sounds and rumours of rebel infiltrations coming in from all sides. McHardy obtained a Beaver of the Army Air Corps and set off on a reconnaissance, returning to find Glennie setting up his headquarters at Brunei town's police station, where there was a conglomeration of the military and civil and 200 rebel prisoners on the tennis courts. A plan was made for a daring fly-in, by five Twin Pioneers, carrying most of A Company, on a grass clearing not far from Panaga police station, west of Seria, and by a Beverley, carrying a tac headquarters, support elements, and a platoon of A Company—ninety men in all—on to a rebel-held aerodrome at Anduki, east of Seria and 10 miles east of the other landing. Grinning excitedly beneath their steel helmets and camouflage trimmings, the men set off in their planes around 1 p.m., with McHardy still in his Beaver to coordinate proceedings.

Piloted by Wing Commander Graves, the leading Twin Pioneer hopped over a high row of trees and made a rough but safe landing on boggy grass, pulling up 10 yards from a road ditch and sign saying 'HALT—Major Road Ahead'. Its twelve Highlanders jumped out and set off, at the double, for Panaga police station, 2 miles distant, while the other four Pioneers swirled in from a different direction, brushing treetops and being delayed, in the case of the last two, by a sudden rainstorm. The Jocks reached and relieved the police station without opposition, catching the rebels quite unawares. However, they encountered resistance at the Telecommunications Centre beyond, and the rebels did not surrender here, with four hostages, until the platoon commander had made an entry from the rear and poked his head through a window, to have his ear nicked by a bullet from inside. The company then set up a road block and settled for the night. They forced seven Shell Company vehicles to a halt and netted nineteen armed rebels from them, of whom two died trying to crash the road block with lights flashing and rifles firing.

The landing at Anduki, which was even more hazardous, was just as successful. Under the direction of a Shell pilot, the Beverley sneaked in low, braked furiously on landing, halted less than halfway down the runway, and disgorged its men, who were standing on the lower deck, at speed. It then roared into flight again, and not until it took off was fire opened at it from the control tower, causing hits but no important damage. By now the control tower itself was under fire. It fell to a brisk platoon attack, yielding two rebels killed and five captured. Leaving some to consolidate on the aerodrome, other Highlanders set off towards Seria and captured a bridge 2 miles away, where they dug in, having forced the occupants of three vehicles into surrender, in one case after a neat hit on a fast departing tyre.

It was a good start, but much remained to be done, and requests were flying fast from Brunei to Singapore, thanks to naval signallers and the wireless equipment on the destroyer *Cavalier*, which brought extra companies of the 1/2nd Gurkhas and Queen's Own Highlanders. Brigadier Patterson, who was himself a Gurkha, had been released from Singapore with his Headquarters 99 Gurkha Brigade, and he took over command of land operations, also from Brunei town, being subordinate to Glennie, who concentrated on inter-service coordination and on political matters, which included keeping the grateful, middle-aged Sultan informed on the state of his realm.

Early on the morning of December 11, B Company and the Assault Pioneer Platoon of the Highlanders were flown into Anduki, being guided in by flares—for the weather was black—lit by the padre: truly a case of 'Lighten our darkness, we beseech Thee, O Lord!' B Company were despatched westwards and by 2 p.m. they had joined up with A after a few brief brushes with rebel groups. They freed a number of Shell employees who had been imprisoned in their own offices, but did no more than seal off the main rebel stronghold, Seria Bazaar, the capture of which without death to the hostages needed careful planning. A Company meanwhile had probed further westwards and driven the rebels from the Sultan's summer palace. A bren and a sten had been used in its defence, and the company commander, Major Cameron, had personally led the assault, first lobbing tear-gas bombs in and, on their failure to eject the rebels, dashing upstairs and with a single shot forcing eight men into surrender. B Company, 1/2nd Gurkhas also entered the battle. They were flown into Anduki with ten Land Rovers and drove 10 miles west of Seria to Kuala Belait, whose police station had fallen to the rebels the previous day. They fought their way into the town just before nightfall and, attacking the police station early next morning, found the rebels gone.

The attack on Seria began later this morning with the occupation of a school and a block of flats overlooking the police station, where the rebels' flag still flew defiantly. An escape route had purposely been left open to them into the jungle, where patrols lurked out of sight. A native police inspector called for a surrender by loud hailer. There was neither sound nor movement in response. The M.M.G. Platoon of the Highlanders moved forward as infantry and at once came under fire from the police station. McHardy called on the air force. Four Hunters screeched in, making frightening dummy runs, one firing its guns into the sea. A section of machine-gunners sneaked up a monsoon drain to within 20 yards of the building and opened fire with rifles, while the platoon commander led another section over a 7-foot wire fence and rushed the back entrance. He burst in and encountered a rebel with his hands up. Two others surrendered with him and two were lying wounded. With them was a Shell Company doctor and a nurse, Miss Jean Scott, who had secured the return of women and children hostages by withholding treatment of the rebel wounded and had herself insisted on remaining at the police station.

The keys were produced, and in the arms kote thirty stiff and haggard Shell employees greeted their liberators with a cheer; in a cell for one man a further sixteen did likewise. They were in their fifth day of captivity under threat of death and were glad to be free.

On this same day, December 12, 42 Commando went into action to liberate the upriver town of Limbang, 12 miles south of Brunei town. Only L Company had as yet arrived and they made the journey in two requisitioned lighters, which had been patched up and were manned by the Royal Navy. They left Brunei at midnight, and under guidance of a civil marine officer and under heavy attack by mosquitoes, they chugged 12 miles up the narrow and winding river. At 5.45 a.m. Limbang came into view, blazing with light. Suddenly the lights went out; darting figures were seen through the gloaming. The leading craft, carrying 5 Troop, headed for a jetty in front of the police station and was greeted with a hail of fire, against which the men's packs were the only shield. Although two marines were killed and others wounded, a landing was made by two sections under heavy covering fire from two machine guns in the other craft. The police station continued to stab out fire, forcing those ashore to take cover, and the craft was cast back into the river. It went upstream now and crunched shore again beyond search of bullet. Troop headquarters and the last section plunged waistdeep through mud and slime to gain the bank, and a troop from the other craft followed.

Now firmly ashore, the commandos mounted a quick and deadly attack on the police station and surrounded the hospital, which was near their landing point. Singing could be heard from inside: 'They'll be wearing bright green bonnets when they come'. This was the first clue that the British residents, of whom there were nine, were still alive—and it transpired that they probably would not have been much longer. The rebels opened fire from the hospital and received a deluge in reply, under cover of which some men burst in and bustled the hostages to the shelter of a back room; 'Out you come, old girl' was the warming greeting accorded the British Resident's wife, who was soon to be dressing the wounds incurred by either side. No sooner had the commandos cleared the hospital than a sudden burst of fire dropped a sergeant and two marines dead, and almost at once two rebels fell dead, spotted behind a hedge from which they had made a daring point blank attack with shotguns. Although the combing of Limbang was a long and difficult task, L Company encountered no further open opposition. They had lost five killed and eight wounded, counting two naval ratings, and themselves killed fifteen rebels in the toughest fight of the revolt.

Westwards the revolt had spread into Sarawak, a process stemmed to a certain extent by the despatch of A Company, 1/2nd Gurkhas, in civil aircraft, to the oil harbour of Miri on December 9. In the drizzling dawn of the eventful 12th a fleet of Shell motor launches brought a fresh battalion here, the 1st/1st Green Jackets, 43rd and 52nd; they had spent a hectic Sunday (the 9th) gathering in their men on Penang island, had made the long journey to Singapore by road and rail, and come thence in the cruiser H.M.S. *Tiger*. Two companies of Green Jackets were now re-embarked in Shell launches to follow the coastline further southwards, B Company for 30 miles, C for 40. The latter reached their destination, Niah, at dusk and were met by a bearded Hemingwayesque surveyor, accompanied by 'forty little dark men with shotguns', whose loyalty he thought had almost reached breaking point. One platoon journeyed further upriver to link up with the loyalists protecting Mrs. Tom Harrisson, whose husband, a famous resistance leader in wartime, had gone to rally the tribes to the British cause.

B Company of the Green Jackets had a harder trip. Their objective was the upriver town of Bekenu, and while one platoon continued by launch, the remainder of the company set off on a trek of 15 miles that was expected to last four hours but took fourteen and kept them marching all night to avoid suspected ambushes. In the morning they saw the rebel flag over what looked like a wooden cricket pavilion but was in fact the government office. An appeal by loud hailer produced a vicious volley, whereupon the platoons sprayed the positions with fire from river and land. They killed five, wounded six, rounded up 328 prisoners, and relieved them of 327 shotguns. This was achieved without loss.

On this same day—December 13—the 12th (Minden) Battery of the 20th Regiment, R.A. were brought as infantry into Kuching, the fair capital of Sarawak, where there was high anxiety about an extension of the revolt under external influences. Next day they were joined by 40 Commando, who had been hurried back from a far distant exercise in their carrier *Albion*. Police launches and native river boats went out to welcome her, with sirens emitting their joy.

With *Albion* came 845 (Wessex) and 846 (Whirlwind) Naval Helicopter Squadrons, and use was immediately made of them, the 1st Green Jackets making the first descent into jungle clearings to cut off rebel groups they had turned into fugitives. The occupation of Muara by the 1/2nd Gurkhas and of Bangar (upriver from Limbang) by 42 Commando, both achieved early on December 14, had freed every town from the rebels' clutch, and it remained now to round up Affandi and his men, of whom there are said to have been 4,000 at the start, men of diverse races and tribes, all imbued with 'anti-imperialist' propaganda. It had taken six days to crush them, thanks to the sense of urgency that had run from Force H.Q. down to company commanders, and this same sense now invigorated the pursuit.

It is, however, easier to put rebels to flight than to round them up, and appreciation of the size and importance of this latter task was displayed in the appointment on December 19 of Major-General W. C. Walker, G.O.C. 17th Gurkha Division and Major-General Brigade of Gurkhas, as Commander British Forces Borneo Territories (which included the police and all services) in place of Glennie and his improvised set-up. Smart, precise, and assertive, Walker established his headquarters at Labuan and cast wide a net into which all the elements of a comprehensive security force were woven. He switched the Green Jackets and 40 Commando to North Borneo and eastern Brunei, where there were strongest signs of rebel activity, and although Sarawak afforded armoured cars little freedom of movement, security there was entrusted to R.H.Q. and C Squadron, Queen's Royal Irish Hussars, who were already represented in Brunei by half B Squadron. In the mountain range that formed Sarawak's eastern border and covered that of Brunei, the little men of Kayan, Kenyah and Iban tribes were fast being organised into irregular bands, working under Mr. Tom Harrisson, to intercept the flight of rebels into Kalimantan. The Sarawak Rangers had also entered the battle, and although most of them were employed in their old rôle of providing trackers for battalions, a platoon operated on its own with considerable success. As further stimulant to tribal resistance, a squadron of 22 S.A.S. Regiment were brought out from England in January 1963. This did not bode well for the rebels.

A large number of them had already slunk back to their kampongs and buried their arms. Others half-heartedly took refuge in the jungle and showed little incentive to fight or run when the patrols closed in on them. 42 Commando found themselves landed with a 'flood' of such fellows, 'a pathetic crowd of hungry, scared and bemused scarecrows'. But there were plenty of tough ones still at large, as the Queen's Own Highlanders discovered when a sentry was wounded by a sniper—their one casualty of the rebellion—and in mid-January torrential rain greatly hampered operations and enforced some diversion of effort to flood relief. Patrols had to take to swimming.

In February there was a general relief. The 1st King's Own Yorkshire Light Infantry—who had been in Malaya on the outbreak of rebellion in 1948 and had returned to join the Commonwealth Brigade—took over the far stretching duties the Queen's Own Highlanders had acquired from Seria; the 1/7th Gurkhas came from Malaya and took over the swamps and jungle south and west of Brunei from the 1/2nd Gurkhas and later from 42 Commando too; and the 2/7th Gurkhas came from Hong Kong and with headquarters at Brunei town extended eastwards as far as the eastern coasts of North Borneo, where they freed the Green Jackets and 40 Commando. It was around Brunei town and in the great steaming, inscrutable mangrove swamps by the River Brunei that the rebel leaders lurked, and much sweat and frustration had already been spilled in the search for them. Some successes by the 1/7th Gurkhas, in which there was some lively action, helped prise open some of the secrets, and in April the Special Branch were able to locate two brothers of Azahari. One fought when his house was raided by the 2/7th and was mortally wounded after himself killing an Army Intelligence officer attached to the Special Branch. The other was caught next day.

The captures accumulated, and information with it, and as dawn broke on May 18 B Company, 2/7th Gurkhas had a recently captured informer with them to guide them down the River Brunei to a rebel camp in a swamp. In league with the Assault Pioneer Platoon, this company had become expert at watermanship in the weeks they had spent afloat, and two platoons glided neatly in to lay a cordon on the land side of the vast expanse of swamp, while the pioneers drew attention to themselves elsewhere on the river by the roar of their engines. Then the company commander, Major Cutfield, took a party in by canoe. For four hours they paddled and waded around the dank morass of swamp. Then they spotted a towel in among the sprawling, serpentlike roots of the mangrove trees. The sound of splashes announced that the rebels were on the alert, and a burst of fire at them merely produced a captive, who said that nine had run away.

On the bank the cut-off men were lined among rubber trees, singly at 100 yards interval. Rifleman Nainabahadur Rai saw four rebels approach but held his fire, not wanting to hit the flushing party. At 50 yards the leader saw him and rushed forward with pistol firing. Nainabahadur put one shot through him and the man behind him, killing them both. The other two made a dash for cover and engaged him with fire from left and right. Nainabahadur dealt first with one and then the other, disabling them both. One of the wounded was Affandi; the others constituted his Army Council. The other fugitives from the hide, who were the next senior in the hierarchy of the rebel army, were found lying in another piece of mangrove.

Their revolt had been brought to a conclusive end, but already British Borneo had come under attack from another, interconnected quarter, setting more taxing problems for the G.O.C. at Labuan and his Commander-in-Chief at Singapore.

II—GUERRILLA INCURSIONS (1963–64)

As the British Army dealt with the rebellion in Brunei, Jakarta radio sent out its warning that volunteers were ready 'to help liberate Kalimantan Utara (British North Borneo) from colonialism'. The need for them to do so was becoming urgent, not only because the rebellion was obviously failing but because the territories were coming due for independence and had expressed a wish to join the 'neo-colonialists' of Malaya in a projected federation. Soekarno was determined that they should fall to a different coloniser, himself.

The 'volunteers' made their debut on Good Friday, April 12, 1963, by attacking the police station of the frontier village of Tebedu in the extreme western district of Sarawak, which was known (rather confusingly for soldiers) as the First Division. It was due south of the capital, Kuching, from which the Queen's Royal Irish Hussars kept watch over a frontier 500 miles long and brought comfort to a diverse and uneasy population with only one squadron of armoured cars, together with the squadron of 22 S.A.S. and a detached company of Gurkhas under command. The report that arrived with breakfast on this gloomy Good Friday showed that the police station had been overrun, with two men killed. Reinforcements were urgently needed to drive the invaders out and to prevent eruptions in their support.

40 Commando and the 2/10th Gurkhas (of 99 Brigade) were alerted and, after some fluctuation of plan, both embarked at Singapore

in the carrier *Albion*, together with Headquarters 3rd Commando Brigade, early on the Saturday. They sailed in on Easter Sunday, just as the commanding officers flew back to Singapore on completing their reconnaissance. The Commando went to Kuching, whence a troop dashed to the frontier with two troops of the Hussars and recaptured Tebedu police station, which the guerrillas abandoned at their approach. The Gurkhas went by helicopter and launch to Sibu, in Sarawak's Third Division, a town near the mouth of the wide, meandering River Rajang, surrounded by Chinese settlements growing rice and rubber.

The threat was both internal and external. The Communists had a Chinese-run clandestine organisation—the C.C.O.—which worked for the same cause as Soekarno, the disruption of British influence, by familiar methods of intimidation. It was strongest around Sibu, and the 2/10th Gurkhas at once made a series of night raids in support of the police, which yielded a capture of weapons and suspects while suggesting that the C.C.O. was not quite so deadly as its Malayan predecessor. Nevertheless it could obviously make a great nuisance of itself in conjunction with external raids, of which 40 Commando had to contend with two before the end of April. On both occasions the raiders withdrew after exchanges of fire that did enough to indicate that they were led by Indonesian regular officers, one of whom left his card. The 2/10th Gurkhas were brought westwards to Sarawak's Second Division, leaving Sibu in the hands of two companies of the 1/10th, brought over from Malaya.

It was a relief for General Walker when the capture of Affandi brought the Brunei revolt to its end on May 18. He was still left with worries enough. The frontier lay open and unmarked across 970 miles of wild and mountainous country, over which raids could, and undoubtedly would, be made without warning at any point, and the coastline was very much longer and just as vulnerable. The total area to be protected was slightly larger than England and Scotland, and there were only five battalions (including the commando) available, controlled by a brigade headquarters at Kuching and another at Brunei, and with the need for a regular system of reliefs over an interminable period, there was no immediate prospect of any great increase. Three battalions had been sent out during the revolt as a reserve, but only the 1st Royal Leicestershire at Hong Kong had stayed.

There were many similarities to the Malayan rebellion, and it was as well that Walker had been long and closely involved in it, for little had been done to perpetuate the lessons learnt. He had on his arrival issued a directive listing five ingredients of success: unified operations; timely and accurate information; speed, mobility, and flexibility; security of bases, both forward and back; and domination of the jungle. A month later he had issued a sixth, which more than any other bore the stamp of its originator, Sir Gerald Templer: winning the hearts and minds of the people. All six were of course interdependent. What it boiled down to was that the first great need was for confidence, the second, a product of it, good intelligence, and the third speed into action.

It followed that in league with the police the battalions had to get to know the inhabitants and terrain of areas of bewildering dimensions. There were no maps, except of a very small scale, and hardly any roads. There were a number of busy towns and villages in the coastal region and up the main rivers, and they were inhabited predominantly by immigrant Malays and Chinese. The interior was a roadless confusion of jungle and of rivers winding down from the mountains that filled most of North Borneo and in Sarawak formed a narrow range along the top of which ran the frontier. Innumerable village settlements or kampongs were to be found, either by the river or on a hillside, from which tribes-men of many varieties primitively tilled the land around them or went hunting for fish, deer, baboons, porcupine, or ever pervasive snakes. They lived in longhouses, which were made of attap wood, had foetid interiors, and were apt to creak balefully on the stilts that had kept them out of the water for decades. The Iban predominated in Sarawak. They were small, cheerful and indolent people, who neither cut their hair nor dressed above the waist, regardless of sex, except when attired in cere-monial finery. The latter was worn, with bells tinkling, for the gay, heart-warming receptions accorded visiting officers and men, who would be primed with rice-wine and invited to do a solo dance.

Rivers gave the jungle tribesmen their one tenuous link with the out-side world, and the troops reached them by river, using launches or longboats provided, complete with crews, by willing contractors. Rivers also gave the land its enchantment and in their lower reaches provided a parade of all the races, Chinese, Malay, Iban and European, plying their water trades with the rhythmic lethargy demanded by the climate. The troops joined the concourse on the water and soon acquired the know-how not to look out of place. It was important to make full use of the rivers for supply purposes in order to conserve the aircraft for operations, particularly helicopters of the R.N. and the R.A.F. for which the infantry were always clamouring, with the result that the number soon advanced to sixty but would never be enough, although an R.A.F. Belvedere could carry 15 men. The R.A.S.C., both British and Gurkha working in conjunction with the Royal Engineers, therefore built up an elaborate water transport service. Labuan had the only port where ocean-going vessels could unload, and from here the supplies were despatched by coastal craft to Brunei, Seria, Kuching and Tawau, and thence by a motley of impressed boats to various upriver towns. It was very much an improvised service, which of course grew in sophistication until eventually hovercraft were introduced, jarring the timeless serenity of the scene but easing the problems of the suppliers.

Mention has been made of the enlistment of tribesmen as irregulars to intercept fugitive rebels during the rounding-up operations. It was decided, in the face of opposition from a number of resident Europeans, to extend this system into a properly organised home guard, known as the Border Scouts, whose main function would be to give warning of enemy incursions and who would of course be under temptation to join them. The Scouts were issued with rifles and uniforms and trained by pairs of N.C.O.s who lived in the longhouses with them. It was the function of the scouts to give warning of the incursions over the border, and, across the wild mountainous centre of the frontier, they worked in close conjunction with 22 S.A.S., whose headquarters came out from England to take command of its own squadron already there, of the Gurkha Parachute Company, of the Guards Independent Parachute Company, and of the Australian and New Zealand squadrons who were later to relieve some of the others for alternate tours. Pairs of these adventurous men lived for months on end in complete isolation, except by radio transmitter. A few would be lost without trace, but they made a great contribution by filling the tribesmen with their own cheerful, dauntless spirit and thus building a barrier along 500 miles of frontier.

Many other things were done to win the battle of the hearts and minds. The kampongs were frequently visited by soldiers and administrators alike, and aid was given them to improve their agriculture, marketing and basic facilities, and to teach them to help themselves. Medical attention was the greatest need of all, and the R.A.M.C. and battalion teams spent long hours working where doctors had never stepped before. They made their weekly rounds by helicopter, a vehicle that was to become very familiar to hundreds of people who had never seen a car. Regimental bands made their visits too, livening the village scene. But much more important than material aid, smiles and display, were the steps taken to build up confidence in the troops' determination to protect the villages against vindictive guerrilla bands and at the same time to preserve them from the horror of a battle. This at times meant a reduction in the killing ground allotted to artillery, mortars and machine-guns, for as Walker wrote subsequently, 'It was indelibly inscribed on our minds that one civilian killed by us would do more harm than ten killed by the enemy'.

Initially, battalions operated in much the same way as they had done

in Malaya. Company bases were established, at distances varying between 10 and 100 miles apart, and patrols set forth in search of the
enemy, taking five days' rations with them and replenishing by air or
local supply. Hills or hillocks were plentiful in most parts, and with the
tops of them cleared, control sets, of much improved penetration, had
far less difficulty in maintaining touch with these patrols than during
the Malayan operation. Areas were larger and rest in shorter supply.
But reliefs were more frequent, with tours varying between four and
seven months according to the district and the base of the troops.

Not until mid-August did the guerillas make a deep incursion, and it
was directed on Song, a riverside town in the sparsely populated Third
Division of Sarawak. The 2/6th Gurkhas were in occupation here,
having come from Hong Kong, and were stretched north-eastwards all
the way to Tawau, excluding a part of the Fourth Division, for which
the British battalion at Seria was responsible together with internal
security duties along the coast, a rôle that passed from the K.O.Y.L.I.
back to the Queen's Own Highlanders and in August on to the 1st Green
Jackets. First news of the guerrillas' coming was brought by an Iban
who had been captured and had escaped. A patrol from the farspread
2/6th bumped them in great strength and in an attempt to outflank them
its British subaltern was wounded and later killed, after a brave lone
fight while awaiting evacuation. This was on the 18th, and on the 23rd
the 1/2nd Gurkhas made their first return to Borneo, being flown into
Sibu, which was itself in some disorder, following the arrival of a U.N.
fact-finding team. Put on the trail of the gang by the head of a longhouse,
a platoon made contact after boating, wading and plunging through
desperately thick secondary jungle. They killed six after a tense fire
fight and drove others into encircling ambushes, in one of which the
bearded leader was slain. Some certainly escaped, others may have
starved.

On September 16 Sarawak and North Borneo gained their independence, the latter taking the name of Sabah, and both joined the new
Federation of Malaysia, which also included the newly independent
Singapore. Only Brunei elected to retain its old status, that of a British
protectorate. Elsewhere the British ceased to be defending their own
territory and instead undertook the task for an ally. This called for a
delicate exercise in tact, and it also put Walker under two masters, the
Malaysian National Defence Council at Kuala Lumpur for general
policy and the C.-in-C. Far East for operations.

Soekarno was incensed, and to add further fuel to his rage, the
United Nations Commission confirmed that the new countries had
chosen their destiny by a fair electoral process. He promised a 'terrible

confrontation' and roused the mob to such fury at Jakarta that every window of the British Embassy was smashed by stones, while the assistant military attaché, Major Roderic Walker, marched up and down inside the compound playing his bagpipes, impervious to the missiles and the febrile yelling. But two days later, following the withdrawal of the Malayan ambassador, the British Embassy came under fiercer attack. It was sacked and burned, and its inmates were rescued, bruised and bleeding, by a dozen brave Indonesian soldiers. The British Government followed the instructions given their soldiers and eschewed rash retaliation, merely demanding an assurance that such barbaric behaviour should cease.

Malaya was swift to make a contribution to the defence of the new federated territory. The 3rd Battalion The Royal Malay Regiment took over the eastern end of Sabah's frontier, and the 5th Battalion came to Sarawak's First Division, enabling 40 Commando (who alternated with 42) to close up in the coastal sector. Practically all the officers in these battalions were Malays, and they tended to regard their federated territory as a colony. Armoured cars, artillery and aircraft were also forthcoming. Further reinforcements were offered by Australia and New Zealand, and the finest contribution to be made was a squadron of Australian engineers, for whom the claims of air supply, accommodation, and defence works were in shrill competition.

There was also an organisational change in September. Headquarters 99 Gurkha Brigade returned to Singapore, and Brigadier Glennie returned to Brunei, to act as deputy to Walker, with responsibility for operations in Brunei and Sabah, while Sarawak remained under the control of 3 Commando Brigade.

The first blow against Malaysian territory in the undeclared war of the now official confrontation was again directed against Sarawak's Third Division, in an even more remote and mountainous part. On September 28 a surprise attack, under cover of mortars, was made on a supervised Border Scouts' post 30 miles inside the border, and so complete was its success that news of it did not reach the 1/2nd Gurkhas until two days later. The Gurkhas had been improving their techniques. Troops were flown in by helicopter astride the suspected return route of the raiders, and so skilled was their approach over the foliage canopy that on the evening of their arrival they ambushed two longboats crammed with gangsters in midstream. Twenty-six were thought to have died and none to have survived. A medium machine-gun was wrested from another gangster killed in a separate clash, and five more dead were found at an abandoned camp, together with the mutilated remains of some Border Scouts.

There were splutters along the entire frontier during the next three months, with pressure mounting on the two extremes, where there was greatest ease of access by sea from Indonesia and where two towns, Kuching in the west and Tawau in the east, lay dangerously close to the frontier. The largest incursion, which was uncharacteristically irresolute, was into Sarawak's Second Division and it crumpled rapidly when confronted by the Border Scouts and 1/10th Gurkhas.

Meanwhile the Communists stepped up their underground operations, keeping the troops busy on search operations around the coastal areas, and in November overhead activity began as well, in the form of buzzing by Indonesian Mustang aircraft over villages and company bases. This was all part of the war of nerves, and the British refused to be provoked into firing at them or flying over Indonesian territory, even after an Auster had been shot down by Bofors fire when near the frontier in the extreme west. It contained a chaplain making his Christmas rounds, and he died of his wounds.

During the last three days of 1963 there were two large incursions at the extremities. In the west, where 40 Commando had 60 miles of coast to guard and 88 of frontier, the guerrillas, reckoned a hundred strong, rapidly retreated after a clash in which they killed a corporal and left two dead of their own. In the east they were very much more successful, penetrating 20 miles into Sabah and surprising a half-company of the 3rd Royal Malay at their base camp at Kalabatan. They inflicted heavy loss on them, both physically and morally. The situation was serious.

Walker asked for the 1/10th Gurkhas, who had returned to their camp at Malacca after relief in Sarawak. They were flown in on January 5, 1964 and were at once dispersed by naval helicopters to sniff out the raiders' most likely lines of retreat, using every tracker available. The first contact was made on the 6th, and on the 7th twelve of the raiders were netted, nine of them killed in a spirited attack led by a Gurkha lieutenant. But four Gurkhas were killed this day, one of them by a falling tree, an ever present risk when landing zones had to be cleared. The pressure was intense, with the helicopters tirelessly shifting parties of Gurkhas to form an intricate web around the jungly hills and valleys and seal every escape route, and with soldiers, sailors and airmen performing prodigies of improvisation to keep the troops supported and supplied. Steadily, remorselessly, and with minimum publicity, the guerrillas were hunted down.

On January 22 the 1st Royal Leicestershire chimed in with a good success. They had come from Hong Kong at the end of September and relieved the 2/6th Gurkhas astride the Sarawak-Sabah border, where they had already had some successful encounters. Now a sergeant with a small patrol discovered the location of a guerrilla band and launched a surprise attack which left him in possession of seven dead and a heap of weapons and ammunition.

On January 23 Soekarno proclaimed a cease-fire as a prelude to negotiations, thus making the first admission that he had been at war. It made little difference. Raiders still crossed the border, and the 1/10th Gurkhas carried on with their interception operation until they had accounted for a hundred of the estimated 120 that had created such alarm. Such was the reward for mobility, flexibility, and tenacity, and it was to earn Lieutenant-Colonel Burnett a lone D.S.O. as a battalion commander in Borneo. It also gave scope for speculation. Seven of the captives and one of the dead were identified as regular Indonesian soldiers.

It was obvious that Soekarno—or 'the Mad Doctor' in British Army parlance—could not abandon his 'terrible confrontation' and likely that, copying Grivas's methods, he had announced the cease-fire in order to regroup for his next move. Negotiations with Malaysia, conducted at foreign minister level, merely hardened the animosity between the two. Indonesia had been worsted in the first two, clandestine rounds of the contest, thanks largely to the speed with which British troops had been deployed and the confidence generated in the people. It was up to Soekarno to start the third.

III—THE REGULARS INVADE (1964–66)

There was a hardening of the command structure following the predictable breakdown of negotiations in February 1964. Most of Sabah became the responsibility of the 5th Malaysian Brigade, under a Malay commander, who had his headquarters at Tawau and had two Malay battalions under command together with the 1/10th Gurkhas, still on duty along the frontier and by the southern coast. Headquarters 51st Gurkha Brigade was committed, as strategic reserve from England, to Brunei, whence it took command of the K.O.Y.L.I., who had returned to the Seria district and Fourth Division of Sarawak, and of the 2/7th Gurkhas, who were astride the Sarawak–Sabah border on second tour, having relieved the Royal Leicesters. Headquarters 99th Gurkha Brigade had relieved the 3rd Commando at Kuching in January and had 42 Commando on the coast, the 5th Royal Malay next them in Sarawak's First Division, the 2/10th Gurkhas (on second tour) in the Second Division, and the 1/6th Gurkhas, newly arrived from England, in the Third, together with the 1/7th (also on second tour) near the coast and 22 S.A.S. along the mountainous frontier. It was now a full divisional organisation, and the new G.O.C. 17th Gurkha Division, Major-General P. M. Hunt, who was a Cameron Highlander by origin, was assigned command, becoming deputy to Walker in place of the faithful Glennie, who once again faded from the scene. Hunt established his headquarters alongside Walker's at Labuan, working in the same relationship as that between Patterson and Glennie in the early days.

The 2/10th Gurkhas, in Sarawak's Second Division, were the first to discover the new pattern of enemy activity. The frontier ran along a sharp, rocky, dominating ridge, and from a veritable pinnacle on the western extremity of the division smoke was seen rising on the evening of March 6, 1964. A platoon of A Company was sent off to investigate. The area was practically uninhabited, but there were a number of tracks, and on the morning of the 7th the platoon moved up two of them, left and right of the pinnacle, to ambush its occupants. The section on the right reported the sound of broadcast music and voices, and the company commander decided on an enveloping attack round this flank. But it was on the left flank that the battle opened, and with a shot that killed the section commander from short range. There was a fierce little fight over his body, in which the remainder of the section repelled attack.

This hastened the other, predominant wing into action, and again the Gurkhas lost a man killed by a burst of machine-gun fire in the early exchanges. It was obvious now that they were up against something more formidable than mere guerrillas, and the sheer rock rising to the pinnacle made the prospect of assault a forbidding one. There was no hesitation. The troublesome outpost was put to flight, leaving behind one dead soldier in the camouflage smock, high black boots, peaked-cap and American equipment of the Indonesian Army. The leading Gurkhas then crept round the face of the pinnacle, with bullets smacking the rock above them, while another platoon laboured painfully through jungle thorn round its rear. Finding the main pinnacle too steep to climb, the two leading sections attacked the enemy in position along a continuation of the ridge. With machine-gun bullets flying at them from front and rear, they darted between the rocks yelling 'Ayo Gurkhali!' with a corporal at their head. A lance-corporal fell mortally wounded and two other men were wounded, and then the enemy withdrew, narrowly escaping encirclement from the other platoon by good use of their machine-guns. Grenades were now hurled up on to the main position, and this too was soon captured, but there was no dead or wounded left on it, although bloodstains showed the damage done.

A captured nominal roll showed the position to have been held by forty regulars of 328 Raider Battalion, and later reports put their casualties at five killed and five wounded. As much courage must have been displayed in the withdrawal as in the attack, but while the Gurkhas' dead and wounded were swiftly evacuated by helicopters with stretchers lashed to their under-shafts, the radioed plea for help from the Indonesian side was answered (according to a Border Scout interpreter) with, 'Get on with it; there are plenty more where they came from.'

The next time the Indonesians were reported to be back on the ridge, 16 miles eastwards, A Company of the 2/10th smote them again, with an array of fire support that throws revealing light on the impact of that first, chance encounter. Two French anti-tank guided missile projectors, known as S.S.11s, opened proceedings from Wessex helicopters, by special permission of the Chief of Defence Staff, Earl Mountbatten, and a troop of 105-mm. field guns, of 45 Light Regiment, continued the pounding, accompanied by two 76-mm. guns in the Saladins of the Heavy Troop, B Squadron, Queen's Royal Irish Hussars. The Gurkhas had an exceptionally difficult climb and were relieved to encounter only minor opposition. Two camps were found, displaying signs of hasty evacuation, and a third position was won after a brief fire fight. Two soldiers lay dead inside them.

On the day of this attack, March 31, an incursion was reported on the eastern end of the 2/10th Gurkhas' division, 60 miles distant. It had been made by a company of the Black Cobra Battalion, thirty-six strong, and there had been indications of its coming, with the result that C Company was deployed near the frontier, ready to sever lines of retreat, and B Company was waiting further back to block approaches, but the country was exceptionally close and jagged, calling for the employment of many more troops. Every available man of the 2/10th was turned out, regardless of employment, leaving only A Company committed to the other half of the division. The Gurkha Parachute Company was brought in, together with the whole of 845 Helicopter Squadron, R.N. The newly formed Sarawak Police Field Force also joined in, and so too did the Border Scouts. The Wessex helicopters were used to entrap, confuse, harry and kill, dropping ambush parties in an ever changing pattern, simulating drops at other places, and pumping explosive bullets from their Brownings into areas unoccupied by troops.

The first contact did not come until April 7, when the Black Cobras, already in retreat, lost three killed in an ambush and scattered, leaving thirty packs on the ground. There was a swift accumulation of kills, four dying when they themselves ambushed a pair of Gurkhas. By the end of the month fourteen had been killed and seven captured, and only six were reported still to be at large. Having lived on practically nothing for three weeks, these six at last fell into the hands of Ibans. Unfortunately for them, their captors were head-hunters and chopped theirs off. The new owners of the heads allowed them to be sent to Kuching for identification and they were put on a plane for return to them by parachute. By a rare mistake in despatch they descended with the rations eagerly awaited by C Company whose men had been living on one meal a day to avoid disclosure of their positions by air supply. The company commander was not amused.

With such a huge frontage to choose from it was unwise of the Indonesian commander to pick as his first opponents a battalion that had the knowledge of its sector gleaned from six months of continual occupation and, like all Gurkha battalions, had many veterans in its ranks who had long experience of jungle warfare and were imbued with the offensive spirit that springs from confidence in their skill at arms. However, the Indonesian regulars had shown themselves tougher opponents than the guerrillas, and with a lavish supply of automatic weapons and vast numbers to draw on—their country had 100,000,000 inhabitants and an army said to number 300,000, reared on a successful guerrilla campaign waged against the Dutch—they presented a sombre menace, especially at the type of insidious, limited warfare Soekarno obviously had in mind. The respect they commanded was to be seen in the new look of the allied positions. Companies had in general been moved nearer the frontier and most had two bases, sited as a rule on hilltops with prodigious fortifications making amends for lack of concealment. They were surrounded by multiple coils of dannert wire and thousands of needlesharp spikes, which were cut from bamboo and known as panjis, and inside them were gun emplacements, mortar emplacements, and elaborate excavations with ample overhead cover, which was shaped very often on the lines of a pagoda, giving the impression of a weird, tumbledown Buddhist settlement. From these bases patrols went forth and established their own temporary, carefully concealed bases, and from here they operated for periods of up to twenty days, living frugally and from local resources to restrict to the minimum the need for air supply.

The companies had their helicopter 'pads' but their routine weekly rations were dropped by parachute to conserve the precious helicopters. The battalion bases were also on air supply, as much to deprive the enemy of the opportunity to ambush convoys as to avoid overstrain of the very few roads and tracks available, and they had landing grounds for Beavers and Twin Pioneers, the levelling of which was high on the priority list of the overworked squadrons of Royal Engineers, Gurkha

Engineers, and Australian Engineers, the latter on loan from the 28th Commonwealth Brigade. Some even had space for a Hastings to land, and all throbbed with the bustle peculiar to air terminals as helicopters spiralled in and wheeled aircraft took off with a roar and rush of air.

For the first time since Korea the Royal Artillery had an important part to play with their main armament. The company bases had to be supported, and there was no means of doing this except from within them. Each was therefore provided with a single 105-mm. howitzer, brought in by Belvedere helicopter, and they were sited in section pairs, mutually supporting each other from twin bases: a system pioneered by the 45th Regiment in July 1964. Thus, as in the infantry, junior ranks bore heavy responsibility, and a battery might be spread over a frontage of 90 miles. Great care had to be taken over ranging, so as not to disturb the people. Plenty of infantry tasks also fell to the gunners, as they had done in the earlier days of the campaign, and there were never any surplus men to be found on a gun site. Boating patrols were undertaken too; indeed the gunners lived up to their tradition of ubiquity and many regiments were represented, both British and Commonwealth, performing many different tasks. There was a troop of 5·5-inch medium guns for long range harrassing, a radar troop, a sound ranging troop, and around the ports anti-aircraft guns pointed skywards, both heavy and light. As further mark of preparedness, coils of wire surrounded every detachment, whether of gunners, sappers, drivers, mechanics, or ordnance storemen, and there were sand-bagged positions inside them for the occupants to man. The sultry, steamy air of North Borneo exuded a strong whiff of war.

In April 1964 the 2/2nd Gurkhas became the last of the eight Gurkha battalions to be committed by taking over the Second Division of Sarawak from the 2/10th. On their left flank, in the Third Division, the situation had been quieter since the 1/7th Gurkhas won a spirited little battle on an island against some reinforcements for the C.C.O. brought in by sea. The Third Division could be left to one battalion and the S.A.S. But in the First Division on their right, where the frontier was nearest the sea and facilities for approach from the Indonesian side were at their best, the pressure was steadily mounting. The 1/6th Gurkhas came here in May, after inauguration in the Third Division, and took over the coastal sector from 42 Commando. On June 21 they had one of the hardest fights of the campaign. The Indonesians were bumped on the border hills west of Lundu and the 1/16th lost seven men killed and four wounded before they drove them off. Again the Indonesians evacuated their dead and wounded, leaving the Gurkhas with two prisoners and an estimated tally of fifteen kills. The garrison of the First Division had now been raised to three battalions, the 1st Green Jackets being inserted in the centre in early June.

There were by now three British battalions in the line. The 1st Argyll and Sutherland Highlanders had come out with their families in January, replacing the Queen's Own Highlanders in Selerang Barracks, Singapore, and in late April they took over Seria and the Fourth Division on completion of the K.O.Y.L.I.'s second and final tour. They had to wait until August 3 for their first success, which was gained by the swift interception of a rare raiding party that dropped some mortar bombs on a post. Two tracker teams were dropped by helicopter, each under a sergeant with a dog and an Iban. One team scored two kills, the other four, the latter being the highest possible.

The 1st Royal Ulster Rifles took over the Third Division near the end of May, having come, as the Royal Leicesters before them, for a year's tour that began in Hong Kong. Like all new battalions from now onwards, their companies had each done an intensive course at the Jungle Warfare School in Johore. In August they did an exchange with the 4th Royal Malay, taking over the eastern sector of the First Division and at once noticed a quickening of the tempo. The Green Jackets, on their right, were in their third and final tour. They found it quite the liveliest and gained a number of successes intercepting the return of short penetrating raiding parties. Their best produced six kills, gained by a team that descended through the treetops down 200 feet of rope. The Green Jackets were relieved near the end of October, having rather exceeded the four months that were standard for a British battalion based permanently on Malaya. The excursionists from England did a single, much longer tour, never less than six months.

Soekarno and the Tungku Abdul Rahman attended a 'summit' meeting in mid-June. It produced nothing more than another bogus cease-fire and a reiteration of Soekarno's vow to 'crush Malaysia'. His latest device for fulfilling it revealed itself on August 17 in a landing on the south coast of Singapore. It was effectively crushed by the Malaysian Army, in the persons of the 4th Federal Infantry Brigade, who had just quelled some furious rioting by the Chinese population of Singapore. There was thus no great disruption to the routine of the troops on relief from Borneo.

However, on September 2 a large force of parachutists was reported to have descended into the Labis area of Johore, and this was serious. For the second time within nine months an emergency summons reached the 1/10th Gurkhas in Malacca. They were rushed to the area by lorry and—after sorting out a mass of wild rumours—made their first contact and first capture on September 7. After a month's feverish activity, with police, helicopters, Malay and New Zealand troops joining in the search, ninety-two out of an established force of ninety-six para-troopers were either dead or prisoner. The great majority had fallen to the 1/10th, at a cost to them of a British officer and a rifleman killed, and no sooner were they back in barracks than they were called out again to cope with a force of fifty that had landed up the River Kesang. They arrived to find them already captured. The Indonesians had been told that they would be warmly welcomed by the people and had lost heart when they found this was untrue.

Other attempts on the mainland were to follow. Although they caused anxiety enough at G.H.Q. Malaysia proved herself capable of self-defence.

The reliefs continued their uneven course, with the comic little river motor vessel, H.M.S. *Auby*, which could carry only half a battalion, taking the leviathan's share of the transportation duty between Singapore and Kuching. Certainly it was around Kuching that the troops were most needed. For the most part the ground is flat in the First Division, broken by sharp ridges and little hillocks which, although covered in thick undergrowth and bamboo, afforded good observation for marauders. There were many kampongs amid the thicket growing rubber, pepper or tapioca, and a maze of tracks, along which the Indonesians were apt to stalk in the late afternoon to lord it over the people before disappearing in the night. A proliferation of ever twisting rivers and streams hampered the task of interception and the wading of them called for many feats of strength and daring.

The Ulsters, in the eastern sector of the First Division, had a number of minor successes, which made the enemy much less conspicuous, but the fiercest action in their area was fought by ten Gurkhas attached from the 2/10th, who were by the coast. These men held a temporary platoon base from which an ambush party had departed, and on the afternoon of October 5 they withstood three determined assaults, each made by about fifty men, each from a different direction, and each supported by heavy but inaccurate machine-gun and light mortar fire. The last came nearest to success and ended, as darkness was falling, with the Gurkhas hurling grenades at Indonesians bravely lugging their casualties away a few yards from the platoon post. The Gurkhas had holes through their hats, water bottles, and equipment and were almost out of ammunition, but were themselves all untouched. The first D.C.M. of the campaign went to Sergeant Barmalal Limbu, their leader. A single gun of the 45th Light Regiment had fired 155 rounds in support of his detachment.

Intelligence now reported a very powerful build-up against Sarawak's First Division. It was decided to increase its garrison to five battalions, all holding sectors of the frontier, and to rely on the mobile use of reserves to contain any large penetration. In order to ease the strain on 99 Brigade, the command of which passed in December 1964 from Brigadier Patterson to the former Seaforth Highlander, Brigadier W. W. Cheyne, the Second and Third Divisions were formed into a separate sector, controlled from Sibu. Headquarters 3 Commando Brigade temporarily took on this commitment in mid-January 1965, and on March 22 it was transferred to a well-known traveller from England, Headquarters 19 Infantry Brigade. Thus the West Brigade (as it was commonly called) had five battalions on a front of 181 miles, the Mid West Brigade two battalions and the mixed squadrons of 22 S.A.S. on a front of 442 miles, the Central Brigade two—of which one, the 2/6th Gurkhas, had been in permanent residence at Seria, complete with families, since September 1964—for a frontage of 267 miles, and the East Brigade three and a front of 81 miles, together with 500 miles of coast. A thirteenth battalion arrived in January 1965, coming straight from England to do jungle training at Kota Belud in Sabah as a prelude to taking over the front of the East Brigade. This was the 1st Gordon Highlanders. There were two armoured car regiments, performing a variety of tasks on wheels, foot and afloat; one was British and one Malaysian, the former passing from the Queen's Royal Irish Hussars to the 4th R.T.R. in September 1964. The artillery strength was two and a half regiments, part Malaysian, mainly British, and there were three squadrons of field engineers.

All this, together with minesweepers and patrol boats, seventy helicopters and forty fixed wing aircraft, two battalions' worth of police field force, 1,500 border scouts, and a highly effective joint signals' service, was handed in March 1965 by General Walker over to Major-General G. H. Lea, a graduate from the Lancashire Fusiliers who, like Walker, had won a D.S.O. as a commanding officer in Malaya, in his case of 22 S.A.S. If still small and short of many essentials, the force had grown greatly, both in size and prowess, in the course of two years, and even as Walker left the prospect was being improved by a sudden conversion to lighter equipment for the infantry soldier. It included the American armalite rifle—an automatic weapon highly lethal at close range—the 88-mm. mortar, the Carl Gustav rocket launcher, and the General Purpose Machine Gun in place of those two old faithfuls, the Bren and the Vickers. The deadly anti-personnel Claymore mines and seismic intruder detectors were issued, and so were a new Australian-designed jungle kit and special rations, all lightening the soldier's load. Battalions also received their own Army Air Corps Platoon, consisting of two Sioux helicopters, and at Brigade level an officer and N.C.O. specially trained in psychological warfare concentrated on lowering the enemy's morale by the crafty dissemination of propaganda. Although on a parsimonious scale by American standards, every possible agency was employed to sap the Indonesian ambition.

The build-up in the First Division was completed at the end of January 1965 when the Ulsters ended a successful, casualty-free tour of eight months by handing the left sector over to two battalions, the Argylls and the 1/6th Gurkhas. On their right were the 1st Scots Guards, who had replaced the K.O.Y.L.I. in the 28th Commonwealth Brigade and had been patrolling the Thailand border before coming to Borneo in January. Other Commonwealth battalions followed them, the 1st Royal New Zealand Regiment taking over the Second Division in January and the 3rd Royal Australian coming to the First in early March, thus easing the pressure on the British Army, which also had heavy commitments in Aden. The Australians took over from the 1/7th Gurkhas just after the latter had ended four months of comparative inaction by smashing a force on the border, with most effective artillery support, and inflicting loss claimed at twenty-three killed without harm to themselves. Further right, by the coast, the 2/10th had as usual been busy. They three times thumped the enemy hard, but encountered lively resistance and might themselves have been thumped if the Indonesians' marksmanship had matched their tactics.

The 2nd Parachute were sent from England for a short tour and after six weeks jungle training in Malaya took over the eastern sector of the First Division in mid-March, relieving the Argylls, who were switched to the coastal sector. A helicopter crash—an amazingly rare occurrence —caused them their first losses, to the extent of an officer and four men killed. Then on April 27 they were the recipient of the Indonesians' most ambitious venture of the campaign, a direct attack on a company base. It belonged to B Company on a hilltop at Plaman Mapu and was held by Company Headquarters and a weak platoon. They came under fire in the pre-dawn gloom from light mortars and rocket launchers and the infantry rushed in close behind the crash. A mortar position of the paras was overrun. A section counterattacked at once and drove the enemy out. There was a pause of some 20 minutes and then another crash, followed by a great rush of forms through the gloaming and a deafening shindy of shot and bomb from both sides. The Indonesians penetrated the inner wire and made an entry into a trench. With his company commander twice hit beside him and with one eye blinded by a splinter, C. S. M. Williams grabbed a machine-gun from a wounded soldier and pumped lead into the enemy. Another scratch counterattack was mounted, and now the forms were to be seen scrambling downhill, dragging dead and wounded with them. They left two dead behind them and many blood trails. Two men of the paras lay dead or dying and eight were wounded, including the A.C.C. cook, who had manned his post resolutely and, like most present, had had a stormy baptism of fire, calmly endured.

The assault force made good their escape, encumbered though they were, according to locals, with a long column of dead and wounded. The 2nd Para had to wait until mid-May before making an effective counter thrust. They first drove back a force of seventy that had made their presence known to villagers, obviously with the intention of ambushing the interception force. Their flanks had therefore to be carefully established, and with admirable aid from their artillery the paras inflicted heavy losses in a series of turning movements, although again the enemy took their dead and wounded away. The paras lost one killed. They had greater success a week later. Border Scouts reported an intrusion by a hundred raiders and seven platoons were at once dropped by helicopter and rope at pre-selected places on the ridge behind them, and by skimming in behind the ridge, following the line of every contour, and by diversionary flights around the raiders, they arrived unnoticed. Indeed, one section were still getting into position when they were approached by a platoon of Indonesians, whose leader waved in greeting when he spotted them 20 yards away, only to undergo pitiful change of expression before the bullets ripped him and a dozen of his men. In a subsequent ambush, shortly before the paras' relief at the end of June, a half-platoon claimed sixteen killed, either by automatic fire or claymore mine. Probably there was some double counting, for as usual there was little chance to check before the Indonesians launched a counterattack, which was broken up by five well placed rounds from an Australian section of 105-mms.

Since they were themselves in the habit of lobbing mortar bombs into kampongs from across the border, the Indonesians could not expect their enemies to be over conscientious in observing a frontier line that was not marked anyway, and they were made to learn with pain that they could not sit behind it, preparing their raids, with complete immunity. The Australians struck them a lethal blow in this same month of June, and so too did the Argylls. The latter was delivered by a platoon dropped by helicopter and supported by a 105-mm. gun also brought forward by helicopter. The ambush was laid some distance from the point of the platoon's descent, and in the course of two days' fighting the Argylls claimed eleven kills for the loss of one man wounded by a bullet that pierced his hand and rifle butt. The Indonesians retaliated with a bloody raid on a village deep inside the First Division, in which the C.C.O.

played a prominent part, and the 2/2nd Gurkhas, who relieved the Argylls on the coastal sector, were kept very busy both forward and back.

Outside the First Division there was most action at the junction between Sabah and Sarawak, a sector that included a part of Brunei as well. The 1/2nd and 2/7th Gurkhas were in alternate occupation here for two years and had some spirited actions. The 1/2nd had four men wounded by mortar fire when ejecting a raiding party fifty strong soon after their arrival in 1964; during a subsequent tour in 1965 they twice hit the enemy really hard, counting fourteen dead after a combined attack and ambush operation and thirteen dead, with twenty-two weapons recovered, after a river ambush. The 2/7th's best effort was an attack for which they manhandled their mortars over a long distance; although the enemy were dug in with plenty of mortars and machine-guns in support, they took the position without loss and claimed fifteen killed. On the right of this sector the 2/6th Gurkhas, based on Seria, did an operational stint of thirteen months on end, with frontier responsibility for Sarawak's Fourth Division. They had occasional clashes and twice ejected large raiding groups.

To revert to the First Division, when the Scots Guards completed their four months tour in May 1965, having gained a few successes, they were relieved by the 1st/2nd Green Jackets, K.R.R.C., who had come to Penang in place of the 1st, and by the end of June the 1st/3rd Green Jackets, Rifle Brigade, were also in the line, two sectors left of the 2nd, having replaced the Ulsters as battalion based on Hong Kong. The 2nd and 3rd Green Jackets enhanced the reputation already made by the 1st, the K.R.R.C. (or 60th) having two particularly fine successes. The first was gained by a company that made a two-day march through fiendish jungle and then lay up for over two days with an ambush set. At last the enemy—camouflage smocked regulars—walked into it and seven were felled by the opening burst. A further seven, it was subsequently established, died in the desperate fighting that ensued before the company made their retreat through the jungle carrying their one casualty with them. The second was the investment by two companies of an enemy base next a border village. One crossed a river which had swollen to a depth of 8 feet and had to be swum against a fast current; this was achieved, and after a night march both companies were in position. Action began with the destruction of an Indonesian river patrol, whereupon mortar fire from the enemy camp was answered by some accurate rounds from a 105-mm. gun. This produced a wild exodus, and the 60th had some good targets, as Indonesians scuttled up the rides they covered. The river had further swollen when the company returned, yet there were no casualties, either to men or weapons, except for six unfortunates who went down with the dread leptospirosis, a rat-borne disease caught from immersion in water, or from drinking it.

During this tour the 60th claimed a total of forty-three confirmed enemy dead and many other probables, for a loss of only one rifleman killed and two wounded. The Rifle Brigade were not so fortunate, losing five killed in battle accidents or by enemy action, but they had one bright success when a platoon caught a party of the enemy at bivouac, killing eight of its members and wounding a further five. Their sector, the most eastern of the First Division, had quietened considerably, and time and again patrols returned from long excursions 'tired but unblooded'.

There was still plenty happening nearer the coast, and when the 2/10th Gurkhas came to the Bau sector, second from the west, they found the Indonesians in strength astride the border and dealt them some shattering blows. The first was on August 28 when a fortified platoon base was located and swept away in a dawn attack which caught the enemy completely unawares and forced them to leave twenty dead on the position. Two Gurkhas were killed. This was followed by two ambushes which yielded kills of nine and fourteen, two complete parties.

These successes were evenly distributed between D, A, and B Companies respectively. C's turn came on November 21, when the Indonesians were located digging in on top of a sheer-sided hill. A razor-backed spur leading up to it was covered in secondary jungle, and the Gurkhas at once carved themselves a tunnel through it while listening to the digging up above. In the lead was Lance-Corporal Rambahadur Limbu and his machine-gun group, and he crawled to ten yards of the position before being seen by a sentry with a machine-gun. The sentry fired, hit the man next Rambahadur, and was instantly killed by the youthful lance-corporal as he made the first entry into the trench system. Others followed as fast as the tunnel would allow and began to fight their way with grenades from trench to trench, as heavy machine-gun fire whipped the open top of the ridge from the further extreme. Having moved his gun forward and wishing to notify his platoon commander, Rambahadur leapt out of his trench to report the fact, and as he stood fully exposed he saw both his machine-gunners hit hard. He tried first to crawl back, with bullets churning the dust up all round him, then got up and ran, carried one of his men to safety down the hill, and returned in short rushes to remove the other. This he also achieved by a miracle of survival, for the bullets were sweeping the ground in great volume. He came back again and brought his machine-gun very effectively into action to support his platoon.

After an hour's grim work with grenade, bayonet and bullet, the

Gurkhas had gained the ridge and had twenty-four enemy dead around them. Three counterattacks were attempted, from south, west and north, and each was smashed, with some aid from artillery. The company then withdrew. They had suffered three killed and two wounded, one of them badly. A 5-mile trek across very rough country followed, and to complement the valour of Rambahadur, the life of the wounded man was finally saved after ten hours of stretcher carrying, three hours of saline administration by the medical officer, walking beside the stretcher, and a pre-dawn flight by helicopter.

Rambahadur was awarded the Victoria Cross and sent to England to receive it from the Queen.

On October 1 the Communists attempted a *coup d'état* at Jakarta and failed. The C.C.O.'s ambitions towards the same end were simultaneously crushed by a large round-up in which the 2/2nd Gurkhas played a leading part in the First Division's coastal sector, aided by a company of the 1/7th. This was followed by a marked slackening of activity, from both across the border and in the Chinese dominated districts. The worst menace was anti-personnel mines, laid by sneak parties of raiders on tracks near the frontier. These caused the loss of a number of feet and some hectic deeds of first aid and porterage in the removal of an unfortunate loser to the nearest helicopter pad. They put a new, sickly element into patrolling, while making it all the more important.

In other respects there was nothing much to do but to keep the people happy and maintain the pattern of reliefs. The two Commandos had each done a spell on the Sabah frontier astride 1964 and 1965, and since this involved plenty of boating in a variety of harbour vessels and assault craft, to patrol the many swamps and creeks, they were well suited to the task. In May 1965 they had returned to Sarawak's First Division, still taking alternate tours, and had left Sabah in the keeping of Scotland, first in the persons of the Gordons and from September 1965 to January 1966 of the Scots Guards, who had a company of the 1st Irish Guards permanently attached and a platoon on loan from the garrison battalion at Hong Kong, the 1st South Wales Borderers, thus forming a rare Celtic union.

Scotland gained a third representative when the 1st King's Own Scottish Borderers arrived in October after a training period in Malaya, to complete the unique triple event of active service in Korea, Malaya and Borneo. They had come for a six-months' tour in the Third Division, and beside them in the Second were the 1st Malaysian Rangers, who had been newly raised by British and Malay officers from a nucleus of Sarawak Rangers. Control of this Mid West Sector passed, in this same month of October 1965, from Headquarters 19th Brigade to that of the 5th, which had been removed from Germany eighteen months earlier in an attempt to ease the strain on the hard pressed new model army.

To revert to the Gordons, they relieved the 2/6th Gurkhas operationally in October, after only a month's rest, although leaving them in their quarters at Seria and the Sultan's summer palace which provided a sumptuous officers' mess. The Gordons returned to Scotland in February. Their training camp in Sabah—Paradise Camp—had been taken over by the 1st Durham Light Infantry in October, and in January 1966 the D.L.I. became operational in the eastern sector of the First Division.

Their neighbours here were the Argylls, who had begun their third tour in November, thus emulating only the 1st Green Jackets among British infantry battalions. In late February there was a sudden, abrupt quickening of the tempo, coinciding with a political tempest in Jakarta. Tracks of large parties come from across the border were reported by the Scouts. The D.L.I. had a fleeting contact, and on the 26th they ambushed a regular Indonesian platoon, killing six of its men, but themselves losing a private killed and four wounded when heavy mortar fire came down on them as the enemy withdrew. The Argylls reported a large party near Tebedu. They drifted into the area of the 2/7th Gurkhas on their right and were estimated at fifty strong, a mixture of Indonesian commandos and C.C.O. terrorists, with women among them. They proved a tough bunch. A company of the 1/10th Gurkhas, brought in to aid the 2/7th, lost one killed and five wounded in two sharp clashes that started the fragmentation of the raider group. The 2/7th then conducted a prolonged strangulation operation in conjunction with their neighbouring battalions, the guns and scout cars of the 4th R.T.R., harrassing fire by 40th Light Regiment, search and interrogation squads of the Police Field Force, spotter planes of the Air Corps, and flares, broadcasts, and of course helicopter lifts provided by the R.A.F. The stubborn, stoic infiltrators were given no rest by day or night, and near the end of March the last of them were rounded up by the police inside a resettlement compound for Chinese.

The 1/10th Gurkhas, who had taken the Bau district over from the 2/10th, were meanwhile engaged in a resumption of the border war. A brilliant success was gained by their D Company in early March. One platoon caught an enemy platoon in an ambush, made obvious withdrawal, and induced the relieving enemy force to walk into the fire of a second platoon that had remained hidden all the time. The company suffered no loss and claimed thirty-seven kills, the highest in any action of the campaign. Major Pike became the only company commander to win the D.S.O. during the campaign.

Near the end of March this same company lost four men killed by one Indonesian soldier and had two others wounded in a very fierce surprise encounter when the whole battalion were trying to envelop a large enemy force located elsewhere. The intruders were forced into retreat, leaving thirteen dead and carrying many wounded with them, and a quick adjustment was made to the battalion plan in order to cut them off. It was brought to frustration by a message from Whitehall ordering the 1/10th to desist. They returned growling, to hand over the fight against curb and enemy to the 4th Royal Australian.

Soekarno's 'terrible confrontration' had by now rebounded upon himself. After a month of crisis and rioting he was relegated on March 12 to the rôle of a puppet, still styled President. A soldier, General Suharto, won the executive control and wrought terrible, bloody vengeance on all Communists for having so nearly dragged the country to disaster. It was the turn of the Chinese Embassy now to be ransacked and burned. Peace feelers went out to Kuala Lumpur and on June 1 an agreement provisionally ending the confrontation was signed at Bangkok. Soekarno refused to ratify it, but could not prevent its confirmation by formal agreement signed by the foreign ministers at Jakarta on August 11.

The British undertook to withdraw their troops from Malaysian Borneo by the end of September, and as they began to arrange details of their departure the border raiders came to life again for a farewell kick. First reports of an incursion came on July 29, when tracks of 'fifty plus' were spotted by a Gurkha Parachute Company patrol on border duty in the mountains of Sarawak's Fifth Division. The 1/7th Gurkhas were in operational charge, and at once every available man was summoned to net the invaders. A Gurkha officer and a few men of the Recce Platoon made the first contact, finding the enemy—they appear to have been guerrillas—in a valley two miles inside Sarawak and at once charging them in the face of a hail of bullets that scored two minor nicks. This split the guerrillas into two groups, and full pressure by ground and air resources was applied on the untrammelled mountain sides. Lack of food eventually had its effect, and by September 3 forty-six of the guerrillas had been accounted for, a very large proportion captured, the leader among them, showing that ardour no longer burned so high. The remaining four penetrated to Brunei, where they were picked up by the newly formed Royal Brunei Regiment.

The British withdrawal was by now well under way, and among the departing battalions were two new ones. The 1st Royal Hampshire came from Hong Kong and in mid June took the Sabah frontier over from the 2nd Royal Green Jackets (now converted to a battalion of a new regiment) whose one loss in this sector had been that of a foot belonging to an Iban tracker, for whom a subscription of £600 was raised within the battalion. The 1st Queen's Own Buffs took over the Serian sector of the First Division in mid-July, to become the fifteenth British battalion to play an operational part. One more, the 1st Royal Warwickshire Fusiliers, followed them to Sabah's jungle training camp, but were too late to become operationally involved. Meanwhile the armoured role had been handed over by the 4th R.T.R. to squadrons of the Queen's Dragoon Guards, the Life Guards, and the 5th R.T.R. just before the final phase. The gunners' representatives had numbered no less than fourteen regiments and four independent batteries. They included the 26th Field Regiment, the 20th Medium, the 4th, 6th, 29th Commando, 40th (who spent twelve months in the line), 45th, 49th and 95th Commando Light Regiments, the 12th, 16th, and 22nd Air Defence Regiments, the 94th Locating Regiment, and elements of the 3rd R.H.A.

The brunt, no one would deny, had been borne by the eight Gurkha battalions and the two commandos, and appropriately the first two in at the start of the confrontation proper, the 2/10th Gurkhas and 40 Commando, were among the last to leave Sarawak, having each completed five tours, some lasting six months or more. Including the Brunei revolt, the Gurkhas had suffered forty-three killed and eight-seven wounded; the Commandos sixteen killed and twenty-six wounded; and the British battalions and ancillaries sixteen killed and fifty-one wounded. Yet the Gurkhas were far from overjoyed that it was over. 'It was a sad time', reported the 1/7th when in mid-October they completed the hand-over to the Malaysian Army and wedged themselves aboard 'our dear old friend', *Auby.*

Thus ended what must surely rank as the British Army's neatest achievement during the post-war years. What might so easily have been an interminable embroilment in the jungle, the kampongs, the villages and towns, with an ever swelling flow of blood and hate, had been brought to a happy end in little more than three years. This had been achieved because the army had won the confidence of the inhabitants and gained complete mastery over a brave and tough, if not very ably led, enemy. They had combined kindness to the defended with aggression against the attackers, two virtues not always regarded as compatible, and it had all been done with a lack of self advertisement, which must have had a deflating effect on the enemy and in which the British press played a cooperative part. Mr. Denis Healey, the Minister of Defence for the second half of the confrontation, had good reason to predict in the House of Commons: 'In the history books it will be recorded as one of the most efficient uses of military force in the history of the world'.

It was an adjunct to the policy of self-effacement that operational decorations were awarded stintingly. However, now that victory was won Lea had the extremely rare distinction, for a major-general, of being made a K.C.B. Walker, who had laid the foundations so firmly and precisely, would also receive this honour, but not until he had risen to higher rank.

15

Africa

(1957-70)

THE earliest colonial war fought by the British Army was in
Africa and is commemorated by the battle honour Tangier,
1662–80. There were no further British military adventures in the
continent until the nineteenth century, when what might be termed the
fight for possession was spread between 1801 and 1901. It was followed
by the fight for retention, which was divided between the two world
wars and resulted in an enlargement of the British holding, and then
came the fight for stability, wherein the British Army were engaged in
suppressing the Shifta bandits in Eritrea, in trying to hold Egypt to a
satisfactory settlement, and in quelling the Mau Mau in Kenya, as
already described in this book. The fourth and final phase, which is the
subject of this chapter, was that of emergence, when the British Army's
main task was to assist the colonies in their leap to independence.

The first to emerge, by a gradual but not always smooth process, was
the Gold Coast Colony, which became the independent state of Ghana
on March 6, 1957. This of course started the rush, and Nigeria reached
independence on October 1, 1960, being joined by the former mandated territory, the Northern Cameroons on January 1, 1961. Sierra
Leone followed on 27 April 1961. The old Royal West African Frontier
Force was divided up to form the armies of the new Dominions, and
British officers were seconded with them to continue what had so far
been a grindingly methodical transfer of responsibility to African
officers. The only involvement of British troops was in the provision
of a battalion for peacekeeping during the plebiscite held to decide the
future of the North and South Cameroons, which elected to go in
different directions. This provided the 1st King's Own Royal Border
Regiment with some pleasantly varied and widespread duties from

September 1960 to May 1961 and the 1st Grenadier Guards from then until October.

Civil war had meanwhile broken out in the Congo. It began in July 1960, and in the same month the United Nations decided to intervene. Among the first on the scene was Major-General H. T. Alexander, a small and lively officer late of the Cameronians, who was seconded as Ghana's Chief of Defence Staff and at an early stage was sent by President Nkrumah to find if a Ghanaian contingent could be accepted. Being ahead of any official United Nations commander, he made valiant efforts on his own initiative to pluck a little order out of the rampant chaos, and on subsequent visits, after the despatch of Ghanaian troops, he more than once played a prominent part in easing crises. His exploits were well publicised, as also were those of a Major Lawson, who was serving with the Nigerian contingent and had a wonderful knack of restoring calm to perilous situations by his own unruffled, unarmed presence. Lawson won the D.S.O., as also did a Lieutenant-Colonel Price of the S.W.B., and the M.C. was won by four British officers similarly seconded. But it was a war in which the Africans, not unnaturally, wanted the limelight. In September 1961 Alexander was told that it was 'politically imperative' that a Ghanaian should hold command and was instantly dismissed. His subordinate British officers were relegated to advisory roles. Prestige mattered more than efficiency to the young nations, and there was a lesson here that required to be digested more speedily than soldiers would think wise.

Kenya had by now been transformed from a scene of war to a strategic base, and without damage to nationalist sentiment. Its possibilities as such, which had beckoned planners since 1942, were well demonstrated towards the close of the Mau Mau campaign when the last British battalions taking part, the 1st Gloucestershire and the 1st King's Shropshire Light Infantry, were flown off to Arabia in April and November 1956, bringing about the disbandment of 49 Brigade. The K.S.L.I. soon returned to Kenya, and in 1958 they made another excursion northwards, this time to Aden. New barracks were meanwhile being built at Kawaha, 8 miles west of Nairobi, and in December 1958 Headquarters 24th Infantry Brigade arrived to take occupation and to swell the size of its command to a brigade group, with an artillery regiment but no armour.

The logical culmination was the strategic reorientation effected in March 1961, under which Headquarters Middle East Command was transferred to Aden, controlling the south-north shaft running through the east side of Africa to the Persian Gulf. In July of that year the 24th Brigade were rushed from one end of the shaft to the other, from Kenya to Kuwait, as related in Chapter 12, and the 19th Brigade came from England to replace them as strategic reserve. The 2nd Coldstream Guards, of 24 Brigade, left a two-company detachment in Kenya, and in September they trod fresh territory for the British Army, going to the island of Zanzibar to relieve a battalion of the King's African Rifles that had successfully quelled some fierce disturbances produced by an election.

In the autumn of this eventful year, as 24 Brigade were returning to Kenya, a number of rivers broke their banks and bridges, filling vast areas of Kenya with swirling chocolate-coloured water. The army and R.A.F. launched a great relief operation, with the latter keeping districts on air supply for weeks. The Royal Engineers shouldered the main military burden, being raised from squadron to regimental strength by the arrival of most of the 36th Corps Engineer Regiment from England. Great exertions were made over a period of almost six months, sometimes by a complete troop engaged on the reconstruction of a major bridge, more often by detachments of a corporal and a few sappers working with local labour to open routes over debris-littered culverts and across streams swollen to torrents. Some were marooned by reflooding but carried on under supply by helicopter.

In 1963 there was a sudden call for another pioneering trip. There was trouble in Swaziland, a small British colonial territory enveloped within the eastern boundary of South Africa. A general strike was called on June 10, in demand for a quicker rate of constitutional advance, and 3,000 men marched menacingly on the Resident Commissioner in the little capital town of Mbabane and fought a battle with the police. On the 12th the 1st Gordon Highlanders were warned to fly from Eastleigh aerodrome, Nairobi, by Beverley and Argosy, and on the morning of the 13th they began to arrive at Matsapa aerodrome. They speedily brought order to Mbabane and, without dispersing, prepared to make a swoop on Havelock, an asbestos mining centre, some 12 miles away and 6,000 feet above sea level. This was the strikers' strong-hold.

Lieutenant-Colonel Napier obtained some lorries for his men and set off in the earliest, bitterly cold hours of June 17. After over an hour of strained climbing the lorries were halted 3 miles short of Havelock, and the men got out, wearing gymn shoes. By dawn they had surrounded the shack houses of the defiant ones, and soon afterwards they thwarted an attempt at escape. The police made the arrests they wanted with unaccustomed ease, and the Gordons returned to Mbabane to receive a rapturous welcome from the security committee. After dark they set forth again and applied similar treatment to a sugar plantation, and the only thing then left to cope with was a propaganda campaign, launched

413

by leaflet, to the effect that the British soldiers had come to kill the people, just as they had been killing the Mau Mau. The Gordons had only to show themselves to the people to prove the untruth of this, and this they did with their pipers well to the fore, spreading joy round many a kraal. They returned in August, leaving the 1st Loyals, who had flown from Cyprus, in charge of the most genial of the British Army's far flung commitments in Africa.

East Africa, panting in the steps of West, was now harvesting its hastily sown crop of independence. Tanganyika gathered it in December 1961, Uganda in October 1962, and Zanzibar in December 1963. Ceremonial conferment on Zanzibar was made by the Duke of Edinburgh at midnight on December 9, and he then journeyed to Nairobi for the proudest and most emotional since India of all transfers of powers, that to Kenya, made at midnight on December 11 in the presence of pardoned Mau Mau generals. Except in the case of Zanzibar, converted battalions of the former King's African Rifles took part in these ceremonies, and they still had British officers in command. Africanisation had come late and with a rush, leaving the senior appointments in British hands and the junior ones in very inexperienced African hands. There were also a number of British warrant and non-commissioned officers still seconded.

Agreement had been reached for the British troops to remain for a year in Kenya, and East African Command was renamed British Land Forces Kenya. Its G.O.C. was Major-General I. H. Freeland, late the Royal Norfolk, and in command of 24 Brigade was Brigadier D. L. Lloyd Owen, late the Queens. A sudden flush of crises descended on their heads a month after Kenya had celebrated independence, and although no definite connection was traced between them, they must undoubtedly have been set off as it were by sympathetic detonation. 24 Brigade consisted of the 2nd Scots Guards and 1st Staffordshire at Kahawa and the 3rd RHA (less a battery in Aden) at Gilgil with the Gordons, who were in process of returning home without relief.

The first alarm arrived at 5 a.m. on January 12, 1964: there was trouble in Zanzibar. It was in fact a rising against the Sultan and the 2nd Scots Guards, who had made an enjoyable visit to the island the previous August to supervise elections, stood by to fly to the Sultan's aid. The British Government ruled against intervention, and the Scots Guards flew instead to Aden, where they were due to be exercised, leaving the Sultan to the mercy of triumphant revolutionaries, who were breaking up everything Arab and Asian. The safety of the British community was in jeopardy, and the Staffords, standing by in place of the Scots Guards, flew a company to Mombasa, where they embarked in the frigate H.M.S. *Rhyll,* merely to wait, as it turned out. The Sultan made his escape by air, being admitted by President Nyerere to Tanganyika, thence to be transferred to that popular sanctuary for deposed monarchs, England. The danger to British life subsided.

The next call for help came from President Nyerere himself, and the first stutters of it reached Kenya in the early hours of January 20. The men of the 1st Tanganyika Rifles, quartered near the capital, Dar-es-Salaam, had risen against their British officers, had locked them up, seized the airport, and arrested the acting British High Commissioner as well. Again there was scurrying within 24 Brigade, and the remaining two companies of Gordons had to be diverted from journeying homewards to stand by at airport and in ship to move in with the Staffords. But the mutineers held the airport at Dar-es-Salaam, and they despatched from it the British officers and N.C.O.s both of the 1st and 2nd Battalions—some thirty from each—complete with families, sending them to Nairobi, where they arrived safely. A certain Eliza Kavana was proclaimed army commander in place of Brigadier Sholto Douglas. However, Nyerere retained control of government and bravely broadcast about the 'day of great disgrace to our nation' and formally made appeal to Britain for help.

It had already been decided at H.Q. Middle East Command at Aden, where Lieutenant-General Sir Charles Harington (who had been the last commander of 49 Brigade in Kenya), was C.-in-C., that it was a task for 45 Commando, who combined operational and reserve duties in Aden. Hastily embarked on the carrier H.M.S. *Centaur* with their comrades of 815 Naval Helicopter Squadron and some scout cars of the 16th/5th Lancers, they set sail at midnight on January 20 and on the 24th lay off Dar-es-Salaam. That evening a launch was sent to a secret rendezvous and came back with Brigadier Douglas, who had been in hiding. At first light on the 25th he accompanied Z Company in a helicopter lift to a football field next the mutineers' barracks, while a gunboat put down diversionary fire to a flank. With all weapons blazing, the commandos rushed and seized the barrack entrance. Douglas thereupon called for a surrender by loud hailer. He was answered by a burst of firing, to which the commandos retaliated by demolishing the front of the guard room with an anti-tank rocket. It produced a sad stream of askaris, emerging with hands up until no one remained inside the barrack buildings, except for three dead and six wounded. The helicopters meanwhile were completing the lift of the commando, so that the town could be dominated and the remnant of the mutineers rounded up. Since many had broken out of barracks, this latter task called for extensive searching.

The Scots Guards had returned to Kenya from Aden by January 22, and for twenty-four hours 24 Brigade was able to relax, with no one at shorter notice than four hours. Then at 6 p.m. on the 23rd a report arrived of trouble from another direction: there were mutinous stirrings in Uganda and the Prime Minister, Dr. Milton Obote, had asked Britain for aid. The Staffords, less two of their own companies and with Right Flank Company, 2nd Scots Guards, under command, were airborne by 9 p.m. and soon after 11 they began to arrive at Entebbe, where they were met by the army commander, Colonel J. M. A. Tillett, who now took the British troops under command.

The trouble was at Jinja, 70 miles away, where the 1st Uganda Rifles, with a large element of the embryo 2nd, were in the throes of agitated upheaval that had not yet erupted into violence against their officers or the large British community in the district. The men had been addressed on the 23rd by the Minister of Internal Affairs, Mr. Onama, and had given him rough treatment. They mounted their own guards on the armoury and shooed away the British staff, who assembled in the orderly room, whence the commanding officer kept in touch with Entebbe by telephone. It was agreed that the mutineers would have to be forcibly disarmed in the early hours of the 25th.

Leaving the Scots Guards company to hold the aerodrome at Entebbe, Lieutenant-Colonel Stuckey of the Staffords set off around midnight on the 24th with his men riding in an assortment of vans and buses acquired through contractors. He was met a few miles short of Jinja by two British company commanders of the Rifles who had broken out of camp. They advised a rush on wheels in place of the encirclement on foot Stuckey had planned. There had been rowdy and bombastic meetings in the camp, but all had been quiet since 12.30 a.m. The convoy sped on, its lights visible from the camp 5 miles away. At 4.45 the leading vehicles drove into the camp without evoking even a challenge. The guard room was entered and its occupants surprised, and at the same time a cordon was thrown round the camp. As dawn broke the mutineers found themselves surrounded by bayonets, each with a face behind it expressing the compelling stubbornness of Staffordshire. They gave in without a fight, and the troops were left with the task of removing a huge stock of weapons.

Kenya itself was by now astir. The first warning came immediately after the call from Uganda on the evening of the 23rd, and its sender was the British commanding officer of a battalion bearing its old K.A.R. number, the 11th Kenya Rifles, stationed at Lanet, near Nanyuki. It was 20 miles from Gilgil camp, and the 3rd R.H.A. were ordered to send a battery from there to the neighbourhood in readiness. Its men had a night of discomfort without summons. Next day a clandestine reconnaissance was made of the barracks and a plan made for swift response. This consisted of the entry of two gunner sergeants on a simulated social visit to British colleagues in the Kenya Rifles sergeants' mess; they took with them a radio set in link with D Battery, who, 75 men strong, moved to within 2 miles of the camp as darkness fell.

At 8.15 p.m. the signal for help was received from the sergeants' mess. The battery were in their vehicles for a debussing practice and reached the camp in under five minutes. They gained the guardroom and a party rushed off for the armoury, where all the weapons had been stored. This too they gained, only to find that it had been broken into. 280 weapons had in fact been removed, including ten bren guns. A vibrant crackle of bullets from the ammunition magazine 300 yards away showed that the mutineers were in deadly earnest. The horse gunners swiftly launched an infantry attack and captured the magazine, killing one of the mutineers as he ran off laden with ammunition and wounding another. But beyond was a concrete monsoon ditch, and from this the mutineers emitted a heavy volume of fire. The battery secured other objectives, such as the officers' mess and telephone exchange, while African officers made prolonged and brave attempts to persuade their men to give up.

At 9.30 p.m. Lieutenant-Colonel Victory of 3rd R.H.A. arrived with H.Q. and C Batteries and a few Sappers and Gordon Highlanders. He decided to contain the mutineers overnight and make a phased clearance of the camp in the morning; he was influenced by the presence in among the mutinous soldiers of their wives and children, casualties to whom could spread dire repercussions throughout Kenya. His clearance operation began well, men coming out of a barrack block, from which a few shots had been heard, in response to an appeal by loud hailer. There were shouts now from the main resistance centre and requests for a parley. A long verbal exchange took place, with the mood of the mutineers fluctuating like a cork on a choppy sea. They agreed at last to lay down their arms—provided they could do so supervised only by their own officers. After pondering this teasing proposition Victory agreed to give the African officers their chance and withdrew his men out of sight. He was nearly proved right, but not quite—for after seven-eighths of the men had with many delays handed their weapons over there was a sudden change of tide, a grab to regain possession, and shots of defiance from those still armed.

The gunners redeployed and, with fire from their scout cars, scotched an attempt by the mutineers to break out of camp. But the latter had captured the armoury and D Battery had to make another attack on it, led by two scout cars of the R.E. and covered by fire from a flanking barrack road. Vehicles and men went in at speed and caught the mutineers off guard, one of them having a bren kicked from his grasp as he fumbled with the mechanism. There were a few final shots, then silence as the gunners searched the barracks and chivvied downcast askaris into a cage by the armoury.

The whole of 24 Brigade was now committed, with the Scots Guards guarding places of importance in Nairobi; such Gordons as remained similarly employed in Mombasa; and even the Field Workshops performing infantry duties. 41 Commando flew out from England, arriving during the night of the 25th. Kenya simmered down, and on the 30th the 41st went on to Tanganyika to free the 45th and complete their task of rounding up fugitive mutineers.

It was a service that could be rendered only once. The rundown continued, and at the end of October 1964 Headquarters 24 Brigade left Kenya for Aden, leaving the Staffords to complete the withdrawal. The last rites were performed at Nairobi civil airport on December 10. C Company, 1st Staffords exchanged ceremonial compliments with a detachment of the 3rd Kenya Rifles, and Jomo Kenyatta, who was then President designate, paid tribute to the British soldier, thanking him in particular for his 'willing and valued cooperation' when the country was struck by flood and famine. These were rewarding words from a former enemy.

Swaziland still had its battalion of infantry, and in December 1965 the commitment was extended to Bechuanaland, whither the 1st Gloucestershire rushed a company over Christmas to guard the B.B.C. radio station against sparks set off by Rhodesia's defiant declaration of independence. The duty later provided pleasant diversion for a company of the 1st South Wales Borderers from anti-terrorist duty in Aden, until they left in August 1967, after Bechuanaland had become the Republic of Botswana. Swaziland too was nearing independence, and at the end of 1966 the 1st Royal Irish Fusiliers brought to a close the British Army's brief sojourn in the 'Jewel of Africa'.

The only part of Africa left with a British garrison was also the only territory won from the Axis powers exclusively by British arms, Libya. It was therefore of some sentimental value, and it was also of great practical value for training, drawing frequent visits by troops from Germany and Britain. Its strategic value was hampered by political restrictions, as had been revealed at the time of the Suez crisis, since when the main function of the garrison had been to safeguard the regime of King Idris, with whom the treaty of occupation had been signed in 1953. The troops had also given the country physical assistance, notably

in combating the plague of locusts, which almost brought disaster in
1955. The garrison was at its largest in 1958, when the United Arab
Republic threatened to expand northwards and westwards, and subsequently it was steadily reduced, until Benghazi was evacuated in
1967, leaving only a company from Gibraltar at Tobruk and a troop of
armour at the near-by R.A.F. station, El Adem, which as a staging post
dwindled in importance with the dwindling of commitments.

On September 1, 1969, the military turned and overthrew their King,
setting up the type of dictatorship that the British had in the past
striven to avert. The right of the revolutionaries to abrogate the treaty
was not disputed, and the process of evacuation was soon put in train.
A great quantity of stores was removed ahead of schedule, thwarting
Libyan hopes of some pickings, and on March 20, 1970, the last British
plane left El Adem, carrying a company of the 3rd Para, who had taken
over from B Squadron, 17th/21st Lancers. The final departure was made
from Tobruk, under R.A.F. command, on March 26. The Army's
representatives, a company of the 3rd Royal Regiment of Fusiliers, from
Gibraltar, quietly covered the withdrawal without fuss or incident.

It was the first time Britain had no permanent military foothold in
Africa since a garrison for the Cape of Good Hope was provided in 1806.
The soldiers had gone, but their influence is to be seen in the national
armies of many of the new states, and they themselves are still to be seen
from time to time. Some come for training in Kenya—a treat which
many enjoy—and others, not as a rule dressed as soldiers, come on tasks
of construction. Much had already been done in Kenya, such as a rescue
operation by Royal Engineers to save a ruptured pipeline deep in the
forest and thus restore Nairobi's water supply; an attempt by 16th
Air Despatch Company R.T.C. to seed clouds with salt for some much
needed rainwater; and the construction of many bridges for agricultural
purposes. Now as the last garrison in Africa withdrew, sappers were
prospecting for water on the Kenya–Somaliland border and rebuilding
a major bridge for the Emperor of Ethiopia. The British Army can claim
to have done much constructive work for Africa, and if that performed
by the sappers is the easiest to see, the foundations were laid by the
infantry.

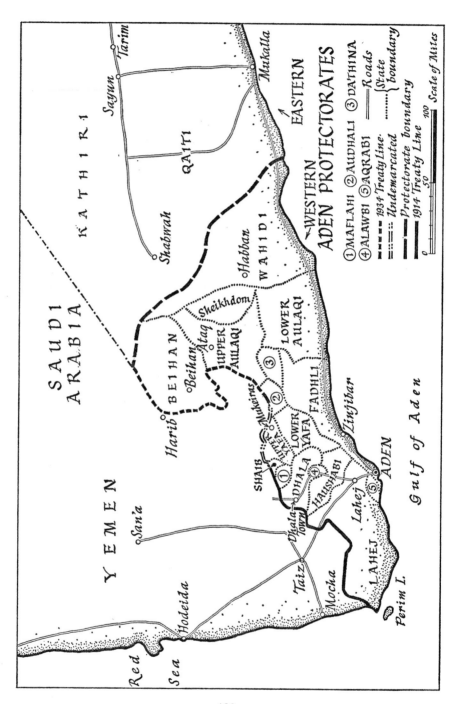

WESTERN
ADEN PROTECTORATES

①MAFLAHI ②AUDHALI ③DA'THINA
④ALAWBI ⑤AQRABI

Roads
State boundary
1934 Treaty Line
Undemarcated
Protectorate boundary
1914 Treaty Line

Scale of Miles
0   50   100

EASTERN

SAUDI ARABIA

K A T H I R I

QA'ITI

Tarim
Sayun
Mukalla

Shabwah

Habban

WAHIDI

Sheikhdom

LOWER AULAQI

Ataq
UPPER AULAQI

Beihan
BEIHAN
Harib

Mukeiras

FADHLI

③
②
UPPER YAFA
SHA'IB
LOWER YAFA
①
DHALA
④
HAUSHABI
⑤

Zinjibar

ADEN

YEMEN

San'a

Dhala Town

Taiz

Mocha

Hodeida

Red Sea

LAHEJ
Lahej

LAHEJ

Perim I.

Gulf of Aden

420

16

Aden

I—THE BORDER WAR (1955-58)

ADEN became British in January 1839. A Captain Haines of the Indian Marine effected the seizure of its glaring rocks, allegedly as retribution for the maltreatment of shipwrecked clients of an Indian line, in truth because a coaling station for the new steamers was wanted. Haines was aware that the 'little village' he found had once been one of the jewels of the Queen of Sheba, lying at the end of the Incense Way, the main trade route to the East, and that 'in the reign of Constantine this town possessed unrivalled celebrity for its impenetrable fortifications, its flourishing trade, and the glorious haven it offered to vessels from all quarters of the globe. How lamentable is the present contrast!' Yet he was not alone in coveting it. Mohammed Aly, Egypt's great imperialist ruler, was in process of subduing the Yemen and protested to Britain that Aden formed part of it. The claim could be muted for a time but never silenced.

The rocks are five miles wide and in their centre is a flat hollow formed by volcanic eruption, on which a town was to be built, named Crater. An isthmus, one mile wide, connects the rocks with the mainland, and five miles westwards there is a similar rocky promontory known as Little Aden. Possession was taken of a strip of mainland connecting the two to form what was eventually to become a Crown colony. Inland, claiming independence from the Yemen, were the sultanate of Lahej, of which Aden had been part, and a number of amirates and sheikhdoms lying hugger-mugger and usually a-snarl over the fertile coastal plain and over the jagged mountains that made imperialist expansion from the Yemen a near impossibility for Mohammed Aly's men. With tact and the minimum expense Britain made treaties with the rulers, bribing them with arms to keep the peace, and eventually they were formed into an enormous protectorate, split into

421

two divisions. Eighteen tribal territories around Aden were formed into the Western Aden Protectorate, covering 400 miles of coast and stretching less than 100 inland, except on the east side, and five much larger, better developed, and more distinguished territories formed the Eastern Aden Protectorate.

As Aden regained some of its lost importance, thanks to the ships that called for refuelling, the British Army had three times to repel invaders: Turks in 1901 and again in 1915, when they reached the very gates of Aden, and Yemenis in 1920, who had entered Dhala and put the Amir to flight. In 1928 the Trenchard scheme was implemented, and the army thankfully handed over what had been regarded as a punishment station to the Royal Air Force. A few light bombs, dropped after two warnings and inspections to ensure the absence of women and children, drained the ardour from the rebellious next time there was an incursion from the Yemen.

Regarded initially as an adjunct of India, Aden did not come under the Colonial Office until 1937, and only now was any attempt made to lift the protected territories out of the erosion of their medieval feudalism. The first essential was to instil a measure of law and order. A regular native force, the Aden Protectorate Levies, was therefore raised by the Air Officer Commanding, with R.A.F. officers in command. A gendarmerie, the Government Guard, was also formed, and great square forts were built for its detachments. Its men were government-paid and locally enlisted and were separate from—and often rivals of—the tribal guards, which were the private armies of the sultans and amirs. They too were subsidised out of government funds, but the money went no further and the R.A.F. had still to rely on their aeroplanes, and a few rough landing grounds, to control the country.

While the inhabitants of the Protectorate were wild and rugged, those of Aden were regarded as the most docile of the whole Empire. However, trade brought in many immigrants, Arab, Asian, Jewish and European, and in December 1947 Aden suddenly showed itself as capable of eruption as any other part of combustible Arabia. Violence was sparked off by fear of the Jews, following their advance towards nationhood in Palestine. No less than 122 people were killed—76 of them Jews—in four days of assault, arson and looting. Two squadrons of the Levies, with a British Army officer in command, intervened pluckily but with marked partiality towards their compatriots, and order was not finally restored until naval parties had been landed from two destroyers and a detachment of the 2nd North Staffordshire brought in from Egypt. Calm returned and the R.A.F. reassumed full responsibility as military guardians of colony and protectorate.

In the torrid hinterland belligerence between tribes and factions had for centuries been endemic but its practitioners had not been taken very seriously by the British authorities and those who opposed the Pax Britannica went by the milk-sop name of dissidents, much as if their opposition was confined to verbal protest. As the British were pushed into retreat at Abadan and in Egypt, the dissidents became more daring, egged on by the Iman of the Yemen, and eventually they refused to submit to the Trenchard treatment of air control. They showed their defiance in the sultanate of Upper Aulaqi, 170 miles north-east of Aden, where a fort was besieged at Robat, and instead of sitting in the mountains waiting to be warned and bombed, the besiegers lay up by the supply route, where they were safe from bombing, and inflicted heavy loss on the Levies who escorted the convoys. The climax came on June 15, 1955, when two R.A.F. officers, one of them a wing commander, were killed in an ambush near the fort. The Levies lost eleven killed in all and suffered even heavier loss to their morale. Again an appeal for help was made to the Army.

Egypt, from which the evacuation was in midstream, was the natural source, and the 1st Seaforth Highlanders were selected for despatch, in company with a squadron of the Life Guards and a troop of Royal Engineers. Command was assigned to Brigadier J. A. R. Robertson, who was removed with a skeleton headquarters from 51 Brigade—just as was to happen two years later when there was trouble in Oman (as already described on page 354). He was a Gurkha with plenty of experience of frontier warfare in Waziristan, and his choice indicates the awareness at Middle East Command that the terrain and situation were very similar.

The troops arrived by air on the first days of July, and the main body of the Seaforth, with some fresh Levy squadrons, were flown on to Ataq, where the R.A.F. had constructed one of nine airfields in the protectorate. Unfortunately it could not receive Hastings aircraft, and the Life Guards had therefore to take their Ferret scout cars, which had extra armour hastily fitted to keep out high angle fire, overland. Twenty three-ton lorries went with them, and it proved a nightmare introduction to the heritage of air control, an absence of roads. To avoid the troubled district the convoy took a route that started along the coast and was 345 miles long, with encumbrances varying from sea water, soft sand, volcanic rock, and boulders along the narrow troughs of wadis. Having left Aden just before midnight on the Sunday, July 3, they reached Ataq after dark on the Thursday, July 7, to find that the only difficulty the Highlanders had as yet encountered was to gain a place at the well in competition with women and goats. Two scout cars and seven three-tonners had been left behind stranded. Their drivers and escorts were consigned to the care of tribal guards, and one pair were set upon by Bedouin. An R.A.F. Regiment driver was badly wounded and his Seaforth companion killed, presumably for the £120 that each of their rifles could fetch.

Robat is some 40 miles south-east of Ataq, and on July 9 the Seaforth made a toilsome advance towards it, picquetting the heights as they progressed, until securing a base 7 miles short of it. Next morning Lincoln bombers plastered the entrance to the jagged defile ahead. The Life Guards and Levies then probed warily forward, passed the burnt-out vehicles that gave testimony to the Levies' recent tragedy, and relieved the Government Guards in the fort. One burst of fire had been enough to scatter the only apparent opposition. More shots were subsequently fired at fleeting forms on the hilltops, and a few were received in exchange. Such was apt to be the pattern when it was open to the enemy either to resist or melt away.

On July 23 the Seaforth with squadrons of the R.A.F. Regiment and Levies under command, were required to open up another rebel-dominated route, running along a track from Lodar to Mafidh, south of Ataq. They twice came under fire, at about 5 p.m. on the 23rd and 24th, losing one killed and two wounded. On each occasion the opposition evaporated once the Seaforth brought their mortars and machine-guns into action and toiled upwards to the troublesome peaks. The old Frontier rules still applied: it was a case of spilling a pint of sweat to save an ounce of blood.

Certainly it was an exhilarating experience to reach the peaks, to breathe the raw mountain air, which was in such contrast with the prickly humidity of Aden itself, and to gaze around on the rugged grandeur of a land as harsh and untamable as its inhabitants. For the Seaforth there was the added thrill of being first there, which more than compensated for the discomfort that went with it, such as living in two-men bivouacs with scorpions as tormentors. They marvelled and were marvelled at, and inquisitiveness rapidly turned to friendship, particularly with their woad-painted, half-clad colleagues of the tribal guards and with hawk-faced sheikhs proud of their Mausers or more ancient firing pieces but eager to explore the possibilities of enlarging their armouries from British sources. The biggest treat, for a large party of officers and men, was a visit at the Sharif's invitation to Beihan, the most northerly territory of the Protectorate, jutting into the Yemen. An exuberant volley greeted the British soldiers, fired indiscriminately by the great crowd come to welcome them, and there was then the ceremonial slaying of a calf, a great feast eaten barefoot seated on cushions, and a performance by dancing girls, which was accompanied by jangling from the chains of manacled prisoners who had been brought along apparently for a sort of bon-bon before punishment. The Seaforth, by way of a counterattack, then produced their pipers.

Aggressive stirrings from the Yemen were meanwhile beginning to be felt further westwards, and no sooner had Brigadier Robertson and his soldiers departed in October than others came in to replace them, with the main function of bolstering the four battalions of the Aden Protectorate Levies the R.A.F. had raised. The infantry rôle was undertaken initially by troops from Kenya, where the situation was improving, first by the 1st King's Own Yorkshire Light Infantry and from April 1956 the 1st Gloucestershire. Both had their headquarters at Aden and maintained detachments either at Mukeiras or Dhala. From Malaya the 15th/19th Hussars sent a squadron of scout cars permanently on detachment for escort duty, and an army headquarters, under a brigadier, was set up as a permanent adjunct of the A.O.C.'s headquarters by Steamer Point, where two old guns stood as a reminder that the army had been in occupation before. For the time being the R.A.F. Regiment remained in control of the Levies, jealous guardian of the child it had reared. The soldiers for their part gazed with some jealousy on the splendid accommodation the R.A.F. occupied alongside Khormaksar aerodrome, next to which a camp had been built for the army on the swampy isthmus just below the rocks of Aden.

The first battalion to stay in Aden for more than a few months was the 1st Queen's Own Cameron Highlanders, who arrived from Korea in September 1956 and replaced the Gloucesters, who had been drawn to the Persian Gulf. On November 5 the 1st Durham Light Infantry were rushed out to join them, flying from England via West and East Africa, in order to preserve the peace during the Suez crisis. Their presence, as it turned out, was not required in Aden, but just before their return home in February they had a lively time in Beihan helping the Levies to keep a pass open close to the Yemeni border.

Around Dhala there was even more activity. Since December the Camerons had had a company in residence there alongside the company garrison of Levies. It lay at the end of the famous Incense Way, the route built for camel caravans that was to become familiar to British soldiers. From Aden it ran, without too many bumps, over the plain through Lahaj and then through the foothills of the mountain range before plunging into the valley in which Thumier lay. This was an important Government Guard garrison station, lying in the midst of the territory of the Quteibi tribe, whose members had a long and proud history of brigandage. Apart from a few improvements made by sappers after the First World War, the road was in the same state as in the days before the birth of Mohammed, and in the ascent from Thumier to the plateau on which Dhala stands lorries had to crawl round hairpin bends designed for the manoeuvring capacity of a camel. The dust-coated soldiers inside them seemed to be in permanent suspension over the cliff's edge, and as if to remind them that there were other dangers the bren-gunner sat hunched over the cab, ever on the look-out, and the machine-guns in the scout cars weaved to and fro, sniffing for bandits. It was a journey of 83 miles from Aden and needed to be spread over two days, with the night spent deployed in hedgehog formation.

Dhala itself consisted of a few houses that had been hand-hewn out of the rock, all looking like prisons, the Amir's palace included. Beyond there is a great escarpment rising to the Jihafi massif, which is some 3,000 feet above the town and over 7,000 above sea level and was adjacent to the frontier. It was on this plateau that the Camerons came into action in support of the Levies in late January 1957. Coincidental with a claim to the United Nations for the possession of Aden, Yemeni soldiers crossed the border and opened fire on guard posts, the Amir's palace and the airfield, even bringing a few shells down. The Levies' company from Aden drove them back after a night move to Sanah, but needed help in clearing them from a ridge by the border. B Company of the Camerons were therefore summoned, and having brought mortars and machine-guns into position, they made a dawn attack with all weapons blazing. The Yemenis fired back without scoring a hit and withdrew to positions on the border, and the Camerons likewise were pulled back.

No sooner had the situation quietened on the Jihafi than a routine patrol of the Camerons met trouble south of Dhala. The men were emerging from a defile well spaced in single file, with the company commander, Major Grant, studying his map at their head. Suddenly there was a crackle of fire from a hill to their right and almost every man of the leading section was hit. Grant had his binoculars smashed and his chest lacerated, the corporal and a private were dead, and four others wounded. An attack was speedily mounted, and the Camerons soon gained the hill—without finding trace of any enemy upon it.

A series of sweeps, with reinforcements participating, restored the Dhala area to a state of outward calm, and during the remainder of their long, eighteen months' tour the Camerons had little trouble, either in the Protectorate or in Aden itself, apart from receiving the occasional pot shot in convoy. But there were signs of trouble brewing, particularly in and around Aden itself, where Nasser's agents were busy converting Britain's humiliation over the Suez affair to hatred and defiance. There was plenty of good material for subversion here, since Aden's prosperity had produced a great influx of workers, mostly Yemenis, whose favourite pastime was striking. Approaching 200,000, the Colony's polyglot population had doubled itself since the war and was still on the rampage.

The 1st Buffs, who relieved the Camerons in March 1958, were kept busy at both ends of their territory. Their first task was to make a swoop on the town of Lahej, from which three advisers of the absentee Sultan, the Jifri brothers, were exercising such a subversive influence that it had been decided to use strong-arm tactics to protect Lahej from the Egyptian embrace. The Buffs arrived unheralded before dawn on April 18, surrounded the barracks without opposition from the Sultan's little army, and enabled one of the brothers to be arrested, the others having fled to Cairo. A flag march on wheels, traditional remedy for political malaise, was then conducted along the camel tracks and dried river beds of the sultanate.

A general strike in Aden, the Queen's Birthday parade, and another invasion of Dhala had also to be attended to, and to aid the Buffs the 1st King's Shropshire Light Infantry (less two companies) were flown in from Kenya, and the 1st York and Lancaster were brought from England for a more permanent share of duties. Crisis had been fomenting at Dhala since April 19, when the resident political officer, Mr. Fitzroy Somerset, visited a Government Guard fortress at As Sarir, on the Jihafi plateau, and was there encircled and besieged by Yemenis and rebellious tribesmen. Three times the resident company of Levies attempted to relieve him, but each time—probably through no fault of the men—they failed to overpower the fire they encountered and returned to camp. The Levies had, in 1957, been transferred from R.A.F. control to that of the Army!

The Levies' company was replaced by another and the K.S.L.I. moved in to camp beside the Buffs' resident company, while the papers in Britain made the most of a situation that seemed to have sprung from the adventurous, far distant days of the Bengal Lancer and the North-West Frontier. A coordinated attack, under K.S.L.I. command, was made on April 30, Somerset's twelfth day of siege. C Company of the K.S.L.I. opened proceedings with a diversionary movement through Dhala itself, whence they aimed a left hook towards As Sarir with support from the 13th/18th Hussars, who had taken over the armoured car rôle. For political reasons, 3 Company, 1st Levies had to have the major rôle, and they headed for a goat track up the Jihafi escarpment, taking the direct route due westwards from the airfield. A Company, 1st Buffs, followed these lean, turbaned men, and ahead of them fell bombs from Shackletons and 75-mm. shells from a section of a troop that had for over a year been provided by the 33rd Parachute Field Regiment. There were roars, shudders and raucous cracks, then silence as the Levies began their climb.

The enemy had not been frightened away, and with their opening fusillade they caught the Buffs in the open and hit four of them, one mortally. This was the start of a very hard fight for the summit, of which the Levies, under Major Boucher-Myers, of the East Lancashire, nobly bore the brunt. The mere climb of nearly 2,000 feet up a slippery precipitous track called for feat enough in the broiling heat. The Levies climbed fighting, driving back riflemen in khaki drill and galabiyas with aid from some accurate strikes by Venom fighters, and within four hours they had gained a foothold at the top of the pass, for a loss of some seven casualties. A platoon of Buffs, who had been more heavily laden, then captured one further pimple and at length silenced the fire from a ridge beyond, enabling air-dropped supplies to be retrieved and the advance to be continued. As Sarir was a further two miles on, and Boucher-Myers reached the fort just as night was falling, and just after the guard of honour detailed to greet him had been stood down in despair of his coming. He won the D.S.O.

Some punitive bombing of the barracks at Kataba, just inside the Yemen, and a series of searches restored Dhala to its normal state of suppressed belligerence, enabling the K.S.L.I. to return to Kenya. But near the end of May the Yemenis turned their attention to Mukeiras, and the York and Lancasters sent a company to reinforce the Levies there and to take permanent residence at this oasis perch, 7,000 feet up, which in default of any road communication had an airfield attainable by Beverleys and was to be the most popular station in the whole of Arabia. After a number of minor forays, the Yemenis were very hard smitten by the 75-mm. guns of the para troop, combined with machine-guns and mortars, in an operation staged by the York and Lancaster company.

Another commitment that fell to the York and Lancasters was to police Lahej following the desertion of most of its army and the consequent banishment of the Sultan. This again raised the need for a third battalion, and after the 1st Royal Lincolnshire had temporarily filled the gap during their return journey from Malaya, the 1st Prince of Wales's Own Regiment of Yorkshire arrived from England in September on their first voyage as such. One of their first tasks was to escort homewards a host of Yemenis sentenced to deporation after some violent rioting in Crater, which the Buffs helped the police to quell. Again the cauldron simmered down.

II—THE MESHES OF THE WEB (1958-63)

For the next five years there was comparative quiet, at least from the viewpoint of the British Army. With the departure of the York and Lancasters in December 1958 the garrison was reduced to two battalions. The Buffs were subsequently relieved by the 1st Northamptonshire; and the Prince of Wales's Own—after delivering a smarting blow to the Yemenis at Mukeiras—likewise by the 1st Royal Warwickshire. There was further reduction of a sort when the latter went on to Hong Kong at the end of April 1960, for their relieving unit, 45 Commando, had commitments as a strategic reserve, although keeping a company at Dhala. They were based on Little Aden, where the B.P. Oil Company made air-conditioned accommodation available and, unlike Army units, they stayed there for an indefinite period by exchanging individuals with units at home, in the manner of the old Cardwell System. The garrison battalion, which kept a company at Mukeiras, occupied quarters by Khormaksar, known as Waterloo Lines, which were becoming quite comfortable. The rôle was undertaken by the 1st Royal Highland Fusiliers through most of 1960, thereafter by the 1st Queen's Royal Surreys until February 1962, and by the 1st King's Own Scottish Borderers from then until February 1964. The lengthening tour is an indication of the greater stability and comfort; and indeed Aden was now a family station for the infantry. Although internal security was the main preoccupation, imposing aggravating restrictions on training, there were few calls to arms, and even in the rioting that greeted anti-strike legislation, the Royal Highland Fusiliers had to do no more than display themselves and make crafty manoeuvres to double their apparent number.

The building of a road to Mukeiras was an exacting commitment for the Royal Engineers, keeping a troop fully occupied through most of 1959 and 1960. The tribesmen showed their hostility at first, killing a sapper and wounding another in an ambush in the autumn of 1959, but the project gained increasing favour as its commercial advantages became apparent, and there was as much rejoicing in native as in military circles when it was completed near the close of 1960.

A squadron of armoured cars and a battery of field artillery were also kept busy and alert in support of the Levies, of whom three battalions were deployed upcountry and a fourth in reserve at Little Aden. The battery was initially provided by the 14th Field and from 1960 by the 3rd R.H.A., based on Kenya, and the Life Guards, Royals, 11th

Hussars, Queen's Royal Irish Hussars, 9th/12th Royal Lancers and
4th R.T.R. were consecutively to be seen patrolling the hinterland in
their armoured cars between 1958 and the end of 1963. The Queen's
Own Hussars, 17th/21st Lancers, Carabiniers and Royal Scots Greys
made use of the excellent facilities for tank training while standing by on
strategic reserve duties, with other members of their regiments at
Bahrain, Hong Kong, or waiting in readiness at sea.

The British Government were meanwhile wrestling with the teasing
political and strategic problems Aden posed, and in the process they
weaved a web from which there was to be no release except by brazen
flight. The first manifestation of their political plans came on February
11, 1959, when with much ceremony six states of the Western Protectorate were merged, at their own wish, into what was later to be called
the Federation of Southern Arabia. Four more, including Lahej, joined
during the year that followed. Federation of course gave the states
greater security, when added to the continued guarantee of British
protection, and its benefits were to be seen in Malaya, although there
was the difference that the states there had the wealth and sophistication
to stand on their own feet. Both the Imam of the Yemen and President
Nasser were virulent in their opposition to the Federation from the start,
and the aggressive gestures from the Yemen had undoubtedly been
launched with the object of disrupting it in embryo.

Aden itself was gradually dragged towards the Federation despite
fierce opposition within the colony, both on political and economic
grounds, against union with these scions of feudalism and poverty. The
opposition became much fiercer in September 1962, when following the
death of the tyrannical Imam of the Yemen, General Sallal seized power
from his son, declaring a republic, and Egyptian troops were rushed to
his support. They did not have much success in subduing the royalist
remnant, but did much to inflame the nationalist passion in Aden and to
harden the issue as between the advance of pan-Arab republicanism and
the archaic rule of Britain's protégés, the sultans and amirs. The British
Government came firmly down on the side of their protégés, hoping to
lead them to more liberal ways. Recognition of the Yemeni Republic was
withheld, and on January 18, 1963, Aden was drawn, kicking, into the
Federation, on a vote passed by the Legislative Council on the day
before Sallal's coup. Once in the Federation, there was no way out
except by force.

As a further stimulant to their opponents, the Government were
forced to place increasing reliance on Aden for strategic purposes,
largely because there was so much hostile air space between Cyprus and
the Persian Gulf. The first development was the conversion of the Air

Headquarters, whose sphere had always stretched far beyond the Protectorate, into the integrated all-service Headquarters British Forces Arabian Peninsula; it was the first of its kind and was opened by the C.I.G.S., Field Marshal Templer, on April 1, 1958. It rapidly expanded and on March 1, 1961, was converted into no less than the Middle East Command. This in fact involved little more than the extension of its dominion down the east part of Africa as far as Swaziland. An airman, Air Marshal Sir Charles Elworthy, remained C.-in-C., with a major-general commanding land forces.

Militarily, the sense of this arrangement was demonstrated by the speed with which a force was landed in Kuwait in July 1961. But experience in Palestine, Egypt and Cyprus had shown that nothing inflamed the anger of nationalists more than to see their country used for the military designs of an 'imperialist', and the Middle East Command had long enjoyed the dubious prestige of being their favourite Aunt Sally; a command by any other name would smell, not as sweet, but perhaps less acrid. Inevitably the requirements for base facilities grew, as for the commando, tank squadron, and all their ancillaries brought there for strategic purposes. The infantry reserve was based on Kenya, but with his 'wind of change' speech in February 1960 Mr. Macmillan as good as gave notice that a new home would soon have to be found for it. Short of keeping its three battalions on a desert island or aboard carriers, Aden was the only place left for them, and to Aden they were in due course consigned, as if on the assumption that this part was immune from the wind of change. Thus what had originally been no more than a strategic staging post acquired the added functions of command centre and base. There was dire political peril in such overloading.

The Levies meanwhile were being forged as the main shield against it. Since November 1961 they had been placed under the operational control of the Federation and renamed the Federal Regular Army— which of course was abbreviated to F.R.A. They showed themselves well able to keep the peace on the border and in the hinterland, par-ticularly with the continued support of their British armoured cars and gunners, the latter of whom put their 105-mm. howitzers, each portable in a modified Land Rover, to chastening use against errant tribesmen. The R.A.F. also continued to provide effective support, and in August 1963 they introduced a new element into mountain fighting by the provision of two Belvedere helicopters for an operation by the 1st F.R.A. against a murderous group of tribesmen near Ataq. The result was that five prisoners were netted, almost a unique occurrence. Meantime Arab officers were beginning to replace British ones, until by 1965 they would hold command even of the battalions.

It was, however, quite impossible for the F.R.A. and their colleagues of the National (formerly Government) Guard to seal the indefinite Yemeni frontier, and ever since the Egyptians had had access to the other side of it a steady stream of arms, ammunition, and mines came trickling through to those areas where nothing much prospered except brigandage. Training courses were held in the Yemen, and just to make sure that the weapons were put to the use required by the Egyptians and their Russian mentors one hostage was retained, so it was said, for every ten rifles issued. In Aden itself—which was now officially a State (as opposed to a colony), self-governing in internal matters outside the realm of security—the Yemeni population had risen to 80,000, over a third of the whole, and it was easy enough to issue them with explosives with which to add sting to the verbal offensive that was storming unchecked across Southern Arabia, in wave after monotonous wave, from Cairo radio.

Being unmarked and in many places undecided, the Yemeni border was of course open to flux from either direction, and in June 1963 a party of servicemen and servicewomen, on an adventure training expedition from Command Headquarters, flowed disastrously off course, with the result that they were fired upon by soldiers, losing four killed, two wounded, and twenty-one captured, out of fifty-five in all. The Egyptians made the most of the capture, blaring humiliation upon the British through their radio, and ten days elapsed before they would let the captives free, in response to pressure which the Foreign Office was obliged to exert vicariously, having no representative at the court of the Yemen Republic.

This no doubt further emboldened hostile tribesmen, of whom the most menacing were the Quteibi, the inhabitants of the mountain fastnesses known as Radfan, from which they had for centuries preyed upon travellers along the Dhala road. They became increasingly aggressive as 1963 progressed, causing much tribulation with the mines they laid not only on the road itself but on tracks used by Federal forces for routine reliefs. Their territory was their own wild, unknown domain, inaccessible by wheeled vehicle, and from reports of political officers and military intelligence officers it was estimated that it contained over 6,000 armed men. It was bad for the morale of the Federal men to have this great prickly hedgehog in their midst, and an agricultural case could also be made for taming it, for fertile soil lay among the mountains, awaiting access from the Dhala road for development. The Federal Government were eager enough to launch an operation, but they required the support of the British, and in London there was understandable dread of involvement in any venture that might swell the cry of the anti-imperialist pack. However, the British had brought the Federation into being. . . .

The final goad was provided by a grenade that was tossed towards the High Commissioner of the Federation, Sir Kennedy Trevaskis, and a group of his ministers, who were about to embark for London at Aden civil airport on December 10, 1963. Trevaskis was saved by his aide, George Henderson, who himself died of wounds and was one of fifty-five casualties. The Federal Government declared a state of emergency, and the British Government gave their support to the occupation of Radfan.

III—THE RADFAN WAR (1964)

It was the first time the Federal Regular Army had concentrated at brigade strength. The 2nd, 3rd, and 4th Battalions were all engaged, leaving only the 1st to garrison the rest of the Federation and at the same time shed a cadre for the raising of the 5th. They had a troop of Centurion tanks in support, provided by the 16th/5th Queen's Royal Lancers, a battery of 105-mm. guns of the 3rd R.H.A., and a troop of the 12th Field Squadron, R.E.; the R.A.F. made available Hunter fighters, Shackleton bombers, and two of their four Belvedere helicopters, and the Royal Navy provided six Wessex helicopters. The aim was 'to carry out a demonstration in force' and without knowing much about the rebel strongholds Brigadier J. D. Lunt, commanding the F.R.A., made his main objective the Bakri Ridge, about 8 miles east of the Dhala road at Thumier.

The operation began on January 4, 1964, with the dropping of a picquetting party by a Belvedere and some hits on the Belvedere bringing the next. This led to the abrupt withdrawal of all helicopters and an argument about risk, which was finally settled in favour of the F.R.A. on the grounds that the operation must go on, with the qualification that risk must be kept to the minimum not only to preserve precious men and machines but to deny Cairo radio food that could be richly spiced. Thus were the guide lines for this operation and its successors belatedly established, and in the meantime further picquets had climbed their hilltops, where they were engaged and outnumbered by groups of tribesmen as well armed as they. (The F.R.A. did not have the self-loading rifle or the general purpose machine-gun.) Two of three picquets were forced into retreat.

The F.R.A. redeemed this inauspicious start. By a series of determined, methodical advances they gained the Bakri Ridge in the course of fourteen days, and by January 31 the sappers had built a road to the

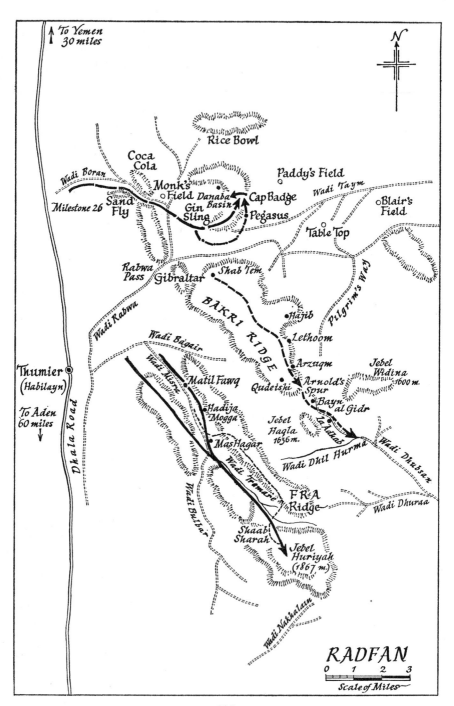

To Yemen
30 miles

N

Rice Bowl

Coca
Cola

Paddy's Field

Wadi Boran

Monk's
Field *Danaba* **Cap Badge**
Basin

Wadi Taym

Blair's
Field

Milestone 26
Sand
Fly
Gin
Sling
Pegasus

Table Top

Rabwa
Pass
Gibraltar
Shab Tem

Wadi Rabwa

BAKRI RIDGE

Pilgrim's Way

Hajib

Lethoom

Wadi Bagair

Wadi Misra

Arzuqm

Jebel
Widina
1600 m.

Thumier
(Habilayn)

Matil Fawq

Qudeishi

Arnold's
Spur

Dhala Road

To Aden
60 miles

Hadija
Mogga

Bayn
al Gidr

Jebel
Haqla
1636 m.

Mas Hagar

Wadi Trmase

La Adlas

Wadi Dhil Hurma

Wadi Dhubsar

Wadi Butbar

F·R·A
Ridge

Wadi Dhuraa

Shaabi
Sharah

Jebel
Huriyah
(1867 m.)

Wadi Nakhalain

RADFAN

0   1   2   3

Scale of Miles

434

ridge up the Wadi Rabwa, making the first insolent blemish across a country of stark unbridled magnificence. The advance was now continued to bring the fertile Danaba Basin and Wadi Taym under military control. This was achieved without difficulty. The F.R.A. had subdued most of Radfan at a cost of only five killed and twelve wounded.

The 1st F.R.A. meanwhile were becoming grievously overstrained in trying to keep the rest of the Federation peaceful. It became essential to free the other battalions, who had admirably achieved their allotted task of staging a demonstration. They were therefore withdrawn from Radfan.

The withdrawal was converted by Cairo radio into a humiliating defeat and the tribesmen resumed their offensive with greater gusto and greater weight of fire than ever before. The Yemenis even chimed in with a couple of air raids, to which the R.A.F. retaliated, in response to a plea from the Federal Government, drawing shrill charges of aggression that reached the Security Council. It was reported now that Egyptian-trained commandos were operating in Radfan, and certainly more and more tribesmen were defecting to their side. The Federal Government appealed to the British for the direct military aid to which they were entitled under treaty obligations, and the British were bound to comply, aware though they were of the dire political peril. The meshes of the web were beginning to cling.

Militarily the request was almost as embarrassing as politically. In its final months before conversion to the Army Department on April 1, 1964, the War Office had disposed of its home-based reserve, the 51st Brigade, to Borneo, after the 1/6th Gurkhas had visited Aden for some training; it had committed most of the 3rd Division to war prevention in Cyprus; it had seen the Middle East reserve, the 24th Brigade, tied to the defence of the new African states; and it had been compelled to remove the 5th Brigade from Rhine Army to form a stopgap reserve. All that could be spared for the Middle East—whose C.-in-C. was now a soldier, Lieutenant-General Sir Charles Harington—was A Squadron, 22 S.A.S., who flew off at once with their usual ready-for-anything verve, and the 1st King's Own Scottish Borderers, who were ordered back to Aden only three months after being relieved by the 1st/1st East Anglian (Royal Norfolk and Suffolk).

In the absence of 24 Brigade, a scratch force had to be formed under command of the newly installed Aden Garrison commander, Brigadier R. L. Hargroves, who thus had rapidly to switch his thoughts from town to country and scrounge officers and men for an improvised shoe-string headquarters. He had 45 Commando, recently returned from Tanganyika, available for a spearhead role, coupled with B Company,

3rd Parachute Regiment, sent down from Bahrain. He was also allotted the 1st and 2nd F.R.A., both depleted by the demands of the 5th; D Squadron, 4th R.T.R. (armoured cars); J Battery, 3rd R.H.A.; 2 Troop, 12th Field Squadron; and 653 Squadron, Army Air Corps. Although heavily committed in Aden until the arrival of the K.O.S.B., the East Anglians were required to provide a company for the organisation and defence of a base at Thumier.

Hargroves' aim, as defined by the G.O.C. Land Forces Middle East, Major-General J. H. Cubbon, was simply 'to end the operations of dissidents' in a defined area, and a political directive gave him guidance on the pressure that could, and could not, be exerted to make them desist. It was left to him to decide on his objectives, and he chose two towering features north of Bakri Ridge, from which the camel route to the Yemen and two fertile belts could be dominated. One was christened Cap Badge, the other (more northerly) Rice Bowl. No one knew how strongly they were held, and as a bitter taste of the capabilities of the rebels, Hargroves saw the Brigade Major and D.A.A. & Q.M.G. of the F.R.A. blown to their death in a Land Rover just ahead of him when helping him with his reconnaissance. This was on April 25.

The plan suffered restriction from the medical insistence that each soldier must be provided with two gallons of water a day—for the heat was approaching the intense period and memories of Kuwait were still fresh in mind. This tied the pitifully few Belvedere helicopters to a supply rôle, and the idea of using them for a swift assault was abandoned. None the less it was decided that both Rice Bowl and Cap Badge should be captured by a sudden sally during the night April 30/May 1, the former after a march of 7 miles by the commandos, the latter after a parachute descent by the paras.

The opening move was made by an officer and nine men of the S.A.S. who had only just arrived from England. Their task was to mark a dropping zone for the paratroops at the foot of Cap Badge, and to start them on their journey they were deposited in rebel-held territory by Scout helicopters of the A.A.C. under cover of artillery fire. This was successfully done as light was fading on April 29, and the men spent the night on the march towards the dropping zone.

Next morning a platoon of East Anglians headed up the Wadi Rabwa north-eastwards from Thumier, supported by three armoured car troops of the 4th R.T.R. and the battery of field guns. This move was intended partly as a diversion, partly as a means of getting the guns into position to support the main attack. The force reached their objective in the afternoon, after having to remove a newly constructed barrier of rocks under accurate fire, which wounded six men, the platoon commander among them, before being silenced by the 76-mm. guns on the Saladins and the 105s of the R.H.A. Desultory sniping continued.

Meanwhile the S.A.S. party had been detected as they lay in a sangar awaiting the return of darkness. The rebels quickly gathered all round them, and a desperate battle ensued, in which Hunter fighters zoomed in with their cannon, the pilots speaking directly to the officer on the ground by a combined wireless-telephone-wireless link through S.A.S. H.Q. and air control at Thumier. The rebels persisted, despite heavy casualties, and as evening approached it became clear that there could be no hope of the party reaching the intended dropping zone, even if they could survive the enveloping attack. Another lot set out in a pair of Scout helicopters, but the air was thick with bullets, forcing their return, holed and torn. From B Company 3rd Para, assembled in their 'chalks' at Khormaksar aerodrome, came the offer to descend with DZ unmarked. It was vetoed by the G.O.C. and instead the paras were piled into lorries and rushed off on the 60-mile journey to Thumier. They arrived at 2 a.m., thence to plan an overland assault on Cap Badge.

Instead of going as far as Rice Bowl, 45 Commando were ordered to consolidate on two sharp intermediary features, named Coca Cola and Sand Fly, some 3 miles west of Cap Badge. They had since nightfall been marching from the west, each man with three water bottles from which he took periodic sips. It was a difficult approach from this direction, and as the companies clambered along in single file they could feel the sweat on their backs and the cool of night on their cheeks. As had happened at Nizwa in 1958 they found the enemy had retired for a night's rest in a village, yet even so prospects of reaching Rice Bowl before dawn were receding when around midnight the leading companies received the orders changing the plan. Z Company had in any case planned to occupy Sand Fly and were soon on it. X had to scale an unreconnoitred precipice to reach the top of Coca Cola. Being an expert mountaineer, the company commander made the climb, fixed a rope to a bush, and one by one the men heaved themselves up. It was a nasty surprise for the rebels to find themselves fired at from these features next morning, but they might have had a worse one.

As for the S.A.S. marking party, seven returned through the East Anglians' lines soon after daybreak, having broken from their besiegers' clutch in darkness. There had been no contact with them since their radio operator had been killed before nightfall, and they had also lost their commander, Captain Edwards of the Somerset and Cornwall Light Infantry, killed soon after ordering the break-out. The headless bodies of these two men were later to be found buried, after a Yemeni broadcast had announced that the heads were displayed on stakes in the Yemen, a fact reported publicly by the G.O.C. Land Forces, denied by the American representative in the Yemen, and consequently the cause of unwarranted criticism of the G.O.C. in the Commons.

The next two days were spent in bringing up the remainder of the East Anglians, who had now been relieved in Aden by the K.O.S.B., and in the remaking of the track up the Wadi Rabwa so that the guns could be brought further forward. After dark on May 3, 45 Commando handed their positions over to the East Anglians and set off for the great towering slab named Cap Badge, while B Company 3 Para, under their command, began a right flanking movement to climb the jebel from the east. By another marvellous feat of climbing the commandos reached the summit by daybreak, again without meeting opposition. The paras were less lucky. They were impeded by unsuspected obstacles and by the need to evade rebel parties heard in the night, and consequently were caught with the far-stretching sandy mass of the jebel glaring down at them when dawn broke. Fire was opened at them from some blocks of brick that constituted a village on the lower slopes, later to be christened Pegasus. The paras attacked at once, with their company commander, Major Walter, at their head, and drove the enemy out. Then a counter-attack came in from behind them, only to be scotched by the rear platoon at fearful cost to the rebels.

Sensibly, the rebels reverted now to their traditional tactic of sniping, using well concealed positions overlooking the paras, and since the slope was too steep for either the commandos on the summit or the guns to bring fire down on them, they had considerable success, killing an officer and a private and wounding six others. The paras' predicament was eased to a certain extent by some skilful air strikes and by a daring resupply fly-in by two A.A.C. Beavers. Then the reserve company of 45 Commando were lifted to the top of Cap Badge by helicopter, and from there they began to descend the slope, subjecting the rebels to the overhead treatment with a much heavier volume of fire than they were capable of. Predictably they melted away, bringing an end to what for every paratrooper except Walter and his C.S.M. had been a hectic baptism of fire.

Aircraft now dropped leaflets telling the tribes to go, the area having been proscribed by decree. Patrols found all dwelling places deserted, except by flies. The East Anglians moved into the flat and fertile Wadi Taym, east of Cap Badge, relying on helicopters to bring them their supplies, and their Land Rovers too, while the sappers laboured in the broiling heat to make the Rabwa Pass navigable by jeeps and to build a road of greater capacity from due west through the Wadi Boran.

Although Rice Bowl still lay untamed and untackled further northwards, Hargroves and his improvised 'Radforce' could scarcely have done more 'to end the operations of dissidents'. But Radfan, like alcohol, always beckoned the consumer onwards—and certainly there could be no turning back after all the trouble caused by the F.R.A.'s withdrawal. The Army Department scratched around its larder and produced further aid so that the area under control could be enlarged.

The first requirement was to return Hargroves and his dauntless staff back to their offices in Aden, and to this end Brigadier C. H. ('Monkey') Blacker arrived from Northern Ireland with Headquarters 39th Infantry Brigade. They took over command at Thumier on May 11, on the day after the rebels had sprung to life again with a determined attack on the camp there, which was repulsed by a picquet of the K.O.S.B. The 1st Royal Scots were also warned for air despatch from Britain, and Headquarters and a second company of the 3rd Para were brought in from Bahrain. The Far East Command was ordered to lend a troop of 5·5-inch guns of 170 Battery, 45th Regiment, required for their greater range. The troop travelled on the carrier *Centaur*, and with them came a naval squadron of Wessex helicopters. Helicopters were as bread to the starving, and although the cries from Borneo were the most compelling, those from Aden had to be heeded too.

A week was devoted to acclimatisation, the building of tracks and airfields to ease the strain on the overworked helicopters, a rest for the commandos and para company, and the accumulation of information by patrolling and other means. It appeared that the Bakri Ridge was again swarming with rebels and as a preliminary to their subjugation Blacker turned to the arm to which he had belonged, armour, for a show of strength up a wadi running parallel to it, the Wadi Misra. It was carried out on May 19 by D Squadron, 4th R.T.R. with under command a troop of the 16th/5th Lancers' Centurions and a scout car troop of the F.R.A. The going was worse than anticipated, and in three hours the vehicles laboured only two miles up the wadi, where the rebels were rash enough to give the Lancers the chance to let fly with their 105-mm. guns and claim the first shots fired at the Queen's enemies by a British tank since Korea. Then there was a rainstorm, and the armour was called back to avoid being cut off by the floodwater that was mounting at torrential speed behind them. Another great victory against the imperialists could be claimed.

Meanwhile the 3rd Para, finding fewer rebels on the Bakri Ridge than had been reported, had begun to take possession of this 5-mile long, sharp-sided feature. They made their first, deep penetration along it on the night of the 18th/19th, using a goat track from the north. They met no opposition, and this was fortunate, for the men even of the leading company carried burdens of up to 90 lb. and the other company had the rôle of fighting porters, returning for more supplies—mostly water— once a lie-up position had been consolidated. Not until the following evening did they have their first brush with a rebel band, and on the 20th the ridge was cleared almost to its end on the northern side, thanks to some thrustful work by the Anti-Tank Platoon under C.S.M. 'Nobby' Arnold, which gained the first three prisoners of the campaign and the designation of the furthermost spur as Arnold's Spur. A battalion attack had then to be mounted on some blockhouses standing on a prominence at the end of the ridge. They had fifty-odd defenders, armed with automatics and rifles, and they endured with great fortitude the shelling that the exertions of the sappers made possible and the rockets from Hunter fighters. But they did not stay long when the red berets of C Company—bush hats were discarded at the greater altitude —came bobbing in among them to the accompaniment of a savage rattle of fire. Several dead were found on the position, and below there was an extraordinary network of tunnels, affording means of escape. By dawn on May 24 the paras were masters of the whole ridge.

Just to prove that there was no place the rebels could call their own, Blacker's men drove deep into the shafts of rock and sun-baked mud around Bakri Ridge. On May 24 the 4th R.T.R. staged a more successful demonstration, this time up the Wadi Nakhalain, from the south-west, with a company of East Anglians under command. Then on the night of the 25th/26th the 3rd Para continued in a south-easterly direction down a precipice into the slab-sided Wadi Dhubsan, while also scaling the Jebel Haqla on the south side of the wadi. The final part of the descent had to be by rope, and among the first down was the commanding officer, Lieutenant-Colonel Farrar-Hockley, late the Gloucesters.

By dawn the paras were firmly established across the wide flat floor of the wadi without dispute by any tribesman. X Company, 45 Commando now began to advance down it under para command, picquetting the lower part of the glaring slopes on either side. When half-way to the end they spotted some rebels high above them and claimed two hits with a burst. A vicious crackle burst upon them in response, first from the slope ahead, then from the flank, and later from the rear as well. There were six automatics in the chorus, according to a paratroop estimate. Farrar-Hockley went forward in a Scout helicopter that had been landed with great difficulty on the wadi floor. It had even greater difficulty in making its next landing, having overshot the leading troops, been peppered with bullets, and hobbled back just within the commandos' gains, with one officer wounded. A Company, 3rd Para now began to work round the left flank of X Company; C similarly cleared the right flank from the Jebel Haqla; air strikes, 5·5-inch shells and mortar bombs crumpled the localities from which the rebels were thought most likely to be firing and X Company themselves plugged grimly on, easing their peril by capturing a blockhouse. Around 2 p.m. the clatter subsided, the rebels having decided that it was time to give up. They had killed X Company's radio operator, almost killed the second-in-command, and wounded one other.

The troops were to have returned to the Bakri Ridge that night, but the helicopter could not be left and was in no state to take the air. Two R.E.M.E. fitters were flown in and next morning saw their patient fly away; recovery under fire had been a routine task for the R.E.M.E. ever since there had been a company of British infantry at Dhala, and this time they had not been under fire, tempting though the target was. The troops could now toil back up the precipitous slope to Bakri.

Blacker had one final objective, the Jebel Huriyah, which at 5,500 feet is the highest peak in Radfan, lying due south of the Bakri Ridge and accessible along a line of jagged wadis and ridges running parallel to it. 10 miles of this forbidding terrain had to be crossed, and the task was assigned to the East Anglians and the 2nd F.R.A. Between May 31 and June 5, they advanced 7 miles, laboriously picquetting the heights between the cultivated but quite deserted Wadis Misra and Tremare, and actively obstructed only by a mine, which upset a Land Rover and wounded a by-stander, who unlike the driver had no sandbagging to protect him. The East Anglians were to make the assault on the great jebel, and as a preliminary the 2nd F.R.A., who had been advancing along the ridge on the East Anglians' left, swung right-handed on June 7 to cross a valley and seize a feature with some blockhouses on it, named Shaab Sharah. At about 10 a.m. they came under heavy fire from here, as they began the descent into the valley. The enemy had three machine-guns and perhaps forty rifles, and it was decided to blast them out before the F.R.A. continued their exposed advance. Hunter aircraft, the battery of 105s, and the troop of 5·5s rained their fury upon them, but amazingly the rebels stuck it out until nightfall.

A fresh company of the F.R.A. were brought up for a dawn attack on Shaab Sharah. It met no opposition. The East Anglians passed through, striving methodically forward up exhaustingly jagged slopes. They made the final assault on the night June 10/11, under the light of flares dropped by Shackletons and with a formidable array of fire support on call. By 4.50 a.m. the summit was theirs, with the street lights of Aden twinkling at them 40 miles away, and around midday a sniper offered the one brief poop of opposition, to be silenced by a massed crumping from the hungry mortars. The rebels' stand at Shaab Sharah had been as unwise as it had been brave, and it clearly plunged them into a wave of defeatism.

There were to be no more deliberate attacks. The army had in the course of six weeks driven the tribesmen from their mountain strongholds and shown that the weapons provided by the Egyptians were of no avail when the British were provoked into retaliating with their full land and air power, jerky though it might be in attaining momentum. But it was a war that could not be ended merely by the capture of objectives, however great their prestige value. An enormous area had been occupied and had now to be kept under control, and the K.O.S.B., who had taken over the northern sector, from the Rabwa Pass to the Wadi Taym, had already been finding that the task could be made hazardous and exasperating by a few determined intruders enjoying the freedom of movement that the wild mountainous terrain would always confer. The tribes might be temporarily subdued, but the instigation from across the Yemeni border was for ever on the increase, and there was evidence of immigrant guerrillas, dressed in green drill uniform, whom the army called 'Red Wolves' to distinguish them from the resident tribesmen warriors who relished the nickname 'Wolves of Radfan'.

The R.A.F. were meanwhile trying out their traditional remedy, air control, in areas not occupied by the army, mainly to the east of the Bakri Ridge and to the south-east round the Jebel Radfan itself, which was of less tactical importance than the Jebel Huriyah. Although they undoubtedly did much to bring the tribes to heel, it was decided to extend the area of army control and towards the end of June the K.O.S.B., who had been relieved in the northern sector by the Royal Scots on the 9th, moved up the hilly Pilgrim's Way, southwards from the Wadi Taym, in conjunction with the 1st F.R.A. The climax came when the latter took temporary possession of the great steepling pinnacle, Jebel Widina, after a very skilful climb.

This jebel was handed back for watch and ward by the R.A.F. and reoccupied on occasions, the next being in August, when the East Anglians were required to seize it, operating from the Bakri Ridge. They achieved this by flying in by helicopter at night without lights, and since one of the two Scouts allotted broke down it had all to be done by a single shuttle service, four men at a time. The build-up was mounted at the rate of one load every eight minutes, with thirty seconds allowed for embarkation and five for discharge: an all-army effort, of which both pilot and passengers had good reason to be proud, and a new venture in night operations.

There were three battalion areas to be controlled, the northern one from the Rabwa Pass to Wadi Taym, the south-east one from Bakri

Ridge to the Pilgrim's Way, and the south-west one from the Wadi Misrah to the Jebel Huriyah. An F.R.A. battalion looked after the latter, and, including 45 Commando, there were three British battalions left to guard the other two and garrison Aden, for the K.O.S.B. returned to England and the 3rd Para to Bahrain astride July and August. They also had to provide a company for defence duty at the Thumier base— which was renamed Habilayn in order to dissociate the inhabitants of Thumier from participation in the war—and companies at Dhala and Mukeiras.

The upcountry commitment was of course more popular than the dreary internal security guards and picquets in and around Aden, even before the latter became dangerous. There was infinite scope for leadership by lance-corporals and subalterns alike in the task of detecting and outwitting the bands that roved the great mountains and the crevices and terraced plots of cultivation lying between them. Minelaying and sniping in the late afternoon, when night was near at hand to cover retreat, were the rebels' favourite ploys, and machine-guns were often used in the sniping, usually at long range. There was intense patrolling against them, in which many a lesson was learned and many a boy turned into man. The policy was to smite the rebels with the maximum weight of fire from guns and mortars whenever any were located, and this in turn called for a high standard of communications and of fire direction by junior leaders. The S.A.S. were the most expert at this, and many rebel bands were bewildered, demoralised and shrivelled by the shells that seemed to follow them around under the guidance of some magical demon, which in fact were the eyes of a patrol on long range penetration.

The Radfan operations, from their start, attracted great publicity, and the troops manning the more accessible positions in bare buff and bush hats were gazed upon and quizzed by a constant flow of visitors, generals, politicians, journalists, and both British and German television teams. Much was done to make the positions habitable, particularly in the valley of the Danaba Basin and Wadi Taym, where the heat was at its most scorching. Four camps were built on little prominences here, named Monk's Field, Paddy's Field, Table Top, and Blair's Field, the first being named after one of the officers killed by a mine on April 25, the fourth after Blacker's successor as brigade commander. Each had its own airstrip, to which fresh rations were brought each morning, and its own shower baths, two of them drawing from outside water points. Up the crags such as Gibraltar, towering over the Rabwa Pass, there were cable supply services linked with the roads along which wheeled vehicles made their first ever incursions into the tribal domains. Certainly the infantry were in debt to the tireless sappers. But the greater the

443

development, the greater the incentive and opportunity to strike at the intruders, and it had constantly to be emphasised to the troops that the object of making them comfortable in camp was to increase their endurance on patrol.

The need to win the hearts and minds of the people was not forgotten, although the task was made harder than in Borneo by the innate turbulence of the tribesmen, a lack of funds, and the lead, which was never adequately challenged, gained by the Egyptian imperialists in the matter of broadcast propaganda. Sufficient persuasion was nevertheless exerted to cause most of the tribes to ask for terms by the end of October. It looked as if the Radfan operations had gained real success.

Also in October the 24th Brigade evacuated Kenya and took over the Radfan commitment from the 39th, thus forfeiting its function as a reserve from the moment of its arrival at Aden. In fact only Brigade Headquarters came, having left its units to journey homewards from Kenya independently. Maintaining a Tac H.Q. at Habilayn, it was based on Little Aden, as also were 45 Commando, the 10th Royal Hussars who had taken over the armoured car rôle from the 4th R.T.R. in August, the 19th Light Regiment, who replaced the 3rd R.H.A. in 24 Brigade, and the 2nd Coldstream Guards, who joined the brigade in place of the 2nd Scots Guards and formed a welcome reinforcement. In Aden itself, when not upcountry under 24 Brigade, the 1st Royal Anglian (as the 1st/1st East Anglian has become) enjoyed the comfort of Waterloo Lines as the permanent, family-accompanied garrison battalion, and the Royal Scots were alongside them in the transit camp and discomfort.

Having undertaken to make South Arabia fully independent by 1968 and at the same time to maintain the Middle East base, with £20 million allotted for quartering and installations, the Tories had by now been obliged to hand government over to Labour. The new Colonial Secretary, Mr. Anthony Greenwood, early announced that he would visit Aden in November, and as greeting for him the Egyptian-sponsored National Liberation Front opened a terrorist offensive that had obviously long been planned. Among its first casualties was the newly arrived adjutant of the Coldstream, who lost a leg when his Land Rover hit a mine and would have lost his life but for the courage of his driver in warding off marauders. By the end of the year the number had risen to two servicemen killed and thirty-four wounded, by mine, grenade, or bullet. It was a bad Christmas, with an R.A.F. officer's daughter killed by a grenade thrown into his quarter and an Arab Special Branch officer shot dead. A new phase had begun, making Radfan alluring by contrast.

Although the emergency was now officially entering its second year, the command organisation was cumbersome and confusing. In overall charge of defence and internal security was the High Commissioner of the Federation of South Arabia, and it is indicative of the British Government's hope that tact and reason would yet prevail that on Trevaskis's retirement on January 20, 1965, another civilian administrator, Sir Richard Turnbull, was appointed, and indeed extracted from retirement to succeed him. He lived in Government House, Steamer Point, and had an office in the newly built Federal capital at Al Ittihad, on the border of Aden State midway between Aden and Little Aden. The Commander-in-Chief Middle East gave him such assistance with operations as he required, delegating control to his G.O.C. Land Forces at their combined headquarters at Steamer Point. Internal security was in turn delegated to the commander Aden Garrison, or Aden Brigade as it was to be renamed, with a new headquarters in Singapore Lines at the southern end of the isthmus, or in the case of Little Aden to the commander 24 Brigade, who also had responsibility for upcountry operations and was constantly exchanging troops with the commander Aden Brigade. Both of course were in concert with the civil and police chiefs in their localities, but there was a sad lack of coordination in that most crucial of all departments, Intelligence, until at last a brigadier was appointed Director early in 1965. He established his centre at Steamer Point.

In early March an ardent nationalist, and unashamed ally of Nasser in his war of attrition against the Federation, was appointed Chief Minister of Aden by the electoral process with which the British were proud to invest the constitution of an ex-colony. His name was Abdul Mackawee. Thus every measure of security decreed by the High Commissioner, even the continuation of the state of emergency, was opposed and criticised by the head of the state most affected, and of course every wild charge against the troops was substantiated and embellished by governmental announcement. The prospect, always dim, of any cooperation from the non-European inhabitants of Aden faded to nothing. The terrorists, as ever, made the 'traitors and collaborators' their first target, and there was no incentive whatever to risk identification as such with independence promised for the Federation by 1968. Policemen were 'executed', not as yet in large numbers, but enough to cause the steady erosion of the morale of a force that in the past had been efficient

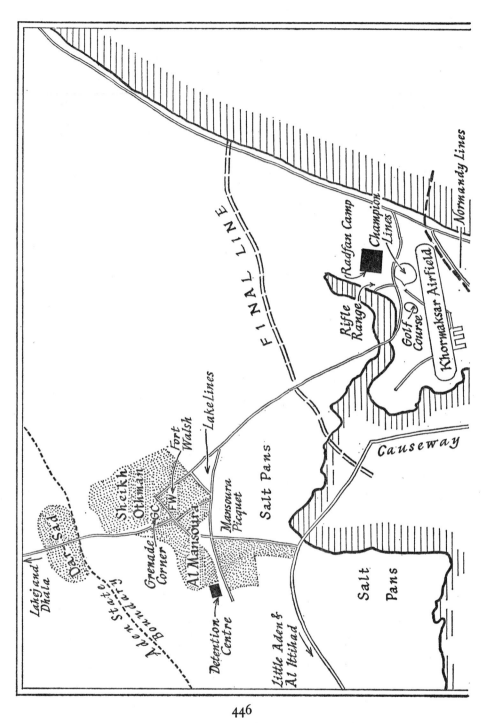

Lakejand Dhala

Dar Sad

Aden State Boundary

Sheikh Othman

Grenade Corner

GC

FW

Fort Walsh

Al Mansoura

Detention Centre

Little Aden & Al Ittihad

Lake Lines

Mansoura Picquet

Salt Pans

Salt Pans

FINAL LINE

Causeway

Rifle Range

Radfan Camp

Champion Lines

Golf Course

Khormaksar Airfield

Normandy Lines

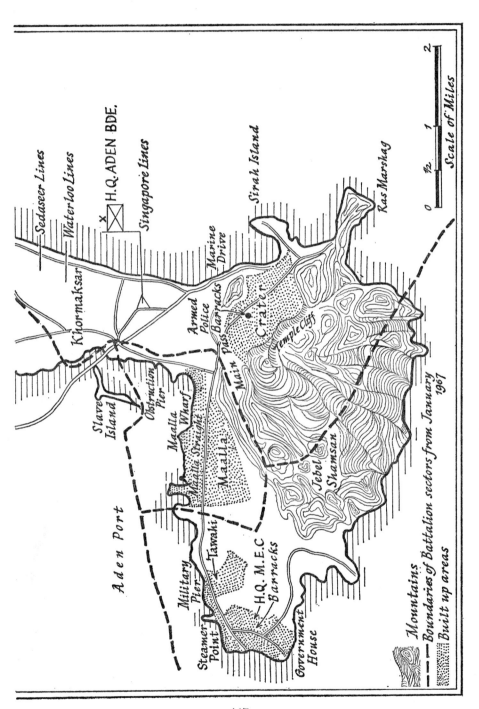

Sedaseer Lines
Waterloo Lines
X H.Q. ADEN BDE.
Singapore Lines
Khormaksar
Marine Drive
Crater
Sirah Island
Temple Cliff
Ras Marshag
Armed Police Barracks
Main Pass Barracks
Obstruction Pier
Slave Island
Maalla Wharf
Maalla Straight
Maalla
Jebel Shamsan
Aden Port
Military Pier
Tawahi
Steamer Point
H.Q. M.E.C Barracks
Government House

Mountains
Boundaries of Battalion sectors from January 1967
Built up areas

0   ½   1   2
Scale of Miles

447

and effective. Information became as rare as water in the desert, and the security forces were helpless without it.

There was greatest scope for terrorism in Sheikh Othman, the town north of the isthmus just inside Aden state. It afforded easy access for infiltrators from the Yemen and a maze of shacks and closely huddled houses from which to toss grenades at the upcountry traffic from Little Aden, Al Ittihad, or Aden itself, all of which had to pass through this ramshackle township. A western adjunct of the town, named Al Mansoura, contained the detention centre, and its inmates had plenty of friends around the periphery ever alert for a chance to strike the guards. A battalion could speedily be absorbed on static and mobile duties in and around Sheikh Othman, on guards, picquets and permanent check points, and on swoops and searches in quest of information, which were motivated as a rule by no more than a hunch and the urge to deny the terrorists a monopoly of the initiative.

Further southwards the task of sealing off the isthmus by static check points and patrols was a heavy consumer of troops, and Khormaksar Aerodrome, with its two miles of runways and its civil and military installations, stretched the R.A.F. Regiment to, and at times beyond, the limit of their resources. On the peninsula itself there were three separate townships containing good storage facilities for dynamite. The ever sultry Crater on the east side had the reputation of being the most turbulent, but the mountain barriers around it at least limited the approaches to passes from the north-west and north-east side and, like the police barracks in the centre, facilitated the task of control. Maalla posed a more worrying problem. It was sprawled on either side of the road to Steamer Point for over a mile and consisted of both flats and hugger-mugger houses. A large number of the 9,000 members of service families lived here, and guarding them was a heavy, worrying commitment. Further westwards, adjacent to the port, was the town of Tawahi, which with its shops, restaurants and hotels had been developed for tourists and been laden with the slum quarters of the vendors who preyed upon them. Steamer Point adjoined the town and above it were the stately and not-so-stately buildings used by the Aden Government and the Middle East Command. Guards for the latter and its road route to the north formed another heavy commitment.

Obviously more troops were needed, and in April 1965 the total garrison was raised to five battalions, and the Aden Brigade to three, by the despatch of the 1st Royal Sussex from Malta for a six-months tour, brought to strength by a large draft of Territorial 'Ever-Readies'. A new camp at the northern end of the isthmus, named Radfan, was built for them, and as comrades in Aden they had two battalions of the Royal

Anglian, for the 4th (Leicestershire) had arrived from England in February to relieve the Royal Scots, also for a six-months' tour. A company of the Parachute Regiment from Bahrain, where in April the 1st relieved the 3rd, further eased the burden, but it was increased again by the despatch of a company of Coldstreamers in May to quieten a disturbance in Mauritius. The 19th Light Regiment contributed a battery for internal security duties, and the 10th Hussars, and the resident tank regiment, the 5th Royal Inniskilling Dragoon Guards (who had relieved the 16th/5th in December) also made their contributions.

On June 5 Major-General J. E. F. Willoughby, late the Middlesex Regiment, had the appointment of Security Commander superimposed on that of G.O.C. Land Forces, which he had assumed from Cubbon in May. This made for greater cohesion, not only between the 24th and Aden Brigades, but between the military, government, police and intelligence chiefs, and the naval and air commanders as well, both of whom were naturally anxious about the safety of their holdings and the operational availability of their men. Willoughby had representatives of them all on his Operational Executive, which met almost daily.

Shortly after Willoughby's appointment a rare success was achieved, thanks to the brave opportunism of 2nd Lieutenant Hawkins of the 1st Royal Anglian. He was passing through Tawahi in a Land Rover with two men when he heard two explosions and later saw three men leap into a car and drive furiously off. He gave chase and chivvied the car up back streets to a dead-end. The men leapt out. Hawkins ran after them, grabbed one, and brought him down. He now sent both his men off to summon help while he sat on his prisoner's chest with revolver drawn, keeping guard over both the man and the car. People surrounded him, increasingly aggressive; he could have as easily been overpowered as poor Moorhouse of the West Yorks at Port Said. But relief arrived in time, and from both the man and the car a great deal of evidence accrued, for which many fruitless hours of patrolling and searching had been spent and from which many other arrests followed, incapacitating a complete terrorist cell for six months. The explosions that started the sequence were of grenades thrown through the window of the Seamen's Mission.

It will be noted that this coup—which gained an incongruous M.B.E. for Hawkins, since troops in Aden state were not on active serivce—was achieved without the discharge of a shot, although the fugitives were armed. The troops were allowed to use their weapons only in self-defence, and although the need to do so was expressly left to split-second judgment of 'the senior officer on the spot' and each soldier had a missive in his paybook telling him, 'If you act in good faith you need not fear the consequences', there was always a strong inhibition against firing. It was to endure the test of increasing provocations, of which the worst early examples were a grenade that wounded six officers dining al fresco in the Command headquarters mess at Tarshyne and one into the camp cinema at Waterloo Lines, which wounded fourteen.

Upcountry the tribes in Radfan had shown an increasing willingness to come to terms, and the Royal Engineers were hard at it improving the road through the Rabwa Pass and planning various developments, such as school construction, for which money was made available as part of a belated 'hearts and minds' campaign. There were sharp reactions against these peaceful endeavours from across the border. Near the end of March 1965 the 2nd Coldstream lost three killed on the Dhala road by a direct hit by a mortar bomb on a mortar pit, and there were four wounded, including a gunner major, before the raiders were driven off. On April 12 a very hot attack came in on the base camp from which 50 Field Squadron R.E. were working, and it was not beaten back until a warrant officer and sergeant had been killed and five others wounded. The warrant officer was one of the 'ever-Readies', a territorial soldier who had made himself available for six months' regular service if, as had happened in this year of heavy operational strain, there were insufficient regulars to bring units to strength. The sergeant belonged to the R.A.P.C.; everyone had been in the firing line.

Intense patrol activity was meanwhile maintained from the Radfan position, and so many targets were found for the artillery that in a six weeks tour a battery attached to the 19th Light from the 7th Para fired 2,954 rounds. The most successful ambush in this period was laid by the 1st Royal Sussex on July 6, operating from Monk's Field. It produced four kills and two wounded, a high score against these wily men of the mountains. The territorials with the Royal Sussex were well to the fore, and among them was the patrol commander, Lieutenant Smith, who won the M.C., and the only man to receive wound.

Between August and October 1965 there was a succession of reliefs. The first to go were the 4th Royal Anglian who were replaced for a nine-months' tour by another battalion that had seen service in Borneo and since been in England, the 1st King's Own Yorkshire Light Infantry; the 1st Prince of Wales's Own Regiment of Yorkshire then came to relieve the 1st Royal Anglian, who had had a hard nineteen months, for a year's duty from Waterloo Lines; the 1st Welsh Guards also came for a year, taking the 2nd Coldstream's place in 24 Brigade; and the 1st Coldstream Guards came from Libya, where they were on exercise from Rhine Army, for a six-months' tour in place of the Royal Sussex. The 10th Hussars handed the armoured car rôle over to the 4th/7th Royal

Dragoon Guards, the 19th Light the gunner rôle to the 1st R.H.A., and at the end of the year the 5th Dragoon Guards the tank rôle to the 1st R.T.R. 45 Commando, as ever, soldiered on, sustained by an internal rotation of reliefs.

In the midst of the change-over of units a political decision of great consequence was taken. It followed the murders of two eminent Britons, one a police superintendent, the other the Speaker of Aden's Legislative Council. Both were shot in Crater, and the only comment from Mackawee was a protest against the curfew ordered. Then a grenade exploded amidst a party of British schoolchildren, injuring five without drawing any expression of governmental regret. On September 26 the High Commissioner dissolved the Aden Government and assumed direct rule. A strike was called in protest, and rioting broke out in Crater, providing the Prince of Wales's Own with their first harsh taste of crowd control in support of the police—a test made all the more trying by the hordes of children who were incited to bombard them. Federal troops were brought in to assist in the enforcement of a curfew, making their first entry into Aden as such. The town was subdued, with 760 arrested, of whom a third were deported to the Yemen. Selective arrests of leaders were also made, with charges under the emergency rules to follow, and two newspapers were banned. The Federal Government had at last been authorised to use the stick to bring its one rebellious member to heel.

Among British troops in Aden there was joy at a measure regarded as long overdue, and it certainly eased their problems for the time being. For the British Government it was a sad, retrograde step. They were fully enmeshed now in the web woven by their predecessors, and as from Palestine in 1947 their one concern was escape. The decision was announced in February 1966. Not only was the Federation to be made politically independent by 1968 but militarily as well. The Middle East Command and all its forces, which once again had become fully committed to the defence of their base, were to be removed. To the Federal rulers the news spelt betrayal and doom.

Although there was in theory nothing more to be achieved from killing British soldiers, the attacks steadily increased their momentum as part of the battle for possession of the holdings that had virtually been put on offer to the strongest grabber. In fact only six servicemen were killed in Aden throughout 1965 and only five in 1966, but the wounded amounted to 83 and 218 respectively, showing both the increase in activity and the success achieved by the armour plating, sandbags, and improvised guards used to protect troops travelling in vehicles. Grenades thrown at these vehicles were the commonest form of attack and though they might cause hurt by disabling a vehicle they were nearly always deprived of lethal effect.

The troops were at their most vulnerable when patrolling streets after being brought in to enforce a curfew, and although again the grenades tossed at them seldom killed they often maimed. It was a tense, eerie duty. The men of a patrol supported each other from either side of a street, ready to bring instant fire on every possible direction of attack and covered from behind by a sniper on a roof or an armoured car. A gunman would have little chance against them and waited instead to catch a soldier off duty, preferably when isolated in disregard of security regulations. But for the grenade throwers—or 'Cairo Grenadiers'— every door and window presented opportunity for an unseen attack, and after some ludicrously amateur efforts to begin with they gained increasing expertise. There appears to have been no satisfactory alternative to foot patrolling; armoured cars had neither the powers of detection nor speed of reaction to keep a town under tight control.

Rocket launchers made their first appearance in 1965, and in 1966 they gave way to mortars, which were easier to conceal, had greater range, and could cause plenty of anxiety, however indiscriminate their use. Baits were used to lure troops into ambushes, such as the discharge of fire-arms or the apparently panicky flight of a vehicle up a back street.

There was scope for retaliation at this game, and the Prince of Wales's Own, as the battalion in longest residence, had most practice and most successes, largely because of the willingness of Major Tillotson to be used as a bait. But there could be no substitute for searches as the primary means of curbing terrorism. In order to channel entrants into Aden through the four check points, the 1st Coldstream built a wire barricade of 11 miles along a perimeter including Sheikh Othman, and the daily average through these points was 4,500 men and 500 vehicles. All had to be searched, and the most likely place for a find was the innards of a car, a tyre, a dustcart, pot, melon, or even a camel. Snap searches of houses were ceaselessly conducted and yielded the occasional rich dividend, usually from the information of a terrorist netted in the process. Thus the Welsh Guards unearthed an arms cache in Tawahi in July 1966, and in the months that followed two larger and very heartening hauls were made by more recently arrived battalions, the 1st Cameronians and the 3rd Royal Anglian.

Upcountry the tempo of attacks similarly increased, both on the frontier and in Radfan. The camp was frequently mortared, and in a particularly heavy concentration in March the Welsh Guards lost five men wounded, two N.C.O.'s among them and would have had a post overrun but for the resolution of a guardsman. In this same tour a company claimed six killed in repulsing an attack in the Wadi Taym. Such attacks were made at night and preceded by a sharp stonk from rocket launchers and mortars, and at least one would be bound to be made on one position or another during a battalion's five-week tour. Casualties steadily mounted, maintaining an average of just over two a week during 1966, and rebels would be killed in their twos and threes, occasionally with a higher score at Dhala. In July a half-platoon of the Prince of Wales's Own had a very tough fight with a somewhat larger enemy party whom they ambushed near Habilayn; they had four casualties and claimed to have inflicted seven after the subaltern in command had thrown all his grenades.

A new development in December sharpened the ferocity of the struggle. The hitherto allied 'liberation fronts', known as N.L.F. and F.L.O.S.Y. (South Yemen), quarrelled and from now on were in vicious rivalry, trying to outdo each other in atrocities against the British and their stooges and waging war between themselves. Egypt backed the less aggressive, Flosy.

To cope with the added menace the Aden Brigade was enlarged to four battalions at the start of that most turbulent of years, 1967. The ending of the Borneo war had somewhat eased the strain on the Army as a whole, and there were more battalions available in Britain to sustain a swift rotation of reliefs. Thus the 1st Coldstream were returned to Rhine Army in April 1966 on relief at Radfan Camp by the 1st Somerset and Cornwall Light Infantry, who were themselves relieved in October by the 3rd Royal Anglian (16th/44th Foot). The Cameronians had taken Singapore Lines over from the K.O.Y.L.I. in May; in September, after all but a year in occupation, the Prince of Wales's Own handed Waterloo Lines over to the 1st Royal Northumberland Fusiliers. The battalion that came in January, 1967, bringing the Aden total to four, was the 1st South Wales Borderers. Single companies were also provided in rotation by battalions in other parts of the East, by the 1st Gloucestershire, the 1st Royal Irish Fusiliers, the 1st Loyals, and from February 1967 by the 1st King's Own Royal Border Regiment from Bahrain.

From Little Aden 45 Commando and the 1st R.H.A. continued to provide their share of field and internal security duties. The armoured car rôle passed in September 1966 from the 4th/7th to the Queen's Dragoon Guards, with a squadron permanently allotted to the Aden Brigade, which now had no other armour. The Welsh Guards, after a varied and eventful year's service, were relieved in October by the 1st Irish Guards, and scarcely had the latter completed the week's acclimatisation, which was allotted but seldom completed without interference, than they were whisked off by sea to make a landing by helicopter in the Eastern Aden Protectorate, where they successfully netted yet another 'liberation army' in embryo.

The Aden Brigade took tighter control of the situation after demonstrations staged by the N.L.F. in January had revealed the weakening resolve of the police. Instead of being in support, the soldiers were now to take control as soon as danger threatened, on the issue of codeword Amber by the Security Commander; instead of awaiting the call to disperse assemblies forbidden by emergency regulations, they were to take the initiative in preventing them. Their duties, as in Cyprus, became nearer those of policemen, but they retained the equipment of soldiers, for bullets and grenades were as likely to fly as marbles and stones. The police, both civil and armed gendarmerie, still had their parts to play, but would be in support of the soldiers once Amber was received.

The first big test of this organisation came on February 11, the anniversary of the formation of the Federation, which both the N.L.F. and Flosy promised to make 'The Day of the Volcano'. The troops deployed the day before, the Royal Anglians in Sheikh Othman, the Fifth Fusiliers in Crater, the S.W.B. in Maalla, and the Cameronians in Tawahi and Steamer Point, and by the prompt arrest of curfew breakers the volcano was kept from erupting. On the 12th the curfew was lifted and now the troops came under attack both by mobs and armed gangsters, but the former were dispersed by a combination of firmness and restraint and the latter subdued by the prompt return of fire, often from places never known to the aggressors. Three gangsters were killed and eleven captured during the exchanges.

The Aden Brigade had given an impressive display of their authority and set the pattern for subsequent events, with battalions remaining in their allotted areas and leaving the upcountry duties to 24 Brigade, except for the Mukeiras company. The Cameronians, soon after the February confrontation, handed the western area over to the 1st Lancashire and returned to Scotland.

The rival insurgent groups meanwhile concentrated on the murder of each other or of 'all traitors to the cause', of whom the favourite target, and the most vulnerable to intimidation, were members of the Federal Government. There were also some deadly bomb attacks on British civilians. However, the troops struck back at times, and by telescopic observation from Mount Shamsan, above Tawahi, the Lancashires picked out a number of grenadiers in the act of throwing and ringleaders in the act of rousing their rabbles. These men would then sit innocently at café tables, still under the eagle eye from the eyrie, and here they would to their amazement be arrested by patrols swiftly directed by wireless.

Preceded by a mighty rainstorm, which switched the British military effort to a herculean feat of rescue and road clearance, a United Nations three-man mission of investigation arrived on April 2, to be treated to a competition in chaos between N.L.F. and Flosy. The delegates shut themselves in their hotel and stayed there, while the security forces, already deployed in readiness, withstood and eventually subdued an orgy of rioting and attacks by grenade and bullet. Twenty-four times the Fifth Fusiliers came under attack in Crater, losing only four men wounded. At Sheikh Othman the fury was even fiercer. The Royal Anglians and armoured cars of the Q.D.G. had first to relieve the police station from siege by a hooligan mob, and a few days later, when a measure of quiet had been restored, they had to form a shield for the one and only visit made by the United Nations' men, to the Al Mansoura detention centre. They provoked pandemonium inside and constant shooting from without and had finally to be rushed back to their hotel by the Q.D.G. A similar operation was needed to get them to Khormaksar aerodrome on the 7th for their departure, in a state of petulant relief. Eighteen servicemen were wounded during this week of furore. They killed eight gangsters by selective firing and wounded seven, resisting at all times the temptation to open up indiscriminately.

Later this month the spotlight was diverted back to Radfan, where a patrol of the Irish Guards had a hot clash with the enemy, both losing four killed. The 1st R.H.A. lost three killed at the same time.

On April 30 the terrorists of Sheikh Othman achieved their biggest killing of all by blowing up a school bus for Arab children, killing nine of them and the driver and maiming a further fourteen. It was as well that plans were ready for the evacuation of service families, of whom most belonged to the R.A.F. and Middle East staff, and it began on May 1. It was spread over two-and-a-half months and, while removing a load of anxiety, it left its own problem in the denial of 3,100 flats and houses to squatter snipers. Changes of appointment in this same month also presaged the coming departure. The first on May 12, was a routine change of Security Commander, Major-General P. T. Tower replacing Willoughby, whose success in holding the insurgents in check was to be recognised by knighthood. Tower was an artillery man, come from the Directorate of Public Relations, and his C.-in-C. was Admiral Sir Michael Le Fanu, who had succeeded Harington early in 1966. The second change was of considerable political significance. Sir Richard Turnbull was succeeded as High Commissioner by Sir Humphrey Trevelyan, who made it known that he had come to ensure an orderly withdrawal of the British forces and leave, if he possibly could, some form of order in their place. 45 Commando made a rapid switch to full ceremonial in honour of the departing Turnbull, and the Fusiliers provided a welcome for Trevelyan by beating Retreat at Steamer Point.

Near the end of May the 1st Parachute relieved the 3rd Royal Anglian at Radfan Camp, and within a week they were called into Sheikh Othman in anticipation of a strike. By first light on June 1 they were in occupation of the police station and had sections on seven rooftops. One had an early target when three men were seen running towards the mosque after a grenade had exploded near a patrol; the first two were dropped dead by one shot at each, and the third ran into a shop and was shot through its window. Widespread fire was now opened on the paras, showing that they had forestalled a takeover bid. One was killed in a rooftop post and four were wounded, and many another had a narrow escape, for there were other, higher rooftops available to the attackers—'We have just been grenaded. No casualties. Just one or two headaches', reported a corporal after a grenade had exploded inside his position. The enemy fire subsided at length under the weight of retaliation, but remained intermittent until dark, by which time the paras had taken five prisoners and claimed a further five killed. There had been some very heavy firing.

To take a firmer hold on Sheikh Othman and thus dominate the route to the north, Lieutenant-Colonel Walsh, of the 1st Para, established his headquarters in a high, disused building overlooking 'grenade corner' and thoroughly sandbagged it in overnight. It, the police station, and other adjacent posts received a constant barrage of rockets and bombs, but thanks to skilfully devised protective skirting only a few casualties were incurred. It was a great gain for the convoys to have this town firmly held at last, and it proved well worth the expenditure in manpower, which included a squadron of the Q.D.G., a company of the King's Own Border, and temporarily one of the Irish Guards as well.

War now flared in the Sinai desert, bringing the Israeli Army a sensational six-day victory between June 3–9. This plunged all Arabs into anguish and increased the nationalist fervour against the British, whom Nasser accused of aiding Israel. It speeded the disintegration of the Federal Government, already demoralised by murderous intimidation by the N.L.F. and the pending collapse of British support, and in turn aggravated the strain on the morale of its hitherto faithful servant, the South Arabian Army, as which the F.R.A. was renamed on June 1. Command of it was soon to fall to an Arab in succession to the man who had commanded the 1st East Anglians in the Radfan, Brigadier

J. B. Dye, and in many quarters there was no confidence at all in the commander designate. Rumours were rife, and one that gained currency was that the British had turned against the S.A.A. and opened fire on its men. It had awful consequences, which fell in a torrent of disaster on June 20.

First to be smitten were nineteen men of the Royal Corps of Transport riding in a 3-ton lorry past the Federal Guard camp, Champion Lines, just north of Khormaksar aerodrome, towards the adjacent Radfan Camp. They were ripped at close range by machine-gun fire, quite without warning, and in a trice lost eight killed and eight wounded. Two Adeni policemen and a British Public Works employee were killed almost simultaneously as they travelled along this road in two cars, and a subaltern of the Lancashires was also killed while manning the defences of Radfan Camp, where he was on detachment.

To C Company, 1st King's Own Border, under command 1st Para, fell the daunting task of subduing the mutineers without, if possible, firing at them. Accompanied by a troop of A Squadron, Queen's Dragoon Guards, they promptly set off from Radfan Camp in 3-tonners and were shot up before they debussed, losing one killed and eight wounded. There was horror and confusion, under oppressive, humid heat, outside the entrance to the Arab-held camp, and yet even as a party was being organised to locate and dress the wounded, a platoon made a dash for the guard room, covered only by small arms fire from the armoured cars and without firing themselves. They reached it safely and rescued some British and Arab officers made prisoner by the men. The other platoons passed through, bound for other parts of the camp, from which a fierce crackle of fire was coming. It died down when the Arab soldiers saw the British coming at them without any intention of firing, and the only further casualties were four paratroopers wounded as they arrived to help in the casualty evacuation. It was a marvellous achievement, which restored confidence in the British throughout the Federal forces and gained an M.C. for the company commander, Major Miller, an award for which previously only those on active service upcountry were eligible.

Unfortunately the affair sparked off fresh rumours that flew to the Aden Armed Police in their barracks in Crater and filled them with fear of an attack by the British. British troops used these barracks when there was trouble in Crater, and soon after midday on the 20th the commander of the responsible company, Y of the Fifth Fusiliers, drove towards them, not realising that a patrol sent ahead had taken a different route. He was in a Land Rover with five of his men, and behind came another with a major and two men of the 1st Argyll and Sutherland

Highlanders, who were shortly to relieve the Fusiliers, having spent eight months in England since their return from the Far East.

The party were blasted by fire at point-blank range from the police barracks. All were killed except for one Fusilier Storey, who escaped with bullet wounds in arm and thigh, shot one of the policemen when he reached cover, and after a series of adventures was eventually given protection by a senior Arab police officer, taken inside the barracks, where he saw the bodies of his comrades removed by lorry, and was evacuated by ambulance under an amnesty agreement after being well cared for by the police. The subaltern who had taken the first patrol went back into the town with three of his own men and two armoured cars. He was drawn into a heavy fire fight with the policemen and sent the armoured cars back for help. He and his men were never seen again alive.

As the black smoke billowed from the smashed Land Rovers, another blaze was started high up on the southern rim of the actual crater, named Temple Cliff. An army Sioux helicopter had been lifting a two-man observation picquet on to it when it had been hit by bullets and forced down in flames. The pilot was trapped inside with a bullet through his knee, and one of his passengers lay in a crumpled heap where he had been ejected. The other, Fusilier Duffy, emerged shaken and badly cut, then suddenly realising the pilot's plight, leapt into the flames and dragged him out. He returned and hauled the wireless set out just before the plane exploded. He then stood guard over his companions, treated their wounds, and reported the situation. He won a lone D.C.M.

An attempt was now made to enter Crater by the road from the north-east. A Saladin of the Q.D.G. led, with troops behind in an armoured vehicle. It drew such a volume of fire that its machine-gun, the sight of its 76-mm. gun, its turret hatch, and brakes were all put out of action, and the attempt was abandoned. Two further entries by armoured cars were made, one in the afternoon, the other after dark. The first was forced back with periscope smashed and commander and gunner wounded, and the second was met by rockets and intense automatic fire from an ambush position. It too had to be brought back, leaving twelve bodies in the hands of the enemy.

With twenty-two killed in all and thirty-one wounded, and a citadel of great importance lost to an unsuspected enemy, it was a black day for the British Army, blacker even than the day of death by fire in Cyprus in July 1956. The military instinct was to counterattack immediately, under cover of the hitherto forbidden heavy armament of the Saladins, but there were grave political risks in attacking Federal forces in a crowded town and the military instinct had for the time being to bow

to the political. The soldiers fretted and sighed. They had been hampered all along by what they regarded as absurd concessions to their
opponents, and this was the most infuriating, indeed humiliating, of all.
Crater was merely sealed off, and although the bodies were handed over
to the British by the mutinous police, the morale of the troops, which
had been wonderfully high, turned to sullen.

It was in this brief, bleak period, as previously arranged, that the
British handed over their upcountry commitments to the South
Arabian Army. The event was preceded, four weeks earlier, by another
misfortune for the men who had shed such sweat and blood in opening
up Radfan and keeping the roads free of mines. A working party of the
39th Field Company, R.E., were ambushed in convoy and lost two
killed and ten wounded before the guerrillas were dispersed by Hunter
aircraft, directed by a wounded subaltern. Now, on June 25, they made
their last, laborious search for mines and back came the longest occupants, 45 Commando, after a hand-over which included ceremonial
exchanges and was clouded only by the scowl on the face of the relieving
commander. The squadron of S.A.S. went shortly ahead of the commandos, after an innings as long, and the last battery out belonged
to the 47th Light Regiment, who had relieved the 1st R.H.A. that
month. Irish Guardsmen toiled up hills on familiar picquetting duties,
the Q.D.G. acted as shepherds, and the R.E.M.E. stood by to rescue
the crocks. From Mukeiras a company of the Fifth Fusiliers returned by
air. It was farewell to the mountains and to the type of adventure for
which most men had joined the army. Twenty-four of them had died
sampling it since the Radfan operations began.

The 24th Brigade remained in Little Aden, and although the insurgents' urge to blow up the oil pipeline and other of B.P.'s installations
kept plenty of troops occupied there, more were now available for
duties in 'big' Aden. There were further reinforcements from England
following the police mutiny. The Argylls duly relieved the Royal
Northumberland Fusiliers, who had lost nine killed (all on June 20)
and thirty-five wounded in nine months. The 1st Prince of Wales's
Own were rushed out on the heels of the Argylls, arriving between June
27–29 for their third tour of Aden; the first troops left Colchester
within four hours of receiving warning. Thus there were seven battalions within Aden state, and the equivalent of an eighth was supplied
separately by the King's Own Border company, two batteries of the
47th Light on infantry duty, and a squadron of the 5th R.T.R., similarly
converted for a four-months' tour.

Tower had strength enough now to swamp and dominate Crater,
where rebel flags were flying and looting was rife, and he planned to do

it gradually, without causing further damage to the morale of the police and Federal forces in general. The Argylls, who had taken over responsibility for Crater, were meanwhile itching to gain revenge for their losses and had to be restrained. Intelligence, acquired from some skilful clandestine patrolling, suggested that resistance might be slight, and after 45 Commando had chipped away at some snipers around the Main Pass, which covered the entrance from the west, the Argylls came in from the north-east and south-east approaches as darkness fell on July 3. They advanced on a two-company frontage to the skirl of their pipes, and with them went A Squadron, Q.D.G., flying the red and white hackles of the Fifth Fusiliers on their aerials. A few shots were fired from a palace of the Sultan of Lahej, nothing else, and by 3 a.m. the Argylls were secure on their second and final objective, which was well short of the armed police barracks. A ceremonial reveille, played by pipes and drums, roused the inhabitants when daylight came. From the Q.D.G. went a signal to the Fusiliers: 'Your hackles fly again in Crater'.

It was an act of redemption, carried out with impressive panache and announced dramatically to the world, for the Argylls' Lieutenant-Colonel Mitchell, who had risen rapidly to command from brevet rank, had a most unusual (for a soldier) flair for publicity, as one result of which he was accorded the inappropriate nickname of 'Mad Mitch' by a reporter hungry for colourful embellishment. He came at a time when the troops were suffering from a lack of self-advertisement, through fear of further inflaming the Arab passion, and certainly the light focussed upon the Argylls by their commanding officer's efforts—and magnified by their own splendid bearing—shone all the brighter by contrast. Mitchell was undoubtedly motivated by pride in regiment, without which no battalion could for long have endured Aden at its hottest, and with the future of his regiment in jeopardy it was good policy to publicise achievements. However, by stressing how expert his men were at killing, he obscured some of the other, more important qualities required for police operations and did not make the task of those holding together the fragile threads of civil-military-police cooperation any easier.

The real test in Crater was in fact yet to come, and it was passed successfully thanks to Tower's policy of gradualism, by which he combined further limited nocturnal advances with parleys and enabled the Argylls to gain unopposed occupation of the whole of Crater, including the armed police barracks, with the consent of the hitherto mutinous policemen. On July 13 he held a ceremonial inspection of the latter in their own barracks: a gesture of forgiveness which was to simplify the soldiers' task and of which officers of the Argylls showed their opinion by refusing to shake hands with any of the police officers. Crater was to erupt less frequently from now on. Free from the other commitments that had stretched the Fusiliers, the Argylls kept a tight hold on the town, drawing the predictable, strident protests against their alleged brutality in general but no specific complaints in response to invitations made by themselves.

Towards the end of June the Middle East Command was given November 20 as the planning date for the final withdrawal, which was over a month earlier than originally understood. This involved some hectic staff work, which paradoxically had been simplified by a strike earlier in June that had paralysed Aden port and necessitated a complete military takeover. The Royal Corps of Transport took control with aid from a company of the Royal Pioneer Corps sent from England and members of the other services. It was through this port organisation that the stores were evacuated. The men went by tactical transport aircraft from Khormaksar, staging at Bahrain for a transfer to passenger planes.

Operationally, the problem was simplified by the tighter control the military had gradually been compelled to take and the measures by which the mutinies in the Federal Guard and the Aden Police had been quelled without making these forces ineffective. It was a question now of battening down and restricting recreational movement to the minimum until the time came to pull out, a comparatively easy task compared with the long grind of keeping options open for a more responsible transfer of government. August was a month of fury, in which 762 terrorist incidents were recorded. Perhaps twenty caused casualties to British troops, including three deliberate murders. They drew belated recognition from the Ministry of Defence that the troops were officially on active service.

Little Aden was the first to be evacuated. The Irish Guards, who had performed a marvellous variety of duties, from excursions to the East Protectorate to dock labour duty in Aden, left in August followed by H.Q. 24 Brigade and the 47th Light Regiment, less one battery for duty with 45 Commando in 'big' Aden. On September 13 the Queen's Own Hussars, who had relieved the Q.D.G. in July, handed protection of the oil installations and the rest of Little Aden over to the S.A.A. and with solemn exchange of compliments drove off.

There was no need now to remain in Sheikh Othman, where a tremendous battle between N.L.F. and Flosy had been raging without interference from the British. Taking advantage of a lull in the fighting, the 1st Para handed over their constantly bombarded posts to the S.A.A. in the early hours of September 24 and slipped back to a line covering the neck of the isthmus, which had rapidly been put into a fully fortified state. They had lost three killed and twenty-one wounded at Sheikh Othman and could claim, with King's Own Border assistance, thirty-two terrorists killed and thirteen wounded. The Lancashires went with them. They had handed the Steamer Point-Tawahi area over to the Prince of Wales's Own in July to relieve 1st Para of that other great terrorists' Aunt Sally, Al Mansoura. They were now free to return home after eight exacting months' service, which had cost them five killed and forty wounded and been stoically endured by the young soldiers in particular, of whom they had 200 in their 'teens. Six combat decorations were to fall to the Lancashires, among them a D.S.O. for their Lieutenant-Colonel Downward, a distinction emulated only by Walsh of the 1st Para in Aden state. Downward had, incidentally, also acted as brigade commander for the re-occupation of Crater, during a brief recuperative period of leave for Brigadier R. C. P. Jefferies, of the Royal Irish Fusiliers, who for twenty-one months bore the strain of commanding Aden Brigade.

45 Commando had meanwhile taken Maalla over from the South Wales Borderers, who had kept it subdued for seven and a half months and by kills or captures eliminated thirty-nine terrorists, and on October 11 42 Commando arrived from Singapore to use their carrier *Albion* as a mobile base from which to relieve the Prince of Wales's Own at Tawahi and Steamer Point, where they had had to contend, among other nuisances, with some sharp, though not very lethal mortar attacks. The ships and aeroplanes meanwhile maintained a swift rate of discharge, and by October 28 H.Q. Middle East Command had shrunk from a strength of 800 to 45, in which diminished form it moved to Khormaksar for the final act of dissolution.

The N.L.F. had by now frightened away or exterminated every one of the Federal rulers and were fast winning the battle against Flosy for possession of Aden, making a sudden decisive onslaught just after an official announcement from Britain, made on November 2, had given closer clue to the date of departure. On November 6 the S.A.A., who still under Brigadier Dye had remained wonderfully firm and impartial amid the chaos around them, declared the N.L.F. the winners and pledged them their support, simultaneously intervening with some powerful thumps to end the slaughter the rivals were inflicting on each other in Sheikh Othman. On the 13th the British Government agreed to negotiate with the N.L.F., and terrorist attacks came to an end. It remained for Trevelyan, who had won the admiration of servicemen, to concoct a formula for the orderly transfer of what power remained in his hands.

He was ready by November 26, in the earliest hours of which three battalions of the S.A.A., now styled the Arab Armed Forces in Occupied South Yemen, relieved 42 and 45 Commandos in Maalla and Tawahi and the Argylls in Crater. Only at the last was there any ceremony, which was filmed for television; the Argylls had lost a further two killed since their tragic preliminary and twenty-four wounded, a number by mortar bombs. Soon the N.L.F. flags were waving everywhere, proclaiming the birth of The People's Republic of South Yemen. But one part of urban Aden remained in British keeping. C Company, 1st King's Own Border were at Steamer Point and they stayed there until next day, when Sir Humphrey Trevelyan handed over the keys of Government House and moved on to the carrier *Eagle*.

He departed next day, the 28th, from Khormaksar aerodrome, and representatives of the remnant left to guard it paraded to honour him: of the ever faithful 45 Commando, who stood on the right as representing the Royal Navy; of A Squadron, Queen's Own Hussars; C Company, 1st King's Own Border; and of the R.A.F. Regiment, while Hunter fighters zoomed overhead in salute. The Royal Marine band from *Eagle*, who had done much to boost the morale of the troops in some pretty uncomfortable places, played 'Fings Ain't Wot They Used To Be' as the High Commissioner climbed into his plane. 42 Commando meanwhile, with their own 8 (Alma) Battery, 95th Commando Light Regiment in support, were manning the defence line across the top of the isthmus, which they had recently taken over from 1st Para. Fifty years previously the British had confronted the Turks from the same positions.

Next day, Wednesday the 29th, a rush of aircraft brought the last of the arduous, far-stretching duties performed by the R.A.F. from Khormaksar to a close soon after noon, the King's Own Border company having the well deserved distinction of being the last army unit to leave. The final lift was made by naval helicopters, carrying 42 Commando straight from their positions to their carrier, *Albion*. The last, carrying the Commanding Officer, flew off at 3 p.m. just behind one carrying Major-General Tower to H.M.S. *Intrepid*, flagship of the C.-in-C., Admiral Le Fanu. Here the Middle East Command, and with it British responsibility for Aden, remained officially in business until closing down at midnight.

It was a neat task of extrication, carried out with the professionalism gleaned from years of hard experience. Its brightest feature from the military viewpoint, as in India, was the cooperation provided by the national army that the British had reared and seen, at one awful moment, turn against them. Its restitution was something of a triumph, both for the restraint of the British soldiers, the pluck of the Arab officers, and the leadership of Brigadier Dye, who did not hand over until just before the departure and whose successor, Colonel Muhammed Ahmad, came to bid the British commanders a touching farewell. It was thanks to the Arab soldiers they had trained that the British did not have to hand their old colony over to complete anarchy, and even though the new government was to hound and execute the 'traitors' who had worked for the Federal cause, there was at least some form of order to show for all the pelting—with words, bullets, and bombs—that the British troops had so stoically endured. They had enabled their political masters to achieve a better solution than they deserved.

The cost in Aden State, since December 1963, was sixty-eight soldiers killed, and without the twenty-two slain in a single day this would have been a remarkably low figure. According to operational returns officially announced for the British forces in Aden state, 669 were wounded—a figure reduced to 322 by army returns through administrative sources, which presumably only includes men sent to hospital long enough to be struck off the strength of their units. For a glimpse of two of them we may turn to General Willoughby, writing in a foreword to Julian Paget's *Last Post* of a visit he made to hospital after a bomb episode in Crater: 'They were aged 18 and 19. Neither had a word of complaint. Both were blind, and one had lost his right hand. What could one say to these two? What could one do, except to go back to one's room to be alone for a while?'

17

The Lone Sentry

(1966-70)

W ITH the evacuation of Aden, it could be claimed, an era had
ended. But eras do not end neatly to suit the convenience of
writers, and within two months of the retreat from Aden calls for help
were heard from an island in the midst of the Indian Ocean, Mauritius,
where a state of emergency was declared on January 21, 1968. The 2nd
Coldstream had sent a company there from Aden in 1965, but responsibility for it had perforce been transferred to the Far East Command,
and a company group of the 1st King's Shropshire Light Infantry were
brought in from Malacca, where they belonged to the Commonwealth
Brigade. Warned in the early hours of the 22nd, when at no special
state of readiness, they drove 150 miles to Changi airport and then
rode 4,400 miles in two Hercules aircraft, staging at the Maldive island
of Gan. On that very evening of the 22nd they were out on patrol in the
streets of Mauritius.

It was a question of keeping Creoles and Moslems apart and it called
for the familiar tasks of curfew enforcement, searches for weapons, and
showing the flag. A second company of the K.S.L.I. had to be summoned and was not released until after the grant of independence to
Mauritius, without royal ceremony, on March 12. A single company
detachment remained until the end of 1968, and there were scenes of
great emotion when these men of the 3rd Light Infantry, as the K.S.L.I.
had become, departed, for they had done an immense amount of work
for the people, both old and young. It won them presentations from
the Prime Minister, Dr. Sir Seewoosagur Ramgoolam, and the Wilkin-
son Company's Sword of Peace, awarded for outstanding work in
fostering good relations with the peoples of occupied countries.

Although few places were left under British rule, they still contained
potential for trouble; the most combustible was to be found in Hong

465

Kong, where there had been a spate of violence between May and November 1967. In common only with Gibraltar, the garrison at Hong Kong had remained constant in size. It had been reduced to four battalions by the exodus to Korea in August 1950, and it had remained at four until the Borneo campaign, when it rose to five, of which three were Gurkhas of the 48th Brigade, with armour reduced from a regiment to a squadron. The police were tough and efficient, and during the riots staged by the Red Chinese in May and June the troops had little to do except stand by at immediate readiness.

On July 8 the frontier erupted. A village police post was attacked by armed militiamen and a raving mass, with regular troops in menacing support. Five policemen were killed in an attempt at relief. With the reluctant consent of the Governor, the 1/10th Gurkhas and a troop of Life Guards were ordered forward to remove the intruders, using the absolute minimum of force. They were met by machine-gun fire and went to ground until it ended without firing a round. They relieved the police post and dug in around it, with many a weapon trained on them. This was the start of two months of electric tension, shared by the 1/10th, 1/7th, 1/6th, and 2/7th Gurkhas, the latter brought in from Malaya, doing frontier duty in pairs. They had to resist many assaults by hysterical youths, either with tear gas or in dire crisis with phosphorous grenades, but always refraining from rifle fire. One night in August Lieutenant-Colonel McAlister of the 1/10th was grabbed with the district officer after a parley that had already lasted eight hours, and four hours of frightening scuffling and confusion passed before their release. A police officer on a subsequent occasion was less fortunate and had to make his own escape from imprisonment. However the tension gradually subsided, and by December it was no longer necessary for soldiers to be entrenched along the frontier line.

Twice previously the army had been called in to help subdue riots in Hong Kong, although these had not attained the violence achieved by the 'Red Guards' in 1967. Just as important was the relief and construction work done by the soldiers for the community. Ravages wrought by typhoons, floods and forest fires have all been redeemed, the latter calling for a feat of immense exertion by a mule company of the R.T.C. in bringing the ingredients for the construction of great water storage tanks to the top of a bleak frontier hill. There can be no part of the world more saturated by the sweat of British soldiers than these steeps in the New Territories.

Stormy though the scene will no doubt remain in this part of the dwindled Empire, it is unlikely that the problems encountered in Aden will recur here or anywhere else, for the reason that the soldiers would have the vast majority of the people on their side. Aden can therefore rightly be said to have ended an era, the era of voluntary release from British rule, and it is worth pausing to consider the overall part played by the British Army in the process, bearing in mind the obligation long accepted by the British to leave stable and democratic governments behind them. The essential claim that can surely be made is that the army did all that was asked of it by the politicians, at times more. The failures were the result of reluctance to enlarge the army's commitments, invariably because of the cost.

Thus the Punjab was plunged into hideous massacre which could surely have been averted, or at least greatly lessened, by leaving the British Army in occupation of it for, say, a year. Palestine was surrendered to what may become a hundred years of warfare because the troops were not required to stay until a frontier settlement had been agreed, which admittedly would have been a taxing task but one in which help might have been forthcoming from the United Nations at a much earlier stage than occurred. Over Egypt the army made the best of a bad political job, taking the initiative in arranging terms for a departure that in itself was satisfactorily carried out, and even if the return journey was a fiasco, at least the soldiers did what the political leaders expected of them. In Kenya and in Cyprus there was firm political resolve to reach a fair settlement, and in each the army thwarted a take-over by force. But in Aden there was resolve only to get out, and the marvel was that the army left behind them the means of preserving order.

It is of interest, and surely no coincidence, that in the Middle East, where Britain's greatest wartime victories had been won, the army's post-war role was to pull chestnut after chestnut out of the fire. There were some painful burns, which were felt most sharply by the troops on the spot, and many of them might have been avoided but for the belief, stemming from the wartime victories, that a powerful military presence had to be maintained in the Middle East. On the other hand defeat in the Far East had left the prestige of the British at its lowest ebb, and in place of the weary yet confident conservatism that tinted the outlook from Cairo, there had to be humble beginnings. There was greater sympathy with people who had known occupation by a cruel foe, and from the partnership eventually forged the army's greatest post-war successes emerged. There were plenty of adventurers keen to take the place of the Japanese, and the parts played by the soldiers in stemming the onslaught on South Korea and in preserving first Malaya and then Malaysia from the grasp of tyrants must rank as the British Army's finest achievements at any time of technical peace.

During the years of triumph in Borneo the axe was beginning another bout of chipping at Whitehall. The Labour Government were resolved to reduce expenditure on defence from 7 to 5 per cent and it was with this morbid brief that Mr. Denis Winston Healey began a term as Minister of Defence which was to outspan even that of the first, Winston Churchill, and was to be marked by as tight a hold over the service chiefs. With Aden and Borneo in simultaneous furore, there could be no immediate prospect of reducing the Regular Army, and he therefore made his first military target the Territorials. As first announced in July 1965, and subsequently enlarged upon, the Territorial Army and Army Emergency Reserve were together to be converted into the Army Volunteer Reserve, with a reduction in strength from 120,000 to 50,000. The new role was merely reinforcement of the Regular Army, and in place of the eight divisions that had formed the T.A. only eighteen battalions of infantry (of which three were Para and two S.A.S.) one regiment of armour, and five of artillery were to be maintained, each with the primary function of bringing regular units up to operational strength. 72 per cent of the A.V.R. was to consist of specialist units, R.E., Signals or services, needed for war but not essential in peacetime.

The amazing reason given for the disbandment of the T.A. was that the only type of war envisaged was a quick nuclear one, on the likelihood of which the Tory Government had been criticised by Labour for placing too much store, although they had not based their plans solely on it, as was now the case. What was more amazing than the rashness of the assumption was the fact that the T.A. had been trained, as a subsidiary role, in combating the devastation of a nuclear attack and were spread all over Britain ready to play a part of most crucial importance if the ghastly need arose. It was said to be too expensive to modernise their equipment, although the need for it was not explained. In the event a motion rejecting the reorganisation was defeated in the Commons by only one vote, and strong pressure exerted on behalf of the T.A. obtained the retention of most of the battalions as a glorified home guard. Such battalions were named Territorial battalions and placed in Category T. & A.V.R. III. The reinforcement ones were in T. & A.V.R. II and named Volunteer battalions, although their role was very different from that of the old Volunteers. T. & A.V.R. I contained the 'Ever-Readies', individuals and specialised units liable to call-up without proclamation.

The forming of the élite Volunteer battalions provided an additional spur towards the evolution of the large regiment, since there was to be one to each of the thirteen brigades or regiments, raising invidious problems of identity and homogeneity for those that remained brigades.

Labour ministers had shown themselves no keener to interfere in this matter than their predecessors, the policy of the Army Board being still to coax without coercing. It was known that there were to be further reductions, and consequently debate raged throughout the Infantry, and this was unsettling, particularly since the advocates of the large regiments had officialdom on their side and its opponents therefore risked being branded as reactionaries, to the possible detriment of their prospects. Opposition was fiercest in Scotland, where mutters of 'tribalism' were overpowered by warnings about the 'big brother watching you'. Scotland, paradoxically enough, could claim to have been the cradle of the large regiment. The Highland Regiment and the Lowland Regiment had been in existence during the Second World War, both displaying their own badges, for the training and holding of recruits.

In the event only three of the brigades opted for conversion, and two of them, the East Anglian and the Green Jacket, had been organised for it since the early days of the 1957 reforms. The Royal Anglian Regiment was formed on September 1, 1964, and The Royal Green Jackets on January 1, 1966. The Home Counties followed, being influenced among other factors by the Reserve Army reorganisation; they became The Queen's Regiment on the eccentric date of December 31, 1966. Now the Army Board turned from coaxing to intimidation. With the Borneo war ended and a date agreed for the evacuation of Aden, reduction, which had long been threatened, could begin and the share allotted to the Infantry was eight battalions. Instead of carefully considering the case for each regiment, the planners merely selected eight brigades—the Lowland, Lancastrian, Fusilier, Light Infantry, Yorkshire, Mercian, Welsh, and Northern Irish—and nominated the junior regiment of each for elimination, leaving it to the Council of Colonels of each to decide whether the loss should be shared. (Technically, the battalion, not its regiment, was nominated, but a regiment without a regular battalion is a lifeless thing.) All eight of these regiments had escaped amalgamation in 1957, and three had happily raised 2nd battalions in 1952.

There were three courses open to the Councils of Colonels and the decisions were divided between them in the ratio of three, three, two. The Fusilier, Light Infantry, and North Irish Brigades opted for conversion to large regiments, and thus the Lancashire Fusiliers—an elderly junior, 280-year-old, in whose ranks nineteen V.C.s had been won—the Durham Light Infantry, and the Royal Irish Fusiliers were able to see their traditions perpetuated before the battalions that had built them up became extinct; for the Irish it was a case of 'Faugh a

Ballagh'—Clear the Way—once again, but it is doubtful whether the people of Durham were ever persuaded that their beloved 'Faithfuls' could live on under any other name. An amalgamation was arranged for the Loyal (North Lancashire) with a regiment recently born of amalgamation, the Lancashire (Prince of Wales's Volunteers); for the Sherwood Foresters (Nottinghamshire and Derbyshire) with a regiment whose territory did not even adjoin theirs, the Worcestershire; and for the Welch with the South Wales Borderers, a union to be blessed with the accolade of Royal. The decision made for the other two, and accepted by themselves that others should live on unscathed, was death. The 1st Cameronians (Scottish Rifles)—the 26th or Covenanters, who had been faithfully serving their Sovereign ever since 1689—met their end unflinchingly in a requiem parade, held at Edinburgh on May 14, 1968, and the 1st York and Lancaster—the 65th Foot, and to some 'the Young and Lovelies'—made a similar brave departure from the scene at their camp at North Weald, Essex, far from home, on December 14, 1968.

The announcement of the cuts, which was made in July 1967, caused remarkably little public comment, and the measure that went with it none at all. The powers of bondage assigned the brigades under the 1957 reforms—common eligibility for service, a single promotion roll, a centralised depot and, most binding of all, a common cap badge—were to be transferred to a new administrative grouping containing two or three large regiments or brigades, the division. The object was to save men and money and to widen prospects of promotion; it was a time when the merits of mergers were being widely proclaimed, and the army could not ignore the demands of efficiency and the shrill cliché-cry, 'cost effectiveness'. There was of course another sort of cost that could not be measured by a chartered accountant. Regiments that had themselves voluntarily formed combines to escape from the soulless grasp of the brigade were caught at once beneath a larger net, which could drag men together from as far apart as Londonderry and Hull, or Nottingham and Bournemouth, switch them around at random to suit the convenience of the staff, and would stamp them all with a common badge. Ten years earlier the regiments had been self-sufficient with a single depot for one regular battalion and strong ties with the county; they had then been pushed into league with two or three others because this was regarded as the ideal, viable size; and now they were told that to be viable the organisation had to support upwards of six battalions, never less. It was a bewildering situation, and although Mr. Healey claimed that he intended to 'preserve the best features of the Infantry regimental system' there was good cause for cynicism. The county system had virtually been scrapped, and with it went not only a source of strength in peacetime but the framework for expansion at time of war.

Details of the divisional groupings can be seen in Appendix A. It will be noted that the only brigade that could claim antiquity as such, the Brigade of Guards, could not avoid the indignity of being renamed the Guards Division. Whether its regiments would be allowed to retain the freedom to wear their own cap badges remained to be seen.

The Infantry of course was not the only arm affected by the 1967 cuts. Armour was taxed to the tune of three regiments, and static employment at the Centre at Bovington was to remove one other regiment from the operational list. The 5th Royal Tank Regiment was assigned to disbandment as one of the three; the 10th Royal Hussars was merged with the 11th or 'Cherrypickers', a pair that had been standing like rocks against the tide of amalgamation; and the third was deferred for further consideration. Only the 1st and 2nd Dragoons—the Royals and the Royal Scots Greys—remained untouched out of the twenty-eight cavalry regiments first assailed by the axe in 1922, and the 2nd were allowed to live precariously on, for the Royals were dragged upwards to become Household Cavalry by fusion with the Blues. The Royal Artillery lost four regiments, among them the 6th and 18th Light, and the Royal Engineers the equivalent of three squadrons.

The C.G.S. at this time was General Cassels, the last of the Chiefs with experience of commanding a division in war. As field commander in Palestine, Korea, Malaya, and Germany, he had made as large a contribution to the achievements of the post-war army as any man and knew the quality of its many components. It was sad for him, having at last reached the top, to be confronted with the depressing task of reduction—whereas his predecessors, Field Marshals Festing and Hull, had by contrast been engrossed with the far more intriguing problems of stretching limited resources to meet ever growing demands.

Warning that further reductions would follow came from the Prime Minister, when he announced emergency financial measures on January 16, 1968. In among domestic targets for retrenchment were the Brigade of Gurkhas (the only brigade allowed to retain this title), the T. & A.V.R. III, and all military commitments east of Suez except for the garrison at Hong Kong. It was not for soldiers to say what parts of the world they should be asked to defend. At the same time they had made great and well rewarded sacrifices for the people of Malaysia in particular, and they could be excused a sigh at seeing them abandoned with lack of compassion merely to make the domestic cuts more acceptable to selfish people at home. One Minister of State, Miss Jennie Lee, cast revealing light on the motive by publicly withdrawing her threat to resign over the prescription charges because of the defence cuts that went with it. Probably she did not wish the Malaysian people to succumb to tyranny, but merely could not rid herself of the long indoctrinated delusion that the soldiers were there for the sole purpose of preserving a veneer of imperial grandeur.

The army, in particular the infantry, fell into a state of sullen brooding. There seemed little point in soldiering on when the old commitments were in process of dissolution and old institutions were being chopped up and bound together into bundles displaying garish new labels. There was a bad slump in recruiting and a rush of applications for retirement from officers.

One strange manifestation of the prevailing discontent was a leader in *The Times* which had the unmistakable tone of official sponsorship. And it was a petulant tone, expressing aggravation with the 'political tribalism which has dogged and inhibited previous attempts—by all governments—to reshape the infantry into a more flexible arm than the rigid regimental system makes possible in a dwindling Army.' No attempt was made to explain why a firmer line had not been taken against the tribalism, and a sense of failure in this respect presumably accounted for the petulance. There was no discussion of the merits of a large regimental system over the divisional one, nor of the feasibility of a looser grouping, as exercised by the brigades prior to 1957. The leader ended, like a scolding nannie, with a threat. After a warning about the powers of the new divisional headquarters, the regiments were told that 'if they show signs of that restrictiveness in recruiting and cross-posting which had made the old-style infantry so difficult to organize, then clearly a corps of infantry will have to come.'

Among the protests that this article drew was one from Field Marshal Templer, who expressed himself 'deeply shocked at the implications in the final sentence'. 'Do you not realise,' he asked, 'that the Regimental system of the British Army is and always has been the envy of the world? I know this very well from innumerable talks with senior officers of other countries, including the United States.' His own regiment, it is worth noting, was one of those that had secured its survival in modified form by accepting the evolution of the large regiment.

This was in the summer, and one of the causes of upset was that one regiment, the Argyll and Sutherland Highlanders, had decided to fight their battle in the open. The Highland Council of Colonels were resolved to oppose any internal merging, just as the 91st Argylls and 93rd Sutherland Highlanders would without doubt have stood firm against it in 1881 if they had been allowed any say in the matter. It was agreed therefore that the Argylls must die unless they could save themselves by their own exertions. Certainly they made a brave and stirring attempt, as befitted a regiment with a fine fighting record. Over a million signatures were collected. But there was an unstated complement to the slogan, 'Save the Argylls,' and it was 'Shoot someone else'. Probably very few serving infantrymen were among the million, certainly none from the regiments that had accepted the invitation to merge into large ones. If the invitation had at an early stage been converted to order the fuss would have been avoided, and there would have been no cause for what an Argyll officer had on a previous occasion (the departure for Korea) described as 'bags of ballyhoo'.

Having chosen to stand or fall alone, the Argylls had as little chance of swaying their masters as the H.L.I. in 1957. All six of the brigades or large regiments untouched the previous year were to be shorn of one battalion, and on July 11, 1968, the fatal details were announced. There was a furore in Parliament over the choice of the Argylls, none over the junior battalions of the Queen's Regiment, the Royal Anglian Regiment, and the Royal Green Jackets, although these battalions had gained great renown respectively as the Middlesex, a regiment famed for living up to the nickname won at Albuhera, Die-Hards; the Royal Leicesters or Tigers, the old 17th Foot, whose earliest battle honour was Namur 1695; and the Rifle Brigade, the élite of Moore's army in its earliest days and an élite corps ever since, the only regiment always to have worn green. Their traditions of course were safe in the keeping of the regiments they had joined. In the Wessex Brigade the junior was spared, being the already amalgamated Duke of Edinburgh's (Berkshire and Wiltshire), and the hitherto untouched Gloucestershire and the Royal Hampshire were joined together in a union lavishly splashed with honours, old and new; it was an option of a type not open to the Lancastrian the previous year. The other reduction, first in precedence, was in the Guards Division, and the victim was the 282-year-old 2nd Battalion Scots Guards.

As for the Gurkhas, each of their four regiments was to be reduced to one battalion, by separate decree, between 1968 and 1971, and in the event the 2/2nd was to gain a timely reprieve. Only the Parachute Regiment, with its three battalions and Guards company, escaped unscathed 'for special operational reasons'. This was not very popular among those chosen for elimination because they were the most junior, and there was a feeling too that the advent of the helicopter had made parajumping a superfluous skill. On the other hand, the paras had certainly proved their worth in the post-war years.

The Royal Armoured Corps, Royal Artillery and Royal Engineers were each skinned of a regiment or its equivalent, and in each case the decision was deferred. The cry now, though raised less stridently, was 'Save the Royal Scots Greys', and certainly a strong case could be made for the retention intact of this one cavalry regiment that Scotland could claim as her own. But there was to be no avoiding the fate that had befallen every other regiment of the old Cavalry of the Line, although the Life Guards remained serene and did not stoop as the Blues had done the year before. The Greys, after a year's anxious deliberation, were paired with a regiment of Dragoon Guards whose previous amalgamation was obscured in the title of 3rd Carabiniers. (The Carabiniers had been the 6th.) This meant unwanted promotion for the Royal Scots Greys.

The totals left in the army Healey trimmed would come to fifty battalions of infantry (including the Gurkhas but not the 22 S.A.S.), nineteen regiments of armour, and twenty-nine of artillery. Of these, seventeen battalions and thirteen armoured regiments were with Rhine Army, each division having only two British brigades, of which one, the 6th Infantry, had since 1967 been stationed in England, although still part of Rhine Army, as a means of saving money. Nine battalions and one armoured regiment would suffice for the other overseas commitments, divided between Hong Kong and Mediterranean stations. This leaves twenty-four battalions and five armoured regiments (of which one and two are tied to a static training role) available to the home command, a figure higher than in any other post-war period except the rundown days of 1948 and the period of brief bounty that followed the evacuation of Egypt.

Again Britain had an equivalent of the old pre-war field force at home, and for the control of it the Army Strategic Command was formed on April 1, 1968, with headquarters near Salisbury, as previously occupied by the now enlarged Southern Command. Its main component was the 3rd Infantry Division (5th, 19th, and 24th Brigades), 16th Para Brigade, and 22 S.A.S. who together formed an airportable force available as an immediate reserve for N.A.T.O. at any point required. As an untied reserve the 5th Infantry Division was reborn (for the second time since the war) also on April 1, 1968, bravely striking out against the current of reduction; its brigades were the 2nd (which could claim, alone with the 24th, full continuity since war ended in 1945), the recently resurrected 8th, and the 39th, spread from Dover to Derry. Also available were the Royal Marine commandos, reduced from five to four, numbered 40, 41, 42, and 45.

The home-based troops had plenty of opportunity to make overseas excursions for training, but a yearning could be felt for the old days of adventure. The army in other words was in search of a role, like the country as a whole, and the idea under fomentation in many high-ranking minds was that aid to the civil community should provide the new sense of purpose required. A great deal had already been done in this sphere. Indeed it had provided the key to success in Malaya and Borneo, as has already been related, and mention has also been made of feats of rescue and construction in Africa, Hong Kong and the Caribbean, which brought as much political benefit to Britain as material benefit to the people. Other rescue work was performed outside areas of British occupation, as by the thirty gunners who took their vehicles to the Ionian Islands after the earthquake there in 1953; the party of sappers who supervised the erection of Nissen huts after the Skopje earthquake in Yugoslavia in 1963; and the sapper squadron and the field ambulance who went to Vientiane, in Laos, to repair the human and material damage wrought by flood in 1966. In England troops have often been called out on emergency aid. Relief work after the tidal disaster of February 1953 was their biggest achievement, and among others only slightly less exacting have been visits to the docks to work under the jeering eyes of striking professionals. Aid has also been given for many routine development tasks, ranging from work on an oil palm plantation in the Far East, to airstrip construction in the Caribbean, to bridge building and agricultural assistance in home commands. In 1968 a pamphlet was issued to civil authorities and social organisations, listing the types of assistance the services could provide, and it appears to be from this that Giles the cartoonist conceived a new idea in one-upmanship, the employment by the Joneses of Life Guardsmen in full regalia in place of the denim-clad fatiguemen next door.

The danger of employing troops on public utility work is that it might impede their training for what must always be their first and foremost role, defence against aggression, and with sudden starkness, in August 1968, came realisation that there was still a need for them in this role. The Soviet Government were forced to make public display of that predatory instinct of which politicians and journalists in England so seldom dared to speak. Czechoslovakia was invaded and the world trembled. Militarily, it was a brilliant operation, carried out with such speed that the Czechs had no chance to appeal to the outside world and no one could do anything to save them. The British Government were vehement in protest, but as if to prove that they had no intention of running any risk on behalf of the suppressed they brought the brief lifespan of the reprieved territorials, the T. & A.V.R. III, to its end in early 1969. However the regulars had been put on their toes, and it had become apparent that there was as much danger of Europe's slithering into an old-fashioned type of war as being drenched by a nuclear horror-splash. There was to be no more filching from Rhine Army, at any rate for the time being.

Contemplation of this prospect, and of recruiting figures, too, may have brought realisation that efficiency was not the only thing that mattered. Anyway on February 27, 1969, the Army Board issued an order of great consequence, showing that they were after all genuine in their intention to preserve the regimental system. Instead of being branded as mere ciphers of a division, the infantry regiments were allowed to wear their own cap badges. This meant that those who had become large regiments could retain the badges around which such pains had been taken to build up the new esprit. The others could discard their brigade badges, ordered in 1957, and either bring back their old ones or, if an amalgamation, have new ones made. Out of sixty-four cap badges on display in 1957, only eight could return with prospect of permanence, and six belonged to regiments for whose integrity others had chosen extinction: the Royal Scots and the King's Own Scottish Borderers from the Lowlands, the Green Howards and the Duke of Wellington's from Yorkshire, and the Black Watch and the Gordon Highlanders from the Highlands. The two others were the Cheshire Regiment and the Royal Welch Fusiliers, and subsequently the Gloucestershire, and in diminished form, the Royal Hampshire and the Argylls were also to gain admittance to the list.

Cynics may sneer at the effect of a mere emblem and regard this order as a retrograde step. Certainly it cannot be denied that a battalion reflects the personality of its commanding officer more strongly than the traditions with which it may be imbued. But the commanding officer, if he is wise, will call on every aid to build morale, and the intimate pride of belonging to a regiment can be a powerful support when under ordeal by fire and steel. This surely was proved in Korea within the Middlesex, Argylls, Gloucesters, Ulsters, Borderers and Duke's, to mention only a few, well distributed round Britain. They had to face the toughest test, and it is for the toughest that an army should always be prepared; who can say, with over half the countries of the world under dictators, that such a test shall not recur? Undoubtedly the same intimate pride sustained, as two examples, the Suffolks in Malaya and the South Staffords in Cyprus in the more complex tests not only of courage but of patience, vigilance, skill at arms, and tact. It was to be seen again in Aden, displayed both by old regiments and those recently born of amalgamation, such as the Royal Anglians, the Lancashires, and the peerless company of the King's Own Border who gained as much by restraint as has ever been won by fire power.

Here at least was recognition that this individual intimacy, which may be aggravating to outsiders but embraces those temporarily drawn into its fold, should live on, and on a lower key the restoration of the cap badge would act as a safeguard against the indiscriminate cross-posting of men between regiments widely separated territorially. It had its counterpart in the measures taken to ease the clutch of the group system in 1951, and it seems to have had the same effect, for whether or not by coincidence there was a rise in recruiting during the spring of 1969. The army seemed to be straightening to its full height again, and presiding over the revival, making this great concession to infantry pride, was an artilleryman, General Sir Geoffrey ('George') Baker.

It was he who had wrestled with the complexities of the Eoka rising in Cyprus as Field Marshal Harding's Chief of Staff, when for almost the first time in its history the army had to be employed as an auxiliary police force, armed with batons and shields. It is doubtful whether he can have imagined that the experience would be of much value to him when he took office as C.G.S. in February 1968, three months after the surrender of what appeared to be the last of the great imperial policing tasks. Then came the riots in Northern Ireland, and all of a sudden the army was landed with its heaviest commitment since Cyprus and one posing many similar problems.

It seemed almost unbelievable that it could happen in a part of the United Kingdom. Admittedly there had long been sandbags and wire around the barracks by the Southern Irish border, but the country had seemed so peaceful that the resident brigade had been used as a source of reinforcement for overseas, sinking at times to only one battalion, and even losing its headquarters (that of the 39th, which had gone there after evacuating Kenya in 1956) when there was an emergency requirement in Radfan. As the Royal Ulster Constabulary slowly wilted under days of bombardment by brick and petrol bomb, there were leaders in some of Britain's papers giving dire warnings against the employment of troops. But the poor policemen could not stick it forever, and on August 14, 1969, those hardy veterans of Aden, the 1st Prince of Wales's Own, entered Londonderry, not to support, but to relieve the police. They came armed with shields and batons. The correspondent of the *Guardian*, which paper had been strong in its advocacy against committing the troops, reported an immediate lowering of the tension, and wrote in admiration of the 'benign surveillance' the Yorkshiremen exerted over the troubled part of the city.

Now Belfast was ablaze, and on the evening of the 15th the 2nd Queen's (former Queen's Own Buffs) and the recently amalgamated 1st Royal Regiment of Wales entered the Falls and Shankill districts of the city with smoke billowing from many a fire around them. They marched in grimly, in box formations, equipped for battle (although all as riflemen), and they had the task of placing themselves between the warring factions, just as many of them had done in Cyprus or British Guiana. It was done with surprisingly little difficulty, although there was some sniping and one Welsh soldier was wounded. The troops had to stick it without firing back—unless someone was seen in the act of firing. There were some horrifying scenes of devastation, and the eager, welcoming hands stretched out to them made it clear enough to the troops that their stay would have to be a long one.

With a population of almost 400,000 (against Derry's 56,000) Belfast was the heaviest consumer of troops of any town the army had had to police, and bulky though it was by former standards, the strategic reserve was soon whittled to half strength. The 3rd Light Infantry (the former K.S.L.I., and the last engaged on a policing operation) swiftly joined the Belfast garrison; H.Q. 24 Brigade took over responsibility for Londonderry from the 39th and received the 1st Queen's in place of the Prince of Wales's Own, who had completed four months's duty as emergency reinforcements, and also the 2nd Grenadier Guards; the 1st Royal Hampshire and the 1st Royal Green Jackets had also arrived by August 20; in September the resident 1st Light Infantry relieved the Royal Regiment of Wales on return from an exercise in Kenya and the arrival of the 2nd made the Light Infantry involvement complete; 41 Commando came in near the end of September, and the 1st Parachute on October 12, bringing the infantry strength to its maximum of ten battalions. There were representatives here of all types of regiment, the old and the new, the large, the merged and the small, most with new badges and one, the Royal Hampshire, with an old one restored for what was expected to be a brief outing before fusion with another. The 17th/21st Lancers, as the resident regiment, had the main armoured role, with heavy commitments on the frontier as well as in the cities, and the Life Guards sent a squadron out to join them. The 3rd Field Squadron R.E. came at an early stage for the many tasks of clearance and construction.

On August 19 the G.O.C. Northern Ireland, Lieutenant-General Sir Ian Freeland (late of Kenya Land Forces), was made fully responsible for security, with both police and military under his command. Plenty of generals had been in a similar situation, but few can have known it quite so inflammable, with so much depending on the confidence the troops could engender in people filled with fear, hatred, suspicion and superstition.

The Hampshires had to fire a volley of tear-gas C.S. shells to protect

Belfast Catholics from a Protestant onslaught, and not until September 18, after days of street diplomacy, were the former persuaded to allow the removal of their barricades after the soldiers had built a dividing wire fence, which they patrolled.

Diplomacy was not enough. The 'Prots' launched an onslaught on the Saturday night, September 27, and for three successive week-ends the troops in Belfast had to endure assault by petrol bombs, bricks, sheet glass, slates, ball bearings, shot and, latterly, bullets. They could not fire at the attackers, except with gas shells, and could do little at first except stand their ground and send rescue parties to burning houses. A means had to be found of catching without killing, and for this purpose —in defiance of all the old principles of 'duties in aid'—strong-arm groups were formed, ready to rush in with clubs and grab a ringleader. They made their debut on the night of October 11 in what proved the most ferocious fight of all. It was in the Shankill district of Belfast, and the brunt was borne by the 3rd Light Infantry and 41 Commando, with the Life Guards, 2nd Queen's, and a company of the 1st Light Infantry in support.

It fell to the 3rd L.I. to ward off an advance by thousands of Protestants, making a thunderous noise, on Catholic Unity Walk Flats, and their correspondent to *The Silver Bugle* found it 'difficult to describe this utterly incredible scene in a British city: a howling drunken mob, half-bricks and broken flagstones bouncing down the street, petrol bombs, and now automatic weapons joining in the fray'. The Light Infantrymen stood their ground, fired some tear-gas shells, and released the 'heavy' squad, who soon returned clutching some writhing toughs. There was no abating of the fury, and when a platoon tried to come up from behind the crowd, riding in Saracens, they were surrounded and had great difficulty in extricating themselves. The Saracens, manned by Life Guardsmen, had greater success in a subsequent frontal advance in which they smashed through a barricade of cars.

Not until after midnight, when the men had been under fire and suffering casualties for over an hour, were orders received to return the fire, and it was done by marksmen under close supervision, firing only at snipers seen to be firing. A George Medal was won by one of the marksmen, Private James, for his patient and fearless exposure to fire for over four hours, undaunted by having his rifle butt smashed by a bullet. Sergeant Power gained the B.E.M. for leading fifteen charges with his 'heavy' squad, in the face of close range fire from which almost half his men received wounds. And for Lieutenant-Colonel Ballenden, commanding, there was an O.B.E. for the gallantry with which he personally inspired his men wherever the fury was hottest. Dawn had broken before at last it subsided, and the soldiers and police were left alone on the streets to survey the heaps of debris that had been missiles and the charring and scars inflicted by petrol bomb and bullet.

A policeman and two rioters were killed during this night, and sixty-six other casualties were reported, of whom twenty-two were soldiers, despite the splinter-proof vests (similar to those first worn in Korea) of which there had been issue. During the whole week-end, which included a further foray on the Sunday, the 3rd L.I. had twenty men shot, of whom fourteen were admitted to hospital. They reckoned to have been the recipients of 1,000 rounds of small arms fire and 200 petrol bombs, plus half the pavement of Shankill Road. In return they fired 68 bullets and 394 tear-gas shells, and—most important of all—they made seventy arrests. They had ceased to be 'Dad's army'.

There had been criticism that the army had been too conciliatory, but now a decisive victory had been gained, leading to some easing of the strain of keeping watch and administering to the people's needs, which reduced to a debilitating minimum the hours of rest in billets of crude austerity. The 3rd Light Infantry, who may have had the toughest scrap but certainly had no monopoly of the fighting or the hardship, were relieved by the 1st R.H.A. in mid-November, having served only three months, in place of the four that was made standard for an un-accompanied tour, because of their recent return from the Far East and the place they had more easily pacified, Mauritius. 41 Commando were at the same time relieved by other substitute infantrymen, the 33rd Wing, R.A.F. Regiment, who had a battery of the 47th Light Regiment attached, as also did the 1st R.H.A. By mid-January 1970 the garrison had been reduced from ten to seven battalions, and the troops had begun to dismantle some of the barriers, as gingerly as if they were made of glass, not knowing whether peace had been achieved or merely a lull.

It turned out to be a lull, and from Easter onwards the sudden out-bursts of violence flared with sickening regularity, changing pattern from the wild abandon of the earlier riots to what appeared to be deliberate and skilfully managed attempts to provoke the troops to violent retalia-tion and thus spoil the effect of all the work they performed for a com-munity that had long since ceased to diplay any gratitude towards them. The soldiers had been landed with a task that threatened to last as long and to make as heavy demands on patience and stamina as any they had tackled, and whereas their lives had been in greater danger in former encounters with terrorists, their bodies had never before been hit so often or by so wide a range of missiles. The 1st Gloucestershire, 1st Grenadier Guards, 1st Royal Highland Fusiliers, and the 2nd Parachute continued the rotation of reliefs, and in March Rhine Army took a permanent share of the burden by the despatch of the 1st Royal Scots and subsequently of the 1st King's Own Scottish Borderers, who in May replaced the recently arrived 42nd Medium Regiment as the eighth battalion of the garrison. Rhine Army received some redress through the return of its 6th Infantry Brigade, which with four others of armour and infantry was reorganised on a 'square' basis, that is of two units of each. At least no one could accuse Rhine Army of being stagnant.

The arrival of 45 Commando in early June gave further strength to Northern Ireland, and a discovery made by the Royal Scots this month led to the influx of the 16th Light Air Defence Regiment, 1st Green Howards, 3rd Royal Green Jackets, 1st Devon and Dorset (from Malta), 2nd Scots Guards, 1st Black Watch, two squadrons of Life Guards, and one of the Royal Scots Greys, together with Headquarters 5th and 24th Brigade, the latter of whom had been relieved at Derry by the family-accompanied Headquarters 8th Brigade. They were flown in, in the course of four days astride June and July, to take part in a large search and cordon operation, of which the main role was borne as usual by the 39th Brigade, whose Brigadier P. Hudson, late Rifle Brigade, must have had more battalions under his command than any other brigadier in history. It was the first time the army had taken the initiative, and it resulted in some sharp fighting, the capture of over a hundred weapons, and the voicing of sufficient anger from Irish Republican Army sources to show that a telling blow had been struck.

By gradual stages the garrison was slimmed again to eight battalions and an armoured regiment from its maximum of fifteen and two. It was sustained on short tour (from April 1970) by the 1st Cheshire, 5th Light Regiment, 1st Queen's Lancashire, 1st Royal Regiment of Fusiliers, 2nd Coldstream Guards, 42nd Medium Regiment, 1st King's, 3rd R.H.A., 2nd Royal Anglian, and the 1st Royal Regiment of Wales, the last of whom arrived from Germany in October, thirteen months after their first, brief tour had ended. 41 Commando also achieved two brief tours, and in 1971 the Royal Highland Fusiliers would become the first to begin a full four-months tour for the second time. Of the permanent, family-accompanied battalions, the 1st L.I. were relieved by the 3rd Queen's in April 1970 and in September the 2nd Queen's were relieved by the 1st Para, having spent thirteen months on continual watch in Belfast or at immediate readiness to rush from their barracks in armoured carriers and cut off raiding gangsters before they could evaporate up side streets. At the end of July the 1st Royal Anglian took up permanent duty as guardians of Derry under the permanent H.Q. 8 Brigade, and the 17th/21st Lancers stayed on to patrol the province and cities as the oldest military inhabitants.

Meanwhile a Conservative Government had come to power, committed to renewing obligations east of Suez and to reconsidering the fate of the Argylls. They decided that a single battalion group, based on Singapore, would be sufficient for the first, and for its provision they turned to the most obvious source, the Brigade of Gurkhas. Their solution to the second problem was to give all units condemned under the 1968 cuts the option of survival at company or equivalent strength. It was not explained what the function of these companies would be or why, if they were really needed, they should be optional. Nor was it explained why the survival of six companies was thought preferable to that of a complete battalion, except that each is intended to be a candidate for expansion if sufficient men can be recruited within its division. Certainly there will be widespread rejoicing if any can expand.

Naturally the units faced with disbandment chose to survive as sub-units. The tricky problem faced the two pairs earmarked for amalgamation, and a swift and agonising decision had to be made by the pair due for conversion, after most elaborate preparations, to The Royal Regiment of Gloucestershire and Hampshire on September 5, 1970, less than a month's after the Government's decision. In the event the Royal Hampshires, being a few years junior, accepted shrinkage to a company that the Gloucesters might survive as a whole. The Royal Scots Greys on the other hand successfully held out for amalgamation, reckoning it preferable to save The Royal Scots Dragoon Guards rather than continue on their own in shrivelled form.

It is much to be hoped that the Royal Hampshires will not have cause to regret the decision which, in the peculiar manner long shown in such matters, was left to them to make. They have to battle against a tide that has been steadily eroding the Army's strength for fifty years; it was due to sink to 166, 100 under Mr. Healey's forecast for April 1971 and is likely to be some 8,000 lower in fact, and this despite the raising of a six-year recruit's weekly wage to £18·90np. (or £15·25np. after deduction for board and lodging) which is some advance on the £1·40np. on offer in 1948. Only by achieving the near miracle of turning the tide can the independent companies feel at all secure.

Yet affairs in Northern Ireland have at least shown that there is still a task for the British soldier and have restored the iron into his soul. Many people have awoken to the seldom realised truth that he has saved many more lives than he has taken, and in the early days of the emergency tribute was paid him from many unexpected quarters. A fair sample came from Mr. G. Fitt, a Republican Labour M.P. for Belfast, in the Commons: 'I cannot find words of praise high enough to commend the actions of the British troops since they arrived in the streets of Belfast.

Had they not arrived many hundreds of people would have lost their lives.'

Equally impressed was a brigadier making a duty visit to Belfast from the Ministry of Defence. He was impressed by the vastness of the stricken area and the blackness of the dereliction, and most of all by the size of the undertaking thrust upon the troops. To eke out a meagre quota of reliefs, single sentries did duty on the dannert coils stretched across the street ends by the 'peace line', and watching a young soldier at this duty the brigadier marvelled at the stature of the man, at the mixture of authority and kindliness with which he prevented strollers from becoming loiterers. Though the task screamed for two sentries, the peace of Belfast seemed secure on this one pair of shoulders.

Thus stands the British soldier of today, yesterday, and tomorrow. It has become a tradition that the Army must always be overstretched, just as peaceful governments must always see their expectations outpaced by the march of events. One man has therefore to suffice in place of two, and a battalion is assigned a commitment broad enough for a brigade. Such has been the recurring pattern over the past twenty-five years. It has been accepted without complaint by officers and men, and indeed they would appear to be at their happiest when thrust into some hazardous situation and presented with a task of awesome dimensions. The lone sentry of Belfast seems well aware of this great tradition, and we can confidently leave the reputation of the British Army in his keeping.

Appendix A

Organisation

I—THE REGULAR ARMY IN 1949
(i.e. after the post-war cuts)

Round brackets are used when the words are part of the regiment's official title. Square brackets are used for the Infantry regiments' original numbers of Foot.

Mounted Troops
The Life Guards *Also armoured*
Royal Horse Guards (The Blues) *Also armoured*
King's Troop, Royal Horse Artillery

Royal Armoured Corps
1st King's Dragoon Guards
The Queen's Bays (2nd Dragoon Guards)
3rd Carabiniers (Prince of Wales's Dragoon Guards)
4th/7th Royal Dragoon Guards
5th Royal Inniskilling Dragoon Guards
1st The Royal Dragoons
The Royal Scots Greys (2nd Dragoons)
3rd The King's Own Hussars
4th Queen's Own Hussars
7th Queen's Own Hussars
8th King's Royal Irish Hussars
9th Queen's Royal Lancers
10th Royal Hussars (Prince of Wales's Own)
11th Hussars (Prince Albert's Own)
12th Royal Lancers (Prince of Wales's)
13th/18th Royal Hussars (Queen Mary's Own)
14th/20th King's Hussars
15th/19th The King's Royal Hussars
16th/5th The Queen's Royal Lancers
17th/21st Lancers
Royal Tank Regiment *Eight regts.*

Appendix A

Supporting Arms

Royal Regiment of Artillery *Sixty-nine regts, incl. R.H.A.*
Corps of Royal Engineers
Royal Corps of Signals

Foot Guards

Grenadier Guards *Three bns.*
Coldstream Guards *Three bns.*
Scots Guards *Two bns.*
Irish Guards
Welsh Guards

Infantry

The Royal Scots (The Royal Regiment) [1]
The Queen's Royal Regiment (West Surrey) [2]
The Buffs (Royal East Kent Regiment) [3]
The King's Own Royal Regiment (Lancaster) [4]
The Royal Northumberland Fusiliers [5]
The Royal Warwickshire Regiment [6]
The Royal Fusiliers (City of London Regiment) [7]
The King's Regiment (Liverpool) [8]
The Royal Norfolk Regiment [9]
The Royal Lincolnshire Regiment [10]
The Devonshire Regiment [11]
The Suffolk Regiment [12]
The Somerset Light Infantry (Prince Albert's) [13]
The West Yorkshire Regiment (The Prince of Wales's Own) [14]
The East Yorkshire Regiment (The Duke of Yorks' Own) [15]
The Bedfordshire and Hertfordshire Regiment [16]
The Royal Leicestershire Regiment [17]
The Green Howards (Alexandra, Princess of Wales's Own Yorkshire
    Regiment) [19]
The Lancashire Fusiliers [20]
The Royal Scots Fusiliers [21]
The Cheshire Regiment [22]
The Royal Welch Fusiliers [23]
The South Wales Borderers [24]
The King's Own Scottish Borderers [25]
The Cameronians (Scottish Rifles) [26 and 90]
The Royal Inniskilling Fusiliers [27 and 108]
The Gloucestershire Regiment [28 and 61]
The Worcestershire Regiment [29 and 36]
The East Lancashire Regiment [30 and 59]

The East Surrey Regiment [31 and 70]
The Duke of Cornwall's Light Infantry [32 and 46]
The Duke of Wellington's Regiment (West Riding) [33 and 76]
The Border Regiment [34 and 55]
The Royal Sussex Regiment [35 and 107]
The Royal Hampshire Regiment [37 and 67]
The South Staffordshire Regiment [38 and 80]
The Dorset Regiment [39 and 54]
The South Lancashire Regiment (The Prince of Wales's Volunteers)
  [40 and 82]
The Welch Regiment [41 and 69]
The Black Watch (Royal Highland Regiment) [42 and 73]
The Oxfordshire and Buckinghamshire Light Infantry [43 and 52]
The Essex Regiment [44 and 56]
The Sherwood Foresters (Nottinghamshire and Derbyshire Regiment)
  [45 and 95]
The Loyal Regiment (North Lancashire) [47 and 81]
The Northamptonshire Regiment [48 and 58]
The Royal Berkshire Regiment (Princess Charlotte of Wales's) [49 and
  66]
The Queen's Own Royal West Kent Regiment [50 and 97]
The King's Own Yorkshire Light Infantry [51 and 105]
The King's Shropshire Light Infantry [53 and 85]
The Middlesex Regiment (Duke of Cambridge's Own) [57 and 77]
The King's Royal Rifle Corps [60]
The Wiltshire Regiment (Duke of Edinburgh's) [62 and 99]
The Manchester Regiment [63 and 96]
The North Staffordshire Regiment (The Prince of Wales's) [64 and
  98]
The York and Lancaster Regiment [65 and 84]
The Durham Light Infantry [68 and 106]
The Highland Light Infantry (City of Glasgow Regiment) [71 and 74]
Seaforth Highlanders (Ross-shire Buffs, The Duke of Albany's) [72
  and 78]
The Gordon Highlanders [75 and 92]
The Queen's Own Cameron Highlanders [79]
The Royal Ulster Rifles [83 and 86]
The Royal Irish Fusiliers (Princess Victoria's) [87 and 89]
The Argyll and Sutherland Highlanders (Princess Louise's) [91 and
  93]
The Parachute Regiment *Three bns. and Guards coy.*
The Rifle Brigade (Prince Consort's Own)

Appendix A

Army Air Corps

Glider Pilot Regiment *At cadre strength*
Special Air Service *No regular unit until 1950*

The Brigade of Gurkhas

2nd King Edward VII's Own Gurkha Rifles (The Sirmoor Rifles) *Two bns.*
6th Gurkha Rifles *Two bns.*
7th Gurkha Rifles *Two bns.*
10th Gurkha Rifles *Two bns.*
Gurkha Engineers

Services

Royal Army Chaplains' Department
Royal Army Service Corps
Royal Army Medical Corps
Royal Army Ordnance Corps
Corps of Royal Electrical and Mechanical Engineers
Corps of Royal Military Police
Royal Army Pay Corps
Royal Army Veterinary Corps
Small Arms School Corps
Military Provost Staff Corps
Royal Army Educational Corps
Royal Army Dental Corps
Royal Pioneer Corps
Intelligence Corps
Army Physical Training Corps
Army Catering Corps
General Service Corps
Queen Alexandra's Imperial Military Nursing Service
Queen Alexandra's Royal Army Nursing Corps
Women's Royal Army Corps

II—THE REGULAR ARMY IN 1971

(i.e. on completion of cuts ordered in 1968 and modified in 1970)

Mounted Troops

The Life Guards *Also armoured* .
The Blues and Royals (Royal Horse Guards and 1st Dragoons) *Also armoured, formed 1969*
King's Troop, Royal Horse Artillery

Royal Armoured Corps

1st The Queen's Dragoon Guards *Formed 1959*
The Royal Scots Dragoon Guards (Carabiniers and Greys) *Forming July 1971*
4th/7th Royal Dragoon Guards
5th Royal Inniskilling Dragoon Guards
The Queen's Own Hussars [3rd and 7th] *Formed 1959*
The Queen's Royal Irish Hussars [4th and 8th] *Formed 1958*
9th/12th Royal Lancers (Prince of Wales's) *Formed 1960*
The Royal Hussars (Prince of Wales's Own) [10th and 11th] *Formed 1969*
13th/18th Royal Hussars (Queen Mary's Own)
14th/20th King's Hussars
15th/19th The King's Royal Hussars
16th/5th The Queen's Royal Lancers
17th/21st Lancers
Royal Tank Regiment *Four regts.*
Parachute Squadron, Royal Armoured Corps *Formed 1964*

Supporting Arms

The Royal Regiment of Artillery *Twenty-nine regts. and three btys.*
The Corps of Royal Engineers
The Royal Corps of Signals

The Guards Division

Grenadier Guards *Two bns.*
Coldstream Guards *Two bns.*
Scots Guards *One bn. and one coy.*
Irish Guards
Welsh Guards

The Scottish Division

The Royal Scots (The Royal Regiment) [1]
The Royal Highland Fusiliers (Princess Margaret's Own Glasgow and Ayrshire Regiment [21, 71 and 74] *Formed 1959*
The King's Own Scottish Borderers [25]
The Black Watch (Royal Highland Regiment) [42 and 73]
Queen's Own Highlanders (Seaforth and Camerons) [72, 78 and 79] *Formed 1961*
The Gordon Highlanders [75 and 92]
The Argyll and Sutherland Highlanders (Princess Louise's) [91 and 93] *Reduced to single coy. 1971*
Still listed but no longer effective:
The Cameronians (Scottish Rifles) [26 and 90] *reg. bn. disbanded 1968*

Appendix A

The Queen's Division

The Queen's Regiment [2, 3, 31, 35, 50, 57, 70, 77, 97 and 107] *Three bns and one coy. Formed in 1966 by conversion of:*
Headquarters Home Counties Brigade
The Queen's Royal Surrey Regiment [2, 31 and 70] *Formed, 1959*
The Queen's Own Buffs, The Royal Kent Regiment [3, 50 and 97] *Formed 1961*
The Royal Sussex Regiment [35 and 107]
The Middlesex Regiment (Duke of Cambridge's Own) [57 and 77]
The Royal Regiment of Fusiliers [5, 6, 7 and 20] *Three battalions Formed in 1968 by conversion of:*
Headquarters Fusilier Brigade
The Royal Northumberland Fusiliers [5]
The Royal Warwickshire Fusiliers [6] *Renamed 1963*
The Royal Fusiliers (City of London Regiment) [7]
The Lancashire Fusiliers [20]
The Royal Anglian Regiment [9, 10, 12, 16, 17, 44, 48, 56, and 58] *Three battalions and one company. Formed in 1964 by conversion of:*
Headquarters East Anglian Brigade
1st East Anglian Regiment (Royal Norfolk and Suffolk) [9 and 12] *Formed 1959*
2nd East Anglian Regiment (Duchess of Gloucester's Own Royal Lincolnshire and Northamptonshire) [10, 48 and 58] *Formed 1960*
3rd East Anglian Regiment (16th/44th Foot) *Formed 1958*
The Royal Leicestershire Regiment [17]

The King's Division

The King's Own Royal Border Regiment [4, 34 and 55] *Formed 1959*
The King's Regiment [8, 63 and 96] *Formed in 1958 as* The King's Regiment (Manchester and Liverpool)
The Prince of Wales's Own Regiment of Yorkshire [14 and 15] *Formed 1958*
The Green Howards (Alexandra, Princess of Wales's Own Yorkshire Regiment) [19]
The Royal Irish Rangers (27th (Inniskilling), 83rd and 87th) *Two battalions. Formed in 1968 by conversion of:*
Headquarters North Irish Brigade
The Royal Inniskilling Fusiliers [27 and 108]
The Royal Ulster Rifles [83 and 87]
The Royal Irish Fusiliers (Princess Victoria's) [87 and 89]

The Queen's Lancashire Regiment [30, 40, 47, 59, 81 and 82]
Formed in 1970 by the amalgamation of:
    The Lancashire Regiment (Prince of Wales's Volunteers) [30, 40, 59 and 82] *Formed 1958*
    The Loyal Regiment (North Lancashire) [47 and 81]
The Duke of Wellington's Regiment (West Riding) [33 and 76]
Still listed but no longer effective:
The York and Lancaster Regiment [65 and 84] *Reg. bn. disbanded 1968*

The Prince of Wales's Division

The Devonshire and Dorset Regiment [11, 39 and 54] *Formed 1958*
The Cheshire Regiment [22]
The Royal Welch Fusiliers [23]
The Royal Regiment of Wales (24th/41st Foot) *Formed 1969*
The Gloucestershire Regiment [28 and 61]
The Worcestershire and Sherwood Foresters Regiment (29th/45th Foot) *Formed 1970*
The Royal Hampshire Regiment [37 and 67] *Reduced to single coy. 1970*
The Staffordshire Regiment (The Prince of Wales's) [38, 64, 80 and 98] *Formed 1959*
The Duke of Edinburgh's Royal Regiment (Berkshire and Wiltshire) [49, 62, 66 and 99] *Formed 1959*

The Light Division

The Light Infantry [13, 32, 46, 51, 53, 68, 85, 105 and 106] *Three bns. Formed in 1968 by conversion of:*
    Headquarters Light Infantry Brigade
    The Somerset and Cornwall Light Infantry [13, 32 and 46] *Formed 1959*
    The Kings' Own Yorkshire Light Infantry [51 and 105]
    The King's Shropshire Light Infantry [53 and 85]
    The Durham Light Infantry [68 and 106]
The Royal Green Jackets *Two bns. and one coy.*
Formed in 1966 by conversion of:
    Headquarters Green Jacket Brigade
    1st Green Jackets, 43rd and 52nd *Renamed 1958*
    2nd Green Jackets, The King's Royal Rifle Corps *Renamed 1958*
    3rd Green Jackets, The Rifle Brigade *Renamed 1958*

Airborne

The Parachute Regiment *Three bns. and Guards coy.*
22 Special Air Service Regiment
Army Air Corps *Reconstituted 1957*

Appendix A

The Brigade of Gurkhas

2nd King Edward VII's Own Gurkha Rifles (The Sirmoor Rifles)
Two Bns.
6th Queen Elizabeth's Own Gurkha Rifles *Renamed 1959*
7th Duke of Edinburgh's Own Gurkha Rifles *Renamed 1959*
10th Princess Mary's Own Gurkha Rifles *Renamed 1950*
Gurkha Engineers
Gurkha Signals
Gurkha Transport Regiment

Services

Royal Army Chaplains' Department
Royal Corps of Transport *Renamed 1965*
Royal Army Medical Corps
Royal Army Ordnance Corps
Corps of Royal Electrical and Mechanical Engineers
Corps of Royal Military Police
Royal Army Pay Corps
Royal Army Veterinary Corps
Small Arms School Corps
Military Provost Staff Corps
Royal Army Educational Corps
Royal Army Dental Corps
Royal Pioneer Corps
Intelligence Corps
Army Physical Training Corps
Army Catering Corps
General Service Corps
Queen Alexandra's Royal Army Nursing Corps
Women's Royal Army Corps

Appendix B

Appointments

I—*Executives*

Minister of Defence (since integration)

April–October 1964	Rt. Hon. G. E. P. Thorneycroft, MP
October 1964–1970	Rt. Hon. D. W. Healey, MBE, MP
from June 1970	Rt. Hon. Lord Carrington, KCMG, MC

Chief of Defence Staff

1957–1959	Marshal of the R.A.F. Sir William Dickson, GCB, KBE, DSO, AFC
1959–1965	Admiral of the Fleet Earl Mountbatten of Burma, KG, PC, GCB, OM, GCSI, GCE, DSO
1965–1967	Field Marshal Sir Richard Hull, GCB, DSO
from 1967	Marshal of the R.A.F. Sir Charles Elworthy, GCB, CBE, DSO, MVO, DFC, AFC

Secretary of State for War

July 1945–1946	Rt. Hon. J. J. Lawson, MP
October 1946–1947	Rt. Hon. F. J. Bellenger, MP
October 1947–1950	Rt. Hon. E. Shinwell, MP
February 1950–1951	Rt. Hon. E. J. St. L. Strachey, MP
October 1951–1956	Rt. Hon. A. H. Head, CBE, MC, MP
October 1956–1958	Rt. Hon. J. H. Hare, OBE, MP
January 1958–1960	Rt. Hon. A. C. J. Soames, CBE, MP
July 1960–1963	Rt. Hon. J. D. Profumo, OBE, MP
June–October 1963	Rt. Hon. J. B. Godber, MP
October 1963–1964	Rt. Hon. J. E. Ramsden, MP

Minister of Defence for the Army

April–October 1964	Rt. Hon. J. E. Ramsden, MP
October 1964–1965	Rt. Hon. F. W. Mulley, MP
December 1965–1967	Rt. Hon. G. W. Reynolds, MP

Under-Secretary of State for Defence for the Army

January 1967–1969	Mr. H. J. Boyden, MP

October 1969–1970	Mr. I. S. Richard, MP
from June 1970	Mr. I. H. J. L. Gilmour, MP

Chief of the Imperial General Staff

1941–1946	Field Marshal Viscount Alanbrooke, KG, GCB, OM, GCVO, DSO (late R.A.)
June 1946–1948	Field Marshal Viscount Montgomery of Alamein, KG, GCB, DSO (late Inf.)
November 1948–1952	Field Marshal Sir William Slim, GCB, GCMG, GBE, DSO, MC (late Gurkhas)
November 1952–1955	Field Marshal Sir John Harding, GCB, CBE, DSO, MC (late Inf.)
September 1955–1958	Field Marshal Sir Gerald Templer, GCB, GCMG, KBE, DSO (late Inf.)
September 1958–1961	Field Marshal Sir Francis Festing, GCB, KBE, DSO (late Inf.)
November 1961–1964	General Sir Richard Hull, GCB, DSO (late R.A.C.)

Chief of General Staff

April 1964–1965	Field Marshal Sir Richard Hull, GCB, DSO
February 1965–1968	Field Marshal Sir James Cassels, GCB, KBE, DSO (late Inf.)
from March 1968	General Sir Geoffrey Baker, GCB, CMG, CBE, MC (late R.A.)

Adjutant-General

1941–1946	General Sir Ronald Adam, Bt., GCB, DSO, OBE (late R.A.)
June 1946–1947	General Sir Richard O'Connor, GCB, DSO, MC (late Inf.)
September 1947–1950	General Sir James Steele, GCB, KBE, DSO, MC (late Inf.)
September 1950–1953	General Sir John Crocker, GCB, KBE, DSO, MC (late R.A.C.)
September 1953–1956	General Sir Cameron Nicholson, GCB, KBE, DSO, MC (late R.A.)
November 1956–1959	General Sir Charles Loewen, GCB, KBE, DSO (late R.A.)
August 1959–1960	General Sir Hugh Stockwell, GCB, KBE, DSO (late Inf.)
July 1960–1963	General Sir Richard Goodbody, GCB, KBE, DSO (late R.A.)
June 1963–1964	General Sir James Cassels, GCB, KBE, DSO (late Inf.)

493

October 1964–1967	General Sir Reginald Hewetson, GCB, CBE, DSO (late R.A.)
October 1967–1970	General Sir Geoffrey Musson, KCB, CBE, DSO (late Inf.)
from June 1970	General Sir John Mogg, KCB, CBE, DSO (late Inf.)

Quarter-Master-General

1941–1946	General Sir Thomas Riddell-Webster, GCB, DSO (late Inf.)
February 1946–1947	General Sir Daril Watson, GCB, CBE, MC (late Inf.)
June 1947–1950	General Sir Sidney Kirkman, GCB, KBE, MC (late R.A.)
June 1950–1952	General Sir Ivor Thomas, GCB, KBE, DSO, MC (late R.A.)
August 1952–1955	General Sir Ouvry Roberts, GCB, KBE, DSO, MA (late R.E.)
June 1955–1956	Lieutenant-General Sir Maurice Chilton, KBE, CB (late R.A.)
December 1956–1958	General Sir Nevil Brownjohn, GBE, KCB, CMG, MC (late R.E.)
November 1958–1961	General Sir Cecil Sugden, GBE, KCB (late R.E.)
November 1961–1965	General Sir Gerald Lathbury, GCB, DSO, MBE (late Inf.)
January 1965–1966	General Sir Charles Richardson, GCB, CBE, DSO (late R.E.)
August 1966–1969	General Sir Alan Jolly, GCB, CBE, DSO, (late R.A.C.)
from September 1969	General Sir Antony Read, KCB, CBE, DSO, MC (late Inf.)

II—Commanders-in-Chief Overseas

Middle East Land Forces

1944–1946	General Sir Bernard Paget, GCB, DSO, MC (late Inf.)
June 1946–1947	General Sir Miles Dempsey, GBE, KCB, DSO, MC (late Inf.)
June 1947–1950	General Sir John Crocker, GCB, KBE, DSO MC (late R.A.C.)
July 1950–1953	General Sir Brian Robertson, Bt., GCB, KCMG, KCVO, DSO, MC (late R.E.)
April–September 1953	General Sir Cameron Nicholson, KCB, KBE, DSO, MC (late R.A.)

September 1953–1957   General Sir Charles Keightley, GCB, KBE, DSO (late R.A.C.)

January 1957–1958   Lieutenant-General Sir Geoffrey Bourne, KCB, KBE, CMG (late R.A.)

January 1958–1960   Lieutenant-General Sir Roger Bower, KCB, KBE (late Inf.)

Middle East Command (inter-service)

May 1960–1961   General Sir Dudley Ward, GCB, KBE, DSO (late Inf.)

June 1963–1966   Lieutenant-General Sir Charles Harington, KCB, CBE, DSO, MC (late Inf.)

Near East Command (inter service)

March 1961–1962   General Sir Dudley Ward, GCB, KBE, DSO (late Inf.)

Near East Command (inter-service)

February 1947–1949   General Sir Neil Ritchie, GBE, KCB, DSO, MC (late Inf.)

July 1949–1951   General Sir John Harding, GCB, CBE, DSO, MC (late Inf.)

February 1951–1953   General Sir Charles Keightley, GCB, KBE, DSO, (late R.A.C.)

September 1953–1956   General Sir Charles Loewen, GCB, KBE, DSO (late R.A.)

August 1956–1958   General Sir Francis Festing, GCB, KBE, DSO (late Inf.)

June 1958–1961   General Sir Richard Hull, GCB, DSO (late R.A.C.)

June 1961–1962   Lieutenant-General Sir Nigel Poett, KCB, DSO (late Inf.)

Far East Command (inter-service)

February 1967–1969   General Sir Michael Carver, KCB, CBE, DSO, MC (late R.A.C.)

British Forces Germany

November 1947–1949   General Sir Brian Robertson, Bt., GBE, KCMG, KCVO, DSO, MC (late R.E.)

British Army of the Rhine

September 1949–1951   Lieutenant-General Sir Charles Keightley, KCB, KBE, DSO (late R.A.C.)

August 1951–1952   General Sir John Harding, GCB, CBE, DSO, MC (late Inf.)

September 1952–1956	General Sir Richard Gale, GCB, KBE, DSO, MC (late Inf.)
January 1957–1960	General Sir Dudley Ward, GCB, KBE, DSO (late Inf.)
January 1960–1963	General Sir James Cassels, GCB, KBE, DSO (late Inf.)
April 1963–1966	General Sir William Stirling, GCB, CBE, DSO (late R.A.)
April 1966–1968	General Sir John Hackett, GCB, CBE, DSO, MC, MA (late R.A.C.)
July 1968–1970	General Sir Desmond Fitzpatrick, KCB, DSO, MBE, MC (late R.A.C.)
from December 1970	Lieutenant-General Sir Peter Hunt, KCB, DSO, OBE (late Inf.)

East Africa

June 1953–1955	General Sir George Erskine, GCB, KBE, DSO (late Inf.)
May 1955–1957	Lieutenant-General Sir Gerald Lathbury, KCB, DSO, MBE (late Inf.)

III—Inter-Allied Commands

Chairman, Commanders-in-Chief Committee, Western Union

November 1948–1951	Field Marshal Viscount Montgomery of Alamein, KG, GCB, DSO (late Inf.)

Deputy Supreme Allied Commander, Europe

April 1951–1958	Field Marshal Viscount Montgomery
September 1958–1960	General Sir Richard Gale, GCB, KBE, DSO, MC (late Inf.)
September 1960–1963	General Sir Hugh Stockwell, GCB, KBE, DSO (late Inf.)
December 1963–1967	Marshal of the R.A.F. Sir Thomas Pike, GCB, CBE, DFC
March 1967–1970	General Sir Robert Bray, GBE, KCB, DSO (late Inf.)
from December 1970	General Sir Desmond Fitzpatrick, GCB, DSO, MBE, MC (late R.A.C.)

Commander-in-Chief Northern Army Group

Appointment held by C.-in-C. British Army of the Rhine since November 29, 1952

Commander-in-Chief Allied Forces Northern Europe

April 1953–1956	General Sir Robert Mansergh, GCB, KBE, MC (late R.A.)
January 1956–1958	Lieutenant-General Sir Cecil Sugden, KCB, CBE, (late R.E.)
July 1958–1961	General Sir Horatius Murray, GCB, KBE, DSO (late Inf.)
July 1961–1963	General Sir Harold Pyman, GBE, KCB, DSO, MA (late R.A.C.)
November 1963–1967	General Sir Robert Bray, GBE, KCB, DSO (late Inf.)
February 1967–1969	General Sir Kenneth Darling, KCB, CBE, DSO (late Inf.)
from August 1969	General Sir Walter Walker, KCB, CBE, DSO (late Gurkhas)

Appendix C

Honours and Awards

I—Battle Honours in Korea

Honour	Dates of battle	Awarded to
Naktong Bridgehead	September 16–25, 1950	Middlesex Regiment
Chongju	October 25–30, 1950	Middlesex
Pakchon	November 4–5, 1950	Argyll and Sutherland Highlanders
Chongchon II	November 25–30, 1950	Middlesex
Seoul	January 2–4, 1951	8th King's Royal Irish Hussars, Royal Northumberland Fusiliers, Royal Ulster Rifles
Chuam-Ni	February 14–17, 1951	Middlesex
Hill 327	February 16–20, 1951	8th Hussars, Gloucestershire Regiment
Kapyong-Chon	April 3–16, 1951	Middlesex
Imjin	April 22–25, 1951	8th Hussars, R.N.F., Gloucesters, R.U.R.
Kapyong	April 22–25, 1951	Middlesex
Kowang-San	October 3–12, 1951	8th Hussars, R.N.F., King's Own Scottish Borderers, King's Shropshire Light Infantry
Maryang-San	November 4–6, 1951	Royal Leicestershire Regiment, K.O.S.B.
Hill 227 I	November 17–19, 1951	K.S.L.I.
The Hook, 1952	November 18–19, 1952	5th Royal Inniskilling Dragoon Guards, Black Watch

Appendix C

The Hook, 1953	May 28–29, 1953	King's Regiment, Duke of Wellington's Regiment
Korea, 1950–51		8th Hussars, R.N.F., Gloucesters, Middlesex, R.U.R., A.&S.H.
Korea, 1951–53		Royal Tank Regiment
Korea, 1951–52		5th D.G., Royal Norfolk Regiment, Royal Leicesters, K.O.S.B., Welch Regiment, K.S.L.I.
Korea, 1952–53		Royal Fusiliers, King's, Duke's, Black Watch, Durham Light Infantry

II—Campaign Medals

General Service Medal 1918–62 (ribbon: purple with green stripe down centre).

Clasps since 1945:

South East Asia 1945–46 (for service in Java or Sumatra between September 3, 1945 and November 30, 1946, or in French Indo-China between September 3, 1945, and January 28, 1946).

Bomb and Mine Clearance 1945–49 (for clearance work in the British Isles).

Palestine 1945–48 (for service between September 27, 1945, and June 30, 1948).

Malaya (for service between June 16, 1948, and July 31, 1960).

Cyprus (for 120 days' service between April 1, 1955, and April 18, 1959).

Near East (for service in Egypt between October 31 and December 22, 1956).

Arabian Peninsula (for 30 days' service in Aden Colony, Aden Protectorate, Muscat and Oman, or the Persian Gulf States between January 1, 1957, and June 30, 1960).

Brunei (for service in Northern Borneo between December 8 and 23, 1962).

Africa General Service Medal (ribbon: yellow with black borders and two narrow green stripes).

Clasp since 1945:
Kenya (for 91 days' service between October 21, 1952, and November 17, 1956).

Korea Medal (ribbon: yellow with two blue stripes, for service between July 2, 1950, and July 27, 1953).

General Service Medal 1962 (ribbon: purple with green edges).
Clasps:
Borneo (for 30 days' service between December 24, 1962, and a date to be decided).
Radfan (for 14 days' service between April 25 and July 31, 1964).
South Arabia (for 30 days' service in the Federation of South Arabia between August 1, 1964, and November 30, 1967).
Malay Peninsula (for 30 days' service between August 17, 1964, and June 12, 1965).

United Nations Medal for Korea (ribbon: light blue and white stripes for service between June 27, 1950, and July 24, 1954).

United Nations Medal for Congo (ribbon: United Nations blue with a broad green central stripe flanked by two narrow white stripes, for 90 days' service between July 10, 1960, and a date to be decided).

United Nations Medal for Cyprus (ribbon: United Nations blue with a central wide white stripe which is flanked by two dark blue stripes, for 30 days' service between March 27, 1964, and March 26, 1965, or 90 days' service between March 27, 1965, and a date to be decided).

Commonwealth Medals
Officers and men seconded to Commonwealth forces were granted Independence Medals, when eligible, and the following campaign medals:
Federation of Malaya Active Service Medal.
Ghana Congo Medal.
Sierra Leone General Service Medal (for service in the Congo).
The Uniformed Services Malaysia.
The Brunei Service Medal
The Dhofar Campaign Medal (for service with the Sultan of Muscat and Oman's Forces).
Kenya Campaign Medal (for service against the Somali Shifta).

Appendix C

III—Personal Awards

(The date in brackets is that of notification in the *London Gazette*; page reference is given when the individual is mentioned in the text.)

Victoria Cross

Korea:

Major K. Muir, 1st Argyll and Sutherland Highlanders—posthumous (5.1.51) (pp. 142–3).

Lieutenant-Colonel J. P. Carne, DSO, 1st Gloucestershire (27.10.53) (pp. 172–5).

Lieutenant K. P. E. Curtis, D.C.L.I., with 1st Gloucestershire—posthumous (1.12.53) (p. 170).

Private W. Speakman, Black Watch, with 1st King's Own Scottish Borderers (28.12.51) (pp. 192–3).

Borneo:

Lance-Corporal Rambahadur Limbu, 2/10th Princess Mary's Own Gurkha Rifles (22.4.66) (pp. 405–6).

George Cross

England:

Major K. A. Biggs, R.A.O.C.

Staff Sergeant G. Rogerson, R.A.O.C. (both 11.10.46, for saving ammunition from railway trucks that were blazing and exploding, with much loss of life).

Korea:

Lieutenant T. E. Waters, West Yorks, with 1st Gloucesters—posthumous (13.4.54) (p. 176).

Fusilier D. G. Kinne, 1st Royal Northumerland Fusiliers (13.4.54) (p. 208).

Austria:

Lieutenant M. P. Benner, R.E.—posthumous (17.6.46, for a vain attempt to save the life of a sapper during a mountaineering exercise).

Distinguished Service Order

Palestine:

Lieutenant-Colonel T. H. Birkbeck, DSO, Border, with 2/3rd Parachute—bar (15.10.48) (p. 53).

Lieutenant-Colonel H. C. Blackden, S.W.B., with Transjordan Frontier Force (15.10.48) (p. 50).

Malaya:

Captain A. F. E. Lucas, Royal Berkshire, with 1st Devons (12.8.49) (p. 88).

Major E. Gopsill, MC, 1/6th Gurkhas (21.3.50).

Lieutenant-Colonel E. P. Townsend, 1/6th Gurkhas (11.4.50).

Major P. Richardson, 1/2nd Gurkhas (11.4.50) (p. 90).

Major S. J. Causley, 26th Field Regiment, R.A. (19.5.50).

Lieutenant-Colonel J. W. Stephens, 1/2nd Gurkhas (19.5.50).

Lieutenant-Colonel I. L. Wight, 1st Suffolk (7.7.50) (p. 92).

Lieutenant-Colonel R. G. V. FitzGeorge-Balfour, CBE, MC, 2nd Coldstream Guards (24.10.50) (p. 93).

Lieutenant-Colonel C. C. Graham, OBE, 1/10th Gurkhas (24.10.50).

Lieutenant-Colonel J. S. Sanderson, OBE, 2nd Scots Guards (24.10.50).

Lieutenant-Colonel J. M. Hepper, R.A., with 1/7th Gurkhas (19.10.51).

Lieutenant-Colonel W. M. Henning, 1st Cameronians (4.4.52).

Lieutenant-Colonel E. D. Murray, OBE, 2/7th Gurkhas (4.4.52).

Lieutenant-Colonel P. A. Morcombe, OBE, 1st Suffolk (21.10.52).

Major S. B. Purne Rai, OBE, MC, OBE, 1/10th Gurkhas (1.5.53).

Lieutenant-Colonel W. C. Walker, DSO, OBE, 1/6th Gurkhas—bar (30.10.53).

Lieutenant-Colonel J. H. Allford, 2/7th Gurkhas (29.6.54).

Brigadier C. S. Howard, OBE, 26th Gurkha Brigade (26.10.54).

Lieutenant-Colonel P. H. Man, OBE, MC, 1st Royal Hampshire (8.5.56).

Lieutenant-Colonel G. H. W. Goode, OBE, Queen's, with 1st North Rhodesian (8.5.56).

Lieutenant-Colonel D. L. Powell-Jones, OBE, 2/6th Gurkhas (8.5.56).

Brigadier H. T. Alexander, OBE, 26th Gurkha Brigade (28.5.57).

Lieutenant-Colonel G. H. Lea, Lancashire Fusiliers, with 22nd S.A.S. (20.12.57).

Lieutenant-Colonel R. C. H. Miers, DSO, OBE, 1st South Wales Borderers—bar (20.12.57).

Lieutenant-Colonel A. W. N. L. Vickers, OBE, 1/2nd Gurkhas (20.12.57).

Korea:

Lieutenant-Colonel A. M. Man, OBE, 1st Middlesex (12.12.50) (p. 141).

Lieutenant-Colonel G. L. Neilson, 1st Argyll and Sutherland Highlanders (12.12.50) (p. 145).

Major R. M. Pratt, 1st Royal Northumberland Fus. (17.4.51) (p. 156).

Major J. K. H. Shaw, MC, 1st Royal Ulster Rifles (17.4.51) (p. 159).

A/Lieutenant-Colonel D. B. Drysdale, MBE, RM, 41 Independent Commando (18.5.51).

Major P. H. Huth, MC, 8th Hussars (1.6.51) (pp. 179–80).

Major H. J. Winn, MC, 1st Royal Northumberland Fusiliers (29.6.51) (p. 173).

Major H. M. Gaffikin, 1st Royal Ulster Rifles (10.7.51) (pp. 158–9).

Major C. H. Mitchell, 1st Royal Northumberland Fusiliers (10.7.51).

Lieutenant-Colonel J. P. Carne, 1st Gloucesters (13.6.51).

Lieutenant-Colonel K. O. N. Foster, 1st Royal Northumberland Fusiliers (13.7.51).

Brigadier T. Brodie, CBE, 29th Infantry Brigade (7.9.51).

Captain A. H. Farrar-Hockley, MC, 1st Gloucesters (8.12.53) (p. 175).

Major E. D. Harding, 1st Gloucesters (8.12.53) (p. 172).

Captain E. T. G. Shuldham, R.M., 41 Independent Commando (3.9.52).

Major W. G. O. Butler, MC, 8th Hussars (30.11.51).

Major W. J. Cottle, 1st K.S.L.I. (30.11.51) (p. 189).

Lieutenant-Colonel J. F. M. MacDonald, OBE, 1st K.O.S.B. (30.11.51).

Major P. F. St. C. Harrison, 1st K.O.S.B. (28.12.51) (pp. 193–4).

2nd Lieutenant W. Purves, 1st K.O.S.B. (28.12.51) (pp. 193–4).

Major P. H. V. de Clermont, 8th Hussars (29.4.52).

Major R. C. Robertson-Macleod, MC, TD, 1st K.O.S.B. (29.4.52) (pp. 193–4).

Major T. J. Jackson, 1st Welch (29.8.52) (p. 199).

Lieutenant-Colonel P. N. M. Moore, DSO, MC, 28th Field Engineer Regiment, R.E.—2nd bar (10.10.52) (p. 185).

Major D. G. M. Fletcher, 28th Field Engineer Regiment, R.E. (10.10.52).

Lieutenant-Colonel V. W. Barlow, DSO, OBE, 1st K.S.L.I.—bar (10.10.52).

Lieutenant-Colonel G. E. P. Hutchins, 1st Royal Leicesters (10.10.52).

Lieutenant-Colonel D. H. Tadman, OBE, 1st K.O.S.B. (10.10.52).

Major A. D. H. Irwin, MC, 1st Black Watch (9.1.53) (pp. 202–3).

Major B. D. Chapman, 1st Royal Norfolk (24.4.53).

Lieutenant-Colonel H. H. Deane, 1st Welch (24.4.53).

Major A. G. Roberts, 1st Welch (24.4.53).

Major R. A. Pont, 14th Field Regiment, R.A. (24.4.53).

Major J. M. H. Hailes, 1093 Independent A.O.P. Flight, R.A. (24.4.53).

Lieutenant-Colonel D. M. C. Rose, DSO, 1st Black Watch—bar (1.6.53).

Lieutenant-Colonel F. R. St. P. Bunbury, DSO, 1st Duke of Wellington's—bar (7.7.53) (p. 205).

Major L. F. H. Kershaw, 1st Duke of Wellington's (7.7.53) (p. 205).

Lieutenant-Colonel P. J. Jeffreys, DSO, OBE, 1st Durham Light Infantry—bar (8.12.53).

Lieutenant-Colonel T. G. Brennan, CBE, 20th Field Regiment, R.A. (8.12.53).

Brigadier D. A. Kendrew, CBE, DSO, 29th Infantry Brigade—3rd bar (8.12.53).

Major-General M. M. A. R. West, CB, DSO, 1st Commonwealth Division—2nd bar (8.12.53).

Kenya:

Major M. C. Hastings, 1st Devons (1.1.55) (pp. 284–5).

Egypt, Port Said:

Lieutenant-General Sir Hugh Stockwell, KCB, KBE, DSO, Allied Land Forces—bar (13.6.57).

Brigadier M. A. H. Butler, DSO, MC, 16th Parachute Brigade—bar (13.6.57).

Lieutenant-Colonel P. E. Crook, OBE, Royal West Kent, with 3rd Parachute (13.6.57).

Brigadier R. W. Madoc, 3rd Commando Brigade (13.6.57).

Lieutenant-Colonel D. G. Tweed, R.M., 40 Commando (13.6.57).

Cyprus:

Lieutenant-Colonel N. H. Tailyour, DSO, R.M., 45 Commando—bar (25.1.57).

Lieutenant-Colonel H. E. N. Bredin, DSO, MC, R.U.R., with 2nd Parachute—2nd bar (23.7.57).

Lieutenant-Colonel J. D. King-Martin, MC, 50th Medium Regiment R.A. (23.7.57).

Aden Protectorate:

Major B. W. S. Boucher-Myers, Lancashire, with Aden Protectorate Levies (25.11.58) (p. 428).

Muscat and Oman:

Lieutenant-Colonel A. J. Deane-Drummond, MC, Royal Signals, with 22nd S.A.S. (25.8.59) (p. 358).

Congo:

Lieutenant-Colonel R. E. C. Price, S.W.B., with 4th Queen's Own Nigerian (22.12.61).

Major R. G. Lawson, R.T.R., with H.Q. 3rd Nigerian Brigade (30.3.62).

Borneo:

Brigadier A. G. Patterson, OBE, MC, 99th Gurkha Brigade (14.2.64).

Lieutenant-Colonel E. J. S. Burnett, MBE, MC, 1/10th Gurkhas (17.11.64) (p. 394).

Major-General W. C. Walker, CB, CBE, DSO, British Commonwealth Forces—2nd bar (16.2.65).

Brigadier W. W. Cheyne, OBE, 99th Gurkha Brigade (24.5.66).

Major C. J. Pike, 1/10th Gurkhas (9.12.66) (p. 408).

Radfan:

Lieutenant-Colonel A. H. Farrar-Hockley, DSO, MC, 3rd Parachute—bar (4.5.65) (p. 440).

Aden:

Lieutenant-Colonel M. J. H. Walsh, 1st Parachute (23.1.68) (p. 456).

Lieutenant-Colonel P. A. Downward, DFC, 1st Lancashire (23.1.68) (p. 462).

Appendix D

Casualties

The following figures have been obtained from official sources. They do not include Royal Marine commandos. It is understood that the number of wounded is that detained in hospital, a lower figure than reported operationally.

Campaign			Killed		Wounded	
			Officers	Soldiers	Officers	Soldiers
Indonesia		1945–46	28[1]	22	NOT KNOWN	
Palestine		1945–48	20	203	51	427
Malaya	1948–61	British units:	60	280	77	536
		Brigade of Gurkhas:	20[2]	149	30[2]	278
Korea		1950–53	86	779	185	2404
Egypt		1951–54	54[3]		NOT KNOWN	
Kenya		1952–56	5	7	21	48
Cyprus		1955–58	7	72	28	386
Egypt		1956	3	9	10	53
Borneo & Malaya		1962–66				
		British units:	1	15	3	33
		Brigade of Gurkhas:	3 (Brit.)	40[4]	4 (Brit.)	83[4]
Radfan		1964–67	2	22	8	180
Aden		1964–67	12	56	20	302[5]

[1] Includes British officers in Indian units.

[2] Including 10 British officers.

[3] All services, officers and men.

[4] includes Gurkha officers.

[5] 669 were reported wounded (officers and men) under operational returns.

Appendix E

Sources

Page ref.

I must acknowledge as a start the use made of *Keesing's Contemporary Archives*, which are digests of press reports. These volumes have provided the framework of events round which I have built, and I am much indebted to them.

Chapter 1—Redeployment for Peace

4   Details of operations in the Far East come from the Official History, *The War Against Japan*, Vol. V.

5   see *The Memoirs of Field Marshal Montgomery* (Collins, 1958).

6   The figures were kindly provided by the Director of Army Public Relations.

12–13   For the distribution of units I have relied on the location lists kindly provided by the regiments.

14   see p. 483 of *The Memoirs of Field Marshal Montgomery*.

Chapter 2—India

John Connell's *Auchinleck* (Cassell, 1959) formed a valuable background.

16   For the Bombay mutiny I have drawn on Brigadier W. E. Underhill's *The Royal Leicestershire Regiment* (1928–56), and for that at Lahore on private sources and on Lieutenant-General Sir Francis Tuker's *While Memory Serves* (Cassell, 1950), which was also my main source for the Calcutta killings and for extracts from Major Livermore's account.

20   For the arrival and departure of General Whistler, see Sir John Smyth's *Bolo Whistler* (Muller, 1967).

21   Mark Henniker's words—he is now Brigadier Sir Mark Henniker, Bart.—appear in his story 'The Last of the Many', which is one of nineteen, all told by soldiers of post-war experiences, in *The Unquiet Peace* (Allan Wingate, 1957), edited by Maurice Tugwell. I have made wide use of this

book, and in this instance obtained private elucidation on certain points from Sir Mark Henniker.

23–4   Information on the plight of the Gurkhas was provided privately by two officers serving with them.

24–5   For the departures I have relied on the magazines of the regiments concerned, also on Smyth's *Bolo Whistler*.

Chapter 3—Palestine

No comprehensive account of this campaign has hitherto been written, although the 6th Airborne's story is fully told in Major R. D. Wilson's *Cordon and Search* (Gale & Polden, 1949) and light on the 1st Division's part is thrown by General Sir Richard Gale in his *Call To Arms* (Hutchinson, 1968), similarly on the 3rd Division's in Smyth's *Bolo Whistler*. For background I have used John Marlowe's *Rebellion in Palestine* (Cresset Press, 1946). *The Memoirs of Field Marshal Montgomery* are revealing and controversial on Palestine, being based on impressions made during fleeting visits.

I have received valuable help from Generals Sir Alan Cunningham, Sir Evelyn Barker, and Sir Gordon MacMillan, who all kindly gave me interviews and made much information available.

32–3   Details of 8th Para's action were kindly provided by Colonel G. Hewetson to supplement Wilson's *Search and Cordon*, from which much material for Parts II and III was drawn. Also of value: Search Operations in Palestine, from *The Army Quarterly*, 1948, by the present Lieutenant-General Sir R. N. Anderson, who was then commanding a brigade.

38–9   M. Begin, leader of the Irgun, has told his story in *The Revolt* (W. H. Allen, 1951) and it has flavoured my account of the blowing-up of the King David Hotel and the subsequent search of Tel Aviv.

52   The I.O. of the 1st Para Brigade was Maurice Tugwell, who tells his story in *The Unquiet Peace*.

53   This story also comes from *The Unquiet Peace*, as told by Guy Hatch.

For the final phase valuable contributions came from *The Household Brigade Magazine*, *The H.L.I. Chronicle*, *The Thin Red Line*, the King's Royal Rifle Corps, and privately from General Sir Charles Jones, who commanded the 2nd Brigade.

Chapter 4—Europe

Lieutenant-General Sir Otway Herbert gave me some very helpful information to supplement that found in Robert Rodrigo's *Berlin Airlift* (Cassell, 1960), the Air Ministry's *Berlin Airlift* (1949), and Brigadier A. M. Stewart's Operation Plainfare in *The Royal Engineers' Journal*. Regimental sources were also fruitful, and for the build-up of Rhine Army I am indebted to information from Headquarters 4th Division.

Chapter 5—Malaya

There is plenty of good outline material, notably Brigadier R. L. Clutterbuck's highly authoritative *The Long, Long War* (Cassell, 1967), which is particularly good for its insight into the rebel movement, Julian Paget's *Counter-Insurgency Campaigning* (Faber, 1967), and Edgar O'Ballance's *Malaya: The Counter-Insurgent War* (Faber, 1966). Colonial Office Annual Reports have also been a great stand-by, and for deeper penetration into administrative problems I used Vernon Bartlett's *Report from Malaya* (Verschoyle, 1954).

For the military build-up I am indebted to regimental sources, most of all to *The Kukri*, the Gurkhas' annual, which has been of great value, and to private contributions from General Sir Neil Ritchie, Major-General R. C. O. Hedley, Colonel I. G. Pine-Coffin, late the Devons, and Colonel C. J. Kidston-Montgomerie, late the 4th Hussars. Of regimental accounts, Major J. B. Oldfield's full-length *The Green Howards in Malaya* (Gale & Polden, 1953), *2nd Battalion Scots Guards Tour in Malaya*, 1948–1951, and an appendix to Lieutenant-Colonel H. D. Chaplin's *The Queen's Own Royal West Kent Regiment*, 1920–50 (Michael Joseph, 1954) have been of most value. The personal experiences respectively of brigade, battalion, and company commander are admirably told in Mark Henniker's *Red Shadow over Malaya* (Blackwood, 1955), Richard Miers' *Shoot to Kill* (Faber, 1959), and Arthur Campbell's *Jungle Green* (Allen & Unwin, 1953). Brigadier A. E. C. Bredin's *The Happy Warriors* (Blackmore Press, 1961) tells of the Gurkhas' activities, from both personal and general viewpoints, and of many extracts from magazines I found Major R. E. R. Robinson's Reflections of a Company Commander (in *The Army Quarterly*) and Group-Captain K. R. C. Slater's Air Operations in Malaya, 1953–56 (in the *Journal of the R.U.S.I.*) of particular value.

78	I was myself the witness of this scene.
87	Major J. M. Sutro provided me with details.
92	Brigadier I. L. Wight provided me with details.
94	Most details of this affair were obtained from the official Report of the Singapore Riots Enquiry Commission.
98	Maurice Tugwell, who was with the Royal West Kent, describes this action in *The Unquiet Peace*.
101–2	Professor C. Northcote Parkinson, who was living in Malaya, provides a deep and vivid picture in his *Templer in Malaya* (Donald Moore, 1954).
108	Details were obtained from *The Suffolk Regimental Gazette*.
109	Tedford tells his story in *The Unquiet Peace*.
115	I have relied on Clutterbuck (quoted above) for estimates of the rebel strength.
120	This action is well described in *The Royal Hampshire Regiment Journal*.

Chapter 6—Korea

For no other chapter was information easier to accumulate. Brigadier C. N. Barclay has written a semi-official account of the whole campaign in *The First Commonwealth Division* (Gale & Polden, 1954) and of wider scope, there is Brigadier-General S. L. A. Marshall's *The Military History of the Korean War* (Franklin Watts, U.S.A., 1963). Tim Carew has contributed a lively picture of the fighting in his *The Korean War* (Cassell, 1967). There are some excellent regimental accounts, sometimes as separate editions, as Lieutenant-Colonel G. I. Malcolm's *The Argylls in Korea* (Thomas Nelson, 1952), *The Royal Ulster Rifles in Korea* (Wm. Mullan, 1953), and special supplements to the *Journal of the 8th King's Royal Irish Hussars* and the Royal Norfolk's *Britannia*. The doings of others have been faithfully recorded as routine reports in such magazines as *The Die-Hard, St. George's Gazette, Back Badge, The Borderer, The K.S.L.I. Regimental Journal, The Red Hackle, The Iron Duke*, and *The Kingsman*. I am also indebted to Major-General B. A. Coad for help over the Battles of the Naktong Bridgehead and Pakchon and to Major-General T. Brodie over that of the Imjin.

163	General Coad wrote these words as a foreword to *The Argylls in Korea*.

Additional sources used for the Imjin battle were A. H. Farrar-Hockley's *The Edge of the Sword* (Muller, 1954) E. J. Kahn's article No One But The Glosters from *The New Yorker*, and a very good private account written and lent by Brigadier Maris Young, late of the 45th Field Regiment.

174 The relaying of Brigadier Brodie's last message is as reported in *Back Badge* and agreed by him.

204 Winston Churchill's words are to be found in *The River War*, following the battle of Abu Klea.

Chapter 7—Regimental Revival

I am indebted to help received from a former Director of Infantry, Major-General C. B. Fairbanks. I obtained details of strengths from the White Papers, Statements Relating to Defence, presented for approval of estimates.

Chapter 8—Egypt

Material for Part I has been drawn largely from private sources, many of them first tapped for one of my previous books, *Objective: Egypt* (Muller, 1966). The late General Sir George Erskine, his former Chief of Staff, Major-General R. F. K. Goldsmith, General Lord Robertson of Oakridge, and Major-General F. R. G. Matthews (who was G.O.C. 1st Division) come within this category. I acquired further material for *The Farewell Years: The Buffs*, 1948–67, of which use has been made, particularly that from Brigadier J. W. Tweedie. More recent contributions have been made by Major-General R. K. Exham, who commanded 3rd Brigade, and his brigade major at that time, Lieutenant-Colonel R. F. Nixon, who has kindly supplied a number of missing links. The Lancashire Fusiliers' part, both in October 1951 and January 1952, is described in some detail in *The Gallipolli Gazette* and has been supplemented by officers who were there. *The Household Brigade Magazine* was also a useful source.

217 Lord Attlee's words come from Francis Williams's *A Prime Minister Remembers* (Heinemann, 1961).

217 Although not witnessed by him, the severing of the military policeman's head was reported from a reliable and responsible source.

236–5 Details of the departure are as privately related by Brigadier J. H. S. Lacey.

Of the published work used for Parts II–IV, three articles

by General Sir Hugh Stockwell, telling his own story in the *Sunday Telegraph* of October–November 1966, are revealing and informative, without contradicting such standard works previously studied as Lieutenant-Colonel A. J. Barker's *Suez—The Seven Day War* (Faber, 1964), and the official *Despatch by General Sir Charles Keightley* (London Gazette, 1957) on the military side, and on the political Sir Anthony Eden's *Full Circle* (Cassell, 1960), Merry and Serge Bromberger's *Secrets of Suez* (Pan Books, 1957)—a book of many truths and some inaccuracies—and Terence Robertson's *Crisis—Inside Story of the Suez Conspiracy* (Hutchinson, 1965). Valuable private contributions were made by Major-General M. A. H. Butler (as he then was), Brigadier Lacey, Lieutenant-Colonel T. H. Gibbon, of the 6th R.T.R., and a number of others.

242–3 For the interception over the Egyptian coast, see Eden's *Full Circle*, p. 524.

247 The action by 3rd Para is well described in *Pegasus*, in an account written by Lieutenant-Colonel Crook, and in a subaltern's account in *The Unquiet Peace*, C. A. Hogg's Sound and Fury. Captain de Klee described his advance up the causeway in *The Household Brigade Magazine*, under the title A Jump with the French. Admiral Sir Manley Power provided the information about the offer of marines.

253 Captain D. M. J. Clark, a gunner who accompanied 42 Commando ashore, has provided a vivid account of his experiences in *Suez Touchdown* (Peter Davies, 1964).

260 The quote from Lieutenant-Colonel Bredin appears in the Brombergers' *Secrets of Suez*.

261 The bulk of this part was gleaned from an account in *The Unquiet Peace* by Edward Fursdon, who was D.A.A. & Q.M.G. of 19th Brigade and from the magazines of regiments engaged, together with sources already notified.

Chapter 9—Kenya

One has the rare advantage of drawing on the accounts of the two C.-in-C's, General Erskine's *The Kenya Emergency* and General Lathbury's article in *The Oxfordshire and Buckinghamshire Light Infantry Chronicle*, The Security Forces in the Kenya Emergency, and there is also an excellent book on the campaign as a whole in Fred Madjalany's *State of Emergency* (Longman, 1962). Battalions' doings are fully recorded in the aforementioned *The Buffs*, 1948–67 and in *The Mau Mau Emergency, Kenya; 1st Bn., The Devonshire Regiment*, and others are well covered in their regimental magazines. Major F. E. Kitson's exciting *Gangs and Counter-Gangs* (Barrie & Rockcliff, 1960) was also of great value.

281   Brigadier Tweedie's words are from a letter written to the author.

Chapter 10—Cyprus

In contrast with Kenya, material on the operational aspect, viewed overall, is in short supply, the best being in Julian Paget's *Counter-Insurgency Campaigning* (already mentioned) which is particularly sound on the organisational side. For background of course there is Laurence Durrell's classic *Bitter Lemons* (Faber, 1964), from which quotations appear on pages 297 and 298–9.

I have had to lean heavily on private contributors and am especially grateful to General Sir Geoffrey Baker, who provided me with much useful information, and to one of his successors as Chief of Staff, Major-General P. Gleadell. Two former brigade commanders, General Sir Antony Read and Major-General J. A. R. Robertson, have also been very helpful, and for enlightenment on the strategic problems of 1958 I am indebted to Lieutenant-General Sir Roger Bower. Field Marshal Lord Harding kindly put me right on certain details, as also on the evacuation of Egypt.

Nearly all regimental magazines cover the campaign well and have been my main source for the build-up and deployment. I am much indebted to Major R. St. G. G. Bartelot, of the Royal Artillery Institution, and to Colonel R. H. Senior, of the Royal Artillery Record Office, for help in tracing the movements of gunner regiments.

It has been of great advantage to have the enemy's story, as told ln detail in *The Memoirs of General Grivas* (Longman, 1964). It will be apparent where it has been used.

293   see André Maurois' *Disraeli* (Bodley Head, 1927) p. 297.

295   Captain J. N. Elderkin wrote a good account of this in his article, In Aid of the Civil Power in *The Royal Engineers Journal*.

301   Major Coombe's story appears in *The Unquiet Peace*.

303   The method used here by the Royal Norfolks was related to me privately.

320   from an account by Private Hicks in *The Oxfordshire and Buckinghamshire Light Infantry Chronicle*.

For the Aftermath I drew on Brigadier Michael Harbottle's *The Impartial Soldier* (Oxford University Press, 1970) and some very good regimental accounts.

Chapter 11—The New Model

Details of the amalgamations were obtained from the White Paper, The Future Organisation of the Army (Cmnd. 230, July 1957). The brief, guide-lines, and recommendation of the infantry committee come from Sir John Smyth's *Bolo Whistler* (as under chapter 2). Also used: Anthony Varrier's *An Army for the Sixties* (Secker & Warburg, 1966).

338   The story of the picture's crash was kindly related by Field Marshal Templer himself.

340–4   Gleaned from public reports and private sources.

Chapter 12—Arabia

351   Good background to the operations in Oman was provided by P. S. Allfree's *War Lords of Oman* (Robert Hale, 1967), by an officer who was seconded both to the Trucial Scouts and the Sultan's Forces. Major W. O. Little's article in *The Army Quarterly*, named Oman Redivivus, covers the reoccupation of the Buraimi Oasis. J. Morris's *Sultan in Oman* (Faber, 1957) vividly covers subsequent developments.

355   I have relied on the Cameronians' magazine, *The Covenanter*, on information provided privately by Major-General Robertson, and on another source.

357–8   Colonel Smiley wrote a good account of the recapture of the Jebel in *The Journal of the R.U.S.I.*, entitled Muscat and Oman. Further lively details were obtained from Major K. W. D. Diacre's contribution to *The Household Brigade Magazine* as commander of the Life Guards detachment, and from Lieutenant P. S. Mongor's to the *Royal Army Service Corps Review*.

359   My account of the Kuwait landing is based on information obtained privately and from regimental sources, with *The Globe and Laurel* being of particular aid among the latter. Heat casualty figures were provided by official sources, although I was not allowed access to the Army Operational Research Establishment's report. However, the gist of it was provided by Gillian King in her Chatham House essay, Imperial Outpost—Aden.

Chapter 13—The Caribbean

Regimental and corps journals form the entire structure of this chapter within the framework provided by *Keesings Archives*.

Chapter 14—Borneo

Although there is a dearth of published material covering the campaign as a whole, there are some excellent accounts in regimental magazines, particularly of the opening actions described in *The Kukri, The Queen's Own Highlander, The Globe and Laurel*, and *The 1st Green Jackets Chronicle*. The *Kukri* also contains a report by General Walker, and another, longer article by him, covering his full tenure of command, appeared in *The Round Table* of January 1969, entitled How Borneo Was Won. For their private contributions in filling in gaps I am much indebted to Brigadier J. B. A. Glennie, Lieutenant-Colonel J. A. I. Fillingham, who had the 2/10th Gurkhas, Brigadier J. M. Strawson, who had the Queen's Royal Irish Hussars, Brigadier F. S. Eiloart, who was C.R.A., Major-General J. Harington, who was Chief of Staff Far East Command, Brigadier E. N. W. Bramall, who had the 2nd Royal Green Jackets, Lieutenant-Colonel M. R. Wallace, who had the Argylls, and Major-General H. R. S. Pain, who had the 5th Infantry Brigade.

Chapter 15—Africa

412 Major-General Alexander has described his experiences in his *African Tightrope* (Pall Mall Press, 1965).

413 The Sappers' relief operations are well described by Lieutenant-Colonel F. W. E. Fursdon in *The Royal Engineers Journal*, March 1964.

413 The details are from *The Tiger and Sphinx*.

414 For the sequence of events within the 24th Brigade I am indebted to Major-General Lloyd Owen, and for help over the story of the Jinja mutiny to Colonel Tillett. An account of the latter, written by Major J. M. Greny, who was with the Uganda Rifles, was also of value. 45 Commando's action is well described in *The Globe and Laurel*.

416–7 The commander of D Battery, Major I. C. Lambie, wrote an account, The Lanet Mutiny, which was published in *The Journal of the Royal Artillery*.

Chapter 16—Aden

I built up Part I and II from regimental sources and from

Brigadier G. S. Heathcote's penetrating article in *The Journal of the R.U.S.I.*, May 1968, Aden—A Reason Why.

422   The Colonial Office Report (no. 233) gives details.

423   Fortunately Major Diacre was in command of the Life Guards (as in Oman) and he wrote his story this time for *The Army Quarterly*. Information provided privately by Major-General Robertson was also of much value, together with an account by a Seaforth company commander, Captain R. J. R. Campbell.

426   as related privately by Major Grant to the author.

427–8   Written accounts both by Major Boucher-Myears and by Major Semmence of the Buffs were drawn upon.

Julian Paget's *Last Post: Aden, 1963–67* (Faber, 1969) was published at a convenient time for me. I have drawn freely on this book for the political background, the Radfan operations, and the struggle in Aden itself, and the author has been very co-operative in enlarging on certain points. There are some good regimental accounts of the Radfan fighting, notably in *Pegasus*, and Lieutenant-Colonel T. M. P. Stevens and Major M. E. B. Banks, both of 45 Commando, have contributions respectively in *The Journal of the R.U.S.I.* and *Brassey's Annual*.

I have relied on Paget and regimental sources for Part IV and have also consulted Colin Mitchell's *Having Been A Soldier* (Hamilton, 1969).

Chapter 17—The Lone Sentry

466   *The Kukri* is my source for the Hong Kong eruptions.

Details of reductions have been drawn from Supplementary Statements on Defence Policy.

475   The pamphlet referred to is *Military Aid to the Civil Community in the United Kingdom*. Hugh Hanning's *The Peaceful Use of Military Forces* (Praeger Special Studies, 1967) provides an interesting guide to the aid that has already been given, on a world-wide basis.

478–81   I am grateful to the Army Public Relations Department for details of the build-up in Northern Ireland and to *The Silver Bugle* for those of the 3rd Light Infantry's action.

483   The brigadier referred to is now Major-General A. J. Woodrow and was then Director of Army Public Relations. His impressions are as privately related.

Index

531